The Ethics o

The Ethics of War

Classic and Contemporary Readings

Edited by Gregory M. Reichberg,
Henrik Syse, and Endre Begby

Blackwell
Publishing

Editorial material and organization © 2006 by Blackwell Publishing Ltd

BLACKWELL PUBLISHING
350 Main Street, Malden, MA 02148-5020, USA
9600 Garsington Road, Oxford OX4 2DQ, UK
550 Swanston Street, Carlton, Victoria 3053, Australia

The right of Gregory M. Reichberg, Henrik Syse, and Endre Begby to be identified as the Authors of the Editorial Material in this Work has been asserted in accordance with the UK Copyright, Designs, and Patents Act 1988.

First published 2006 by Blackwell Publishing Ltd

3   2010

Library of Congress Cataloging-in-Publication Data

The ethics of war : classic and contemporary readings / edited by Gregory M. Reichberg, Henrik Syse, and Endre Begby.
    p. cm.
  Includes bibliographical references and index.
  ISBN-13: 978-1-4051-2377-8 (hardcover : alk. paper)
  ISBN-10: 1-4051-2377-X (hardcover : alk. paper)
  ISBN-13: 978-1-4051-2378-5 (pbk. : alk. paper)
  ISBN-10: 1-4051-2378-8 (pbk. : alk. paper) 1. War—Moral and ethical aspects. 2. Military ethics. I. Reichberg, Gregory M. II. Syse, Henrik, 1966– III. Begby, Endre.

  U22.E86 2006
  172'.42—dc22

2005037647

A catalogue record for this title is available from the British Library.

Set in 10/13pt Galliard
by Graphicraft Limited, Hong Kong
Printed and bound in the United States of America
by Sheridan Books, Inc.

The publisher's policy is to use permanent paper from mills that operate a sustainable forestry policy, and which has been manufactured from pulp processed using acid-free and elementary chlorine-free practices. Furthermore, the publisher ensures that the text paper and cover board used have met acceptable environmental accreditation standards.

For further information on
Blackwell Publishing, visit our website:
www.blackwellpublishing.com

Contents

Preface

No doubt, some wars have been fought for the sake of justice and peace. But regardless of idealistic aims and even occasional just outcomes, wars *always* cause fear, suffering, and destruction. War is that human activity which, in the words of Augustine, brings the most sorrow to our minds and makes us confess that we are indeed miserable creatures. Augustine simultaneously insisted, however, that adherence to sound moral norms – on the part of rulers as well as ordinary soldiers – can do much to lessen the worst ills of war.

It is easy to be skeptical of the body of literature claiming to clarify an ethical stance toward war. After all, most traditional narratives of war portray glorious displays of battlefield bravery. Less frequently do we find nuanced accounts of the hardships of the soldiers who fought in those battles, or of the civilians who were made to suffer the consequences. Admittedly, writings on war – journalistic, literary, and philosophical – have changed significantly over the last 150 to 200 years, at least since the Crimean war (1854–6), with an increasing number of critical accounts, and an enhanced sensitivity to the concrete sufferings of individual human beings. Historically, however, it is undeniable that the ideas of honor, glory, and moral superiority have overshadowed the innumerable wrongs and injustices caused by wars.

Still – notwithstanding the seemingly insensitive or even callous view of war cultivated in earlier times – a rich body of literature has nevertheless emerged over the past two and a half millennia on the moral challenges posed by violent conflict. A long line of serious thinkers have persuasively argued that the hardships of war are of a kind that compels us to reflect on them as a *moral problem*, even if wars can also bring glory or be politically expedient. This varied history of moral reflection on war has indeed also exerted considerable influence on political decision-making and military practice. Modern international law of war, for instance, would be unthinkable without it.

The basic impetus for the thinkers who have reflected on the ethics of war can be summed up thus: since wars arise in large measure by human volition, we can be expected to exercise at least some measure of control with respect both to their inception and to the way in which they are fought. This being the case, we find ourselves confronted with four fundamental questions:

- Can human beings ever take part in war without seriously violating our moral obligations or destroying our moral character?
- When and under what conditions can war be rightly initiated?
- How can war be fought so that our most basic moral standards are not violated?
- What should be done to ensure a lasting peace once the hostilities are over?

Philosophers, theologians, jurists, political theorists, historians, and military strategists have been grappling with questions such as these for well over two thousand years. The largest body of writings on the ethics of war has appeared in the West, under the combined influence of Greek and Roman humanism, Christianity, and, more recently, secular conceptions of sovereignty, democracy, and political rights. Given the rich diversity of these writings, as well as the many common points of reference shared by the authors in this tradition, we have thought it best to limit the scope of this book to this Western framework, lest we spread our attention too widely and thinly. This is not to say that non-Western cultures have produced little in the way of ethical reflection on war. On the contrary, important contributions may also be found within Middle Eastern and Asian cultures. In recent years scholars have carried out serious research on the ethics of war in, *inter alia*, Islam, Taoism, and Buddhism.[1] We can only hope that our work here will complement theirs in a useful way, and that future collections will gather texts from non-Western traditions in much the same way we have done here.

We believe that this collection will prove useful to many students, teachers, and researchers. For years, lecturers across a number of fields – military studies, political science, law, philosophy, and theology – have had to struggle to find the relevant texts when teaching on the moral problems of war. Many have been forced to copy pages from numerous scattered and often hard-to-find sources, or simply to fall back on a relatively small number of canonical texts, in the hope that these will suffice. Likewise, scholars doing historical or systematic research on the ethics and laws of war could attest that a considerable number of key texts remained untranslated into English, or, in some cases, were difficult to find even in the original Latin. The chief purpose of the present volume has been to remedy this situation by collecting under a single cover the most important and influential texts on the ethics of war.

A few terminological and philosophical reflections are in order. Most readers will be familiar with the expression "just war." It comes from the Latin *iustum bellum*, which has been used since Roman times to signify the kind of war that

---

[1]   See, for instance, Torkel Brekke (ed.), *The Ethics of War in Asian Civilizations* (London: Routledge, 2006).

may be deemed morally permissible. Writers who work from this standpoint – the just war tradition – make a conscious attempt to formulate what ethical criteria must be met if a war is to be termed "just."

However, the parameters of the just war tradition are in fact quite broad; this tradition encompasses thinkers who wrote under often varied circumstances, across different centuries; while they often built on their predecessors' ideas, they could also be opposed to each other in both substance and style. Thus, as our selections show, we must not think of "just war" as one static idea or set of criteria, but rather as a living tradition in constant development.

Furthermore, not all the thinkers represented in this volume fall under the "just war" rubric. While we have not attempted to provide full coverage of, for instance, the realist or pacifist traditions – that must be reserved for another project – we have offered a representative sampling of texts from alternative approaches.

Most obvious are those who tend toward pacifism (such as Erasmus and Bertrand Russell) or those who write from – or about – a realist or "realpolitik" point of view (e.g. Thucydides, Machiavelli, and Hobbes). These authors place themselves outside of what we would normally call "the ethics of war," inasmuch as they typically deny that there can be such a thing. Yet we have included them in this volume because the reader should be aware of their existence as important standpoints against which the "just war" view must always contend and be compared.

There are, however, two other standpoints that clearly fall within the ethics of war, yet have defining characteristics that set them apart from the just war tradition. One is the "regular war"[2] view – represented by, among others, Raphaël Fulgosius and Alberico Gentili – for whom the idea of "just cause" is held not to be a decisive factor when judging war ethically. In line with what would later be termed "raison d'état," these thinkers argued that every sovereign political unit has an inherent right to make use of violent force when such a resort is deemed necessary. Yet, in continuity with later developments in international law, they maintained that once war is under way there are norms that should be upheld by *both* sides. War was thereby conceptualized as a kind of contest between equal parties who should both (or all) be held to certain standards of right conduct, and to whom the same set of privileges would apply. Only in the eighteenth century, with thinkers such as Wolff and Vattel (although their writings were to a certain extent prefigured by Grotius, writing in the century before), were attempts made to coordinate the *just war* and *regular war* views into a systematic whole. In the preceding centuries, the two often coexisted – sometimes within one and the same author, as in the writings of Christine de Pizan – without an express recognition of their basic difference.

---

[2] On the notion of "regular war," see Peter Haggenmacher, "Just War and Regular War in Sixteenth-Century Spanish Doctrine," *International Revue of the Red Cross*, 290 (September–October 1992), pp. 434–45.

Secondly, there is also the tradition which goes under the name of "perpetual peace," represented most famously by Dante Alighieri in the fourteenth century and Immanuel Kant in the late eighteenth. Perpetual peace thinkers typically hold that the just war view is at once too optimistic in thinking that war can effectively be regulated by moral norms and values, and too pessimistic in presupposing that war is an inexpugnable part of the human condition. Instead, they advocate a new set of political structures (notably an international body to adjudicate disputes between states), which, if effectively implemented, will conduce to rendering war obsolete.

Finally, the reader should note that this is not a book on the contemporary *law of armed conflict*, about which several excellent anthologies have already been published.[3] While the thinkers represented in this volume have influenced – sometimes directly but more often indirectly – the emergence of positive norms such as we find in the Hague Rules of Land Warfare and Geneva Conventions, the kind of argumentation represented herein is of a different nature than what may be found in the current discourse on international law. This is not to say, however, that legal perspectives are absent from this volume. In fact, quite a few of the texts from the medieval and early modern periods were written by lawyers (e.g. Gratian, Raymond of Peñafort, Innocent IV, Bartolus, Gentili, and Grotius) who made important contributions to the development of legal thinking about war. It remains true, nevertheless, that, unlike their modern counterparts, these legal theorists did not presuppose a sharp line of division between law and ethics. Most often they may be found blending the two orders of discourse; and for this reason we have seen fit to include them in the present volume.

A note on the chapters: we have furnished each of these with a commentary. Sometimes this is limited to an introduction that offers the reader essential information on the historical and philosophical context for the text in question; at other times we provide a running commentary that is interspersed between the different selections. In either case, our aim has been to place the selections in their proper perspective and to suggest some ways of reading the texts. On occasions where a given text has been subject to an interpretative dispute, we have usually refrained from taking sides in the argument – that must be left to the reader.

We have excerpted from well-respected translations and editions of the texts in question. We have also commissioned some translations especially for this volume,[4] thus making a number of important Latin texts available in English for the first time. In cases where we have excerpted from long and complex works, discerning what to include, in light of rather strict space constraints, has been a very challenging

---

[3] For instance, Adam Roberts and Richard Guelff (eds.), *Documents on the Laws of War*, 3rd edn. (Oxford: Oxford University Press, 2000).

[4] Chapters 10 (Gratian and the Decretists), 12 (Raymond of Peñafort and William of Rennes), 13 (Innocent IV), 14 (Alexander of Hales), 15 (Hostiensis), 18 (Bartolus of Saxoferrato), 20 (Raphaël Fulgosius), 22 (Cajetan), and 28 (Luis de Molina).

task. While delicate choices were unavoidable, we have sought, for each chapter of this book, to assemble a set of selections that offer a balanced understanding of what each author stood for and how each went about formulating his or her respective stance. We hope that you, the reader, will find some merit in our efforts.

Editors' Note

In assembling these texts our goal has been to track each author's main line of argument on issues of war and peace. In some cases this has involved reproducing a single block of continuous text. In other cases, this result has been achieved by drawing together texts from several different works or, on occasion, by cutting and pasting many passages from a single work of much larger scope. Omissions within a text are marked by ellipses, except as regards author and translator footnotes, which have generally not been retained in this anthology. We have taken care to reproduce these texts exactly as they stand in the source (which in each instance is indicated at the start of the reading), although for purposes of continuity from chapter to chapter we have occasionally modified spelling, formatting, and abbreviations. Likewise, some of the translations have been modified. This has especially been the case with older translations of Latin works, which, in the cases indicated, have been amended in the light of recent scholarship, as well as to render key terms consistent from one chapter to the next.

There will inevitably be some disagreement about which texts should have been included in this anthology. In view of possible future printings, we, the editors, would greatly appreciate if you, our readers, would convey to us your reactions and any recommendations for inclusion or deletion.

Acknowledgments

A large volume of this kind would not have been possible without the active support we have received from many quarters.

Preparation of this volume has depended heavily on the generosity of our funders, the Earhart Foundation, the Research Council of Norway, and the Norwegian Defense Ministry. We have also benefited greatly from the infrastructure and collegiality afforded to us by the International Peace Research Institute, Oslo (PRIO), and the Ethics Program at the University of Oslo.

PRIO's head librarian, Odvar Leine, was extremely diligent in locating the many texts needed for this anthology. Copying all of the anthology's texts and scanning them into electronic format required many hours of hard work by our research assistants, Tor Rikard Evensen, Kristoffer Lidén, and Tonje Paulsen. In addition, we have received much valuable advice from PRIO's language editor, John Carville.

Identifying the relevant sources was facilitated by valuable suggestions from Martin Cook, Dieter Janssen, Kristoffer Lidén, Jean-Christophe Merle, Delphine Thivet, and several anonymous reviewers.

The logistics of bringing this volume to press has been greatly aided by the cheerful and able assistance of our colleagues at Blackwell: Jeff Dean, Danielle Descoteaux, Simon Eckley, and Jenny Phillips. Likewise, we gratefully acknowledge the diligent efforts of our copy-editors, Pandora Kerr Frost and Valery Rose, who, in the face of a very tight production schedule, succeeded in bringing order to a large and complex manuscript.

With the exception of the newly translated material, all of the selections in this volume have been taken from previously published sources. Every effort has been made to secure the necessary permissions. We appreciate the copyright holders' willingness to allow these texts to appear in the present volume. A special thanks is due to the Clarendon Press (Oxford), which published the monumental series "The Classics of International Law," from which many of our Latin translations are taken.

This volume would have been much impoverished had it not been for the dedication and skill of our two translators, Robert Andrews and Peter Haggenmacher, who were aided in their work by Gerard Etzkorn.

Peter Haggenmacher, Professor of International Law at the Graduate Institute of International Studies, Geneva, must be singled out for his many contributions to this undertaking. His writings on the history of normative thinking about war have served as an inestimable guide in the preparation of the present volume; he provided us with photocopies of numerous hard-to-find Latin texts, which later served as a basis for the translations that followed; he offered much sound advice on the individual chapters; and in one case (chapter 10 on Gratian and the Decretists) he painstakingly assembled the selections and contributed much of the introduction.

To all of the above, we, the editors, express our heartfelt thanks.

The editors and publisher gratefully acknowledge the permission granted to reproduce the copyright material in this book:

Chapter 1: Thucydides, "The Peloponnesian War," pp. 40–1, 43–5, 176–9, 180–3, 350–1, 352–6, from Robert B. Strassler (ed.), *The Landmark Thucydides*, trans. Richard Crawley (New York: Touchstone, 1998).

Chapter 2: Plato, "Alcibiades," pp. 180–3, and "Laches," pp. 256–7, from Thomas L. Pangle (ed.), *The Roots of Political Philosophy: Ten Forgotten Socratic Dialogues* (Ithaca, NY: Cornell University Press, 1987). © 1987 by Cornell University. Reprinted by permission of the publisher, Cornell University Press.

Plato, "The Republic," pp. 50, 95, 150–1, from *The Republic of Plato*, trans. Allan Bloom (New York: Basic Books, 1968); © 1968 by Allan Bloom.

Plato, "Laws," pp. 7, 10, 358, from *The Laws of Plato*, trans. Thomas L. Pangle (Chicago: University of Chicago Press, 1980). © 1980 by Basic Books, Inc., University of Chicago Press edition 1988.

Chapter 3: Aristotle, "Nicomachean Ethics," pp. 1760–4, 1790–1; "Politics," pp. 1991–2, 1994, 2017, 2102–3, 2111–12, 2115–17, 2085; "Rhetoric," p. 2162, from Jonathan Barnes (ed.), *The Complete Works of Aristotle: The Revised Oxford Translation*, Bollingen Series LXXI, vol. 2 (Princeton, NJ: Princeton University Press, 1984). © 1984 by The Jowett Copyright Trustees. Reprinted by permission of Princeton University Press.

Chapter 4: Dionysius of Halicarnassus, pp. 521, 523, 525, 527, from *The Roman Antiquities of Dionysius of Halicarnassus*, vol. 1, Loeb Classical Library vol. 319 (Cambridge, MA: Harvard University Press, 1937). © 1937 by the President and Fellows of Harvard College. Reprinted by permission of the publishers and the Trustees of the Loeb Classical Library. The Loeb Classical Library® is a registered trademark of the President and Fellows of Harvard College.

Chapter 5: Cicero, pp. 14–19, 21–2, 25–8, 29–32, 108–11, from M. T. Griffin and E. M. Atkins (eds.), *On Duties* (Cambridge: Cambridge University Press, 1991). © 1991 by Cambridge University Press. Reprinted by permission of the publisher.

Chapter 6: Early Church Fathers, pp. 34–5, 41–2, 43–4, 54–5, 59, 62–3, 67–8, 98, 99, 101–2, 103, 109, from Louis J. Swift (ed.), *The Early Fathers on War and Military Service* (Wilmington, DE: Michael Glazier, 1983). © 1983 by Louis J. Swift. Reprinted by permission of the author.

Early Church Fathers, pp. 23–4, 82, from Philip Schaff and Henry Wace (eds.), *A Select Library of Nicene and Post-Nicene Fathers of the Christian Church*, Second Series, vol. 10 (Grand Rapids, MI: William B. Eerdmans, [1896] 1955). © 1955 by William B. Eerdmans.

Chapter 7: Augustine, pp. 32, 108, 112–13, 127–8, 149–50, 152–3, 213–15, 216–17, 219–20, 221–2, 222–3, 225–6, 231–2, 234–5, 238–9, 245, 246, 247, from Ernest L. Fortin and Douglas Kries (eds.), *Augustine: Political Writings* (Indianapolis: Hackett, 1994). © 1994 by Hackett Publishing Company, Inc. Reprinted by permission of the publisher. All rights reserved.

Augustine, pp. 115, 118, 122, 135, 138, 155, from Louis J. Swift (ed.), *The Early Fathers on War and Military Service* (Wilmington, DE: Michael Glazier, 1983). © 1983 by Michael Glazier, Inc.

Augustine, pp. 10, 12–13, from *The City of God*, trans. Henry Bettenson (London: Penguin, 1984). © 1984 by Penguin.

Augustine, "Letter 185, to Boniface," pp. 641, 642, from Philip Schaff (ed.), *A Select Library of the Nicene and Post-Nicene Fathers of the Christian Church*, Second Series, vol. 4 (Grand Rapids, MI: William B. Eerdmans, [1887] 1956). © 1956 by William B. Eerdmans.

Chapter 8: Medieval Peace Movements, pp. 19–21, from R. G. D. Laffan (ed.), *Select Documents of European History, 800–1492* (New York: Henry Holt, 1929); reproduced in Udo Heyn, *Peacemaking in Medieval Europe: A Historical and Bibliographical Guide* (Claremont, CA: Regina Books, 1997).

Medieval Peace Movements, pp. 195–213, from H. J. Schroeder (ed.), *Disciplinary Decrees of the General Councils: Text, Translation and Commentary* (St. Louis: B. Herder, 1937); reproduced online at: www.fordham.edu/halsall/basis/lateran2.html.

Chapter 9: The Crusades, pp. 54–6, 59–61, 71–2, from R. G. D. Laffan (ed.), *Select Documents of European History*, vol. I: *800–1492* (New York: Henry Holt, 1929).

Chapter 10: Gratian and the Decretists, *Decretum*, Leipzig: Tauchnitz (1879); *Decretum Divi Gratiani . . . una cum glossis & thematibus prudentum, & doctorum suffragio combrobatis* (Lyon, 1554). Translation © 2006 by Blackwell Publishing Ltd.

Chapter 11: John of Salisbury, pp. 173–4, 180–1, lxxiii–lxxiv, 335–6, 350, 351–2, 356–7, 368–9, 372–3, from John Dickinson (ed.), *Policraticus: The Statesman's Book of John of Salisbury* (New York: Russell and Russell, [1927] 1963). © 1927 by Alfred A. Knopf, Inc.; © 1955 by Lindsay Rogers. Reissue © 1963 by Russell & Russell, Inc.

Chapter 12: Raymond of Peñafort and William of Rennes, pp. 184–8 from Raymundus de Pennafort, *Summa de poenitentia, et matrimonio, cum glossis Ioannis de Friburgo* [= William of Rennes], Rome, 1603. Translation © 2006 by Blackwell Publishing Ltd.

Chapter 13: Innocent IV, *Apparatus in quinque libros Decretalium*, Lyon, 1535. Translation © 2006 by Blackwell Publishing Ltd.

Chapter 14: Alexander of Hales, *Summa theologica seu sic ab origine dicta* "Summa fratris Alexandri," vol. 4, pp. 683–6 (Florence: Quaracchi, 1948). Translation © 2006 by Blackwell Publishing Ltd.

Chapter 15: Hostiensis, *Summa aurea*, Venice, 1574. Translation © 2006 by Blackwell Publishing Ltd.

Chapter 16: Thomas Aquinas, pp. 1212–13, 1308–10, 1353–60, 1402–3, 1465–6, 1704, 1988–9 from *Summa theologica*, trans. Fathers of the English Dominican Province, revised (available online at http://www.ccel.org/a/aquinas/summa/home.html). Benziger Brothers, 1920, reissued by Benziger, 1948, reprinted by Christian Classics 1981.

Thomas Aquinas, *Scripta super libros sententiarum, II*, pp. 72, 72–4, 74–5, from R. W. Dyson (ed.), *St Thomas Aquinas: Political Writings* (Cambridge: Cambridge University Press, 2002). © 2002 by Cambridge University Press.

Thomas Aquinas, pp. 56–61, from *On the Governance of Rulers* [*De Regimine Principum*], trans. Gerald B. Phelan (London and New York: Pontifical Institute of Medieval Studies, published by Sheed and Ward, 1938). © 1936, 1948 by the Pontifical Institute of Medieval Studies, Toronto. Reprinted by permission of the publisher.

Chapter 17: Dante Alighieri, pp. 46–9, 51, 53, 55, 57, 59, 61, 63, 83, 85 from *Dante's "Monarchia,"* trans. Richard Kay (Toronto: Pontifical Institute of Medieval Studies, 1998). © 1998 by the Pontifical Institute of Medieval Studies, Toronto. Reprinted by permission.

Chapter 18: Bartolus of Saxoferrato, *Secunda super Digesto novo* (Lyon, 1533). Translation © 2006 by Blackwell Publishing Ltd.

Chapter 19: Christine de Pizan, pp. 14–19, 24–5, 58–60, 152–3, 161–6, 169–72, 176–8, 180–1, 152–3, 161–6, 169–72, 176–8, 180–1, 190 from Charity Cannon Willard (ed.), *The Book of Deeds of Arms and of Chivalry* (University Park: Pennsylvania State University Press, 1999). © 1999 by The Pennsylvania State University. Reprinted by permission of Pennsylvania State University Press.

Christine de Pizan, pp. 239–40, from Renate Blumenfeld-Kosinski (trans.), *The Selected Writings of Christine de Pizan* (New York: W. W. Norton, 1997). © 1997 by W. W. Norton & Company. Reprinted by permission of the publisher.

Chapter 20: Raphaël Fulgosius, *In primam Pandectarum partem Commentaria* (Lyon, 1554). Translation © 2006 by Blackwell Publishing Ltd.

Chapter 21: Erasmus of Rotterdam, pp. 199–288, from Neil M. Cheshire and Michael J. Heath (trans.), *The Collected Works of Erasmus*, vol. 27 (Toronto: University of Toronto Press, 1986). © 1986 by University of Toronto Press. Reprinted by permission of the publisher.

Chapter 22: Cajetan, *Sancti Thomae Aquinatis Doctoris Angelici Opera Omnia iussu impensaque Leonis XIII, cum commentariis Thomae de Vio Caietani Ordinis Praedicatorum*, volume 8 (Rome: Editori di San Tommaso, 1895). Translation © 2006 by Blackwell Publishing Ltd.

Cajetan, *Summula Caietani* (Lyon: A. de Harsy, 1581). Translation © 2006 by Blackwell Publishing Ltd.

Chapter 23: Niccolò Machiavelli, pp. 14–15, 20–1, 35, 37–8, 61, 103, from *The Prince*, trans. Harvey C. Mansfield, Jr. (Chicago: University of Chicago Press, 1985). © 1985 by The University of Chicago. Reprinted by permission of University of Chicago Press.

Niccolò Machiavelli, pp. 459–60, 515, from Bernard Crick (ed.), *Niccolò Machiavelli: The Discourses* (London: Penguin, 1970). © 1970 by Penguin.

Chapter 24: Thomas More, pp. 105–15 from *Utopia*, trans. Clarence H. Miller (New Haven and London: Yale University Press, 2001). © 2001 by Yale University Press. Reprinted by permission of the publisher.

Chapter 25: Martin Luther, pp. 124–6, from Walther I. Brandt (ed.), *Luther's Works*, vol. 45: *The Christian in Society, II* (Philadelphia: Fortress Press, 1962). © 1962 by Fortress Press. Reprinted by permission of Augsberg Fortress.

Martin Luther, pp. 94–6, 105, 121, 123, 125–7, 129–31, 164–6, from Robert C. Schulz (ed.), *Luther's Works*, vol. 46: *The Christian in Society, III* (Philadelphia: Fortress Press, 1967). © 1967 by Fortress Press. Reprinted by permission of Augsberg Fortress.

John Calvin, pp. 1499–1501 from John T. McNeill (ed.), *Calvin: Institutes of the Christian Religion*, vol. 2 (Philadelphia: The Westminster Press, 1960). © 1960 by W. L. Jenkins. Reprinted by permission of Westminster John Knox Press.

Chapter 26: Radical reformers: pp. 52–5, 58–9, 118–21, 176–7, 178, from Michael G. Baylor (ed. and trans.), *The Radical Reformation* (Cambridge: Cambridge University Press, 1991). © 1991 by Cambridge University Press. Reprinted by permission of the publisher.

John Knox, pp. 84–5, 110–11, from Roger A. Mason (ed.), *On Rebellion* (Cambridge: Cambridge University Press, 1994). © 1994 by Cambridge University Press. Reprinted by permission of the publisher.

Chapter 27: Francisco de Vitoria, "On the American Indians," pp. 233–4, 237–8, 250–2, 264–5, 269–75, 277–92, and "On the Law of War," pp. 295–327, from Anthony Pagden and Jeremy Lawrance (eds.), *Francisco de Vitoria: Political Writings* (Cambridge: Cambridge University Press, 1991). © 1991 by Cambridge University Press. Reprinted by permission of the publisher.

Chapter 28: Luis de Molina, pp. 227–9 from *De iustitia et iure opera omnia* (Geneva: M. M. Bousquet, 1733). © 2006 by Blackwell Publishing Ltd.

Chapter 29: Francisco Suárez, pp. 800–9, 815–41, 843–55, from *Selections from Three Works of Francisco Suárez, SJ*, trans. Gwladys L. Williams, The Classics of International Law, vol. 2 (Oxford: The Clarendon Press, 1944). © 1944 by The Carnegie Endowment for International Peace. Reprinted by permission of the publisher.

Chapter 30: Alberico Gentili, pp. 12–13, 15, 31–3, 38–9, 55–7, 61–2, 64–6, from *De iure belli libri tres*, trans. John C. Rolfe, The Classics of International Law, vol. 2 (Oxford: The Clarendon Press, 1933). © 1933 by The Carnegie Endowment for International Peace. Reprinted by permission of the publisher.

Chapter 31: Johannes Althusius, pp. 88–9, 186–9, 195–7, 199, from Frederick S. Carney (ed. and trans.), *Politica* (Indianapolis: Liberty Fund, 1995). © 1964 by Frederick S. Carney. © 1995 by Liberty Fund, Inc. Reprinted by permission of the publisher.

Chapter 32: Hugo Grotius, pp. 9–13, 15–22, 33–4, 51–4, 91–2, 97–103, 138–9, 164–6, 169–74, 176, 179, 184–5, 462, 502–8, 546–52, 556–7, 559–60, 565–8, 574–6, 578–93, 595, 599–601, 630–3, 639, 641–50, 656–7, 716, 718–19, 722–3, 729–44, 746–8, 751–2, 804, 814, 817, 860–2, from *De iure belli ac pacis*, trans. Francis W. Kelsey, The Classics of International Law, vol. 2 (Oxford: The Clarendon Press, 1925).

Chapter 33: Thomas Hobbes, pp. 21–2, 23–4, 30–1, from Richard Tuck and Michael Silverthorne (eds.), *On the Citizen* (Cambridge: Cambridge University Press, 1998). Editorial matter and translation © 1998 by Cambridge University Press. Reprinted by permision of the publisher.

    Thomas Hobbes, pp. 89–91, 484–6, from Richard Tuck (ed.), *Leviathan* (Cambridge: Cambridge University Press, 1991).

    Thomas Hobbes, pp. 103–4, from J. C. A. Gaskin (ed.), *The Elements of Law Natural and Politic*, Part I: *Human Nature*, and Part II: *De Corpore Politico* (Oxford: Oxford University Press, 1994).

Chapter 34: Baruch Spinoza, pp. 698–700, from Michael Morgan (ed.), *Spinoza: Complete Works* (Indianapolis: Hackett, 2002). © 2002 by Hackett Publishing Company, Inc. Reprinted by permission of the publisher. All rights reserved.

Chapter 35: Samuel Pufendorf, pp. 118, 119, 168–72, from James Tully (ed.), *On the Duty of Man and Citizen According to Natural Law* (Cambridge: Cambridge University Press, 1991). © 1991 by Cambridge University Press. Reprinted by permission of the publisher.

Samuel Pufendorf, pp. 1298–9, 1301, from *De jure naturae et gentium libri octo*, vol. 2, trans. C. H. Oldfather and W. A. Oldfather (Oxford: The Clarendon Press,1934). © 1934 by The Clarendon Press.

Chapter 36: John Locke, pp. 118–19, 124, 125–7, 206–11, 213, 232–3, from *Two Treatises of Government* (London: Everyman's Library, 1924).

Chapter 37: Christian von Wolff, pp. 295–6, 325, 326, 327, 328, 403, 408, 409–10, 411–12, 454–5, from *Ius gentium methodo scientifica pertractatum*, trans. Joseph H. Drake, The Classics of International Law, vol. 2 (Oxford: The Clarendon Press, 1934). © 1934 by The Carnegie Endowment for International Peace. Reprinted by permission of the publisher.

Chapter 38: Montesquieu, pp. 7–8, 138–40, 224–5, from Anne M. Cohler, Basia Carolyn Miller and Harold Samuel Stone (ed. and trans.), *The Spirit of the Laws* (Cambridge: Cambridge University Press, 1989). © 1989 by Cambridge University Press. Reprinted by permission of the publisher.

Chapter 39: Jean-Jacques Rousseau, pp. 185, 186–7, 187–8, 188–9, 190, 191, 193, 194, 194–6, 197, 200–1, 203–4, 205, 206–7, 208, 208–9, 211–13, 213–15, 219–20, 222–3, 224–5, 227, 228–9, from Grace G. Roosevelt, *Reading Rousseau in the Nuclear Age* (Philadelphia, PA: Temple University Press, 1990). © 1990 by Temple University. Reprinted by permission of Temple University Press. All rights reserved.

Chapter 40: Emer de Vattel, pp. 6–7, 13–14, 235–6, 243, 248–53, 279–80, 293–4, 304–6, 336–40, from *The Law of Nations or the Principles of Natural Law, Applied to the Conduct and to the Affairs of Nations and of Sovereigns*, trans. Charles G. Fenwick, The Classics of International Law, vol. 3 (Washington, CD: Carnegie Institution, 1916).

Chapter 41: Immanuel Kant, pp. 96–7, 98, 99–100, 102, 103–5, 105–8, 112–13, 114, 116, 116–19, 121–5, 169–70, from Hans Reiss (ed.), *Kant: Political Writings*, 2nd edn., trans. H. B. Nisbet (Cambridge: Cambridge University Press, 1991). © 1991 by Cambridge University Press. Reprinted by permission of the publisher.

Chapter 42: G. W. F. Hegel, pp. 208, 209–10, 212–15, 215, 217, 218–19, 295–7, from *Hegel's Philosophy of Right*, trans. T. M. Knox (Oxford: Clarendon Press, 1967). © 1967 by Oxford University Press. Reprinted by permission of the publisher.

Chapter 43: Carl von Clausewitz, pp. 75–6, 86–7, 101–2, 102–4, 105–6, 107–8, from Michael Howard and Peter Paret (ed. and trans.), *On War* (Princeton, NJ: Princeton University Press, 1976). © 1976 by Princeton University Press; renewed 2004 by Princeton University Press. Reprinted by permission of Princeton University Press.

Chapter 44: Daniel Webster, "From a letter of American Secretary of State Daniel Webster to British Ambassador Henry Fox, dated 24 April, 1841," pp. 1132–3, and 1137–8, from *British and Foreign State Papers, 1840–1841*, vol. XXIX (London: James Ridgway and Sons, 1857).

Chapter 45: Francis Lieber, "Instructions for the Government of Armies of the United States in the Field," promulgated as General Orders No. 100 by President Lincoln, April 24, 1863. Available at: http://www.yale.edu/lawweb/avalon/lieber.htm; website accessed May 2004.
    Elihu Root, pp. 90, 91, 93, 95, 144, from *Addresses on International Subjects*, ed. Robert Bacon and James Brown Scott (Freeport: Books for Libraries Press, [1916] 1969).

Chapter 46: John Stuart Mill, pp. 158–9, 166–77, 196–7, 202–5, from *Dissertations and Discussions: Political, Philosophical, and Historical*, vol. 3 (London: Longman, Green, Reader and Dyer, 1867).

Chapter 47: Karl Marx and Friedrich Engels, pp. 94–5, from C. J. Arthur (ed.), *The German Ideology* (London: Lawrence & Wishart, 1970). © 1970 by Lawrence & Wishart).
    Karl Marx and Friedrich Engels, pp. 40, 44–5, 638, from *Selected Works*, vol. 1 (Moscow: Foreign Languages Publishing House, 1955). © 1955 by Foreign Languages Publishing House.
    Friedrich Engels, pp. 184, 189, from *Herr Eugen Dühring's Revolution in Science (Anti-Dühring)*, trans. Emile Burns (New York: International Publishers, 1939). © 1939 by International Publishers.

Chapter 48: Woodrow Wilson, pp. 302–5, 307–8, 317, 322–3, 326, 329–30, from August Heckscher (ed.), *The Politics of Woodrow Wilson* (New York: Harper & Brothers, 1956).

Chapter 49: Bertrand Russell, pp. 29–32 (pp. 18–23 in second edition, 2001), from *Common Sense and Nuclear Warfare* (London: George Allen & Unwin; 2nd edn. Routledge, 1959, 2001). © 2001 by The Bertrand Russell Peace Foundation Ltd. Reprinted by permission of Routledge, an imprint of the Taylor & Francis Group.

Chapter 50: Hans Kelsen, pp. 330–4, 336–9, 341, from *General Theory of Law and State*, trans. Anders Wedberg (Cambridge, MA: Harvard University Press, 1945). ©

1945 by Hans Kelsen. Reprinted by permission of The Hans Kelsen-Institut, Vienna, Austria.

Chapter 51: Paul Ramsey, pp. 215, 216, 221–2, 224, 236–7, 242–3, 249–58, from *The Just War: Force and Political Responsibility* (Lanham, MD: University Press of America, 1983; first published New York: Charles Scribner & Sons, 1968). © 1968, 1983 by Paul Ramsey. "The Limits of Nuclear War" first appeared in a pamphlet published by The Council on Religion and International Affairs, 170 East 64th Street, New York, 1965. Reprinted by permission of the Carnegie Council on Ethics and International Affairs.

Chapter 52: G. E. M. Anscombe, pp. 53, 54–5, 57–8, 63, 66–7, 74–5, 78–9, from *Collected Philosophical Papers of G. E. M. Anscombe*, vol. 3: *Ethics, Religion and Politics* (Oxford: Basil Blackwell, 1981). "The Justice of the Present Law Examined" was first published as a pamphlet by G. E. M. Anscombe and Norman Daniel and published by the authors (Oxford, 1939); "Mr Truman's Degree" was first published as a pamphlet by G. E. M. Anscombe (Oxford, 1957); "War and Murder" first appeared in Walter Stein (ed.), *Nuclear Weapons: A Catholic Response* (London: New York, 1961).

Chapter 53: John Rawls, "Fifty Years after Hiroshima," pp. 565–72, from Samuel Freeman (ed.), *John Rawls: Collected Papers* (Cambridge, MA: Harvard University Press, 1999). © 1999 by the President and Fellows of Harvard College. Reprinted by permission of Harvard University Press.

Chapter 54: Michael Walzer, "Chapter 12," pp. 197–206, from *Just and Unjust Wars: A Moral Argument with Historical Illustrations*, 2nd edn. (New York: Basic Books, 1977, 2nd edn., 1992). © 1977 by Basic Books. Reprinted by permission of Basic Books, a member of Perseus Books, LLC.

Chapter 55: Thomas Nagel, "War and Massacre," pp. 123–44, from *Philosophy and Public Affairs* (Oxford: Basil Blackwell, 1972). © 1972 by Philosophy and Public Affairs. Reprinted by permission of Blackwell Publishing Ltd.

Chapter 56: James Turner Johnson, "Does Defense of Values by Force Remain a Moral Possibility?" pp. 3–4, 7–8, 10–11, from Lloyd J. Matthews and Dale E. Brown (eds.), *The Parameters of Military Ethics* (Washington, DC: Pergamon-Brassey's, 1989). © 1985 by Parameters. Originally published (under a slightly different title) in the Spring 1985 issue of *Parameters*. Reprinted by permission of the US Army War College.

James Turner Johnson, "Maintaining the Protection of Non-Combatants," pp. 444–7, from *Journal of Peace Research*, 37 (no. 4). © 2000 by International Peace Research Institute (Oslo) PRIO. Reprinted by permission of Sage Publications Ltd.

Chapter 57: National Conference of Catholic Bishops, pp. iii, 6–7, 28–34, 39, 46–51, 56, 59, from *The Challenge of Peace: God's Promise and Our Response*, A Pastoral Letter on War and Peace, May 3, 1983 (Washington, DC: Office of Publishing Services, United States Catholic Conference, 1983). Available online at http://www.osjspm.org/cst/cp.htm. © 1983 by The National Conference of Catholic Bishops. Reprinted by permission of USCCB Publishing.

National Conference of Catholic Bishops, pp. 452–4, from *The Harvest of Justice is Sown in Peace*, *Origins*, 23 (no. 26). Available online at: http://www.nccbuscc.org/sdwp/harvest.htm. © 1993 by The National Conference of Catholic Bishops.

Chapter 58: Kofi Annan, "Two Concepts of Sovereignty," pp. 49–50, from *The Economist*, 352, September 18, 1999. © 1999 by The Economist Newspaper Ltd, London. Reprinted by permission of *The Economist*.

Kofi Annan, the 1998 Ditchley Foundation Lecture: "Intervention." Available from http://www.un.org/News/Press/docs/1998/19980626.sgsg6613.r1.html. © 1998 by The United Nations. Reprinted by permission.

Part I

Ancient and Early Christian

1

Thucydides
(ca. 460–ca. 400 BC)

War and Power

You know as well as we do that right, as the world goes, is only in question between equals in power, while the strong do what they can and the weak suffer what they must.

The Athenians to the Melians, in *The Peloponnesian War*

The first author within the Western tradition to address seriously the relationship between ethics and war was the historian Thucydides. It may come as a surprise that we turn to a historian rather than a philosopher for the beginnings of the ethics of war. And, indeed, there is not much in Thucydides's work that systematically considers when and how it is right to wage war. Yet, Thucydides writes about the most famous armed contest of his time in a way that brings the moral questions about war to the fore, directly and indirectly. If we want to look for a work that starkly portrays the moral issues that confront us in warfare, we need look no further than this most renowned of the Greek historians of antiquity.

Given his stark portrayals of the brutality of war, with seemingly little or no moral evaluation, Thucydides has often been considered a political realist, not an idealist or "just war" thinker. However, his habit of giving us both sides of the story through opposing speeches, and his underlying lament about the futility of much of the fighting, conveys a very real sense of moral engagement.

The topic of Thucydides's monumental work is the Peloponnesian War, a military contest between Sparta and Athens, supported by their respective allies. Athens was the most successful and expansive of the Greek city-states, famous for its philosophy, literature, and urban culture. After helping to defeat the Persians in 479 BC, Athens took the leading role within the so-called Delian League. Initially, its strength and vitality were valued by the other cities of the League. However, by the 430s the power of Athens came to be viewed with suspicion, a defensive wall around Athens and its seaport Piraeus – a wall that would make the Athenians more immune to attack than the other cities – being one of several thorns in the eye. Sparta took the lead among a group of cities that aimed to forestall the expansive imperialism of the Athenians. They went to war in 431, in what was seen by the Spartans and their allies as a necessary, preventive strike.

While Thucydides rarely takes sides, his portrayals of the Athenians are especially vivid, showing many Athenian politicians and generals to be unbending realists: the powerful cannot help but fight wars in order to pursue their ambitions and conquer more territory. It is not as if the Athenians pause to consider whether it is morally rightful to expand their might. This is simply what powerful cities do. In that sense, many of Sparta's fears – and its reasons for going to war in the first place – are vindicated by Thucydides's text. Yet, this does not mean that there exists no room for choice, if we take seriously the way in which Thucydides describes the problems facing the actors. In reporting (or reconstructing) speeches and dialogues, we do come to see the moral dimension of the problems being presented, and we come to envision the different ways in which they could have been solved.

Let us start by looking at the war's initiation. In 432, the Spartans and their allies presented three grievances against Athens, all of which they believed were violations of a treaty the two parties had entered into 14 years earlier. One of these concerned the help Athens had given the oligarchic faction in the island of Corcyra against Corinth, a Spartan friend and ally. The Corinthians eagerly encouraged the Spartans to lead an attack against the Athenians in a classic statement of the idea of preventive war: even if we face no *imminent* danger to our own city-states from the enemy, they argued, this enemy has nevertheless shown us hostile intent, and his attitude and plans are such that an armed conflict on a large scale is ultimately inevitable. It is therefore best to act before it is too late, while the initiative is still on our side.

Ambassadors for the Athenians were also present at the meeting in Sparta where the Corinthians and Spartans debated their grievances. They reply in true Athenian fashion: justice has no part in this; the central issue is power, and Athens merely behaves like any powerful city would do. We first hear the Corinthians conclude their case, after having described the ever-present bellicosity of the Athenians:

From *The Peloponnesian War*, bk. 1, chaps. 71–2, 76, 78[1]

71 "Such is Athens, your antagonist. And yet, Spartans, you still delay, and fail to see that peace stays longest with those who are not more careful to use their power justly than to show their determination not to submit to injustice. On the contrary, your ideal of fair dealing is based on the principle

---

[1] From Richard Crawley's translation, revised and edited by Robert P. Strassler, in *The Landmark Thucydides* (New York: Touchstone, 1998), pp. 40–1, 43–5.

that if you do not injure others, you need not risk your own fortunes in preventing others from injuring you. Now you could scarcely have succeeded in such a policy even with a neighbor like yourselves; but in the present instance, as we have just shown, your habits are old-fashioned as compared with theirs. It is the law, as in the arts so in politics, that improvements ever prevail; and though fixed usages may be best for undisturbed communities, constant necessities of action must be accompanied by the constant improvement of methods. Thus it happens that the vast experience of Athens has carried her further than you on the path of innovation."

"Here, at least, let your procrastination end. For the present, assist your allies and Potidaea in particular, as you promised, by a speedy invasion of Attica, and do not sacrifice friends and kindred to their bitterest enemies, and drive the rest of us in despair to some other alliance. Such a step would not be condemned either by the gods who received our oaths, or by the men who witnessed them. The blame for a breach of a treaty cannot be laid on the people whom desertion compels to seek new relations, but on the power that fails to assist its confederate. But if only you will act, we will stand by you; it would be unnatural for us to change, and never should we meet with such a congenial ally. For these reasons choose the right course, and endeavor not to let the Peloponnesus under your supremacy degenerate from the prestige that it enjoyed under that of your ancestors."

72 Such were the words of the Corinthians. There happened to be Athenian envoys present at Sparta on other business. On hearing the speeches they thought themselves called upon to come before the Spartans. Their intention was not to offer a defense on any of the charges which the cities brought against them, but to show on a comprehensive view that it was not a matter to be hastily decided on, but one that demanded further consideration. There was also a wish to call attention to the great power of Athens, and to refresh the memory of the old and enlighten the ignorance of the young, from a notion that their words might have the effect of inducing them to prefer tranquillity to war. So they came to the Spartans and said that they too, if there was no objection, wished to speak to their assembly. They replied by inviting them to come forward. The Athenians advanced, and spoke as follows:

76 ". . . You, at all events, Spartans, have used your supremacy to settle the states in the Peloponnesus as is agreeable to you. And if at the period of which we were speaking [i.e. after the war with the Persians] you had persevered to the end of the matter, and had incurred hatred in your command, we are sure that you would have made yourselves just as galling to the allies, and would have been forced to choose between a strong government and danger to yourselves. It follows that it was not a very remarkable action, or contrary to the common practice of mankind, if we

did accept an empire that was offered to us, and refused to give it up under the pressure of three of the strongest motives, fear, honor, and interest. And it was not we who set the example, for it has always been the law that the weaker should be subject to the stronger. Besides, we believed ourselves to be worthy of our position, and so you thought us till now, when calculations of interest have made you take up the cry of justice – a consideration which no one ever yet brought forward to hinder his ambition when he had a chance of gaining anything by might. And praise is due to all who, if not so superior to human nature as to refuse dominion, yet respect justice more than their position compels them to."

"We imagine that our moderation would be best demonstrated by the conduct of who should be placed in our position; but even our equity has very unreasonably subjected us to condemnation instead of approval." . . .

78 ". . . It is a common mistake in going to war to begin at the wrong end, to act first, and wait for disaster to discuss the matter. But we are not yet by any means so misguided, nor, so far as we can see, are you; accordingly, while it is still open to us both to choose aright, we bid you not to dissolve the treaty, or to break your oaths, but to have our differences settled by arbitration according to our agreement. Or else we take the gods who heard the oaths to witness, and if you begin hostilities, whatever line of action you choose, we will endeavor to defend ourselves against you."

79 Such were the words of the Athenians. After the Spartans had heard the complaints of the allies against the Athenians, and the observations of the latter, they made all withdraw, and consulted by themselves on the question before them. The opinions of the majority all led to the same conclusion; the Athenians were open aggressors, and war must be declared at once.

In spite of calls for moderation from the Spartan king Archidamus, the decision is upheld and war is declared.

In what follows we reproduce speeches in which Thucydides portrays the stark moral choices that confront the various parties at war. First, he takes us to a debate in Athens concerning the city of Mytilene on the island of Lesbos. In 427, the Athenians had resolved to put to death all males of military age in the city, and to enslave the rest of the population, in order to punish the Mytilenians for their rebellion against Athenian rule. However, when some Athenians expressed second thoughts about the decision, another assembly was called and new speeches were made. Diodotus's speech in defense of the Mytilenians is of particular interest. He begs for clemency and moderation by appealing strictly to self-interest. We suspect that he could also have made a plea based on ethical considerations, but that he finds the appeal to self-interest much more effective in the political climate of the day.

From *The Peloponnesian War*, bk. 3, chaps. 36–42, 44–49[2]

36 ... The morrow brought repentance with it and reflection on the horrid cruelty of a decree which condemned a whole city to the fate merited only by the guilty. This was no sooner perceived by the Mytilenian ambassadors at Athens and their Athenian supporters than they moved the authorities to put the question again to the vote; which they the more easily consented to do, as they themselves plainly saw that most of the citizens wished someone to give them an opportunity for reconsidering the matter. An assembly was therefore at once called, and after much expression of opinion upon both sides, Cleon son of Cleaenetus, the same who had carried the former motion of putting the Mytilenians to death, the most violent man at Athens, and at that time by far the most powerful with The People, came forward again and spoke as follows:

> **37** "I have often before now been convinced that a democracy is incapable of empire, and never more so than by your present change of mind in the matter of Mytilene. Fears or plots being unknown to you in your daily relations with each other, you feel just the same with regard to your allies, and never reflect that the mistakes into which you may be led by listening to their appeals, or by giving way to your own compassion, are full of danger to yourselves, and bring you no thanks for your weakness from your allies; entirely forgetting that your empire is a despotism and your subjects disaffected conspirators, whose obedience is insured not by your suicidal concessions, but by the superiority given you by your own strength and not their loyalty. The most alarming feature in the case is the constant change of measures with which we appear to be threatened, and our seeming ignorance of the fact that bad laws which are never changed are better for a city than good ones that have no authority; that unlearned loyalty is more serviceable than quick-witted insubordination; and that ordinary men usually manage public affairs better than their more gifted fellows. The latter are always wanting to appear wiser than the laws, and to overrule every proposition brought forward, thinking that they cannot show their wit in more important matters, and by such behavior too often ruin their country; while those who mistrust their own cleverness are content to be less learned than the laws, and less able to pick holes in the speech of a good speaker; and being fair judges rather than rival athletes, generally conduct affairs successfully. These we ought to imitate, instead of being led on by cleverness and intellectual rivalry to advise the people against our real opinions."
>
> **38** "For myself, I adhere to my former opinion, and wonder at those who have proposed to reopen the case of the Mytilenians, and who are thus

[2] Ibid., pp. 176–9, 180–3.

causing a delay which is all in favor of the guilty, by making the sufferer proceed against the offender with the edge of his anger blunted; although where vengeance follows most closely upon the wrong, it best equals it and most amply requites it. I wonder also who will be the man who will maintain the contrary, and will pretend to show that the crimes of the Mytilenians are of service to us, and our misfortunes injurious to the allies. . . ."

39 "In order to keep you from this, I proceed to show that no one state has ever injured you as much as Mytilene. I can make allowance for those who revolt because they cannot bear our empire, or who have been forced to do so by the enemy. But for those who possessed an island with fortifications; who could fear our enemies only by sea, and there had their own force of triremes to protect them; who were independent and held in the highest honor by you – to act as these have done, this is not revolt – revolt implies oppression; it is deliberate and wanton aggression; an attempt to ruin us by siding with our bitterest enemies; a worse offense than a war undertaken on their own account in the acquisition of power. The fate of those of their neighbors who had already rebelled and had been subdued, was no lesson to them; their own prosperity could not dissuade them from affronting danger; but blindly confident in the future, and full of hopes beyond their power though not beyond their ambition, they declared war and made their decision to prefer might to right, their attack being determined not by provocation but by the moment which seemed propitious. The truth is that great good fortune coming suddenly and unexpectedly tends to make a people insolent: in most cases it is safer for mankind to have success in reason than out of reason; and it is easier for them, one may say, to stave off adversity than to preserve prosperity. Our mistake has been to distinguish the Mytilenians as we have done: had they been long ago treated like the rest, they never would have so far forgotten themselves, human nature being as surely made arrogant by consideration, as it is awed by firmness. Let them now therefore be punished as their crime requires, and do not, while you condemn the aristocracy, absolve the people. This is certain, that all attacked you without distinction, although they might have come over to us, and been now again in possession of their city. But no, they thought it safer to throw in their lot with the aristocracy and so joined their rebellion! Consider therefore! If you subject to the same punishment the ally who is forced to rebel by the enemy, and him who does so by his own free choice, which of them, think you, is there that will not rebel upon the slightest pretext; when the reward of success is freedom, and the penalty of failure nothing so very terrible? We meanwhile shall have to risk our money and our lives against one state after another; and if successful, shall receive a ruined city from which we can no longer draw the revenue upon which our strength depends; while if unsuccessful, we shall have an enemy the more upon our hands, and shall spend the time that might be employed in combating our existing foes in warring with our own allies."

40 "No hope, therefore, must be held out to the Mytilenians, that their rhetoric may inspire or money purchase the mercy due to human infirmity. Their offense was not involuntary, but of malice and deliberate; and mercy is only for unwilling offenders. I therefore now as before persist against your reversing your first decision, or giving way to the three failings most fatal to empire – pity, sentiment, and indulgence. Compassion is due to those who can reciprocate the feeling, not to those who will never pity us in return, but are our natural and necessary foes: the orators who charm us with sentiment may find other less important arenas for their talents, in the place of one where the city pays a heavy penalty for a momentary pleasure, themselves receiving fine acknowledgments for their fine phrases; while indulgence should be shown toward those who will be our friends in future, instead of toward men who will remain just what they were, and as much our enemies as before. . . ."

41 Such were the words of Cleon. After him Diodotus son of Eucrates, who had also in the previous assembly spoken most strongly against putting the Mytilenians to death, came forward and spoke as follows:

42 "I do not blame the persons who have reopened the case of the Mytilenians, nor do I approve the protests which we have heard against important questions being frequently debated. I think the two things most opposed to good counsel are haste and passion; haste usually goes hand in hand with folly, passion with coarseness and narrowness of mind. . . ."

44 ". . . I have not come forward either to oppose or to accuse in the matter of Mytilene; indeed, the question before us as sensible men is not their guilt, but our interests. Though I prove them ever so guilty, I shall not, therefore, advise their death, unless it be expedient; nor though they should have claims to indulgence, shall I recommend it, unless it be clearly for the good of the country. I consider that we are deliberating for the future more than for the present; and where Cleon is so positive as to the useful deterrent effects that will follow from making rebellion a capital offense, I who consider the interests of the future quite as much as he, as positively maintain the contrary. And I require you not to reject my useful considerations for his specious ones: his speech may have the attraction of seeming the more just in your present temper against Mytilene; but we are not in a court of justice, but in a political assembly; and the question is not justice, but how to make the Mytilenians useful to Athens."

45 "Now of course communities have enacted the penalty of death for many offenses far lighter than this: still hope leads men to venture; and no one ever yet put himself in peril without the inward conviction that he would succeed in his design. Again, was there ever [a] city rebelling that did not believe that it possessed either in itself or in its alliances resources adequate to the enterprise? All, states and individuals, are alike prone to err, and there is no law that will prevent them; or why should men have exhausted the list of punishments in search of enactments to protect them from evildoers? It is probable that in early times the penalties for the greatest offenses were less severe, and that, as these were disregarded, the penalty of death has been by degrees in most cases arrived at, which is itself disregarded in like manner. Either then some means of terror more terrible than this must be discovered, or it must be admitted that this restraint is useless; and that as long as poverty gives men the courage of necessity, or plenty fills them with the ambition which belongs to insolence and pride, and each of the other conditions of life remains subjugated to some fatal and master passion, so long will the impulse never be wanting to drive men into danger. Hope also and greed, the one leading and the other following, the one conceiving the attempt, the other suggesting the facility of succeeding, cause the widest ruin, and, although invisible agents, are far stronger than the dangers that are seen. Fortune, too, powerfully helps the delusion, and by the unexpected aid that she sometimes lends, tempts men to venture with inferior means; and this is especially the case with communities, because the stakes played for are the highest, freedom or empire, and, when all are acting together, each man irrationally magnifies his own capacity. In short, it is impossible to prevent, and only great simplicity can hope to prevent, human nature doing what it has once set its mind upon, by force of law or by any other deterrent force whatsoever."

46 "We must not, therefore, commit ourselves to a false policy through a belief in the efficacy of the punishment of death, or exclude rebels from the hope of repentance and an early atonement of their error. Consider a moment! At present, if a city that has already revolted perceive that it cannot succeed, it will come to terms while it is still able to refund expenses, and pay tribute afterwards. In the other case, what city think you would not prepare better than is now done, and hold out to the last against its besiegers, if it is all one whether it surrender late or soon? And how can it be otherwise than hurtful to us to be put to the expense of a siege, because surrender is out of the question; and if we take the city, to receive a ruined city from which we can no longer draw the revenue which forms our real strength against the enemy? We must not, therefore, sit as strict judges of the offenders to our own prejudice, but rather see how by moderate chastisements we may be enabled to benefit in future by the revenue-producing powers of our dependencies; and we must make up our minds to look for our protection not to legal terrors but to careful administration. At present we do exactly the opposite. When a free community, held in subjection by force, rises, as is only natural, and asserts its independence, it is no sooner reduced than we fancy ourselves obliged to punish it severely; although the right course with freemen is not to chastise them rigorously when they do rise, but rigorously to watch them before they rise, and to prevent their ever entertaining the idea, and, the insurrection suppressed, to make as few responsible for it as possible."

47 "Only consider what a blunder you would commit in doing as Cleon recommends. As things are at present, in all the cities The People is your friend, and either does not revolt with the oligarchy, or, if forced to do so, becomes at once the enemy of the insurgents; so that in the war with the hostile city you have the masses on your side. But if you butcher The People of Mytilene, who had nothing to do with the revolt, and who, as soon as they got arms, of their own motion surrendered the city, first you will commit the crime of killing your benefactors; and next you will play directly into the hands of the higher classes, who when they induce their cities to rise, will immediately have The People on their side, through your having announced in advance the same punishment for those who are guilty and for those who are not. On the contrary, even if they were guilty, you ought to seem not to notice it, in order to avoid alienating the only class still friendly to us. In short, I consider it far more useful for the preservation of our empire to put up with injustice voluntarily, than to put to death, however justly, those whom it is our interest to keep alive. As for Cleon's idea that in punishment the claims of justice and expediency can both be satisfied, facts do not confirm the possibility of such a combination."

48 "Confess, therefore, that this is the wisest course, and without conceding too much either to pity or to indulgence, by neither of which motives do I any more than Cleon wish you to be influenced, upon the plain merits of the case before you, be persuaded by me to try calmly those of the Mytilenians whom Paches sent off as guilty, and to leave the rest undisturbed. This is at once best for the future, and most terrible to your enemies at the present moment; inasmuch as good policy against an adversary is superior to the blind attacks of brute force."

49 Such were the words of Diodotus. The two opinions thus expressed were the ones that most directly contradicted each other; and the Athenians, notwithstanding their change of feeling, now proceeded to a vote in which the show of hands was almost equal, although the motion of Diodotus carried the day. Another trireme was at once sent off in haste, for fear that the first might reach Lesbos in the interval, and the city be found destroyed; the first ship having about a day and a night's start. Wine and barley-cakes were provided for the vessel by the Mytilenian ambassadors, and great promises made if they arrived in time; which caused the men to use such diligence upon the voyage that they took their meals of barley-cakes kneaded with oil and wine as they rowed, and only slept by turns while the others were at the oar. Luckily they met with no contrary wind, and the first ship making no haste upon so horrid an errand, while the second pressed on in the manner described, the first arrived so little before them that Paches had only just had time to read the decree, and to prepare to execute the sentence, when the second put into port and prevented the massacre. The danger of Mytilene had indeed been great.

The most famous section in Thucydides's *History* is probably the Melian dialogue, which vividly records the encounter between Athenian diplomats and the inhabitants of the island of Melos in 416.

The speeches of the Melians portray their wish to preserve their neutrality and freedom, and their stance comes across as both courageous and admirable. The Athenian diplomats for their part do not challenge the moral validity of the Melian ideals, but merely point out that their city is by far the stronger. Justice, they say, cannot exist between two parties so unequal.

Thucydides seems to suggest, however, that there is a moral dimension even to the Athenian claim. The Melians are urged to adopt a course of action that will save their lives and in the long run secure their well-being. The Athenians are convinced that their rule will not have to be a harsh one, and that the Melians, by submitting to them, will be rewarded with many benefits. The argument is thus framed in terms of mutual self-interest: the Athenians will gain an acquiescent ally, and the Melians will save their lives and property. But our conclusion as readers is unavoidable: the Athenians come off as unjustifiably harsh, and the end result – the mass killing of Melian males and the violent enslavement of the rest of the population – seems an incredibly brutal punishment for the Melians' sincere wish to remain free and independent.

From *The Peloponnesian War*, bk. 5, chaps. 84, 89–114[3]

84 The Athenians also made an expedition against the isle of Melos with thirty ships of their own, six Chian, and two Lesbian vessels, sixteen hundred hoplites, three hundred archers, and twenty mounted archers from Athens, and about fifteen hundred hoplites from the allies and the islanders. The Melians are a colony of Sparta that would not submit to the Athenians like the other islanders, and at first remained neutral and took no part in the struggle, but afterwards upon the Athenians using violence and plundering their territory, assumed an attitude of open hostility. Cleomedes son of Lycomedes, and Tisias son of Tisimachus, the generals, encamping in their territory with the above armament,

---

3   Ibid., pp. 350–1, 352–6.

before doing any harm to their land, sent envoys to negotiate. These the Melians did not bring before the people, but bade them state the object of their mission to the magistrates and the few; upon which the Athenian envoys spoke as follows:

89 *Athenians*:   ". . . [W]e shall not trouble you with specious pretenses – either of how we have a right to our empire because we overthrew the Mede, or are now attacking you because of wrong that you have done us – and make a long speech which would not be believed; and in return we hope that you, instead of thinking to influence us by saying that you did not join the Spartans, although [you were] their colonists, or that you have done us no wrong, will aim at what is feasible, holding in view the real sentiments of us both; since you know as well as we do that right, as the world goes, is only in question between equals in power, while the strong do what they can and the weak suffer what they must."

90 *Melians*:   "As we think, at any rate, it is expedient – we speak as we are obliged, since you enjoin us to let right alone and talk only of interest – that you should not destroy what is our common protection, namely, the privilege of being allowed in danger to invoke what is fair and right, and even to profit by arguments not strictly valid if they can be persuasive. And you are as much interested in this as any, as your fall would be a signal for the heaviest vengeance and an example for the world to meditate upon."

91 *Athenians*:   "The end of our empire, if end it should, does not frighten us: a rival empire like Sparta, even if Sparta was our real antagonist, is not so terrible to the vanquished as subjects who by themselves attack and overpower their rulers. This, however, is a risk that we are content to take. We will now proceed to show you that we have come here in the interest of our empire, and that we shall say what we are now going to say, for the preservation of your country; as we would desire to exercise that empire over you without trouble, and see you preserved for the good of us both."

92 *Melians*:   "And how, pray, could it turn out as good for us to serve as for you to rule?"

93 *Athenians*:   "Because you would have the advantage of submitting before suffering the worst, and we should gain by not destroying you."

94 *Melians*:   "So you would not consent to our being neutral, friends instead of enemies, but allies of neither side."

95 *Athenians*:   "No; for your hostility cannot so much hurt us as your friendship will be an argument to our subjects of our weakness, and your enmity of our power."

96 *Melians*:   "Is that your subjects' idea of equity, to put those who have nothing to do with you in the same category with peoples that are most of them your own colonists, and some conquered rebels?"

97 *Athenians*: "As far as right goes they think one has as much of it as the other, and that if any maintain their independence it is because they are strong, and that if we do not molest them it is because we are afraid; so that besides extending our empire we should gain in security by your subjection; the fact that you are islanders and weaker than others rendering it all the more important that you should not succeed in thwarting the masters of the sea."

98 *Melians*: "But do you consider that there is no security in the policy which we indicate? For here again if you debar us from talking about justice and invite us to obey your interest, we also must explain ours, and try to persuade you, if the two happen to coincide. How can you avoid making enemies of all existing neutrals who shall look at our case and conclude from it that one day or another you will attack them? And what is this but to make greater the enemies that you have already, and to force others to become so who would otherwise have never thought of it?"

99 *Athenians*: "Why, the fact is that mainlanders generally give us but little alarm; the liberty which they enjoy will long prevent their taking precautions against us; it is rather islanders like yourselves, outside our empire, and subjects smarting under the yoke, who would be the most likely to take a rash step and lead themselves and us into obvious danger."

100 *Melians*: "Well then, if you risk so much to retain your empire, and your subjects to get rid of it, it were surely great baseness and cowardice in us who are still free not to try everything that can be tried, before submitting to your yoke."

101 *Athenians*: "Not if you are well advised, the contest not being an equal one, with honor as the prize and shame as the penalty, but a question of self-preservation and of not resisting those who are far stronger than you are."

102 *Melians*: "But we know that the fortune of war is sometimes more impartial than the disproportion of numbers might lead one to suppose; to submit is to give ourselves over to despair, while action still preserves for us a hope that we may stand erect."

103 *Athenians*: "Hope, danger's comforter, may be indulged in by those who have abundant resources, if not without loss, at all events without ruin; but its nature is to be extravagant, and those who go so far as to stake their all upon the venture see it in its true colors only when they are ruined; but so long as the discovery would enable them to guard against it, it is never found wanting. Let not this be the case with you, who are weak and hang on a single turn of the scale; nor be like the vulgar, who, abandoning such security as human means may still afford, when visible hopes fail them in extremity, turn to the invisible, to prophecies and oracles, and other such inventions that delude men with hopes to their destruction."

104 *Melians*: "You may be sure that we are as well aware as you of the difficulty of contending against your power and fortune, unless the terms be equal. But we trust that the gods may grant us fortune as good as yours, since we are just men fighting against unjust, and that what we want in power will be made up by the alliance of the Spartans, who are bound, if only for very shame, to come to the aid of their kindred. Our confidence, therefore, after all is not so utterly irrational."

105 *Athenians*: "When you speak of the favor of the gods, we may as fairly hope for that as yourselves; neither our pretensions nor our conduct being in any way contrary to what men believe of the gods, or practice among themselves. Of the gods we believe, and of men we know, that by a necessary law of their nature they rule wherever they can. And it is not as if we were the first to make this law, or to act upon it when made: we found it existing before us, and shall leave it to exist forever after us; all we do is to make use of it, knowing that you and everybody else, having the same power as we have, would do the same as we do. Thus, as far as the gods are concerned, we have no fear and no reason to fear that we shall be at a disadvantage. But when we come to your notion about the Spartans, which leads you to believe that shame will make them help you, here we bless your simplicity but do not envy your folly. The Spartans, when their own interests or their country's laws are in question, are the worthiest men alive; of their conduct toward others much might be said, but no clearer idea of it could be given than by shortly saying that of all the men we know they are most conspicuous in considering what is agreeable honorable, and what is expedient just. Such a way of thinking does not promise much for the safety which you now unreasonably count upon.

106 *Melians*: "But it is for this very reason that we now trust to their respect for expediency to prevent them from betraying the Melians, their colonists, and thereby losing the confidence of their friends in Hellas and helping their enemies."

107 *Athenians*: "Then you do not adopt the view that expediency goes with security, while justice and honor cannot be followed without danger; and danger the Spartans generally court as little as possible."

108 *Melians*: "But we believe that they would be more likely to face even danger for our sake, and with more confidence than for others, as our nearness to the Peloponnesus makes it easier for them to act; and our common blood insures our fidelity."

109 *Athenians*: "Yes, but what an intending ally trusts to is not the goodwill of those who ask his aid, but a decided superiority of power for action; and the Spartans look to this even more than others. At least, such is their distrust of their home resources that it is only with numerous allies that they attack a neighbor; now is it likely that while we are masters of the sea they will cross over to an island?"

110 *Melians*: "But they would have others to send. The Cretan sea is a wide one, and it is more difficult for those who command it to intercept others, than for those who wish to elude them to do so safely. And should the Spartans miscarry in this, they would fall upon your land, and upon those left of your allies whom Brasidas did not reach; and instead of places which are not yours, you will have to fight for your own country and your own confederacy."

111 *Athenians*: "Some diversion of the kind you speak of you may one day experience, only to learn, as others have done, that the Athenians never once yet withdrew from a siege for fear of any. But we are struck by the fact, that after saying you would consult for the safety of your country, in all this discussion you have mentioned nothing which men might trust in and think to be saved by. Your strongest arguments depend upon hope and the future, and your actual resources are too scanty, as compared with those arrayed against you, for you to come out victorious. You will therefore show great blindness of judgment, unless, after allowing us to retire, you can find some counsel more prudent than this. You will surely not be caught by that idea of disgrace, which in dangers that are disgraceful, and at the same time too plain to be mistaken, proves so fatal to mankind; since in too many cases the very men that have their eyes perfectly open to what they are rushing into, let the thing called disgrace, by the mere influence of a seductive name, lead them on to a point at which they become so enslaved by the phrase as in fact to fall willfully into hopeless disaster, and incur disgrace more disgraceful as the companion of error, than when it comes as the result of misfortune. This, if you are well advised, you will guard against; and you will not think it dishonorable to submit to the greatest city in Hellas, when it makes you the moderate offer of becoming its tributary ally, without ceasing to enjoy the country that belongs to you; nor when you have the choice given you between war and security, will you be so blinded as to choose the worse. And it is certain that those who do not yield to their equals, who keep terms with their superiors, and are moderate toward their inferiors, on the whole succeed best. Think over the matter, therefore, after our withdrawal, and reflect once and again that it is for your country that you are consulting, that you have not more than one, and that upon this one deliberation depends its prosperity or ruin."

112 The Athenians now withdrew from the conference; and the Melians, left to themselves, came to a decision corresponding to what they had maintained in the discussion, and answered, "Our resolution, Athenians, is the same as it was at first. We will not in a moment deprive of freedom a city that has been inhabited these seven hundred years; but we put our trust in the fortune by which the gods have preserved it until now, and in the help of men, that is, of the Spartans; and so we will try and save ourselves. Meanwhile we invite you to allow us to be friends to you and foes to neither party, and to retire from our country after making such a treaty as shall seem fit to us both."

113 Such was the answer of the Melians. The Athenians now departing from the conference said, "Well, you alone, as it seems to us, judging from these resolutions, regard what is future as more certain than what is before your eyes, and what is out of sight, in your eagerness, as already coming to pass; and as you have staked most on, and trusted most in, the Spartans, your fortune, and your hopes, so will you be most completely deceived."

114 The Athenian envoys now returned to the army; and as the Melians showed no signs of yielding, the generals at once commenced hostilities, and built a wall around the Melians, dividing the work among the different states. Subsequently the Athenians returned home with most of their army, leaving behind them a certain number of their own citizens and of the allies to keep guard by land and sea. The force thus left stayed on and besieged the place.

2

Plato (427–347 BC)

Tempering War among the Greeks

The best, however, is neither war nor civil war – the necessity for these things is to be regretted – but rather peace and at the same time goodwill towards one another.

Laws

Plato – alongside his teacher Socrates and his student Aristotle, the most famous of the ancient Greek philosophers – writes surprisingly little about war. Surprisingly, indeed, since the conversations and speeches of Socrates that Plato reports (or invents) are supposed to have taken place right before, during, or immediately after the Peloponnesian War – that terrible contest, so eloquently described by the historian Thucydides, which shook the foundations of Greek culture in general and Athenian pride in particular.

We may suspect, however, that the question of war is closer to Plato's mind than it seems at first glance. His concern for a well-ordered city, which values education, virtue, and the rule of the best men (and, in the *Republic*, women), is a concern for *peace*, and, thereby, for the cessation of war. Plato may write little explicitly about war because he wants to turn his readers' attention to the requirements of peace. As a background relief, then, war may after all loom large in Plato's political thought.

While he believes that politics and philosophy should both be pursued for the sake of peace, not war, Plato is no pacifist. He holds that a well-founded city must be prepared for war, and that great importance should be attached to the right education of soldiers. The dialogue *Statesman* contains a telling passage (at 307e–308a) about how too much peacefulness and tranquillity, on the one hand, and too much readiness for war, on the other, are both inimical to the good of the city. Plato is indicating that there exists a golden mean between too much and too little when it comes to war and military matters. He is more of an idealist than Thucydides before him – and also more of an explicit critic of both the realism of Athens and the military virtues of Sparta – but he harbors no hopes of a city that can eschew preparation for and occasional participation in war. The recurring point in Plato's dialogues is that war should not be considered apart from justice. In this sense, he is indeed one of the originators of the just-war idea.

Plato's moral and political dialogues are all deeply concerned with the search for the proper sort of virtue, and the need for institutions and teachers who apply themselves to the care and quality of the soul. Correct behavior in war, as well as prudent decisions about when to wage war, can only be ensured if the actors in question are guided by the right sort of education. This education must be grounded in knowledge about what virtues are essential for each task, and how these virtues can be developed. For Plato, this is the task of the true philosopher.

Alcibiades

Alcibiades is, alongside the philosopher Parmenides and the poet Aristophanes, probably the most famous of Socrates's interlocutors. We know him from Thucydides's *History of the Peloponnesian War*, where he figures prominently as one of the most important generals of Athens. Among students of philosophy, Alcibiades is famous for his "drunken speech" toward the end of Plato's dialogue *Symposium*. But there is also a dialogue bearing his name, which "was held in the greatest esteem in the Platonic school of antiquity"; indeed, it was considered by the Neoplatonist Iamblichus as containing "the whole philosophy of Plato, as in a seed."[1]

Alcibiades was clearly one of the most gifted of all Athenian politicians and generals, and Socrates seems at one time to have regarded him as his favorite student and "beloved." But Alcibiades somehow failed to learn Socrates's lessons. For while brilliant, he lacked moderation, and was involved in several hapless military and political adventures. He almost ended his career with the Athenians when he, amid great controversy, was relieved of his duty just before the spectacular Athenian defeat at Sicily. Shortly thereafter, he switched sides to the Spartans and became, in the eyes of many, a traitor to Athens. In 411 BC, however, he was again restored to prominence and actually led the Athenian forces toward the end of the Pelop-onnesian War, which ended in defeat for the Athenians. While neither of them ever became traitors, Alcibiades's story recalls more recent military figures such as Patton and MacArthur; brilliant men whose lack of moderation led them to make fateful decisions or consider plans that were unwise and not conducive to peace.

It is a young and highly ambitious Alcibiades we encounter in the dialogue bearing his name; indeed, he aims to become a leader of Athens, surpassing even

---

[1] See Steven Forde, "Commentary on *Alcibiades I*," in Thomas L. Pangle (ed.), *The Roots of Political Philosophy: Ten Forgotten Socratic Dialogues* (Ithaca, NY: Cornell University Press, 1987), p. 222. It should be added here that there is also a second, possibly apocryphal, dialogue named after Alcibiades, often referred to as *Alcibiades II* or *Alcibiades Minor*.

the great Pericles in renown. But if he is to become a politician – that is, an advisor to the Athenian people – what is the subject matter he needs to learn?

This is where war enters the picture. Socrates's probing questioning leads Alcibiades, first, to assert that the most important domain of political deliberation is that pertaining to war and peace, and secondly, that such deliberations must be informed by considerations of justice.

From Plato, *Alcibiades I*, 107c–109d[2]

Soc[rates]: Then what will they be considering when you get up to advise them – if you are to be right in doing so?

Alc[ibiades]: Their own affairs, Socrates.

Soc.: Those concerning shipbuilding, you mean – what sort of ships they ought to build?

Alc.: Not I, Socrates.

Soc.: For I suppose you do not have a knowledge of shipbuilding. Is this the cause or something else?

Alc.: No, this.

Soc.: But what do you mean? When they are deliberating on what sort of affairs of their own?

Alc.: When they are deliberating on war, Socrates, or on peace, or some other of the city's affairs.

Soc.: You mean, therefore, when they deliberate concerning whom they ought to make peace with, and whom war, and in what manner?

Alc.: Yes.

Soc.: Ought it not to be with those with whom it is better to do so?

Alc.: Yes.

Soc.: And at whatever time is better?

Alc.: Certainly.

Soc.: And for as much time as is better?

Alc.: Yes.

Soc.: Now, if the Athenians were to deliberate with whom they ought to wrestle and with whom they ought to spar and in what manner, would you or a trainer advise them better?

Alc.: A trainer, surely.

Soc.: Can you tell me, then, what the trainer would look to in advising them with whom they should or should not wrestle, and when, and in what manner? I'm referring to some such thing as the following: should they wrestle with those with whom it is better to do so or not?

Alc.: Yes.

---

2 From Carnes Lord's translation, in Pangle (ed.), *The Roots of Political Philosophy*, pp. 180–3.

Soc.: And as much as is better?

Alc.: As much.

Soc.: And also at whatever time is better?

Alc.: Certainly.

Soc.: Now, one who sings must sometimes accompany the song with cithara playing and dancing?

Alc.: He must.

Soc.: And at whatever time is better?

Alc.: Yes.

Soc.: And as much as is better?

Alc.: I agree.

Soc.: Now, what of this? Since you used the term "better" in the case both of cithara playing to accompany a song and of wrestling, what do you call "better" in cithara playing – in the way I call it in wrestling "gymnastical"? What do you call it in that case?

Alc.: I cannot bring it to mind.

Soc.: Well, try to imitate me. For presumably what I answered is, what is correct in every instance, and what is correct is surely what comes about according to art – or is it not?

Alc.: Yes.

Soc.: Was the art not gymnastic?

Alc.: What else?

Soc.: I said that the better in wrestling is gymnastical.

Alc.: You did.

Soc.: Didn't I speak in a fine way?

Alc.: It seems so to me at least.

Soc.: Come, then, and tell me yourself – for presumably it would suit you as well to converse in a fine way – what the art is, first of all, to which correct cithara playing, singing and dancing belong. What is it called as a whole? You still cannot say?

Alc.: No, indeed.

Soc.: Then try it this way. Who are the goddesses to whom the art belongs?

Alc.: Do you mean the Muses, Socrates?

Soc.: I do. Now, consider: what name deriving from them does the art have?

Alc.: It seems to me you are speaking of music.

Soc.: That is what I'm speaking of. Now, what is it that comes about correctly in accordance with this? Just as in the other case, in gymnastic, I told you what is correct in accordance with the art, so too here, then – what do you say? How does it come about?

Alc.: Musically, it seems to me.

Soc.: You speak well. Come, then, with respect to what is better in waging war or keeping peace, what term do you use for better in this sense? Just as you said what the better is in each of the other cases – that it is the more musical or in the other case the more gymnastical – try to say what the better is here.

Alc.:   Nothing occurs to me.

Soc.:   But what a shameful thing! If it was about food you were speaking and advising – that this is better than that and at this time and so much of it – and someone then asked you, "What do you mean by better, Alcibiades?" you could say in this case that it is the healthier, even though you do not claim to be a doctor. Yet concerning something that you claim to be knowledgeable about and will get up to give advice on as one who knows, aren't you ashamed to have nothing to say, as it appears you do not, when you are asked about this? Or does it not appear shameful?

Alc.:   Very much so.

Soc.:   Consider, then, and be eager to tell me; the better in keeping peace and waging war with whom one should – to what does this refer?

Alc.:   I am considering but cannot bring it to mind.

Soc.:   Don't you know that when we make war we begin to wage war after accusing each other of some affront and what term we use when we begin?

Alc.:   I do – we say we have been deceived, or done violence to, or deprived of something.

Soc.:   Stop there. How are we affronted in each of these cases? Try to tell me what difference there is between one way and another.

Alc.:   By "way," Socrates, do you mean justly or unjustly?

Soc.:   This very thing.

Alc.:   Certainly they are wholly and entirely different.

Soc.:   Now, what of this? Whom will you advise the Athenians to wage war against, those behaving unjustly or those practicing the just things?

Alc.:   What you are asking is a terrible thing; for even if someone had it in his mind that war ought to be waged against those practicing the just things, he would not admit to it, at least.

Soc.:   For this is not lawful, it would appear.

Alc.:   No indeed, nor does it seem to be anything noble.

Soc.:   Is it with a view to this kind of justice, therefore, that you too will make your speeches?

Alc.:   Necessarily.

Soc.:   Then that "better" in relation to waging or not waging war against those we ought or ought not and when we ought or ought not, which I was just asking about – does it happen to be anything other than the more just? Or not?

Alc.:   It appears so, at any rate.

Soc.:   Yet how is this, dear Alcibiades? Has it escaped you that you have no knowledge of this, or did it escape me that you were learning and going to a teacher who taught you to recognize the more just and the more unjust? And who is this? Tell me as well, so that you can introduce me and I too can become his pupil.

Alc.: You are mocking, Socrates.

Laches

A similar emphasis on the connection between military force and the virtue of justice is found in the dialogue *Laches*. Socrates here converses with Nicias and Laches, two Athenian generals, about the usefulness of education in the military arts. Socrates steers the conversation toward a discussion about the virtue most related to military matters, *courage*. However, he warns against the dangers of possessing courage without having internalized other virtues, such as moderation, justice, and not least prudence (or practical wisdom). Without proper guidance from the other virtues, courage can lead one astray.

In the section that comes just before the following excerpt, Socrates points out to Laches that courage may be exhibited under several different circumstances: fighting in wars, fighting against desires, fighting against pain or fear, and so on. These are all *instances* of courage, but what do they have in common? In a word, what is the *essence* of courage?

From Plato, *Laches*, 191e–192d[3]

Soc[rates]: Then you in turn try, Laches, to speak of courage in this way: what power is it that is the same in pleasure and in pain and in all those things in which we were just now saying it exists, and that is therefore called courage?

Lach[es]: In my opinion, then, it is a certain steadfastness of the soul, if one must say about courage what it is by nature in all cases.

Soc.: Indeed one must, at least if we are to answer for ourselves what is asked. Now then, it looks this way to me at least: not quite all steadfastness, I think, appears to you to be courage. I make that conjecture from this: I pretty much know, Laches, that you hold courage to be among the altogether noble things.

Lach.: Know well, then, that it is among the noblest.

Soc.: So then, is steadfastness accompanied by prudence noble and good?

Lach.: Certainly.

Soc.: And what about it accompanied by folly? As the opposite of this, isn't it harmful and evildoing?

Lach.: Yes.

[3] From James H. Nichols Jr.'s translation, in Pangle (ed.), *The Roots of Political Philosophy*, pp. 256–7.

Soc.:   Will you then assert that such a thing, which is evildoing and harmful, is something noble?

Lach.:   It would certainly not be just, at any rate, Socrates.

Soc.:   You will therefore not agree that steadfastness of this sort, at any rate, is courage, since it is not noble, and courage is a noble thing.

Lach.:   What you say is true.

Soc.:   Prudent steadfastness, therefore, would be courage, according to your argument.

This is not the dialogue's final attempt to define courage, and even the formula of "prudent steadfastness" is shown to be inconsistent with certain commonsense opinions about courage that Socrates is reluctant to jettison. Yet, the crucial moral link between courage and prudence, or between virtue and war-making, is nowhere questioned as such. It is clear that fostering courage without any regard for prudence – which, as the highest practical virtue, certainly encompasses proper concern for justice and moderation as well – is downright dangerous and is of no help in fighting wars.

Republic

The large dialogue known as the *Republic*, Plato's most famous work on politics, tries to come to grips with the virtue of justice, by envisioning an ideal city. While this city seems possible only in speech, it nonetheless remains important as a guide to the virtuous political life – and as a key to understanding what justice truly is.

Plato distinguishes between three main social classes in the city: the rulers (ideally philosophers), the soldiers (or auxiliaries), and the remaining population – artisans, farmers, merchants, and so on. The first two classes are treated together under the name of guardians, and much time is spent discussing their qualities. The guardians must look to the city's protection, and cultivate those qualities that make them apt to be protectors. Plato clearly sees the danger of military personnel lacking proper training, and he fears the creation of a soldier class which may turn on the city and its citizens. Thus, the education and integration of soldiers in society is a basic building-block of Plato's ideal city.

From Plato, *Republic*, bk. III, 416a–c[4]

"Surely the most terrible and shameful thing of all is for shepherds to rear dogs as auxiliaries for the flocks in such a way that due to licentiousness, hunger or some

---

[4] From Allan Bloom's translation, in Plato, *The Republic of Plato* (New York: Basic Books, 1968), p. 95. The "I" in this first-person narrative refers to Socrates.

other bad habit, they themselves undertake to do harm to the sheep and instead of dogs become like wolves," [I said].

"Terrible," [Glaucon said]. "Of course."

"Mustn't we in every way guard against the auxiliaries doing anything like that to the citizens, since they are stronger than they, becoming like savage masters instead of well-meaning allies?"

"Yes," he said. "We must."

"And wouldn't they have been provided with the very finest safeguard if they had been really finely educated?"

"But they have been," he said.

And I said, "It's not fit to be too sure about that, my dear Glaucon. However, it is fit to be sure about what we were saying a while ago, that they must get the right education, whatever it is, if they're going to have what's most important for being tame with each other and those who are guarded by them."

The topic of war in the *Republic* is inextricably linked to Socrates's questioning about education and the inward disposition of the soul. This link is established as Socrates and his young companion Glaucon (Plato's older brother) discuss the characteristics of what they term the "luxurious city" – a city which goes beyond the rudiments of that quite austere community which Socrates initially described as the "healthy" and "true" city (372e) – which is dismissed by Glaucon as a city fit for pigs rather than humans. It is here that the dialogue first introduces the topic of war. Glaucon favors the luxurious city, which will include intellectual and cultural life, as well as many amenities that the citizens would not enjoy in Socrates's "healthy" city. Yet, he concedes, this larger and more sophisticated city will also be forced into war in a quest to satisfy the demands of its growth. It is not, then, prior transgressions of justice that characterize the enemy in such wars; they will merely be the possessors of land and property, which the citizens of the luxurious city need in order to satisfy their ever more luxurious habits. This fact again highlights the need for moderation, which we have already encountered above in the *Alcibiades I*. Indeed, Socrates boldly states, in the unrestrained appetites that are typical of the luxurious city we discover the origins of war:

From Plato, *Republic*, bk. II, 373d–e[5]

"Then must we cut off a piece of our neighbors' land, if we are going to have sufficient for pasture and tillage, and they in turn from ours, if they let themselves go to the unlimited acquisition of money, overstepping the boundary of the necessary?"

---

[5]   Ibid., p. 50.

"Quite necessarily, Socrates," he said.

"After that, won't we go to war as a consequence, Glaucon? Or how will it be?"

"Like that," he said.

"And let's not yet say whether war works evil or good," I said, "but only this much, that we have in its turn found the origin of war – in those things whose presence in cities most of all produces evils both private and public."

"Most certainly."

Unchecked desires lead to the pursuit of luxury rather than the pursuit of true virtue. This hunt for comfort and luxury, in turn, leads to the creation of a large army and a class of guardians, required for the acquisition and defense of all the goods of the city.

At this point, however, an interesting twist occurs. Through the ideals laid out for the guardian class, austerity is actually reintroduced into the city (cf. book II, 374b–e, and book III, 386b, 399e). By means of a well-regulated mythology to guide the education of the guardians, we see a groundwork for the ideal city emerging out of what was originally a city preoccupied with the pursuit of luxury rather than virtue. In this discussion of the education of the guardians, courage plays a central role (in book II, 375a, and book III, 386b), and its connection to prudence is stressed (in book II, 376b–c), as it was in the *Laches*.

The doctrine that subsequently crystallizes is that war arises from a lack of harmony among the soul's desires. The way to remedy this disharmony is the proper education of soldiers, not the abolition of the military class altogether. Thus, what we today call "military ethics" plays a crucial role in the development of Plato's ideal city. Without it, Socrates would have been forced to abandon the luxurious city and instead settle for that more austere community with little or no room for philosophy or leisure.

Further, in book V of the *Republic*, Socrates and Glaucon discuss a topic which is central to the ethics of war. Drawing a distinction between Greeks and "barbarians" – literally, people whose language we do not understand – the discussion concludes with a set of particularly strong moral restrictions that should apply in fighting fellow Greeks.[6] The implied criticism of military conduct during the Peloponnesian War is not to be missed.

In the discussion, the following elements provide the nodes of a code of military conduct applying in wars between the Greeks:

[6] This naturally raises the question about what is permitted in fighting non-Greeks, who are spoken of as "enemies by nature." For an argument that both Socrates and Plato (as well as Aristotle) indirectly criticized the narrowness of Greek pride and self-centeredness in their own time, holding out for a more cosmopolitan view of man, see Thomas L. Pangle and Peter J. Ahrensdorf, *Justice Among Nations* (Lawrence: University Press of Kansas, 1999), pp. 46–50, with reference to, inter alia, Aristotle's *Politics*, 1279a–81a, and Plato's *Laws*, 713a–18c, 886a, 903b–5c.

(a) pillage and ravaging of lands is to be avoided;
(b) only those actually responsible for the dispute are to be seen or treated as enemies;
(c) no enslavement or killing of the defeated is permitted following war;
(d) the dispute must be conducted in a way that allows for a just and mutually acceptable peace, so that a state of war does not continue interminably.

Thus, appearing several centuries before an organized teaching about ethical conduct in war had been formulated, Plato offers to us recognizable criteria of just conduct in war, criteria which were subsequently absorbed in the tradition's emphasis on proportionate use of force, right intention, and the aim of peace.

From Plato, *Republic*, bk. V, 470c–1c[7]

"[W]hen Greeks fight with barbarians and barbarians with Greeks, we'll assert they are at war and are enemies by nature, and this hatred must be called war; while when Greeks do any such thing to Greeks, we'll say that they are by nature friends, but in this case Greece is sick and factious, and this kind of hatred must be called faction."

"I, for one," he said, "agree to consider it in that way."

"Now observe," I said, "in what is nowadays understood to be faction, that wherever such a thing occurs and a city is split, if each side wastes the fields and burns the houses of the others, it seems that the faction is a wicked thing and that the members of neither side are lovers of their city. For, otherwise, they would never have dared to ravage their nurse and mother. But it seems to be moderate for the victors to take away the harvest of the vanquished, and to have the frame of mind of men who will be reconciled and not always be at war."

"This frame of mind," he said, "belongs to far tamer men than the other."

"Now what about this?" I said. "Won't the city you are founding be Greek?"

"It must be," he said.

"Then won't they be good and tame?"

"Very much so."

"And won't they be lovers of the Greeks? Won't they consider Greece their own and hold the common holy places along with the other Greeks?"

"Very much so."

"Won't they consider differences with Greeks – their kin – to be faction and not even use the name war?"

"Of course."

"And they will have their differences like men who, after all, will be reconciled."

"Most certainly."

---

[7] Plato, *The Republic of Plato*, pp. 150–1.

"Then they'll correct their opponents in a kindly way, not punishing them with a view to slavery or destruction, acting as correctors, not enemies."

"That's what they'll do," he said.

"Therefore, as Greeks, they won't ravage Greece or burn houses, nor will they agree that in any city all are their enemies – men, women, and children – but that there are always a few enemies who are to blame for the differences. And, on all these grounds, they won't be willing to ravage lands or tear down houses, since the many are friendly; and they'll keep up the quarrel until those to blame are compelled to pay the penalty by the blameless ones who are suffering."

"I for one," he said, "agree that our citizens must behave this way toward their opponents; and toward the barbarians they must behave as the Greeks do now toward one another."

"So, shall we also give this law to the guardians – neither waste countryside nor burn houses?"

"Let it be given," he said.

Laws

Plato's final work, the gigantic *Laws*, contains several passages pertaining to war. As we enter the dialogue below, the Cretan Kleinias has just related the laws of Crete to an old Athenian Stranger (presumably Plato's mouthpiece, in the absence of Socrates). Kleinias explains that a state of war naturally exists between all cities, and that, as a consequence, the laws of Crete were framed primarily with a view to war. The Athenian Stranger questions this view (which is said to be common to the Cretans and the Lacedaimonians, i.e. Spartans) and insists that the best laws are framed with a view to peace.

From Plato, *Laws*, bk. I, 628c–e[8]

Ath[enian Stranger]:   And doesn't everyone set up all his lawful customs for the sake of what is best?

Kl[einias]:   How could he not?

Ath.:   The best, however, is neither war nor civil war – the necessity for these things is to be regretted – but rather peace and at the same time goodwill towards one another. Moreover, it is likely that even that victory of the city over itself belonged not to the best things but to the necessary things. To think otherwise is as if someone held that a sick body, after it had received a medical purgation, were in the best active condition, and never

---

[8]   From Thomas L. Pangle's translation, in Plato, *The Laws of Plato* (Chicago: University of Chicago Press, 1980), p. 7.

turned his mind to a body which had no need of such remedies at all. Likewise, with regard to the happiness of a city or of a private person, anyone who thought this way would never become a correct statesman, if he looked first and only to external wars, and would never become a law-giver in the strict sense, if he didn't legislate the things of war for the sake of peace rather than the things of peace for the sake of what pertains to war.

Peace is properly speaking the state in which virtue may fully develop – hence, excellence in war can never be more than a part of virtue; moreover, it can only be the "lowest" and "smallest" part (630e–1a). Thus, if the laws of Crete are truly good laws, they cannot be framed with a view to war. A somewhat puzzling exchange follows about the relationship between external wars and civil wars, in which the latter are said to be harsher and thus to require more virtue than the former. While it is not crystal clear to what extent this changes the Athenian's view of preparation for war, it reinforces the teaching, intimated earlier in dia-logues such as *Laches*, that warlike courage is only a part of virtue, and that – especially in the lawgiver – it must be subordinated to the other virtues.

From Plato, *Laws*, bk. I, 631c–d[9]

Ath[enian Stranger]: . . . Prudence, in turn, is first and leader among the divine goods. Second after intelligence comes a moderate disposition of the soul, and from these two mixed with courage comes justice, in third place. Courage is fourth. All of these last goods are by nature placed prior in rank to [the human goods: health, beauty, strength, and wealth], and this is the rank they should be placed in by the legislator.

After these introductory remarks, the dialogue focuses mainly on the laws and requirements of peace, yet the question of preparation for war does not fall from view. Most importantly, ethically speaking, is the insistence in book XII that wars are no private matter and may be undertaken only by legitimate authority:

From Plato, *Laws*, bk. XII, 955b–c[10]

Ath[enian Stranger]: . . . Everyone is to consider the same person a friend or enemy as the city does, and if someone should make peace or war with

[9] Ibid., p. 10.
[10] Ibid., p. 358.

certain parties in private, apart from the community, the penalty is to be death. . . . If some part of the city should by itself make peace or war with certain parties, the Generals are to bring those responsible for this action into court, and the judicial penalty for someone who is convicted shall be death.

The importance of legitimate authority is reinforced by a later passage in Book XII (942a–5b, not reproduced here) where the Athenian Stranger states that military organization at all levels must look toward the rightful ruler, adding that commonality in action and spirit is the backbone of a rightful military order. This discussion of legitimate authority and military order is nested, we should note, within the concluding part of the *Laws*, which lays out how the rule of law should be overseen by the best men of the city (the "Nocturnal Council" or "Council of Elders"). Although the ambition of the *Republic* to create the perfect city led by the philosopher-king has been abandoned, it is made clear that the authority directing military affairs must be a just and deeply pious one, which would exclude the pursuit of extravagant, self-serving, or overly violent military campaigns.

3

Aristotle (384–322 BC)

Courage, Slavery, and Citizen Soldiers

[M]ost of these military states are safe only while they are at war, but fall when they have acquired their empire; like unused iron they lose their edge in time of peace. And for this the legislator is to blame, he never having taught them how to lead the life of peace.

Politics

Plato's most famous student, and tutor to Alexander the Great (who was one of the most important military commanders of Greek antiquity), Aristotle discussed peace and war at several junctures during his long career as a philosopher. While allusions to military matters can be found throughout his writings, it was chiefly in his lectures on ethical and political topics that he paused to reflect on this theme. Firm in the conviction that war-making should be ordained to the higher demands of justice – a view that he articulated in criticism of the Spartan culture of war – Aristotle would exercise a formative influence on subsequent just war thinking. This influence revolved principally around three topics: his treatment of courage, as well as the distinction between natural and legal justice, both advanced in the *Nicomachean Ethics* and in the discussion of slavery which appears in the *Politics*. In addition, Aristotle's comments on the dangers inherent in tyranny and civil war, would, like Plato's earlier admonitions, serve as a point of reference to a wide range of thinkers, well up to the present day.

We begin with a selection of passages from the *Nicomachean Ethics*.[1] After opening sections on happiness (bk. I), the general theory of virtue (bk. II), and human responsibility (bk. III, chaps. 1–6), Aristotle turns his attention to the particular *virtues* (termed "excellences" in the translation used here). An inward principle of upright action, a virtue is defined as a "mean of excellence" between two extremes: excess and deficiency. The virtue of courage is assigned the task of

[1] Translation from *The Complete Works of Aristotle*, vol. 2, ed. Jonathan Barnes (Princeton, NJ: Princeton University Press, 1984).

regulating actions carried out in the face of fear, most especially the fear of death. "Such eventualities," Aristotle notes, "are usually brought about by war." Courage – a mean situated between the opposing extremes of cowardice and recklessness – thereby provides Aristotle with an opportunity to comment on the military profession. Fundamental to his treatment is the idea that virtuous bravery consists in something quite different than sheer fearlessness on the battlefield. The soldier's assessment of the moral purpose behind his fighting – and of whether this purpose is something he should rightly be willing to die for – is an integral aspect of true courage. Aristotle finds this ideal best exemplified by citizen-soldiers; of professional soldiers (mercenaries) he took a rather dim view.

From *Nicomachean Ethics*, bk. III, chaps. 5–9 (1115ᵃ3–17ᵇ23)[2]

5 Let us take up the several excellences, however, and say which they are and what sort of things they are concerned with and how they are concerned with them; at the same time it will become plain how many they are. And first let us speak of courage.

6 That it is a mean with regard to fear and confidence has already been made evident; and plainly the things we fear are terrible things, and these are, to speak without qualification, evils; for which reason people even define fear as expectation of evil. Now we fear all evils, e.g. disgrace, poverty, disease, friendlessness, death, but the brave man is not thought to be concerned with all; for to fear some things is even right and noble, and it is base not to fear them – e.g. disgrace; he who fears this is good and modest, and he who does not is shameless. He is, however, by some people called brave, by an extension of the word; for he has in him something which is like the brave man, since the brave man also is a fearless person. Poverty and disease we perhaps ought not to fear, nor in general the things that do not proceed from vice and are not due to a man himself. But not even the man who is fearless of these is brave. Yet we apply the word to him also in virtue of a similarity; for some who in the dangers of war are cowards are liberal and are confident in face of the loss of money. Nor is a man a coward if he fears insult to his wife and children or envy or anything of the kind; nor brave if he is confident when he is about to be flogged. With what sort of terrible things, then, is the brave man concerned? Surely with the greatest; for no one is more likely than he to stand his ground against what is dreadful. Now death is the most terrible of all things; for it is the end, and nothing is thought to be any longer either good or bad for the dead. But the brave man would not seem to be concerned even with death in *all* circumstances, e.g. at sea or in disease. In what circumstances, then? Surely in the noblest. Now such deaths are

---

[2]   Ibid., pp. 1760–4.

those in battle; for these take place in the greatest and noblest danger. And this agrees with the ways in which honours are bestowed in city-states and at the courts of monarchs. Properly, then, he will be called brave who is fearless in face of a noble death, and of all emergencies that involve death; and the emergencies of war are in the highest degree of this kind. Yet at sea also, and in disease, the brave man is fearless, but not in the same way as the seamen; for he has given up hope for safety, and is disliking the thought of death in this shape, while they are hopeful because of their experience. At the same time, we show courage in situations where there is the opportunity of showing prowess or where death is noble; but in these forms of death neither of these conditions is fulfilled.

7 What is terrible is not the same for all men; but we say there are things terrible even beyond human strength. These, then, are terrible to everyone – at least to every sensible man; but the terrible things that are *not* beyond human strength differ in magnitude and degree, and so too do the things that inspire confidence. Now the brave man is as dauntless as man may be. Therefore, while he will fear even the things that are not beyond human strength, he will fear them as he ought and as reason directs, and he will face them for the sake of what is noble; for this is the end of excellence. But it is possible to fear these more, or less, and again to fear things that are not terrible as if they were. Of the faults that are committed one consists in fearing what one should not, another in fearing as we should not, another in fearing when we should not, and so on; and so too with respect to the things that inspire confidence. The man, then, who faces and who fears the right things and with the right aim, in the right way and at the right time, and who feels confidence under the corresponding conditions, is brave; for the brave man feels and acts according to the merits of the case and in whatever way reason directs. Now the end of every activity is conformity to the corresponding state. This is true, therefore, of the brave man as well as of others. But courage is noble. Therefore the end also is noble; for each thing is defined by its end. Therefore it is for a noble end that the brave man endures and acts as courage directs.

Of those who go to excess he who exceeds in fearlessness has no name (we have said previously that many states have no names), but he would be a sort of madman or insensible person if he feared nothing, neither earthquakes nor the waves, as they say the Celts do not; while the man who exceeds in confidence about what really is terrible is rash. The rash man, however, is also thought to be boastful and only a pretender to courage; at all events, as the brave man *is* with regard to what is terrible, so the rash man wishes to *appear*; and so he imitates him in situations where he can. Hence also most of them are a mixture of rashness and cowardice; for, while in these situations they display confidence, they do not hold their ground against what is really terrible. The man who exceeds in fear is a coward; for he fears both what he ought not and as he ought not, and all the similar characterizations attach to him. He is lacking also in confidence; but he is more conspicuous for his excess of fear in painful situations. The coward, then, is a despairing sort of person; for he fears everything. The brave man, on the other hand, has the opposite disposition; for confidence is the mark of a hopeful disposition. The coward, the rash man, and the brave man, then, are concerned with the same objects but are differently disposed towards them; for the first two exceed and fall short, while the third holds the middle, which is the right, position; and rash men are precipitate, and wish for dangers beforehand but draw back when they are in them, while brave men are keen in the moment of action, but quiet beforehand.

As we have said, then, courage is a mean with respect to things that inspire confidence or fear, in the circumstances that have been stated; and it chooses or endures things because it is noble to do so, or because it is base not to do so. But to die to escape from poverty or love or anything painful is not the mark of a brave man, but rather of a coward; for it is softness to fly from what is troublesome, and such a man endures death not because it is noble but to fly from evil.

8 Courage, then, is something of this sort, but the name is also applied to five other kinds. (1) First comes political courage; for this is most like true courage. Citizens seem to face dangers because of the penalties imposed by the laws and the reproaches they would otherwise incur, and because of the honours they win by such action; and therefore those peoples seem to be bravest among whom cowards are held in dishonour and brave men in honour. This is the kind of courage that Homer depicts, e.g. in Diomede and in Hector:

> First will Polydamas be to heap reproach on me then;[3]

and

> For Hector one day 'mid the Trojans shall utter his vaulting harangue:
> "Afraid was Tydeides, and fled from my face,"[4]

This kind of courage is most like that which we described earlier, because it is due to excellence; for it is due to shame and to desire of a noble object (i.e. honour) and avoidance of disgrace, which is ignoble. One might rank in the same class even those who are compelled by their rulers; but they are inferior, inasmuch as they act not from shame but from fear, and to avoid not what is disgraceful but what is painful; for their masters compel them, as Hector does:

> But if I shall spy any dastard that cowers far from the fight,
> Vainly will such an one hope to escape from the dogs.[5]

And those who give them their posts, and beat them if they retreat, do the same, and so do those who draw them up with trenches or something of the sort

---

[3]   *Iliad*, XXII 100.
[4]   *Iliad*, VIII 148.
[5]   See *Iliad*, II 391; XV 348.

behind them; all of these apply compulsion. But one ought to be brave not under compulsion but because it is noble to be so.

(2) Experience with regard to particular facts is also thought to be courage; this is indeed the reason why Socrates thought courage was knowledge. Other people exhibit this quality in other dangers, and soldiers exhibit it in the dangers of war; for there seem to be many empty alarms in war, of which these have had the most comprehensive experience; therefore they seem brave, because the others do not know the nature of the facts. Again, their experience makes them most capable of doing without being done to, since they can use their arms and have the kind that are likely to be best both for doing and for not being done to; therefore they fight like armed men against unarmed or like trained athletes against amateurs; for in such contests too it is not the bravest men that fight best, but those who are strongest and have their bodies in the best condition. Soldiers turn cowards, however, when the danger puts too great a strain on them and they are inferior in numbers and equipment; for they are the first to fly, while citizen-forces die at their posts, as in fact happened at the temple of Hermes. For to the latter flight is disgraceful and death is preferable to safety on those terms; while the former from the very beginning faced the danger on the assumption that they were stronger, and when they know the facts they fly, fearing death more than disgrace; but the brave man is not that sort of person.

(3) Passion also is sometimes reckoned as courage; those who act from passion, like wild beasts rushing at those who have wounded them, are thought to be brave, because brave men also are passionate; for passion above all things is eager to rush on danger, and hence Homer's "put strength into his passion" and "aroused their spirit and passion" and "bitter spirit in his nostrils" and "his blood boiled."[6] For all such expressions seem to indicate the stirring and onset of passion. Now brave men act for the sake of the noble, but passion aids them; while wild beasts act under the influence of pain; for they attack because they have been wounded or because they are afraid, since if they are in a forest they do not come near one. Thus they are not brave because, driven by pain and passion, they rush on danger without foreseeing any of the perils, since at that rate even asses would be brave when they are hungry; for blows will not drive them from their food; and lust also makes adulterers do many daring things. [Those creatures are not brave, then, which are driven on to danger by pain or passion.][7] The courage that is due to passion seems to be the most natural, and to be courage if choice and aim be added.

Men, then, as well as beasts, suffer pain when they are angry, and are pleased when they exact their revenge; those who fight for these reasons, however, are pugnacious but not brave; for they do not act for the sake of the noble nor as reason directs, but from feeling; they have, however, something akin to courage.

---

[6]   See *Iliad*, V 470; XI 11; XVI 529; *Odyssey*, XXIV 318.
[7]   [*Translator's note:*] Excised in Bywater.

(4) Nor are sanguine people brave; for they are confident in danger only because they have conquered often and against many foes. Yet they closely resemble brave men, because both are confident; but brave men are confident for the reasons stated earlier, while these are so because they think they are the strongest and can suffer nothing. (Drunken men also behave in this way; they become sanguine.) When their adventures do not succeed, however, they run away; but it was the mark of a brave man to face things that are, and seem, terrible for a man, because it is noble to do so and disgraceful not to do so. Hence also it is thought the mark of a braver man to be fearless and undisturbed in sudden alarms than to be so in those that are foreseen; for it must have proceeded more from a state of character, because less from preparation; for acts that are foreseen may be chosen by calculation and reason, but sudden actions in accordance with one's state of character.

(5) People who are ignorant also appear brave, and they are not far removed from those of a sanguine temper, but are inferior inasmuch as they have no self-reliance while these have. Hence also the sanguine hold their ground for a time; but those who have been deceived fly if they know or suspect that things are different as happened to the Argives when they fell in with the Spartans and took them for Sicyonians.

9 We have, then, described the character both of brave men and of those who are thought to be brave.

Though courage is concerned with confidence and fear, it is not concerned with both alike, but more with the things that inspire fear; for he who is undisturbed in face of these and bears himself as he should towards these is more truly brave than the man who does so towards the things that inspire confidence. It is for facing what is painful, then, as has been said, that men are called brave. Hence also courage involves pain, and is justly praised; for it is harder to face what is painful than to abstain from what is pleasant. Yet the end which courage sets before it would seem to be pleasant, but to be concealed by the attending circumstances, as happens also in athletic contests; for the end at which boxers aim is pleasant – the crown and the honours – but the blows they take are distressing to flesh and blood, and painful, and so is their whole exertion; and because the blows and the exertions are many the end, which is but small, appears to have nothing pleasant in it. And so, if the case of courage is similar, death and wounds will be painful to the brave man and against his will, but he will face them because it is noble to do so or because it is base not to do so. And the more he is possessed of excellence in its entirety and the happier he is, the more he will be pained at the thought of death; for life is best worth living for such a man, and he is knowingly losing the greatest goods, and this is painful. But he is none the less brave, and perhaps all the more so, because he chooses noble deeds of war at that cost. It is not the case, then, with all the excellences that the exercise of them is pleasant, except in so far as it reaches its end. But it is quite possible that the best soldiers may be not men of this sort but those who are less brave but have no other good; for these are ready to face danger, and they sell their life for trifling gains.

So much, then, for courage; it is not difficult to grasp its nature in outline; at any rate, from what has been said.

In what follows, Aristotle distinguishes between two forms of justice that are operative in the political realm: *natural* and *legal* justice. Proponents of the medieval natural law tradition found in this distinction a teaching about global justice: natural justice refers to a set of norms that are applicable throughout the broad diversity of human cultures, while the norms of legal justice are tightly circumscribed by the institutions proper to the geographical and historical setting of each particular nation. Whether or not this was Aristotle's intended meaning is today the subject of considerable debate. The influence of this text on the development of just war thinking is nevertheless indisputable. The idea that statesmen, in making decisions about war and peace, should advert to the *ius gentium*, a common law of nations, has this text as one of its principal sources.

From *Nicomachean Ethics*, bk. V, chap. 7 (1134^{b}18–5^{a}5)[8]

7 Of political justice part is natural, part legal, – natural, that which everywhere has the same force and does not exist by people's thinking this or that; legal, that which is originally indifferent, but when it has been laid down is not indifferent, e.g. that a prisoner's ransom shall be a mina, or that a goat and not two sheep shall be sacrificed, and again all the laws that are passed for particular cases, e.g. that sacrifice shall be made in honour of Brasidas, and the provisions of decrees. Now some think that all justice is of this sort, because that which is by nature is unchangeable and has everywhere the same force (as fire burns both here and in Persia), while they see change in the things recognized as just. This, however, is not true in this unqualified way, but is true in a sense; or rather, with the gods it is perhaps not true at all, while with us there is something that is just even by nature, yet all of it is changeable; but still some is by nature, some not by nature. It is evident which sort of thing, among things capable of being otherwise, is by nature, and which is not but is legal and conventional assuming that both are equally changeable. And in all other things the same distinction will apply; by nature the right hand is stronger, yet it is possible that all men should come to be ambidextrous. The things which are just by virtue of convention and expediency are like measures; for wine and corn measures are not everywhere equal, but larger in wholesale and smaller in retail markets. Similarly, the things which are just not by nature but by

---

[8] Ibid., pp. 1790–1.

human enactment are not everywhere the same, since constitutions also are not the same, though there is but one which is everywhere by nature the best.

In Ancient Greece it was customary to enslave communities that were defeated in war. Applied especially in the wars that the Greek city-states waged against outsiders (whom they termed *barbarians*), this practice was continued by the Romans; it persisted well into the Christian era. In the *Politics* Aristotle drew a distinction – much debated by later thinkers – between individuals who by their low mental endowments are naturally fit to be slaves ("natural slaves") and individuals who are taken into permanent captivity as a result of then-accepted conventions of war (the latter were accordingly termed "slaves by convention"). The impetus behind Aristotle's teaching was two-pronged. On the one hand, it represented an attempt to limit the practice of slavery by demonstrating the injustice of enslaving individuals otherwise fit for a free life, but who, by ill-fortune, had been captured in war. Aristotle observed that this injustice was doubly great when the victor was in fact fighting on behalf of an unjust cause. It was to demonstrate the injustice of this conventional slavery that Aristotle contrasted it with the condition of natural slavery, which in his eyes was just. Moreover, in his opinion, those individuals who refused to recognize their natural incapacity for self-government could legitimately be made the targets of war. "This sort of war is by nature just," he writes, thus being one of the first to introduce into Greek philosophy the notion of a "just cause" for war. The condition of natural slavery was, however, not purely and simply equivalent to exploitation. By reason of their very limited mental abilities, Aristotle though that slaves stood to benefit from being ruled by another; the master should thereby take care to govern his slaves humanely, with an eye not only to his own advantage but also to their good. Whether or not this condition of natural slavery could rightly characterize an entire populace is not openly stated in the text, nor is it excluded either. Centuries later, some Christian thinkers would accordingly appeal to Aristotle's defense of natural slavery in the *Politics* as rationale for enslaving the native populations of the newly discovered Americas. This line of argumentation was nevertheless sharply contested by Francisco de Vitoria,[9] among others.

Aristotle discussed slavery in a section of the *Politics* that was devoted to "household management." In ancient Greece, households were made up of free persons and slaves. Heading the household was the master, and the slave was counted among his possessions. After defining the slave as an "animate instrument" of the master ($1253^{b}25$–30), Aristotle tells us that he will investigate whether anyone is "intended by nature to be a slave, and for whom such a condition is expedient and right, or rather is not all slavery a violation of nature?"

---

[9]   See chap. 27, this volume.

From *Politics*, bk. I, chaps. 6–8 (1255^{a}5–6^{b}25)[10]

[T]he words slavery and slave are used in two senses. There is a slave or slavery by convention as well as by nature. The convention is a sort of agreement – the convention by which whatever is taken in war is supposed to belong to the victors. But this right many jurists impeach, as they would an orator who brought forward an unconstitutional measure: they detest the notion that, because one man has the power of doing violence and is superior in brute strength, another shall be his slave and subject. Even among philosophers there is a difference of opinion. The origin of the dispute, and what makes the views invade each other's territory, is as follows: in some sense excellence, when furnished with means, has actually the greatest power of exercising force: and as superior power is only found where there is superior excellence of some kind, power seems to imply excellence, and the dispute to be simply one about justice (for it is due to one party identifying justice with goodwill, while the other identifies it with the mere rule of the stronger). If these views are thus set out separately, the other views have no force or plausibility against the view that the superior in excellence ought to rule, or be master. Others, clinging, as they think, simply to a principle of justice (for convention is a sort of justice), assume that slavery in accordance with the custom of war is just, but at the same moment they deny this. For what if the cause of the war be unjust? And again, no one would ever say that he is a slave who is unworthy to be a slave. Were this the case, men of the highest rank would be slaves and the children of slaves if they or their parents chanced to have been taken captive and sold. That is why people do not like to call themselves slaves but confine the term to foreigners. Yet, in using this language, they really mean the natural slave of whom we spoke at first; for it must be admitted that some are slaves everywhere, others nowhere. The same principle applies to nobility. People regard themselves as noble everywhere, and not only in their own country, but they deem foreigners noble only when at home, thereby implying that there are two sorts of nobility and freedom, the one absolute, the other relative. The Helen of Theodectes says:

> Who would presume to call me servant who am on both sides sprung from the stem
> of the Gods?

What does this mean but that they distinguish freedom and slavery, noble and humble birth, by the two principles of good and evil? They think that as men and animals beget men and animals, so from good men a good man springs. Nature intends to do this often but cannot.

We see then that there is some foundation for this difference of opinion, and that all are not either slaves by nature or freemen by nature, and also that there is

---

[10] *The Complete Works of Aristotle*, vol. 2 (ed. Barnes), pp. 1991–2, 1994.

in some cases a marked distinction between the two classes, rendering it expedient and right for the one to be slaves and the others to be masters: the one practising obedience, the others exercising the authority and lordship which nature intended them to have. The abuse of this authority is injurious to both; for the interests of part and whole, of body and soul, are the same, and the slave is a part of the master, a living but separated part of his bodily frame. Hence, where the relation of master and slave between them is natural they are friends and have a common interest, but where it rests merely on convention and force the reverse is true. . . .

. . . There is likewise a science of the master, which teaches the use of slaves; for the master as such is concerned, not with the acquisition, but with the use of them. Yet this science is not anything great or wonderful; for the master need only know how to order that which the slave must know how to execute. Hence those who are in a position which places them above toil have stewards who attend to their households while they occupy themselves with philosophy or with politics. But the art of acquiring slaves, I mean of justly acquiring them, differs both from the art of the master and the art of slave, being a species of hunting or war. . . .

. . . And so, from one point of view, the art of war is a natural art of acquisition, for the art of acquisition includes hunting, an art which we ought to practise against wild beasts, and against men who, though intended to be governed, will not submit; for war of such kind is naturally just.

In discussing how laws ought to be framed and the commonwealth governed, Aristotle was sharply critical of the Spartan practice of organizing their political life especially with a view to war. In this context he makes a number of significant comments on the proper place of "warlike pursuits" within a finely governed political community. Military prowess is not an end in itself; rather it should be cultivated in order to defend one's nation and in the broader interests of peace.

From *Politics*, bk. II, chap. 9 (1271^{b}1–^{b}11)[11]

The charge which Plato brings, in the *Laws*, against the intention of the legislator, is likewise justified; the whole constitution has regard to one part of excellence only – the excellence of the soldier, which gives victory in war. So long as they were at war, therefore, their power was preserved, but when they had attained empire they fell, for of the arts of peace they knew nothing, and have never engaged in any employment higher than war. There is another error, equally great, into which they have fallen. Although they truly think that the goods for which men contend are to be acquired by excellence rather than by vice, they err in supposing that these goods are to be preferred to the excellence which gains them.

[11] Ibid., p. 2017.

From *Politics*, bk. VII, chap. 2 (1324^{b}2–5^{a}10)[12]

Others, again, are of the opinion that arbitrary and tyrannical rule alone makes for happiness; indeed, in some states the entire aim both of the laws and of the constitution is to give men despotic power over their neighbours. And, therefore, although in most cities the laws may be said generally to be in a chaotic state, still, if they aim at anything, they aim at the maintenance of power: thus in Lacedaemon and Crete the system of education and the greater part of the laws are framed with a view to war. And in all nations which are able to gratify their ambition military power is held in esteem, for example among the Scythians and Persians and Thracians and Celts. In some nations there are even laws tending to stimulate the warlike virtues, as at Carthage, where we are told that men obtain the honour of wearing as many armlets as they have served campaigns. There was once a law in Macedonia that he who had not killed an enemy should wear a halter, and among the Scythians no one who had not slain his man was allowed to drink out of the cup which was handed round at a certain feast. Among the Iberians, a warlike nation, the number of enemies whom a man has slain is indicated by the number of obelisks which are fixed in the earth round his tomb; and there are numerous practices among other nations of a like kind, some of them established by law and others by custom. Yet to a reflecting mind it must appear very strange that the statesman should be always considering how he can dominate and tyrannize over others, whether they are willing or not. How can that which is not even lawful be the business of the statesman or the legislator? Unlawful it certainly is to rule without regard to justice, for there may be might where there is no right. The other arts and sciences offer no parallel; a physician is not expected to persuade or coerce his patients, nor a pilot the passengers in his ship. Yet most men appear to think that the art of despotic government is statesmanship, and what men affirm to be unjust and inexpedient in their own case they are not ashamed of practising towards others; they demand just rule for themselves, but where other men are concerned they care nothing about it. Such behaviour is irrational; unless the one party is, and the other is not, born to serve, in which case men have a right to command, not indeed all their fellows, but only those who are intended to be subjects; just as we ought not to hunt men, whether for food or sacrifice, but only those animals which may be hunted for food or sacrifice, that is to say, such wild animals as are eatable. And surely there may be a city happy in isolation, which we will assume to be well governed (for it is quite possible that a city thus isolated might be well-administered and have good laws); but such a city would not be constituted with any view to war or the conquest of enemies – all that sort of thing must be excluded. Hence we see very plainly that warlike pursuits, although generally to be deemed honourable, are

---

[12]   Ibid., pp. 2102–3.

not the supreme end of all things, but only means. And the good lawgiver should inquire how states and races of men and communities may participate in a good life, and in the happiness which is attainable by them.

From *Politics*, bk. VII, chap. 11 (1330^b32–1^a18)[13]

As to walls, those who say that cities making any pretension to military virtue should not have them, are quite out of date in their notions; and they may see the cities which prided themselves on this fancy confuted by facts. True, there is little courage shown in seeking for safety behind a rampart when an enemy is similar in character and not much superior in number; but the superiority of the besiegers may be and often is too much both for ordinary human valour and for that which is found only in a few; and if they are to be saved and to escape defeat and outrage, the strongest wall will be the truest soldierly precaution, more especially now that missiles and siege engines have been brought to such perfection. To have no walls would be as foolish as to choose a site for a town in an exposed country, and to level the heights; or as if an individual were to leave his house unwalled, lest the inmates should become cowards. Nor must we forget that those who have their cities surrounded by walls may either take advantage of them or not, but cities which are unwalled have no choice.

If our conclusions are just, not only should cities have walls, but care should be taken to make them ornamental, as well as useful for warlike purposes, and adapted to resist modern inventions. For as the assailants of a city do all they can to gain an advantage, so the defenders should make use of any means of defence which have been already discovered, and should devise and invent others, for when men are well prepared no enemy even thinks of attacking them.

From *Politics*, bk. VII, chaps. 14–15 (1333^a31–4^b1)[14]

The whole of life is further divided into two parts, business and leisure, war and peace, and of actions some aim at what is necessary and useful, and some at what is honourable. And the preference given to one or the other class of actions must necessarily be like the preference given to one or other part of the soul and its actions over the other; there must be war for the sake of peace, business for the sake of leisure, things useful and necessary for the sake of things honourable. All these points the statesman should keep in view when he frames his laws; he should consider the parts of the soul and their functions, and above all the better and the end; he should also remember the diversities of human lives and actions.

---

[13] Ibid., pp. 2111–12.
[14] Ibid., pp. 2115–17.

For men must be able to engage in business and go to war, but leisure and peace are better; they must do what is necessary and indeed what is useful, but what is honourable is better. On such principles children and persons of every age which requires education should be trained. Whereas even the Greeks of the present day who are reputed to be best governed, and the legislators who gave them their constitutions, do not appear to have framed their governments with a regard to the best end, or to have given them laws and education with a view to all the excellences, but in a vulgar spirit have fallen back on those which promised to be more useful and profitable. Many modern writers have taken a similar view: they commend the Lacedaemonian constitution, and praise the legislator for making conquest and war his sole aim, a doctrine which may be refuted by argument and has long ago been refuted by facts. For most men desire empire in the hope of accumulating the goods of fortune; and on this ground Thibron and all those who have written about the Lacedaemonian constitution have praised their legislator, because the Lacedaemonians, by being trained to meet dangers, gained great power. But surely they are not a happy people now that their empire has passed away, nor was their legislator right. How ridiculous is the result, if, while they are continuing in the observance of his laws and no one interferes with them, they have lost the better part of life! These writers further err about the sort of government which the legislator should approve, for the government of freemen is nobler and implies more excellence than despotic government. Neither is a city to be deemed happy or a legislator to be praised because he trains his citizens to conquer and obtain dominion over their neighbours, for there is great harm in this. On a similar principle any citizen who could, should obviously try to obtain the power in his own state – the crime which the Lacedaemonians accuse king Pausanias of attempting, although he had such great honour already. No such principle and no law having this object is either statesmanlike or useful or right. For the same things are best both for individuals and for states, and these are the things which the legislator ought to implant in the minds of his citizens. Neither should men study war with a view to the enslavement of those who do not deserve to be enslaved; but first of all they should provide against their own enslavement, and in the second place obtain empire for the good of the governed, and not for the sake of exercising a general despotism, and in the third place they should seek to be masters only over those who deserve to be slaves. Facts, as well as arguments, prove that the legislator should direct all his military and other measures to the provision of leisure and the establishment of peace. For most of these military states are safe only while they are at war, but fall when they have acquired their empire; like unused iron they lose their edge in time of peace. And for this the legislator is to blame, he never having taught them how to lead the life of peace.

15 Since the end of individuals and of states is the same, the end of the best man and of the best constitution must also be the same; it is therefore evident that there ought to exist in both of them the excellences of leisure; for peace, as has been often repeated, is the end of war, and leisure of toil. But leisure and cultivation may be promoted not only by those excellences which are practised in leisure, but also by some of those which are useful to business. For many necessaries of life have to be supplied before we can have leisure. Therefore a city must be temperate and brave, and able to endure: for truly, as the proverb says, "There is no leisure for slaves," and those who cannot face danger like men are the slaves of any invader. Courage and endurance are required for business and philosophy for leisure, temperance and justice for both, and more especially in times of peace and leisure, for war compels men to be just and temperate, whereas the enjoyment of good fortune and the leisure which comes with peace tend to make them insolent. Those then who seem to be the best-off and to be in the possession of every good, have special need of justice and temperance – for example, those (if such there be, as the poets say) who dwell in the Islands of the Blest; they above all will need philosophy and temperance and justice, and all the more the more leisure they have, living in the midst of abundance. There is no difficulty in seeing why the state that would be happy and good ought to have these excellences. If it is disgraceful in men not to be able to use the goods of life, it is peculiarly disgraceful not to be able to use them in time of leisure – to show excellent qualities in action and war, and when they have peace and leisure to be no better than slaves. That is why we should not practise excellence after the manner of the Lacedaemonians. For they, while agreeing with other men in their conception of the highest goods, differ from the rest of mankind in thinking that they are to be obtained by the practice of a single excellence.

Aristotle considered tyranny to be the worst possible form of government. In the following passage he details some of the strategies that tyrants use to maintain their hold on power. This provides Aristotle with an opportunity to explain why tyrannies are more prone to violent conflict than other forms of civil rule.

From *Politics*, bk. V, chap. 11 (1313ª34–ᵇ32)[15]

[One of the ways in which tyrannies are preserved] is the old traditional method in which most tyrants administer their government. Of such arts Periander of Corinth is said to have been the great master, and many similar devices may be gathered from the Persians in the administration of their government. There are firstly the prescriptions mentioned some distance back, for the preservation of a tyranny, in so far as this is possible; viz. that the tyrant should lop off those who are too high; he must put to death men of spirit; he must not allow common meals, clubs, education, and the like; he must be upon his guard against anything

---

[15]   Ibid., p. 2085.

which is likely to inspire either courage or confidence among his subjects; he must prohibit schools or other meetings for discussion, and he must take every means to prevent people from knowing one another (for acquaintance begets mutual confidence). Further, he must compel all persons staying in the city to appear in public and live at his gates; then he will know what they are doing: if they are always kept under, they will learn to be humble. In short, he should practise these and the like Persian and barbaric arts, which all have the same object. A tyrant should also endeavour to know what each of his subjects says or does, and should employ spies, like the "female detectives" at Syracuse, and the eavesdroppers whom Hiero was in the habit of sending to any place of resort or meeting; for the fear of informers prevents people from speaking their minds, and if they do, they are more easily found out. Another art of the tyrant is to sow quarrels among the citizens; friends should be embroiled with friends, the people with the notables, and the rich with one another. Also he should impoverish his subjects; he thus provides against the maintenance of a guard by the citizens, and the people, having to keep hard at work, are prevented from conspiring. The Pyramids of Egypt afford an example of this policy; also the offerings of the family of Cypselus, and the building of the temple of Olympian Zeus by the Peisistratidae, and the great Polycratean monuments at Samos; all these works were alike intended to occupy the people and keep them poor. Another practice of tyrants is to multiply taxes, after the manner of Dionysius at Syracuse, who contrived that within five years his subjects should bring into the treasury their whole property. The tyrant is also fond of making war in order that his subjects may have something to do and be always in want of a leader. And whereas the power of a king is preserved by his friends, the characteristic of a tyrant is to distrust his friends, because he knows that all men want to overthrow him, and they above all have the power to do so.

This concluding passage, taken from the *Rhetoric*, shows that Aristotle was not unconcerned with the pragmatic aspects of decision-making about war and peace. Leaders must take care to acquire the skills requisite for an effective exercise of statecraft.

From *Rhetoric*, bk. I, chap. 4 (1359^{b}34–60^{a}12)[16]

As to Peace and War, he must know the extent of the military strength of his country, both actual and potential, and also the nature of that actual and potential strength; and further, what wars his country has waged, and how it has waged them. He must know these facts not only about his own country, but also about

---

[16]   Translation from *The Complete Works of Aristotle*, vol. 2 (ed. Barnes), p. 2162.

neighbouring countries; and also about countries with which war is likely, in order that peace may be maintained with those stronger than his own, and that his own may have power to make war or not against those that are weaker. He should know, too, whether the military power of another country is like or unlike that of his own; for this is a matter that may affect their relative strength. With that end in view he must, besides, have studied the wars of other countries as well as those of his own, and the way they ended; similar causes are likely to have similar results.

With regard to National Defence he ought to know all about the methods of defence in actual use, and also the strength and character of the defensive force and the positions of the forts – this last means that he must be well acquainted with the lie of the country – in order that a garrison may be increased if it is too small or removed if it is not wanted, and that the strategic points may be guarded with special care.

4

Roman Law of War and Peace (Seventh Century BC –First Century AD)

Ius Fetiale

> It is their duty to take care that the Romans do not enter upon an unjust war against any city in alliance with them.
>
> Dionysius of Halicarnassus, *The Roman Antiquities*

In ancient Rome, the fetials (*fetiales*) were a college of priests who had special responsibility for maintaining peaceful relations among the Latins. They would oversee the making of treaties, declarations of war, and other such functions. Deliberations about war were expected to pass through these priests, who would seek a judgment of the gods about the justice of the proposed course of action. If it was decided that a grave breach of the peace had in fact occurred, such that a just war would be warranted, the fetials would first approach the guilty city to demand redress. If, after a certain lapse of time, no satisfaction was given, war could begin.

It has often been said that the Roman state religion was "primarily legalistic, much more concerned with formalities and observances than with beliefs or personal piety."[1] This holds true as well for the Roman conception of war, wherein issues of justice were closely identified with adherence to legal form. A war would be considered just when it was carried out in conformity with the proper set of religious laws (*ius fetiale*). Declarations of war "were cast in the form of a lawsuit,"[2] in which the verdict transmitted by the fetials was meant to decide on the question whether the war *could* rightly be waged. Whether or not a war *should* be waged (to enforce the verdict) would then be the matter for a new

---

[1] Alan Watson, *International Law in Archaic Rome: War and Religion* (Baltimore: Johns Hopkins University Press, 1993), p. xiii.
[2] Ibid., p. 11.

decision, to be rendered by the king, the senate, or even (in later periods) the entire people.

The practice of using fetials is thought to have begun during the regal period (753–509 BC). In what follows, the Greek historian Dionysius of Halicarnassus (who lived in Rome during the first century BC), describes how the college of the fetials was instituted under the reign of King Numa. This passage provides an excellent outline of the fetials' nature and function.

From Dionysius of Halicarnassus (ca. 60–5 BC), *The Roman Antiquities*, bk. II, chap. 72[3]

The seventh division of his sacred institutions was devoted to the college of the *fetiales*; these may be called in Greek *eirênodikai* or "arbiters of peace." . . . It was instituted by Numa when he was upon the point of making war on the people of Fidenae, who had raided and ravaged his territories, in order to see whether they would come to an accommodation with him without war; and that is what they actually did, being constrained by necessity. But since the college of the *fetiales* is not in use among the Greeks, I think it incumbent on me to relate how many and how great affairs fall under its jurisdiction, to the end that those who are unacquainted with the piety practised by the Romans of those times may not be surprised to find that all their wars had the most successful outcome; for it will appear that the origins and motives of them all were most holy, and for this reason especially the gods were propitious to them in the dangers that attended them. The multitude of duties, to be sure, that fall within the province of these *fetiales* make it no easy matter to enumerate them all; but to indicate them by a summary outline, they are as follows: It is their duty to take care that the Romans do not enter upon an unjust war against any city in alliance with them, and if others begin the violation of treaties against them, to go as ambassadors and first make formal demand for justice, and then, if the others refuse to comply with their demands, to sanction war. In like manner, if any people in alliance with the Romans complain of having been injured by them and demand justice, these men are to determine whether they have suffered anything in violation of their alliance; and if they find their complaints well grounded, they are to seize the accused and deliver them up to the injured parties. They are also to take cognizance of the crimes committed against ambassadors, to take care that treaties are religiously observed, to make peace, and if they find that peace has been made otherwise than is prescribed by the holy laws, to set it aside; and to inquire into and expiate the transgressions of the generals in so far as they relate to oaths and treaties,

---

[3]   English translation (with facing Greek text) by Ernest Cary of *The Roman Antiquities of Dionysius of Halicarnassus*, Loeb Classical Library, vol. 319 (Cambridge, MA: Harvard University Press, 1937), vol. I, pp. 521, 523, 525, 527.

concerning which I shall speak in the proper places. As to the functions they performed in the quality of heralds when they went to demand justice of any city thought to have injured the Romans (for these things also are worthy of our knowledge, since they were carried out with great regard to both religion and justice), I have received the following account: One of these *fetiales*, chosen by his colleagues, wearing his sacred robes and insignia to distinguish him from all others, proceeded towards the city whose inhabitants had done the injury; and, stopping at the border, he called upon Jupiter and the rest of the gods to witness that he was come to demand justice on behalf of the Roman State. Thereupon he took an oath that he was going to a city that had done an injury; and having uttered the most dreadful imprecations against himself and Rome, if what he averred was not true, he then entered their borders. Afterwards, he called to witness the first person he met, whether it was one of the countrymen or one of the townspeople, and having repeated the same imprecations, he advanced towards the city. And before he entered it he called to witness in the same manner the gatekeeper or the first person he met at the gates, after which he proceeded to the forum; and taking his stand there, he discussed with the magistrates the reasons for his coming, adding everywhere the same oaths and imprecations. If, then, they were disposed to offer satisfaction by delivering up the guilty, he departed as a friend, taking leave of friends, carrying the prisoners with him. Or, if they desired time to deliberate, he allowed them ten days, after which he returned and waited till they had made this request three times. But after the expiration of the thirty days, if the city still persisted in refusing to grant him justice, he called both the celestial and infernal gods to witness and went away, saying no more than this, that the Roman State would deliberate at its leisure concerning these people. Afterwards he, together with the other *fetiales*, appeared before the senate and declared that they had done everything that was ordained by the holy laws, and that, if the senators wished to vote for war, there would be no obstacle on the part of the gods. But if any of these things was omitted, neither the senate nor the people had the power to vote for war. Such, then, is the account we have received concerning the *fetiales*.

5

Cicero (106–43 BC)

Civic Virtue as the Foundation of Peace

It is not, therefore, those who inflict injury, but those who prevent it, whom we should consider the men of courage and great spirit.

On Duties

It is fashionable these days to question the originality and scholarly substance of the works of Marcus Tullius Cicero, Roman orator and statesman. This is not the place to take issue with such a contention, but suffice it to say that Cicero's historical significance more than warrants his inclusion in this volume. Cicero held public office at a crucial time in Roman, and thereby also Western, history. He was well versed in Greek philosophy, and was among the first to write a scholarly treatise in Latin. He would also exercise considerable influence on a host of later thinkers, Augustine and Isidore, to name but two, and he was the most widely read authority on both philosophy and rhetoric in the Latin world for more than a millennium. Thus, in addition to being a significant political figure, he is also an important link in the transition from ancient to medieval political philosophy.

Cicero's political career was remarkable not only for the speed with which he rose to power, but also for the fact that he was the first of his family to take up public office. This was a rare thing in the Roman Empire, where political power was in large measure hereditary. Upon his appointment to consulship in 63 BC, the apex of his career, he was noted for his reasoned judgment and moderate politics. These were tumultuous times, however, and Cicero would quickly see his political fortunes change: he was exiled in 58, and upon his return eighteen months later he chose to pursue politics by way of words rather than action. Practically all his theoretical works were written between 55 and 43, when he was executed for his political affiliations.

The most well-known and widely quoted saying of Cicero about war is no doubt "Silent enim leges inter arma" (or in short form: "Inter arma, silent leges"). This adage, normally translated "In times of war, the laws fall silent," appears in

Cicero's famous speech in defense of Titus Annius Milo in 52 BC, known as *Pro Milone*. (Milo, a companion of Cicero, had been accused of the murder of a political rival, Publius Clodius.) However, the quote does not well represent Cicero's more considered views on war. To the contrary, his views on the use of armed force were colored by Stoic natural-law ideas and his belief in a common humanity. Thus, in staunch contrast to the tenor of his most famous quote, Cicero is in fact one of the first thinkers to insist on the need for developing a legal and normative framework for war.

Cicero's most famous work, *On Duties*[1] [*De Officiis*], was written not fully a year before his death. Conceived as a tutorial book addressed to his son Marcus, it is a large work, dealing with all aspects of statesmanship. Of particular interest to us here is the way it reflects the multicultural composition of the Roman Empire. In a way different from his philosophical predecessors in the Platonic school, Cicero calls for liberality and even toleration. As such, *On Duties* can be seen as an ambitious attempt to lift the moral–political teachings of the ancient Greek philosophers out of the narrow confines of the city-state and into the cosmopolitan setting of the Roman Empire. Refracted through the teachings of the Roman Stoics, the dictates of morality apply no longer only to a privileged group of people (be they Greeks or Romans), but in principle to all of mankind. The circumstances of war, as we shall see, provide no exception.

It is not, though, as if such cosmopolitan ambitions were peculiar to Cicero. Like any great thinker, his work reflects and expounds upon ideas that were largely implicit in the political culture of his time. Contemporary juridical thought, in particular, provides a touchstone for Cicero, and to some extent his work can be seen as an attempt to provide philosophical justification for the precepts and practices already codified in Roman law.

In the following passage from book I of *On Duties*, Cicero states his general presumption against war: war should only be undertaken with the aim of peace. We can also see outlined a number of the ideas that would come to influence the Western discourse about war: war must be a last resort, it must be preceded by a formal declaration and only after demands for reparation have not been met, and prisoners of war must be treated fairly. War, then, is not, morally speaking, a world apart: it does not excuse treacherous or deceitful acts.

From *On Duties*, bk. I, sections 34–41[2]

(34) Something else that must very much be preserved in public affairs is the justice of warfare. There are two types of conflict: the one proceeds by debate, the other by force. Since the former is the proper concern of a man, but the latter

[1] Cicero, *On Duties*, ed. M. T. Griffin and E. M. Atkins (Cambridge: Cambridge University Press, 1991).
[2] Ibid., pp. 14–19.

of beasts, one should only resort to the latter if one may not employ the former. (35) Wars, then, ought to be undertaken for this purpose, that we may live in peace, without injustice; and once victory has been secured, those who were not cruel or savage in warfare should be spared. Thus, our forefathers even received the Tusculani, the Aequi, the Volsci, the Sabini and the Hernici into citizenship. On the other hand they utterly destroyed Carthage and Numantia. I would prefer that they had not destroyed Corinth; but I believe that they had some specific purpose in doing so, in particular in view of its advantageous situation, to prevent the location itself from being some day an incitement to war.

In my opinion, our concern should always be for a peace that will have nothing to do with treachery. If I had been followed in this we would still have some republican government (if perhaps not the very best); whereas now we have none. And while you must have concern for those whom you have conquered by force, you must also take in those who have laid down their arms and seek refuge in the faith of generals, although a battering ram may have crashed against their wall. In this matter, justice was respected so greatly among our countrymen that the very men who had received into their good faith cities or peoples conquered in war would, by the custom of our forefathers, become their patrons.

(36) Indeed, a fair code of warfare has been drawn up, in full accordance with religious scruple, in the fetial laws of the Roman people. From this we can grasp that no war is just unless it is waged after a formal demand for restoration, or unless it has been formally announced and declared beforehand. When Popilius was general in charge of a province, Cato's son was serving as a novice soldier in his army. Popilius then decided to dismiss one of the legions, and included in the dismissal the young Cato, who was serving in that legion. But when, out of love of fighting, he remained in the army, Cato wrote to Popilius saying that if he allowed him to stay in the army he should bind him by a fresh military oath, since he could not in justice fight the enemy when his former oath had become void. Such was their extreme scrupulousness when making war. (37) There actually exists a letter of the Elder Marcus Cato to the younger Marcus, in which he writes that he has heard that his son, who was serving in Macedonia in the war against Perseus, had been discharged by the consul. He warns him therefore to be careful not to enter battle. For, he says, it is not lawful for one who is not a soldier to fight with the enemy.

A further point is that the name given to someone who ought properly to have been called a foe (*perduellis*), is in fact *hostis*. I notice that the grimness of the fact is lessened by the gentleness of the word. For *hostis* meant to our forefathers he whom we now call a stranger. The Twelve Tables show this: for example, "a day appointed for trial with a *hostis*"; and again, "'right of ownership cannot be alienated in favour of a *hostis*." What greater courteousness could there be than to call him against whom you are waging war by so tender a name? Long usage, however, has made the name harsher; for the word has abandoned the stranger, and now makes its proper home with him who bears arms against you.

(38) When, then, we are fighting for empire and seeking glory through warfare, those grounds that I mentioned a little above as just grounds for war should be wholly present. But wars in which the goal is the glory of empire are waged less bitterly. For just as in civilian matters we may compete in one way with an enemy, in another with a rival (for the latter contest is for honour and standing, the former for one's civic life or reputation), similarly the wars against the Celtiberi and the Cimbri were waged with enemies: the question was not who would rule, but who would exist. With the Latins, Sabini, Samnites, Carthaginians and Pyrrhus, on the other hand, the dispute was over empire. The Carthaginians were breakers of truces, and Hannibal was cruel, but the others were more just. . . .

(39) If any individuals have been constrained by circumstance to promise anything to an enemy, they must keep faith even in that. Indeed, Regulus did so when he was captured by the Carthaginians in the First Punic war and was sent to Rome for the purpose of arranging an exchange of captives, having vowed that he would return. For first of all, upon his arrival he proposed in the senate that the captives should not be returned; and then when his friends and relatives were trying to keep him, he preferred to go back to his punishment than to break the faith he had given to an enemy.

(40) In the Second Punic war, after the battle of Cannae, Hannibal sent to Rome ten men, bound by a solemn oath that they would return if they did not succeed in arranging for those whom the Romans had captured to be ransomed. The censors disfranchised all of them for the rest of their lives, on the grounds that they had broken their oath. They treated similarly one of them who incurred blame by fraudulently evading his solemn oath. For after leaving the camp with Hannibal's permission, he returned a little later saying that he had forgotten something or other. He then considered that he had released himself from his oath on leaving the camp; but he had done so only in word and not in fact. For on the question of keeping faith, you must always think of what you meant, not of what you said.

Another very great example of justice towards an enemy was established by our forefathers when a deserter from Pyrrhus promised the senate that he would kill the king by giving him poison. Fabricius and the senate returned him to Pyrrhus. In this way, they did not give approval to the killing in a criminal way of even a powerful enemy, and one who was waging war unprovoked. (41) Enough has been said about the duties of war.

Let us remember also that justice must be maintained even towards the lowliest. The lowliest condition and fortune is that of slaves; the instruction we are given to treat them as if they were employees is good advice: that one should require work from them, and grant to them just treatment.

There are two ways in which injustice may be done, either through force or through deceit; and deceit seems to belong to a little fox, force to a lion. Both of them seem most alien to a human being; but deceit deserves a greater hatred. And out of all injustice, nothing deserves punishment more than that of men who, just at the time when they are most betraying trust, act in such a way that they might appear to be good men.

Still from book I, the following passage exhibits the universal aspirations of Cicero's philosophy. Although he clearly favors the fellowship of family and immediate community and in the end asserts that "of all fellowships none is more serious, and none dearer, than that of each of us with the republic" (bk. I, section 57), it is evident that Cicero thinks the moral fellowship of mankind should know no boundaries.

From bk. I, sections 50–2[3]

(50) ... Perhaps, though, we should examine more thoroughly what are the natural principles of human fellowship and community. First is something that is seen in the fellowship of the entire human race. For its bonding consists of reason and speech, which reconcile men to one another, through teaching, learning, communicating, debating and making judgements, and unite them in a kind of natural fellowship. It is this that most distances us from the nature of other animals. To them we often impute courage, as with horses or lions, but we do not impute to them justice, fairness or goodness. For they have no share in reason and speech.

(51) The most widespread fellowship existing among men is that of all with all others. Here we must preserve the communal sharing of all the things that nature brings forth for the common use of mankind, in such a way that whatever is assigned by statutes and civil law should remain in such possession as those laws may have laid down, but the rest should be regarded as the Greek proverb has it: everything is common among friends. ...

... (52) Therefore such things as the following are to be shared: one should not keep others from fresh water, should allow them to take fire from your fire, should give trustworthy counsel to someone who is seeking advice; for they are useful to those who receive them and cause no trouble to the giver. We should therefore both make use of them and always be contributing something to the common benefit. Since, though, the resources of individuals are small, but the mass of those who are in need is infinitely great, general liberality must be measured according to the limit laid down by Ennius, that his own light shine no less; then we shall still be capable of being liberal to those close to us.

Cicero then turns to the connections between justice and courage, exploring themes similar to those we have already encountered in Plato and Aristotle:

---

[3]   Ibid., pp. 21–2.

From bk. I, sections 61–2, 65–6, 68[4]

(61) ... The very fact that the statues we look upon are usually in military dress bears witness to our devotion to military glory.

(62) However, if the loftiness of spirit that reveals itself amid danger and toil is empty of justice, if it fights not for the common safety but for its own advantages, it is a vice. It is not merely unvirtuous; it is rather a savagery which repels all civilized feeling. Therefore the Stoics define courage well when they call it the virtue which fights on behalf of fairness. For that reason no one has won praise who has pursued the glory of courage by treachery and cunning; for nothing can be honourable from which justice is absent. (63) Therefore Plato's words are splendid: "Knowledge," he said, "if separated from justice, should indeed be termed craftiness rather than wisdom." But furthermore, a spirit which is ready to face danger, but is driven by selfish desire rather than the common benefit should be called not courage, but audacity. Therefore we require men who are brave and of great spirit also to be good and straightforward, friends of truth and not in the least deceitful: such are the central qualities for which justice is praised. ...

(65) It is not, therefore, those who inflict injury, but those who prevent it, whom we should consider the men of courage and great spirit. A true and wise greatness of spirit judges that deeds and not glory are the basis of the honourableness that nature most seeks. It prefers not to seem pre-eminent but to be so: he who is carried by the foolishness of the ignorant mob should not be counted a great man. Furthermore, the loftier a man's spirit, the more easily he is driven by desire for glory to injustice. This is slippery ground indeed: scarcely a man can be found who, when he has undertaken toil and confronted dangers, does not yearn for glory as a kind of payment for his achievements.

(66) A brave and great spirit is in general seen in two things. One lies in disdain for things external, in the conviction that a man should admire, should choose, should pursue nothing except what is honourable and seemly, and should yield to no man, nor to agitation of the spirit, nor to fortune. The second thing is that you should, in the spirit I have described, do deeds which are great, certainly, but above all beneficial, and you should vigorously undertake difficult and laborious tasks which endanger both life itself and much that concerns life. ...

(68) It is not consistent for a man who is not broken by fear to be broken by desires, nor for one who has proved himself unconquered by toil to be conquered by pleasure. Therefore you must avoid these, and shun also the desire for money. Nothing is more the mark of a mean and petty spirit than to love riches; nothing more honourable and more magnificent than to despise money if you are without it, but if you have it to devote it to liberality and beneficence. Beware also the desire for glory, as I have said. For it destroys the liberty for which men of great

---

[4] Ibid., pp. 25–8.

spirit ought to be in competition. Nor should you seek military commands. In fact sometimes these should be refused and sometimes even resigned. . . .

After discussing the relations between justice and courage, Cicero turns to the relations between military and civic virtues. He steadfastly maintains that the virtues of public office are more worthy of our respect than those of the military profession.

From bk. I, sections 74–5, 77–9[5]

(74) Most men consider that military affairs are of greater significance than civic; I must deflate that opinion. For men have not infrequently sought war out of desire for glory. This has most often been true of men of great spirit and talent, and all the more so if military service suits them and they love the business of warfare. However, if we are prepared to judge the matter correctly, many achievements of civic life have proved greater and more famous than those of war.

(75) Themistocles may rightly be praised, and his name possess greater renown than Solon's, Salamis may be summoned as a witness to a famous victory, which may indeed be ranked above the counsel that Solon showed when he instituted the Areopagus; in fact, however, the latter should be judged no less splendid than the former. For the former benefit was a single one; the latter will serve the city for ever: by that counsel the very laws of the Athenians and their ancestral institutions are preserved. Themistocles could claim to have helped the Areopagus in nothing; the Areopagus, however, might truly claim to have assisted him: the very war was waged according to the counsel of the senate that Solon had established. . . .

(77) The best expression of all this is the verse which, I gather, is often attacked by shameless and envious men:

> Let arms yield to the toga, and laurels to laudation.

To mention no others, when I held the helm of the republic, did not arms then yield to the toga? Never was there more serious danger to the republic than then, and never was there greater quiet. Through my vigilance and my counsel the very arms swiftly slipped and fell from the hands of the most audacious citizens. Was any achievement of war ever so great? What military triumph can stand comparison? (78) I am allowed to boast to you, Marcus my son. For yours it is both to inherit my glory and to imitate my deeds. Pompey himself, indeed, whose military exploits won lavish praise, paid me the tribute of saying in the hearing of many that he would have won his third triumph in vain had my service to the

5   Ibid., pp. 29–32.

republic not ensured that he had somewhere to celebrate it. Therefore the courageous deeds of civilians are not inferior to those of soldiers. Indeed the former should be given even more effort and devotion than the latter.

(79) That honourableness that we seek from a lofty and magnificent spirit is in general produced not by bodily strength, but by strength of spirit. However, we must exercise the body, training it so that when it has to attend to business or endure hard work it is able to obey counsel and reason. The honourableness that we seek depends entirely upon the concern and reflection of the spirit. In this field the civilians who are in charge of public affairs provide no less a benefit than those who wage war. And so it is by often their counsel that a war may be avoided or terminated, and sometimes declared; it was through Marcus Cato's counsel that the Third Punic war was declared, and his authority had effect even after his death. (80) We must therefore value the reason which makes decisions above the courage which makes battle; yet we must be careful to do that because we have reasoned about what is beneficial, and not merely for the sake of avoiding war. Moreover, war should always be undertaken in such a way that one is seen to be aiming only at peace.

Turning now to book III of *On Duties*, we revisit the issue of civic justice. Cicero writes in a time when civil wars ravaged the empire and is concerned with reviving the virtues of citizenship and the sense of communal fellowship.

From bk. III, sections 21–4, 26–32[6]

(21) Now then: for one man to take something from another and to increase his own advantage at the cost of another's disadvantage is more contrary to nature than death, than poverty, than pain and than anything else that may happen to his body or external possessions. In the first place, it destroys the common life and fellowship of men: for if we are so minded that any one man will use theft or violence against another for his own profit, then necessarily the thing that is most of all in accordance with nature will be shattered, that is the fellowship of the human race. (22) Suppose that each limb were disposed to think that it would be able to grow strong by taking over to itself its neighbour's strength; necessarily the whole body would weaken and die. In the same way, if each one of us were to snatch for himself the advantages other men have and take what he could for his own profit, then necessarily fellowship and community among men would be overthrown. It is permitted to us – nature does not oppose it – that each man should prefer to secure for himself rather than for another anything connected with the necessities of life. However, nature does not allow us to increase our means, our resources and our wealth by despoiling others.

6 Ibid., pp. 108–11.

(23) The same thing is established not only in nature, that is in the law of nations, but also in the laws of individual peoples, through which the political community of individual cities is maintained: one is not allowed to harm another for the sake of one's own advantage. For the laws have as their object and desire that the bonds between citizens should be unharmed. If anyone tears them apart, they restrain him by death, by exile, by chains or by fine. Nature's reason itself, which is divine and human law, achieves this object to a far greater extent. Whoever is willing to obey it (everyone will obey it who wants to live in accordance with nature) will never act so as to seek what is another's, nor to appropriate for himself something that he has taken from someone else. (24) For loftiness and greatness of spirit, and, indeed, friendliness, justice and liberality, are far more in accordance with nature than pleasure, than life, than riches. Indeed to disdain these, when comparing them with the common benefit, and value them as nothing, is the mark of a great and lofty spirit. On the other hand, for anyone to take from someone else for the sake of his own advantage is more contrary to nature than death or pain or anything else of the type. . . .

(26) Again, if a man acts violently against someone else in order to secure some advantage himself, he either considers that he is doing nothing contrary to nature, or else he judges that death, poverty, pain, and the loss of children, relations or friends are more to be avoided than the doing of an injustice to someone. If he thinks that acting violently against other men involves doing nothing contrary to nature – then how can you argue with him? For he takes all the "human" out of a human. If, on the other hand, he thinks that such action should be avoided, but that death, poverty and pain are far worse, his error is that he counts a failing of body or fortune as more serious than any failing of spirit.

Therefore all men should have this one object, that the benefit of each individual and the benefit of all together should be the same. If anyone arrogates it to himself, all human intercourse will be dissolved. (27) Furthermore, if nature prescribes that one man should want to consider the interests of another, whoever he may be, for the very reason that he is a man, it is necessary, according to the same nature, that what is beneficial to all is something common. If that is so, then we are all constrained by one and the same law of nature; and if that also is true, then we are certainly forbidden by the law of nature from acting violently against another person. The first claim is indeed true; therefore the last is true.

(28) Now surely it is absurd to say, as some do, that they would not deprive a parent or brother of anything for their own advantage, but that there is another rationale for the rest of the citizens. Such men decree that no justice and no fellowship exist among citizens for the sake of common benefit, an opinion that breaks up all fellowship in the city. There are others again who say that account should be taken of other citizens, but deny it in the case of foreigners; such men tear apart the common fellowship of the human race. When that is removed then kindness, liberality, goodness and justice are utterly destroyed. Those who destroy them must be judged irreverent even in respect of the immortal gods; for

the fellowship among mankind that they overturn was established by the gods; and the tightest bond of that fellowship is that it be thought more contrary to nature for one man to deprive another for the sake of his own advantage than to endure every disadvantage, whether it affects externals or the body or even the spirit itself – so long as it is free from injustice. For that single virtue is the mistress and queen of virtues.

(29) But perhaps someone might object: would not a wise man, if he is dying of hunger, steal food from another man, if he could benefit no one? Not at all; for my life is not more beneficial to me than to be so disposed in spirit that I would not do violence to anyone for my own advantage. What if a good man were to be able to rob of his clothes Phalaris, a cruel and monstrous tyrant, to prevent himself from dying of cold? Might he not do it?

Such questions are very easy to decide. (30) For if it is for your own benefit that you deprive even someone who is of no benefit whatsoever, you will have acted inhumanly and against the law of nature. If, however, you are the kind of person who, if you were to remain alive, could bring great benefit to the political community and to human fellowship, and if *for that reason* you deprive someone else of something, that is not a matter for rebuke. In situations that are not of that kind, however, each man should endure disadvantage to himself rather than diminish the advantages that someone else enjoys. Illness, want or anything else of that sort are not, then, more contrary to nature than to take or to covet that which belongs to another. The neglect of the common benefit is, on the other hand, contrary to nature; for it is unjust. (31) Therefore the law of nature itself, which preserves and maintains that which is beneficial to men, will undoubtedly decree that the necessities of life should be transferred from an inactive and useless person to someone who is wise, good and brave, who, if he were to die, would greatly detract from the common benefit; he must, however, do this in such a way that he does not, out of self-esteem or self-love, find a pretext for injustice. In this way he will always discharge his duty by having consideration for what is beneficial to mankind and to human fellowship, which I so frequently mention.

(32) Now it is very easy to make a judgement in the case of Phalaris. For there can be no fellowship between us and tyrants – on the contrary there is a complete estrangement – and it is not contrary to nature to rob a man, if you are able, whom it is honourable to kill. Indeed, the whole pestilential and irreverent class ought to be expelled from the community of mankind.

We may be a bit surprised at Cicero's summary treatment of the thorny issue of tyrannicide in this last section. It must, however, be read against the backdrop of the murder of Caesar, which had occurred that same year. Cicero was eager to show his support for Caesar's assassins, hoping thereby to regain his political influence. His plan backfired, however, and the following year he was himself executed.

6

Early Church Fathers (Second to Fourth Centuries)

Pacifism and Defense of the Innocent

> The glory that courage brings resides not only in the strength of arm and body but in the virtue of the soul, and the essence of the virtue is not to be found in inflicting injury but in preventing it.
>
> Ambrose, *On the Duties of the Clergy*

Much of what later came to be thought of as just war theory took shape in the first centuries of the Christian era. Interestingly, this is not because questions about war and military service played a prominent role among the early Christian writers – quite the opposite. Rather, their views on the ethics of war took shape as a by-product of sustained reflections on the overall relationship between moral commitments, on the one hand, and political reality, on the other.

As Christians, they were certainly *in* this world, as Jesus himself had been, aiming to spread the gospel and set an example of peacefulness and love. But they were also living in eschatological expectation of a life *outside* this world. Indeed, many early Christians expected the return of the Savior to be imminent and thus cared little for the demands of this world.

As Romans, they were peaceful and obedient inhabitants of the Roman territory, giving to Caesar what was Caesar's, but simultaneously they were a minority – sometimes even a persecuted minority – with ambitions and hopes that were in real conflict with those of the Roman regime.

These are merely some of the tensions found in the relationship of the early Christian communities to the temporal authorities of Rome. As time went by, the nature of these tensions changed. The hopes for an immediate return of Christ were gradually replaced by an attitude of patience and acceptance of this world as a place of pilgrimage. And as the number of Christians grew and their numbers were taken from all walks of life, the sense of isolation and distinctness from the rest of society decreased. As ever more soldiers, bureaucrats, and politicians converted, Christians could hardly sustain a view of themselves as existing totally apart from the affairs of the state.

Nonetheless, it is reasonable to say that during the first three centuries AD, the mainstream of Christianity adopted what we could call a moderate pacifist stance. This pacifism had two sources of inspiration: Christ's clear injunctions to non-violence in the New Testament, and the view that the world is evil and will soon wither away. Both of these sources were challenged, however: First, there were many signs in the Bible, especially in the Old Testament, but also in the New, that use of military force could be acceptable, sometimes even honorable and willed by God. And second, there was no evident promise in the Scriptures that the Second Coming would be immediate, nor an injunction that Christians should not play an active, or at least an acquiescing, role in this world.

Overall, the self-understanding of Christianity up until the accession of Constantine to the throne – and the accompanying rise of the Christian religion from a faith for outsiders to an official, state-approved church – was one of detachment and skepticism toward the violent weapons of this world, combined with an acceptance of this world as a place where faith, hope, and charity could be displayed. This attitude also forms the backbone of the pacifism of this era. Mostly, this is not an *absolute* pacifism, but an expression of resistance against the evils of this world, including not least the idolatrous practices and frequent brutality associated with Roman military life. Christian apologists were trying to give witness to the pagans that Christianity represented something new, peaceful, and harmonious, frequently citing the saying from Isaiah (2:4) that swords will be turned into plowshares. Yet at the same time, they wanted to show that they were obedient and useful members of their society, able to contribute to all the tasks demanded by that society, within certain limits. Once again, the saying from Isaiah was pertinent: the rejection of the sword was not destructive but constructive, contributing to the well-being of society as a whole.

As mentioned, obedience to the rulers of this world had its limits. For many influential Christian thinkers in the pre-Constantine era, these limits precluded – or at least severely limited – rightful participation in armed battle. It is important to note, however, that since military service in the Roman Empire was, for most people, not mandatory, this stance did not require stark disobedience, merely passive resistance. Later, after the rise of Christianity to a place of prominence within the Roman Empire, these moral limits remained much the same, but they now had different implications, allowing support for participation in war as long as the war was truly just.

It should be noted that through most of this period, at least from the 170s onward, Christians *did* participate in the armed forces.[1] While many of these were no doubt already soldiers when they converted, it is also likely that some enlisted even after conversion. Thus, however strongly we wish to emphasize the pacifism of the early church, there is no doubt that Christian participation in military affairs was not unheard of. Even Tertullian, who for the most part endorses a pacifist position, acknowledges that Christians serve in the army as good Romans (cf. *Apology*, 42.2–3). And his contemporary Clement of Alexandria, another mostly pacifist voice, exhorts soldier converts to obey the military commander as long as he gives just commands (cf. *Exhortation to the Greeks*, X.100.2).

In the following we include statements from five important early theologians reflecting on military service. From Justin Martyr (ca. 100–ca. 160), via Tertullian (ca.160–ca. 220), Origen (ca. 185–ca. 254), and Lactantius (ca. 240–ca. 320), to Ambrose (ca. 339–397), we see a range of attitudes being displayed. Tertullian and Origen come across as the most principled pacifists, while Ambrose stands as a precursor to Augustine, supporting the idea of just wars, and addressing many of the issues that are inevitably raised when Christians come to contemplate the awful responsibility of actually commanding the use of armed force, rather than being critical outsiders who can afford to see the politics of this world as a matter of little concern. As for Justin Martyr and Lactantius, while extolling the virtue of peace that is to be the hallmark of Christians, they fail to enunciate an absolute rejection of the use of armed force.

From Justin Martyr, *First Apology*, chap. 39[2]

When the Prophetic Spirit speaks and foretells the future, he says, "The Law shall come out of Sion and the Lord's word from Jerusalem. And he will judge the Gentiles and reproach many people, and they will beat the swords into plows and their spears into pruning hooks. And nation will not raise its sword against nation, and they will no longer learn the arts of war" (Isaiah 2:4). You can believe that this prophecy, too, was fulfilled. For twelve men, ignorant and unskilled in speaking as they were, went out from Jerusalem to the world, and with the help of God announced to every race of men that they had been sent by Christ to teach the word of God to everyone, and we who formerly killed

---

[1] See James Turner Johnson, *The Quest for Peace* (Princeton, NJ: Princeton University Press, 1987), chap. 1, for a thorough discussion of military practices among early Christians. Johnson thereby argues against older standard accounts such as that of Ronald H. Bainton in *Christian Attitudes towards War and Peace* (New York: Abingdon Press, 1960), which claimed that the pacifism of the early church was quite absolute and strongly condemned all participation in the military.

[2] From Louis J. Swift (ed. and trans.), *The Early Fathers on War and Military Service* (Wilmington, DE: Michael Glazier, 1983), pp. 34–5. In putting together this chapter, which consists of disparate texts from a large number of authors, we are indebted to Dr. Swift's fine collection of texts.

one another not only refuse to make war on our enemies but in order to avoid lying to our interrogators or deceiving them, we freely go to our deaths confessing Christ.

From Tertullian, *On Idolatry*, chap. 19[3]

But the question now is whether a member of the faithful can become a soldier and whether a soldier can be admitted to the Faith even if he is a member of the rank and file who are not required to offer sacrifice or decide capital cases. There can be no compatibility between an oath made to God and one made to man, between the standard of Christ and that of the devil, between the camp of light and the camp of darkness. The soul cannot be beholden to two masters, God and Caesar. Moses, to be sure, carried a rod; Aaron wore a military belt and John had a breast plate. If one wants to play around with the topic, Jesus, son of Nun [i.e. Joshua] led an army and the Jewish nation went to war. But how will a Christian do so? Indeed how will he serve in the army even during peacetime without the sword that Jesus Christ has taken away? Even if soldiers came to John and got advice on how they ought to act, even if the centurion became a believer, the Lord, by taking away Peter's sword, disarmed every soldier thereafter. We are not allowed to wear any uniform that symbolizes a sinful act.

From Tertullian, *On the Crown*, chap. 11[4]

Will a son of peace who should not even go to court take part in battle[?] Will a man who does not avenge wrongs done to himself have any part in chains, prisons, tortures and punishments[?] Will he perform guard duty for anyone other than Christ, or will he do so on the Lord's day when he is not doing it for Christ Himself[?] Will he stand guard at the temples which he has forsworn[?] Will he go to a banquet at places where the Apostle disapproves of it? . . . By looking around one can see how many other forms of wrongdoing are involved in fulfilling the duties of military camps, things which must be considered violations of God's law. Carrying the title "Christian" from the camp of life to the camp of darkness is itself a violation.

The situation is different if the faith comes to a man after he is in the army, as with the soldiers whom John admitted to baptism and the converted centurion whom Christ praised and the one whom Peter instructed in the faith. Nonetheless, once a man has accepted the faith and has been marked with its seal, he must immediately leave the service, as many have done, or he has to engage in all

---

[3]   Ibid., pp. 41–2.
[4]   Ibid., pp. 43–4.

kinds of quibbling to avoid offending God in ways that are forbidden to men even outside the service. Or, finally, he will have to endure for God what civilian members of the faith have been no less willing to accept. Military service offers neither impunity for wrongdoing nor immunity from martyrdom. The Gospel is one and the same for Christians everywhere. Jesus will deny everyone who denies Him and will acknowledge everyone who acknowledges Him. He will save the life that has been given up for his Name's sake but will destroy the one that was saved at the expense of his Name for money's sake. . . . [W]e must either refuse offices in order to avoid falling into sin or we must undergo martyrdom in order to be freed from these obligations.

The following excerpt is from the Alexandrian theologian Origen's apologetic work *Contra Celsum* (Against Celsus). Celsus was a pagan writer who, in the late second century, wrote the treatise *A True Discourse*, attacking Christianity. One of his points of attack concentrated on the weakening of the empire that would follow if everyone lived by the example of the Christians and deserted all earthly affairs. (This shows that at least one prominent writer held that Christians actually did renounce military life and similar exigencies of life in the Roman Empire.) Writing in the ensuing century, Origen replies forcefully to these charges. Note that Origen holds that the non-violent contributions of the Christians, chiefly prayer, actually do contribute positively to the waging of just war. Hence, while he urges that Christians should not take part in battle, he does not dismiss all use of armed force as necessarily wrong.

From Origen, *Against Celsus*, bk. 8, chap. 73[5]

Celsus goes on to encourage us "to assist the emperor with all our strength, to work with him on just undertakings, to fight for him and to serve in his army, if he requires it, either as a soldier or a general." To this we should reply that when the occasion arises, we provide the emperors with divine assistance, as it were, by putting on the "armor of God" (Ephesians 6:11). We do so in obedience to the voice of the Apostle who says "My advice is that first and foremost you offer prayers, supplications, petitions and thanksgiving for all men, especially for the emperors, and all those in authority" (1 Timothy 2:1–2). To be sure, the more pious a man is the more effectively does he assist the emperors – more so than the troops that go out and kill as many of the enemy as possible on the battleline. This would be our answer to those who are strangers to our faith and who ask us to take up arms and to kill men for the common good. Even in your religion priests attached to certain images and guardians of temples which are dedicated

---

[5] Ibid., pp. 54–5.

to what you believe are gods should keep their right hand undefiled for sacrifice so as to make their usual offerings to beings that you consider deities with hands that are free of blood and murder. And, of course, in war time you do not enlist your priests. If this is a reasonable procedure, how much more so is it for Christians to fight as priests and worshippers of God while others fight as soldiers[?] Though they keep their right hands clean, the Christians fight through their prayers to God on behalf of those doing battle in a just cause and on behalf of an emperor who is ruling justly in order that all opposition and hostility toward those who are acting rightly may be eliminated. What is more, by overcoming with our prayers all the demons who incite wars, who violate oaths and who disturb the peace we help emperors more than those who are supposedly doing the fighting. . . . [W]e do battle on [the emperor's] behalf by raising a special army of piety through our petitions to God.

In discussing the role of violence in Biblical history, Origen (in *Against Celsus*, 3.8 and 7.26) draws a sharp distinction between the anti-violent origins of Christianity and the violent historical situation surrounding the Jews of the Old Testament. He holds that the former has superseded the latter as a moral ideal. Origen also insists on reading the Old Testament account of wars allegorically.

From Origen, *Homilies on Joshua,* bk. 15, chap. 1[6]

Unless those carnal wars [i.e. of the Old Testament] were a symbol of spiritual wars, I do not think that the Jewish historical books would ever have been passed down to the Apostles to be read by Christ's followers in their churches . . . Thus, the Apostle, being aware that physical wars are no longer to be waged by us but that our struggles are to be only battles of the soul against spiritual adversaries, gives orders to the soldiers of Christ like a military commander when he says, "Put on the armor of God so as to be able to hold your ground against the wiles of the devil" (Ephesians 6:11).

The North African Christian apologist Lactantius addressed military matters in writing, both in the years leading up to and in the years following the accession of Constantine to the throne. His early remarks display a strong pacifist tendency, but in the service of the emperor who has vowed to defend Christianity, his views change. Both of the following excerpts are from his *Divine Institutes*, the first being from the period before Constantine's accession to the throne, while the second was clearly added at a later date.

---

[6] Ibid., p. 59.

From Lactantius, *Divine Institutes,* bk. 6, chap. 20[7]

It is not right for those who are striving to stay on the path of virtue to become associated with this kind of wholesale slaughter [i.e. of the gladiatorial combats, which many Christian writers roundly criticized] or to take part in it. For when God forbids killing, [H]e is not only ordering us to avoid armed robbery, which is contrary even to public law, but He is forbidding what men regard as ethical. Thus, it is not right for a just man to serve in the army since justice itself is his form of service. Nor is it right for a just man to charge someone with a capital crime. It does not matter whether you kill a man with the sword or with a word since it is killing itself that is prohibited. And so there must be no exception to this command of God. Killing a human being whom God willed to be inviolable, is always wrong.

From Lactantius, *Divine Institutes,* bk. 1, chap. 1 [added to the work after its original composition][8]

Now we take up our task under your auspices, O Constantine, greatest of emperors, the first of Roman princes to cast aside error and to acknowledge and honor the majesty of the one true God. For when that most happy day dawned all over the world, when the all high God raised you to the heights of power, you inaugurated your rule – desirable and beneficial as it is to all men – with a noble beginning. You brought back justice, which had been overturned and blotted out, and you expiated the horrible crimes of other rulers. . . . On those who continue to afflict the just in other parts of the world that same omnipotent Father will wreak vengeance for their wrongdoing. The more delayed that vengeance is the more severe it will be, for just as He is a most indulgent Father toward good men, so, too, is [H]e a very strict judge toward the wicked. In my desire to see to it that God be revered and worshipped, whom should I call upon, whom should I speak to but the man who has restored justice and wisdom to human affairs[?]

In Lactantius, and somewhat later in the church historian Eusebius, we can see the kind of intense Christian loyalty to the Empire (later to be tempered by Augustine) that was engendered by Constantine's accession to the throne. Henceforth, the pacifist attitudes expressed by earlier Christian writers become much rarer, and in its place the idea of just war (*iustum bellum*) gains acceptance. The most influential teaching on justice and war from this era comes from Augustine, whom we will discuss in the next chapter. But even before him some of the Greek theologians – among them Athanasius (296–373) – and not least the

---

[7] Ibid., pp. 62–3.
[8] Ibid., pp. 67–8.

Latin theologian and bishop Ambrose of Milan formulated noteworthy ideas about licit warfare.[9]

In Ambrose we see that the preoccupation with virtue and right living, so central to the earlier writers, still holds pride of place. But now, exerting oneself for one's homeland, even by armed force, has become a duty. While Ambrose, like Augustine after him, denounces personal self-defense as immoral, he praises sacrifice on behalf of the innocent and the common good – if necessary by means of war – as long as agreements are kept and rules respected, so that no unfair advantage is secured. Ambrose insists that the New Testament injunctions to love one's enemy and turn the other cheek are fully valid, even in war, and hence one should not be informed by a hatred of evildoers or an urge to kill. The good Christian hates evil, not evildoers.

From Ambrose, *On the Duties of the Clergy*, bk. 1, chap. 28.139–41[10]

139. How great a thing justice is can be gathered from the fact that there is no place, nor person, nor time with which it has nothing to do. It must even be preserved in all dealings with enemies. For instance, if the day or the spot for a battle has been agreed upon with them, it would be considered an act against justice to occupy the spot beforehand, to anticipate the time. . . .

140. If, then, justice is binding, even in war, how much more ought we to observe it in time of peace. . . . [F]aith and justice should be observed even in war; and . . . it could not but be a disgraceful thing if faith were violated.

141. So also the ancients used to give their foes a less harsh name, and called them strangers. For enemies used to be called strangers after the customs of old.

From Ambrose, *On the Duties of the Clergy*, bk. 1, chap. 36.179[11]

The glory that courage brings resides not only in the strength of arm and body but in the virtue of the soul, and the essence of the virtue is not to be found in inflicting injury but in preventing it. For anyone who does not prevent an injury to a companion, if he can do so, is as much at fault as he who inflicts it. Following this principle Holy Moses provided an early proof of his courage. For when he saw a Jew being injured by an Egyptian, he defended his countryman to the point of killing the Egyptian and hiding him in the sand.

[9] See also Johnson, *The Quest for Peace*, pp. 53 ff.
[10] This excerpt taken from Philip Schaff and Henry Wace (eds.), *A Select Library of Nicene and Post-Nicene Fathers of the Christian Church*, Second Series, vol. 10, trans. H. de Romestin, ass. by E. de Romestin and H. T. F. Duckworth (Grand Rapids, MI: William B. Eerdmans, [1896] 1955), pp. 23–4. Ambrose is here inspired by and refers to Cicero's *De Officiis*, bk. 1 (see chap. 5, this volume).
[11] Swift, *The Early Fathers*, pp. 101–2.

From Ambrose, *Discourse on Psalm 118*, bk. 15, chap. 22[12]

Therefore, it was not evildoers, but evil words that David hated, for when he said, "I have hated evil" he did not add the word "man." Given the fact that Christ says in the Gospel, "Love your enemies" (Matthew 5:44) and the Apostle says, "Bless those who persecute you, and do not curse them" (Romans 12:4), what excuse will a man living according to the principles of the Gospel have for hating wrongdoers? You should interpret the words as meaning that he hated evil itself rather than evildoers, who, despite their actions, are subject to conversion through the preaching of the gospel.

From Ambrose, *Discourse on Luke*, bk. 5, chap. 58[13]

Unless you first free yourself from all stain of sin so as to prevent your interior disposition from giving rise to dissension and strife, you cannot provide a remedy for others. In the area of peace begin with yourself so that when you have established peace there, you can take it to others. For how can you purify the heart of others unless you have done the same to yourself first[?]

From Ambrose, *On the Duties of the Clergy*, bk. 3, chap. 3.23[14]

There is nothing that goes against nature as much as doing violence to another person for the sake of one's own advantage. Natural feeling argues that we ought to look out for everyone else, to lighten the other man's burdens and to expend our efforts on his behalf. Any man wins a glorious reputation for himself if he strives for universal peace at personal risk to himself. Everyone believes it is much more commendable to protect one's own country from destruction than to protect oneself from danger and that exerting oneself for one's country is much superior to leading a peaceful life of leisure with all the pleasures it involves.

From Ambrose, *On the Duties of the Clergy*, bk. 3, chap. 15.91[15]

It is related as a memorable deed of a Roman general,[16] that when the physician of a hostile king came to him and promised to give him poison, he sent him back

---

[12]   Ibid., p. 103.
[13]   Ibid., p. 109.
[14]   Ibid., p. 98.
[15]   Schaff and Wace (eds.), *A Select Library*, p. 82.
[16]   [*Editor's footnote 3, p. 82:*] This affair happened in the war which Pyrrhus waged against the Roman people. Caius Fabricius was the general who refused to take advantage of the base offer.

bound to the enemy. In truth, it is a noble thing for a man to refuse to gain the victory by foul acts, after he has entered on the struggle for power. He did not consider virtue to lie in victory, but declared that to be a shameful victory unless it was gained with honour.

From Ambrose, *On Tobias*, bk. 15, chap. 51[17]

Consider the text of the Law: "You will not exact interest from your brothers; you will exact it from a foreigner" (Deuteronomy, 23:19–20). At that time who was a foreigner if not Amalech, Ammoreaus or other such enemies? From such people the Law says, "Exact interest." That is to say, you can legitimately demand interest from someone whom you have every right to wish harm to and against whom you can lawfully wage war.

While this last quote seems to make any and every "foreigner" a potential enemy, Ambrose also holds that war is justified only when it either punishes wrongdoing, is defensive, or – in the case of several Old Testament wars – aims to take possession of territory promised by God (cf. *On the Duties of the Clergy*, bk. 1, chaps. 27 and 35, bk. 3, chaps. 8 and 19; discussed in Swift [ed. and trans.], p. 100). This is indeed the general tenor of Ambrose's teaching on war: war is never just when waged for self-interest, lust, or worldly ambition, and must never be waged with a wicked intention or a hateful heart. Ambrose, like Augustine after him, is less clear when it comes to waging war for the sake of spreading the true faith – in his treatise *Of the Christian Faith* he encourages the Emperor (in 378) to fight the Goths with religious zeal, comparing the Goths to the frightful Gog of Ezekiel 39. However, the disastrous defeat of the Roman army at Hadrianople seems to have tempered such triumphalism in Ambrose (see Swift [ed. and trans.], p. 106). While he seems sometimes to have advocated the use of violence against non-believers, he also criticizes excessive use of force and indeed heavily rebukes the Emperor Theodosius in 390 for the cruelty with which he had punished a revolt at Thessalonica.

In short, in Ambrose there is no full-fledged, consistent teaching on war, but rather an expression of the peace-oriented virtue ethics of the early Christians, applied to an era of Christian rule. This era does require the use of the sword, but Ambrose holds out hope and indeed requires that this must not endanger the virtues of the true Christian.

---

[17] Swift, *The Early Fathers*, p. 99.

7

Augustine (354–430)

Just War in the Service of Peace

Peace is not sought in order to provoke war, but war is waged in order to attain peace. Be a peacemaker, then, even by fighting, so that through your victory you might bring those whom you defeat to the advantages of peace.

Letter 189, to Boniface

Saint Augustine, bishop of Hippo in North Africa in the early fifth century and one of the most productive and influential theologians the church has ever produced, has often been called the founder of the just war tradition. Our previous chapters show this to be at least inaccurate, if not untrue. Augustine built on an existing body of work by earlier theologians, as well as by pre-Christian Greek and Latin philosophers – in this field as in so many others.

Moreover, Augustine did not systematize his disparate thoughts on war to any significant extent; his remarks on war, peace, and conflict are scattered throughout his extremely voluminous work. It would be the task of later thinkers – Gratian and his successors most notably – to shape Augustine's moral intuitions into a doctrine of just war.

Nonetheless, Augustine deserves his high reputation, if not as the originator, then at least as the prism through which earlier just war ideas are refracted and transmitted to the Middle Ages and modern times. While all but ignored in Eastern Orthodoxy, Augustine is probably the single most influential theologian within both the Catholic and most of the Protestant churches. In formulating their views on war, canon lawyers, scholastic theologians, Reformation thinkers, and a vast array of modern Christian thinkers have all referred to Augustine and used his language and ideas.

Augustine is strikingly nuanced in his views about war. Although he considers military force morally justified in certain cases, he never stops lamenting the fact that such violence has to be used at all. He defends just wars, but never with a light heart. In reading his statements, some will no doubt label him inconsistent since he sometimes defends what he at other times attacks. But many if not most of Augustine's reflections on political matters were written in direct response to ongoing events, and they were thus tailored to meet the concrete challenges he faced. Indeed, we should not look for absolute consistency in a collection of writings that spans five decades, and which replies to the most diverse of political quandaries.

The following selections are organized under three headings: (1) the reluctant just war theorist, (2) criteria for the use of force, and (3) force in the service of religion.

There are a large number of passages in Augustine's writings that deal directly or indirectly with warfare, and we cannot possibly cover them all here. The excerpts below suffice, however, to provide an overall picture of Augustine's views about war. These are also the passages which later theologians and jurists would most often cite in their own more systematic writings about war.

The Reluctant Just War Theorist

Augustine is not enthusiastic about political affairs and the accompanying necessity of waging war. While Aristotle emphasized the intimate connection between political institutions and human flourishing – a view that would later influence Thomas Aquinas – Augustine was less sanguine about the value of the temporal order for human happiness. According to Augustine, only those things that relate to mankind's salvation can be deemed truly meaningful, and thus, political institutions are foundationally important only insofar as they contribute to that aim. This view is reflected in Augustine's famous teaching of "the two cities," the City of God and the Earthly City, which are guided by "two loves": love of God (leading naturally to love of one's neighbor) and love of self. He famously says in his *City of God* (*De civitate Dei*): "The two cities, therefore, were created by two loves: the earthly city by love of oneself, even to the point of contempt for God; the heavenly city by the love of God, even to the point of contempt for oneself."[1]

The teaching of the two cities leads Augustine to take a less than enthusiastic approach to political affairs. Having to use violent force to keep the peace in this world is not something the wise or pious man does gladly, but merely out of necessity:

---

[1] From *City of God*, bk. XIV, chap. 28, p. 108. This page reference, and the majority of page references below, are to Ernest L. Fortin and Douglas Kries (eds.), *Augustine: Political Writings*, trans. Michael W. Tkacz and Douglas Kries (Indianapolis: Hackett, 1994).

From *City of God*, bk. IV, chap. 15[2]

Let our opponents consider the possibility that rejoicing over the extent of their reign is not appropriate for good men. To be sure, the iniquity of those against whom just wars were waged helped the empire to grow, because it surely would have stayed small if its neighbors were peaceful and just and did not, through wrongdoing, provoke war. Human affairs would have been happier that way. All kingdoms would have been small, enjoying concord with their neighbors. There would thus have been many kingdoms of peoples in the world, just as there are many homes of citizens in a city.

Waging war and extending the empire by subduing peoples is therefore viewed as happiness by the wicked, but as a necessity by the good. But because it would be worse if wrongdoers dominated those who are more just, it is not inappropriate to call even this necessity "happiness." Nevertheless, without doubt it is a better happiness to have concord with a good neighbor than to subjugate a bad one through war. It is a wicked prayer to wish for someone to hate or to fear so that there might be someone to conquer. If, then, by waging just wars, not impious or iniquitous ones, the Romans were able to acquire such a large empire, should not "the iniquity of foreigners" be worshipped like some goddess? Indeed, we see how much assistance she has given to the extension of the empire, making others into wrongdoers so that there might be someone to wage just wars against in order that the empire might grow.

From *City of God*, bk. XIX, chap. 7[3]

They say, however, that the wise man will wage only just wars – as if, mindful that he is human, he would not much rather lament that he is subject to the necessity of waging just wars. If they were not just, he would not be required to wage them, and thus he would be free of the necessity of war. It is the iniquity on the part of the adversary that forces a just war upon the wise man. Even if it did not give rise to the necessity of war, such iniquity must certainly be lamented by a human being since it belongs to human beings. Therefore, let anyone who reflects with sorrow upon these evils so great, so horrid, and so savage, confess that he is miserable. Anyone, however, who either permits or considers these things without sorrow in mind is certainly much more miserable, since he thinks himself happy because he has lost human feeling.

Augustine does not describe the horror of war primarily in terms of human suffering – although that certainly plays a part – but more in terms of virtue and

[2] Ibid., p. 32.
[3] Ibid., p. 149.

vice. War distracts pious human beings from the path of virtue and opens up a Pandora's box of vices; and, furthermore, there is no real virtue or glory to be had in waging war.

From *Against Faustus the Manichean*, bk. XXII, chap. 74[4]

What is it about war that is to be blamed? Is it that those who will die someday are killed so that those who will conquer might dominate in peace? This is the complaint of the timid, not of the religious. The desire for harming, the cruelty of revenge, the restless and implacable mind, the savageness of revolting, the lust for dominating, and similar things – these are what are justly blamed in wars. Often, so that such things might also be justly punished, certain wars that must be waged against the violence of those resisting are commanded by God or some other legitimate ruler and are undertaken by the good.

From *City of God*, bk. III, chap. 14[5]

This lust to dominate inflicts great evils on the human race and wears it down. Overwhelmed by it Rome exulted in her victory over Alba and used the term glory to describe the accolades she received for her crime because, as our Scriptures say, "in the desire of his heart the sinner wins praise and the wrongdoer is commended" (Psalm 10:3). Tear away the false and misleading disguise so that we may see the facts as they are. Let no one say to me, "This man or that one is great because he fought with so and so and beat him." Gladiators, too, are victorious. Their kind of cruelty also wins praise as its reward, but I think it is better to suffer the consequences of any kind of lethargy than to seek glory in that kind of fighting.

From *Letter 138, to Marcellinus*[6]

These precepts about patience that we have been discussing must always be observed with respect to one's interior disposition, and a spirit of benevolence must always permeate the will so as to avoid returning evil for evil. . . . [I]f the earthly city observes Christian principles, even its wars will be waged with the benevolent purpose that better provision might be made for the defeated to live harmoniously together in justice and godliness.

[4] Ibid., pp. 221–2.
[5] From Louis J. Swift (ed. and trans.), *The Early Fathers on War and Military Service* (Wilmington, DE: Michael Glazier, 1983), p. 118.
[6] Ibid., p. 122.

Yet, war is not sinful *per se*, as becomes clear in a letter Augustine writes to Boniface, a Roman governor in North Africa.

From *Letter 189, to Boniface*[7]

Do not think that it is impossible for anyone serving in the military to please God. Among those who did so was the holy David, to whom the Lord gave such great testimony. Among them also were many just men of that time. Among them also was the centurion who said to the Lord, "I am not worthy that you should enter under my roof, but only say the word and my servant will be healed; for I, too, am a man under authority and have soldiers under me: I say to one, 'go,' and he goes, and to another, 'come,' and he comes, and to my servant, 'do this,' and he does it.' " And the Lord said about him, "Amen, I say to you, I have not found such faith in Israel" (Matthew 8:8–10). . . . Among them also were those soldiers who came to John to be baptized. John was the holy precursor of the Lord and friend of the bridegroom. The Lord himself said of him, "There has arisen no one born of woman greater than John the Baptist" (Matthew 11:11). When they asked him what they should do, he replied to them, "Terrorize no one, accuse no one falsely, and be content with your pay" (Luke 3:14). He surely did not prohibit them from serving in the military when he commanded them to be content with their pay.

Those who serve God with the highest discipline of chastity, renouncing all worldly actions, indeed have a greater place before God. "Yet everyone," as the apostle says, "has his own proper gift from God, one after this manner, another after that" (1 Corinthians 7:7). Some, then, fight for you against invisible enemies by praying; you toil for them against visible barbarians by fighting. Would that there were one faith in all, for there would be both less toiling and the devil with his angels would be more easily overcome! Yet, because it is necessary in this world that the citizens of the kingdom of heaven are troubled by temptations among the erring and impious in order that they might be tried and tested as gold in the furnace (Proverbs 17:3), we should not want to live with only the holy and the just before the time in order that we might deserve to receive that life in its own time.

It is also noteworthy, but hardly surprising in light of his preoccupation with virtue, that Augustine questions the honorability of self-defense. While not primarily targeting military self-defense, the following famous passage from *On Free Choice of the Will (De libero arbitrio)* – which also introduces the distinction between human law and divine (or natural) law, so important for the later development of international law – emphasizes that force should primarily be used for

[7] Fortin and Kries (eds.), *Augustine: Political Writings*, pp. 219–20.

the defense of others.[8] This is a more rigorous view than later theologians like Aquinas would espouse. The latter viewed private self-defense as fully justifiable (see chap. 16, pp. 190–1 this volume, on Aquinas). Augustine's praise of forceful action in defense of *others*, echoing the earlier thought of his mentor Ambrose, would many centuries later provide a foundation for military action in support of innocent third parties – so-called humanitarian intervention.

From *On Free Choice of the Will*, bk. I, chaps. 5–6[9]

Augustine: It seems to me that it should first be discussed whether either an attacking enemy or a plotting assassin may be killed in defense of one's life, liberty, or chastity without any lust being involved.

Evodius: How can I declare that those who fight in defense of such things as these, which can be lost against their will, are free from lust? Or if such things cannot be lost against their will, why is it necessary to go so far as to kill a human being in defense of them?

Augustine: Then the law is not just which allows a traveler to kill a robber in order to avoid being killed by him. Nor is the law just which allows any man or woman, if able, to slay a violent rapist before the rape is committed. Also, a soldier is commanded by law to kill the enemy; if he refrains from such killing he is punished by his commander. What shall we dare say: that these laws are unjust, or rather that they are not laws? For it seems to me that an unjust law is not a law.

Evodius: I notice that the law is sufficiently protected against an accusation of this kind. The law gives license to lesser wrongdoings among the people it governs so that the greater ones might not be committed. The death of an unjust aggressor is a lesser evil than that of a man who is only defending himself. It is much more horrible that a human being should be violated against his will than that a violent attacker should be killed by his intended victim.

   Moreover, in killing an enemy the soldier acts as an agent of the law. That is why he can easily fulfill his duty without lust. And the law itself, which was enacted for the protection of the people, cannot be accused of lust, since the legislator, assuming that he enacted it at God's command, that is, in accordance with the mandates of eternal justice, was able to do so without any lust at all. And even if the law was decreed with a measure of lust, it does not follow that it must be obeyed out of lust, for a good

---

[8]   According to this view, soldiers fighting for their city or state in self-defense should not be seen as acting in personal self-defense, but rather as representatives of their city or state fighting for the common good and in defense of the innocent.

[9]   Fortin and Kries (eds.), *Augustine: Political Writings*, pp. 213–15, 216–17.

law can be enacted by a bad man. For the sake of argument, suppose that a man who has become a tyrant accepts a bribe from another man who, in his own interest, wants him to pass a law prohibiting the taking of any woman by force, even with a view to marriage. The law will not be evil simply for its having been enacted by an unjust and corrupt man. One can, therefore, obey without lust the law that, for the protection of the citizens, commands the use of violence to repel the violent attack of an enemy. The same can be said for all agents who are subject by law to some higher authority.

Still, I fail to see how these people are blameless because the law is blameless, for the law does not oblige them to kill but only leaves it in their power to do so. Hence, they are free not to kill anyone for the sake of things that can be lost against their will and thus should not be loved. Concerning life, some people may perhaps wonder whether it is not in some way removed from the soul when the body dies. If, however, life can be removed from the soul, then it should be despised; if it cannot, then there is nothing to fear. Concerning chastity, though, who would doubt but that it is located in the soul itself, seeing that it is a virtue? Hence, it cannot be wrenched away from someone by a violent rapist. Whatever he who was killed was about to wrench away was such that it was not in our control, and so I do not understand how we can call it our own. Consequently, I do not blame the law that permits such attackers to be killed, but I do not see how I might defend those who kill them.

Augustine: Much less can I see why you seek a defense for people whom no law holds to be guilty.

Evodius: No law, perhaps, among the ones that are manifest and read by human beings. I do not know whether or not, if divine providence administers all things, they might be held guilty by some stronger and most secret law. Before that law, how are those people free from sin who are defiled by human killing for the sake of things that ought to be despised? Therefore, it seems to me that the law written to govern a people is right to permit these things, and also that divine providence rightly punishes them. The human law deals with crimes that need to be punished if peace is to be maintained among ignorant human beings and does so to the extent that those matters can be regulated by man. The other sins have other suitable penalties, from which, it seems to me, only Wisdom can free us.

Augustine: I laud and approve this distinction of yours. . . . Therefore, if it is agreeable to you, let us call that law "temporal" which, although it is just, can nevertheless justly be changed in the course of time.

Evodius: Let us call it so.

Augustine: What about the law called the "supreme reason," which must always be observed and in virtue of which the wicked deserve misery and the good a life of happiness, and in virtue of which, moreover, the law that we agreed to call "temporal" is rightly enacted and rightly changed? Can that law of supreme reason seem to any intelligent being to be other than incommutable and eternal? Can it ever be unjust that the wicked be miserable and the good happy? Or that a moderate and venerable people choose their own magistrates, but a dissolute and iniquitous people be deprived of this privilege?

Evodius: I see that this is an eternal and unchangeable law.

Augustine insists that the aim of war must be peace. There is nothing paradoxical in this, since all human beings strive for peace in what they do, even in war. The challenge is to pursue the right and enduring kind of peace. There is a lower peace, which merely entails enforcement of someone's arbitrary will by force. And there is a higher peace, which consists in concord and order. It is this latter peace that must be sought for a war to be just:

From *City of God*, bk. XV, chap. 4[10]

The earthly city will not last forever, for when it is condemned to final punishment, it will cease to be a city. It possesses its own good here and now, and it is made joyful through its association with the joy that may be derived from such things. Because its good is not the sort of good that causes no difficulties for its lovers, this city is most often divided against itself by lawsuits, wars, and conflicts, and by victories that either cause death or are themselves subject to death. Out of whichever part of itself that has risen up to wage war against another part of itself, this city seeks to be the conqueror of peoples while being itself the captive of vices. If indeed its pride is elevated because it conquers, then its victory causes death. If, however, considering the common circumstances and vicissitudes of human life, the earthly city is troubled by possible adversities more than it is inflated by the successes that have already occurred, then its victory is itself subject to death, for it will not be able to dominate permanently those whom it was able to subjugate through conquest.

Nevertheless, it is not right to say that the things this city desires are not good, because, in its own human way, it is better by desiring them, for in order to obtain these base things, it desires a certain earthly peace. This peace it strives to obtain through war. If it triumphs and there is no one left to resist, there will be peace, which the parts of the city struggling against each other did not have before, for they were struggling miserably in a condition of scarcity in order to obtain the things they could not all have. Exhausting wars try to obtain this peace, and whatever achieves it is considered a glorious victory.

[10] Ibid., pp. 112–13.

When, however, those fighting with the more just cause triumph, who doubts that the victory should be celebrated and that the hoped-for peace has arrived? These things are good and without doubt they are gifts of God. If, however, to the neglect of better goods, the ones pertaining to the city on high, where victory will be secure in the eternal and highest peace, these lower goods are desired in such a way that they are believed to be the only goods, or else are loved more than the goods believed to be better, then misery necessarily follows and the misery that was already present increases.

From *City of God*, bk. XIX, chap. 11[11]

Because the name "peace" is also frequently used with respect to things which are subject to death, where there certainly is no eternal life, we prefer to call the end of this city, where its highest good will be, "eternal life" rather than "peace." Of this end the apostle says, "Now, indeed, having been liberated from sin and having become servants of God, you will have your reward in sanctification, your true end in eternal life" (Romans 6:22).

On the other hand, "eternal life" could be taken by those who are not familiar with the Sacred Scriptures to include also the life of the wicked. One might think this either because certain philosophers profess the immortality of the soul, or also because our faith professes the unending punishment of the impious, who certainly could not be eternally tormented unless they also lived eternally.

So that it can be understood more easily by all, it must be said that the end of this city, in which it will have its highest good, is either "peace in eternal life" or "eternal life in peace." Peace is such a great good that even with respect to earthly and mortal things, nothing is heard with greater pleasure, nothing desired more longingly, and in the end, nothing better can be found. If I wish to speak of it somewhat longer I will not, I think, be burdensome to readers, both because my subject is the end of this city and because of the very sweetness of peace, which is dear to all.

From *City of God*, bk. XIX, chap.12[12]

Anyone who pays any attention to human affairs and our common human nature, recognizes as I do that just as there is no one who does not wish to be joyful, so there is no one who does not wish to have peace. Indeed, even those who want war want nothing other than to achieve victory; by warring, therefore, they

---

[11]   Ibid., pp. 149–50.
[12]   Ibid., pp. 150, 152–3.

desire to attain a glorious peace. What else is victory, unless triumphing over the opposition? When this has happened, there will be peace. Therefore, even those who are eager to exercise the military virtues by commanding or fighting wage war with the intention of peace. Consequently, the desired end of war is peace, for everyone seeks peace, even by waging war, but no one seeks war by making peace. . . .

After all, even the evil wage war for the sake of the peace of their own associates, and they would want to make everyone their own, if they could, so that everyone and everything would be enslaved to one individual. How would that happen if they did not consent to his peace, either through love or fear? In this manner, pride imitates God in a distorted way. It hates equality with partners under God, but wants to impose its own domination upon its partners in place of God. Consequently, it hates the just peace of God and loves its own iniquitous peace. Nevertheless, it is not able not to love some sort of peace. Truly, there is no defect so contrary to nature that it wipes away even the last vestiges of nature. Accordingly, he who knows to prefer the upright to the deformed, and the ordered to the distorted, sees that the peace of the iniquitous, in comparison to the peace of the just, should not be called "peace" at all. However, it is necessary that even what is distorted be at peace in some way with a part of the things in which it exists or from which it is established. Otherwise, it would not exist at all.

From *Letter 189, to Boniface*[13]

Therefore, when you are arming for battle, think first that even your bodily strength is a gift of God. In this way, you will not think of using the gift of God against God. When fidelity is promised it must be kept, even to an enemy against whom war is being waged. How much more must it be kept with a friend for whom the war is fought! The will should be concerned with peace and necessity with war, so that God might liberate us from necessity and preserve us in peace. Peace is not sought in order to provoke war, but war is waged in order to attain peace. Be a peacemaker, then, even by fighting, so that through your victory you might bring those whom you defeat to the advantages of peace. "Blessed are the peacemakers," says the Lord, "for they will be called children of God" (Matthew 5:9). If human peace is so sweet for attaining the temporal well-being of mortals, how much more sweet is divine peace for attaining the eternal well-being of the angels! Let necessity slay the warring foe, not your will. As violence is returned to one who rebels and resists, so should mercy be to one who has been conquered or captured, especially when there is no fear of a disturbance of peace.

[13] Ibid., p. 220.

From *Letter 229, to Darius*[14]

Preventing war through persuasion and seeking or attaining peace through peaceful means rather than through war are more glorious things than slaying men with the sword. If those who engage in combat are good men, they are undoubtedly striving for peace, but they do so by shedding blood; your charge [as ambassador], however, was to prevent bloodshed. That is your good fortune in contrast to the others who are required to kill.

However, complete peace can never be found in this world.

From *City of God*, bk. XVII, chap. 13[15]

Whoever hopes for so great a good as is promised to David in this world and on this earth shows all the understanding of a fool. Does anyone really think that the promise of such a good was fulfilled in the peace that existed during the reign of Solomon? Through that excellent proclamation Scripture surely prizes the peace of Solomon as a shadow of a future event. Still, the idea that the promise to David was fulfilled in the reign of Solomon is carefully precluded when, after the passage says, "And the son of iniquity will not approach to humiliate him," it immediately adds, "as he has done from the beginning, from the days in which I established judges over my people Israel" (2 Samuel 7:10–11). Now, judges had been established over that people from the time that they received the land of the promise, before there began to be kings in Israel. Also, the son of iniquity – that is, the foreign enemy – certainly did humiliate them during the intervals of time of which we read that peace alternated with war. Yet, longer periods of peace are found than the one enjoyed by Solomon, who reigned for forty years. Under that judge called Ehud there were eighty years of peace.

Thus, dismiss the thought that this promise given to David predicts the reign of Solomon, much less that of any other king, for none of them reigned in peace as long as Solomon. Never did that people possess the kingdom so securely that it did not have to worry about being overrun by enemies, for due to the great vicissitudes of human events no people has ever been granted such security that they did not dread attacks hostile to this life. Therefore, that place which is promised to be such a peaceful and secure dwelling is eternal, and is owed to the eternal ones in Jerusalem, the free mother. In that place will dwell those who are truly the people of Israel, for the name Israel is understood to mean "seeing God." In this journey full of hardships, the pious soul must be led, through faith, by a longing for that reward.

---

[14]   Swift (ed. and trans.), *The Early Fathers*, p. 115.
[15]   Fortin and Kries (eds.), *Augustine: Political Writings*, pp. 127–8.

Criteria for Waging a Just War

Augustine never wrote a separate treatise on war in which he laid out the criteria that must be fulfilled for a war to be just. However, directly and indirectly, his writings foreshadow the three *ius ad bellum* criteria of rightful (or legitimate) authority, just cause, and right intention, and even hint at the connection between the latter and what would later come to be called *ius in bello*.

Augustine is clear, albeit brief, on the importance of rightful authority. He is famous for having emphasized the significance of original sin for human existence and argues that political authority was instituted by God partly as a punishment for sin, partly to keep the peace of this world. Political authority includes the authority to use armed force. If all human beings were to have such authority, to use at their own discretion and whim, there would be no end to war and conflict. As William Stevenson has said, "God did not create human lusts, but once foreseen, God 'used' them, in the *form* of political authority, both to control the chaos engendered by sin and to punish sinners."[16]

Augustine's statements on authority and war must also be read in light of claims from the Manicheans (among them the theologian Faustus) that the Biblical God himself was *not* a rightful authority, since in the Old Testament he seems to have commanded acts that were cruel and excessively violent. The Manicheans – a Gnostic movement which was considered heretical by Augustine and the mainstream church – claimed that there was a contradiction between the bellicose attitudes of the Old Testament and the pacific spirit of the new. To Augustine, there was no such contradiction, since it is not war in itself that is to be feared, but malice and hatred.

From *Against Faustus the Manichean*, bk. XXII, chaps. 74–5, 78[17]

At this point, however, it would be tedious, and unnecessary, to enter into a discussion about just and unjust wars, for it makes a great difference by which causes and under which authorities men undertake the wars that must be waged. The natural order, which is suited to the peace of mortal things, requires that the authority and deliberation for undertaking war be under the control of a leader, and also that, in the executing of military commands, soldiers serve peace and the common well-being. Moreover, it is wrong to doubt that a war which must be waged, undertaken under the authority of God, whether in order to constrain, crush, or subjugate the pride of mortals, is undertaken rightly,

---

[16] William R. Stevenson, *Christian Love and Just War* (Macon, GA: Mercer University Press, 1987), p. 62.

[17] Fortin and Kries (eds.), *Augustine: Political Writings*, pp. 222–3, 225–6.

since even a war which is waged out of human desire can do no harm to the incorruptible God or to his saints. Insofar as the patience of the saints is tried and their souls humbled, and they suffer fatherly correction, they are benefited rather than harmed. No one can have any power over them except what has been given to him from above (see John 19:11); for, "There is no power except from God" (Romans 13:1), who either commands or permits it.

Therefore, a just man, if he should happen to serve as a soldier under a human king who is sacrilegious, could rightly wage war at the king's command, maintaining the order of civic peace, for what he is commanded to do is not contrary to the sure precepts of God, or else it is not sure whether it is or not. In this latter case, perhaps the iniquity of giving the orders will make the king guilty while the rank of a servant in the civil order will show the soldier to be innocent. Since all this is true about a just man serving a sacrilegious human king, how much more innocently may the man who wages war at God's command be occupied in the administration of wars? After all, everyone who serves God knows that he can never command what is evil. . . .

It is, therefore, malicious to blame Moses for waging war since he ought to be blamed less if he were to wage war on his own accord than if he were not to do so when God commanded it. Moreover, to dare to blame God himself because he commanded such things, or not to believe that a just and good God was able to command such things, is the mark of a human being, to put it mildly, unable to consider that for divine providence, extending in time through all things high and low, what arises is not a novelty and what dies does not vanish, but all things, individually, in their own order of natures or merits, either give way or succeed or abide. Furthermore, a correct human will is joined to divine law and inordinate human desire is checked by the order of divine law, so that a good man wills nothing other than what is commanded and a wicked man can do nothing more than what is permitted, and he can do that only in such a way that he cannot accomplish without punishment what he wills unjustly.

Augustine was not very elaborate in his comments on just cause. Nevertheless, he did exert a great influence on later thinkers, who would often cite the following passage on the connection between war, justice, and punishment.

From *Questions on the Heptateuch*, bk. VI, chap. 10[18]

As a rule just wars are defined as those which avenge injuries, if some nation or state against whom one is waging war has neglected to punish a wrong committed by its citizens, or to return something that was wrongfully taken.

---

[18] Swift (ed. and trans.), *The Early Fathers*, p. 135.

He adds in the same place the following, pertaining to the right conduct of just war.

From *Questions on the Heptateuch*, bk. VI, chap. 10[19]

[S]uch things [as ambushes] are legitimate for those who are engaged in a just war. In these matters the only thing a righteous man has to worry about is that the just war is waged by someone who has the right to do so because not all men have that right. Once an individual has undertaken this kind of war, it does not matter at all, as far as justice is concerned, whether he wins victory in open combat or through ruses.

Beyond this, Augustine does not enter into much detail when it comes to right conduct in war. However, several remarks give us an indication of the direction of his thoughts, even on this matter. He insists, as we have seen, that agreements should be kept, even with one's enemies, and that mercy should be shown (cf. *Letter 189*). And his general emphasis on right intention, virtue, love for the enemy, and the quest for peace as hallmarks of the Christian, can be read as injunctions against cruelty. Moreover, he criticizes others for wrongful conduct in war, as he contrasts the spirit of the Christians with what he sees as the barbarous customs of war among both Greeks and Romans, as related by Virgil, Sallust, and others. He contrasts their cruelty with the way in which fleeing people had been able to gather in the larger churches when the latter were being used as sanctuaries during Alaric's attack on Rome in 410. Here Augustine formulates an idea that had already been put into practice, and which we will see returning in different fashions later in the just war tradition: that of prohibitions against certain kinds of violence (in this case, against the use of force in holy places), in order to provide refuge for innocent victims of war.

From *City of God*, bk. I, chaps. 4, 6, 7[20]

[A] place consecrated to so great a goddess [Juno] was chosen [according to Virgil, *Aeneid*, 2.761 ff.], not as a place from which prisoners might not lawfully be taken out, but as a place where the victors might at pleasure shut up their captives. This sanctuary was not the temple of any common god of the lower order of deities, but that of the sister and wife of Jove himself, the queen of all

---

[19]   Ibid., p. 138.
[20]   From Augustine, *City of God*, trans. Henry Bettenson (London: Penguin, 1984), pp. 10, 12–13.

the gods. Now contrast it with the memorial shrines of our apostles. To the former were taken the spoils from the burning temples and gods, not to be given to the vanquished, but to be divided among the victors; to the latter was carried, with honour and most scrupulous reverence, all that belonged to those places which was found elsewhere. There, freedom was lost; here, it was preserved. There, captives were confined; here, enslavement was forbidden. There, men were herded by foes who exercised their power by sending them into slavery; here, they were conducted by foes who showed their pity by setting them free. In short, the greedy arrogance of the contemptible Greeks chose that temple of Juno for its display; the humble clemency of the barbarians, uncouth as they were, chose those basilicas of Christ. . . .

That great Roman, Marcus Marcellus, who captured the splendid city of Syracuse [in 212 BC], is said [by Livy] to have wept over its coming downfall and to have shed his own tears before shedding Syracusan blood. He also took care to preserve the honour of his enemies, for before he ordered the invasion of the town, the victor issued an edict that no violence should be done to the person of any free citizen. And yet that city was overthrown in the usual manner of warfare, and there is no record of any proclamation by that honourable and merciful commander to order that anyone who fled to this temple or that should be immune from harm. . . .

All the devastation, the butchery, the plundering, the conflagrations, and all the anguish which accompanied the recent disaster at Rome [in 410] were in accordance with the general practice of warfare. But there was something which established a new custom, something which changed the whole aspect of the scene; the savagery of the barbarians took on such an aspect of gentleness that the largest basilicas were selected and set aside to be filled with people to be spared by the enemy. No one was to be violently used there, no one snatched away. . . . This is to be attributed to the name of Christ and the influence of Christianity. . . . Let us hope that no one with any sense will ascribe the credit for this to the brutal nature of the barbarians. Their fierce and savage minds were terrified, restrained, and miraculously controlled by him who long ago said, through his prophet, "I will visit their iniquities with a rod, and their sins with scourges: but I will not disperse my mercy from them" [Psalm 89.33–4].

To sum up: According to Augustine, the one who commands war must have a rightful authority to do so, the war must have a just cause (i.e. be a response to wrongful attack or injury), and be fought with an upright intention, the last precluding savage brutality and the lust to dominate, and commanding respect for holy places (i.e. Christian churches) as sanctuaries. Thus we see that although Augustine does not discuss just war in an organized fashion, nevertheless he does formulate most of the criteria that would become central to the just war idea seven to eight hundred years later.

Force in the Service of Religion

Augustine wavers in his views on defense of religion and the spreading of the gospel as just causes for using armed force. Initially, he seems to have dismissed the idea of using force for the sake of religion – whether defensively or offensively – seeing an inherent contradiction between the peaceful spreading of the word of God through persuasion and the brutal destruction brought about by the use of violent force. He may have been impressed, for instance, (as was Ambrose) by the defeat of the emperor's forces at Hadrianople in 378, which had been preceded by proud proclamations of orthodoxy and injunctions to crush the Goths (who were so-called Arians, and viewed as heretics by the mainstream church) with a triumphant show of force. Whatever the historical background, Augustine's teaching of the two cities implied strong skepticism against tying the health of the church too strongly to the political and military fortunes of the empire.

Confronted with the Donatists, who indeed used violent tactics to spread fear and destruction, Augustine seems to have changed his mind. The Donatists were a rebellious faction of the church, which held that prelates who had previously collaborated with the pagan Roman authorities – and avoided persecution in that way – should be shunned. This conflict had its roots in the early fourth century, but the schism continued well into the fifth, and the fierce violence of the Donatists became increasingly worrisome to both churchly and secular authorities.

From his more general remarks on war and violence, it is clear that Augustine saw the use of armed force, at best, as a tool for keeping peace *in this world*. As such, it had nothing to do with spreading or defending religion. But as Augustine believed that heretics (and especially the Donatists) were indeed threatening the worldly peace, so he came to believe that their subjugation – including the subjugation of their theology – was justified.

In the following excerpts we first see Augustine recommending persuasion over persecution in a relatively early work, *On True Religion*. Then, in two later letters, first to the bishop Vincentius and then to the Roman governor Boniface (with whom Augustine discussed military matters on several occasions), we see that he has changed his position, recommending harsh reactions against the Donatists, and saying that the church may "compel people to come in." However, he could still, even after his change of heart, recommend leniency in dealing with the Donatists and other heretics, thus admitting the limitations and problems associated with the use of armed force. This comes out in a letter to his friend, the imperial commissioner Marcellinus.

From *On True Religion*, bk. XVI, chap. 31[21]

Christ did nothing by force, but did everything by persuading and warning. Indeed, the old slavery having been ended, the time of liberty dawned. Man was already being suitably and profitably persuaded that he had been created with free choice. By performing miracles, Christ instilled faith in the God that he was; by his suffering, he instilled faith in the humanity that he was bearing. Hence, speaking to the crowds as God, he denied his own mother when she was announced to him (Matthew 12:46–50); yet, the Gospel says that as a boy he was subordinate to his parents (Luke 2:51). In his teaching, God appeared; in his stages of growing up, a human being. Also, about to change the water into wine, he said as God, "Go away from me, woman. What do you want of me? My hour is not yet come" (John 2:4). However, when the hour in which he would die as a human being had come, he recognized his mother from the cross and commended her to the disciple whom he loved more than the others (John 19:26–7).

To their ruin, the peoples, followers of pleasures, desired riches; he wanted to be poor. They longed for honors and empires; he did not want to become a king. They thought that the bodily generation of children was a great good; he scorned such a union and such descendants. In their pride, they abhorred insults; he withstood every kind of insult. They judged injuries to be intolerable; what greater injury is there than to be condemned though just and innocent? They cursed bodily pain; he was flogged and tortured. They were afraid to die; he was punished with death. They thought that the cross was the most degrading kind of death; he was crucified. All the things which we, not living rightly, were desiring to have, he deemed of little account by abstaining from them. All the things which we, deviating from the zeal for truth, were desiring to avoid, he destroyed by enduring them. No sin can be committed unless that which he scorned is desired or that which he endured is evaded.

From *Letter 93, to Vincentius*[22]

5. You think that no one ought to be compelled to justice, although you read that the father of the house said to his servants, "Whomever you find, compel to come in" (Luke 14:23). . . . You also think that force should not be used to liberate a human being from disastrous errors, although you see through the most certain examples that God himself does this, and no one's love is more profitable for us than his. You also hear Christ saying, "No one comes to me

---

[21] Fortin and Kries (eds.), *Augustine: Political Writings*, pp. 231–2.
[22] Ibid., pp. 234–5, 238–9.

unless the father draws him" (John 6:44), but that happens in the hearts of all who turn to him through fear of divine wrath. . . .

8. If it were always praiseworthy to suffer persecution, it would have been sufficient for the Lord to say, "Blessed are they who suffer persecution" without adding "for the sake of justice" (Matthew 5:10). Likewise, if it were always culpable to apply persecution, it would not be written in the sacred books, "Anyone slandering his neighbor in secret, him I will persecute" (Psalm 101:5). Therefore, sometimes a person suffering persecution is unjust and a person employing persecution is just.

Clearly, the wicked have always persecuted the good and the good the wicked. The wicked persecute by harming through injustice; the good by advising through discipline. The former persecute without bounds; the latter temperately. The former are enslaved to desire; the latter to charity. One who slaughters does not consider how he hacks, but he who cures does consider how he dissects. The one persecutes what is healthy; the other what is rotting. The impious killed the prophets; the prophets also killed the impious (1 Kings 18:4, 40). The Jews scourged Christ; Christ also scourged the Jews. The apostles were handed over to human power by human beings; the apostles also handed over human beings to the power of Satan (1 Timothy 1:20). In all these matters, what else should be considered except this: who among them acted for the sake of truth and who for the sake of iniquity, who acted for the purpose of harming and who for correction?

17. I have yielded to the evidence placed before me by my colleagues. My original position was that no one should be compelled into the unity of Christ, but that we should act with words, fight with argumentation, and triumph with reason, so that we would not have those whom we knew to be professed heretics pretending to be Catholics. This opinion of mine was not conquered through words being spoken against it but through examples which demonstrate the contrary. First, the example of my own city was placed before me. Although it was totally on the Donatist side, it was turned to Catholic unity through fear of the imperial laws. Now we see that it so detests the destructiveness of your enmity that one might believe that it was never Donatist at all. So many other cities were recounted to me by name that, by means of these instances, I realized that what the Scripture says could also be interpreted correctly with respect to this matter: "Give an opportunity to the wise man, and he will become wiser" (Proverbs 9:9). . . .

How many thought the true church to be the Donatist party simply because security was making them too sluggish, squeamish, and lazy to acknowledge the Catholic truth! How many were barred from entering, having heard the rumors of the slanderers who were saying that we place I know not what upon the altar of God! How many, believing that the party to which a Christian belongs does not matter, thus remained in the party of the Donatists because they were born there and no one was compelling them to leave and pass over to the Catholics!

From *Letter 185, to Boniface*[23]

21. It is indeed better (as no one could ever deny) that men should be led to worship God by teaching, than that they should be driven to it by fear of punishment or pain; but it does not follow that because the former course produces the better men, that therefore those who do not yield to it should be neglected. For many have found advantage (as we have proved, and are daily proving by actual experiment), in being first compelled by fear or pain, so that they might afterwards be influenced by teaching, or might follow out in act what they had already learned in word. Some, indeed, set before us the sentiments of a certain secular author, who said,

> 'Tis well, I ween, by shame the young to train,
> And dread of meanness, rather than by pain.
> > (Terence, *Adelphi*, act I)

This is unquestionably true. But while those are better who are guided aright by love, those are certainly more numerous who are corrected by fear. For, to answer these persons out of their own author, we find him saying in another place:

> Unless by pain and suffering thou art taught,
> Thou canst not guide thyself aright in aught.[24]

But, moreover, holy Scripture has both said concerning the former better class, "There is no fear in love, but perfect love casts out fear;" (1 John 4:18) and also concerning the latter lower class, which furnishes the majority, "An obstinate servant will not be corrected by words: for even if he should understand, he will not obey" (Proverbs 29:19). In saying he "will not be corrected by words," he did not order him to be left to himself, but implied an admonition as to the means whereby he ought to be corrected; otherwise he could not have said, "will not be corrected by words," but without any qualification "will not be corrected." . . . [B]efore the good sons can say they have "a longing to be gone and to be with Christ," (Philippians 1:23), many must first be recalled to their Lord by the stripes of temporal scourging, like evil slaves, and in some degree like good-for-nothing fugitives.

23. Why, therefore, should not the Church use force in compelling her lost sons to return, if the sons compelled others to their destruction? . . . [E]ven men who have not been compelled, but only led astray, are received by their loving

---

[23] From Philip Schaff (ed.), *A Select Library of Nicene and Post-Nicene Fathers of the Christian Church*, vol. 4 (Grand Rapids, MI: William B. Eerdmans, [1887] 1956), pp. 641, 642; this letter translated by J. R. King, revised by C. P. Hartranft; a newer translation has been used for the Biblical quotations.

[24] This quotation has not been found in the extant plays of Terence.

mother with more affection if they are recalled to her bosom through the enforcement of terrible but salutary laws, and are the objects of far more deep congratulation than those whom she had never lost. Is it not a part of the care of the flock, even though not violently forced away, but led astray by tender words and coaxing blandishments, to bring them back to the fold of his master when he has found them, by the fear or even the pain of the whip, if they show symptoms of resistance? . . . But we have shown that Paul was compelled by Christ; therefore, the Church, in trying to compel the Donatists, is following the example of her Lord, though in the first instance she waited in the hopes of needing to compel no one. . . .

24. For in this sense also we may interpret without absurdity the declaration of the blessed Apostle Paul, when he says, "Being ready to punish every disobedience, when your obedience has first been made complete" (2 Corinthians 10:6). Whence also the Lord Himself bids the guests in the first instance to be invited to His great supper, and afterwards compelled; for on His servants making answer to Him, "Lord, what you commanded has been done and still there is room," he said, "Go out to the highways and the hedges and whoever you find compel them to come in" (Luke 14:21–3).

From *Letter 133, to Marcellinus*[25]

I have learned that the Circumcelliones [Donatists] and clerics of the Donatist party of Hippo, whom the administrators of public discipline have brought to judgment for their deeds, have been heard by your Nobility. I have also learned that most of them have confessed to committing the homicide of the Catholic presbyter Restitutus and the beating of another Catholic presbyter, Innocentius, and of ripping out his eye and cutting off his finger. Because of this, I have been overwhelmed with the greatest anxiety that your Excellency might determine that these people should be punished by the laws so severely that their punishment will match their deeds. Therefore, with this letter I beg of you – by your faith, which you have in Christ through the mercy of Christ the Lord himself – by no means do this or allow it to be done.

Although we are able to overlook the annihilation of those who might be regarded as having been brought to trial not by our accusations but by the indictment of those to whom the guardianship of public peace belongs, we still do not want the sufferings of the servants of God to be avenged by retaliatory punishments of an equal degree, as though the punishment and the deed were interchangeable. We are not opposed to wicked human beings being denied the license to commit crimes, but we want that to be the end of it, so that, alive and with their body parts unmutilated, they might either be directed away from

---

[25] Fortin and Kries (eds.), *Augustine: Political Writings*, pp. 245–6, 247.

diseased disturbances to the calm of health by the coercion of the laws or cut off from malicious deeds and turned to some useful deed. This is indeed called "condemnation," but who does not understand that it should be termed a bene-fit rather than a punishment when the audacity of savageness is not set free nor the remedy of repentance taken away?

Fulfill, Christian judge, the duty of a pious father. Be angry at iniquity in such a way that you remember to consider humanity, not cultivating the lust for taking vengeance on the atrocities of sin, but applying your will to healing the wounds of sin. . . .

Finally, you have been sent here for the sake of the church. I declare this course of clemency to be advantageous for the Catholic church; or rather, so that I do not appear to exceed my authority, I declare that this is advantageous for the church attached to the diocese at Hippo Regius. If you do not hear a begging friend, hear the considerations of a bishop. Because I speak to a Christian, I have not spoken arrogantly, especially in such a case as this, in saying that it is appro-priate for you to listen to the command of a bishop, my eminently and deservedly distinguished lord and very dear son.

It is hard to extract a single, consistent Augustinian teaching on the use of force in matters of religion. On the one hand, he did sanction the use of violence against heretics, and argued that they should be "forced" back into the church if they did not come back willingly. On the other hand, he preferred peaceful proselytizing to the use of violence, and he never came to see violence as a natural tool for the defense of the faith. We can only speculate what Augustine would have thought about the Holy Wars and Crusades of a much later age. It is, however, an inescap-able fact that Augustine left posterity with several passages urging that force may be used, if not to instill faith (which has to happen by inward conversion), then at least to bring those who have gone astray back to the rightful path of the church. Although arising concretely from the Donatist struggle, and not meant to address the relationship of Christians to members of other religions, his views were later used to vindicate the defense and sometimes also the spreading of the right faith as a just cause for the use of armed force.

Part II
Medieval

8

Medieval Peace Movements (975–1123)

Religious Limitations on Warfare

We command also that priests, clerics, monks, travelers, merchants, country people going and returning, and those engaged in agriculture, as well as the animals with which they till the soil and that carry the seeds to the field, and also their sheep, shall at all times be secure.

Second Lateran Council

Violence was widespread in medieval Europe. The lack of any centralized authority resulted in an incessant state of conflict between "great and lesser nobles, their mercenaries and personal retainers, and roving bands of criminals."[1] The church sought for ways to restrain this violence. A turning point occurred in 975 when Bishop Guy of Anjou consulted with the knights and peasants of his diocese (assembled in a field near Le Puy, France) about how to keep the peace. As a result of this meeting, he imposed on all soldiers (*milites*) an obligation to respect the property of the church and peasants. Several years later, a group of bishops assembled at Charroux, where they officially proclaimed the "Peace of God" (*Pax Dei*). The bishops ordered all those who carried arms to refrain from damaging churches, pillaging the poor, or causing bodily harm to clerics. Other proclamations followed, culminating in popular meetings where "huge and wildly enthusiastic crowds experienced the assemblies as a covenant of Peace between God and men."[2]

---

[1] Udo Heyn (ed.), *Peacemaking in Medieval Europe: A Historical and Bibliographical Guide* (Claremont CA: Regina Books, 1997), p. 21. The author adds: "Just as lines between the public and private use of force were blurred, so none of these groups were mutually exclusive and none of them strangers to criminal acts. And as most organized fighting, for most of the Middle Ages, emanated in the Germanic custom of settling judicial disputes through *Blutrache* (vendetta) and *faida* (feud), private warfare seemed incessant" (pp. 21–2).

[2] R. Landes and F. Paxton, "Pax Dei," in E. Laszlo and J. Y. Yoo (eds.), *World Encyclopedia of Peace*, vol. 2 (Oxford: Pergamon, 1986), pp. 168–71, on p. 169.

By the mid-eleventh century, the "Peace of God" movement had begun to wane. A new initiative arose on the part of the clergy and the higher nobility to limit warfare to certain times and periods. This was termed the "Truce of God" (*Treuga Dei*). It called for the cessation of warfare during certain days of the week, on specified religious festivals, and even for several weeks during Advent and other periods in the religious calendar. The Truce also adopted the central restrictions of the Peace regarding persons and property that ought not to be attacked. To the list of protected persons and things were added women, travelers, merchants, persons engaged in agriculture, shepherds tending their flocks, animals that are used to till the soil, olive trees, etc. The Truce thus "formed a bridge between the goals of the early Peace movement and the emergence of public institutions for the control of violence."[3] The main tenets of the two movements were summed up at the Second Lateran Council (1123), which also issued a ban on using certain weapons against fellow Christians. This was one of the first attempts at what centuries later would be termed "arms control."

The Peace and Truce of God have given rise to quite different assessments. Some have viewed these movements as a key source for the idea of non-combatant immunity, which over time would develop "into a much more universal concept with far-reaching implications."[4] Others, by contrast, view these movements as the expression of a religious exclusivism, wherein the special protection accorded to clerics and other Christians implicitly validated unrestrained violence against outsiders, Jews and Muslims especially. On this account, the Peace of God prepared the way for the Crusades and other forms of Christian Holy War.[5]

However one interprets the Peace and Truce of God, it cannot be gainsaid that they exerted a formative influence on the later emergence of the just war idea, especially as articulated by canon lawyers such as Gratian, Hostiensis, and their followers. In this chapter we offer a representative sampling of texts on the medieval peace movements, followed by some canons from the second Lateran council.

Peace of God, proclaimed in an assembly at Charroux, 989[6]

I, Gumbald, Archbishop of Aquitania secunda,[7] and all my comprovincial bishops, together with religious clerks and others of both sexes, met at the hall,

---

[3]   Ibid., p. 169.

[4]   James Turner Johnson, *The Quest for Peace* (Princeton, NJ: Princeton University Press, 1987), p. 82. Johnson adds that "[t]his is one of the two core ideas around which the *jus in bello* of just war tradition developed, and both modern humanitarian law of war and moral argument centering on the concept of discrimination are legacies of this slender tenth-century beginning" (ibid.).

[5]   This is the thesis articulated by Tomaž Mastnak, *Crusading Peace: Christendom, the Muslim World, and Western Political Order* (Berkeley: University of California Press, 2002).

[6]   From R. G. D. Laffan (ed.), *Select Documents of European History, 800–1492* (New York: Henry Holt, 1929), p. 19.

[7]   I.e. of Bordeaux.

which is called Karrof.[8] . . . Thus solemnly assembled in God's name we decreed thus:

1. Anathema for violators of churches: if any one breaks into a sacred church, or violently removes anything thence, unless he makes satisfaction, let him be anathema.

2. Anathema for spoilers of the poor: if anyone robs peasants or other poor of a sheep, ox, ass, cow, goat, or pigs, unless by the other's fault, and if he neglect to make full reparation, let him be anathema.

3. Anathema for those who assault the clergy: if anyone attacks, captures or assaults a priest or deacon or any clergyman, who is not carrying arms (that is, shield, sword, coat of mail and helmet), but quietly going on his way or remaining at home, that sacrilegious man shall be held to be cast forth from the holy church of God, unless he makes satisfaction, after the clergyman has been examined by his bishop to see if he was at fault.

The Earliest Truce of God, proclaimed in the diocese of Elne[9] 1027[10]

And so the said bishops, with all the clergy and the faithful people, provided that [1] throughout the whole of the said county[11] and bishopric no one should attack his enemy from the ninth hour[12] on Saturday until the first hour on Monday, so that everyone may perform his religious duties on Sunday. [2] And none shall attack a monk or a clergyman who is unarmed, nor any man going to or coming from a church or a council, nor a man accompanied by a woman. [3] And none shall dare to violate a church or the houses within thirty paces of a church.

Truce of God proclaimed at the Council of Narbonne, August 25, 1054[13]

1. First, we order that no Christian slay his fellow Christian. For he who kills a Christian, without doubt sheds the blood of Christ. If anyone unjustly kills a man, he shall pay the penalty according to the law.

2. We confirm the truce of God, which was long ago established by us and now is broken by evil men. Henceforth it shall be faithfully observed by all.

---

[8] Charroux, not far from Poitiers, Vienne.

[9] Near Perpignan.

[10] Ibid., pp. 19–20.

[11] Roussillon.

[12] Counting from sunrise.

[13] Ibid., pp. 20–1.

Accordingly we adjure in God's name every Christian not to do hurt to any other Christian from sunset on Wednesday till sunrise on Monday.

3. From the first Sunday in Advent till the octave of Epiphany; from the Sunday before Lent till the octave of Easter; from the Sunday before Ascension Day till the octave of Whitsunday; and on the following feasts and their vigils – those of St. Mary, St. John Baptist, apostles, St. Peter in Chains,[14] Justus and Pastor,[15] St. Laurence, St. Michael, All Saints, St. Martin; and in the four periods of Ember Days: we forbid any Christian to attack another Christian during any of the said fasts, feasts and vigils or to insult him or to seize his property. . . .[16]

9. Olive trees, which, we read, were used as a sign that peace had returned to the earth at the time of the flood, and from whose oil the holy chrism is made, shall be so strictly protected that no Christian shall dare to cut them down or injure them or seize their fruit.

10. Sheep and their pastors, while tending them, shall also be under the truce of God on all days in all places.

Canons of the Second Lateran Council, 1123[17]

Canon 11: We command also that priests, clerics, monks, travelers, merchants, country people going and returning, and those engaged in agriculture, as well as the animals with which they till the soil and that carry the seeds to the field, and also their sheep, shall at all times be secure.

Canon 12: We decree that the truce of God be strictly observed by all from the setting of the sun on Wednesday to its rising on Monday, and from Advent to the octave of Epiphany and from Quinquagesma to the octave of Easter. If anyone shall violate it and does not make satisfaction after the third admonition, the bishop shall direct against him the sentence of excommunication and in writing shall announce his action to the neighboring bishops. No bishops shall restore to communion the one excommunicated; indeed every bishop should confirm the sentence made known to him in writing. But if anyone (that is, any bishop) shall dare violate this injunction, he shall jeopardize his order. And since "a threefold cord is less easily broken" (Ecclesiastes 4:12), we command the bishops, having in mind only God and the salvation of the people, and having discarded all tepidity, offer each other mutual counsel and assistance for firmly establishing peace; nor should they be swayed in this by the love or hatred of anybody. But if anyone be found to be tepid in this work of God, let him incur the loss of his dignity. . . .

[14] August 1.
[15] August 6. Two Spaniards of Alcala, martyred about 304.
[16] Clauses 4–8 provide penalties for breaches of the truce.
[17] From H. J. Schroeder (ed.), *Disciplinary Decrees of the General Councils: Text, Translation and Commentary* (St. Louis: B. Herder, 1937), pp. 195–213.

Canon 14: We condemn absolutely those detestable jousts or tournaments in which the knights usually come together by agreement and, to make a show of their strength and boldness, rashly engage in contests which are frequently the cause of death to men and of danger to souls. If anyone taking part in them should meet his death, though penance and the Viaticum shall not be denied him if he asks for them, he shall, however, be deprived of Christian burial.

Canon 15: If anyone at the instigation of the devil incurs the guilt of this sacrilege, namely, that he has laid violent hands on a cleric or monk, he shall be anathematized and no bishop shall dare absolve him, except *mortis urgente periculo*, till he be presented to the Apostolic See and receive its mandate. We command also that no one shall dare lay hands on those who have taken refuge in a church or cemetery. Anyone doing this, let him be excommunicated. . . .

Canon 18: By the authority of God and of the blessed Apostles Peter and Paul we absolutely condemn and prohibit that most wicked, devastating, horrible, and malicious work of incendiaries; for this pest, this hostile waste, surpasses all other depredations. No one is ignorant of how detrimental this is to the people of God and what injury it inflicts on souls and bodies. Every means must be employed, therefore, and no effort must be spared that for the welfare of the people such ruin and such destruction may be eradicated and extirpated. If anyone, therefore, after the promulgation of this prohibition, shall through malice, hatred, or revenge set fire, or cause it to be set, or knowingly by advice or other connivance have part in it, let him be excommunicated. Moreover, when incendiaries die, let them be deprived of Christian burial. Nor shall they be absolved until, as far as they are able, they have made reparation to those injured and have promised under oath to set no more fires. For penance they are to spend one year in the service of God either in Jerusalem or in Spain. . . .

Canon 29: We forbid under penalty of anathema that that deadly and God-detested art of stingers and archers be in the future exercised against Christians and Catholics.

9

The Crusades (Eleventh to Thirteenth Centuries)

Christian Holy War

> Let hatreds cease among you, let your quarrels end, let wars have an end, let all strife and dissension slumber. Take the road to the holy Sepulchre, capture that land from the evil nation and subject it to yourselves.
>
> Pope Urban II's speech at Clermont, declaring the first crusade

Intense controversy surrounds the medieval crusades. There is disagreement as to what constituted a crusade, the motivations behind them, and how they were understood by those who were afflicted by them. But most intensely, there has been, and still is, deep disagreement about the moral status of the crusades. A plethora of different views can be found, from ecstatic accounts of brave and selfless knights to stark denunciations of fanatical and brutal warriors.

Modern Christianity has come to look upon the crusades with great skepticism. The stark indictment of war for the sake of religion pronounced by early modern writers such as Gentili, Vitoria, and Suárez has been combined with a belief in human rights and territorial sovereignty to produce an all but unanimous conclusion among Christians that military crusades are morally wrong.

But in a world where a host of political leaders speak of intervening in other countries and regions to spread democratic values, the crusading spirit – albeit secularized – seems not to be so foreign after all. Furthermore, many modern Muslims hold that the concept of *jihad* (struggle) – while primarily meant to be spiritual, and if related to warfare, mainly defensive – can be used to legitimize religiously inspired struggles. To say that the idea of "holy wars" is dead, an artifact of the past, is thus more than dubious.[1]

For our limited purposes, we do not have to settle on an unequivocal definition of a crusade. Let it suffice to say that the term has most often been used to denote

---

[1] For a comparison between Christian and Muslim attitudes to holy war, see James Turner Johnson, *The Holy War Idea in Western and Islamic Traditions* (University Park: Pennsylvania State University Press, 1997).

a "holy war authorized by the pope, who proclaimed it in the name of God or Christ."[2] The most famous campaigns to go under the name are the medieval wars for the "liberation" of Jerusalem and the Holy Sepulcher (Christ's grave), and one normally enumerates at least seven such crusades from 1095/6 until 1274, although there were other holy wars both before and after that time.

While the crusades against the East were militarily successful at several junctures, Palestine turned out to be too far away from home, and the dangers and enemies too numerous, for any victory to prove stable. Also, the Byzantine Empire came to see the crusades as a nuisance and at times an outright threat, especially since the fourth crusade (1201–4) for all practical purposes was directed against Constantinople rather than Jerusalem. Thus, the crusades utterly failed in uniting Christendom and remained a phenomenon experienced by witnesses as brutal spectacles rather than manifestations of Christian virtue.

Yet, there is little doubt that many of the crusaders, at least at the outset, fought for idealistic purposes informed by piety and humility. Also, recent historical scholarship has found that Christians and Muslims in Palestine and its vicinity managed to live together more peacefully and respectfully than has often been thought, even in the era of the crusades. Certainly, there was indiscriminate violence, legal discrimination against Muslims (including slavery), and a serious lack of understanding for the interests and needs of all those – Muslims and others – who already lived in Asia Minor and Palestine. Indeed, much of what took place is hard to reconcile with the injunction to love one's enemy. Then again, this is true for most wars, not only the crusades. Many historians today concur that the picture that emerges from a close study of the crusading centuries is more nuanced than the extreme images of butchery and fanaticism that have dominated many literary and historical accounts of the period.[3]

It is customary to distinguish between a just war and a holy war. According to modern just war scholarship, a just war is fought for the purposes of defending oneself or other innocent parties against impending or ongoing attack, with the aim of establishing a stable and just peace. A just war, according to this view, is not fought for religious purposes, nor does the concept sanction invasion of other countries in order to enlarge one's own territory or power, even if one is believed to have some distant historical right to that territory. Even among medieval authors, there were those who preferred to understand a just war in such terms – among them, many would claim, Thomas Aquinas. Yet, at the time it seems to have been a widespread view that the crusades were just wars in this sense. That is to say, they were *not* meant to be offensive wars to destroy the heathens or spread the

---

[2]   Louise and Jonathan Riley-Smith, *The Crusades: Idea and Reality, 1095–1274* (London: Edward Arnold, 1981), p. 1.

[3]   The most important collection of texts to bring us such an in-depth and nuanced picture of the crusades is Thomas F. Madden (ed.), *The Crusades: The Essential Readings* (Oxford: Blackwell, 2002). For a detailed account of the relationship between Muslims and Christians during the crusades, see the essays by Nikita Elisséeff and Benjamin Z. Kedar in that volume.

faith. Rather, they were truly just wars, declared by legitimate authority (the pope), and intended to defend Christians against attack and recover the wrongfully seized Holy Land from the Saracens (the latter being the term applied to Muslims). Innocent IV, for instance (see chap. 13, this volume), saw the crusades in those terms.

The beginnings of the first crusade clearly bring out this line of thought: the crusade was intended as a defensive, humanitarian mission to help fellow Christians threatened with death and destruction. No doubt, it also provided an opportunity to people who experienced hardships and frequently fought among themselves, and who were ridden with doubts about their own virtue and salvation, to do something truly idealistic and grand, in unison and for the sake of the church. Certainly, bloodthirsty and greedy dreams of riches, power, and military superiority probably played a part for several crusaders (as well as for some of the popes and emperors who instigated them). But it would be misguided to claim that the crusades were nothing but brutal wars of destruction, fueled by fanatical rage or bigoted ideology. However much we want to distance ourselves from the crusaders today, we should attempt to understand them – and criticize them – with a degree of nuance and historical sensitivity.

The following excerpts display several sides of the crusades. The first is a rendition of Pope Urban II's speech during the Council of Clermont in November 1095, which is famous for setting the agenda for the first crusade against the East. While we have no verbatim report of what Urban said, this rendition by Robert the Monk is believed to contain the gist of his argument. From what we know, it was a very forceful speech, partly given in the Franks' (Frenchmen's) vernacular tongue, intensely inspiring to those present – and to all who later heard it reported.

The second excerpt illustrates the ferocity of the crusaders after they finally reached Jerusalem in 1099. It shows the brutality of the battle with the Saracens, and how little mercy was shown either way.

The third excerpt, on the other hand, shows us the kind of situation in which the crusaders would increasingly find themselves. It was, after all, hard to hold on to the cities and territories that had been seized, and the crusading soldiers and political leaders would increasingly have to negotiate with – and accommodate – local Muslim centers of power. The Treaty of Jaffa in 1229 is a good example. There was considerable disagreement at the time as to whether the treaty – which secured a ten-year truce – was good for the Christians, and many seem to have felt that the emperor who negotiated it, Frederick II, too hastily accepted the terms of the Sultan of Egypt, Malek el Kamil. The account of Hermann von Salza, Grand Master of the Teutonic Knights (one of several military orders established during the crusades), gives a more favorable review of the treaty. He describes the kind of sharing of holy places and access to worship that was prescribed by it; measures that certainly proved to be necessary if the Christians were to have any realistic chance of staying on in Palestine.

Eventually, the crusaders were driven out of the Holy Land in 1291. They could look back upon almost 200 years that had been neither stable nor driven by any unified motivation. Ethically speaking, the crusades were a mixture of high-minded religious ideals and brutal violence – a mixture for which we have little patience today.

From Pope Urban II's speech at Clermont, November 27, 1095, as reported by Robert the Monk[4]

Nation of the Franks, nation beyond the mountains, nation chosen and beloved of God – as is shown by your many works – set apart from all peoples as well by the situation of your lands as by your catholic faith and your respect for [the] Holy Church: to you our speech is directed and for you is our exhortation intended. We wish you to know how sad a cause has brought us to your country, what crisis in the fate of you and of all Christians has drawn us hither.

From the land of Jerusalem and the city of Constantinople a grievous tale has gone forth and often reached our ears, that the people of the kingdom of the Persians, a strange people, a people wholly alienated from God, *a generation that set not their heart aright and whose spirit was not steadfast with God* (Psalm 78:8), have invaded the lands of those Christians and depopulated them with sword, rapine and fire. Some of their captives they have led away to their own country, some they have cruelly slain. The churches of God they have either entirely destroyed or appropriated for the rites of their own religion. . . . The kingdom of the Greeks is now dismembered by them and territory that takes two months to cross is in their possession.

On whom is the task of avenging and recovering this loss incumbent, if not on you, on whom above other nations God has conferred outstanding glory in arms, greatness of soul, agility of body, the power to humble the hairy scalp (cf. Psalm 68:21) of those who resist you? Let the deeds of your ancestors move and incite you to manliness, the virtue and greatness of King Charles the Great, of his son Lewis, and of your other kings, who destroyed the kingdoms of the heathen and extended in them the bounds of the Holy Church. Let our Lord and Saviour's holy Sepulchre, now possessed by unclean nations, specially move you; and the holy places, which are now defiled and polluted with their filth. Oh, bravest of soldiers, descendants of unconquered forefathers, be not degenerate, but recall the valour of your ancestors.

And if love of children, parents and wives hold you back, remember what the Lord says in the Gospel: *He that loveth father or mother more than Me is not*

---

[4]   From R. G. D. Laffan (ed. and trans), *Select Documents of European History*, vol. 1: *800–1492* (New York: Henry Holt, 1929), pp. 54–6. Robert the Monk is, according to Laffan, "believed to have been elected as Abbot of St. Rémi in Rheims in 1094" (p. 54).

worthy of Me (Matthew 10:37). *Everyone that hath forsaken house, or father, or mother, or wife, or children, or lands, for My name's sake, shall receive an hundredfold, and shall inherit eternal life* (Matthew 19:29). Let no possession hold you back, no care for your family. For this land which you inhabit, shut in on all sides by the sea and surrounded by mountain ranges, is overfilled by your numbers. It does not abound in wealth. It supplies scarcely food enough for those who farm it. Hence it is that you fight and devour each other, that you wage wars and often perish by mutual blows. Let hatreds cease among you, let your quarrels end, let wars have an end, let all strife and dissension slumber. Take the road to the holy Sepulchre, capture that land from the evil nation and subject it to yourselves. That land was given by God to the children of Israel as a possession, and, as the Scripture says, *it floweth with milk and honey* (Exodus 3:8).

Jerusalem is the centre of the earth.... She seeks and desires to be freed, and ceases not to implore your aid.... Therefore, undertake this journey for the remission of your sins, assured of the imperishable glory of the kingdom of heaven.

From an account of the capture of Jerusalem, June 7–July 15, 1099[5]

Exulting with joy we reached the city of Jerusalem on Tuesday, June 6, and we besieged it in a wonderful manner....

During the siege we were unable to find any bread to buy for about the space of ten days, until a messenger came from our ships; also we were afflicted by great thirst.... We sewed up skins of oxen and buffaloes in which we brought the water six miles. The water we drank from such receptacles was fetid, and what with foul water and barley bread we daily suffered great affliction and distress. Moreover the Saracens hid near all the springs and wells and ambushed our men, killing and mutilating them and driving off the animals into their dens and caverns.

Then our leaders planned to attack the city with machines, in order to enter it and adore the sepulchre of our Saviour. They made two wooden towers and many other machines.... Day and night on the fourth and fifth days of the week we vigorously attacked the city on all sides; but before we made our assault the bishops and priests persuaded all by their preaching and exhortation that a procession should be made around Jerusalem to God's honour, faithfully accompanied by prayers, alms and fasting.... One of our knights, Letholdus by name, climbed on to the wall of the city. When he reached the top, all the defenders of the city quickly fled along the walls and through the city. Our men followed and pursued them, killing and hacking, as far as the temple of Solomon, and there

---

[5]   Ibid., pp. 59, 60–1; the account is by an unknown author, seemingly an eyewitness, and is taken from the *Gesta Francorum et aliorum Hierosolimitanorum* (1101), one of the oldest accounts we have of the first crusade.

there was such a slaughter that our men were up to their ankles in the enemy's blood. . . .

The emir who commanded the tower of David surrendered to the Count [of St. Gilles] and opened the gate where the pilgrims used to pay tribute. Entering the city, our pilgrims pursued and killed the Saracens up to the temple of Solomon. There the Saracens assembled and resisted fiercely all day, so that the whole temple flowed with their blood. At last the pagans were overcome and our men seized many men and women in the temple, killing them or keeping them alive as they saw fit. On the roof of the temple there was a great crowd of pagans of both sexes, to whom Tancred and Gaston de Beert gave their banners [as a sign of protection]. Then the crusaders scattered throughout the city, seizing gold and silver, horses and mules, and houses full of all sorts of goods. Afterwards our men went rejoicing and weeping for joy to adore the sepulchre of our Saviour Jesus and there discharged their debt to him.

From an account of the Treaty of Jaffa, signed on February 4, 1229[6]

The Sultan of Babylon and his brother, the Sultan called Sceraph, with an innumerable host, were encamped at Gaza, less than a day's march from us; and the Sultan of Damascus, with a large army, was at Neapolis, also a day's march from us. And after negotiations about the restoration of the Holy Land, the Lord Jesus Christ, with His wonted providence, ordained that the Sultan restored to the lord Emperor and to the Christians the holy city of Jerusalem with its appurtenances; except that the monastery, which is called the temple of the Lord, was to be in the keeping of the Saracens, because they had long been accustomed to pray there; and that they should have free access to it and exit from it for purposes of prayer; and that Christians wishing to pray there should likewise have free access to it. They also restored the village called St. George's and the hamlets on either side of the road as far as Jerusalem; as well as Bethlehem and its appurtenances and the hamlets between it and Jerusalem.[7] . . .

Further, neither the said Sultan of Babylon nor any of his subjects is to construct any fortresses or buildings or to strengthen existing ones during the truce, which has been established between the lord Emperor and him for ten years. Also the prisoners who remained in captivity after the loss of Damietta, and those captured in the recent campaigns, are to be restored on both sides.

---

[6] Ibid., pp. 71, 72; from a contemporary letter of Hermann von Salza, Grand Master of the Teutonic Knights, to the Pope. Professor Laffan shows in his commentary, and through a rendition of the text of the treaty interspersed with commentaries by the Patriarch of Jerusalem, that there was disagreement among Christians about the treaty (see ibid., pp. 68–71).

[7] The treaty specified that the Saracens were allowed to go freely to Bethlehem on pilgrimage.

10

Gratian and the Decretists (Twelfth Century)

War and Coercion in the *Decretum*

[T]he point of all soldiering is to resist injury or to carry out vengeance.

Decretum Gratiani

Around 1140 in Bologna a monumental textbook appeared with the title *Concordia discordantium canonum*. Most often referred to simply as the *Decretum Gratiani*, very little is known about its author, a Camaldolese monk named Gratian.[1] The work was quickly accepted as authoritative within the emerging law schools in the Latin West, such as Bologna, Orleans, or Cologne; it was studied and annotated by several generations of canonists (church lawyers) during the second half of the twelfth century. The productions of these Decretists, as they came to be called, also included autonomous commentaries and compendia, but the main result was the *Glossa ordinaria*, a consolidated body of glosses assembled by Johannes Teutonicus (before 1215) and later revised by Bartholomaeus Brixiensis (around 1240). Meanwhile, the interests of the canonists had shifted to the newly gathered collections of decretals (papal pronouncements on canon law) which were in turn glossed and commented by the so-called Decretalists; yet Gratian's massive compilation remained the basic manual on canon law, not only for lawyers but also for theologians, who would find in it abundant materials to organize their own reflections on moral and legal issues.

The *Decretum* consists of three main parts, the second being a voluminous collection of 36 fictitious cases – *causae* – all of which raise a number of legal questions that are discussed by reference to the numerous texts gathered by

---

[1] It has recently been argued that the full text of the *Decretum* was in fact compiled by at least two different twelfth-century scholars. On this, see Anders Winroth, *The Making of Gratian's* Decretum (Cambridge: Cambridge University Press, 2000), chap. 6.

Gratian. These texts are called "canons," although only part of them are canons proper, that is, legal rules emanating from councils or synods; some consist of papal decretals but most are excerpts from the church fathers or other authors. Each canon is headed by a short summary (rubric) which is intended to convey its legal meaning. The link between the canons is established by so-called *dicta Gratiani* (Gratian's own statements), which aim at "harmonizing" them, in line with the overall title of the work.

The lengthy causa 23 is entirely devoted to the topic of recourse to force and armed coercion in a Christian perspective. Much of it is taken from St. Augustine's comments on the use of compulsion by secular and spiritual authorities. Drawing on earlier compilations of patristic literature such as the *Collectio canonum* of Anselm of Lucca or the *Decretum* and *Panormia* of Ivo of Chartres, Gratian set out the key elements which later canonists and theologians would organize into a body of doctrine around the idea of just war.

Causa 23 deals with a case of heresy into which certain bishops had lapsed, and its repression by their Catholic counterparts, acting upon orders by the pope. At first sight this looks more like a police action (wherein disciplinary sanctions are administered within a well-structured organization) than war in the classical sense. Yet, to Gratian and his contemporaries this sort of action very normally qualified as war, owing to the mere fact that it involved an armed contest, whatever the legal status of the parties: it was the tangible reality which the very terms *war* or *guerra* referred to, both deriving from Germanic *werran*, "bring into confusion."[2] This is why all the eight questions Gratian formulates after enunciating the facts of causa 23 have some bearing on the problem of war.[3]

First he asks whether Christians are allowed at all to engage in military service and warfare. Gratian neutralizes the various objections arising from the Gospel by distinguishing between the Christian's inner disposition and his outward action, which may lead him lawfully either to resist injury (*propellere iniuriam*) or to inflict punishment (*vindictam inferre*) – it being understood that, while anyone is allowed to defend himself or others, punishment is reserved to public authorities. This basic distinction between merely defensive and full-fledged offensive war conditions the overall structure of causa 23, and it was to have a lasting effect on the subsequent scholastic doctrine of war.

Gratian's second question then briefly examines the notion of just war. He quotes two definitions which henceforth were to enjoy canonical status: the first

---

[2] *The Oxford Dictionary of English Etymology*, edited by C. T. Onions, with the assistance of G. W. S. Friedrichsen and R. W. Burchfield (Oxford: Clarendon Press, 1966), s.v. *war*.

[3] A French abbot, César-Auguste Horoy, endeavored to present causa 23 as a treatise on Public International Law in a lecture course delivered in the Faculty of Law of Douai in 1884–5. See César-Auguste Horoy, *Droit international et droit des gens public d'après le* Decretum *de Gratien* (Paris: Chevalier-Maresq, 1887). However estimable his efforts – which may have stimulated the renascence of the just war doctrine in the late nineteenth century – they were bound to be anachronistic. As an appendix, the work contains a useful, though often loose, translation of causa 23.

was drawn from the *Etymologies* of Isidore of Seville, the other from a comment of St. Augustine on Joshua. The former stressed the element of authoritative command, the latter the necessity of a material cause of war. Both passages are then supplemented by another quotation from Augustine setting out a case of just war due to denial of innocent passage on foreign territory. The *ius humanae societatis* alleged by Augustine would obtain central importance four centuries later in the *Relectio de Indis* of Francisco de Vitoria.

The idea of human solidarity is again present in the next question which deals with the defense of third persons, here the faithful oppressed by the heretical bishops. More generally this raises the timeless problem of intervention on religious, political, or humanitarian grounds. The situations created by alliances and collective self-defense (as contemplated by article 51 of the United Nations Charter) can also be subsumed under this heading.

Questions IV and V constitute in every respect the center of gravity of the whole causa. By their sheer volume they make up almost half of its length; and their subject matter forms its main theme: the legitimacy for Christians of exerting punishment, including the death penalty. This problem is dealt with in general terms – war is only occasionally touched upon – but the arguments were clearly meant to apply in the context of the causa, and hence to war. This was to have a lasting influence on the subsequent conceptions of just war, which in its full expression involved the idea of just retribution and required corresponding jurisdiction on the part of the just belligerent.

The last three questions revolve around some specific issues that were raised by the case under examination. Question VI deals with the all important problem whether heretics or schismatics may be compelled to revert to the true faith: which is answered in the affirmative on the authority of St. Augustine and his famous *compelle intrare* ("force them to come in," see this volume, pp. 85ff.). Question VII concerns the goods owned by the heretics: as in any just war, Gratian considers them as accruing to the captors; the glossators would, however, add that, if the heretics repent, their goods should be returned to them. The final question deals with the problem of clerics participating in warfare, which was by no means a purely academic question during the Middle Ages. While denying them the right to handle arms and to spill blood, Gratian permits them, if need be, to encourage the soldiery in defending the faithful entrusted to their protection.

As was observed earlier, Gratian hardly ever consulted the original works for his quotations; rather, he would find them in various collections of extracts compiled by his immediate predecessors. His work had nothing in common with a philological exercise. As a result, the texts he quotes would often appear more or less distorted. Paradoxically enough, having become "canons" in this guise, they would yet prevail in law over the original texts, despite their deficiencies. Hence, in this anthology, Augustine's comments on war have sometimes been made to appear twice, first (chapter 7) in a translation based on the proper Latin text, and second (below) in a translation of the corrupt yet canonical version that Gratian made available in the *Decretum*.

A telling example of such a distortion is offered by the canon *Iustum est bellum* (q. II, canon 1) which contains the Ciceronian definition of just war given by Isidore of Seville.[4] In fact the canon draws together two distinct passages of Isidore's *Etymologies*, creating thereby an immediate relationship between just war and the office of the judge, a link that had never been intended by the author.[5] Yet the distortion was not of Gratian's own doing: he merely took over the passage as he found it in the compilations of Ivo of Chartres.[6]

The situation is different with the canon *Quid culpatur* (q. I, canon 4): it considerably alters the original source, one of Augustine's polemical treatises against the Manicheans; but we do not find it in this form in any of the known collections of canons that preceded Gratian. Hence the question arises whether he might have effected these changes himself. The canon reproduces and partly sums up two chapters of the *Contra Faustum manichaeum* (XXII, 74–5) with some significant omissions. Augustine's original argument had focused on the unconditional obedience that is owed to divine injunctions. Thus Moses, far from acting like a brigand when he despoiled the Egyptians, as contended by Faustus, had been fully justified in so doing since he was but executing a command of God. In order to bring this point home, Augustine drew an analogy with the chain of command in human affairs, which could not in his opinion be reasonably disputed. While this had been only a subordinate part in a wider *a fortiori* reasoning, it alone was retained in Gratian's text. Augustine's original argument has practically vanished from it, and the alteration would seem to be the result of a conscious purpose. Indeed a similar change can be observed in the last sentence of this canon, where the relationship to God has equally disappeared. Whoever may be the author of this trimming, both sentences thus isolated could take on an importance of their own in the emerging discussion about the conditions of just war.

The Decretists would in their turn contribute to moving Gratian's excerpts away from their original sources, not by altering the text, but by conferring a renewed

---

[4] Isidore quotes two sentences of Cicero's *De re publica* (III, 35 a): "Those wars are unjust which are undertaken without cause. For aside from vengeance or for the sake of fighting off enemies (*ulciscendi aut propulsandorum hostium causa*) no just war can be waged. – No war is considered just unless it is announced and declared and unless it involves the recovery of property." (English translation from Cicero, *On the Commonwealth and the Laws*, ed. James E. G. Zetzel [Cambridge: Cambridge University Press, 1999], p. 73.) For the relationship between Cicero and Isidore, see Jonathan Barnes, "Cicéron et la guerre juste", *Bulletin de la Société française de Philosophie*, 80 (1986), pp. 37–80. (English summary at pp. 38–9.)

[5] The two passages are, however, part of the same book of this encyclopedic work, book XVIII, which deals with "war and games"; see *Isidori Hispalensis Episcopi Etymologiarum sive Originum libri XX*, ed. W. M. Lindsay, (Oxford: Clarendon Press, 1911), XVIII, I, 2, and XVIII, XV, 6.

[6] Ivo of Chartres, *Decretum*, X, 116, and *Panormia*, VIII, 54.

meaning upon them through their glosses. They would in particular infuse into these excerpts a legal component which had been largely absent from the moral and theological discourse of their authors.

Thus the gloss *Qui repellere possunt*[7] outlines a theory of self-defense which was hardly contemplated in either Gratian's *dicta* or in the texts he adduces from Augustine. The criteria that are set out – immediacy and proportionality – draw mainly on Roman law. This alone enabled these "canons" to become properly operative in legal argumentation.

Similarly, the gloss *Nullus ergo*[8] establishes a link between Augustine's famous sentence reserving the right of war to the authority of princes and the well-known imperial constitution promulgated in AD 364 to the same effect.

Auctoritas principis appears again in the gloss *Bellum dicitur iniustum*[9] as one of five factors the absence of which would render war unjust, the others being *persona*, *res*, *causa*, and *animus*. These five vitiating circumstances would soon be transformed into five positive and cumulative conditions of just war by Raymond of Peñafort. Later in the century Thomas Aquinas would partly recast them into his famous three conditions, *auctoritas principis*, *iusta causa*, and *recta intentio*. Clearly, this edifice was built with conceptual blocks cut out and polished by the Decretists from the texts Gratian had gathered in his *Concordia discordantium canonum*.[10]

In what follows we reproduce a selection of excerpts from the *Decretum*, accompanied by some glosses which, from the beginning of the thirteenth century, appeared alongside Gratian's text. After a prologue which lays out the case that serves as the occasion for the ensuing discussion, causa 23 is divided into questions, which are then subdivided into canons. The canons are numbered, and each is preceded by its rubric, which, in the text below, appears in the left column, set in bold type. Also appearing in the left column are the glosses. Each gloss took as its starting point some word or clause (italicized in the extracts reproduced below) that had appeared in the canon. This word or phrase, much like our modern numerical footnote markers, appears at the beginning of the gloss; by the same token, it could subsequently function as a sort of title by which later authors would identify the gloss, although in some cases that purpose was served by the first words of the gloss itself. Gratian's own statements are preceded by the name "Gratian," set in bold type.

---

[7]   See *Decretum Gratiani*, II, causa 23, q. I, i. pr.

[8]   Causa 23, q. I, can. 4.

[9]   Causa 23, q. II, i. pr.

[10]   For an analysis of the canons and glosses mentioned, and a discussion of the significance of the whole causa 23 for the development of just war doctrine, see Frederick H. Russell, *The Just War in the Middle Ages* (Cambridge: Cambridge University Press, 1975), pp. 55–85; Ernst-Dieter Hehl, *Kirche und Krieg im 12. Jahrhundert. Studien zu kanonischem Recht und politischer Wirklichkeit* (Stuttgart: Anton Hiersemann, 1980), pp. 57–108; Peter Haggenmacher, *Grotius et la doctrine de la guerre juste* (Paris: Presses Universitaires de France, 1983), pp. 23–31; 85–91.

From Gratian, *Decretum*, part II, causa 23, and from Decretists[11]

Certain bishops have fallen into heresy with the people in their charge. They began with threats and tortures to force neighboring Catholics into adopting this heresy. Having learned of this, the pope ordered the Catholic bishops of the neighboring regions, who had received temporal jurisdiction from the emperor, to defend the Catholics from the heretics, and to compel them by any means possible to return to the true faith. The bishops, upon receiving these instructions from the pope, having gathered soldiers, undertook to fight against the heretics, both openly and by ambushes. Finally, several of the heretics having been killed, others having their own as well as their church's property seized, and others having been confined in jail or the workhouse, they were forced to return to the unity of the Catholic faith. At this stage we ask in the first place whether it is a sin to serve as a soldier (*militare*). Second, what sort of war is just, and how the children of Israel fought just wars. Third, whether an injury inflicted upon our associates (*sociorum*) ought to be repelled with arms. Fourth, whether vengeance (*uindicta*) is permissible. Fifth, whether it is a sin for a judge or minister to execute a guilty person. Sixth, whether the wicked may be forced to do good. Seventh, whether heretics ought to be despoiled of their property, and whether he who gains possession of property taken from heretics is to be considered as possessing things belonging to others. Eighth, whether it is permitted to bishops, or any sort of cleric, to take up arms on the authority of the pope or by command of the emperor.

Question I

[a]*Resist injury*] Let us see who may resist violence, and how it may be resisted, and whether only a personal injury may be resisted, or also one against both persons and property. It seems that not only lay persons, but also clerics, may repel violence, against either persons or property. . . . On the contrary side, it seems that clerics may

Gratian: It would seem that it is contrary to the teaching of the Gospel to serve as a soldier, since the point of all soldiering is either to resist injury[a] or to carry out vengeance; but injury is either warded off from one's own person or from one's associates, both of which are prohibited by the law of the Gospel. For it is said: "If

[11] Translation by Peter Haggenmacher and Robert Andrews, from the edition of Emil Friedberg, *Decretum Magistri Gratiani*, in *Corpus Iuris Canonici*, pars prior (Leipzig: Tauchniz, 1879). The glosses are taken from *Decretum Divi Gratiani . . . una cum glossis & thematibus prudentum, & doctorum suffragio comprobatis . . .* (Lyon, 1554).

not. . . . On this point, some people say that nobody is allowed to resist violence by hitting back, but only by impeding it. Others say that lay persons are permitted to hit back, but not clerics. I myself hold that both lay persons and clerics are permitted to hit back; but one has to distinguish, because force is either directed at persons or at property.

If it is directed at persons, then force may be resisted before it strikes. But certain people have contended that no one ought to resist force before it strikes; yet it is permitted to kill an ambusher and anyone who tries to kill you. . . . If, however, someone returns violence, this should be done with the assumption that it is for defense, rather than for revenge . . . , and only if the first attacker intends to strike once more; otherwise, if the attacker does not intend to strike once more and the other person still returns force, this should be seen as revenge rather than resistance to force. And this is what I understand when it is said that force may be resisted "on the spot" (*incontinenti*). It is therefore required that a return blow be in defense, not in revenge . . . , and that self-defense be exercised in moderation (*cum moderamine*). If, however, someone exceeds the bounds of moderation, though not on purpose, he is not to be held liable . . . , even though the decretal *Olim causam* seems to contradict this. Moreover, force may only be resisted with force on the spot. . . .

anyone strikes you on the right cheek, turn to him the other also" (Matthew 5:39); and again: "If anyone forces you to go one mile, go with him two miles" (Matthew 5:41); likewise, the Apostle said to the Romans: "Beloved, never avenge yourselves, but leave it to the wrath of God" (Matthew 12:19): What else, then, is meant by these passages, except that we are barred from resisting injury? §1. Furthermore, when Peter defended his master with a sword, Christ said: "Put your sword into its sheath"; "Do you think that I cannot appeal to my Father, and he will send me more than twelve legions of angels?" (Matthew 26:52). Finally, as is read about St. Andrew, when there was a rush of people to rescue him from the clutches of a wicked judge and to save him from an unjust death, he urged upon them patience, both in word and deed, lest they prevent his martyrdom. What else are we [hereby] incited to do than patiently to endure similar trials? §2. Next it is said in Proverbs:[12] "Vengeance is mine, and I will repay, says the Lord". Likewise, it is said in the Gospel: "Judge not, and you will not be judged" (Matthew 7:11). . . . What else is enjoined by all this if not that punishment of delinquents is to be reserved to divine judgment?

Since therefore, as was stated above, all soldiering seems to aim at resisting an attack or at inflicting vengeance, and since each of these is prohibited by the law of the

---

[12]   No such passage can be found in the book of Proverbs; this may be an allusion to Deuteronomy 32:35.

If on the other hand force is directed against property, then it is permitted to resist, both before the fact and after, but preferably after the fact than before.

Gospel, it appears that it is a sin to serve as a soldier. . . .

Gratian: Here is how we answer these arguments: The precepts of patience have to prevail less in outward deed than in the preparation of the heart.

Hence Augustine said in his *Sermon on the Child of the Centurion*:

Canon 2.
The precepts of patience have to be observed through firmness of the mind, not in outward attitude.

The just and pious man ought to be ready to put up with the malice of those he wants to become good, in order that the number of the good may increase, instead of adding himself by equal malice to the number of the wicked. In sum, these precepts are rather for the preparation of the heart which is internal, than for the deed which is in the open; so that patience and benevolence are to be confined to the secret of the mind, while that has to show in the open what would seem to profit to those we want to become better. . . .

Likewise, [Augustine] to Boniface:

Canon 3.
Many can please God in the profession of arms.

Do not think that none can please God while serving in arms. . . . Therefore keep this in mind first of all, when you prepare to fight, that your valor, including your bodily courage, is a gift of God. Thus you will care not to use a gift of God against the Lord. For, when it has been vowed, faith is to be kept even toward the enemy against whom war is being waged; how much more toward a friend whom one is fighting for? To strive for peace is a matter of willing, but war should be of necessity, so that God may free us from necessity and conserve us in peace. For peace is not pursued in order to wage war, but war is waged in order to gain peace. Be therefore peaceable while you wage war, so that you may in winning lead over to the benefit of peace those whom you defeat. . . . It is therefore necessity, not will, that crushes the fighting enemy. Just as he who fights and resists is checked by violence, mercy is due to the vanquished, to the captive, mostly when no trouble to the peace is to be feared on his part.

Likewise, [Augustine] against the Manicheans:

Canon 4.
What is rightfully to be blamed in war.

What is to be blamed in war? Is it the death of some who are to die in any case, so that others may be forced to peaceful subjection? To reprove this is cowardice, not religion. What is rightly reproved in war are love of mischief, revengeful cruelty, fierce and implacable enmity, wild resistance, lust of power, and such like. And it is generally to punish these things, when force is required to inflict punishment,

[a]Princes]   As below, same Causa, q. II, can. 1. No one, therefore, may go to war without the authorization of the prince (*auctoritate principis*). . . . Likewise a prince of the Church may declare war. . . .

that, in obedience to God or some lawful authority, good men undertake wars, when they find themselves in such a position as regards the conduct of human affairs, that this very position justly compels them either to give such orders or to obey them. Thus John does not order soldiers to lay down their arms, and Christ urges that money be given to Caesar, because soldiers need to get their pay on account of war. For this natural order which seeks the peace of mankind ordains that the authority and resolve to undertake war lie with the princes.[a] §1. But if war is undertaken to serve human greed, this does not trouble the saints, over whom no one can have any power but what is given from above. For there is no power but from God, who either orders or permits. Thus a righteous man, who happens to be serving even under a sacrilegious king, can rightfully engage in combat at his command if, keeping up the order instead of peace,[13] it is either certain that what he is ordered is not contrary to God's law, or it is not certain whether it is [contrary to God's law]. . . .

Gratian: From all this we gather that soldiering is not a sin, and that the precepts of patience are to be observed in the preparation of the heart, not in the ostentation of the body.

Question II

Now, as to what[b]]   War is said to be unjust in five ways: either because of the person (*persona*):

Gratian: Now, as to what[b] constitutes a just war, Isidore in *Twenty Books of Etymologies* says:

---

[13]   *si, vice pacis ordinem servans.* This translation follows the text of Augustine as reproduced by Gratian, or rather, it tries to confer meaning on a passage that is unintelligible. Augustine's original text reads *civicae pacis ordinem servans,* which literally means "preserving the order of civic peace." For reasons set out above (pp. 106–7) our translation must adhere to Gratian's faulty version, which obtained canonical status by its inclusion into the *Decretum.*

thus, if they are ecclesiastic persons, who are not permitted to shed blood. . . . Because of the object (*res*): thus if it is not for the recovery of property or for the defense of the country. . . . By reason of the cause (*causa*): thus, if the fight is by choice, not by necessity. . . . It is unjust because of the state of mind (*animus*): thus, if it is undertaken with the intention of revenge. . . . It is equally unjust if it is initiated without the authorization (*auctoritas*) of the prince. . . .

Canon 1.
What is a just war.

That war is just which is waged by an edict in order to regain what has been stolen or to repel the attack of enemies. A judge is called such because he pronounces justice (*ius dictat*) to the people, or because he adjudicates (*disceptet*) justly. To adjudicate justly is to judge justly. For he is no judge who has no justice within himself.

Likewise, Augustine in *Seven Questions Concerning the Heptateuch* says:

Canon 2.
It is of no concern to justice
whether one fights openly
or by ambushes.

Our Lord God himself gave the order to Joshua to set up an ambush behind him, that is, to arrange his warriors so as to trap the enemy in an ambush. This teaches us that such things are not done unjustly by those who fight a just war; so that the just man doesn't need particularly to worry about this, except that war be undertaken by one who has the right to do so. For this right does not belong to everyone. Yet when a just war is undertaken, it does not affect justice whether one fights openly or by ambushes. Just wars are usually defined as those which have for their end the avenging of injuries, when it is necessary by war to constrain a nation or a city which has either neglected to punish an evil action committed by its citizens, or to restore what has been taken unjustly. But also this kind of war is certainly just which is ordered by God, who knows what is owed to everyone; in which case the leader of the army or the people itself are not to be deemed authors but agents of the war.

Gratian: Since therefore the just war is one which is waged by an edict, or by which injustices are avenged, it is asked how the children of Israel fought just wars.
On this subject, Augustine wrote in his *Questions on [the book of] Numbers* that

Canon 3.
The sons of Israel were refused
innocent passage, and therefore
they waged just wars.

One ought indeed to note how just wars were waged by the sons of Israel against the Amorites. For they were denied innocent passage, which ought to have been granted according to the most equitable law governing human society.

Question III

Gratian: But injury done to associates should not be repelled, as shown by examples and authorities. . . . Thus we also read about the first faithful that they suffered with joy to be robbed of their goods, without asking for any assistance by others; rather, they rejoiced at being found worthy of bearing disgrace in the name of Christ. And the Apostle also advises the Corinthians, in his first epistle to them, patiently to put up with injury and fraud, rather than to scandalize their brethren by asserting their rights. . . . Since therefore he who is being protected from injury by the force of arms is no less scandalized than he whose stolen property is being claimed before a judge, it is evident that armed assistance ought not to be requested. And what ought not to be requested, ought not to be granted in law (*iure*). But on the other hand many things are being regularly (*rite*) granted that are not legally claimed. The virtuous will indeed not regularly (*rite*) claim that an injury be sanctioned, lest he render an evil for an evil; and yet the judge would rightly inflict such punishment; nor [would he do it] if he did not [thereby] render a good deed for an evil one. . . .

Likewise, Ambrose [writes] in the first book of [his work] *On the Duties* [*of Ministers*]:

Canon 5.
He is full of justice who protects his country from the barbarians.

The courage that protects one's country[a] from barbarians in war, or defends the weak in peace, or associates against brigands,[b] is full of justice.

[a]*Country*]   In this case he who kills his own father is not held responsible: as in *Digest*, 11, 7, 35.

[b]*Brigands*]   It is permitted to kill these without the authorization of a judge: as below, same Causa, q. V, canon 17.

Likewise, Ambrose [writes] in the first book of [his work] *On the Duties* [*of Ministers*]:

Canon 7.
He who does not ward off an injury from an associate is similar to him who caused it.

The law of valor lies not in inflicting injury but in repelling it; for he who fails to ward off injury from an associate if he can do so, is quite as blamable as he who inflicts it. It is

[a]*Striking*] Therefore someone can exceed proportionality in defending. Argument against *Decretals*, II, 13, 12, i.f.

here, therefore, that Moses the saint gave the first proofs of his courage at war. For when he saw a Hebrew being mistreated by an Egyptian, he defended him by striking[a] the Egyptian and hiding him in the sand. Solomon too said: Deliver him who is being led to death (Proverbs 24:11).

Question IV

Gratian: Likewise, this Gospel sentence, "He who resorts to the sword shall perish by the sword," that is advanced as an objection, is explained by Augustine in book II [chap. 70] of his *Against Manicheans*:

**Canon 36.
Who should be said to resort to the sword.**

He resorts to the sword[a] who has armed himself to spill the blood of another without the order or assent of a legitimate power.[b]

[a]*He resorts to the sword*] i.e. unjustly.

Gratian [dictum post can. 48]: It has been briefly shown that the good laudably pursue the wicked, and that the wicked damnably pursue the good. . . . It has been shown that vengeance may be exerted. It now remains to show who is to exert it and by what means, and that those who are punished are more cherished than those who remain unpunished: both points are proven with many authorities.

[b]*Power*] For the power of the sword (*potestas gladii*) is derived only from the prince. . . .

Likewise, Augustine [writes] in *On the Lord's Sermon on the Mountain*:

**Canon 51.
Vengeance that aims at correction is not to be prohibited.**

That vengeance which aims at correction is not prohibited; it even belongs to mercy, and it is not in conflict with the attitude whereby he who wants someone to be punished is ready to suffer more from him; but only he is apt to inflict this vengeance who has overcome by the mildness of love that hatred which usually impels those who avenge themselves. Indeed, it is not to be feared that the parents would hate their little son when he is being chidden in order not to sin again. . . . No one should therefore exert vengeance but he on whom regular power has been conferred thereto, and who punishes like a father striking his little child, unable as he is to hate him owing to his age. . . .

Gratian [dictum post can. 54]: From all this we gather that vengeance is to be inflicted not out of passion for vengeance itself, but out of zeal of justice; not in order that hatred be vented, but that evil deeds be corrected. But since retribution is sometimes inflicted by destroying goods, sometimes by flogging, sometimes even by death, we ask whether it is sinful for the judge or his minister to put the guilty to death.

Question V

Gratian: Now, that nobody is allowed to kill anyone is proved by that precept whereby the Lord in the Decalogue prohibited homicide, saying: "Thou shalt not kill." Likewise it is said in the Gospel that "Whoever takes the sword, shall perish by the sword".

Likewise, [it is said by] pope Gregory:

Canon 7.
Those who are accused of shedding blood must be defended by the Church.

Let the Church defend those who are accused of bloodshed, lest it partake in the spilling of blood.

This precept[a]] Thou shalt not kill.

Gratian: Hence it appears that the wicked are to be corrected by flogging, not to be quelled by maiming or temporal death. §1. But an objection arises from what the Lord said to Moses: "Do not suffer evildoers to live" (Exodus 22:18). . . . This precept[a] forbids thus anyone to arm himself by his own authority to inflict death on somebody; it does not forbid putting the culprits to death by the command of the law. For he who in the exercise of public power puts to death the wicked by the command of the law is neither considered a transgressor of this precept nor a stranger to the heavenly fatherland.

Therefore Augustine [wrote] to Publicola:

Canon 8.
It is no sin to kill a man in the exercise of a public function.

As to putting men to death in order that nobody be killed by them, I do not approve of it, except perhaps by a soldier[a] or by someone held thereto owing to a

public function, so that he does not do it for himself but for others, or for the city where he finds himself, having been conferred legitimate power in

[a]*Soldier*] Constituted under some power . . . , unless this happens in a just war. . . .

[b]*Person*] He says this on account of the bishops who are invested with secular jurisdiction, but cannot preside over cases involving blood. . . .

conformity with his person.[b] As to those who are held back by some terror from doing evil, they may themselves draw some benefit from it. Hence it is said: We should not resist evil, lest you take delight in vengeance, which feeds the mind in others' misfortune; yet we should not for all that neglect the correction of evil men. . . .

Gratian: But nobody is allowed by the authority of any law to kill himself.

Hence, Augustine [declares] in the first book of *The City of God*:

Canon 9.
Those who made war with God's authority in no way transgressed the command not to kill.

If someone is not allowed to kill an innocent man by virtue of his private power, without any law granting him the permission to kill, surely he too who kills himself is a murderer, and he becomes all the guiltier in killing himself the more he was innocent with respect to the very plight which led him to think that he had to kill himself. . . . Indeed, when the law says: "Thou shalt not kill," we have to understand the prohibition as being also directed towards us. . . . Nor does he who kills himself kill aught but a man. §4. To be sure, some exceptions to the principle that no one is allowed to kill a man have been made by divine authority itself; in these cases the killing was ordered by God, through a law or a temporary command expressly addressed to a person; he who kills is only the executioner obeying an order, as the sword is an instrument in the hand of him who uses it. And therefore those who waged wars ordered by God never acted against the precept "Thou shalt not kill," as little as those who, invested with public powers, punished criminals with death according to just laws, that is, to the command of supremely just reason. . . .

[Augustine adds] in the same first book [of *The City of God*]:

Canon 13.
The soldier who kills a man in obedience to the powers that be does not commit homicide.

A soldier who kills a man in obedience to the power under which he has been legitimately constituted cannot be accused of homicide under the law of his commonwealth; on the contrary, if he had not done it, he would be guilty of desertion and insubordination. Had he done it on his own initiative and authority, then he would be accused of having spilt human blood. He therefore would be equally punished whether he did it without orders or whether he did it not in spite of orders received.

Likewise [Augustine writes] in the *Questions on Exodus*:

Canon 14.
He is a murderer who willfully
kills those whom the judge
orders to be killed.

When the judge's minister kills him whom the judge ordered to be put to death, he is surely a murderer if he did it willfully (*sponte*), even though he kills someone whom he knows to be doomed to death by the judge.

The same, in the *Questions on Matthew*:

Canon 16.
The duties of revenge can be
fulfilled in good conscience.

The virtuous can fulfill the duties of revenge in good conscience, like the judge, like the law.

The same, to Macedonius:

Canon 17.
He is not iniquitous but
humane who prosecutes crime
in order to liberate man.

He is not prone to iniquity, but rather to humanity who is a prosecutor of crime in order to be a liberator of men.

The same, [in the same letter]:

Canon 18.
Why regal power and legal
tortures have been instituted.

It is not in vain that regal power, the right of the prosecutor, the iron claws of the executioner, the arms of the soldier, the discipline imposed by the ruler, and even the severity of a good father have been instituted; all these means have their measure, their causes, reasons and utilities. While all these things are feared, the wicked are held in check and the good live quietly among the wicked.

Likewise:

Canon 19.
Sometimes he who is the cause
of death is guiltier than he
who inflicted death.

When a man is killed by a man,
there is a great difference whether
this happens with the lust to inflict
harm or to carry off something
unjustly (such as by an enemy or
a brigand); or whether it happens by way of official revenge or obedience
(as with a judge or an executioner); or whether it happens in order to escape
or to give assistance in a case of emergency, as when a brigand is killed by a
traveler or an enemy by a soldier. §1. And sometimes he who was the cause
of death is guiltier than the one who did the killing: as when someone
deceives his guarantor, and the latter incurs the death penalty in his stead.
Not everyone, however, who is the cause of somebody's death is therefore
guilty. . . . Shall we, [to avoid] such deaths being caused to others, have to
consent to crimes, or do away with the punishment of sins, even on the part of
a father – not in order to inflict harm but to exert correction – or refrain from
the works of mercy? When these things happen we owe them human grief, but
we should not, in order to avoid them, quell the will to act righteously.

Likewise, Augustine, *On Free Will,* book I:

Canon 41.
He does not sin who kills a
criminal by virtue of his
functions.

If killing a man is indeed homicide,
it sometimes can happen without
sin. For neither a soldier killing an
enemy, nor a judge or his minister
killing a criminal, nor someone
inadvertently or imprudently throwing a spear would sin, in my opinion, when
they killed a man. Nor are they usually called homicides. – The same, in
Questions on Leviticus: §1. When a man is justly killed, it is the law, not you,
who kills him.

Likewise, pope Nicholas to the army of the Franks:

Canon 46.
Whoever dies in the fight
against the infidels is deserving
of the celestial kingdom.

We want all of you to know
charity, since none of those who
will have faithfully died in this
battle (we say this without wishing
it) shall in the least be denied the
celestial kingdom.

Likewise, Augustine to Boniface:

Canon 48.
The peace of the Church
alleviates the sorrow caused
by those who are lost.

For who of us would have someone
of his enemies, I say not die, but even
lose something? But if the house of
David could not regain peace
otherwise than by the death of

Absalom, his son, in the war he was waging against the father – although the
latter had been at great pains to enjoin his men as far as possible to take him
safe and alive so that he might repent and obtain his pardon from paternal
affection – what else remained than to weep his loss and to soothe his sorrow
at the thought of peace being restored in his kingdom?

    Gratian: If therefore saintly men and public powers waging war did not
transgress that command, "Thou shalt not kill," while inflicting
death on all villains deserving it; if the soldier, acting in obedience to
his authorities, is not guilty of homicide when, following their order, he kills
any villain; if killing murderers and punishing poisoners does not amount to
spilling blood but to serving the law; if the peace of the church allays the
sorrow caused by the lost ones; if those who, inflamed by the zeal of their
Catholic mother, put to death the excommunicated are not considered
homicides – then it is obvious that it is allowed not only to whip but also to
kill the wicked. §1. But it is asked, if some rogues happen to be punished by
persons not invested with legitimate power, whether those by whom they are
punished are guilty of spilling blood.

    Here is what Ambrose writes in this respect:

Canon 49.
Sometimes sins are punished
by peoples impelled by
a divine order.

Sins are remitted by God's word,
which is interpreted by the Levite
and executed by someone. They
are remitted by the office of the
priest and his sacred ministry. Sins are

also punished by men, such as judges acting by virtue of their temporary
power. §1. Sins are also punished by peoples, as we read, since the people of
Israel has often been subdued for its offenses to divine majesty by foreign
nations impelled by divine injunction.

    Gratian: Hence it is to be noted that God sometimes punishes sins
by unknowing [agents], sometimes by knowing ones. He punishes sins
by unknowing ones, as when he at times afflicted the people of Israel
[or] at times led it into captivity by Sennacherib, by Nebuchadnezzar,
by Antiochus, by the Roman emperors, and by various heathen kings. . . . He
punished sins by knowing [agents] as when he wanted to punish the sins of
the Amorites and Canaanites and other peoples whose territory he gave as a
possession to Israel, ordering it also not to spare anyone of them but to put

them all to death. . . . When therefore peoples are thus impelled by divine order to punish sins, as the Jewish people is incited to occupy the promised land and to extirpate the sinful nations, it is without sin that noxious blood is spilled, and what had been wickedly possessed by them becomes the right and property of the good ones. On the other hand, when some are moved by hidden instinct to pursue the wicked, such as Sennacherib and others who pursued the delinquent people, though they are impelled by the operation of hidden instinct to pursue them for their deeds, yet, since their wicked intention does not aim at punishing the sins of the delinquents but at taking their goods and subduing them, they are not free from reprobation. . . . It therefore appears that the wicked are not only flogged but often even destroyed for their sins, sometimes by legitimate powers, sometimes by peoples impelled by divine order. Nor is this contradicted by the fact that Augustine supplicated Marcellinus not to put the Circumcellions to death but to chastise them by flogging. Although he asked by his supplication for their lives to be spared, he did not say that the severity of the laws which punished such deeds by death should not be observed.

Question VI

Gratian: As to the question whether the wicked ought to be compelled to the good, the answer is obvious. The Ancient People was indeed compelled by the fear of punishments to observe the law. In the Gospel, too, the Lord said to his disciples: "Be not afraid of those who kill the body, while they cannot kill the soul, be rather afraid of him" – that is, serve him in awe – "who can kill the soul and the body in hell" (Matthew 10:28). Paul, too, when he persecuted God's church, was blinded on his way and forced to convert to God. . . .

Hence Augustine writes to Boniface:

Canon 1.
The Church must compel the wicked to the good, as Christ compelled Paul.

The schismatics say: To whom did Christ do violence, whom did he compel? Let them take the apostle Paul as an example. Let them recognize in him Christ, first compelling, then teaching; first striking, then comforting. It is indeed remarkable how this man, who came to the Gospel through corporal punishment, was to labor more than all those who were called to the Gospel only through words; and he who was forced to charity by great fear, was to banish fear through his perfect charity. Why therefore should the church not compel the lost sons, when the lost sons compelled others to perdition? Yet, even when those who were not compelled but only seduced, are called back by severe but salutary laws into the bosom of their pious mother, she will lovingly receive them and rejoice much more with them than with those whom she never lost. §1. Is it not part of the vigilance owed by the shepherd even to those sheep who have left their flock and come to be possessed by others – not by being violently drawn off but blandly and softly seduced – once he finds them, to drive them back to the flock under the threat and even the pain of flogging? – Likewise: §2. We have referred to the example of Paul compelled by Christ. The church has therefore imitated her Lord in applying coercion, when she first waited, in order not to compel anybody, so that the prophecies concerning the faith of the kings and peoples might be fulfilled. §3. Nor is it absurd to refer to this apostolic sentence where Saint Paul said: "We are ready to avenge any disobedience, when your obedience will first be complete" (2 Corinthians 10:4). §4. Therefore the Lord himself ordered the guests first to be invited, then to be compelled to his great meal. For when the servants answered him: "Lord, what you ordered has been done and there is still room," he said: "Go out by the ways and paths, and compel whomsoever you meet to enter" (Luke 14:22–3). In those, therefore, who were first gently brought along, prior obedience was fulfilled; but in those who were compelled, disobedience was curbed. – Likewise: §5. If, by the power the church received in its time as a divine gift through the religion and the faith of the kings, those who are found on the ways and paths, that is, in the heresies and schisms, are compelled to enter, they should not reprehend being compelled but rather ask themselves to what purpose they are being compelled. . . .

Gratian [dictum post can. 4]: From all this one gathers that the wicked must be compelled to the good. §1. But it is objected that nobody is to be uselessly compelled to anything. But it is useless to compel anybody to the good, since God disdains forced worship. . . . §5. These [objections] we answer thus: If the wicked were always to suffer unwillingly the good which they are forced to, without ever serving it willingly, they would have been uselessly compelled to it. But since human nature tends to dislike what it gets out of habit and rather likes what it is used to, the wicked have to be removed from evil by the lash of tribulations and called to the good, so that, evil falling into disuse through the fear of punishment, it is rejected, while the good becomes agreeable owing to habit.

Question VII

[a]*But now* Not only heretics, but all enemies may be despoiled of their goods, provided the war is just: and he who takes something becomes by

Gratian: But now[a] we ask whether the heretics are to be deprived of their own and their churches' goods; and whether those who possess what has been

right its owner. . . . But it is licit to deprive heretics of their goods . . . Yet it is better that this happens with the authority of the judge. . . . When therefore a layman is convicted of heresy, his goods are confiscated. . . . And this remains true even if a heretic has sons and relatives. . . . And thus the law which provides that the goods of the heretics devolve on the sons and relatives is corrected. . . . Although the goods have been taken away from the heretics, yet, if they recant, their former goods are restituted to them out of mercy, including the episcopate. . . . Thus he who returns from heresy is in a better position than he who returns from the enemy. For if a deserter freely returns to his people, his life will be spared, but he will be deported to an island. . . .

taken from them must be said to possess things belonging to others.

Gratian: These authorities plainly show that what the heretics possess unrightfully is rightfully taken away from them by the catholics, who therefore are not said to possess things belonging to others.

Question VIII

Gratian: As to bishops or any [other] clerics, it is easy to show that they are not supposed to take up arms, either on their own authority or on the authority of the Roman Pontiff. . . . For anyone apart from him, or the authorization of him who is invested with legitimate power and who does not bear the sword without cause, as says the Apostle, and to whom any being is subjected, anyone, I say, who takes up the sword without this authority shall perish by the sword. . . .

Gratian: Hence also the following has been established in the council of Tribur with respect to those who die in war or in a broil:

Canon 4.
No prayer nor sacrifice is offered for a cleric who dies in war or in a broil.

No cleric whatever having died either in war or in a broil or in tournaments shall be sustained either through sacrifices or prayers, but he shall be handed over to the judge; yet he shall not be deprived of burial.

Gratian: We answer this as follows: Priests may not take up arms themselves; but they are allowed to exhort others to do so in order to defend the oppressed and to fight the enemies of God.

Hence pope Leo IV wrote to emperor Louis: . . .

Canon 8.
The pope has to be the defender
and protector of his flock.

You must know that we shall never suffer our men to be oppressed by anyone; but should there arise some necessity, then we shall presently react, because we have to defend our flock against everybody and be its foremost protectors.

The same, to the army of the Franks:

Canon 9.
He shall obtain the heavenly
kingdom from God who dies
in defense of the Christians.

Having relinquished all fright and terror, do combat with all your strength the enemies of the holy faith and the adversaries of all religions. For, if anyone of you dies, the Almighty knows that he died for the truth of the faith, for the salvation of the country and the defense of the Christians, and he will therefore obtain celestial reward.

Likewise pope Nicholas, in response to the Bulgarians:

Canon 15.
In case of pressing necessity,
it is allowed to go to war
even during Lent.

If there is no urgent necessity, one has to abstain from battle, not only during Lent, but in any time. If however an unavoidable importunity is pressing, there is no doubt that one has to engage in war, even during Lent, for the defense of oneself or of one's country, or of paternal laws; otherwise man might indeed seem to tempt God if, while having the means to do so, he does not take care of his own and others' safety, and does not forestall the damage to the holy religion.

Gratian [dictum post can. 18]: In the pontifical register it can also be read that Saint Gregory ordered the citizens of Tuscany to take up arms against the Lombards and that he decreed that the soldiers be paid. From this example and from the foregoing authorities it appears that priests, though they may not themselves take up arms, are however in a position by their own authority to order either those to whom this office is committed, or anybody, to do so.

Gratian [dictum post can. 28]: The prelates of the Church are therefore allowed, following the example of the Blessed Gregory, to call upon the emperor or any generals to defend the faithful. It is even allowed, with the Blessed Leo, vigorously to exhort anybody to make a defense against the adversaries of the holy faith and to incite everybody to fend off the violence of the infidels. But no bishop is allowed to order spilling of blood on his own or on the emperor's authority.

11

John of Salisbury
(ca. 1115–1180)

The Challenge of Tyranny

> The origin of tyranny is iniquity, and springing from a poisonous root, it is a tree which grows and sprouts into a baleful pestilent growth, and to which the axe must by all means be laid.
>
> *Policraticus*

John of Salisbury combined his career as a man of letters with significant contributions to political drama and courtly intrigue. One of his main associates was the illustrious Thomas Becket, archbishop of Canterbury, who was murdered in his own cathedral as a result of deep divisions over the proper rule of church and state in twelfth-century England. And Becket was not John's only controversial associate.

Yet, although John of Salisbury became involved in a myriad of cabals and intrigues, as a scholar he is remembered as a man of prudence and moderation. Indeed, moderation stands as a unifying theme of his writings on politics, of which his treatise *Policraticus*, completed in 1159, is the most widely read. In it, he urges private, public, and ecclesiastical leaders to show restraint, and to respect the liberty and safety of their subjects. Good leaders are marked by a moderate disposition, never seeking to misuse their power for their own sake, and always striving to make the life of human beings better – not only in the sense of preparing their fellows for eternal life, but also in making the everyday existence of ordinary men and women more secure.[1]

John's political thought aligns itself well with a major trend in twelfth-century European law and political philosophy: it seeks to define the spheres of power within which each ruler should move, and to clarify the often overlapping and sometimes confusing relationships between various power-holders.[2] Having witnessed

---

[1] See Cary Nederman, "Introduction," in John of Salisbury, *Policraticus*, trans. and ed. Cary Nederman (Cambridge: Cambridge University Press, 1990), esp. p. xxiv.
[2] See Harold Berman, *Law and Revolution* (Cambridge, MA: Harward University Press, 1983).

anarchy and civil war under the rule of King Stephen of England (1135–53), John sought to formulate morally edifying advice for virtuous rulers, for the sake of peace and the common good.

For our purposes, John of Salisbury is important because he offers one of the first coherent defenses of an important, yet contested theory of the Middle Ages: the idea that a tyrant can be removed by violent force. John uses the word tyrant to denote a man who rules to his own advantage, outside the bounds of law and morality. According to John, such tyrants might be found in private and ecclesiastical settings, not only on the political scene. In his discussion of tyrannicide, however, it is politics that John mainly has in mind. He leaves political rulers to deal with private tyrants, and the church to chastise ecclesiastical tyrants. For political tyrants, however, such mechanisms are rarely effective, although both private individuals and churchly leaders should try to lead tyrannical rulers to better ways. John's conclusion is that public persons, and in extreme cases even private individuals, may rightly use violence against – and if necessary kill – the political tyrant.

In the centuries to come, John's position on tyrannicide would be subject to lively debate. John does not, however, take a clear-cut and unambiguous stand on the subject. He merely says that in the extreme case where the abuse of power by the political tyrant becomes unbearable, it *may* become the duty of public persons, sometimes even of a private individual, to ensure political change by violent means. Historically, however, in spite of its author's caution, this argument became very significant, since it held forth a possible legitimation of internal warfare (i.e. civil war).[3]

While John is reticent about making tyrannicide an automatic response to illegitimate rule, it is clear that he identifies tyranny as the root cause of war and a host of other evils. Peace would have reigned in the world, had certain individuals not sought to secure their private advantage by dominating other people, thereby rebelling against natural and divine law.

Before presenting our excerpts from John's rightly famous treatment of tyranny and its demise in books III and VIII of the *Policraticus*, we first turn to some passages from book VI, in which he presents his understanding of military power and its proper role in society. We should note that he does not discuss explicitly the morality of going to war or, for that matter, morality *in* war. But the overall political teaching that emerges in these and other passages of the *Policraticus* – namely, that the prince is obliged to defend the people, that he should respect the law, must exhibit moderation, and may shed blood only when necessary for the

---

[3] Jan van Laarhoven has asserted that John's general teaching on obedience to political authority all but abolishes the so-called theory of tyrannicide, and that John's main point is that tyrants will inevitably come to a bad end, not that one should actively seek to kill them. See Jan van Laarhoven, "Thou Shalt *Not* Slay a Tyrant! The So-called Theory of John of Salisbury," in *The World of John of Salisbury*, ed. Michael Wilks (Oxford: Basil Blackwell, 1984).

common good – furnishes a general framework that fits well with the main tenets of the just war tradition as it was developing among jurists and philosophers in John's day and in the centuries to follow.

From *Policraticus,* bk. VI, chaps. 1–2[4]

1 The hand of the commonwealth is either armed or unarmed. The armed hand is that which performs the soldiering of camps and blood; the unarmed is that which administers justice and, keeping holiday from arms, is enlisted in the service of the law. For not those alone do military service for the commonwealth who, protected by helmets and cuirasses, ply their swords or what other weapons you please against the foe, but also the advocates and pleaders of causes who, trusting to the bulwark of their glorious voice, lift up the fallen, refresh the weary; nor do they less serve mankind, than if they were preserving from the foe by the use of weapons the life, hope and posterity of those who are hard-pressed. Publicans, apparitors, and all officers of the law courts may also be said to perform military service. For as some offices are of peace and others of war, so it is necessary that the ones should be performed by one set of officials, the others by another.

The armed hand is employed only against the enemy, the unarmed is stretched out against the citizen also. It is needful that both should be subject to discipline, because both have a noteworthy tendency to viciousness. Besides, the way in which the hands are used bears witness to the character of the head, because, as Wisdom [Proverbs 29:12] says, an unjust king has none but ungodly ministers; and as is the ruler of a state, so are those who inhabit therein. . . .

The hand of each militia, to wit both the armed and the unarmed, is the hand of the prince himself; and unless he restrains both, he is not continent. And in truth the unarmed hand is to be curbed the more tightly for the reason that while the soldiery of arms are enjoined to abstain from extortion and rapine, the unarmed hand is debarred even from taking gifts. But if a lawful penalty is demanded of anyone, if it is a question in other words of exacting or receiving that which is fixed or allowed by law, then there is no ground for punishment or blame. Whatever it is, it cannot properly be called an exaction; nor does it fall into the class of gifts which officials are forbidden to receive.

Because the license of officials has a freer rein in that they can use the pretext of their office to despoil or harass private persons, all usurpations contrary to their official duty must be punished with a proportionately heavier penalty. . . .

2 . . . The control exercised over [the armed hand] is the principal test of the wisdom and justice of the prince. . . . [S]ince works of both peace and war require to be regulated, he ought to be learned both in the law and in military

---

[4] From John of Salisbury, *Policraticus: The Statesman's Book of John of Salisbury,* trans. and ed. John Dickinson (New York: Russell and Russell, [1927] 1963), pp. 173–4, 180–1.

science. . . . [The armed hand is] never fit and vigorous without selection, science, and training. For if any of these is lacking the hand becomes useless and unprofitable; of the three, science and training are the most valuable. For knowledge of military science promotes boldness of strategy. No one fears to do what he feels confident that he has learned to do well. A mere handful of men practiced in the art of war is more likely to be victorious than a rough, untrained multitude, which is always exposed to the danger of slaughter. What made the Romans victorious over all nations? Principally science, training, and the loyal devotion which chosen men paid to the commonwealth in pursuance of their oath.

From *Policraticus,* bk. III, chap. 15[5]

15 . . . To kill a tyrant is not merely lawful, but right and just. For whosoever takes up the sword deserves to perish by the sword. And he is understood to take up the sword who usurps it by his own temerity and who does not receive the power of using it from God. Therefore the law rightly takes arms against him who disarms the laws, and the public power rages in fury against him who strives to bring to nought the public force. And while there are many acts which amount to *lèse majesté,* none is a graver crime than that which is aimed against the body of Justice herself. Tyranny therefore is not merely a public crime, but, if there could be such a thing, a crime more than public. And if in the crime of *lèse majesté* all men are admitted to be prosecutors, how much more should this be true in the case of the crime of subverting the laws which should rule even over emperors? Truly no one will avenge a public enemy, but rather whoever does not seek to bring him to punishment commits an offence against himself and the whole body of the earthly commonwealth.

From *Policraticus,* bk. VIII, chaps. 17–18, 20[6]

17 . . . A tyrant, then, as the philosophers have described him, is one who oppresses the people by rulership based upon force, while he who rules in accordance with the laws is a prince. Law is the gift of god, the model of equity, a standard of justice, a likeness of the divine will, the guardian of well-being, a bond of union and solidarity between peoples, a rule defining duties, a barrier against the vices and the destroyer thereof, a punishment of violence and all wrong-doing. The law is assailed by force or by fraud, and, as it were, either wrecked by the fury of the lion or undermined by the wiles of the serpent. In whatever way this comes to pass, it is plain that it is the grace of God which is being assailed, and that it is

---

[5]   Ibid., pp. lxxiii–lxxiv.
[6]   Ibid., pp. 335–6, 350, 351–2, 356–7, 368–9, 372–3.

God himself who in a sense is challenged to battle. The prince fights for the laws and the liberty of the people; the tyrant thinks nothing done unless he brings the laws to nought and reduces the people to slavery. Hence the prince is a kind of likeness of divinity; and the tyrant, on the contrary, a likeness of the boldness of the Adversary, even of the wickedness of Lucifer, imitating him that sought to build his throne to the north and make himself like unto the Most High, with the exception of His goodness. For had he desired to be like unto Him in goodness, he would never have striven to tear from Him the glory of His power and wisdom. What he more likely did aspire to was to be equal with him in authority to dispense rewards. The prince, as the likeness of the Deity, is to be loved, worshipped and cherished; the tyrant, the likeness of wickedness, is generally to be even killed. The origin of tyranny is iniquity, and springing from a poisonous root, it is a tree which grows and sprouts into a baleful pestilent growth, and to which the axe must by all means be laid. For if iniquity and injustice, banishing charity, had not brought about tyranny, firm concord and perpetual peace would have possessed the peoples of the earth forever, and no one would think of enlarging his boundaries. Then kingdoms would be as friendly and peaceful, according to the authority of the great father Augustine [in *De civitate Dei*, bk. IV, chap. 15], and would enjoy as undisturbed repose, as the separate families in a well-ordered state, or as different persons in the same family; or perhaps, which is even more credible, there would be no kingdoms at all, since it is clear from the ancient historians that in the beginning these were founded by iniquity as presumptuous encroachments against the Lord, or else were extorted from Him. . . .

18 I do not, however, deny that tyrants are the ministers of God, who by His just judgment has willed them to be in the place of highest authority in one sphere or the other, that is to say over souls or over bodies, to the end that by their means the wicked may be punished, and the good chastened and exercised. For the sins of a people cause a hypocrite to reign over them, and, as the Book of Kings bears witness, tyrants were brought into power over the people of Israel by the failings of the priests. . . .

Indeed all power is good since it is from Him from whom alone are all things and from whom cometh only good. But at times it may not be good, but rather evil, to the particular individual who exercises it or to him upon whom it is exercised, though it is good from the universal standpoint, being the act of Him who uses our ills for His own good purposes. Just as in a painting, a black or smutty color or some other such feature, looked at by itself, is ugly, and yet considered as a part of the whole painting is pleasing; so things which separately examined seem foul and evil, yet when related to the whole appear good and fair, since He adapts all things to Himself whose works are all exceeding good. Therefore even the rule of a tyrant, too, is good, although nothing is worse than tyranny. For tyranny is the abuse of power entrusted by God to man. But this evil embraces a vast and varied use of things which are good. For it is clear that tyranny not only exists in the case of princes, but that every one is a tyrant who abuses power that has been conferred upon him from above over those that are subjected to him. . . .

[From what has been pointed out so far] it will readily appear that it has always been lawful to flatter tyrants and to deceive them, and that it has always been an honorable thing to slay them if they can be curbed in no other way. I am not now talking of tyrants in private life, but of those who oppress the commonwealth. For private tyrants can easily be restrained by the public laws which are binding upon the lives of all; but in the case of a priest, even though he acts the tyrant, it is not lawful to employ the material sword against him because of the reverence due to sacred things, unless perchance after he has been unfrocked, he lifts a bloody hand against the Church of God; since the rule always prevails that there ought not be double punishment of one man for the same offence. . . .

20 . . . [T]yrants are demanded, introduced, and raised to power by sin, and are excluded, blotted out, and destroyed by repentance. And even before the time of their kings, as the Book of Judges relates, the children of Israel were time without number in bondage to tyrants, being visited with affliction on many different occasions in accordance with the dispensation of God, and then often, when they cried aloud to the Lord, they were delivered. And when the allotted time of their punishment was fulfilled, they were allowed to cast off the yoke from their necks by the slaughter of their tyrants; nor is blame attached to any of those by whose valor a penitent and humbled people was thus set free, but their memory is preserved in affection by posterity as servants of the Lord. . . .

The histories teach, however, that none should undertake the death of a tyrant who is bound to him by an oath or by the obligation of fealty. . . . [S]ureties for good behavior are justly given even to a tyrant.

But as for the use of poison, although I see it sometimes wrongfully adopted by infidels, I do not read that it is ever permitted by any law. Not that I do not believe that tyrants ought to be removed from our midst, but it should be done without loss of religion and honor. For David, the best of all kings that I have read of, and who, save in the incident of Urias Etheus, walked blamelessly in all things, although he had to endure the most grievous tyrant, and although he often had an opportunity of destroying him, yet preferred to spare him, trusting in the mercy of God, within whose power it was to set him free without sin. He therefore determined to abide in patience until the tyrant should either suffer a change of heart and be visited by God with return of charity, or else should fall in battle, or otherwise meet his end by the just judgment of God. . . . And surely the method of destroying tyrants which is the most useful and the safest, is for those who are oppressed to take refuge humbly in the protection of God's mercy, and lifting up undefiled hands to the Lord, to pray devoutly that the scourge wherewith they are afflicted may be turned aside from them. For the sins of transgressors are the strength of tyrants.

12

Raymond of Peñafort (ca. 1180–1275) and William of Rennes (Thirteenth Century)

The Conditions of Just War, Self-defense, and their Legal Consequences under Penitential Jurisdiction

[T]hose [enemy] subjects who, fearing God more than men, refuse to abet their lord in his unjust war by giving advice, aid, or favor, should not, I believe, in any way be despoiled; for the punishment should smite the authors [of the wrong] and not reach beyond the delinquent's fault

Summa de casibus poenitentiae

Some people say that no one may strike another before he is first struck, which is not true

William of Rennes, *Apparatus ad Summam de casibus*

Born near Barcelona around 1180, Raymond of Peñafort entered the Order of Preachers (Dominicans), and in the course of his long life produced two works that greatly influenced the course of canon law. The first was a compilation of papal decrees that Raymond edited at the request of Pope Gregory IX (hence it was called *The Decretals of Gregory IX*). Upon its publication in 1234 the work quickly became authoritative and was widely cited in the ensuing centuries. The second work, *Summa de casibus poenitentiae*, was authored by Raymond during 1224–6 (and later revised some time between 1234 and 1245), earning him much renown as the "father of casuistry." The *Summa Raymundi* (as it was also called) provided an elementary set of juridical rules, organized around a number of topics, which was intended to serve as a guide for confessors. By virtue of their power to absolve penitents from their sins, confessors exercised a role akin to judges, and were expected to apply the law within a special jurisdiction: the inner domain of conscience (*forum conscientiae* or *forum internum*, as opposed to *forum externum* or *forum contentiosum*). Since many of the individuals who came to confession had contact of one sort or another with problems relating to war, it was natural that this theme would be taken up in Raymond's *Summa*. The main locus of his treatment was a discussion of brigands and incendiaries in book II of this work. By selecting this rubric, Raymond was able to dissociate his analysis of war from the theme of heresy to which it had been closely linked in Gratian's *Decretum*. Drawing on the work of the Decretists, Raymond was one of the first authors to carve out the problem of war as a distinct field of investigation. A whole series of penitential *summae* succeeded the *Raymundina* during the next three centuries, up to the *Summula Caietani*.[1]

Most editions of Raymond's *Summa de casibus poenitentiae* are accompanied by a commentary which, on the question of war in particular, has exercised considerable influence in its own right. Written toward the middle of the thirteenth century by the Dominican William of Rennes,[2] the commentary clarified a number of points which were left undetermined in Raymond's text; in so doing it brought a new technical sophistication to the emergent doctrine of just war.[3]

Raymond's discussion closely follows the *Decretum* glosses *Bellum dicitur iniustum* and *Qui repellere possunt* (reproduced above pp. 109–11), to which he contributes some subtle changes and elaborations. Thus, in §17, whereas the gloss had earlier spoken of five ways in which a war can be *unjust*, Raymond now speaks of five conditions that, cumulatively, must be fulfilled if a war is to be considered *just*. Of these, the authority condition, though mentioned last, was to be the most important

---

[1] See Cajetan, chap. 22 below. On this and parallel developments in "ordinary" canon (and civil) law, epitomized by John of Legnano's *Tractatus de bello*, see Peter Haggenmacher, *Grotius et la doctrine de la guerre juste* (Paris: Presses Universitaires de France, 1983), pp. 33–5; 39–42; 105–7.

[2] Very little is recorded about William's life, apart from the fact that he originated from Rennes and was a Dominican attached to a priory in Dinan (Brittany). The years of his birth and death remain unknown. He has sometimes been wrongly identified with better-known authors such as Pierre Durant. Likewise, William's gloss on the *Summa de casibus* has sometimes been erroneously attributed to John of Freiburg, as for example in the 1603 edition referenced below. This error is explained by the fact that both the *Summa de casibus* and its gloss had long since fallen into disuse when they were first edited in print on the occasion of Raymond's canonization in 1601. This confusion was definitely cleared up by 1715 (on this, see Johann F. von Schulte, *Die Geschichte der Quellen und Literatur des Canonischen Rechts von Gratian bis auf die Gegenwart*, vol. 2 [Stuttgart: Enke, 1877], pp. 413–14).

[3] For a treatment of William's contribution to the development of just war doctrine, see Ludwik Ehrlich, "Guillaume de Rennes et les origines de la science du droit de la guerre" in *Mélanges en l'honneur de Gilbert Gidel* (Paris: Librairie Sirey, 1961), pp. 215–27. Cf. Peter Haggenmacher, *Grotius et la doctrine*, pp. 107–10.

historically, since it would soon become central to the concept of war proper, as distinguished from lesser forms of armed coercion. Its potential preeminence is dimly perceptible already, since authority is the main differentiating factor between war as discussed here (including vindicative power) and purely defensive war (§18). Raymond points out that such authority is possessed both by leaders of the church (who can wage war for the protection of the faith, i.e. the crusades), and by temporal princes. In his gloss, William sought to specify, with respect to the latter, whose authority was to be secured in concrete cases when a conflict arose between different feudal lords. His response makes clear that not only the emperor, but indeed any prince not having a superior, could use force against exterior enemies or rebellious subordinates, and moreover, that this war-making authority could be delegated downwards to properly designated subordinates. William nevertheless added an important qualification: in any case where there exists the possibility of adjudicating the dispute by some judicial process, the resort to force would be justified only after that process had first been attempted and failed. After discussing various applications of this principle, including a vassal's right of resistance against the unjust treatment of his lord, William concluded that even where no means of judicial resolution exist (as in a conflict between a king and the emperor), the offended party should still not resort to war if the other is willing to offer adequate satisfaction. War, on this account, has the character of a last resort; it is legitimate only in cases of true necessity, where arbitration and related measures have proven unsuccessful.

In the next section (§18), Raymond considers another kind of war, one that is waged by lesser lords and even private individuals in self-defense. He argues that such action must aim solely at repelling an attack that is already in progress or about to commence. Defense thereby stands in sharp contrast to revenge; the first looks to the present and near future, while the second imposes a penalty for acts that are past and done. In his gloss on this passage, William sought to expand the notion of justifiable defense beyond the strict limits that had been set by Raymond. The concept of immediacy (defense *in continenti*), which had constituted the core of Raymond's account, should not be taken to imply, William argued, that an attack can legitimately be countered only in the heat of the moment, when it was actually under way or about to begin. On the contrary, a defender could be justified in delaying his armed response – even for a significant period of time provided he did not turn to any other activity – in order to make adequate preparations for countermeasures.

Both authors nevertheless concurred that legitimate self-defense required strict adherence to the rule of proportionality; using more force than was necessary to repel an attack could render the defender liable for the damages caused by his excess. The underlying supposition was that war should be conducted in a spirit of justice and charity, in conformity with the requirements of an upright intention (*animus*). Moreover, in drawing a distinction between offenders (*nocentes*) and the innocent (§§17 and 19), they made clear that the requirements of proportionality and discrimination also applied to the treatment of enemy subjects in a just war. This was a precursor to the modern idea of civilian immunity.

From Raymond of Peñafort, *Summa de casibus poenitentiae*, II, §§17–19; William of Rennes, *Apparatus ad Summam Raymundi*[4]

Raymond of Peñafort

William of Rennes

§17

Regarding princes or knights warring against each other, you have to distinguish, because either the one you are examining has a just quarrel (*guerra*) or war (*bellum*),[5] or not. In the former case, i.e. when he has a just war, and wages it only against offenders (*nocentes*), and he has no wicked intention, then **whatever he captures** from his enemy becomes his own, and he is not held to make restitution. . . .

Now in order to gain complete clarity concerning war, note that five conditions are required for a war to be just, namely person (*persona*), object (*res*), cause (*causa*), state of mind (*animus*), and authority (*auctoritas*): The *person* [engaged in war] must be a secular, for whom it is permitted to shed blood, and not a cleric, for whom this **is prohibited unless under necessity**. . . .
The *object* [of war must be] the recovery of property and the defense of the fatherland. . . . The *cause* [requires] that [the war] be fought out of necessity, so that peace is achieved by the fighting. . . .

"Regarding princes": This is a response to the fifth question [raised above, at §10 (pp. 175–6)]

"whatever he captures": Until he has received satisfaction for all damages and interest, as will be said below in the same [section] at [§19]

"is prohibited": To shed blood and to fight for one's fatherland; yet, the pope and other ecclesiastics who have the right of the sword (*ius gladii*) may authorize their subordinates to fight.

"unless under necessity": Because

---

[4]   Raymundus de Pennafort, *Summa de poenitentia, et matrimonio, cum glossis Ioannis de Friburgo* [=William of Rennes], Rome, 1603, pp. 184–8. Translation by Robert Andrews and Peter Haggenmacher.
[5]   The terms *guerra* and *bellum* are here used as synonyms.

The *state of mind* [requires] that [war be waged] not because of hatred, revenge, or greed, but because of piety, justice, and obedience; [see *Decretum*, part II, causa 23, q. 1, canon *Quid culpatur*] and to serve as a soldier is not wrong, but to do so for the sake of booty **"is a sin,"** etc.;[6] see above, section on homicide, § **What if a cleric**, near the middle. *Authority* [requires] that [war be] waged by the authority of the church, particularly if it is fought for the faith; or **by the authority of the prince**, [according to *Decretum*, part II, causa 23, q. 1, canon *Quid culpatur*, and q. 2, canon 1]. If any of these conditions **be lacking**, the war will be called unjust.

then a cleric may defend himself, even with weapons.

"is a sin, etc.": And below; nor is it a crime to govern a commonwealth; but to govern a commonwealth so as to increase your own riches is condemnable.

"What if a cleric": There it is said that those who raise arms for the sake of obedience, justice, and zeal for the faith are praiseworthy.

"by the authority of the prince": For the emperor says: Absolutely no one is to have the power to make war unless we have been appraised of it and consulted [*Code*, 11, 46, 1].

Whose authority is to be required if the barons subordinate to a count wage war against him, or the counts against their king, or vice versa? Response: A prince who has no superior – whether a king or the emperor – may on his own authority wage war against either his own subordinates or against foreigners, if he has a just cause; he may also grant to his subordinates the authorization to wage war against a foreign prince as well as against his subjects if there is a just cause and it seems to be expedient; but not against his own subordinates, as long as he is able to bring the

---

[6] This quote corresponds to *loc. cit.*, canon 5.

perpetrator to trial, or as long as [the perpetrator] is willing to undergo his judgment (and his [own superior's] judgment if he is an intermediate judge between such a prince and the perpetrator). However, if he cannot bring him to trial, or if he refuses to appear in his court, not only this prince but any prince who has a superior may on his own authority wage war against such a perpetrator (if he is subordinate to the prince immediately or mediately), and authorize the injured party to raise arms against him. If, however, the perpetrator is not subordinate (either immediately or mediately) to a prince who has a superior above himself, this prince cannot authorize his subordinates to raise arms against the perpetrator; in this case the authorization of this superior prince is required, and most of all if the perpetrator belongs immediately or mediately to the jurisdiction of the superior prince. Thus, when a vassal of a count would wage war against the count, the king's authority is required. But, if a count [has grievances] against the king, and the king, having been humbly petitioned by the court of peers (*Pares Curiae*),[7] declines to hear his case, then I believe that [the count] does not sin if he defends his right by arms, with a moderation of blameless defense. Yet he ought not attack the king on his own authority; but the pope, having been appraised of the king's excesses and the king refusing to refrain from

---

[7] Literally, "the peers (equals) of the (lord's) court," that is, all the immediate vassals of a feudal lord or king, who were entitled to be judged by their "peers."

his sins, could excommunicate the king; and if the disobedience continues, he could grant the authority to raise arms against him.

But when a king has a [just] cause of war against the emperor, or vice versa, I believe that neither one nor the other is obliged to seek justice by judicial means, since neither of them has a superior; nonetheless, the victim of an injury would sin in waging war if the perpetrator would offer suitable satisfaction to him according to the judgment of good men, and without the interference of the courts.

"be lacking": What if one [of the conditions for a just war] is lacking? Will he who wages such a war be required to make restitution of whatever he gained from the war? Response: Even though a war is unjust on account of the cause, the state of mind, the person, and the authority, if nevertheless it has a valid object (*res*) because the war is waged for the recovery of property, then he who started the war is not obliged to make restitution of what he [gained] therein, [unless][8] what he took from his adversary or caused him as damages exceeds what the latter had unjustly taken from him or caused him as damages. And this I say following penitential jurisdiction, where a set-off (*compensatio*) is

[8] The text of the 1603 edition does not make sense here (although it seems accurately to reproduce a manuscript tradition, as witnessed by Ms. Basel B.IX.935). The words *accepit: nisi*, which have been inserted, are taken from the *Summa perutilis* of Monaldus (compiled between 1254 and 1274) which closely follows Raymond's *Summa*, combining its text verbatim with William's gloss (see Monaldus, *Summa perutilis* [Paris: P. Baletus, 1516], *De restitutione damnorum in bello iusto facienda*, fol. 217v).

admissible, even between contested and uncontested [claims] (*non liquidi ad liquidum*), which has no place in contentious jurisdiction. Therefore, if someone confesses before the penitential jurisdiction that he took ten of the things belonging to him who manifestly took ten of his things, the penitential judge habitually, and rightly, agrees to the set-off and refrains from ordering [the penitent] to render those ten things, unless his adversary forthwith renders him the ten things he took. The judge will, however, inflict on him a penance for the theft he has committed.

What if a cleric serving in a just war with his lord were to obtain something from that war? Is he held to return it? Response: He can retain it if it is given to him by someone to whom it is permitted to rob. Yet, if the cleric himself robbed, since he sins by robbing, he ought to be induced, under penitential jurisdiction, if he can, to return it to whom he robbed it, if he knows who that is; if he does not know, he should donate it to the poor. For such a cleric does not become the owner of that thing he takes, because just as his lord cannot grant him the authority to wage war, so neither can he grant him the authority to rob. Yet I believe that he may retain the thing thus robbed with the consent of his master, provided, however, that the master consents while the war is still on, because the case is the same as if the master had given [him] that thing.

§18

Yet there seems to be a case in which war might be waged

"Yet there seems to be a case": And this *is indeed so.*

without the special authority of
the prince or the church, namely
for **the recovery of things** and the
defense of the fatherland. For by law it
is permitted for anyone to repel force
with force, immediately (*in continenti*),
and **with the moderation of
blameless defense** (*cum moderamine
inculpatae tutelae*). . . . **Some people
say** that no one is **permitted to repel
force with force** by striking back
(*repercutiendo*), but only by **impeding**
(*impediendo*) **it.** Others say that it is
permissible for the laity to strike back,
but not for clerics. **A third group say**
that it is permitted not only to the
laity but also to clerics to strike back,
but draw a distinction between force
directed against persons or against
property.

"without the special authority":
Yet waged with proper authority.
"To wage war" means here to fight
with weapons defensively, not
offensively.

"for the recovery of things": I
believe that the word "things"
should be taken broadly, to include
not only physical things, but also
injuries. Just as war can be waged for
the sake of movable or immovable
things that are taken away, so may
[war be waged] in order to obtain
satisfaction for injuries inflicted, not
for the lust for revenge but for the
zeal for justice, or to protect one's
interests.

**"with the moderation of blameless
defense":** This moderation has its
place when someone for the reason
of protection, that is, of defending
himself, resists the adversary with such
moderation that that defense or
protection is blameless, that is without
fault, because it does not exceed the
limits (*modum*) of defense, and does
not harm the adversary more
(especially [if it is] on purpose) than
is required [to repel] his violence
(*violentia*).

"Some people say": This opinion was
held by H[uguccio].

**"permitted to repel force with
force":** Without the authorization of
a judge.

"impeding": For example, holding up
an arm or a stick, lest one receive an
injury to the head or body.

"A third group say": Their opinion is the better one.

If [force is directed] against persons, then it may be repelled **before it is applied** (*priusquam sit illata*), though some people say that no one ought to repel force **unless it has been applied** (*nisi illatam*); on the contrary, the law says that it is permissible to kill an ambusher and one who intends to kill, which I understand to hold **if there is no other way** to counter the threat of the ambusher, according to [*Digest*, 9, 2, 4 and 5]. Yet, if someone after [suffering] an act of violence strikes back, and does it immediately, that is, when he sees the other ready to strike again, he is in no way liable, but if he strikes back while the other does not want to hit him again, this is impermissible, because this is not to fend off injury (*repulsio iniurie*) but is for revenge (*vindicta*), which is prohibited for everyone, and most of all for the clergy. . . . It is therefore required that he strike back only **in self-defense** (*defendendo se*), not in revenge. . . . Likewise, it is required that he defend himself with moderation, Decretals, *De restitutione spoliatorum*, chap. *Olim causam*.[10]

Understand that if force is inflicted with weapons (*cum armis*), it may be repelled with weapons; otherwise without weapons. . . . In this matter I take into consideration the abilities of the persons, so that sometimes the small and weak may defend

"before it is applied": One may prevent (*praevenire*) a violent attack before it is inflicted, or repel it.[9]

"unless it has been applied": Some people say that no one may strike another before he is first struck by him, which is not true, as the Master implies by saying, "on the contrary," etc.

"if there is no other way": Than killing him.

"in self-defense": Lest one suffer an injury.

---

[9]   The text here seems to be defective; the translation is tentative.

[10]   See Innocent IV, chap. 13, this volume.

themselves with weapons against the big and strong attacking with raised fist. . . .

If, however, someone exceeds moderation, though not deliberately, then **he is not liable**, except [with respect to the amount of] caution [shown]; see [*Digest*, 9, 2, 52, §1]; if deliberately, then he is liable.

I agree with this latter view, and it is held by almost everybody. As regards its final part, however, I agree with the opinion that holds, with respect to the sentence of excommunication, that if someone defending himself against a cleric goes too far, if this is intentional, he is subject to excommunication; otherwise not. But with respect to satisfaction other[wise due] for excess, or also with respect to penance and irregularity in case perhaps a death resulted from striking back, I believe that it is safer to say **that he is liable; taking however into consideration** whether it is intentional or unintentional. . . .

If force is directed against property, then one is permitted to repel it, whether it has already occurred or is planned, but rather, that is, above all, when it has already occurred; provided this happens **immediately** (*in continenti*), that is, as soon as one knows that the attack has occurred, and before one turns to a **contrary action**. . . .

"he is not liable": To render some satisfaction, according to those [authors]; but according to the Master, he is held to make satisfaction to the injured party, and to make penance with regard to irregularity, as will be discussed below.

"that he is liable": Namely, he who goes too far [in defending himself].

"taking however into consideration": Because [an action] demands a greater penance and satisfaction when it is intentional than when it is unintentional.

"immediately": This immediacy is by no means to be determined as it is in stipulations,[11] where it is not even enough to respond to the stipulation within the same day, as it is said in [*Dig.*, 45, 1, 137] to which the Master refers, but according to the

---

[11] In stipulations, the parties' declarations must be made one immediately after the other, both being present.

quality of the activity, depending on the greater or lesser time required for preparation. Thus, if some nobleman with a whole army invades the territory of another nobleman and occupies a castle or takes booty there to carry it off to his own territory, if the second nobleman upon hearing this, unable to gather troops and recover the booty or liberate the castle immediately, sends messages or envoys to levy an army, though he cannot do so before one week, or two, or more, he is still deemed to defend himself and to liberate the castle and to recover the booty immediately, even if his adversary has already secured it behind his walls.[12] I also believe that, while he is thus pursuing the booty and cannot manage to recover it, perhaps because it has been brought to impregnable places, if he seizes some of the goods of his adversary or his attendants or of those who thwart his pursuit of the goods, he can retain some of their goods and indemnify himself for the losses incurred; just as someone pursuing a thief who takes away his goods may satisfy himself for his loss by taking an equivalent of the goods the thief is drawing or carrying off with him, if he can get hold of it while pursuing him in his flight.

"contrary action": It is not considered to be a "contrary action" if one in the meanwhile eats, drinks, or sleeps, or prepares to drive the

---

[12] Normally this means, under the medieval law of arms, that the ownership of the booty has passed to the captor; as a consequence, any action to recover it goes beyond mere defense. But throughout this text William is reasoning under penitential canon law.

enemy out of an unjustly occupied possession or recover booty brought away by him, even if this preparation demands a period of delay (as has been said); but if one disregards the injury and gives up the intention to pursue one's goods, turning to other occupations, then this is "a contrary action."

And if perhaps, while someone is endeavoring to expel from his possession an enemy who has unjustly or wickedly occupied it, some [of the enemy] get hurt or killed, I believe that he is liable in accordance with what is laid down above **with respect to defense of persons**, and by the same rules. Understand that this applies [only] to the imperfect; by contrast, **the perfect**[13] are not allowed to strike back, which the Lord shows in Matthew 5[:39]: "If anyone strikes you on the right cheek, turn to him the other also". Likewise, in the Epistle to the Romans 12[:19]: "Beloved, never avenge yourselves, but leave it to the wrath of God". And similar passages. They are however permitted to protest the injury, from the example of the Lord in John 18[:22–23], when he was struck in the face: "If I have spoken wrongly, bear witness to the wrong; but if I have spoken rightly, why do you strike me?" . . . Furthermore, it is permitted to ask for an escort,

"with respect to defense of persons": Where a distinction is to be made between exceeding moderation either unintentionally or intentionally.

"the perfect": Who are these [perfect]? Does this include regular clergy who have renounced possessions and even their own will? Response: as perfection has many shapes, such as perfection in respect of sufficiency, order, empire, religion, and some other matters distinguished by the theologians, I believe that here only those are meant who are obliged by vow, precept or law not to retaliate; among these were the apostles and disciples in the primitive Church who were held to non-retaliation by the teachings of the Lord, since the Church was to be

---

[13] "The perfect" (*perfecti*) signified those individuals who, by their professed state of life, were committed to living out the gospel counsels of perfection; first and foremost this included members of religious orders ("religious"), as well as bishops. The "imperfect" (*imperfecti*) designated all lay Christians, who were not required to follow the gospel counsels of perfection. There was some debate about whether ordinary clerics ought to be situated in the category of the "imperfect." This uncertainty is reflected in William's commentary.

following the example of the Apostle, Acts 2[3], whom the tribune [Festus], hearing that an ambush was being laid by the Jews, ordered to be led unharmed by two hundred soldiers to Caesarea. Likewise, one may flee persecution, so that "if they persecute you in one town, flee to the next," [according to] Matthew 10[:23].

From the aforesaid it is sufficiently clear how and when one may wage a war, whether against heretics, pagans, or tyrants and persecutors of Christians. It is equally evident that those who in time of truce seize at sea and on land the goods of the **Saracens** commit robbery, and are thereby obligated to make restitution. They even may be punished by the prince whose truce they violated, except for Templars and the Hospitallers, whom I do not believe to fall under the jurisdiction of princes either in this or other matters, since they are clerics and representatives of the Church, and their Order is specially appointed to this.

propagated and enhanced by blood and martyrdom.

"Saracens": With whom they or their princes have a truce.

§19

As to the question that has been propounded, I say that a knight waging war against another knight is allowed to make his whatever he takes from his enemy or his [enemy's] **abettors** (*vallatoribus*), **until** he deems in conscience to have obtained satisfaction for all the damages **suffered by him**, as well as for his and his men's labor and toil, or until the enemy himself offers a legal settlement or is [otherwise] willing to make satisfaction. But those [enemy]

"As to the question that has been propounded": See above, same title [§10, p. 175] and [175–176].

"abettors": That is, auxiliaries.

"until": And not more, unless it be such an enemy as sins so gravely, either through infidelity or heretical wickedness or some [other] vice, that he deserves to have his goods and those of his men confiscated, to be deprived of his land, and to become a

subjects who, fearing God more than men, refuse to abet their lord in his unjust war by giving advice, aid, or favor, should not, I believe, in any way be despoiled; for the punishment should smite the authors [of the wrong] and not reach beyond the delinquent's fault [*Decretales Gregorii IX*, III, XI, II].[14]

slave of the captors by virtue of a public edict; in which case he can be entirely despoiled and even expelled from the country.

"suffered by him": And by his men, unjustly,[15] through depredations, pillage, as well as arson, havoc, injuries, killings, and whatever else.

What if he who wages a just war sets fires or wrecks havoc, or roots up trees or vineyards in the territory of his adversary or of his [adversary's] men: will he be held responsible in any respect for these actions? Response: he will not be liable for those damages he inflicted in good faith, or from which he could not have abstained without inconvenience, according to the practice and custom of those who fight in good faith. If, however, he inflicted [these damages] with a pernicious and wicked intent, although he could easily have protected his interests otherwise, he will be [held] responsible, and those damages will be set off up to their full amount against [the losses] that have been inflicted on him and his men, and for the part in excess he will be held to give satisfaction to those he damaged.

But he who undertakes an unjust war is liable for all the damages he or his men inflict upon their adversary

---

[14] Raymond's reference shows that his text is but an elliptical rendering of a sentence of this decretal which affirms that "sins (*peccata*) are to 'hold' (*tenere debeant*) their authors, and punishment should not exceed the measure of the wrong as found in the culprit."

[15] The text here says: *etiam iuste, tam in depraedationibus . . .*, which seems contradictory. Ms. Basel B.IX.35 has: *iniuste tam etiam depredacionibus . . .*, which is equally unsatisfactory as to *etiam*, but does make sense as to *iniuste*. This reading is indirectly confirmed by the *Summa Monaldina*, fol. 218r. The *etiam* seems to have crept into the text owing to a copyist's misreading. The original text would seem to have read: *et iniuste, tam depraedationibus. . . .*

and his men. He is also held [to compensate] the damages caused to his own men by the adversary, provided this adversary is justly striking back, unless his men have been helping him in bad faith; in which case they have no legal action against him, since no one should have an action based on his own culpable conduct. Conversely, the nobleman who fights justly is not required to compensate the losses that his men suffer from the adversaries, since they are duty-bound to expose themselves and their goods for their lord; he is not bound, I say, unless he was culpably negligent in defending them.

What if two noblemen negotiate a settlement with respect to their war: can they make a settlement or a transaction concerning the damages incurred by their men without providing for any restitution in favor of those [of their men] who suffered losses? Response: If the settlement is made with the consent of the damaged, it has to be respected; otherwise I do not believe that he who culpably started an unjust war can prejudice his men by his settlement; nay, he is obliged to compensate them out of his own means; unless they are as much at fault as himself, as was said; in which case I believe that, although under contentious jurisdiction he may not be bound toward them in any way for the part they knowingly took in his crime, yet under penitential jurisdiction he is so bound if they did this by his persuasion, and would not have done it otherwise. But he who wages a just war must not negotiate

with his adversary in prejudice to his
men; instead, he has either to
compensate the losses that they
incurred or make sure that they are
compensated by the adversary. This,
however, I understand to hold with
respect to the losses that they suffered
from fires and robberies; but with
respect to the expenses incurred by
joining the army and staying there,
the princes are pretty much in the
habit of compounding (*componere*) or
disregarding (*dissimulare*) them on
their own authority, and this may be
conceded with respect to the aforesaid
damages. If the princes consider for
some plausible reason that they rather
have to remit these than to forgo the
benefit of peace and to incur the
perils of war, since in this case they
are taking care as best they can
of their subjects' interests by
compromising in such a manner,
the subjects are required to consent.
It would be otherwise if from the
beginning they objected to any
settlement unless their damages be
compensated.

If for some just reason the [princes]
consider it expedient, they can
discontinue the war, although perhaps
they may not be in a position to
refund the damages incurred [by their
subjects]; [this is so] because, just as
the authority to engage in the war
rests solely with the princes, likewise
does the authority to desist from it or
to lay down the arms.

13

Innocent IV
(ca. 1180–1254)

The Kinds of Violence and
the Limits of Holy War

It is permissible for anyone to wage war in self-defense or to protect property.
Yet this is not properly called "war," but rather "defense."

Apparatus in quinque libros Decretalium

Innocent IV, born Sinibaldo de Fiesco, was pope from 1243 until his death in 1254. His commentary on the Decretals of Gregory IX (*Apparatus in quinque libros Decretalium*; ca. 1245) earned him much renown as one of the foremost canon lawyers of his time. Innocent, Hostiensis, and other canonists of the period are known as "Decretalists," since their work consisted primarily in commentaries on the contemporary papal legislation, or Decretals.[1]

Innocent's Decretal commentary exercised considerable influence on, inter alia, Aquinas's conception of just war; it was quoted well into the sixteenth century by Vitoria, who adopted Innocent's view that non-Christians could not be denied the natural right of dominion over their own lands.

In what follows, we reproduce three passages from Innocent's *Apparatus*. In the first two (taken from the titles "On the Restitution of Spoils" and "On Oaths") he distinguishes war from other forms of licit violence.

The immediate context for this treatment was the Decretal *Olim causam*, which had been issued by his predecessor Innocent III. The text discussed a case in which certain Templars, who had taken possession of an estate, were forcibly ejected from it by a bishop. This prelate had long since assigned the estate to a congregation

---

[1]   During the twelfth and thirteenth centuries the papal decretals were gathered in several collections, the most important among them being the five *compilationes antiquae* (ca. 1190–1226). These were all superseded by the compilation prepared by Raymond of Peñafort at the request of Pope Gregory IX, who promulgated it in 1234. The *Decretales Gregorii IX* mark a culmination of papal legislative power.

(under certain conditions), while retaining ownership over it. Although "the actual violence used here was probably minimal by contemporary standards, the fact that all the parties were clerics provided Innocent IV with the opportunity to dwell at length on the rights of anyone, even a cleric, to use violence in his own defense."[2] This led him to argue that whereas lower rulers and even private individuals were entitled to use force in self-defense or in the exercise of a jurisdiction, war properly speaking could only be undertaken at the command of a prince who had no superior. And unlike the repression of internal wrongdoing ("police-action" we would now say), Innocent maintained that war is first and foremost directed against external enemies. While recognizing that his contemporaries often employed the term *bellum* to designate lesser forms of violence, Innocent insisted that war, correctly understood, represents something qualitatively different.[3] It is a kind of sanction, one that targets wrongdoers who lie outside the sovereign's domestic jurisdiction, and which allows for a range of acts that go well beyond what may licitly be done in strict self-defense or enforcement of a jurisdiction. In this manner, Innocent "proposed distinctions between the various levels of licit violence that were appropriate to various levels of authority."[4] This gradation of licit violence is taken up again in the Decretal *Sicut et infra*.

In the third passage (Decretal *Quod super his*, under the title "On Vows and the Fulfilling of Vows"), Innocent discusses a number of questions that relate to the theme of Christian holy war. He is chiefly concerned with determining whether, and in what measure, force may be used to recover the Holy Land (i.e. the crusades). Innocent concedes at the outset (n. 1) that the pope may take steps "to defend the Holy Land and all the faithful inhabiting it." He raises a doubt, however, as to whether (generally speaking) Christians may invade and expropriate lands belonging to non-believers. In response, Innocent maintains (n. 3) that by natural law "dominion and jurisdiction is permitted to infidels"; hence their property rights must be respected. After an excursus on the pope's jurisdiction over the infidels,[5] where Innocent famously declares that they may rightly be punished for violating the laws of nature (n. 4), he returns to the question of the crusades in

---

[2]   Frederick H. Russell, *The Just War in the Middle Ages* (Cambridge: Cambridge University Press, 1975), p. 135.

[3]   See Peter Haggenmacher, *Grotius et la doctrine de la guerre juste* (Paris: Presses Universitaires de France, 1983), pp. 112–14, for an analysis of Innocent's teaching on the difference between war and lesser forms of violence. Cf. Russell, *The Just War*, pp. 145–7.

[4]   Russell, *The Just War*, p. 145. This author further comments that "[t]he Decretalists had made the right to take up arms the monopoly of legitimate authority. Now Innocent IV restricted the right to wage just wars to the monopoly of superior authorities while still preserving the right of lords to use violence in their own defense. Military actions of inferior princes remained licit but they did not qualify as just wars. . . . Now wars were clearly set apart from military actions in general, and Innocent and his colleagues could turn to advantage this newly restricted concept of just war when they came to discuss the practical operation of the just war" (ibid., pp. 146–7).

[5]   Innocent also briefly discusses the scope of the pope's jurisdiction over Jews and Christians (nn. 5–6), passages that have not been included.

n. 7. In this central passage, he argues that the occupation of the Holy Land by Saracens is illegitimate, and moreover, that these infidels have been guilty of persecuting Christians. This leads Innocent to conclude that the pope may licitly declare war on them, in the interests of recovering the Holy Land for Christians. Innocent does, however, urge some show of restraint. In particular, he makes clear (n. 8) that non-believers may not be forced to accept the Christian faith. Nor, he maintains, should they be excluded from exercising dominion over the faithful who live on their lands (n. 10), especially if they allow free entry to preachers of the Gospel (n. 9).

Innocent's rather measured discussion of the juridical status of non-Christians is often contrasted with the "less cautious"[6] attitude adopted by Hostiensis. The latter maintained that the infidels possessed no legitimate title to the lands on which they lived; hence Christians could legitimately use force to make these lands their own.[7]

From "On the Restitution of Spoils," Decretal *Olim causam inter vos* (*Decretals*, II, 13, 12), nn. 6–8 (f. 89vb)[8]

[6] For it is permitted to avenge an attack directed against property, and, after loss caused by the theft of property, to regain what is stolen; but after an injury inflicted upon a person it is not permitted to seek vengeance or to return the injury. . . . It is written, "you are not to avenge yourself," unless perhaps in fear of repeated blows.

[7] How was this admissible, since the bishop and canons and Templars were religious persons? This could not happen without [entailing] a canonical sanction. . . . Also because they are not allowed to make war . . . ; while others might be allowed, clerics would not be.

[8] We answer: It is permissible for anyone to wage war in self-defense or to protect property. Nor is this properly called "war" (*bellum*), but rather "defense" (*defensio*). And when someone has been ejected, he may lawfully fight back on the spot (*incontinenti*), that is, before he has turned his attention to other matters. And since this is permitted by law, authorization by the prince is not required. Nor do they [those who fight back to protect their property] incur excommunication, unless they actually lay hands on persons; but not even then, if [the occupants] were unwilling to leave the place without violence, as can be gathered from this

---

[6] This characterization is from Russell, *The Just War*, p. 201.

[7] For a discussion of the relevant passages in the two authors, see J. Muldoon, *Popes, Lawyers, and Infidels: The Church and the Non-Christian World 1250–1550* (Philadelphia: University of Pennsylvania Press, 1979), especially pp. 5–18. For an overview of the Decretalists' thought on the crusades, see Russell, *The Just War*, pp. 195–212. See also chapter 9 (this volume) on the crusades.

[8] *Apparatus in quinque libros Decretalium*, Lyon, 1535. Translated by Robert Andrews and Peter Haggenmacher. The textual references that appear in the Latin text have been omitted here.

place [in the text] . . . or unless they went beyond a proportionate response (*modum excesserint*).

Furthermore, whenever one cannot retrieve one's goods or obtain justice through someone else, it is permitted by the authority of the superior to take up arms and declare war in order to recover one's property – and even to take it back secretly. Nevertheless, if he has a prince above him, he should do it by his authority, and not otherwise. . . . This seems in accordance with justice, for no one may tamper with the law without the authorization of the lawgiver. Now, according to the law no one may occupy [by force] even his own possession. Yet the prince, who is not bound by civil constitutions, may do so without authorization.

Furthermore, we say that if one cannot recover [property] by stealth or violent seizure, one may recover the equivalent by the authorization of a superior. He should, however, beware lest he recover property by a lie, fraud, or calumny without the authorization of a judge, because then he will be obligated to make restitution. Some, however, maintain, and not mistakenly, that even without authorization one can proceed in clandestine fashion as long as one is able to do so without harm or scandal; for if scandal occurs thereby for the wife or servant or anyone else, then the property must be returned in its pristine condition.

We also believe for good reason that a prelate of the church may declare war in his own right and take part in it, but he ought not himself to fight; however he may pursue [the enemy] until he surrenders what is not his, and may urge [his troops] to fight and capture, but not to kill. Nor is there an objection to this in *De homicidio*, next to last chapter; because there [a prelate] had traded blows but did not know whether he had killed anyone, and therefore the matter was to be left to his conscience.

Furthermore, any prelate, if he has temporal jurisdiction, could legitimately take up arms against disobedient subjects as long as he has the legal authority to declare war, or in the aforesaid cases. And even if he does not have the right to declare [war], as long as he has jurisdiction [he may take up arms], because in such cases it is not properly called "war," but rather "execution of jurisdiction" or "justice." . . . Nor are captives in such cases made slaves.

War, properly speaking, can only be declared by a prince who does not have a superior. He can declare war against those who would not be liable to an execution of jurisdiction, for example, against those who fall under the rule of some other prince. Also, for the defense of ancestral laws.

"On Oaths," Decretal *Sicut et infra* (*Decretals*, II, 24, 29) n. 5 (f. 111rb)

Now, in a just war that is made by order of a prince, we say that things taken become the property of the captors, and free men who have been captured become slaves. . . . When a war does not occur by order of the prince, but is otherwise just, as when it is undertaken to defend one's goods or to obtain one's due, then you have to distinguish, because if he who wages such a war has jurisdiction, he may decide that whoever is being invaded be allowed to take and make his the goods of the invader, and even detain the invader until he hands him over to the master. . . . Likewise, if he has not made any constitution on this, he may yet pronounce a condemnation on this invasion as far as it occurs within the bounds of his jurisdiction. . . . If, however, he who wages such a war has no jurisdiction over the adversary and yet fights justly, e.g. because the adversary invades him and he defends himself and his property, then he is allowed to repel violence by violence and in the process strike and kill the assailants, but only within the limits of acceptable defense. . . . In this case, however, he may not seize the goods of his adversary, and appropriate them, nor incarcerate his invader.

"On Vows and the Fulfilling of Vows," decretal *Quod super his* (*Decretals*, III, 34, 8), nn. 1–4, 7–10 (f. 164vb)

[1] There is no doubt that it is licit for the pope, by persuading the faithful and granting indulgences, to defend the Holy Land and all the faithful inhabiting it. But is it ever licit to invade lands which are held or owned by infidels? In response to this we say that "the earth is the Lord's, and the fullness thereof; the world, and all that dwell therein" [Psalm 24:1]. For he is himself the creator of all things. Also, the same God himself subjected the world to the dominion of rational creatures for whom He made all things, as is stated in the first chapter of Genesis [verse 28]. The world was from the beginning held in common, until by the usage of the earliest forefathers it began that some things were appropriated by some, others by others. This was not bad; on the contrary, it was good, because it is natural that property held in common is neglected, and communal property gives rise to discord. From the beginning things belonged to anyone who occupied them, because they belonged to no one except the Lord. Therefore it was licit for anyone to occupy what was not already occupied, but it was not licit to occupy what was occupied by another, because it would be against natural law, which enjoins everyone not to do unto others what one does not wish to be done to oneself. There were also special ownerships established by the divisions made by the earliest forefathers, as is apparent with Abraham and Lot: one received one part of the land, and the other another [Genesis 13:11]. Over persons as slaves, no one had dominion, except by the law of nations or civil law; for by nature all men are free. . . .

[2] God himself is said to have exercised jurisdiction from the beginning. For I read that just and right jurisdiction exists where the sword has been given for revenge. . . . But how it began, I do not know, unless maybe that God gave [the sword] to one or to some in order for them to exercise justice on the delinquents; or that by the law of nature the father had from the beginning all jurisdiction

over his family; though nowadays it is no more, except in few or minor matters. . . . At any rate it is certain that in the beginning God himself exercised jurisdiction. . . . [3] Furthermore, there can be rulers by election, as in the case of Saul and many others. . . .

The aforesaid dominions, possessions, and jurisdictions may licitly and without sin be held by the infidels, for these were ordained not only for the faithful, but for every rational creature, as "He maketh his sun to rise on the good and evil," and "he feeds the fowls of the air," Matthew, chapter 5 near the end [verse 45], and chapter 6 [verse 26]. And therefore we say that it is not legitimate for the pope or the faithful to dispossess the infidels of either dominion or jurisdiction, because they possess them without sin; but we certainly hold that the pope, who is the vicar of Christ, has dominion not only over Christians, but also over all infidels, since Christ had dominion over all, as in the Psalms [72:1]: "Give the king thy judgments, O God." He would not be a diligent father unless his vicar whom he placed on earth would have full power over all. [4] Likewise, he gave to Peter and his successors the keys to the kingdom of heaven, and he said to him, "whatsoever thou shalt bind on earth . . ." [Matthew 16:19]. And elsewhere: "Feed my sheep [John 21:17]." Everyone, both faithful and infidel, are Christ's sheep through creation, although they are not in the sheepfold of the church. From what was said above it is clear that the pope has power and jurisdiction over all – *de jure* even if not *de facto*. Therefore, by this power which the pope has, I believe that a pagan who has no law except the law of nature, if he acts against the law of nature, may be legitimately punished by the pope. I argue from Genesis 19 [verse 25] where you read that the Sodomites who sinned against the laws of nature were punished by God; now since the judgments of God must serve as our model, I do not see why the pope, who is the vicar of Christ, could not do this as well, and indeed should, as long as he has the capacity. And I say the same if they worship idols; for it is natural to worship the one and only God, the creator, and not creatures. . . .

[7] The pope may grant indulgences to those who act to recover the Holy Land, even though the Saracens occupy it. The pope may also declare war and grant indulgences to those who occupy the Holy Land which the infidels illegally possess. All this has a [good] cause, for the pope acts justly when he strives to recover the Holy Land – which is consecrated by the birth, life, and death of Jesus Christ, yet where not Christ but Mohammed is being worshipped – in order that it be inhabited by Christians.

Furthermore, the Holy Land was conquered in a just war by the Roman emperor after the death of Christ. Thus it is legitimate for the pope, by reason of the Roman Empire which he obtained, to return it to his jurisdiction, since it was unjustly expropriated and despoiled by those who have no right to it. This same reason holds for all other lands in which the Roman emperors had jurisdiction, although it might be said that he cannot do it on the basis of this right, that is, by reason of the Roman Empire, because the Church has dominion only in the

West. . . . But if he cannot do it as emperor, he can do it according to the aforesaid reasons. At the very least the emperor can do it in the capacity of the King of Jerusalem, which belongs to him by law – which we believe and ought to believe, since the contrary is not obvious to us.

Yet the pope may also justly lay down rules and decrees against other infidels, who now hold the land where Christian princes had jurisdiction, in order that they do not unjustly persecute the Christians who find themselves under their jurisdiction. What is more, he may even exempt them entirely from their jurisdiction and dominion. . . . Indeed, if they maltreat Christians he may by a pronouncement deprive them of the jurisdiction and dominion they have over Christians, but it would require an extreme necessity to bring this about. The pope ought to put up with them insofar as he can, provided there is no great danger to Christians, or there is no great offense done to them.

[8] Furthermore, although infidels ought not be forced to accept the faith, since everyone's free will ought to be respected, and this conversion should [come about] only by the grace of God . . . yet the pope may command the infidels to admit preachers of the Gospel to the lands under their jurisdiction; for, since every rational creature is created to praise God, they sin if they stop the preachers from preaching, and therefore they ought to be punished.

[9] Now, in all of the aforesaid cases, and others where the pope may command them in some respect, if they do not obey, they ought to be forced by the secular arm; war ought to be declared against them by the pope, and not by others, where someone is seeking his lawful rights.[9] Nor does [Decretum, part II, causa 2, canon 1] go against this, where it is said that it is not up to us to judge about those who are outside; because it means that we are not to judge them by way of excommunication or by compelling them to faith, which they are called to by the sole grace of God. [10] But you will say, why is it not licit for them to reclaim lands such as Italy and others where the infidels [once] had dominion? I respond, because the rulers of those lands and their people have been converted [to Christianity]. I acknowledge that if a people has converted while the rulers remain infidel, the pope could certainly abandon dominion and jurisdiction over the faithful to an infidel ruler, provided he does not unjustly oppress the Christians. Furthermore, a ruler might be forced to accept the price or its equivalent; for someone often loses a possession through no fault of his own. . . . Indeed, a favorable judgment ought to be made for the sake of religion.

But you might ask: Shouldn't the pope accept those who want to preach the law of Muhammad, for the same reasons? I say that he should not. The same

---

[9]   The last part of this sentence reads *ubi quis de iure suo contendit*, which makes little sense. Possibly this is a corruption from *nisi quid de iure suo concederet* (except if he gave up something of his right). Hostiensis echoes this passage by *nisi de iure suo concederet* in *Lectura in decretales*, Hostiensis, *In secundum Decretalium librum commentaria* (Venice, 1581), ad *Decretales* III, 34, 8, n. , n. 23.

judgment does not hold equally for them and us, because they are in error and we follow the path of truth. We hold this resolutely.

You might ask how it can be that the Roman church and all other churches, and all other Christians, licitly possess what they do in the West and elsewhere, since the Roman emperors occupied all these lands violently by force of arms, and so it is certain that they hold them in bad faith. I respond that in general all, both clerics and laity, may hold securely and in good faith all that they hold, because we do not know whether those who occupied the aforesaid [lands] previously were exercising their rights; we ought to believe that they were exercising their rights when they occupied it, because they were perhaps taking back what they had previously lost by violence; or that perhaps they had legitimately received them through gifts and donations, even if there were many rebels whom they had to subdue.

Regarding churches, it is clear that he [the pope] can retain possession, because if it is not certain to whom they belonged prior to occupation, then it reverts to the pope as the vicar of Christ and to the other churches which are possessed by the pope and through his authority; for the pope and the churches possess all things in the name of all men, so that they may come to the aid of anyone in need.

As to the goods of schismatics and heretics, it is permitted to seize them according to the constitutions of the princes, which hold them to be forfeit.

14

Alexander of Hales
(ca. 1185–1245)

Virtuous Dispositions
in Warfare

[I]n the person for whom the war is fought there should be found a just cause, which is the restoration of the good, the suppression of the wicked, and peace for all.

Summa theologica

An Englishman who held a prestigious chair of theology at the University of Paris,[1] Alexander of Hales was one of the first theologians (as opposed to the canonists) in the Latin West to discuss the moral dimensions of war. While adhering closely to the work of Gratian and his commentators, Alexander did nevertheless leave his own distinctive mark on the developing doctrine of just war. His thought on this topic appears in a section of his *Summa theologica* that is devoted to the laws of punishment ("De legibus punitionis"). In keeping with the *Decretum* gloss *Quid culpatur*,[2] Alexander viewed just war first and foremost as a kind of punishment. However, in contradistinction to Gratian, yet in keeping with St. Augustine, he refrained from advancing private self-defense as a rationale for just war.[3]

---

[1] Alexander entered the Franciscan order at around age fifty, after he had already become a professor; in so doing he retained his university position and thereby became the first Franciscan to hold a chair at the University of Paris. It was there that he became the teacher of Bonaventure, Jean de la Rochelle, and other notable Franciscan theologians; for this reason he is often referred to as the founder of the Franciscan school of theology. In addition to his scholarly work, Alexander also engaged in some notable practical endeavors, as, for instance, in 1235 when Henry III of England appointed him to help pursue peace with the French king (see Christopher M. Cullen, "Alexander of Hales," in *A Companion to Philosophy in the Middle Ages*, ed. Jorge J. E. Gracia and Timothy Noone [Oxford: Blackwell Publishing, 2003], pp. 104–8).

[2] See chap. 10, this volume, p. 112.

[3] Even though Alexander mentions the protection of self or associates from attack in one of the initial objections to this article (*contra* no. 1, p. 684), the body of the text focuses exclusively on

Alexander likewise followed St. Augustine in emphasizing the inward dispositions that ought to be cultivated by persons participating in war. He was very
much preoccupied with the *virtues* of those who fight (including the leaders
responsible for the *decision* to fight). His "criteria" for just war are in practice
as much descriptions of the *sort of people* that may take part in war (or who may
command this course of action), as they are of the qualities that should be possessed by them. Hence, in his enumeration of the six ways in which a just war
differs from an unjust war, Alexander noted that the one authorizing such a war
(*iusta auctoritas*, presumably a prince or a judge) should do so with an upright
state of mind (*iustus affectus*), hence, in a spirit of equity and not with a lust for
domination or revenge. Similarly, soldiers should not be moved by an appetite for
gain and other base motives; rather, at all times they should maintain a proper
intention (*debita intentio*). Moreover, clerics should never serve as combatants;
this function was set aside for laymen, who alone possess the requisite condition
(*debita conditio*). Finally, understood as a form of punishment, a war will be
just only when it is directed against persons who are guilty of a blameworthy
offense (*iustum meritum*), and on behalf of those truly possessing a just cause
(*iusta causa*).[4]

From *Summa theologica*, III, n. 466: *Utrum bellare sit licitum* ("Whether war can be licit")[5]

I reply:

To fight a just war is permissible according to divine law, and also from the
command to the kings and sovereigns of the earth.[6] . . .

---

punishment as a rationale for just war. And when Alexander returns to the above objection at the end
of the article (*ad primum*, p. 686), he again emphasizes that only public officials are allowed to
administer punishment. Then, after acknowledging that all persons do nevertheless have a duty to
resist injury, he cites St. Ambrose to the effect that this protective action should be exercised on behalf
of friends or associates, according to the example of Moses (Exodus 2:11–12). Significantly, no
mention is made of self-defense. Among medieval approaches to just war, Alexander's represents
perhaps the purest case of a theory built up around the idea of punition (see Peter Haggenmacher,
Grotius et la doctrine de la guerre juste [Paris: Presses Universitaires de France, 1983], pp. 120–1,
165, and 414); this approach was later pursued more systematically by Cajetan in the sixteenth
century (see chap. 22, this volume).

[4] This is a reference to Gratian's discussion of just war on behalf of associates (*socii*), in *Decretum*,
c. 23, III (see chap. 10, this volume, pp. 114–15).

[5] Alexandri de Hales (Doctor irrefragabilis – the Irrefutable Doctor), *Summa theologica seu sic ab
origine dicta* "Summa fratris Alexandri"), vol. 4 (pp. 683–6) (Florence: Quaracchi, 1948). Translation by Robert Andrews.

[6] Many of Alexander's numerous citations from the *Letter to Boniface* and other texts of St. Augustine
have been omitted here.

To fight an unjust war is forbidden and prohibited, according to Baruch 3:27, where he speaks about the giants of old who were of great stature and expert in war: "God did not choose them, nor give them the way to knowledge, so they perished."

It[7] should be remarked that one can distinguish between a just and an unjust war according to authority (*auctoritatem*), state of mind (*affectum*), intention (*intentionem*), condition (*conditionem*), desert (*meritum*), and cause (*causam*).[8] State of mind and authority should be considered in the person who declares war; condition and intention in the person who fights the war; desert in the person who is warred upon; and the cause in the person for whom the war is fought.

It should be said that for a war to be just requires that the person declaring the war has a just state of mind and a just authority. . . . Just authority . . . is ordained according to what Augustine shows in his writing against the Manicheans.[9] . . .

Furthermore, two things are required of the person who fights the war: rightful intention and rightful condition. Rightful intention, according to what Augustine says in *On the Words of the Lord*,[10] "To fight a war is not an offense, but it is a sin to fight a war for the spoils; it is not to act in criminal fashion for the sake of the republic [i.e. common good], but it is damnable to do so in order to increase your own wealth."

Furthermore, [the person who fights the war must have] a rightful condition, namely that he not be a cleric. Thus in the *Canon* of Pope John [VIII], [Causa] XXIII, question 8,[11] it says, "It pertains to earthly powers to conduct secular warfare, to defend the land, to deal in arms and battles." Likewise in the same work, the Canon of the Council of Meldi,[12] it says, "Whoever is one of the clergy should not take up military arms, because they cannot fight for both God and the secular."

Furthermore, desert on the part of the person who is warred against must be considered, namely that he should justly deserve to be attacked or to suffer persecution. Thus Augustine says in his Letter to Boniface,[13] "It is an unjust persecution which the impious conduct against Christ's Church. He is blessed who is 'persecuted for righteousness' sake',[14] but they are wretched who suffer persecution because of their unrighteousness. So, the former pursues [the goal]

---

[7] The following passage is also translated in Jonathan Barnes, "The Just War" in *The Cambridge History of Later Medieval Philosophy*, ed. Norman Kretzmann, Anthony Kenny, and Jan Pinborg (Cambridge: Cambridge University Press, 1982), pp. 771–84, on p. 773.

[8] Some manuscripts show *ratio* (reason) instead of *causa*.

[9] Augustine *Contra Faustum* XXII, c. 74. In the omitted passage Alexander quotes the *Decretum* canon *Quid culpatur* (see note 2 above).

[10] Pseudo-Augustine *Sermo* 82.

[11] Gratian *Decretum*, causa 23, q. 8, c. 1.

[12] Gratian *Decretum*, causa 23, q. 8, c. 6.

[13] Letter 185.

[14] Matthew 5:10.

lovingly, the latter with rage [or hatred]; the former that he might correct [what is wrong], the latter that he might destroy." . . .

Furthermore, in the person for whom the war is fought there should be found a just cause, which is the restoration of the good, the suppression of the wicked, and peace for all. Augustine says in *Diverse Observations on the Church*:[15] "The truly peaceful servants of God are those who wage war not for motives of aggrandizement, or cruelty, but with the object of securing peace, of punishing evildoers, and of uplifting the good."

---

[15] Not in St. Augustine's extant works, but cited in Thomas Aquinas, *Summa Theologiae* II–II q. 40, and Gratian *Decretum*, Causa 23, q. 1, c. 6.

15

Hostiensis
(ca. 1200–1271)

A Typology of Internal
and External War

[I]t is not permitted to anyone to take up arms to attack another without the authority of law or judge; otherwise he incurs punishment, since he intends to inflict violence.

Summa aurea

The Italian canonist Henry of Susa (Henricus de Segusio) is best known by the name Hostiensis, from the diocese of Ostia in Italy, where he served as Cardinal-Bishop. Author of several highly regarded commentaries on the decretals, his most influential discussion of legal–moral problems relating to war appears in a section of his *Summa aurea* (written 1239–53) entitled "De treuga et pace" (On Truce and Peace). In this commentary he proposed a classification of seven kinds of war. Much cited by subsequent authors,[1] this classification is organized around the principle of legitimate war-making authority. In continuity with the medieval civil lawyers, Hostiensis considers as especially legitimate those wars (e.g. crusades) that Christian princes waged, presumably with the authorization of the pope or emperor, against the Infidels. He termed this kind of war *bellum Romanum* to emphasize its

---

[1] Most famously by John of Legnano (d. 1383) whose *Tractatus de Bello, de Repraesaliis et de Duello* (English translation in the Classics of International Law, 1917) adopted this classification (chap. LXXVI) and made it known to a broader reading public, which included Christine of Pizan (see chapter 19 of this volume). For the most part, however, Hostiensis's classification was soon eclipsed by the set distinctions which, around the same time, were formulated in the *Apparatus* of pope Innocent IV (see chap. 13, this volume). Hostiensis himself, in his last work, *Lectura in Decretales*, adopted Innocent's classification (on this see Peter Haggenmacher, *Grotius et la doctrine de la guerre juste* [Paris: Presses Universitaires de France, 1983], pp. 110–14; cf. Frederick Russell, *The Just War in the Middle Ages* [Cambridge: Cambridge University Press, 1975], who comments that "[b]y viewing situations of both parties in a single war Hostiensis was able to contrast just and unjust wars more effectively" – p. 130).

likeness to the wars, legitimate in his eyes, which ancient Rome waged against foreign peoples (thus considering Christendom as heir to the legal prerogatives of the Roman Empire).

By contrast, Hostiensis condemned as illegitimate the wars that Christian princes waged against each other. His condemnation was not unqualified, however, since alongside the external wars that the emperor could rightly wage against foreign peoples, Hostiensis also recognized that force might legitimately be used within Christendom, to enforce the decision of a judge who possessed the requisite legal authority. Moreover, he even allowed that, on some occasions, arms could be taken up by Christians against other Christians, in order more generally to uphold the authority of the law. Likewise, he acknowledged that even private individuals could justifiably resort to violence in the heat of the moment, so as to defend self or others from unwarranted attack. In contradistinction to the last three modes of just war, Hostiensis maintained that forcible measures would be unjust when undertaken in contempt of a judge's decree, in violation of the law, or by private individuals for reasons other than the press of necessity.

Having distinguished different kinds of wars, just and unjust, Hostiensis next considers whether, and in what measure, the prosecution of hostilities ought to be moderated by a truce. One sort of truce is "conventional"; it arises, he explains, from a mutual agreement of the warring parties, whether they be Christians or infidels. A "canonical" truce, by contrast, applies only to warring relations between Christians. This provides Hostiensis with an opportunity to discuss the rules that had been promulgated within medieval Christendom since the tenth century, under the heading of the Peace and Truce of God.[2]

From *Summa aurea*, On Truce and Peace (*Decretals*, bk. I, tit. 34, columns 356–362)[3]

1 What a truce is.[4]
2 What peace is.

---

[2] See chap. 8, this volume, on Medieval Peace Movements.

[3] *Summa aurea*, Venice, 1574. This commentary is also known as *Summa super titulis Decretalium* or *Summa archiepiscopi*, translation by Robert Andrews and Peter Haggenmacher. Hostiensis's numerous references to civil and canon law have been omitted, although they were integral to his terse notations which, like those of Innocent IV, lie somewhere between twelfth-century glosses and fourteenth-century commentaries. Indeed, while they were as transparent to his medieval readers as Biblical references, they have mostly become opaque to us today. Including these references here would therefore hamper rather than illuminate our understanding of Hostiensis's admittedly elliptic statements.

[4] The articulation presented in this summary slightly diverges from the one figuring in the lemma. The latter, which is obviously Hostiensis's own division, is followed in the text and must therefore be preferred.

3 What a just war is.
4 Unjust war is determined in five ways.
5 How many kinds of truce there are.
6 What a truce effects.

We discussed above the office of ecclesiastical judges, an office which specially concerns the maintaining and restoring of peace between subordinates. . . . And because a truce (*treuga*) leads to peace, we shall consider truce and peace: what is a truce; what is peace; what is a just war; to which kind of war the truce in question relates; how many kinds of truce there are; how a truce functions.

1. What a truce is. The security of persons and things during a predetermined time when a conflict has not yet been settled. In [civil] law it is called "treaty" (*foedus*) or "armistice" (*indutiae*). . . .

2. What peace is. The end of conflict – and yet a truce is called peace at [*Decretum*] causa 23, q. 4, canon 29.[5]

3. What a just war is. The *Decretum* says that it is not sinful to serve as a soldier . . . which is true if [the war] is declared by a prince, as will be discussed hereafter. Likewise [it is not sinful] for the defense of oneself, or for the fatherland, or for ancestral laws. . . .[6]

A just war is therefore one which is conducted according to a perpetual edict of the prince, for the restoration of goods, or for the repulsion of the enemy. . . . And in brief, he is just who takes up the sword with his judge's authority properly intervening, whether by order or consent. . . . Therefore, he who takes up the sword on his own authority is to be smitten by the sword. . . .

There are, however, some who say that a war can be considered unjust in five ways.

First, because of the object (*ratione rei*), if it is not undertaken for the recovery of property or for the defense of the fatherland. . . . Second, on account of the cause, thus if it would be fought voluntarily and not out of necessity. . . . Third, because of the state of mind (*ex animo*), namely when it is conducted out of revenge. . . . Fourth, if it does not have the authority of the prince. . . . Fifth, because of the person, for example a cleric, who may not licitly shed blood, neither by himself nor through another. . . .

Here too there is disagreement. For certain people say that clerics can use only defensive arms, such as a shield or cuirass, but not offensive weapons such as a sword, lance, or blade. Others say that under inescapable necessity any weapons may be used in defense of oneself alone, but not of others. But if there are any

---

[5] It is not clear why Hostiensis refers to this passage.
[6] In the omitted passage Hostiensis discusses whether spoils of war rightly become the captor's property.

other means of avoidance, [weapons] may not be used.... Others say that [clerics] may [use weapons] with the permission of the pope, and otherwise not. Gratian says that they may not [use weapons] personally, but through others ... namely by urging them to fight. John[7] says indistinctly that [clerics] may not [use weapons], whether they are in Holy Orders or not ... unless perhaps for their own defense and under the most violently pressing necessity; and unless against pagans by command of their superior; and unless he has judicial competence. And so they understand the canons which seem to be in contradiction. Or, [weapons may be used] in defense of justice with the consent of the bishop ... but in this case is meant a soldier or other secular official.

Others say indistinctly that clerics may use weapons in defending themselves and their possessions and recovering them ... notwithstanding the canon referred to by John, because it speaks of those who take up arms voluntarily, not out of necessity or for defense: for clerics – especially those who have temporal jurisdiction – are allowed to exhort others to take up arms in defense of the oppressed, and to attack the enemies of God. Likewise, for the peace and defense of oneself and one's fatherland, and the upholding of justice; for war is conducted so that peace may be obtained. ... As the Pope states [*Decretum Gratiani*, part II, causa 23, question 8, canon 8] "You must know that we shall never suffer our men to be oppressed by anyone; but should there arise some necessity, then we shall presently react, because we have to defend our flock against everybody and be its foremost protectors." Nor is there a difficulty with those two canons which follow [*Decr. Gr.*, c. 23, q. 8, can. 19 and 20] because they concern, according to what Gratian says in the passage that follows, the bishop who has no temporal jurisdiction. In the *Constitutions of the Legates of the Holy See*, it is maintained that if a cleric would use a pointed knife without the permission of his bishop, he will not enjoy clerical privilege. ... Nevertheless, regardless of what the *Constitutions* maintain, and of what is said in canon and divine law, the clerics of our day in all and every circumstances have become soldiers.

The [civil] law asserts that those against whom the Roman People declares war, or those [who declare war against] the Roman People, are properly called enemies; others [are called] bandits. ... Thus it seems that the sort of war which princes of today constantly undertake is unjust, and they cannot exempt themselves from their duty of faithfulness even through a defiance (*per diffidantiam*)[8]; for since nature established among us a certain law of kinship, it is impious for a man to ambush a man ... because this law cannot be derogated by any agreement ...

---

[7] Johannes Teutonicus, author of the *glossa ordinaria* to the *Decretum*.

[8] Defiance (*diffidantia* or *diffidatio*) was a formal declaration of hostilities, originally by a vassal against his lord. It implied that the defiant vassal's allegiance and "faith" was openly broken off, so that he could not be accused of "perfidy" or felony when he started his war. Defiance was also used apart from feudal relationships, to the same effect, as hinted at by Hostiensis, who seemed to construe it as a kind of implied agreement between the contending parties.

even if the parties mutually agree . . . for a civil agreement cannot destroy natural principles (*naturalia*). . . . Such persons thus ought to be punished, because wickedness ought not to remain unpunished. . . . And generally it is prohibited to take the law into one's own hands. . . . Nor is it permitted to take up or to bear arms without the knowledge of the emperor . . . , for he who engages in war without order, that is, without a command from the emperor, comes within the provisions of the *Lex Iulia maiestatis*[9] . . . although in a case of urgent necessity, the authorization of an official magistrate would suffice. . . . Yet the emperor usually allows some persons the use of the sash,[10] for the sake of inspecting fields or for some other cause, which however seems to result in no one's injury. . . .

There is, however, a contrary argument in [civil] law, because if we have no pact of friendship with a given nation, these are not for that matter our enemies; yet a free man of ours who comes to them is made their slave, and what of ours comes to them is made theirs; and conversely what of theirs comes to us is made ours. . . . But this may be understood [to be accepted] when it occurs by the authority of a judge, and it is called peace in comparison to war against the enemies of the Roman People. But if someone harbors assassins, from this day forward he is perpetually defied by the Roman People, and his goods can legitimately be seized, and no other defiance is required. It seems therefore in other cases to be required, and from the fact that someone defies another he may legitimately attack him. . . . But this too should be understood when [it occurs by] the authority of law or a judge. If therefore someone captures our man without the authority or consent of a judge, he can be ordered by interdict to produce the free man. As to things, there lies an action at law for things taken by force. . . . But if someone would seize our property by the authority of a judge, he has just cause for its detention, and hence he has an exception. . . . Yet I also say that if one who inflicts an injury suffers an injury [from the injured person who] repels him for the preservation of his body, the one repelling is not responsible. . . . But what if there is no judge available? Then he should appeal to the prince; otherwise he would act illicitly; nor should anyone turn to violence because of a threat to property, unless by the authority of a judge, because one should rather surrender one's cloak after losing one's coat . . . , which I hold to be true, if one could not retain property without danger of someone's death; otherwise, if the danger of death does not threaten, he can retain his property. . . .

But in order that you may have some teaching regarding this matter, you should note that war is considered in several ways.

One [sort of war] is between believers and infidels, and this is a just [sort of war] on the part of the faithful.

---

[9]   This law, which was passed under the emperor Augustus, concerned crimes of *lèse majesté* committed against the Roman state or against the person of the emperor; see *Digest*, 48, 4, and *Codex*, 9, 8. The name *Iulia* is due to the fact that Augustus had been adopted by Julius Cesar, and hence was a member of the *gens Iulia*.

[10]   A symbol of the prince's authority; see *Codex*, 12, 5, 5.

Another sort is between believers[11] on both sides; and this sort may be understood in several ways, because it is undertaken either by the authority of a judge, or by the authority of law, or by one's own will.

If it is undertaken by the authority of a legitimate judge, say because those against whom he grants legitimate authority are immediately subordinate to him, and he has the right of exercising full power of command and he is not a judge (*auctor*) in his own case, nor was just (*nec erat iustum*).[12] ... Therefore an action does not lie against those who are not his subjects, because "the applicant follows the court of the defendant." ... Nor therefore should one be pledged or accused for another ... unless perhaps in the absence of a judge for the injuring party refusing to render justice ..., because one judge would remedy the absence of the other. ... One who does not have full power of command cannot grant this authority. Furthermore, no one will be a judge in his own case. ... Furthermore, an error on the part of the judge will surely not excuse him entirely. ... For even if the error were plausible, satisfaction has to be rendered as soon as it is discovered. ... Nevertheless the presumption is prima facie for the judicial authority, unless the contrary clearly appears. ... Therefore, whoever by a legitimate judicial authority free of error attacks another, attacks justly, whereas the one attacked defends himself unjustly, since his contumacious and presumptuous rebellion is all the more revealed. ...

This will be the same if [war] is undertaken by the authority of the law (*iuris*), namely where it is conceded by law, regarding the one empowered by law, as it is proper to set examples through the law. ...

Likewise, [war is just] in fending off injury to a friend or neighbor. But also a prelate who is empowered to use both swords [namely, spiritual and secular], can and must use both swords against those who would harm his church. ... In these and similar cases, he who uses arms does so justly; and consequently, he who defends himself does so rashly; he would do wisely to amend and correct his life. ...

But if the authority of a judge or law does not intervene, [the war] is unjust on either side regarding the attackers; but regarding the defenders, it is just on either side.[13] ...

Now, to sum up what we have said, one [sort of war] can be called "Roman war" (*bellum Romanum*), namely that which is between believers and infidels; and this sort is just. ... I call it "Roman" because Rome is the head and mother of our faith. ... A second [sort of war] is between believers fighting by the authority of a judge, and this may be called "judicial," and is just. ... A third [sort of war] is waged by believers who are obstinately opposed to a judge; and

---

[11] The text reads *infideles*, which is obviously a misprint for *fideles*.

[12] This phrase is probably corrupted, for it does not make sense in its present form. The comment that follows, which takes up each of the elements in this sentence, suggests that *iustum* should read *errans* or *iniustus*.

[13] This sentence may be spurious, but its general meaning seems to be clear: in the absence of any authorization, the aggressors are wrong, the defenders right, on whichever side they may be.

this sort may be called "presumptuous," and is unjust. A fourth [sort of war] is waged by believers with the authority of law, and this may be called "licit," and is just. A fifth [sort of war] is one which is waged by believers against the authority of law, and this may be called "temerarious," and is unjust. . . . A sixth [sort of war] is one which is waged by believers on their own authority, attacking others; and this may be called "voluntary," and is unjust. A seventh [sort of war] is one which is waged by believers defending themselves with the authority of law against those who attacked willfully, and this may be called "necessary," and is just. . . .

Therefore, in Roman, judicial, legal, and necessary wars one is not obligated to make restitution. But in presumptuous, temerarious, and voluntary wars there is an obligation for anyone concerned to make restitution. . . . What, therefore, of our counts who all day long raise and cause to be raised arms without authority of the prince, and disinherit their own vassals? I do not doubt that they are obligated to make restitution, unless they observe the judicial order, which is that if a vassal wishes to appeal to law, he ought to be heard; if he is obstinate, he ought to be attacked, which can be done by the authority of the law or by order of a judge. . . . Otherwise, if he is obedient, he should not be punished by the sword. . . . For it is not permitted to anyone to take up arms to attack another without the authority of law or judge; otherwise he incurs punishment, since he intends to inflict violence.

As to feudal questions, see the Constitution on Keeping Peace,[14] throughout. Yet, there is a contrary argument in Feudal Constitutions,[15] "Of the investiture accepted by Titius" . . . , but that may be understood [as applying] when the authority of a judge obtains. Therefore if a ruler who is immediately subject to a prince complains about his vassal, and wishes to choose the safer path as to the soul, I advise that he judge not for himself, nor take up arms by authority of the prince, but rather appeal to the diocese of the vassal, who, refusing to obey the admonition [of the bishop], will be excommunicated for this sin. . . . And if he remains excommunicated after one year, he and his property shall be forfeited to the bishop. . . . Thus the secular arm must appeal to its ecclesiastical counterpart. Just as happens conversely. . . . Perhaps this is meant when it is said that "one sword always needs the other."

4. To which kind of war the truce in question relates. Not to Roman war, because this should not be in abeyance even for a day, nor to necessary war, because necessity is not subject to the law. . . . If you understand it of unjust, namely "voluntary," war this may not be waged at any time. . . .

Solution: this can be understood of just war, which, though it is [in principle] at no time to cease, should however not be pursued during the periods and days

---

[14] *Consuetudines feudorum,* lib. II, tit. 27.
[15] Ibid., lib. II, tit. 13.

mentioned in this decretal [*Decr. Greg.*, IX, I, 34, 1, *De treuga et pace*]. The same is implied in the canon *Si nulla*, when it says "If inevitable necessity or importunity is pressing."[16] The same can be understood of unjust war which, though it is at no time to be waged, should however [even] less be pursued during these periods and days than at others.

[The truce in question] can therefore be understood indistinctly of judicial and legal [war], and [equally] of voluntary, presumptuous, and temerarious [war]; not that the pope would approve of such war for that matter; but because, even though it cannot be wholly corrected, men might be mutually restrained.

5. How many kinds of truce there are. Two: conventional and canonical. Conventional is that sort which takes its form from an agreement, just like any contract. . . . And just as the will is law in matters of last will and testament . . . also this [sort of truce] ought to be observed with respect to the enemies of Rome . . . ; you have to understand this [as applying] if the infidel also keeps faith with the believers, otherwise not. . . . Nor does the canon *Noli*[17] constitute an objection, because even if the infidel does not keep faith [with respect to a] canonical [truce], as long as he observes a conventional [truce], it ought to be kept in return. The reason for this is that it is a grave [sin] to betray faith . . . which is called public with respect to "Roman" war. Nay, whenever a conventional truce is broken, it should not be broken [in return] nor avenged [as would ordinarily be the case with broken agreements] according to military law or approved custom.

As to canonical truce, which is the sort of truce discussed here, some enjoy it perpetually, others temporarily. Those who enjoy it perpetually are priests, monks, converts, pilgrims, and peasants with their animals, and all agricultural servants when they are engaged in farming and when they are coming and going. Peasants enjoy this privilege as long as they dwell in agriculture, just as it is with soldiers as long as they serve as soldiers. Thus clerics and monks and converts, as long as they live regularly in churches under canonical rule, enjoy clerical privilege . . . and legates enjoy the privilege while engaged in a legation . . . and likewise animals which belong to farming. . . . However, if they are living a common life with the laity, they rightly are subject to common discipline with [the laity] under [civil] law.

As to temporary [truce], all enjoy it in common, from Wednesday after sunset to Monday before sunrise, Thursday in observance of the Lord's ascension, Friday because of the Lord's passion, Saturday because it is a day of rest, and Sunday because of his resurrection. Likewise from Advent until the octave of Epiphany, and from Septuagesima Sunday until the octave of Easter. Three strings combine to maintain the observance of these truces; diocesan excommunication;

---

[16] *Decretum Gratiani*, pt. II, c. 23, q. 8, can. 15.
[17] *Decretum Gratiani*, pt. II, c. 23, q. 1, can. 3.

confirmation, i.e. approval, and a similar interpretation by neighboring bishops; mutual assistance and counsel to be offered by fellow bishops. . . . But it is asked whether bishops should be declared transgressors if they do not observe these conditions? One can say that they should not, because these things are not borne out by the conduct of those concerned.

6. What does a truce effect? Protection and security, as is clear from its description. And whosoever breaks [the truce] ought to be forced by excommunication to make amends. Also, mutual counsel and assistance by the prelates ought to contribute to the peace and the steadfast observance of the truce. . . . A breaker or violator of the peace ought to be excommunicated, according to the canons . . . and punished by death according to [civil] law.

In summary, it should be known that any prelate, and most of all the bishop, ought to lead the combatants to agreement – beforehand by persuasion and without force, but afterwards by jurisdiction and power. . . . But it is objected that if disputants are reconciled, there are still unpunished crimes; which is against the law. . . . Furthermore, it is fitting that criminal activity be revealed. . . . To this I respond the same as is said above: this takes place in civil cases and in the action for injuries, which anyone is entitled to renounce, as long as there is no injury to the church. . . . And if this happened, it [still] should not have been done. . . . I also understand this to hold in civil actions, observing the aforementioned, namely that in certain cases there can be no settlement. . . . Likewise, I mean this to apply to civil actions in criminal matters; for even if one cannot remit a crime, one can refrain from making an accusation or initiating a civil action. However, those cases in which one can desist from accusation without punishment, and those in which a crime is being abolished will be noted further on. Likewise, a judge will mete out punishment in virtue of his office, as is apparent from what is said below . . . and so misdeeds will not go unpunished.[18]

---

[18] In the remainder of the text, Hostiensis inquires whether or not bishops have a special duty to forgive injuries, rather than punishing them.

16

Thomas Aquinas (ca. 1225–1274)

Just War and Sins against Peace

True peace is only in good men and about good things. The peace of the wicked is not a true peace but a semblance thereof.

Summa theologiae

The influence of Thomas Aquinas on the development of just war thinking has been considerable. This is due in large measure to the elegantly simple presentation that the Dominican friar gave to the ethics of war and peace in his most famous work, the *Summa theologiae*[1] (written 1268–71). From the sixteenth century onwards, this work served as a textbook in theology, around which many professors in the Latin West organized their teaching. By devoting a distinct chapter (termed a *question* – Latin *quaestio* – in the nomenclature of medieval scholasticism) to war in his *Summa*, he thereby put this theme on the map for succeeding generations of thinkers. Aquinas's moral analysis of war is admittedly short, taking up approximately 8 pages in a work over 2,000 pages long. Nevertheless, his identification of "princely authority," "just cause," and "right intention" as the key moral criteria for assessing resort to armed force, remains the basic architecture according to which discussions of just war are carried on even today.

While Aquinas's *question* "On War" (*De bello*) in *Summa theologiae* II–II, q. 40, is the most famous of his writings on this topic, in the same work he also wrote chapters on peace (q. 29), strife (q. 41), sedition (q. 42), military prudence (q. 50, a. 3), killing in self-defense (q. 64, a. 7), coercive force at the service of religion (q. 10, a. 8), and battlefield courage (q. 123, a. 5). In his numerous other writings Aquinas touched on issues relating to war and peace only obliquely. Most significant among these are his treatments of tyrannicide in the *Sentences* commentary and civil insurrection in *On the Governance of Rulers*.

[1] Sometimes called *Summa theologica*.

Aquinas's contribution to the ethics of military force results principally from his deft ordering of ideas taken from earlier authors (principally Augustine and Gratian), thereby providing a compact précis of the emerging medieval consensus on just war. Aquinas's systematic treatment of moral principles (which provides a rich backdrop for his articulation of this idea), allied with his enormous prestige as a theologian, assured that his formulation of this consensus would have a lasting influence, especially from the fifteenth century onwards.

As will become apparent from the texts presented below, Aquinas's comments focus mainly on the legitimacy of *resort* to armed force (now termed *ius ad bello*). The question of how soldiers should conduct themselves in war (now termed *ius in bello*), while not entirely absent from his discussion (see, for example, his discussion of military deception in *Summa theologiae*, II–II, q. 40, a. 3), is given little explicit treatment in his works.

I   Peace and Sins against Peace

"On War" (*De bello*), in *Summa theologiae*, II–II, q. 40, is assuredly the most important text in Aquinas's corpus on the problem of war.[2] This chapter is situated among a group of *questions* which discuss sins against charity (*caritas*), the preeminent Christian virtue. Aquinas conceives of this virtue as the source of several inward dispositions to good acts: love, joy, mercy, and, most importantly for our present purposes, *peace*. Alongside each of these virtuous dispositions, he lists one or several characteristic *sins* (also termed *vices*). Against peace, Aquinas names three sins that involve acts of outward violence: (a) *war*, wherein independent cities or nations engage in open combat; (b) *strife*, wherein several individuals (or small bands of individuals) fight against each other; and (c) *sedition*, wherein one faction in civil society sets itself against the larger community.

In the *Summa* passages that follow, Aquinas uses the literary form of the medieval "disputed question." According to this procedure, the separate chapters (*questions*) are divided into subsections, termed *articles*. Each article is introduced by a set of *objections*, which marshal arguments against the thesis to be defended by Aquinas (some of these have been deleted from the passages reproduced below). Next, with the words *"On the contrary"*, he usually quotes some recognized authority in support of his own position. Then, in a section beginning with the words *"I answer that,"* he presents the main argument to decide the point, and finally, he replies to each of the objections that were raised at the outset.

In *question* 29, Aquinas views peace (*pax*) not solely as the absence of conflict, but especially as a positive good to be pursued by individuals and states alike.

---

[2]   For a treatment of Aquinas's discussion of war in the *Summa theologiae*, see Gregory M. Reichberg, "Is There a 'Presumption against War' in Aquinas's Ethics?" *The Thomist*, 66 (July 2002), pp. 337–67.

After differentiating the inner peace of the soul from the peace which can exist within and between communities (also termed *concord*), he proceeds to distinguish between perfect and imperfect, and true and false peace. The *question* then engages in a reflection on the close link between charity, the highest Christian virtue, and peace. The idea that peace is a positive reality that follows upon a shared sense of belonging, a union of the affections directed toward the common good, is what leads Aquinas to situate his discussion of war (sedition, strife, etc.) within the treatise on charity rather than within his *Summa* treatise on justice. "Peace," he writes, "is the 'work of justice' *indirectly*, insofar as justice removes the obstacles to peace: but it is the work of charity *directly*. . . . For love is a unitive force."

From *Summa theologiae*, II–II[3]

Question 29: On Peace[4]

We must now consider Peace, under which head there are four points of inquiry:

1 Whether peace is the same as concord?
2 Whether all things desire peace?
3 Whether peace is an effect of charity?
4 Whether peace is a virtue?

Article 1: Whether peace is the same as concord?

It would seem that peace is the same as concord.

Obj. 1: For Augustine says (*De civitate Dei*, XIX, 13): "Peace among men is well ordered concord." Now we are speaking here of no other peace than that of men. Therefore peace is the same as concord.

Obj. 2: Further, concord is union of wills. Now the nature of peace consists in such like union, for Dionysius says (*Div. Nom.*, XI) that peace unites all, and makes them of one mind. Therefore peace is the same as concord.

Obj. 3: Further, things whose opposites are identical are themselves identical. Now the one same thing is opposed to concord and peace, viz. dissension; hence

---

[3] These passages from part II–II (Secunda Secundae) of the *Summa theologiae* represent an emended version of St. Thomas Aquinas, *Summa theologica*, trans. Fathers of the English Dominican Province, rev. edn. (orig. published 1920), Benziger Brothers, 1948 (reprinted Westminster, MD: Christian Classics, 1981) available online at: http://www.ccel.org/a/aquinas/summa/home.html. Latin text in *Sancti Thomae Aquinatis Doctoris Angelici Opera Omnia iussu impensaque Leonis XIII*, vols. 8–10 (Rome: Editori di san Tommaso, 1895).

[4] Ibid., pp. 1308–10.

it is written (1 Corinthians 16:33): "God is not the God of dissension but of peace." Therefore peace is the same as concord.

On the contrary, there can be concord in evil between wicked men. But "there is no peace to the wicked" (Isaiah 48:22). Therefore peace is not the same as concord.

I answer that, peace includes concord and adds something thereto. Hence wherever peace is, there is concord, but there is not peace, wherever there is concord, if we give peace its proper meaning.

For concord, properly speaking, is between one man and another, in so far as the wills of various hearts agree together in consenting to the same thing. Now the heart of one man may happen to tend to diverse things, and this in two ways. First, in respect of the diverse appetitive powers: thus the sensitive appetite tends sometimes to that which is opposed to the rational appetite, according to Galatians 5:17: "The flesh lusteth against the spirit." Secondly, in so far as one and the same appetitive power tends to diverse objects of desire, which it cannot obtain all at the same time: so that there must needs be a clashing of the movements of the appetite. Now the union of such movements is essential to peace, because man's heart is not at peace, so long as he has not what he wants, or if, having what he wants, there still remains something for him to want, and which he cannot have at the same time. On the other hand this union is not essential to concord: wherefore concord denotes a union of desires among various persons, while peace denotes, in addition to this union, the union of desires even in one man.

Reply Obj. 1: Augustine is speaking there of that peace which is between one man and another, and he says that this peace is concord, not indeed any kind of concord, but that which is well ordered, through one man agreeing with another in respect of something befitting to both of them. For if one man concord with another, not of his own accord, but through being forced, as it were, by the fear of some evil that besets him, such concord is not really peace, because the order of each concordant is not observed, but is disturbed by some fear-inspiring cause. For this reason he premises that "peace is tranquillity of order," which tranquillity consists in all the appetitive movements in one man being set at rest together.

Reply Obj. 2: If one man consent to the same thing together with another man, his consent is nevertheless not perfectly united to himself, unless at the same time all his appetitive movements be in agreement.

Reply Obj. 3: A twofold dissension is opposed to peace, namely dissension between a man and himself, and dissension between one man and another. The latter alone is opposed to concord.

Article 2: Whether all things desire peace?

It would seem that not all things desire peace.

. . . *Obj. 2:* Desire does not tend to opposite things at the same time. Now many desire war and dissension. Therefore all men do not desire peace.

Obj. 3: Further, good alone is an object of desire. But a certain peace is, seemingly, evil, else Our Lord would not have said (Matthew 10:34): "I came not to send peace." Therefore all things do not desire peace.

Obj. 4: Further, that which all desire seems to be the supreme good which is the last end. But this is not true of peace, since it is attainable even by a wayfarer; else Our Lord would vainly command (Mark 9:49): "Have peace among you." Therefore all things do not desire peace.

On the contrary, Augustine says (*De civ. Dei,* XIX, 12, 14) that "all things desire peace": and Dionysius says the same (*Div. Nom.,* XI).

I answer that, From the very fact that a man desires a certain thing it follows that he desires to obtain what he desires, and, in consequence, to remove whatever may be an obstacle to his obtaining it. Now a man may be hindered from obtaining the good he desires, by a contrary desire either of his own or of some other [person], and both are removed by peace, as stated above. Hence it follows of necessity that whoever desires anything desires peace, in so far as he who desires anything, desires to attain, with tranquillity and without hindrance, that which he desires: and this is what is meant by peace which Augustine defines as (*De civ. Dei,* XIX, 13) "the tranquillity of order."

... *Reply Obj. 2:* Even those who seek war and dissension, desire nothing but peace, which they deem themselves not to have. For as we stated above, there is no peace when a man concords with another man counter to what he would prefer. Consequently men seek by means of war to break this concord, because it is a defective peace, in order that they may obtain peace, where nothing is contrary to their will. Hence all wars are waged that men may find a more perfect peace than that which they had heretofore.

Reply Obj. 3: Peace gives calm and unity to desire. Now just as desire may tend to what is good simply, or to what is good apparently, so too, peace may be either true or apparent. There can be no true peace except where desire is directed to what is truly good, since every evil, though it may appear good in a way, so as to calm desire in some respect, has, nevertheless many defects, which cause desire to remain restless and disturbed. Hence true peace is only in good men and about good things. The peace of the wicked is not a true peace but a semblance thereof, wherefore it is written (Wisdom 14:22): "Whereas they lived in a great war of ignorance, they call so many and so great evils peace."

Reply Obj. 4: Since true peace is only about good things, as the true good is possessed in two ways, perfectly and imperfectly, so there is a twofold true peace. One is perfect peace. It consists in the perfect enjoyment of the supreme good, and unites all of one's desires by giving them rest in one object. This is the ultimate end of the rational creature, according to Psalm 147:3: "Who hath placed peace in thy borders." The other is imperfect peace, which may be had in this world, for though the soul's chief movement finds rest in God, there nevertheless remain certain hindrances within and without which disturb this peace.

Article 3: Whether peace is the proper effect of charity?[5]

It would seem that peace is not the proper effect of charity.

Obj. 1: For one cannot have charity without sanctifying grace. But some have peace who have not sanctifying grace, thus heathens sometimes have peace. Therefore peace is not the effect of charity.

Obj. 2: Further, if a certain thing is caused by charity, its contrary is not compatible with charity. But dissension, which is contrary to peace, is compatible with charity, for we find that even holy doctors, such as Jerome and Augustine, dissented in some of their opinions. We also read that Paul and Barnabas dissented from one another (Acts 15:37). Therefore it seems that peace is not the effect of charity.

Obj. 3: Further, the same thing is not the proper effect of different things. Now peace is the effect of justice, according to Isaiah 32:17: "And the work of justice shall be peace." Therefore it is not the effect of charity.

On the contrary, It is written (Psalm 118:165): "Much peace have they that love Thy Law."

I answer that, Peace implies a twofold union, as stated above (a. 1). The first is the result of one's own desires being directed to one object; while the other results from one's own desire being united with the desire of another [person]: and each of these unions is effected by charity: the first, in so far as man loves God with his whole heart, by referring all things to Him, so that all his desires tend to one object: the second, in so far as we love our neighbor as ourselves, the result being that we wish to fulfil our neighbor's will as though it were our own: hence it is reckoned a sign of friendship if people "make choice of the same things" (*Ethics*, IX, 4), and Cicero says (*De amicitia*) that friends "like and dislike the same things" (Sallust, *Catilin.*).

Reply Obj. 1: Without sin no one falls from a state of sanctifying grace, for it turns man away from his due end by making him place his end in something undue: so that his desire does not cleave chiefly to the true final good, but to some apparent good. Hence, without sanctifying grace, peace is not real but merely apparent.

Reply Obj. 2: As the Philosopher says (*Ethics*, IX, 6) friendship does not involve a concord in opinion, but only concord about such goods as conduce to life, and especially upon such as are important; because dissension in small matters is scarcely accounted dissension. Hence nothing hinders those who have charity from holding different opinions. Nor is this contrary to peace, because opinions pertain to the intellect, which precedes desire, [and it is according to the latter] that [one person] is united [to another] through peace. In like manner if there be concord as to goods of importance, dissension with regard to some that are of

---

[5] Aquinas further elaborates on this theme in *Summa theologiae* II–II, q. 45, a. 6, where he considers how peace flows from the wisdom which is likewise an effect of charity.

little account is not contrary to charity: for such a dissension proceeds from a difference of opinion, because one man thinks that the particular good, which is the object of dissension, belongs to the good about which they agree, while the other thinks that it does not. Accordingly such like dissension about very slight matters and about opinions is inconsistent with a state of perfect peace, wherein the truth will be known fully, and every desire fulfilled; but it is not inconsistent with the imperfect peace of the wayfarer.

Reply Obj. 3: Peace is the "work of justice" indirectly, in so far as justice removes obstacles to peace: but it is the work of charity directly, since charity, according to its very nature, causes peace. For love is "a unitive force" as Dionysius says (*Div. Nom.*, IV): and peace is the union of the appetite's inclinations.

Article 4: Whether peace is a virtue?

It would seem that peace is a virtue.

... *Obj. 3:* Vices are opposed to virtues. But dissensions, which are contrary to peace, are numbered among the vices (Galatians 5:20). Therefore peace is a virtue.

On the contrary, Virtue is not the last end, but the way thereto. But peace is the last end, in a sense, as Augustine says (*De civ. Dei*, XIX, 11). Therefore peace is not a virtue.

I answer that, As stated above (q. 28, a. 4), when a number of acts all proceeding uniformly from an agent, follow one from the other, they all arise from the same virtue, nor do they each have a virtue from which they proceed, as may be seen in corporeal things. For, though fire by heating, both liquefies and rarefies, there are not two powers in fire, one of liquefaction, the other of rarefaction: and fire produces all such actions by its own power of calefaction.

Since then charity causes peace precisely because it is love of God and of our neighbor, as shown above (a. 3), there is no other virtue except charity whose proper act is peace, as we have also said in reference to joy (q. 28, a. 4).

Reply Obj. 3: Several vices are opposed to one virtue in respect of its various acts: so that not only is hatred opposed to charity, in respect of its act which is love, but also sloth and envy, in respect of joy, and dissension in respect of peace.

We turn now to the *questions* in the *Summa* where Aquinas discusses war and related acts of violence. Although war is here treated in the context of sins opposed to charity, he makes clear that this moral condemnation bears only on those wars that are waged without proper warrant, i.e. unjust wars. He leaves open the possibility that recourse to arms may sometimes be justified, and lays out the moral criteria which must be met if such an undertaking is to be deemed morally fitting. In the first article of *question* 40, Aquinas details his thoughts on just war (*iustum bellum*). This is the sole passage in his *corpus* where he explicitly takes up this theme. Subsequent articles in this *question* address issues relating to proper conduct in war. Although Aquinas does not here discuss the problem of non-combatant immunity (see however *Summa*, II–II, q. 64, a. 6, where, without expressly mentioning war, he nevertheless condemns the deliberate killing of innocent people), he does limit participation in war to certain classes of people (priests are excluded by reason of their special role as ministers of Christ). Likewise he notes (a. 3) that certain tactics may not be used in war, and finally in article 4 he acknowledges that some restrictions should be observed with respect to when battles may be fought (although exceptions are allowed). Aquinas thereby echoes the emerging medieval view that even just wars should be waged with appropriate restraint.

Question 40: On War[6]

We must now consider war, under which head there are four points of inquiry:

1 Whether any war is licit?
2 Whether it is licit for clerics to wage war (*bellum*)?
3 Whether it is licit for those waging war to lay ambushes?
4 Whether it is licit to fight on holy days?

Article 1: Whether it is always sinful to wage war?

It would seem that it is always sinful to wage war.

Obj. 1: Because punishment is not inflicted except for sin. Now those who wage war are threatened by Our Lord with punishment, according to Matthew 26:52: "All that take the sword shall perish by the sword." Therefore all war is illicit.

Obj. 2: Further, whatever is contrary to a divine precept is a sin. But war is contrary to a divine precept, for it is written (Matthew 5:39): "But I say to you not to resist evil"; and (Romans 12:19): "Not revenging yourselves, my dearly beloved, but give place unto wrath." Therefore war is always sinful.

Obj. 3: Further, nothing, except sin, is contrary to an act of virtue. But war is contrary to peace. Therefore war is always a sin.

Obj. 4: Further, every exercise of a licit thing is itself licit, as is evident in scientific exercises. But warlike exercises which take place in tournaments are forbidden by the Church, since those who are slain in these trials are deprived of ecclesiastical burial. Therefore it seems that war is purely and simply a sin.

On the contrary, Augustine says in a sermon on the son of the centurion (*Ep. ad Marcel.*, CXXXVIII): "If the Christian Religion forbade war altogether,

[6] Ibid., pp. 1353–7.

those who sought salutary advice in the Gospel would rather have been counselled to cast aside their arms, and to give up soldiering altogether. On the contrary, they were told: 'Do violence to no man . . . and be content with your pay' (Luke 3:14). If he commanded them to be content with their pay, he did not forbid soldiering."

I answer that, In order for a war to be just, three things are required. First, the authority of the prince by whose command the war is to be waged. For it is not the business of a private individual to declare war, because he can pursue his right (*ius suum prosequi*) before the judgment of his superior. Moreover it is not the business of a private person to summon together the people, which has to be done in wartime. And as the care of the common weal is committed to those who are in authority, it is their business to watch over the common weal of the city, kingdom or province subject to them. And just as it is licit for them to have recourse to the material sword in defending the common weal against internal disturbances, as when they punish malefactors, according to the words of the Apostle (Romans 13:4): "He beareth not the sword in vain: for he is God's minister, an avenger to execute wrath upon him that doth evil"; so too, it is their business to have recourse to the sword of war in protecting the common weal against external enemies. Hence it is said to those who are in authority (Psalm 81:4): "Rescue the poor: and deliver the needy out of the hand of the sinner"; and for this reason Augustine says in *Contra Faustum* (XXII, 75): "The natural order conducive to peace among mortals demands that the power to declare and counsel war should be in the hands of those who are princes."

Secondly, a just cause is required, namely that those who are attacked, should be attacked because they deserve it on account of some fault (*culpa*). Wherefore Augustine says . . . (*Questions. in Hept.*, q. X, *super Jos.*): "A just war is wont to be described as one that avenges wrongs, when a nation or state has to be punished, for refusing to make amends for the wrongs inflicted by its subjects, or to restore what it has seized unjustly."

Thirdly, it is necessary that those waging war should have a rightful intention, so that they intend the advancement of good, or the avoidance of evil. . . . For it may happen that the war is declared by the legitimate authority, and for a just cause, and yet be rendered illicit through a vile intention. Hence Augustine says in *Contra Faustum* (XXII, 74): "The passion for inflicting harm, the cruel thirst for vengeance, an implacable and relentless spirit, the fever of revolt, the lust of power, and such like things, all these are rightly condemned in war."

Reply Obj. 1: As Augustine says in *Contra Faustum* (XXII, 70): "To take the sword is to arm oneself in order to take the life of anyone, without the command or permission of superior or lawful authority." On the other hand, to have re-course to the sword (as a private person) by the authority of a prince or judge, or (as a public person) through zeal for justice, and by the authority, so to speak, of God, is not to "take the sword," but to use it as commissioned by another, wherefore it does not deserve punishment. And yet even those who make sinful use of the sword are not always slain with the sword, yet they always perish with their own sword, because, unless they repent, they are punished eternally for their sinful use of the sword.

Reply Obj. 2: Such like precepts, as Augustine observes (*De Serm. Dom. in Monte*, i, 19), should always be borne in readiness of mind, so that we be ready to obey them, and, if necessary, to refrain from resistance or self-defense. Nevertheless it is necessary sometimes for a man to act otherwise for the common good, or for the good of those with whom he is fighting. . . .

Reply Obj. 3: Those who wage war justly aim at peace, and so they are not opposed to peace, except to the evil peace, which Our Lord "came not to send upon earth" (Matthew 10:34). Hence Augustine says (*Ep. ad Bonif.*, CLXXXIX): "We do not seek peace in order to be at war, but we go to war that we may have peace. Be peaceful, therefore, in warring, so that you may vanquish those whom you war against, and bring them to the prosperity of peace."

Reply Obj. 4: Manly exercises in warlike feats of arms are not all forbidden, but those which are inordinate and perilous, and end in slaying or plundering. In olden times warlike exercises presented no such danger, and hence they were called "exercises of arms" or "bloodless wars" Jerome states in an epistle.[7]

Article 2: Whether it is permissible for clerics and bishops to fight (*pugnare*)?

It would seem licit for clerics and bishops to take part in combat.

Obj. 1: For, as stated above (a. 1), wars are licit and just in so far as they protect the poor and the entire common weal from suffering at the hands of the foe. Now this seems to be above all the duty of prelates, as Gregory says (*Hom in Evang.*, XIV). Therefore it is licit for prelates and clerics to fight.

Obj. 2: Further, Pope Leo IV writes ([in Decretum, causa] XXIII, q. 8, can. [7] *Igitur*): "As untoward tidings had frequently come from the Saracen side, some said that the Saracens would come to the port of Rome secretly and covertly; for which reason we commanded our people to gather together, and ordered them to go down to the seashore." Therefore it is licit for bishops to proceed into war (*ad bella procedere*).

Obj. 3: Further, apparently, it comes to the same whether a man does a thing himself, or consents to its being done by another, according to Romans 1:32: "They who do such things, are worthy of death, and not only they that do them, but they also that consent to them that do them." Now those, above all, seem to consent to a thing, who induce others to do it. But it is licit for bishops and clerics to induce others to fight: for it is written ([*Decretum*, causa] XXIII, q. 8, can. [10] *Hortatu*) that Charles went to war with the Lombards at the instance

---

[7]   This is apparently a reference to Vegetius, *De Re militaris*, I.

and entreaty of Adrian, bishop of Rome. Therefore it is licit for them to take part in combat.

Obj. 4: Further, whatever is right and meritorious in itself, is not illicit for prelates and clerics. Now it is sometimes right and meritorious to wage war, for it is written ([*Decretum*, causa] XXIII, q. 8, [can. 9] *Omni timore*) that "if a man die for the true faith, or to save his country, or in defense of Christians, God will give him a heavenly reward." Therefore it is licit for bishops and clerics to wage war.

On the contrary, It was said to Peter as representing bishops and clerics (Matthew 26[52]: "Put up again thy sword into its place." Therefore it is not licit for them to engage in combat.

I answer that, Several things are requisite for the good of a human society: and a number of things are done better and quicker by a number of persons than by one, as the Philosopher observes in the *Politics,* while certain occupations are so inconsistent with one another, that they cannot be fittingly exercised at the same time; wherefore those who are deputed to important duties are forbidden to occupy themselves with things of smaller importance. Thus according to human laws, soldiers who engage in warlike pursuits are forbidden to take part in commerce.

Now warlike pursuits are altogether incompatible with the duties of a bishop and a cleric, for two reasons. The first reason is a general one, because, to wit, warlike pursuits are full of unrest, so that they hinder the mind very much from the contemplation of divine things, the praise of God, and prayers for the people, which belong to the duties of a cleric. Wherefore just as commercial enterprises are forbidden to clerics, because they unsettle the mind too much, so too are warlike pursuits, according to 2 Timothy 2:4: "No man being a soldier to God, entangleth himself with secular business." The second reason is a special one, because, to wit, all the clerical orders are directed to the ministry of the altar, on which the Passion of Christ is represented sacramentally, according to 1 Corinthians 11:26: "As often as you shall eat this bread, and drink the chalice, you shall show the death of the Lord, until He come." Wherefore it is unbecoming for them to slay or shed blood, and it is more fitting that they should be ready to shed their own blood for Christ, so as to imitate in deed what they portray in their ministry. For this reason it has been decreed that those who shed blood, even without sin, become irregular. Now no man who is deputized to some office may licitly do that which renders him unfit for that office. Wherefore it is altogether illicit for clerics to wage war, which is directed to the shedding of blood.

Reply Obj. 1: Prelates ought to withstand not only the wolf who brings spiritual death upon the flock, but also the pillager and the oppressor who work bodily harm; not, however, by having recourse themselves to material arms, but by means of spiritual weapons, according to the saying of the Apostle (2 Corinthians 10:4): "The weapons of our warfare are not carnal, but mighty through God." Such are salutary warnings, devout prayers, and, for those who are obstinate, the sentence of excommunication.

Reply Obj. 2: Prelates and clerics may, by the authority of their superiors, take part in wars, not indeed by taking up arms themselves, but by affording spiritual help to those who fight justly, by exhorting and absolving them, and by other like spiritual helps. Thus in the Old Testament (Joshua 6:4) the priests were commanded to sound the sacred trumpets in the battle. It was for this purpose that bishops or clerics were first allowed to proceed into war: and it is an abuse of this permission, if any of them take up arms themselves.

Reply Obj. 3: As stated above (q. 23, a. 4, ad 2) every power, art or virtue that regards the end, has to dispose that which is directed to the end. Now, among the people of faith, carnal wars should be considered as having for their end the divine spiritual good to which clerics are deputed. Wherefore it is the duty of clerics to dispose and counsel other men in waging just wars. For they are forbidden to take up arms, not as though it were a sin, but because such an occupation is discordant with their role (*personae*).

Reply Obj. 4: Although it is meritorious to wage a just war, nevertheless it is rendered illicit for clerics, by reason of their being deputed to works more meritorious still. Thus the marriage act may be meritorious; and yet it becomes reprehensible in those who have vowed virginity, because they are bound to a yet greater good.

Article 3: Whether it is licit to lay ambushes in war?

It would seem that it is illicit to lay ambushes in war.

Obj. 1: For it is written (Deuteronomy 16:20): "Thou shalt follow justly after that which is just." But ambushes, since they are a kind of deception (*fraudes quaedam*), seem to pertain to injustice. Therefore it is illicit to lay ambushes even in a just war.

Obj. 2: Further, ambushes and deception seem to be opposed to faithfulness even as lies are. But since we are bound to keep faith with all men, it is wrong to lie to anyone, as Augustine states in *Contra Mend.* (chap. XV)]. Therefore, as one is bound to keep faith with one's enemy as Augustine states (*Ep. ad Bonifac.*, CLXXXIX) . . . it seems that it is illicit to lay ambushes for one's enemies.

Obj. 3: Further, it is written (Matthew 7:12): "Whatsoever you would that men should do to you, do you also to them": and we ought to observe this in all our dealings with our neighbor. Now our enemy is our neighbor. Therefore, since no man wishes ambushes or deceptions to be prepared for himself, it seems that no one ought to carry on war by laying ambushes.

On the contrary, Augustine says (*Questions. in Hept.*, q. 10, super Jos.): "Provided the war be just, it is no concern of justice whether it be carried on openly or by ambushes": and he proves this by the authority of the Lord, who commanded Joshua to lay ambushes for the city of Ai (Joshua 8:2).

I answer that, Ambushes aim at misleading (*ad fallendum*) the enemy. Now a man may be misled by another's word or deed in two ways. First, through being told something false, or through the breaking of a promise, and this is always illicit. No one ought to deceive the enemy in this way, for there are certain "rights of war and covenants, which ought to be observed even among enemies," as Ambrose states in *De Officiis.*

Secondly, a man may be misled by what we say or do, because we do not declare our purpose or meaning to him. Now we are not always bound to do this, since even in Sacred Doctrine many things have to be concealed, especially from unbelievers, lest they deride it, according to Matthew 7:6: "Give not that which is holy, to dogs." Wherefore much more ought the plan of campaign to be hidden from the enemy. For this reason among other things that a soldier has to learn is the art of concealing his purpose lest it come to the enemy's knowledge, as stated in the book *Stratagematum* by Frontinus. Such like concealment is what is meant by an ambush which may be licitly employed in a just war.

Nor can these ambushes be properly called deceptions, nor are they contrary to justice or to a well-ordered will. For a man would have an inordinate will if he were unwilling that others should hide anything from him.

This suffices for the Replies to the Objections.

Article 4: Whether it is licit to wage war on holy days?

It would seem illicit to wage war on holy days.

Obj. 1: For holy days are instituted that we may occupy ourselves with the things of God. Hence they are included in the keeping of the Sabbath prescribed Exodus 20:8: for "sabbath" is interpreted "rest." But wars are full of unrest. Therefore by no means is it licit to fight on holy days.

Obj. 2: Further, certain persons are reproached (Isaiah 58:3) because on fast-days "they exacted what was owing to them, were engaged in fighting, and smiting with the fist." Much more, therefore, is it illicit to wage war on holy days.

Obj. 3: Further, no inordinate act should be done to avoid temporal harm. But warring on a holy day seems to be inordinate in itself. Therefore no one should wage war on a holy day even out of the necessity of avoiding temporal harm.

On the contrary, It is written (1 Maccabees 2:41): The Jews rightly determined . . . saying: "Whosoever shall come up against us to fight on the Sabbath, we will fight against him."

I answer that, The observance of holy days is no hindrance to those things which are ordained to man's safety, even that of his body. Hence our Lord argued with the Jews, saying (John 7:23): "Are you angry at me because I have healed the whole man on the Sabbath?" Hence physicians may licitly attend to their patients on holy days. Now there is much more reason for preserving the safety of the common weal (whereby many are saved from being slain, and innumerable evils both temporal and spiritual prevented), than the bodily safety of an individual. Therefore, for the purpose of protecting the common weal of the faithful, it is licit to engage in a just war on holy days, provided there be necessity for doing so: because it would be to tempt God if notwithstanding such a necessity, one were to choose to abstain from war.

However, as soon as the necessity ceases, it is no longer licit to wage war on a holy day, for the reasons given: wherefore this suffices for the Replies to the Objections.

The next passage takes up the problem of violence waged between single individuals, bands of criminals, or militias acting without the sanction of princely authority. The last sort of violence in particular was endemic to medieval society.[8] This *question* reflects the theological efforts then under way to restrict resort to such "private warfare."

Question 41: On Strife[9]

We must now consider strife, under which head there are two points of inquiry:

1   Whether strife (*rixa*) is a sin?
2   Whether it is a daughter of anger?

Article 1: Whether strife is always a sin?

It would seem that strife is not always a sin.

. . . *Obj. 3:* [For] strife seems to be a kind of private war (*bellum particulare*). But war is not always sinful. Therefore strife is not always a sin.

On the contrary, Strife is reckoned among the works of the flesh (Galatians 5:20), and "they who do such things shall not obtain the kingdom of God." Therefore strife is not only sinful, but is even a mortal sin.

I answer that, While contention implies a contradiction of words, strife denotes a certain contradiction of deeds. Wherefore a gloss on Galatians 5:20 says that "strifes are when persons strike one another through anger." Hence strife is a kind of private war, because it takes place between private persons, being declared not by public authority, but rather by an inordinate will. Therefore strife is always sinful. In fact it is a mortal sin in the man who attacks another unjustly, for it is not without mortal sin that one inflicts harm on another even if the deed be done by the hands. But in him who defends himself, it may be without sin, or it may sometimes involve a venial sin, or sometimes a mortal sin; and this depends on his intention and on his manner of defending himself. For if his sole intention be to

[8]   See Richard W. Kaeuper, *War, Justice and Public Order: England and France in the Later Middle Ages* (Oxford: Clarendon Press, 1988), pp. 134–9 ("Medieval Violence").
[9]   Fathers of the Dominican Province, *Summa*, p. 1357.

repel the injury done to him, and he defend himself with due moderation, it is no sin, and one cannot say properly that there is strife on his part. But if, on the other hand, his self-defense be inspired by vengeance and hatred, it is always a sin. It is a venial sin, if a slight movement of hatred or vengeance obtrude itself, or if he does not much exceed moderation in defending himself: but it is a mortal sin if he makes for his assailant with the fixed intention of killing him, or inflicting grievous harm on him. . . .

Reply Obj. 3: In order for a war to be just it must be carried out by authority of the public power, as stated above (q. 40, a. 1); whereas strife proceeds from a private feeling of anger or hatred. For if an officer of a prince or judge, in virtue of their public authority, should attack certain men and these defend themselves, it is not the former who is said to be guilty of strife, but those who resist the public power. Hence it is not those who attack who are guilty of strife and commit sin, but those who defend themselves inordinately.

The next *question* takes up the problem of civil war, wherein there is "violent conflict between mutually dissentient parts of one people, as when one part of the state rises in tumult against another part." As in the earlier *question* on war, here too Aquinas establishes a contrast between just and unjust participation in violence. Wrongful insurrection he terms "sedition" (*seditio*) while justified resistance against abusive or illegitimate authority he accords no special name, describing it simply as "disturbing tyrannical rule" or "the defense of the common good." Aquinas reflected on the permissibility of resistance to tyrannical rule at several different points in his career (see the additional selections reproduced below, section V). The following *question* on sedition represents his final attempt at grappling with this problem.

Question 42: On Sedition[10]

We must now consider sedition, under which head there are two points of inquiry:

1 Whether it is a special sin?
2 Whether it is a mortal sin?

Article 1: Whether sedition is a special sin distinct from other sins?

It would seem that sedition is not a special sin distinct from other sins.

Obj. 1: For, according to Isidore (*Etymol.*, X), "a seditious man is one who sows dissent among minds, and begets discord." Now, by provoking the commission

[10]   Ibid., pp. 1359–60.

of a sin, a man sins by no other kind of sin than that which he provoked. Therefore it seems that sedition is not a special sin distinct from discord.

Obj. 2: Further, sedition denotes a kind of division. Now schism takes its name from scission, as stated above (q. 39, a. 1). Therefore, seemingly, the sin of sedition is not distinct from that of schism.

Obj. 3: Further, every special sin that is distinct from other sins, is either a capital vice, or arises from some capital vice. Now sedition is reckoned neither among the capital vices, nor among those vices which arise from them, as appears from *Moral.*, XXXI, 45, where both kinds of vice are enumerated. Therefore sedition is not a special sin, distinct from other sins.

On the contrary, Seditions are mentioned as distinct from other sins (2 Corinthians 12:20).

I answer that, Sedition is a kind of special sin, having something in common with war and strife, and differing somewhat from them. It has something in common with them, in so far as it implies a certain antagonism, and it differs from them in two points. First, because war and strife denote mutual fighting that actually occurs, whereas sedition may be said to denote both actual combat, and the preparation for such combat; hence a gloss on 2 Corinthians 12:20 says that "seditions are tumults tending to a fight," when, to wit, a number of people make preparations with the intention of fighting. Secondly, these differ in that war, properly speaking, is carried on against external foes, being as it were between one multitude and another,[11] whereas strife is between one individual and another, or between few people on one side and few on the other side, while sedition, in its proper sense, is between mutually dissentient parts of one people, as when one part of the civic community (*civitatis*) rises in tumult against another part. Wherefore, since sedition is opposed to a special kind of good, namely the unity and peace of a multitude, it is a special kind of sin.

Reply Obj. 1: A seditious man is one who incites others to sedition, and since sedition denotes a kind of discord, it follows that a seditious man is one who creates discord, not of any kind, but between the parts of a multitude. And the sin of sedition is not only in him who sows discord, but also in those who dissent from one another inordinately.

---

[11] The way that Aquinas here sets up the respective definitions of sedition and war – the first violating the just concord of citizens within a single political community (an independent city or kingdom), the second violating the concord of two or more independent political communities – suggests that a certain conception of international community lies behind his theory of just war. This conception Aquinas seems to have mentioned explicitly (albeit very briefly) on only one occasion, in the following passage from his *Commentary to the Sentences of Peter Lombard* (IV, d. 24, q. 3, a. 2, qc. 3co): "and between a single bishop and the pope there are other grades of dignities corresponding to the grades of unions insofar as one congregation or community includes another one, as the community of a province includes the community of the city, and the community of the kingdom includes the community of the province, and the *community of the whole world* includes the community of a kingdom" (*et communitas totius mundi communitatem unius regni*) (emphasis added).

Reply Obj. 2: Sedition differs from schism in two respects. First, because schism is opposed to the spiritual unity of the multitude, viz. the unity of the church, whereas sedition is contrary to the temporal or secular unity of the multitude, for instance of a city or kingdom. Secondly, schism does not imply any preparation for bodily combat as sedition does, but only for spiritual dissension.

Reply Obj. 3: Sedition, like schism, is contained under discord, since each is a kind of discord, not between one individual and another, but between the opposing parts of a multitude.

Article 2: Whether sedition is always a mortal sin?

It would seem that sedition is not always a mortal sin.

Obj. 1: For sedition denotes "a tumult tending to a fight" according to the gloss quoted above (a. 1). But fighting is not always a mortal sin, indeed it is sometimes just and licit, as stated above (q. 40, a. 1). Much more, therefore, can sedition be without a mortal sin.

Obj. 2: Further, sedition is a kind of discord, as stated above (a. 1, ad 3). Now discord can be without mortal sin, and sometimes without any sin at all. Therefore sedition can be also.

Obj. 3: Further, it is praiseworthy to deliver a multitude from tyrannical rule. Yet this cannot easily be done without some dissension in the multitude, if one part of the multitude seeks to retain the tyrant, while the rest strive to dethrone him. Therefore there can be sedition without mortal sin.

On the contrary, The Apostle forbids seditions together with other things that are mortal sins (2 Corinthians 12:20).

I answer that, As stated above (a. 1, ad 2) sedition is contrary to the unity of the multitude, viz. the people of a city or kingdom. Now Augustine says in *De civ. Dei,* II, that "wise men understand the word people to designate not any crowd of persons, but the assembly of those who are united together in fellowship recognized by law and for the common good." Wherefore it is evident that the unity to which sedition is opposed is the unity of law and common good: whence it follows manifestly that sedition is opposed to justice and the common good. Therefore by reason of its genus it is a mortal sin, and its gravity will be all the greater according as the common good which it assails surpasses the private good which is assailed by strife.

Accordingly the sin of sedition is first and chiefly in its authors, who sin most grievously; and secondly it is in those who are led by them to disturb the common good. Those, however, who defend the common good, and withstand the seditious party, are not called seditious, likewise as neither are those called strifeful because they defend themselves, as stated above (q. 41, a. 1).

Reply Obj. 1: Combat is licit, provided it be for the common good, as stated above (q. 40, a. 1). But sedition runs counter to the common good of the multitude, so that it is always a mortal sin.

Reply Obj. 2: Discord from what is not manifestly good may be without sin, but discord from what is manifestly good cannot be without sin: and sedition is discord of this kind, for it is contrary to the unity of the multitude, which is a manifest good.

Reply Obj. 3: A tyrannical government is not just, because it is directed, not to the common good, but to the private good of the ruler, as the Philosopher states in *Politics*, III and *Ethics*, VIII. Consequently there is no sedition in disturbing a government of this kind, unless indeed the tyrant's rule be disturbed so inordinately that his subjects suffer greater harm from the consequent disturbance than from the tyrant's government. Indeed it is the tyrant rather that is guilty of sedition, since he encourages discord and sedition among his subjects, that he may lord over them more securely; for this is tyranny, being conducive to the private good of the ruler, and to the injury of the multitude.

II Military Prudence

In his general moral theory, Aquinas held that human decision-making, to be upright, must be informed by the moral virtue of prudence (*prudentia*). In the following passage, he explains how a special mode of this virtue applies to military leaders, insofar as they protect the political community from outward attacks.

Question 50: The Different Kinds of Prudence[12]

Article 4: Whether military prudence should be reckoned a kind of prudence?

It would seem that military prudence should not be reckoned a kind of prudence.

Obj. 1: For prudence is distinct from art, according to *Ethics*, VI. 3. Now military prudence seems to be a kind of art in relation to the things of war, according to the Philosopher (*Ethics*, III. 8). Therefore military prudence should not be accounted a species of prudence.

Obj. 2: Further, just as military business is contained under political affairs, so too are many other matters, such as those of tradesmen, craftsmen, and so forth. But there are no species of prudence corresponding to other affairs in the civic sphere. Neither therefore should any be assigned to military affairs.

Obj. 3: Further, the soldier's bravery counts for a great deal in matters of war. Therefore military prudence pertains to fortitude rather than to prudence.

On the contrary, It is written (Proverbs 24:6): "War is managed by due ordering, and there shall be safety where there are many counsels." Now it belongs to

---

[12] Fathers of the English Dominican Province, *Summa*, pp. 1402–3.

prudence to take counsel. Therefore there is great need in matters of war for that species of prudence which is called military.

I answer that, Whatever things are done according to art or reason, should be made to conform to those which are in accordance with nature, and are established by divine reason. Now nature has a twofold tendency: first, to govern each thing in itself, secondly, to withstand outward assailants and corruptives: and for this reason it has provided animals not only with the concupiscible faculty, whereby they are moved to that which is conducive to their well-being, but also with the irascible power, whereby the animal withstands an assailant. Therefore in those things also which are in accordance with reason, there should be not only political prudence, which disposes in a suitable manner such things as belong to the common good, but also a military prudence, whereby enemy attacks are repelled.

Reply Obj. 1: Military prudence may be an art, in so far as it has certain rules for the right use of certain external things, such as arms and horses, but in so far as it is directed to the common good, it belongs rather to prudence.

Reply Obj. 2: Other matters in the state are directed to the profit of individuals, whereas the business of soldiering is directed to the protection (*tuitionem*) of the entire common good.

Reply Obj. 3: The execution of military service belongs to fortitude, but the direction, especially in so far as it concerns the commander-in-chief, belongs to prudence.

III   Battlefield Courage

Although, as we have seen, Aquinas treats of war primarily within the context of vices opposed to charity, it should not be inferred from this that he disapproved of the military profession. In the following passage he explains how soldiering can in fact be a meritorious pursuit. This shows how distant he was from the pacifism of, for instance, Tertullian and Lactantius, for whom engagement in war could never serve as a context for positing true acts of virtue. Aquinas's brief discussion of battlefield courage (referred to under the Christian name "fortitude") carries the implication that participation in war is not merely permissible, but, if carried out for the common good, it may be deemed both virtuous and meritorious.

Question 123: On Fortitude[13]

Article 5: Whether fortitude is properly about dangers of death in battle?

It seems that fortitude is not properly about dangers of death which arise in battle.

---

[13]   Ibid., p. 1704.

Obj. 1: For martyrs above all are commended for their fortitude. But martyrs are not commended in connection with the things of war. Therefore fortitude is not properly about the dangers of death in battle.

Obj. 2: Further, Ambrose says in *De Officiis*, I, that "fortitude is applicable both to warlike and to civil matters": and Cicero (*De Officiis*, I) under the heading "That it pertains to fortitude to excel in battle rather than in civil life" says: "Although not a few think that the business of war is of greater importance than the affairs of civil life, this opinion must be qualified: and if we wish to judge the matter truly, there are many things in civil life that are more important and more glorious than those connected with war." Now greater fortitude is about greater things. Therefore fortitude is not properly concerned with death in war.

Obj. 3: Further, war is directed to preserving temporal peace of the common weal, for Augustine says (*De civ. Dei*, XIX) that "wars are waged to insure peace." Now it does not seem that one ought to expose oneself to the danger of death for the temporal peace of the common weal, since this same peace is the occasion of much license in morals. Therefore it seems that the virtue of fortitude is not about the danger of death in battle.

On the contrary, The Philosopher says (*Ethics*, III) that fortitude is chiefly about death in war.

I answer that, As stated above (a. 4), fortitude strengthens a man's mind against the greatest danger, which is that of death. Now fortitude is a virtue; and it is essential to virtue ever to tend to good; wherefore it is in order to pursue some good that man does not fly from the danger of death. But the dangers of death arising out of sickness, storms at sea, attacks from robbers, and the like, do not seem to come on a man through his pursuing some good. On the other hand, the dangers of death which occur in war come to man directly on account of some good, because, namely, he defends the common good by a just war. Now a just war may be spoken of in two different ways. First, in a general sense (*generale*), it refers to those [i.e. a group of soldiers] who fight on a line of battle. Secondly, in a particular sense (*particulare*), it refers to [some individual], say a judge or even a private person who does not shirk from rendering a just judgment despite the fear of an impending sword or any other danger, even though it threatens him with death. Consequently, it belongs to fortitude to strengthen the mind against dangers of death, not only such as arise in the war of a group (*in bello communi*), but also as occurs in confrontations of individuals (*in particulari impugnatione*), which, if the word be understood in an extended sense, may likewise be termed war. Accordingly it must be granted that fortitude is properly about the dangers of death occurring in war.

Moreover, a brave man behaves well when confronting the danger of any other kind of death; especially since a man may be in danger of any kind of death on account of virtue: thus may a man not fail to attend on a sick friend through fear of deadly infection, or not refuse to undertake a journey with some pious object in view through fear of shipwreck or robbers.

Reply Obj. 1: Martyrs face the fight that is waged against their own person, and this for the sake of the supreme good which is God; wherefore their fortitude is praised above all. Nor is it outside the genus of fortitude that regards martial actions, for which reason they are said to have been valiant in war.

Reply Obj. 2: Personal and civic affairs are differentiated from the martial affairs (*res bellicas*) that come into play in the wars of a group. However, in personal and civic affairs there are dangers of death that arise out of those conflicts that may be termed as it were "wars of individuals." Hence with regard to these also there may be fortitude properly so called.

Reply Obj. 3: The peace of the common weal is good in itself, nor does it become evil because certain persons make evil use of it. For there are many others who make good use of it; and many evils prevented by it, such as murders and sacrileges, are much greater than those which are occasioned by it, and which belong chiefly to the sins of the flesh.

IV   Private Self-defense

The first of the two passages below (q. 64, a. 7) is focused on the problem of self-defense as exercised by private individuals in peacetime. Aquinas has in mind the situation that can arise when, for example, an ordinary individual is beset by a thieves who threaten him with physical harm. The self-defense which is exercised by soldiers in wartime is, however, mentioned in passing, as a point of contrast. This passage has been credited (somewhat controversially)[14] as the source of what has come to be called "the principle of double effect." This is the idea that agents are not responsible for foreseeable, yet unintended, side-effect harms in the same way that they are responsible for harms that are directly intended. In military jargon this is usually referred to under the heading of "collateral damage." Although Aquinas does not here mention the problem of side-effect harm to non-combatants, later thinkers have used this principle to permit such harm when it occurs within the context of attacks on legitimate military targets.

The second passage below (q. 188, a. 3) distinguishes between defense of self and defense of others. Apparently written apropos of the Templars (a religious order devoted to military affairs), the article makes the point the while defense of self is always permissible (within the bounds of moderation), it is not always obligatory: charity can sometimes direct that one refrain from using violence to protect *oneself*, out of love of the attacker. By contrast, not to use force to defend *others* who are under attack, when one is able to do so, would violate the demands of brotherly love. Aquinas thereby suggests that those with sufficient strength have an *obligation* to protect their fellows in need. This provides an opening into the problem of what is now termed *humanitarian intervention*.

---

[14]   See Gregory M. Reichberg, "Aquinas on Defensive Killing: A Case of Double Effect?" *The Thomist*, 69 (2005), pp. 341–70.

Question 64: On Murder[15]

Article 7: Whether it is permissible to kill a man in self-defense?

It would seem that nobody may licitly kill a man in self-defense.

Obj. 1: For Augustine says to *Publicola* (Ep. XLVII): "I do not agree with the opinion that one may kill a man lest one be killed by him; unless one be a soldier, exercising a public office, so that one does it not for oneself but for others, having the power to do so, provided it be in keeping with one's role." Now he who kills a man in self-defense, kills him lest he be killed by him. Therefore this would seem to be illicit. . . .

Obj. 4: Further, murder is a more grievous sin than fornication or adultery. Now nobody may permissibly commit simple fornication or adultery or any other mortal sin in order to save his own life; since the spiritual life is to be preferred to the life of the body. Therefore no man may licitly take another's life in self-defense in order to save his own life.

Obj. 5: Further, if the tree be evil, so is the fruit, according to Matthew 7:17. Now self-defense itself seems to be illicit, according to Romans 12:19: "Not defending yourselves, my dearly beloved." Therefore its result, which is the slaying of a man, is also illicit.

On the contrary, It is written (Exodus 22:2): "If a thief be found breaking into a house or undermining it, and be wounded so as to die; he that slew him shall not be guilty of blood." Now it is much more licit to defend one's life than one's house. Therefore neither is a man guilty of murder if he kill another in defense of his own life.

I answer that, Nothing hinders a single act from having two effects, only one of which is intended (*in intentione*), while the other is beside the intention (*praeter intentionem*). Now moral acts get their character in accordance what is intended, but not from what is beside the intention, since the latter is incidental. . . . Accordingly, the act of self-defense may have a double effect: the saving of one's life, on the one hand, and the slaying of the attacker, on the other. Since saving one's own life is what is intended, such an act is not therefore illicit, seeing that it is natural to everything to keep itself in existence as far as possible. And yet, though proceeding from a good intention, this act may be rendered illicit, if it be out of proportion to the [intended] end. Thus if a man, in self-defense, uses more than necessary violence, this will be illicit: whereas if he repel force with moderation his defense will be licit, because according to the jurists "it is licit to repel force by force, provided one does not exceed the limits of a blameless defense." Nor is it necessary for salvation that a man omit the act of moderate self-defense

---

[15]   Fathers of the Dominican Province, *Summa*, pp. 1465–6.

in order to avoid killing the other man, since one is bound to take more care of one's own life than of another's. But because it is not licit to kill a human being except by public authority acting for the common good, as stated above (a. 3), it is not licit for a man to intend killing another in self-defense, save for one who has public authority, and who, while intending to kill another in self-defense, refers this to the public good. So it is clearly, for example, in the case of a soldier fighting against the foe, and in the case of a minister of justice fighting against robbers, although even these sin if they be moved by private animosity.

Reply Obj. 1: The words quoted from Augustine refer to the case when one man intends to kill another to save himself from death. The passage quoted in the Second Objection is to be understood in the same sense. Hence he says pointedly, "for the sake of these things," whereby he indicates the intention. . . .

Reply Obj. 4: The act of fornication or adultery is not necessarily directed to the preservation of one's own life, as is the act whence sometimes results the taking of a man's life.

Reply Obj. 5: The defense forbidden in this passage is that which comes from revengeful spite. Hence a gloss says: "Not defending yourselves – that is, not striking your enemy back."

Question 188: Of the Different Kinds of Religious Life[16]

From Article 3: Whether a religious order can be directed to soldiering?

It would seem that no religious order can be directed to soldiering.

Obj. 1: It would seem that no religious order can be directed to soldiering. For all religious orders belong to the state of perfection. Now our Lord said with reference to the perfection of Christian life (Matthew 5:39): "I say to you not to resist evil; but if one strike thee on the right cheek, turn to him also the other," which is inconsistent with the duties of a soldier. Therefore no religious order can be established for soldiering. . . .

On the contrary, Augustine says (Ep. CLXXXIX, *ad Bonifac.*), "Beware of thinking that none of those can please God who handle warlike weapons. Of such was holy David to whom the Lord gave great testimony." Now religious orders are established in order that men may please God. Therefore nothing hinders the establishing of a religious order for the purpose of soldiering.

I answer that, As stated above (a. 2), a religious order may be established not only for the works of the contemplative life, but also for the works of the active life, in so far as they are concerned with helping our neighbor and in the service

---

[16]   Ibid., p. 1989.

of God, but not in so far as they are directed to a worldly object. Now the occupation of soldiering (*officium militare*) may be directed to the assistance of our neighbor not only as regards private persons, but also as regards the defense of the whole common weal. . . .

Reply Obj. 1: Not to resist evil may be understood in two ways. First, in the sense of pardoning the wrong done to oneself, and thus it may pertain to perfection, when it is expedient to act thus for the spiritual welfare of others. Secondly, in the sense of tolerating patiently the wrongs done to others: and this pertains to imperfection, or even to vice, if one be able to resist the wrongdoer in a becoming manner. Hence Ambrose says (*De officiis* [I, 270]): "The courage whereby a man in battle defends his country against barbarians, or protects the weak at home, or his friends against robbers is full of justice." . . .

V   Holy War

Although Aquinas does not here use the expression "holy war," in the following passage from the *Summa theologiae* he discusses whether forcible measures (including war) may be taken against those who resist the teaching and practice of the Christian faith. Justifying the use of force for religious purposes was common among medieval thinkers. Aquinas adopts a restrictive conception as compared to some of his fellow theologians, since, in line with pope Innocent IV (see chap. 13, this volume), he allows only for a defensive employment of such force. In this article he carefully rules out what might be termed "offensive holy war": the use of coercive means to propagate right religion. His teaching on the freedom of religious conscience dictated that non-believers could be induced to embrace the faith not by compulsion but by persuasion only. He maintained, however, that those who had embraced the faith through baptism, yet sought to renounce it or to adopt new teachings (apostates and heretics), could be forcibly compelled to remain within its fold.

Question 10: Unbelief in General[17]

Article 8: Whether unbelievers ought to be compelled to the faith?

It would seem that unbelievers ought by no means to be compelled to the faith.
. . . *Obj. 2:* [For] we read in the *Decretals* (dist. XLV can. [5], De Judaeis): "The holy synod prescribes, with regard to the Jews, that for the future, none are

---

[17]   Ibid., pp. 1212–13.

to be compelled to believe." Therefore, in like manner, neither should unbelievers be compelled to the faith.

Obj. 3: Further, Augustine says (Tract. XXVI *in Joan.*) that "it is possible for a man to do other things against his will, but he cannot believe unless he is willing." Therefore it seems that unbelievers ought not to be compelled to the faith. . . .

On the contrary, It is written (Luke 14:23): "Go out into the highways and hedges; and compel them to come in." Now men enter into the house of God, i.e. into Holy Church, by faith. Therefore some ought to be compelled to the faith.

I answer that, Among unbelievers there are some who have never received the faith, such as the heathens and the Jews: and these are by no means (*nullo modo*) to be compelled to the faith, in order that they may believe, because to believe depends on the will: nevertheless they should be compelled by the faithful, if it be possible to do so, so that they do not hinder the faith, by their blasphemies or their evil persuasions, or even by their open persecutions. It is for this reason that Christ's faithful often wage war with unbelievers, not indeed for the purpose of forcing them to believe, because even if they were to conquer them and take them prisoner, they should still leave them free to believe, if they will, but in order to prevent them from hindering the faith of Christ.

On the other hand, there are unbelievers who at some time have accepted the faith, and professed it, such as heretics and all apostates: such should be submitted even to bodily compulsion, that they may fulfil what they have promised, and hold what they, at one time, received.

. . . *Reply Obj. 2:* Those Jews who have in no way received the faith, should by no means be compelled to the faith: if, however, they have received it, they ought to be compelled to keep it, as is stated in the same chapter.

Reply Obj. 3: Just as taking a vow is a matter of will, and keeping a vow, a matter of obligation, so acceptance of the faith is a matter of the will, whereas keeping the faith, when once one has received it, is a matter of obligation. Wherefore heretics should be compelled to keep the faith. . . .

VI   Tyrannicide

In the following two texts, Aquinas discusses the problem of tyrannicide. The first is taken from one of his earliest writings, the *Commentary on the Sentences of Peter Lombard*. After distinguishing those tyrants who lack a proper title to authority from those others who abuse an authority properly acquired, Aquinas approvingly quotes Cicero to the effect that private individuals may take it upon themselves to depose and if necessary kill the former. The permissibility of tyrannicide was discussed by medieval theologians against the backdrop of St. Paul's admonition in Romans 13:1–2: "Let every person be subordinate to the higher authorities, for there is no authority except from God. . . . Whoever resists authority opposes what God has appointed, and those who oppose it will bring judgment upon themselves."

From *Scripta super libros sententiarum*[18]

Article 2: Whether Christians are bound to obey the secular powers, and tyrants in particular?

It seems that Christians are not bound to obey the secular powers, and tyrants in particular. . . .

Obj. 4: Moreover, anyone can lawfully take back what has been unjustly taken away from him if the opportunity to do so arises. But many secular princes have acquired dominion over their lands by tyrannical invasion. Therefore, when the opportunity of rebellion arises, we are not bound to obey them.

Obj. 5: Moreover, no one is bound to obey someone whom it is lawful, or even praiseworthy, to slay. But Cicero, in *De officiis* (1, 26), defends those who slew Julius Caesar even though he was their friend and relative, because he usurped the rights of empire as a tyrant. We are therefore not bound to obey such persons.

On the contrary, 'Servants, be subject to your masters' (1 Peter 2:18); and further: 'He that resisteth the power, resisteth the ordinance of God' (Romans 13:2).

I answer that, It must be noted that obedience consists in the observance of a command which it is our duty to observe. Now the cause of such duty is an order of authority having the power to coerce not only temporally but also spiritually, in conscience, as the Apostle says at Romans 13:1ff., because the order of authority descends from God, as the Apostle intimates in the same place. And so the Christian is bound to obey it insofar as it is 'of God', and not insofar as it is not. But authority can be said to be not of God for two reasons: either because of the way in which the authority was acquired, or because of the use to which the authority is put. As to the first, there are two ways in which this can be so: either because of a defect of the person, because he is unworthy, or because of a defect in the means by which power was acquired; that is, by violence or simony or some other unlawful mode of acquisition. The first defect is not an impediment to the acquisition of rightful authority; and because authority is always of God according to its form, which is the cause of our duty to obey it, their subjects are always bound to obey such rulers, however unworthy. But the second defect is an impediment to rightful authority, for he who seizes power by violence does not become a ruler or lord truly; and so anyone can reject such authority when the

---

[18]   Bk. II, d. 44, 1. 2; translation taken from R. W. Dyson (ed.), *St Thomas Aquinas: Political Writings* (Cambridge: Cambridge University Press, 2002), pp. 72–4, 74–5.

opportunity arises, unless perhaps the ruler is subsequently made a true lord either by the consent of his subjects or by the authority of a superior.

Now the abuse of authority can be of two kinds. First, when what is commanded by the ruler is contrary to the purpose for which the ruler was appointed: for example, if some sinful act is commanded contrary to the virtue which the ruler is ordained to foster and preserve. In this case, not only is one not bound to obey the ruler, but one is bound not to obey him, as in the case of the holy martyrs who suffered death rather than obey the ungodly commands of tyrants. Second, when what is demanded goes beyond what the order of authority can require: if, for example, a master were to exact a payment which a servant is not bound to give, or something of the kind. In this case the subject is not bound to obey; nor, however, is he bound not to obey. . . .

Reply Obj. 4: Those who achieve ruling power by violence are not truly rulers; hence, nor are their subjects bound to obey them, except in the circumstances already mentioned.

Reply Obj. 5: Cicero was speaking of a case where someone had seized dominion for himself by violence, either against the wishes of his subjects or by coercing them into consenting, and where they had no recourse to a superior by whom judgment might be passed on the invader. In such a case he who delivers his country by slaying a tyrant is to be praised and rewarded.

In a later work, *On the Governance of Rulers*, discussing the case of the tyrant who abuses an authority *rightly acquired*, Aquinas argued that private individuals should sometimes tolerate such tyranny in order to avoid even greater evils. In this respect his position was somewhat more restrictive than the one articulated earlier by John of Salisbury (see chapter 11, this volume).

From *De Regimine Principum*[19]

Indeed, if there be not an excess of tyranny it is more expedient to tolerate for a while the milder tyranny than, by acting against the tyrant, to be involved in many perils which are more grievous than the tyranny itself. For it may happen that those who act against the tyrant are unable to prevail and the tyrant, thus provoked, rages the more. Even if one should be able to prevail against the tyrant, from this fact itself very grave dissensions among the people frequently ensue: the multitude may be broken up by factions either during their revolt against the tyrant, or, concerning the organization of the government, after the tyrant has been overthrown. It also happens that sometimes, while the multitude

---

[19]   From the translation of Gerald B. Phelan, *On the Governance of Rulers* [*De Regimine Principum*], rev. edn. (London: Sheed and Ward, 1938), pp. 56–61.

is driving out the tyrant by the help of some man, he, having received the power, seizes the tyranny, and fearing to suffer from another what he did to his predecessor, oppresses his subjects with a more grievous slavery. For this is wont to happen in tyranny, namely, that the second becomes more grievous than the one preceding, inasmuch as, without abandoning the previous oppressions, he himself thinks up fresh ones from the malice of his heart: whence, in Syracuse, when there was a time that everybody desired the death of Dionysius, a certain old woman kept constantly praying that he might be unharmed and that he might survive her. When the tyrant learned this he asked why she did it. Then she said, "When I was a girl we had a harsh tyrant and I wished for his death; when he was killed, there succeeded him one who was somewhat harsher: I was very eager to see the end of his dominion also: then we began to have a third ruler still more harsh – that was you. So if you should be taken away a worse would succeed in your place."[20]

Now some have been of opinion that if the excess of tyranny is unbearable, it would be an act of virtue for strong men to slay the tyrant and to expose themselves to dangers of death in order to set the multitude free. An example of this occurs even in the Old Testament. For a certain Aioth (Ehud) slew Eglon, King of Moab, who was oppressing the people of God under harsh slavery, with the dagger fastened to his thigh; and he was made a judge of the people (cf. Judges 3:21). But this opinion is not in accord with apostolic teaching. For Peter admonishes us to be reverently subject to our masters, not only to the good and gentle but also to the froward (1 Peter 2:18): "For if one who suffers unjustly bear his trouble for conscience sake, this is a grace" (ibid. 2:19). Wherefore, when many Roman emperors tyrannically persecuted the faith of Christ, a great multitude both of the nobility and of the populace was converted to the faith and they were praised, not for resisting, but for patiently and courageously bearing death for Christ. This is plainly manifested in the case of the holy legion of Thebans.[21] Aioth (Ehud), then, must be considered rather as having slain a foe, than as having assassinated a ruler of the people, though a tyrannical one. Hence even in the Old Testament we read that they who killed Joash, the king of Judah, although he had fallen away from the worship of God, were slain and their children spared according to the precept of the law.[22] It would, moreover, be dangerous both for the multitude and for their rulers if certain persons should attempt on their own private presumption, to kill their governors, even tyrants. For to dangers of this kind, usually the wicked expose themselves more than the good. For the rule of a king, no less than that of a tyrant, is burdensome to the wicked because, according to the words of Solomon, "A wise king scattereth the wicked" (Proverbs 20:26). Consequently, by presumption of this kind, danger

[20]   Valerius Maximus, *Facta et dicta memorabilia*, VI, 2, ext. 2.
[21]   See S. Eucharii, Lugdunensis Episc., *Passio Agaunensium Martyrum*, Migne, Patrol. Lat., vol. 50, coll. 827–32; also Catholic Encyclopedia, I, 205, s.v. Agaunum.
[22]   Cf. IV Kings 14:5, 6.

to the people from the loss of their king would be more imminent than relief through the removal of the tyrant.

Furthermore it rather seems, that to proceed against the cruelty of tyrants is an action to be undertaken, not through the private presumption of a few, but by public authority. First of all, if to provide itself with a king belong to the right of any multitude, it is not unjust that the king set up by that multitude be destroyed or his power restricted if he tyrannically abuse the royal power. It must not be thought that such a multitude is acting unfaithfully in deposing the tyrant, even though it had previously subjected itself to him in perpetuity; because he himself has deserved that the covenant with his subjects should not be kept, since, in ruling the multitude, he did not act faithfully as the office of a king demands. Thus did the Romans cast out from the kingship, Tarquin the Proud, whom they had accepted as their king, because of his tyranny and the tyranny of his sons; and they set up in their place a lesser power, namely, the consular power. So too Domitian, who had succeeded those most moderate Emperors, Vespasian, his father, and Titus, his brother, was slain by the Roman senate when he exercised tyranny, and all that he had wickedly done to the Romans, was justly and profitably, by a decree of the senate, declared null and void.

Thus it came about that Blessed John the Evangelist, the beloved disciple of God, who had been exiled to the island of Patmos by that very Domitian, was sent back to Ephesus by a decree of the senate.

If, however, it pertains to the right of some higher authority to provide a king for a certain multitude, a remedy against the wickedness of a tyrant is to be looked for from him. Thus when Archelaus, who had already begun to reign in Judaea in the place of Herod, his father, was imitating his father's wickedness, a complaint against him having been laid before Caesar Augustus by the Jews, his power was, first of all, diminished by depriving him of his title of king and by dividing one half of his kingdom between his two brothers; later, since he was not restrained from tyranny even by this means, Tiberius Caesar sent him into exile in Lyons, a city of Gaul.

Should no human aid whatsoever against a tyrant be forthcoming, recourse must be had to God, the King of all, who is a helper in due time in tribulation.[23] "For, it lies within His power to turn the cruel heart of the tyrant to mildness" (Proverbs 9:10). In the words of Solomon (Proverbs 21:1): "The heart of the king is in the hand of the Lord, whithersoever He will He shall turn it." He it was who turned into mildness the cruelty of King Ahasuerus, who was preparing death for the Jews.[24] He it was who so transformed the cruel king Nebuchadnezzar that he became a proclaimer of the divine power. "Therefore," he said, "I, Nebuchadnezzar, do now praise and magnify and glorify the King of Heaven: because all his works are true and His ways judgments, and them that walk in

---

[23] Cf. Psalm 9:10.
[24] Cf. Esther 8; 9; 10:1–12.

pride He is able to abase" (Daniel 4:34). Those tyrants, however, whom he deems unworthy of conversion he is able to put out of the way or reduce them to the lowest degree, according to the words of the Wise Man (Ecclesiasticus 10:17): "God hath overturned the thrones of proud princes: and hath set up the meek in their stead." He it was who, seeing the afflicting of his people in Egypt and hearing their cry, hurled the tyrant Pharaoh with his army into the sea.[25] He it was who not only banished from his kingly throne the above mentioned Nebuchadnezzar in his former pride, but also cast him from the fellowship of men and changed him into the likeness of a beast.[26] For also His hand is not shortened that He cannot free His people from tyrants.[27] For by Isaiah[28] He promises to give his people rest from their labour and trouble and harsh slavery in which they had formerly served; and by Ezekiel (34:10) He says, "I will deliver my flock from their mouth," that is from the mouth of shepherds who feed themselves. But to deserve to secure this benefit from God, the people must desist from sin; because by divine permission wicked men receive power to rule as a punishment of sin, as the Lord says by the Prophet Hosea (13:11): "I will give thee a king in my wrath"; and it is said in Job (34:30) that he "maketh a man that is a hypocrite to reign for the sins of the people." Sin must therefore be done away with that the scourge of tyrants may cease.

---

[25]   Cf. Exodus 14:23–8.
[26]   Cf. Daniel 4:28–30.
[27]   Cf. Isaiah 59:1.
[28]   Isaiah 60:1.

17

Dante Alighieri (1265–1321)

Peace by Universal Monarchy

[T]he best condition of the human race depends on a unity of wills. But this cannot be unless there be one will dominating all the others and directing them all to one goal.

Monarchia

Dante the poet was also a political philosopher. In his treatise *Monarchia* (On Monarchy, written ca. 1317), he sought to formulate a solution to the problem of war. There he explains that wars arise when individual princes use arms to settle their competing claims. In the absence of a commonly recognized judge to adjudicate their disputes, these sovereigns conclude that they have no recourse but to press their claims by dint of force. Dante argued that resort to war would no longer be needful if the world's independent princes could be persuaded to place themselves under the authority of a single emperor, who would function as the supreme earthly judge. Possessed of full enforcement powers, his decisions would be imposed without further appeal, thereby preventing serious disputes from disrupting the peace.

Dante did not think it right that this universal monarchy should be *imposed* on the princes of the world. To the contrary, he held this was a matter for their free consent. They would be moved to relinquish the full measure of their sovereignty by the certitude that the universal monarch would *arbitrate* their conflicts with indefectible equity and fairness. This confidence in the monarch originates, not out of a perception of his upright character, but from an awareness of the special characteristics which attach to his *role*. Having no superior, and possessing full plenitude of temporal power, the monarch will have nothing to covet, and no one to compete with; hence his judgments will manifest an unwavering rectitude.

Dante was among the first of Western thinkers to propose a structural solution to the age-old problem of war. Few after him would agree with the specifics of his political program. Nevertheless, his idea of achieving a perpetual peace through the establishment of a universal order, would see many permutations in the centuries to come in the writings of, *inter alia*, Kant and Woodrow Wilson (see chapters 41 and 48).

From *Monarchia*, bk. I[1]

Chapter 10: Mankind Needs a Supreme Judge[2]

1 And wherever there can be a dispute, a judgment ought to be available there. Otherwise something imperfect would exist without the appropriate means of making it perfect, which is impossible, since God and nature does not fail to provide things that are necessary.

2 It is self evident that between any two rulers, neither of whom is subject to the other in any way, a dispute can arise, due either to their own wrongdoing or to that of their subjects. Therefore in such cases there must be a judgment between the rulers.

3 And because neither ruler is able to exercise jurisdiction over the other, since neither one is subject to the other (for a peer does not have power over a peer), there must be a third ruler with a broader jurisdiction that gives him the right to rule over both of them.

4 And this third ruler will either be the monarch or not. If he is, our thesis is proved; if he is not, he himself will similarly have a co-equal who is outside the limits of his jurisdiction, in which case another third ruler will be necessary.

5 And consequently either this process will go on to infinity, which is impossible, or else it will necessarily come at last to the first and highest judge, by whose judgment all disputes may be settled, either directly or indirectly, and this will be the monarch or emperor. Therefore monarchy is necessary to the world. . . .

Chapter 11: Monarchy Maximizes Justice[3]

1 Moreover, the world is best disposed when justice is most powerful in it. . . .

2 Now justice is most powerful only under a monarch: therefore, for the best disposition of the world, there needs to be a monarchy or empire.

---

[1] The English text is taken from *Dante's "Monarchia,"* trans., with a commentary, by Richard Kay (Toronto: Pontifical Institute of Medieval Studies, 1998). This edition includes the full Latin text. For an account of Dante's significance within the history of ethical thinking about war, see James Turner Johnson, *The Quest for Peace* (Princeton, NJ: Princeton University Press, 1987), esp. pp. 113–19. For a more elaborate summary of Dante's argument, the reader may usefully consult Etienne Gilson, *Dante and Philosophy*, trans. D. Moore (New York: Harper & Row, 1949), pp. 162–224.

[2] Kay, *Dante's "Monarchia,"* pp. 46–9.

[3] Ibid., pp. 50–63.

3 In order to make the minor premise of this syllogism clear, it must be understood that justice *per se*, i.e. considered in itself and with regard to its own nature, is a kind of rectitude, which is to say a rule to avoid deviations from the correct way to either one side or the other. Thus considered, justice cannot be either more or less, in the same way that whiteness cannot be either more or less when considered in the abstract. . . .

8 And so the following argument can be made from what has been said above: Justice is most powerful in the world when it is present in the most willing and most powerful subject; only the monarch is such a subject: therefore, justice is most powerful in the world when it is pursued by the sole monarch. . . .

11 In order to make the first part plain, it should be noted that greed is most especially contrary to justice, as Aristotle intimates in the fifth book of the *Nicomachean Ethics*. When greed is altogether absent, nothing remains that is opposed to justice. For this reason, it is the Philosopher's opinion that those things that can be determined by law should never be left to the judge's discretion. Fear of greed makes this precaution necessary, for greed readily perverts the minds of men. The point is that where there is nothing to desire, there can be no greed; for there can be no passions when their objects have been eliminated.

12 But the monarch has nothing he can desire, for his jurisdiction has only the ocean as its boundary, which is not the case with other rulers, whose lands border on one another, as for example those of the king of Castile border on those of the king of Aragon. Hence it follows that the monarch can be the purest human subject of justice.

13 Furthermore, just as even a little bit of greed does to some extent obscure the disposition to do justice, so charity, or rightly ordered love, makes it more clear and keen. Therefore justice can be present most powerfully in a person whose love is ordered rightly. The monarch is such a person; when he exists, therefore, justice is most powerful or can be.

14 That rightly ordered love has the effect stated above, can be shown as follows. Greed rejects with scorn that which is specifically good for man and seeks other things instead. But charity, spurning everything else, seeks God and man, and consequently it seeks the good of man. And since living in peace is the most powerful of human goods – as was said above – and because justice most especially and most powerfully brings this about, it follows that charity most especially makes justice strong; and the more powerful charity is, the stronger will justice be.

15 And the minor premise – that rightly ordered love ought to be present in the monarch most especially of all men – is made plain by the following argument. Every lovable thing is loved so much the more when it is nearest to the lover. But men are nearer to the monarch than to other rulers. Therefore they are loved most especially by him, or at least they ought to be. The first premise is evident if one considers the nature of things passive and active. The second premise is manifestly true because men are not close to other rulers except in part, whereas they are close to the monarch in their entirety.

16 Another proof: Men are close to other rulers through the monarch, but the converse is not true. Thus the care of all men pertains to the monarch directly and primarily, whereas other rulers receive it from the monarch, inasmuch as their office is derived from his, which is supreme.

17 Furthermore, the more universal a cause is, the greater is its causative force, because an inferior cause is not a cause except as the result of a superior cause, as is evident from the *Liber de causis*. And the more a cause is a cause, by so much more does it love its effect, because such love is derived from the cause acting as such.

18 Now, since the monarch is the most universal human cause of men living well, while other rulers cause this thanks to him, as was said above, it follows that he loves the good of men more than any other ruler does.

19 But who would doubt that in the doing of justice the monarch is most powerful, unless he did not understand the word "monarch," since one who is monarch is not able to have enemies.

20 The minor premise of the main syllogism is therefore sufficiently substantiated; hence the main conclusion is certain, namely that it is necessary for the best disposition of the world that there be a monarchy. . . .

Chapter 15: Mankind Needs a Unity of Wills[4]

. . . **8** The foregoing discussion justifies the assumption of another proposition in support of our thesis, so one can argue thus: All concord depends on unity of wills. Now, the best condition of the human race is a kind of concord (for, just as the best condition of one man is a kind of concord because it consists in a harmony between body and soul, so the same is true of a household, a city, and a kingdom, and thus of the whole human race). Therefore, the best condition of the human race depends on a unity of wills.

9 But this cannot be unless there be one will dominating all the others and directing them all to one goal, since the wills of mortals need direction due to the seductive delights of youth, as the Philosopher teaches at the end of the *Nicomachean Ethics*. Nor can this will be one unless there be one ruler of all, whose will can dominate and direct all the others.

10 If all the above deductions are true, which they are, it is necessary for the best condition of the human race that there be a monarch in the world, and consequently monarchy is necessary for the well-being of the world.

---

[4] Ibid., pp. 80–5.

18

Bartolus of Saxoferrato (ca. 1313–1357)

Roman War within Christendom

[W]e should see who may declare war, and what is the effect of a declaration of war. And let us examine this among our peoples.

Secunda super Digesto novo

During the Middle Ages, legal reflection on war was not confined to the work of the canonists. Important contributions on this subject were also made by the "legists" (literally "lawyers"), a group of jurists whose particular field of study was the "laws" of ancient Rome (which were called *leges* as opposed to the *canones* of the church). This body of Roman (or "civil") law consisted of several collections of legal texts compiled by order of emperor Justinian around 530 AD in Constantinople. Among these were mainly the *Institutes*, an elementary textbook; the *Digest*, a collection of legal opinions culled from the great Roman jurisconsults; and the *Codex*, a compilation of imperial legislation. These works were brought to light in Western Europe in the wake of the *Renovatio Imperii Romani* by the German emperors who succeeded to the crumbling Carolingian empire.

The study of the *Corpus Iuris Civilis* was not of merely historical significance to the medieval Romanists. The Holy Roman Empire (as it came to be known) was thought of as a Christian continuation of ancient Rome, and Roman law was deemed to be still in force, although a careful work of interpretation was required to bring it into conformity with contemporary conditions. This was precisely the historical achievement of the medieval legists, who are usually divided into two groups. First came the "glossators," who wrote exegetic annotations ("glosses") on the different parts of the Byzantine compilations. The various glosses soon coalesced into a standard gloss (*glossa ordinaria*), which became an inseparable part of the initial body of texts and conditioned their subsequent reading by the second group of civil lawyers, who wrote ever more extensive comments on the

same Roman "laws" (as they were collectively called, even though they also consisted of legal opinions or didactic passages, apart from laws properly speaking).
These later jurists are therefore called "post-glossators" or "commentators."[1]

Bartolus of Saxoferrato stands out as the most famous of the post-glossators. His
commentary on *Digest*, 49, 15, 24, concerning the Roman conception of enemies
(from a passage in the *Institutes* of Ulpian), contains a noteworthy treatment of
war in relation to the problem of legitimate authority. The immediate context
for this discussion was the law of postliminy, whereby Romans citizens who had
been captured in war would recover their former legal status upon returning
to Roman territory. The *ius postliminii* did not apply in situations other than war,
for instance to persons captured by brigands or pirates, for whom the law did not
dictate a loss of citizenship and freedom. The legal operation of *postliminium* thus
presupposed a very definite understanding of what might count as a war (*bellum*).
This the Romans defined as an armed confrontation with "enemies" (*hostes*), an
independent nation or "people" against whom Rome had publicly declared war,
or who had declared war against Rome. Other sorts of adversaries (criminals guilty
of sedition, for example) would not merit the name "enemy" and the violence
used against them would not be termed "war."

In the following text, Bartolus considers the meaning of the terms *bellum* and
hostis in relation to the political landscape of his day. In contrast to Innocent IV
(who defended the papal position that independent princes possessed legitimate
war-making authority) Bartolus works from the assumption that in Europe only
the Roman emperor (and his Germanic successors) had full authority to declare
war.[2] In practice this raised a difficult set of questions, since the medieval system
of governance allowed cities and feudal jurisdictions various degrees of independence vis-à-vis the Empire. What was the status of the Christian kings, for instance
those ruling over France, who no longer considered themselves subordinate to
the emperor? Should they still be considered members of the Empire such that
the rules of *postliminium* would apply to their respective peoples? Were the rulers
of independent cities (Florence and Pisa are cited as examples) allowed, legally
speaking, to resort to the sword? And which of the peoples who stood wholly

---

[1] See Frederick H. Russell, *The Just War in the Middle Ages* (Cambridge: Cambridge University
Press, 1975), chap. 2, "The Medieval Romanists' Analysis of War" (pp. 40–54) for background on
the glossators and post-glossators; cf. Peter Haggenmacher, *Grotius et la doctrine de la guerre juste*
(Paris: Presses Universitaires de France, 1983), pp. 37–9.

[2] Bartolus was well acquainted with the writings of Innocent IV and other Decretalists. His "public
war" (*bellum publicum*) corresponds to what Innocent had earlier termed "war properly speaking"
(*bellum proprie dictum*). Bartolus likewise adopts Innocent's key claim that legitimate war-making
authority vests in the ruler who has no superior, although he differs from Innocent in identifying this
ruler first and foremost with the emperor. In practice, however, the two jurists are not as far apart as
they may seem, since Bartolus is able to acknowledge that some Italian city-states are independent of
the Empire; hence their rulers have no common superior to whom they could appeal for resolution of
their differences (on this, see Haggenmacher, *Grotius et la doctrine*, p. 116).

outside the Empire (Greeks, Tartars, Turks, Saracens [Muslims], Jews, and Indians) should be considered "enemies" and which not? Finally, by what jurisdiction could lower potentates and even private individuals resort to arms in self-defense? Could this be considered an instance of war? These are the sorts of issues taken up by Bartolus. Together they open a window on the normative status of war-making authority in the (secular) legal literature of fourteenth-century Europe.

From *Secunda super Digesto novo,* ad *Dig.,* 49, 15, 24, foll. 236r-v[3]

On Captives and Postliminy

[Ulpian,[4] *Digest,* 49, 15, 24: "Enemies" are those upon whom the Roman People has publicly declared war, or those who have themselves declared war upon the Roman People; the rest are called brigands or robbers. And therefore someone who has been captured by brigands is not a slave to the brigands, nor is he in need of postliminy; but someone captured by enemies, as by Germans or Parthians, becomes a slave to the enemies, and regains his former condition by postliminy.]

Enemies (nn. 1–16)

This law is divided into four parts: for it explains first who are enemies; second, who are brigands; third, what is the legal condition of captives by brigands; fourth, what is the legal condition of captives by enemies. The second part [starts] at: "the rest"; the third at: "And therefore"; the fourth at: [but someone] "captured by enemies."

On the one side: it would seem that any city would have its enemies, such as those against whom a city declares public war, as says the gloss [to *Dig.,* 49, 15, 21]. I admit that these are enemies; not, however, of the sort to which the laws of captivity and postliminy apply, because they are not [enemies] of the Roman People, but of that city; which is true. I, however, say [1][5] that just as the

---

[3] Lyon: Gryphius, 1533. Translation by Robert Andrews and Peter Haggenmacher. The Latin text includes Bartolus's textual references, which have been omitted here. For an analysis of this text, see Peter Haggenmacher, *Grotius et la doctrine* (Paris: Presses Universitaires de France, 1983), pp. 114–17.

[4] Ulpian, a Syrian jurisconsult writing in the third century AD, became one of the most widely cited authors from Justinian's *Digest* and has been considered, through his influence on medieval law-making and not least due to his concept of natural law, one of the most influential lawyers of all time.

[5] The summaries to which the numbers refer are here omitted, as they merely paraphrase the text for practical purposes; they were added only in the age of printing, probably in the sixteenth century.

enemies of the Roman People lose what depends on the civil law of the Romans, so the enemies of whatever city lose what depends on the civil law proper to that city; thus, if that city would have certain statutes and privileges, such statutes would be of no use to them. This is what I said in the disputation that dealt with the subject matter of banishment. . . .

These things having been stated at the outset, the gloss here says that there are five sorts of peoples. In explaining this I shall not follow the order of the gloss. [2] You should know that there are in principle two sorts of peoples: first, the Roman People; second, foreign peoples, as is proven above [at *Dig.*, 49, 15, 7].

[3] Concerning the first sort I ask, who may be called the Roman People? The gloss says that here it is taken to mean the entire Roman Empire. . . . But you might say: since there are few peoples who obey the Roman Empire, therefore it seems that the Roman People is very small. I answer: There are some peoples who obey the Roman Empire – and these without doubt are among the Roman People – and there are some who do not obey the Roman Empire in all matters, but in some ways, as for example because they live according to the law of the Roman People, and they accept that the Roman emperor is the ruler of all. Such are the cities of Tuscany and Lombardy and others; and these also belong to the Roman People; for when [4] the Roman People exercises jurisdiction over them in some respect, it retains total jurisdiction. . . .

There are some peoples who do not at all obey the emperor (*principi*), nor live according to these laws; and this they claim to do according to a privilege granted by the emperor. These likewise belong to the Roman People, such as Venice does. For since they claim to have this liberty from the Roman Empire by a privilege, in a certain way they hold it precariously, and [the emperor] could revoke this privilege whenever he wishes, since it is permissible for him to alter his will. . . . Moreover, the privilege granted to them ought to be in their interest, so as not to deprive them of Roman citizenship. . . .

There are some people who do not obey the emperor (*principi*), but claim that they have their liberty from him by some contract, such as the provinces which are held by the Roman Church, which were donated by emperor Constantine to the Roman Church with the understanding that the donation holds in such a way that it cannot be revoked. Again I say that they belong to the Roman People, for the Roman Church exercises in those lands a jurisdiction which belonged to the Roman Empire, and they acknowledge this. Therefore they do not cease to be a part of the Roman People, but the administration of these provinces is conceded to someone else. [5] Similarly, jurisdiction over clerics is conceded entirely to the pope; but clerics do not cease to be Roman citizens on this account; by no means, which is apparent since they retain the right of succession. [6] And I say the same about those other kings and princes who deny that they are subordinate to the king of the Romans – such as the king of France, of England, and others; if indeed they admit that [the emperor] is the universal ruler, even though they remove themselves from that universal dominion because of a privilege, or by prescription,[6] or the like, they do not cease to be Roman citizens because of the aforesaid reasons; and according to this almost all peoples who obey the holy mother Church belong to the Roman people. [7] And if someone perhaps were to say that the lord emperor is not the ruler and monarch of the whole world, he would be heretical, because he would speak contrary to the determination of the Church, [and] contrary to the text of the Holy Gospel when it says: "There went out a decree from Caesar Augustus that all the world should be taxed," according to Luke, chapter 2 or 3; and so even Christ recognized the emperor as ruler. The aforesaid is true, unless a public war would be declared against any of the above, because then they would become enemies due to the declaration of war, as I say below.

[8] In the second place I said that the other peoples are foreign. Those are properly foreign peoples who do not acknowledge that the Roman emperor is the universal ruler – such as the Greeks, who do not believe that the Roman emperor is the universal ruler, but instead declare that the emperor of Constantinople is the ruler of the whole world. Next, the Tartars, who declare that the great Khan is the universal ruler. And the Saracens, who say that their ruler is the ruler of the whole world; and the same with the Jews. But among these there is a difference, for some of them are our confederates, as the Greeks were confederates with us against the Turks. There are some of them with whom we are at peace, such as the Tartars, for our merchants travel to them, and theirs to us. There are some with whom we have neither peace nor war, nor anything to do, as with those in India. There are some with whom we have declared war, as with the Saracens, and at present with the Turks. But only few of these foreigners [come] to us.

[9] Having considered these things, we should see who may declare war, and what is the effect of a declared war. And let us examine this among our peoples.

I answer that there is one sort of war which can be declared by any private person, so that in defense or recovery of his property on the spot (*incontinenti*) he can gather people and justly fight against the others. . . . Likewise, you may declare war for the recovery of property after an interval, if there is no judge available for your protection. . . . And although this sort of war is licit, it is not, however, public; and accordingly [those who wage it] are not properly called enemies toward each other. [10] And those captured therein do not thereby belong to the captors, because this requires that there be a public war, as it is said here in the text . . . although the homicides and wounds inflicted on that occasion by the one who makes war licitly are not punished. . . .

[11] Furthermore, anyone having jurisdiction can declare a lawful war in the exercise of his jurisdiction. . . . And although this war is just, it is not, however, public in the way which is meant here. Therefore those who are captured therein

---

[6] "Prescription" is a legal term indicating that an unchallenged legal situation which has prevailed for a given number of years (e.g. regularly drawing water from a well on another's property) has acquired the force of law despite its initial irregularity.

do not belong to the captors, nor do the captives become slaves, unless some law be promulgated on this by the general or the commander or the king who declared the war; this is the opinion held by Innocent [IV]. . . . [12] Therefore, I say that if the ruler of a dukedom or a marquisate declares war against another land, those who are captured do not belong to the captors, and the captives do not become slaves, unless some decree or sentence intervenes over this beforehand. [13] It would seem, however, that if someone is a rebel against an officer or rector of the Church, then he is a rebel against the whole Church, which holds the place of the Empire in these regions; but I shall respond to this below.

[14] A public war is declared in a third way, when it is declared by the Roman People or by the emperor, in whom is invested all of the jurisdiction of the Roman People. . . . Likewise, when someone declares war against the emperor. . . . And therefore I hold that the Italian cities against whom the emperor declared war – such as against the city of Florence and others – are truly enemies of the Empire, and the captives become slaves; and the property which is captured therein belongs to the captors – not meaning thereby the individual captors as such, since in some cases it is sold by public authority, as I shall show below [at *Dig.*, 49, 15, 28].

[15] Concerning the preceding, I ask what happens if some city or land resists an official of the lord emperor or of the supreme pontiff in a land which is under his command: are they because of this truly called enemies? I answer that at times somebody rebels against an official not on account of the official but of the prince; therefore, since he does not want to obey the prince, he seems to rebel against the prince, and to declare war against the prince. And this is what is intended by the aforesaid constitution of emperor [Henry].[7] . . . But if someone should rebel against a governor on account of an action of that governor, because he treats them badly, as do the ducal and marquisate cities, then [these rebels] should not be called enemies of the emperor or the supreme pontiff, but of that governor; and so is intended by what has been said.

[16] Moreover, I ask about those wars which are between cities and cities, whether they might be called enemies of each other, so that the law of captivity and postliminy applies. And it seems that it does not, as appears in the *casus* on [*Dig.*, 49, 15, 21] at the end. But the contrary would seem to hold: nowadays, since every city in itself constitutes a free people, it would seem that the law of captivity and postliminy prevails, just as when there is a conflict between the Roman People and the Saracens.

---

[7] Bartolus clearly refers to emperor Henry VII's constitution *Ad reprimendum* of 1312, already alluded to above, at [1]; see his comment on this constitution in *Consilia, Quaestiones, Tractatus Bartoli*, s.l. 1533, fol. 76v–86r, especially fol. 85r–86r. Yet strangely the emperor appears in this place as *fe*. (*Fe.* in the edition of Venice in 1499) which rather seems to point to Frederic (latinized as Federicus in the Italian manner). But this might just be a copyist's or printer's error for *He.*, faithfully reproduced in subsequent manuscripts or editions.

In brief, when there is a conflict between some cities that are under the same ruler (*domino*), then between them the law of captivity and postliminy does not apply, as in [*Dig.*, 49, 15, 21]. When there is a conflict between two cities that do not recognize any superior, as between the city of Florence and the city of Pisa; and suppose, in order to leave no doubt whatever, that each of these is an enemy of the Empire; then it is certain that, under the law of nations introduced by old custom, the law of captivity and postliminy ought to apply. . . . Yet, according to the usages of modern times and custom long observed among Christians, we do not observe the law of captivity and postliminy as regards persons, nor are captives sold or made slaves; but as to things, we maintain these laws, and this custom ought to be observed. . . .

As to how and by what right war is declared against the Saracens, refer to Innocent [IV] on *Decretals* [III, 34, 8], *De voto*, chapter *Quod super his*.

19

Christine de Pizan (ca. 1364–ca. 1431)

War and Chivalry

> There is absolutely nothing that so needs to be conducted with good judgment as war and battle.
>
> *The Book of Deeds of Arms and of Chivalry*

Chivalry – the word evokes images of brave knights, ladies in distress, and wars fought for noble purposes in a gentlemanly way. To many, chivalric ideals represent the most romantic and desirable elements of the High and Late Middle Ages, vividly portrayed in tales of courtly love written by the likes of Chrétien de Troyes and Andreas Capellanus, and of later sages such as Sir Walter Scott (but also boldly parodied and criticized in Cervantes's immortal tale of Don Quixote from the seventeenth century and by the British comedy troupe Monty Python closer to our own time).

The intensely mythical aura surrounding chivalry makes it hard to distinguish fact from fiction. However, there is little doubt that chivalric ideals of bravery, restraint, and nobility were experienced as very real by many military men in the period from the twelfth through the sixteenth centuries, and these ideals would in turn influence the way in which warfare was understood and portrayed among academic writers. Crucially, chivalric writings included detailed and then quite novel reflections on what we today term *ius in bello* – right conduct in war – and they may be credited with giving this theme a prominence that it had not previously enjoyed within the just war tradition.

One of the best representatives of the chivalric approach to military ethics is the French writer Christine de Pizan. Her writings on the subject stand as an eloquent summary of the military code of honor that had already circulated in Europe since the twelfth century. Yet her work is distinctive in the care that she exhibits for ordinary men and women, and her desire to see them protected from the ravages of war.

We should note, however, that in showcasing Christine's perspectives on chivalry, we are in effect also including insights from three other authors who were important sources for her thought, and to whom she often referred.

First, there was the Roman writer Vegetius (fourth century AD), whose treatise on military matters *Epitoma rei militaris* (or *De rei militaris*) was popular throughout the Latin Middle Ages. For Christine, Vegetius was more a source of knowledge on military tactics and strategy than on ethics and chivalric ideals. Yet his influence even in ethics should be mentioned, since she returns time and again to the opposition which he emphasized between smartness and cunning on the one hand, and rashness and shallow virility on the other.

Second, there was the Italian jurist John of Legnano (d. 1383), whose *Tractatus de bello* supplied Christine with a conception of just war. Christine may even have been acquainted personally with John, through her father, since the two men had likely moved in the same academic circles during their time together at the University of Bologna.

And finally there is Honoré Bonet (or Bouvet), ca. 1340–1410, whose *Arbre de batailles* (*Tree of Battles*) summed up the most crucial tenets of chivalry. The work also presented John of Legnano's conception of just war principles to a French audience. The two final parts of Christine's book on chivalry and warfare are constructed as a dialogue with a wise old man who, albeit unnamed, is undoubtedly Honoré Bonet. Despite her high regard for Bonet, Christine nevertheless departed from him in one important respect. Bonet viewed war as a noble human pursuit and had relatively little to say about the many evils which inevitably follow in its wake. Christine, by contrast, was more attuned to the dark side of war: she provided vivid depictions of the suffering and greed which accompany the waging of even just wars. Although she follows Bonet in praising the good things done by chivalrous knights and soldiers, and stresses that the evils of war should not lead us to condemning war as such, she is more skeptical towards the use of military force than Bonet.[1]

Christine was also distinctive by virtue of the audience that she chose to address. Rather than writing for professors of theology, law, or philosophy, she sought first and foremost to convey chivalric ideals to military men of action.

Christine experienced several profound disappointments in her long career as a writer, most especially in seeing the French mired in internal quarrels and losing the famous Battle of Agincourt in 1415 against the English. But she seems never to

---

[1] See James Turner Johnson, *Ideology, Reason, and the Limitation of War* (Princeton, NJ: Princeton University Press, 1975), pp. 67–73, for an excellent portrayal of Bonet's seeming enthusiasm about war. It should be noted that Christine's regrets about war are even more obvious in other works of hers, such as in her poetic and forceful lamentations on the civil war in France, written under the title of *La Lamentation sur les maux de France* (also called *La Lamentation sur la guerre civile*). We are grateful to Kate Forhan for pointing this out.

have lost faith in the ideals of restraint, piety, and respect for the common man and woman that she understood to be the essence of the chivalric tradition.

The excerpts below are taken mainly from her *Book of Deeds of Arms and of Chivalry* (ca. 1410) although we also include some passages from a later work, *The Book of Peace* (ca. 1412). The former presents lofty ideals in combination with very concrete guidelines. Indeed, in this tension we find the essence of chivalry: It was a tradition rooted in the ideals of a select group of noblemen, who saw themselves as fighting war for the sake of piety, right, and noble damsels in distress – ideals far from the reality of the ill-trained mercenaries and profit-seekers who increasingly played a role in medieval warfare. Yet, these chivalric ideals were not without effect on the military practice of the day and, more importantly still, would exert a notable influence on the formation of military norms in later periods. Thanks to writers such as Honoré Bonet and Christine de Pizan, abstract principles of right conduct in war were usefully applied to a set of highly concrete issues. Indeed, without the tradition of chivalry, the modern science of international law would have lacked a vital resource in formulating what today are termed "laws of war": a set of rules that are meant to guide the actions of all combatants on the battlefield. The fact that they are meant to apply equally to all combatants, and as such do not first ask the question about which party to the conflict has the just cause for fighting, makes it reasonable to call Christine as much a proponent of the "regular war" idea as a traditional "just war" thinker. (For more on the distinction between regular war and just war, see chap. 20, this volume, on Raphaël Fulgosius.)

The first group of excerpts is drawn mainly from part I of Christine's book on chivalry. These passages discuss just and unjust resort to arms, the good and bad behavior of military leaders, and the conduct of negotiations. Much of the remainder of the first part (not included here) recounts advice from Vegetius on the best use of troops and the preparations for battle. Part II, also omitted, contains lessons drawn from Roman history and further advice from Vegetius on military matters, with an emphasis on equipment and logistics.

Note that Christine's category of political leaders with a legitimate authority to wage war is somewhat broader than what was commonly found among medieval just war theorists (see pt. I, chap. 3, below) and even includes landed lords with temporal authority. This probably reflects an important aspect of the political practice of her day, as Christine saw it, with a very real need to face up to the many bands of mercenary robbers who illegitimately waged *de facto* wars. However, her requirement that any war-making authority must be sovereign within his realm is the same that we find in other thinkers of her time, and she is clearly critical of those who act outside of their temporal jurisdiction in declaring war.[2]

---

[2]   This was usefully pointed out by Dr. Kate Forhan in a paper on Christine de Pizan and Geoffrey Chaucer, presented at the American Political Science Association Annual Meeting in 2000, to be published in Gregory Reichberg and Henrik Syse (eds.), *Ethics, Nationalism, and Just War: Medieval and Contemporary Perspectives* (Washington, DC: Catholic University of America Press, forthcoming).

From *The Book of Deeds of Arms and of Chivalry,* pt. I, chaps. 2–5, 7, 20[3]

2 ... [I]n order that this present work may not be accused by some envious people of being the product of idleness and a waste of time, as if it dealt with illicit matters, it is of primary concern to learn whether wars and battles, deeds of arms and of chivalry, of which we hope to speak, are to be considered just matters or not, for in the exercise of arms many great wrongs, extortions, and grievous deeds are committed, as well as rapine, killings, forced executions, and arson; all of these may well seem to some detestable and improper. For this reason, in answer to this question, it seems manifest that wars undertaken for a just cause are permitted by God. We have proof of this in several places in Holy Writ. ... As for the evils committed outside what is right in war, as the authorities say, these are not the result of what is right in war, but of the evil will of people who misuse war. I hope, with God's help, to touch on matters that are limited by civil law and also canon law in the exercise of arms.

3 ... If it is lawful for each person to engage in war to preserve his own right, then it would seem reasonable that any man could start a war; but to point out the truth to those who might err on this point, it should be understood that there is no doubt in law, or in laws, that the undertaking of war or battle for whatever reason belongs to no one except to sovereign princes, which is to say, emperors, kings, dukes, and other landed lords who are duly and rightfully heads of temporal jurisdictions. No baron, or any other person, however great he may be, may undertake war without the express permission and will of his sovereign lord. That this law is right is demonstrated by plain reason, for if it were otherwise, of what use would the sovereign princes be, who were not set up except to do right for and on behalf of their subjects who might be oppressed by some extortion, to defend them and keep them as the good shepherd risks his life for his flock? For this reason, the subject must turn to his lord as to his refuge whenever he is harmed in some way, and the good lord will take up arms for him, if need be. This is to say that he will help him, by virtue of his power, to maintain his rights, either by justice or recourse to arms.

4 As it belongs to sovereign princes to undertake and carry on wars and battles, we must now consider the causes by which, according to lawful means, they may be initiated and pursued. In this regard one is well advised, it seems to me, to remember that five grounds are commonly held to be the basis of wars, three of

---

[3] From Christine de Pizan, *The Book of Deeds of Arms and of Chivalry* (orig. title: *Le Livre des fais d'armes et de la chevalerie*), ed. Charity Cannon Willard, trans. Sumner Willard (University Park: Pennsylvania State University Press, 1999), pp. 14, 15–18, 19, 24, 25, 58, 59–60. We are also indebted to this edition for useful perspectives on Christine's sources and ideas.

which rest on law and the remaining two on will. The first lawful ground on
which wars may be undertaken or pursued is to maintain law and justice; the
second is to counteract evildoers who befoul, injure, and oppress the land and
the people; and the third is to recover lands, lordships, and other things stolen
or usurped for an unjust cause by others who are under the jurisdiction of the
prince, the country, or its subjects. As for the two of will, one is to avenge any
loss or damage incurred, the other to conquer and take over foreign lands or
lordships.

Returning to the first of these points, which concerns justice, it should be
remembered that there are three chief causes under which a king or prince is
empowered to undertake and carry out wars and battles. The first is to uphold
and defend the Church and its patrimony against anyone who would defile it; this
is expected of all Christian princes. The second is to act on behalf of a vassal, if he
should require it, in cases where the prince must settle a quarrel and is duly
obliged to bring about an agreement among various parties, but then only if the
adversary proves to be intractable. And third, the prince, if it pleases him, may
justly go to the aid of any other prince, baron, or other ally and friend of his, or
to help any country or land, if the need arises and if the quarrel is just. In this
point are included widows, orphans, and all who are unjustly trampled under
foot by another power.

For this purpose, and likewise for the other two aforementioned purposes, that
is, to counteract evildoers and to recover lost property, it is not only permissible
for the prince to start a war or to maintain it, indeed he is obliged to do so,
through the obligation incurred by his title to lordship and jurisdiction in accordance with his proper duty.

As for the other two points, the one regarding revenge for some damage or
loss inflicted by another prince, the other regarding acquisition of foreign lands
without title to them – even though conquerors in the past, such as Alexander,
the Romans, and others have done so, and have been praised and accorded chivalric
titles, as have those who wreaked vengeance upon their enemies, for better or for
worse – despite the fact that such actions are commonly undertaken, I do not find
in divine law or in any other text, for causes such as these without any other
ground, that it is acceptable to start any kind of war or battle upon any Christian
land, but rather the contrary.

For according to God's law it is not proper for man either to seize or to usurp
anything belonging to another, or even to covet it. Likewise, vengeance is reserved
for God alone, and in no way does any man have the right to carry it out.

Thus, to set forth our ideas on this subject more clearly, and to answer any
questions that might arise, it is true that it is lawful for any prince to keep for
himself the same right that is granted to others. As for what the just prince would
do if he considered himself wronged by some other power, should he simply
depart, in order to obey divine law, without taking any further actions? In God's
name, no, for divine law does not deny justice, but rather mandates that it should

be carried out and requires punishment for misdeeds. In order that a prince may go about this matter justly, he will follow this course: he will gather together a great council of wise men in his parliament, or in that of his sovereign if he is a subject, and not only will he assemble those of his own realm, but in order that there be no suspicion of favor, he will also call upon some from foreign countries that are known not to take sides, elder statesmen as well as legal advisors and others; he will propose or have proposed the whole matter in full without holding anything back, for God cannot be deceived, everything according to what may be right or wrong, and he will conclude by saying that he wishes to recount everything and hold to the determination of doing right. In short, by these points the affair will be put to order, clearly seen and discussed, and if through such a process it appears that his cause is just, he will summon his adversary to demand of him restitution and amends for his injuries and the wrong done him. Now if it comes about that the adversary in question puts up a defense and tries to contradict what has been said, let him be heard fully without special favor, but also without willfulness or spite. If these things are duly carried out, as the law requires, then the just prince may surely undertake war, which on no account should be called vengeance, but rather the complete carrying out of due justice.

5 As it is licit for a prince to engage in wars and battles, pursuing them for the reasons mentioned above, and as these are great and weighty matters that touch the lives, the blood, and the honor and the fortunes of an infinite number of people, it is necessary to look closely into the matter, for without such a look no such thing should be undertaken, nor should it be undertaken lightly by anyone without experience. . . .

Therefore, it is necessary for the prince to be wise, or at the very least be disposed to use wise counsel, for as Plato said, fortunate is the country where the wise govern, for otherwise it is cursed, as Holy Scripture also testifies. There is absolutely nothing that so needs to be conducted with good judgment as war and battle, as will be seen later. No mistake made in any other circumstances is less possible to repair than one committed by force of arms and by a battle badly conducted. . . .

7 . . . It should also be noted that in [the selection of a constable to serve as master of the King's cavalry] greater attention should be given to perfection of skill in arms, along with the virtues and the character and good bearing that should accompany this, than to exalted lineage or noble blood, although if both were to be found in the same person it would be very useful, for the simple reason that the nobler the blood, the greater the esteem in which he would be held in exercising his office, a quality necessary to every leader. . . . [I]t would be a matter for reproach, however distinguished the blood, to give the charge to an ignorant person, especially where subtlety, good sense, and experience are more needed than even the number of troops or any other kind of force. . . .

It should also be remembered that according to the customs of gentility and true nobility a leader must observe in the conduct of arms in any circumstance that may arise all that good breeding requires, if he wishes to gain due honor and praise, meaning that even to his enemies he must be upright and truthful in act and judgment wherever required. Along with this, he will honor those who are good and meritorious as he would wish to be honored by them. This custom was observed by the valiant King Pyrrhus of Macedonia, who gained great praise because, having observed so many brave deeds among the Romans, he honored them greatly when they came to him as envoys, even though they were his bitter enemies, and he even gave those killed in battle an honorable burial. Concerning the nobility of that king and his great openheartedness it is further written that he held the Romans in such great respect that he did not even wish to retain the prisoners captured in battle, but rather released them freely. . . .

20 . . . Now let us consider another situation: on a field of battle, where two armies are drawn up with great effort on both sides to engage in a day of battle, for certain reasons they instead enter into discussion of a treaty and peace. It thus becomes necessary to keep in mind what has already been said, that the commander must be wise enough that in all matters he can work to his best advantage. . . .

[I]f the pope has sent a representative to bring about peace, or another prince or lord inspired by good will (although he should have first approached the prince) has intervened, or in the event that you yourself are the prince, you should in such circumstances explain thoroughly the action, case, right, or just quarrel that you have for making war against the opponent, so that the arbitrator in question, who would like to end this conflict without bloodshed, may be well advised to have presented to you sufficient amends and satisfaction, pointing out to the enemy their great wrong. Likewise, if the enemy insists on having the greater right, do not be so blind that this will prevent you from submitting to what is reasonable. If you believe that in certain matters you are right and in others not, you should be the more willing to consent to the treaty and allow a part of the demands of the others without dishonoring yourself, if you can do better by giving up something that is really your right.

Let us suppose further that the enemy army is smaller, and that yours is increased in numbers and strength and the other diminished through some misfortune, so that they fear battle and thus wish to negotiate and achieve peace, making you good offers in order better to establish their rights and to avoid bloodshed; what would you do then? Or even if they were inspired to want peace, though their strength was more or less the equal of yours, should you be so proud as to make them think that as they would be at a disadvantage if it came to battle, you would by no means wish to come to an agreement? Even so that the more offers that were made, the more difficult you would be? No, indeed, for you would scarcely find that in refusing just offers, however right they might be, however large the number of men with reference to fewer, that misfortune might not overcome them in the end; for it seems that in such a case God would have it in for those who refuse, and so punish them. But you must look at this carefully, for there is a danger that you may be deceived treacherously by dishonest means, under the pretense of discussing peace. How can you recognize this? In God's name, by conjecture, you can have the appearance of suspecting this and being on your guard, whereby, if it should happen that the idea of entering into a treaty should come from one of your own men, by his condition you can consider what might be the cause that has moved him to wish for a treaty; for if he is wise, prudent, and with a just conscience, and you know him to be thus, you should not be surprised that such a man would willingly look for a way to avoid bloodshed by a good and honorable treaty and that there should be peace. But if it is a man not usually to be found in such a situation, lacking in courage although he may be clever and speak well, you may conclude that this could come from cowardliness, but even so you should not entirely discard his arguments, but rather consider if these are good and whether they resound to your honor and profit.

In parts III and IV, Christine addresses a "master" – Christine's most important mentor in matters of chivalry and war, namely, Honoré Bonet (although, as we will see, he remains unnamed). Several of Christine's chapters closely follow Bonet's treatment in his *Tree of Battles*, although there are also passages original to Christine. In the course of these pages, we come to see the essence of the *ius in bello*, as it was understood in the early fifteenth century, with an emphasis on the protection of non-combatants, the fair treatment of prisoners, the proper payment of soldiers, and the keeping of promises.

We should note that Christine is not as specific about what constitutes non-combatant status as her mentor Bonet had been. Yet it is clear that she agrees with him in holding farmers, clergymen, women, children, and the working poor who take no part in the war, to be people who should not be hurt or intentionally harassed. Likewise, prisoners of war were to be treated humanely.

There is some ambiguity in Christine as to whether non-combatants who actively support a prince who wages an unjust war should be shielded – first it seems not, but then she immediately adds a general exhortation to restraint of force towards all those who are not warriors (see pt. III, chap. 18, below).

From *The Book of Deeds of Arms and of Chivalry*, pt. III, chaps. 7, 12–14, 17–18, 21, 23[4]

7 Master, if I understand you correctly, all subjects are bound to go to war with their lord if they are called upon to do so, not at their expense but accepting their

[4] Ibid., pp. 152–3, 161–2, 163–4, 165–6, 169, 170, 171–2, 176–8, 180–1.

lord's wages.[5] If you please, I have another question. I ask you whether men-at-arms, from the same place or perhaps strangers, may properly and without burdening the soul accept wages from lords, towns, or countries to which they are neither native nor subject, even though such is the generally accepted custom. It would seem not, in view of the fact that war involves killing others and various other kinds of evil, things forbidden among Christians by God's law.

To this question, friend, I answer as follows: You yourself have touched on it enough at the beginning of this book, that every man may go to a just war and accept wages for serving there. For a just war may keep on to recover what is right, of which the limits may not be overstepped by any means, which is to say, by pillaging friendly lands and various other sorts of grievances that men-at-arms carry out frequently, thereby misbehaving seriously. This is unjust and is not sanctioned by law, yet it is allowed. For it is in the very execution of justice that God suffers and permits it, to the end that wrong may be made right, even though God suffers wars to be fought sometimes against all right and reason; this is like the scourge of God and the punishment for the sins of the people.

But to return to the first question: I say to you that every man who quite properly wishes to expose himself to war should, before he becomes involved, be well informed of the nature of the quarrel in order to know whether the challenge is just or not. If you ask me how he shall be able to know this, as all parties that wage war insist that their cause is just, let him inquire if this war has first been judged by competent jurists or lawyers, or whether it may be for the cause of defense, for all wars are just in case of defense, which is to say, defending one's country when it is attacked. In this matter the warrior should be well informed before he engages in it. You should know that if the quarrel is unjust, he that exposes himself in it condemns his soul; and if he dies in such a state, he will go the way of perdition without great repentance through divine grace at the last. But many make light of this, for there are plenty who care not a whit what the quarrel is, so long as they have good wages and may commit robbery. Alas, the sorrowful payment often arrives, for a single stroke suddenly struck can send them to hell forever. And along with this, all, or most of them, forget that those who pass in the exercise of arms the limits of proper warfare, whatever the quarrel, just or not, as limited by law, condemn themselves to perdition. . . .

---

[5] Elsewhere in the book, Christine admits one morally based exception to this general duty, namely, when the emperor makes war on the pope: "Thus the subjects should not in these circumstances properly obey the summons to war if they do not wish to disobey God in persecuting His church" (pt. III, chap. 2, pp. 145–6). From what is said further down in chap. 7, it seems that each soldier ought also to examine the causes of the war – not only in the case of war against the church – to know that it is a just war. But Christine does not elaborate on this idea or turn it into a general doctrine of legitimate disobedience. In general, one is obliged to obey one's sovereign prince. What she seems to have primarily in mind in chap. 7 are professional knights or soldiers who offer their services to various courts and princes: these are required to make sure that the cause for which they enlist their services is a legitimate one.

12 Master, I recall that you once said that a man may injure another in self-defense. As all blows and injuries are sometimes called acts of war, I wish to put this question to you: A man has injured another, and soon after striking the blow, he flees as far as he can. But the injured party goes after him, overtakes him, and injures him. I ask you whether the pursuer should be punished. From what you have said, it would seem not, in view of the fact that he did not exceed the limits of justice. As he was the first one to be assaulted, he has the right of self-defense and should be excused, even if he has killed his adversary. Also he did not wait, for if he had waited until another day, I would not say this, for that would be vengeance.

I answer that the case you bring up is quite different from just defense, which is privileged. This is to say that according to law, as the first assailant fled after delivering the blow, the law does not permit the injured one to pursue him and injure him in turn; for this he deserves to be punished. But it is true that the first one did the other a great disservice, and whether the second deserves a greater or lesser punishment is a matter of disagreement among the masters. Yet there can be no doubt that the first movement caused by being assaulted and by the heat of the moment excuses a great deal, for which the second should be only moderately punished. But if he had killed the other when the other struck the first blow, and it can be proved that said other struck first, justice has no part in the affair, because he was struck by a sword. To protect one's life the law permits one to kill another. If you tell me that perhaps the assailant had no intention of killing, I reply that the one struck did not know this, and blows are not struck according to a pattern. One strikes only to kill, so that the first to strike may be first killed. But notwithstanding these matters, from conscience a man must make every effort not to kill another. Nothing is so displeasing to God as that a man should kill his fellow. He is the judge of all things, who punishes everything according to its due, nor can anything be hidden or concealed from Him. . . .

13 I would put to you another question, different from the last one: is it reasonable and right for a king or prince to resort to trickery to subdue and overcome his enemy, whether in battle or elsewhere? The answer would appear to be no, considering what is right and reasonable. It is in no way right for someone to deceive another. Furthermore, any person who has a just quarrel ought to have good hope in God, whose good fortune should be with him if he pursues his objective with effort and diligence. Therefore, he who has a just quarrel should follow, it would seem, a straight path in war without resorting to wiles.

Daughter and dear friend, you speak very well, but nevertheless I must point out that in accordance with the laws of arms, what is indeed more important, according to God and Holy Scripture, is that one should conquer one's enemy by ruse, wiles, or tricks without doing wrong in arms, seeing that war is judged and involves both sides, and so it is true that this is possible. Even our Lord gave an example of this, when he ordered and showed Joshua how by wile he could surprise his enemies. Such tactics are commonly used to help in arms. But I must confess that there are certain kinds of tricks that are unacceptable and forbidden in deeds of arms as well as in all other cases. For instance, were I to assure somebody that if he came to see me in an allotted place, I would be there to speak with him, and he came according to my assurance, and I surprised him there by some trick to harm him or kill or capture him, such an act would be right evil treason. Or if by feigned truce or peace I should take my advantage to injure another when his guard is down and he thinks he is safe, in all such cases I would do evil and bring dishonor and reproof on myself. In these cases I would do wrong, to my great dishonor, reproach, and sin. Therefore the law says that as faith is given to one's enemy, it should be respected. But it is another matter if a valiant man-at-arms or some wise commander knows how to set up ambushes the enemy must pass through, not being on his guard, or other sorts of tricks, provided these are not contrary to promises or assurances that have been given. And nothing is to be said about the reason you give, that one should wait on God, although basically I agree with you. But however much right is on the side of the king of France against the English king, or in another such case, he must help to sustain his own cause, and so it is that whenever with intelligence and diligence men do their duty, they should put their hope in God that He will allow the matter to be brought to a good and suitable conclusion.

14 ... Now, Master, hear me out if you are so disposed: if men-at-arms are given wages and there is no irregularity in their payment, can they, in addition to their wages, take supplies from the countryside, and take anything else, as they commonly do nowadays in France?

I assure you absolutely not, for such things have nothing to do with war but are wicked and violent extortions visited on common people. As you yourself have said before, a prince who is bent on waging a just war should take into account beforehand where and how it will be financed. Above all he must give the order that his men are to be well paid, so that they may pay properly for their necessities and whatever they take. It would also be just to punish those who take anything without paying for it. But by way of argument you might say to me: True, but what of the unexpected case in which the enemy came into the land suddenly, requiring a sudden defense before the prince had set aside a sufficient amount of money to pay the men month by month, so that in his treasury there were not sufficient funds?

I assure you that in every case of need they must do the best they can, even if in this case the prince might be excused for allowing them to take only absolute necessities on their way to sustain life, causing the least possible grief to the poor laborers. ...

17 Master, as we have turned to the subject of prisoners of war, I ask you whether a captured commander, or some important man, who has been very damaging to his captor or could be so if he escaped, can rightfully be put to death, for according to the law of nature it would appear so, as everything tends to destroy its opposite.

Certainly, friend, I answer that even though civil law says that one who is captured in battle is serf or slave of the one who takes him, he should not be killed. The decree affirms this by saying that as soon as a man is in prison, mercy is due him. Then it follows that if mercy is due him, how may he be put to death without wrong being done him?

But there is more to be said. Another decree states that if one man overcomes another, he is obliged to pardon him, especially his life. So I say to you that it is against right and gentility to slay the one who gives himself up. And the man's relatives might pursue the killer for doing wrong. But if a prince should take charge of him and remove him from the hands of the one who had captured him, and if for a good reason the prince, being advised that great harm might come to him and his own land if he let the prisoner go, should have him put to death, he had well deserved it, but otherwise it would be inhuman and excessively cruel. But if you tell me that the ancients had a law permitting them to kill their prisoners if they liked, or to sell them as slaves or put them to work in their service, I reply to you that among Christians, where the law is based on mercy and pity, it is not proper to use such tyranny, for it is denounced and reproved. . . .

I understand you very well, Master, but now tell me, as we Christians have now abandoned the laws of the ancients that permitted placing in servitude or slaying their prisoners, I ask you whether a demand may be made of a prisoner for gold or silver or some other thing of value of the sort that is customary in matters of war. For if I rightly remember, you have said before that mercy is properly due a prisoner. It seems to me that as this is a right, it would be a wrong to make him pay a ransom, as in this way he is not being shown mercy.

I say to you in further response that truly mercy is due him in two regards: this is to say that his life should be spared, and more important, the master is obliged to defend his prisoner against anyone else who would harm him. Likewise, mercy is due a man-at-arms who should have on him at the time of his capture all his valuables, which failing such exercise of mercy would all be for the captor. But according to written law the captor should act so that in exacting ransom, which is permitted according to military custom, especially when one nation is fighting against another, as French against English, and others likewise, care should be taken that the ransom is not so excessive that the man is ruined by it, his wife and children destroyed and reduced to poverty. That would be tyranny against conscience and all military custom, . . .

18 I ask you whether a king or prince, when warring against another, even though the war may be just, has the right to overrun the enemy land and take prisoner all manner of people, including common people, that is, peasants, shepherds, and such like; it would appear not. Why should they bear the burden of the profession of arms, of which they know nothing? It is not for them to pass judgment about war; common people are not called on to bear arms; rather, it is distasteful to them, for they say they want to live in peace and ask no more. They should be free, it seems to me, just as all priests and churchmen are, because their estate is outside military activity. What honor can accrue to a prince in killing, overrunning, or seizing people who have never borne arms nor could make use of them, or poor innocent people who do nothing but till the land and watch over animals?

To this I would answer with a supposition like this: Let us suppose that the people of England wished not to aid their king in injuring the king of France, and the French fell upon them instantly, with right and reason on their side. In accordance with lawful practice they should not in any way cause bodily harm to, or injure the property of, such people or those who did not come to aid the king, offering either goods or counsel. But if the subjects of that king or of another in a similar situation, be they poor or rich, farmers or anything else, give aid and comfort to maintain the war, according to military right the French may overrun their country and seize what they find, that is to say, prisoners of whatever class, and all manner of things, without being obliged by any law to return the same. For I tell you that this is determined as a matter of law, the law of war. For if a war is judged by the counselors of both kings or princes, the men-at-arms are free to dominate each other. And occasionally the poor and simple folk, who do not bear arms, are injured – and it cannot be otherwise, for weeds cannot be separated from good plants, because they are so close together that the good ones suffer. But in truth it is right that the valiant and good gentlemen-at-arms must take every precaution not to destroy the poor and simple folk, or suffer them to be tyrannized or mistreated, for they are Christians and not Saracens. And if I have said that pity is due some, remember that not less is due the others; those who engage in warfare may be hurt, but the humble and peaceful should be shielded from their force.

21 . . . Then tell me, if a Frenchman had taken the child of an Englishman, could he rightfully ask ransom for him? It would seem so, as someone who can do the largest thing can do the least, and he could indeed imprison the father if necessary. Why should he not then do the same with the son? Likewise and more important, as he could indeed take the possessions of the father, should the son be included among them?

I tell you with certainty that the child cannot and should not rightfully be imprisoned, for reason does not agree that innocence should be trifled with; for it is evident that the child is innocent and not guilty in anything connected with war. Nor has he helped with either advice or possessions, for he does not have any. Therefore he should not suffer the pain of something he is not guilty of.

True, Master, but suppose that the child in question were rich in his own right, left without father or mother, should he then pay? For perhaps his guardians would pay a subsidy from his possessions to help to maintain the war.

I still say no, for whatever his guardians might pay, it would not be at the wishes of the child, who has not reached the age of discretion.

Nevertheless, Master, that law is not well observed today.

I confess to you, fair friend, that no longer are the noble early rights preserved that the valiant warriors observed. Those who follow the military custom in the present time abuse it through the enormous greed that overcomes them. They should be ashamed to imprison women, children, helpless and old people. And what has been done by the English should be considered especially blameworthy, as carried on while fortune was favorable to them in the kingdom of France, where they didn't spare women or maidens, important, ordinary, or small, when they captured fortresses, but put to ransom all they found there, though it was a great shame for them to take those who could not avenge themselves. The capture of the fortress should have sufficed, and the ladies should have been allowed to go free. But what has happened to these warriors subsequently could and should be an example to other warriors to do otherwise, for thanks be to God they no longer have the power to imprison anyone. For rest assured that what has been wrongly acquired cannot be possessed a long time by those who have taken it or by their heirs.

Now let us consider another question: A blind man is captured by a man-at-arms. Should he be retained in prison?

I tell you that if a blind man has taken it into his head to want to be a man-at-arms and has done so, he deserves worse than another. I can prove this by Holy Scripture, where it tells how Cain killed Abel, his brother, and how a blind man named Lameth took a bow and arrow and went about woods and hedges shooting wild animals; so he struck by chance Cain and killed him. Then God said that Cain's crime should be punished seven times over, but the sin of Lameth should be punished seventy-six times. Thus it appears that taking on a task of which one is not capable is often folly. But if a simple blind person is captured, he deserves pity. If he formerly had his sight and had been a man-at-arms in the war, so that he gave advice to the English about waging battles or mounting assaults or some other stratagem, he can rightfully be held for ransom.

23[6] Now I will pose another question, which in the case of prisoners of war has a number of precedents. I am supposing that a knight has captured his enemy in battle and has put him in a castle or some other prison. My question is whether this prisoner, if he sees an opportunity, by some trick or by cleverness, to get away, can properly do so according to the law of war. I doubt this for several reasons, one of them that he has given his word, so he cannot leave without

---

[6]   In this chapter, the sequence of the paragraphs has been altered, in order to make the overall argument clearer. The paragraph beginning with "If the gentleman . . ." can be found on p. 181 in the Willard translation; the paragraph beginning with "[There are, however,] some reservations . . ." comes slightly before that and can be found on pp. 180–1 in the Willard translation.

perjuring himself, which is something the law does not permit. Another reason is that it is not permitted that one do to another something he would not want to have done to himself, and he would not want his prisoner to do such a thing. So he breaks this law in doing this. Another reason is that he is like a servant and in the power of another until he is free of his ransom, so he does wrong, it would seem, in that he takes something that is not his own, which cannot properly be done. . . .

[This question] needs to be decided according to the circumstances. . . .

If the gentleman has sworn to remain in prison, and his captor gives him enough to eat and drink and adequate lodging, and is willing to discuss with him a reasonable ransom when the time comes, and assures him that from the prison he will not suffer death or damage to his body or his health, such a prisoner breaks his word and does wrong, against military custom and to his dishonor, if, despite being well guarded, he escapes. For if he is a gentleman, he should do what is expected of him. . . .

[There are, however,] some reservations you should understand, which is to say that the master should not do him any harm in a proper prison, as is set forth by law, for I agree that if he were to be held so closely and so mistreated that his life and health were threatened, and all this were inhuman and cruel – or if the captor was unwilling to accept a reasonable ransom that had been offered several times – it would be sensible for him to find a way to escape, nor should it in any way be considered improper. Likewise, if the said captor were so cruel that he had the habit of killing or torturing his prisoners or making them languish in prison, or subjecting them to other such hardships as are against gentlemanly custom, anyone held by such a man would not be obliged to keep his word to him if there were some way he could escape, for his given word assumes that the captor is lord of the prisoner through military custom, and that the captor should treat him humanely, as is his right, and not treat him like an animal, or worse than a Saracen or Jew, who should not be treated so badly that it gives them reason to despair. For this reason I say to you that the one who first breaks and oversteps the custom deserves to be treated likewise.

Part IV deals, among other issues, with the question of "safe-conducts," agreements to respect an enemy's safe passage through one's territory. Here Christine writes that even Saracens (Muslims) should be allowed safe conduct under certain circumstances. Conceding such an immunity to a Saracen seems to have been quite unusual at the time, as evidenced by the fact that Christine finds it necessary to argue for this point.[7] The Saracens were considered to be a particularly pernicious enemy to whom the ordinary rules of war did not apply.

[7]   For a discussion of medieval Christian attitudes toward Muslims, see Tomaž Mastnak, *Crusading Peace: Christendom, the Muslim World, and Western Political Order* (Berkeley, University of California Press, 2002).

From *The Book of Deeds of Arms and of Chivalry,* pt. IV, ch. 3[8]

3 [Should safe-conduct be guaranteed to a Saracen, who is an enemy of the church?]

. . . Saracens are not merely at war with one Christian, but with all. The law says that something that affects all must be approved by all, for otherwise it is worthless. But there is another matter to consider, which is that the safe-conduct has been given for a good reason, to discuss and arrange the ransom of some lord, knight, or any other who is a prisoner in their hands, or for any other just and reasonable matter. Do not doubt then that not only the subjects of this king but generally all Christians by whom he must pass should let him go securely for two principal reasons: One is so that among themselves they cannot say that there is so little faith and love among us Christians that we are unwilling to further deliverance to those who have fallen into Saracen hands through Christian faith. The other is that if the Saracens who came here were treated rudely by Christians, supposing they came on business, or an embassy, or for some other just reason, they in turn could take advantage of our Christians. For such a reason they often go among them. So their rights should be observed as we would wish ours to be.

A few years after writing her book on chivalry, Christine produced a new work on war and peace in which she urged her French countrymen to unite against their common enemy, the English, instead of fighting each other. The *Book of Peace* offers a heartfelt lamentation on the evils which follow from civil war. Yet in writing this book Christine does not exalt or in any way promote war against external enemies. Indeed, she argues that even international war should be engaged in only when absolutely necessary. In this particular passage we see Christine enumerating the evil desires that lead to war – thereby summing up those tendencies that are directly opposed to peace.

From *The Book of Peace*, bk. II, chap. 4[9]

4 [The causes of war are] hatred, envy, vengeance, and greed. [War comes about] through some particular hatred or enmity that has some reason, such as the woman Herod kept, who was his brother's wife, something which St. John the Baptist reproached him with; for this reason she succeeded in having his head cut off. An example of envy is when Cain killed Abel because he was better;

---

[8] Willard and Willard (trans. and ed.), *The Book of Deeds*, p. 190.

[9] From *The Selected Writings of Christine de Pizan*, ed. Renate Blumenfeld-Kosinski, trans. Renate Blumenfeld-Kosinski and Kevin Brownlee (New York: W. W. Norton, 1997), pp. 239–40.

and also the envy of Joseph's brothers. An example of vengeance is when Jacob's children killed the king who had raped their sister. Greed was when Ahab condemned Naboth to death in order to get his vineyard, or when David wanted to have Uriah's wife and made him die through flattery. The following events were also caused by greed: when the false servants of King Darius killed him (because they wanted to please King Alexander) and wanted to have a reward; or those who killed the valiant knight Pompey in order to please Caesar.

Although such evil deeds are sometimes done in response to certain rumors circulating in the world and done for justice – or made to look as if they were done for justice – one should not give in to such desires. For Seneca says that a man overcome by anger, hatred, or greed sees and hears nothing, does not think or say anything, except through his madness; he pays no heed to his conscience or any danger. And Cato spoke the truth when he said that anger and greed blind a man to such an extent that he does not see the law, but the law sees him very well; that is, he does not see the risk he takes with regard to justice when he translates his evil intentions into deeds. These are horrible faults in those that give themselves over to them, and especially for true princes, not tyrants, who should possess true nobility and to whom Ovid says: "Be victorious over your heart, you man who wants to conquer everything." And similarly Seneca says: "You who want to subdue everything, submit first to reason, and when reason rules you, you will be the ruler; but when your will governs you, you will be ruled over."[10]

---

[10]   For most of these quotes, Christine's source is Brunetto Latini's *Li Livres dou tresor* [Book of the Treasure], a popular thirteenth-century encyclopedic work.

20

Raphaël Fulgosius (1367–1427)

Just War Reduced to Public War

[I]n public war no distinction should be made as to which side wages an unjust war.

In primam Pandectarum partem Commentaria

The main concern of the medieval just war theorists was with determining the conditions governing resort to force on the one hand, and the legal effects produced by war on the other. The latter were called "rights of war" (*iura belli*); these, however, should not be confused with the legal regulation of war – our current *ius in bello* – which at the time was a rather secondary matter.

Among theologians and canonists the dominant view (in line with the teaching of Augustine, Gratian, and Thomas Aquinas) was that war should be viewed solely as a unilateral proceeding in which a belligerent party was empowered to enforce its rightful claim or to sanction an injury caused it by the other party.[1] The legal effects of such a just war were strictly conditioned by the underlying cause and therefore could only benefit the righteous belligerent. On this conception, the unrighteous adversary was not even deemed a belligerent; he was merely the rebellious object of armed coercion.

But war could also be conceptualized as a contest between equal belligerents who both, owing to their sovereign status, enjoyed a similar capacity to wage war, regardless of the cause that had prompted the conflict. As in a duel, they were

---

[1] See in particular, Augustine, *De civitate Dei*, XIX, 7 (see chap. 7, this volume, p. 72), Gratian, *Decretum* pt. II, causa 23, questions 4 and 5 (see chap. 10, this volume, pp. 115–21), and Thomas Aquinas, *Summa theologiae* II–II, q. 40, a. 1 (see chap. 16, this volume, pp. 176–8). The Spanish scholastic Domingo Bañez (1528–1604) later referred to the idea of a unilateral right of war (*ius belli*) as an *axiom* for jurists and theologians alike (cited by Peter Haggenmacher, *Grotius et la doctrine de la guerre juste* [Paris: Presses Universitaires de France, 1983], p. 203, n. 868).

both entitled to exercise the same legal prerogatives against each other. War thus became in itself a source of legal effects which would apply indifferently on both sides, especially with respect to patrimonial rights (territorial conquest, booty, ransom). This had in fact been the conception of the Roman jurisconsults, and it should normally have prevailed among their medieval successors when they were confronted with the Byzantine civil law compilations. Yet, given the dominant just war conception, these bilateral rights of war were not openly acknowledged before the end of the Middle Ages.

The Italian commentator Raphaël Fulgosius was the first author explicitly to spell out the legal conception underlying the Roman texts. He did so in an analysis of a passage by Hermogenianus (*Dig.*, 1, 1, 5), in which the jurisconsult had illustrated the notion of *ius gentium* by enumerating some of its specific institutions. Among these, war figured in the first place to the surprise of the medieval glossators, who considered it strange that an evil like war should be countenanced by law. This is why they interpreted the passage by specifying that only "licit" war was properly authorized by *ius gentium*, i.e. a war declared by the Roman people or the emperor, or a war of self-defense (gloss *Ergo ius gentium*, ad *Dig.*, 1, 1, 5). Such a restriction was clearly inconsistent not only with the text of Hermogenianus, but also with other passages in the *Digest* where no distinction had been made between just and unjust wars.

This is precisely the point raised by Fulgosius, who reinterpreted the idea of unilaterally "just" war as a bilaterally "public" war. According to this conception, both belligerents were recognized as having equal rights of war inasmuch as they were independent peoples or kings, whose very status precluded any reference to a just cause. In the absence of a common judge, war was deemed the final arbiter of their conflict, and victory became by itself the source of a new legal situation.[2] While he thus re-established a link with the Roman conception of war, Fulgosius also became a remote ancestor of the classical concept of regular war as codified in the Hague Regulations of 1899/1907.

From Fulgosius, *In primam Pandectarum partem Commentaria*, ad *Dig.*, 1, 1, 5[3]

But since belligerents happen to acquire property and make slaves on both sides – as shown below in [*Dig.*, 49, 15, 19] and [*Dig.*, 49, 15, 5], – how is it that the

[2] For an outline of Fulgosius's argumentation, see Haggenmacher, *Grotius et la doctrine*, pp. 203–6 and 284–8. Cf. Haggenmacher, "Just War and Regular War in Sixteenth Century Spanish Doctrine," *International Revue of the Red Cross*, 290 (September–October 1992), pp. 434–45, where the author discusses the idea of regular war. For a defense of this idea, in opposition to the traditional notion of just war, see Carl Schmitt, *The Nomos of the Earth in the International Law of the Jus publicum Europaeum*, trans. G. L. Ulmen (New York: Telos Press, 2003), pt. III, chap. 2, pp. 152–71.

[3] Lyon 1554. Translated by Robert Andrews and Peter Haggenmacher.

one who wages an unjust war acquires the ownership of the things he captures through his unjust action? I respond that, as it was uncertain which side waged war rightfully, and as there was no common judge above the parties by whom this could be ascertained in terms of civil law, the nations with the best of reasons decided that war would be the judge in this matter; i.e. that whatever would be captured in war or through war should become the property of the capturing party, as if it had been adjudicated by a judge; see *Institutes* [4, 17, §7], and this of Lucan: "Let war be the judge."[4] And again: "To him who is armed, one yields all if one refuses his due."[5] For victory in war comes about as it were by the judgment of God, because God is a righteous and just judge of all, as Lucan likewise testifies: "The victorious cause pleased the gods,"[6] just after having said: "Who more rightly raised arms? It is impious to decide; each one appeals to a great judge."[7] For the war which we are discussing took place only between independent nations and kings, as in the said law *Postliminii* [*Dig.*, 49, 15, 5, i. pr]. And this is how one ought to temper what John [the Teutonic] noted with respect to the canon *Ius gentium*, in the first distinction of [Gratian's] *Decretum*: in public war no distinction should be made as to which side wages an unjust war in order to deny it the acquisition of persons and things taken from the opposite side. For how can it be known, and who is to be the judge in this matter, deciding that one side wages a just war, the other an unjust war. . . . Nothing more should therefore be asked than whether the war was just, that is, public, and whether it was declared by someone who could do so, that is, an independent nation or an independent king. And so is also to be understood the gloss to the said canon *Ius gentium*. And the law *Nihil interest* [*Dig.*, 49, 15, 26], which is alleged by that very gloss of the *Decretum*, also speaks of licit or just war, that is, of public war declared by him who can declare it. . . . For my part I hold that the war which is spoken of here, from which flow captivity and postliminy, is that sort only which is declared between independent nations or kings, in conformity with the said laws *Hostes* [*Dig.*, 49, 15, 24] and *Postliminium* [*Dig.*, 49, 15, 19, i.pr.], without any inquiry into the cause for which the war was begun, nor about whose cause is just.

---

[4] Lucan, *Bellum civile* (*Pharsalia*), I, 227.

[5] Ibid., I, 348–9.

[6] Ibid., I, 128. This verse – famously quoted by Lamartine when addressing the French National Assembly in 1848 – ends thus: ". . . the vanquished [cause pleased] Cato."

[7] Ibid., I, 127–8. The "great judges" are Cato on the one hand, the gods on the other; see note 6, above.

Part III

Late Scholastic and Reformation

21

Erasmus of Rotterdam (1466–1536)

The Spurious "Right to War"

[T]he Christian prince must be suspicious about his "rights," and then, if they are established beyond doubt, he must ask himself whether they have to be vindicated to the great detriment of the whole world.

The Education of a Christian Prince

Desiderius Erasmus, or Erasmus of Rotterdam, received his early training in theology and was ordained as a priest in 1492. However, frustrations with scholasticism and monastic life soon turned him over to classical studies, where, along with Thomas More, he would instigate a wave of Christian thinking infused with the humanist ideals of the Renaissance. His studies led him to produce, among other things, a refined Greek edition of the New Testament (published in 1516), setting new standards for biblical scholarship. Initially, his alienation from Catholic philosophy also saw him cautiously sympathize with the reformist theology of Martin Luther, but as the Reformation movement turned more political, Erasmus's sympathy gradually waned.

Alongside his most famous works, such as the popular satire *In Praise of Folly* (1512) and his anti-Lutheran polemic *On Free Will* (1524), Erasmus also wrote a number of shorter and longer pieces passionately advocating a pacifist position and scolding the militant practices of the Christian Empire.[1] Here Erasmus is concerned to counter the Aristotelian influence that was absorbed and cultivated in the works of Thomas Aquinas, from which flows also the modern articulation of the just war doctrine. As a classicist himself, Erasmus was by no means in principle opposed to non-Christian sources informing Christian thought; his concern is rather about the specific way in which scholastic philosophy administered this heritage, placing the Greek philosophers practically on a par with the authority of the

---

[1] For instance *Dulce Bellum Inexpertis*, or "War is sweet to those who have not tried it" (added to the 1515 version of his *Adages*), and *The Complaint of Peace* (1517).

Bible.[2] In particular, he finds the doctrine of just war fatally subversive of Christ's teachings of charity and peace.

The Education of a Christian Prince[3]

In the following, we will be excerpting from the final chapter of Erasmus's work *The Education of a Christian Prince* (1516). This work stands in a venerable tradition, stretching back at least to Cicero's *De Officiis*, of writing (usually unsolicited) "instruction manuals" on good governance, addressed to rulers and contenders. Only three years earlier, Niccolò Machiavelli had written *The Prince*,[4] dedicated to Lorenzo Medici, which remains by far the best-known such work from the period. Erasmus's contribution carried a dedication to the Dutch-born Prince Charles, subsequently Emperor Charles V, and provides a fitting contrast to our excerpts from Machiavelli's more famous work.

From *The Education of a Christian Prince*[5]

On Starting War

Although the prince will never make any decision hastily, he will never be more hesitant or more circumspect than in starting a war; other actions have their different disadvantages, but war always brings about the wreck of everything that is good, and the tide of war overflows with everything that is worst; what is more, there is no evil that persists so stubbornly. War breeds war; from a small war a greater is born, from one, two; a war that begins as a game becomes bloody and serious; the plague of war, breaking out in one place, infects neighbours too and, indeed, even those far from the scene.

The good prince will never start a war at all unless, after everything else has been tried, it cannot by any means be avoided. If we were all agreed on this, there would hardly ever be a war among men. In the end, if so pernicious a thing cannot be avoided, the prince's first concern should be to fight with the least possible harm to his subjects, at the lowest cost in Christian blood, and to end it as quickly as possible.

---

[2] In *Dulce Bellum Inexpertis* he records his frustration that it is now "regarded as sacrilege for anyone to speak about Christian scriptures without having crammed himself 'up to the ears' as they say with nonsense out of Aristotle, or rather out of the sophists" (Margaret Mann Phillips, *The "Adages" of Erasmus: A Study with Translations*, [Cambridge: Cambridge University Press, 1964], p. 332).

[3] English translation by Neil M. Cheshire and Michael J. Heath, reprinted in Lisa Jardine (ed.), *The Education of a Christian Prince* (Cambridge: Cambridge University Press, 1997).

[4] Although Machiavelli's work was not published until 1532.

[5] Ibid., pp. 102–4.

The truly Christian prince will first ponder how much difference there is between man, a creature born to peace and good will, and wild animals and beasts, born to pillage and war, and in addition how much difference there is between a man and a Christian. He should then consider how desirable, how honourable, how wholesome a thing is peace; on the other hand, how calamitous as well as wicked a thing is war, and how even the most just of wars brings with it a train of evils – if indeed any war can really be called just. Finally, putting aside all emotion, let him apply just a little reason to the problem by counting up the true cost of the war and deciding whether the object he seeks to achieve by it is worth that much, even if he were certain of victory, which does not always favour even the best of causes. Weigh up the anxieties, expense, dangers, the long and difficult preparations. You must call in a barbarian rabble, made up of all the worst scoundrels, and, if you want to be thought more of a man than the rival prince, you have to flatter and defer to these mercenaries, even after paying them, although there is no class of men more abject and indeed more damnable. Nothing is more precious to the good prince than that his people should be as virtuous as possible. But could there be a greater and more immediate threat to morality than war? The prince should pray for nothing more fervently than to see his subjects secure and prosperous in every way. But while he is learning to wage war, he is compelled to expose young men to all kinds of peril and to make countless orphans, widows, and childless old people, and to reduce countless others to beggary and misery, often in a single hour.

The world will have paid too high a price to make princes wise, if they insist on learning by experience how dreadful war is, so that as old men they can say: 'I never thought war could be so pernicious.' But, immortal God! what incalculable suffering has it cost the whole world to teach you that truism! One day the prince will realise that it was pointless to extend the frontiers of his kingdom and that what seemed at the outset to be a profitable enterprise has resulted in terrible loss to him; but before then many thousands of men have been either killed or maimed. These things would be better learnt from books, from the reminiscences of old men, or from the tribulations of neighbours. For years now this prince or that has been fighting for this or that realm: how much greater are their losses than their gains!

The good prince will arrange these matters so that they will be settled once and for all. A policy adopted on impulse will seem satisfactory for as long as the impulse has hold of you; a policy adopted after due consideration, and which satisfies you as a young man, will satisfy you as an old man too. This is never more relevant than when starting a war.

Erasmus then turns to a topic close to his heart: war among Christians. As he queries in *Dulce Bellum Inexpertis*: "how did we get it into our heads that Christian should draw a bloody sword on Christian? If one brother kills another, it is called fratricide. But a Christian is nearer allied to another Christian than any brother can be, unless the bonds of nature are closer than those of Christ!"[6] Erasmus uses this insight as a basis for warning against the uses and abuses of the concept of a "right" – and derivatively, that of a rightful cause of war – that was made so important in the just war tradition. Whether or not there may exist a just cause of war – Erasmus apparently wants to stay agnostic on the issue – we must be mindful of the way in which princes use these purported rights as pretexts to wage wars ultimately harming only the innocent.

From *The Education of a Christian Prince*[7]

Plato calls it sedition, not war, when Greek fights Greek, and advises that, if this does occur, the war must be fought with the utmost restraint. What word, then, do we think should be used when Christian draws the sword against Christian, since they are bound to one another by so many ties? What shall we say when the cruellest wars, prolonged for year after year, are fought on some slender pretext, some private quarrel, a foolish or immature ambition?

Some princes deceive themselves as follows: 'Some wars are entirely just, and I have just cause for starting one.' First, I will suspend judgment on whether any war is entirely just; but who is there who does not think his cause just? Amid so many shifts and changes in human affairs, amid the making and breaking of so many agreements and treaties, how could anyone not find a pretext, if any sort of pretext is enough to start a war?

It can be argued that papal laws do not condemn all war. Augustine too approves it somewhere. Again, St Bernard praises some soldiers. True enough, but Christ himself, and Peter, and Paul, always teach the opposite. Why does their authority carry less weight than that of Augustine or Bernard? Augustine does not disapprove of war in one or two passages, but the whole philosophy of Christ argues against war. Nowhere do the Apostles approve it, and as for those holy doctors who are alleged to have approved of war in one or two passages, how many passages are there where they condemn and curse it? Why do we gloss over all these and seize on the bits which support our wickedness? In fact, anyone who examines the matter more closely will find that none of them approves of the kind of war which is usually fought today.

Certain arts, such as astrology and what is called alchemy, were banned by law because they were too close to fraud and were generally managed by trickery, even if it were possible for a man to practise them honestly. This would be far more justifiable in the case of wars, even if some of them might be just – although

---

[6]   In Phillips, *The "Adages" of Erasmus*, p. 327.
[7]   Jardine (ed.), *The Education*, pp. 104–6.

with the world in its present state, I am not sure that any of that kind could be found, that is, wars not caused by ambition, anger, arrogance, lust, or greed. It often happens that the leaders of men, more extravagant than their private resources will allow, will take a chance to stir up war in order to boost their own finances, even by pillaging their own people. This is sometimes done by princes in collusion with one another, on some trumped-up pretext, in order to weaken the people and to strengthen their own position at the expense of the state. For these reasons the good Christian prince must be suspicious of all wars, however just.

Some, of course, will protest that they cannot give up their rights. First of all, these 'rights', if acquired by marriage, are largely the prince's private concern; how unjust it would be, while pursuing these rights, to inflict enormous damage on the people, and to pillage the whole kingdom, bringing it to the brink of disaster, while pursuing some small addition to his own possessions. Why should it affect the population as a whole when one prince offends another in some trifling matter, and a personal one at that, connected with a marriage or something similar?

The good prince uses the public interest as a yardstick in every field, otherwise he is no prince. He has not the same rights over men as over cattle. Government depends to a large extent on the consent of the people, which was what created kings in the first place. If some dispute arises between princes, why do they not take it to arbitration instead? There are plenty of bishops, abbots, scholars, plenty of grave magistrates whose verdict would settle the matter more satisfactorily than all this carnage, pillaging, and universal calamity.

First of all, the Christian prince must be suspicious about his 'rights', and then, if they are established beyond doubt, he must ask himself whether they have to be vindicated to the great detriment of the whole world. Wise men prefer sometimes to lose a case rather than pursue it, because they see that it will cost less to do so. I believe that the emperor would prefer to give up rather than pursue the rights to the ancient monarchy which jurists have conferred on him in their writings.

But, people will say, if no one pursues his rights will anything be safe? Let the prince pursue his rights by all means, if it is to the state's advantage, so long as his rights do not cost his subjects too dear. After all, is anything ever safe nowadays when everyone pursues his rights to the letter? We see wars causing wars, wars following wars, and no limit or end to these upheavals. It is clear enough that nothing is achieved by these methods, and so other remedies should be tried. Even between the best of friends the relationship will not last long without some give and take. A husband often overlooks some fault in his wife to avoid disturbing their harmony. What can war produce except war? But consideration breeds consideration, and fairness, fairness.

The godly and merciful prince will also be influenced by seeing that the greatest part of all the great evils which every war entails falls on people unconnected with the war, who least deserve to suffer these calamities.

Finally, Erasmus takes issue with the role played by the clergy in inciting and legitimizing the military efforts of princes. It produces an absurd spectacle, he says, when both sides to a war claim the blessing of Christ, "as if [Christ is] fighting against himself."[8] Those who point to the many divinely ordained wars of the Old Testament forget precisely the difference that Christ's message of peace and charity makes. Indeed, great reluctance should also be shown before taking up arms against non-Christians, bearing in mind that Christianity was originally spread by peaceful means: "Perhaps it should not be defended by other means than those which created and spread it."[9]

From *The Education of a Christian Prince*[10]

Even if we allow that some wars are just, yet since we see that all mankind is plagued by this madness, it should be the role of wise priests to turn the minds of people and princes to other things. Nowadays we often see them as very firebrands of war. Bishops are not ashamed to frequent the camp; the cross is there, the body of Christ is there, the heavenly sacraments become mixed up in this worse than hellish business, and the symbols of perfect charity are brought into these bloody conflicts. Still more absurd, Christ is present in both camps, as if fighting against himself. It is not enough for war to be permitted between Christians; it must also be accorded the supreme honour.

If the teaching of Christ does not always and everywhere attack warfare, if my opponents can find one passage approving war, then let us fight as Christians. The Hebrews were allowed to engage in war, but with God's permission. On the other hand, our Oracle, which re-echoes again and again in the pages of the Gospel, argues against war – and yet we make war with more wild enthusiasm than the Hebrews. David was beloved of God for his other virtues, and yet he was forbidden to build his temple for the simple reason that he was a man of blood, that is, a warrior – God chose the peaceful Solomon for this task. If such things happened among the Jews, what will become of us Christians? They had only the shadow of Solomon, we have the true Solomon, Christ, the lover of peace, who reconciles all things in heaven and on earth.

However, I do not think, either, that war against the Turks should be hastily undertaken, remembering first of all that the kingdom of Christ was created, spread, and secured by very different means. Perhaps it should not be defended by other means than those which created and spread it. In addition we can see that wars of this kind have too frequently been made an excuse to fleece the Christian people – and then nothing else has been done. If it is done for the faith, this has been

---

[8]   Erasmus, *The Education*, p. 108.
[9]   Ibid.
[10] Ibid., pp. 108–9.

increased and enhanced by the suffering of martyrs, not by military force; if the battle is for power, wealth, and possessions, we must constantly consider whether such a course does not savour too little of Christianity. Indeed, judging by the people who fight this kind of war nowadays, it is more likely that we shall turn into Turks than that our efforts will make them into Christians. Let us first make sure that we are truly Christian ourselves and then, if it seems appropriate, let us attack the Turks.

22

Cajetan (1468–1534)

War and Vindicative Justice

A just combat is an act of vindicative justice.

Summula Caietani

The Dominican theologian (and cardinal) Thomas de Vio is best known by the name Cajetan, after his native Italian city of Gaeta. A pivotal figure in the development of scholastic thinking in general, and about just war in particular, his writings were frequently cited by thinkers such as Vitoria, Molina, Suárez, and Grotius. Cajetan's influence was largely due to his Commentary on the *Summa theologiae* of Thomas Aquinas (completed 1517), which circulated widely and even achieved something of an official status when, under the authority of Pope Leo XIII, it was published alongside the *Summa theologiae* in the standard ("Leonine") edition of Aquinas's works. In this commentary, Cajetan offered a detailed treatment of legitimate war-making authority, the first of the famous three requirements of a just war set out by Aquinas in article 1 of *question* 40 *De bello*.

Central to Cajetan's account was the distinction (not explicitly formulated by Aquinas) between two kinds of war, defensive and offensive. Defensive war required no special appeal to legitimate authority; political leaders of lower status, or even private individuals, were permitted by natural law to resort to such force in case of urgent need. Offensive war, by contrast, was more a matter of choice than of necessity. This mode of warfare Cajetan equated with the administration of punitive justice. No political community could be deemed self-sufficient (a "perfect commonwealth") if it did not possess the power to exact just revenge against its internal and external foes. The authority to wage war against *external* wrongdoers, in particular, he viewed as the distinctive mark of a fully independent commonwealth. Despite the medieval cast of his work, in it we can already detect a glimmer of the new European system of independent sovereign states.

Cajetan provided further elucidations on the idea of just war in a later work, the *Summula* (1524). This, as its name suggests, was a compendium of brief discussions, written especially for the use of confessors, on selected topics in canon law. In a section entitled "When war should be called just or unjust, licit or illicit,"

Cajetan, after recalling Aquinas's three well-known conditions, emphasizes the importance of right intention (a condition which had been somewhat neglected in earlier treatments), especially with respect to the participation of subjects or mercenaries in a war of doubtful legitimacy. He then launches into a discussion of the particular case of a (wrongful) belligerent who makes his (righteous) opponent a last-minute offer of satisfaction: until what point in time is the latter obligated to accept the offer? Clearly, Cajetan argues, if armed hostilities have not yet commenced, the aggrieved party does indeed have an obligation to accept such an offer. By contrast, once hostilities have begun, the juridical situation is no longer the same. At this stage no offer of settlement, however complete, need be accepted. To elucidate this point, Cajetan describes offensive war as a criminal proceeding, in which the just belligerent takes on the office of both prosecutor and judge. Ordinarily equals, one sovereign indeed can come to have authority over another by reason of the latter's fault. On this account, just war is first and foremost an exercise in "vindicative justice" (*iustitia vindicativa*). This punitive finality of war, which had been a lingering issue in the whole of just war thinking ever since Augustine, thus became paramount in Cajetan's theory. Later thinkers, such as Vitoria, Molina, and Wolff distanced themselves from Cajetan's rather exclusive focus on punishment, so as also to account for other possible finalities of just warfare.[1] Finally, in his last set of considerations, Cajetan touches on the *ius in bello*: which categories of persons among the enemy population are to bear the losses incurred by the just belligerent's action? This raises the problem of the "innocents," which would be widely explored by the sixteenth-century Spanish theologians.

From Commentary to *Summa theologiae* II–II, q. 40, a. 1[2]

In the first article of question 40, concerning the first requirement for a just war,[3] a doubt occurs whether the name "prince" should be understood in this place only of those princes who have no superior. And this seems to be the case because those who have a superior can turn to the superior and seek justice before him (*coram eo*[4]), a reason the text has similarly given in speaking about private individuals.

[1]   See Peter Haggenmacher, *Grotius et la doctrine de la guerre juste* (Paris: Presses Universitaires de France, 1983), pp. 126–31 and 417–26, for a contrast between Cajetan and later scholastics (especially Vitoria and Molina) on the relationship between war and punishment.

[2]   Translation by Robert Andrews and Peter Haggenmacher. Latin text: *Sancti Thomae Aquinatis Doctoris Angelici Opera Omnia iussu impensaque Leonis XIII, cum commentariis Thomae de Vio Caietani Ordinis Praedicatorum*, vol. 8 (Rome: Editori di San Tommaso, 1895), pp. 313–14.

[3]   Aquinas opens his famous discussion of just war (see chap. 16, this volume) by listing three requirements that must be met: sovereign authority, just cause, and right intention.

[4]   Aquinas writes "before the judgment of his superior," *quia potest ius suum in iudicio superioris prosequi*.

This is confirmed: because otherwise the authority of the superior would be flouted. For if it be permitted to any prince to wage war against another, it would also be permitted to any prince to pronounce in his own case against another prince; and so the flouted authority would be circumvented.

Against this, however, the term "prince," as discussed in the text, is distinguished from a private person; this is evident in the text. Yet it is certain that not every such prince lacks a superior.

Moreover, it is said in the text that those appropriately use the sword to make war against foreigners who are competent to use the sword against countrymen. But [to exercise this competence] against countrymen, there is no need for the prince to be without a superior, nor therefore [is this a prerequisite] for waging war.

In order to ascertain the authority needed to wage war, it should be understood that this is not a discussion of defensive war, namely when someone makes a war in defense against a war made on himself; for any people has a natural right to do this. But here the concern is with declaring war: what authority is required for this? And, although there are different opinions in this matter, there is only one right answer, if we correctly approach the issue.

Since war is an invasion of a commonwealth (*reipublicae*), and is actively pursued (wars waged by a commonwealth being legitimate with respect to [the condition of] authority), there is as much difference between the authority behind the sword of war and a private sword as there is between public and private interest with regard to the right of defense and the right to seek revenge. For a private person has but the right "to repel force by force with the moderation of blameless defense."[5] But it is beyond "the moderation of blameless defense" for a private person to seek revenge for himself or others, just as it is not permitted for a private person to kill the killer of his own father. The commonwealth, however, in defense of its members and itself is allowed not only to repel force with moderate force, but also to exact revenge for injuries to itself or its members – not only against its subjects, but also against foreigners.

As to its own subjects, this is evident, because punitive justice is the sole right of the commonwealth. As to foreigners in turn this is proved by the fact that a commonwealth should be "sufficient unto itself", according to *Politics* book III.[6] If, however, a commonwealth could not legitimately revenge itself against peoples and princes, it would surely be imperfect and defective. For tyrants and rapacious villains, murderers, robbers, and any other people causing injury to the citizens of a foreign commonwealth would remain naturally unpunished, and natural reason would come to fail in these necessary matters. For under natural law different commonwealths need not share a mutual prince. If one should oppress another's citizens by plundering and injuring them, and the innocent commonwealth could not avenge itself and its citizens by fighting against the oppressor, then unpunished

---

[5]   That is, in modern terms, with proportionate force.
[6]   Aristotle, *Politics*, III, 1, 1280^{b}33–5.

evils would naturally remain, and natural reason, which is of a greater ambit providentially than the natural instinct of animals, would be deficient by not providing the commonwealth with the power of revenge. This is testified to by the story of Jonathan and Simon against the sons of Iambri, in vengeance for the blood of their brother John, in 1 Maccabees 9[:35]. This seems to be approved by the common practice of all nations, as though it were a natural right. Thomas's words in the text obviously have this meaning, with the authority of St. Augustine.

This same point is proved in another way: If a commonwealth could not declare war, but to bring about that effect was in need of a superior, then this would be (1) either a superior with respect only to itself, or (2) with respect to the one against whom war was to be waged; or (3) with respect to both. There would be no need of a superior with respect only to itself, since any commonwealth is so constituted that it cannot provide for everything by itself but instead depends on somebody else, namely a king. This is because the king is a part of that commonwealth, since he is its head. Thus, this argument does not claim that the commonwealth cannot [declare war], but only that an imperfect commonwealth cannot do so without its head.

And this is why, dear reader, you ought to be completely clear that we are talking about a *perfect* commonwealth here.

Nor would there be need of the superior of him against whom the war is to be waged. This is because, as mostly happens, he lacks a superior or, if he has one, [the superior] may be an accomplice in neglecting to sanction his injustice. Also, because if justice is hoped for before war is declared, justice should be sought from his superior, because the plaintiff follows the court of the respondent (as did the people of Israel, seeking justice from the tribe of Benjamin for [the crime of] the people of Gibeah, Judges 20[:12]). And if [the superior] provides justice, war should not be waged; and if he neglects to do so, war may be waged. However this is not in order to secure the authority to declare war (since the superior of the enemy does not grant this, nor is this asked), but in order for the acts of the active ones to be realized in the one passively disposed. For the one passively disposed is confronting a just war because he refuses to offer satisfaction.

Nor is there need for a superior over both sides, first because this would only be accidental, and then because it has not been shown that either side is in need of such authority.

When therefore it is said that to declare a just war the authority of the prince is required, this should be understood either of a perfect commonwealth, or of someone perfectly standing for a commonwealth (*perfecte gerente vices reipublicae*), as for example kings or other similar rulers. Thereby the arguments on both sides can be solved.

In response to the argument concerning princes who lack a superior, we say that there is this difference between a public and a private person that, being a member of a commonwealth (for man is a political animal), a private person has a proper superior to whom he can appeal for revenge against his enemies domestic or foreign; and hence by his very nature he has no vindicative authority (*auctoritatem vindicativam*). The commonwealth itself, however, or the prince, because it is so endowed by the perfection of nature, as has been shown, has vindicative authority, and so it is not necessary that it appeal to a superior for such authority. The argument of the text [of Aquinas] optimally applies to a private person, not to a public one; for the former is a part and the latter the whole, as has been said.

With respect to the confirmation, we say that there are two sorts of princes. Some are indeed heads and rulers unconditionally, perfectly standing for a commonwealth. Others are heads and rulers conditionally, imperfectly standing for a commonwealth. The former have vindicative authority internally and externally; the latter have it only insofar as it is delegated to them. In this second order are counts, marquises, and dukes, who are parts of a single kingdom. The king, however, is the head and ruler not only of the kingdom, but also of any of its commonwealths; the other nobility are heads and rulers only conditionally. As a sign of this, all the commonwealths of a kingdom participate in one royal tribunal, and all pay the royal taxes. Also included in this order is any community which falls under another as under a king, as would seem to be the case for the Roman church. In the first order are generally all kings and completely independent communities. The case is clear with such communities, for each of them is a perfect commonwealth. The same applies to kings, because "kingdom" signifies a perfect commonwealth, and the king stands for it perfectly; albeit in some cases statutes are such that kings are kings in name only; but we are speaking of kings who are rulers unconditionally.

From the distinction thus made among princes, it is clear that those who from an imperfection of their dominion have a superior cannot declare war without the authority of their superior. In so doing they would be injurious to him by usurping their superior's authority and behaving like unconditional heads and rulers of the commonwealth, which they are not. Those rulers who are perfectly heads and rulers, even if they have a superior such as the emperor, commit no injury to his authority by declaring war, since they are only exercising their right. They are indeed under the emperor like a perfect universal cause under another, more universal, cause; and this is not like something imperfect under something perfect, as would be the case with those of the second order. Or, rather, they are under him in a qualified way, not unconditionally.

This seems rather to stem from old custom, for the unicity of the emperor and his dominion belongs to positive law,[7] because no natural principle nor authority of Sacred Scripture forces all parts of the earth, nor all the nations of one part, to elect a single temporal prince, which is obvious; temporal principality depends naturally on the election of someone, unless he be a tyrant. So since it is based on positive law, custom may abrogate and supersede it. Because of this, princes and

---

[7]   Positive law – a law of human origin, including custom – is here contrasted with natural and divine law, which are beyond human command.

commonwealths which, by most ancient custom are in the habit of using their authority to declare war, may make use of that right, provided they were and are *bona fide* in peaceful possession. I add this specification because of those who usurp this by virtue of their superior force, and who, rebelling against their rulers, could not or cannot be coerced.

In response to the arguments concerning all princes, we say as to the first one: it is true that the text [of Aquinas] takes "prince" to mean a public person, and this in contrast to a private person; yet it does not consider the public person as imperfect, but as perfect. Therefore the text only extends to perfect princes.

In response to the second argument, it belongs to the same [authority], by the nature of the office, [to raise the sword] against both natives and foreigners. There are many, however, who may use the sword by commission against natives but are not allowed to declare war against foreigners, as is the case for governors, cities, and many rulers who in their territories judge in capital cases, for this authority is easier for perfect princes to concede than the authority [to declare war] against foreigners. The text therefore speaks of those who operate by proper authority; not all rulers are of this sort, but only perfect rulers.

In the same article, concerning the justice of the cause of war,[8] note that, because friends and allies are considered to be one, the just cause for declaring a war holds good for the revenge of allies. Similarly, a prince can invite allies and foreigners to wage war no less than he can hire foreign ministers for the exercise of justice at home.

In the same article, concerning the rightness of intention,[9] it should be known that, just as the judges' executioners commit a mortal sin if they kill in hate or savageness one rightly condemned, but are not to be held liable to make restitution for the wounds or garments of the executed, likewise, soldiers waging a just war and carrying off booty conceded to them sin owing to their evil intent, but are not held liable to make restitution. . . .[10]

From *Summula*, "When war should be called just or unjust, licit or illicit"[11]

It is certain that unjust war, in itself, is a mortal sin. Concerning this it should first be investigated what are the conditions which render a war unjust. Since a just war requires three things, namely first, a just cause for going to war, secondly,

---

[8] This is a reference to *iusta causa*, the second of the three conditions for a just war mentioned by Aquinas in the article under discussion.

[9] *Recta intentio*, Aquinas's third condition for a just war.

[10] The text concludes with further responses to objections raised in Aquinas's text.

[11] Translation by Robert Andrew and Peter Haggenmacher. Latin text: *Summula Caietani*, "Bellum quando dicatur iustum, vel iniustum, licitum vel illicitum," (Lyon: A. de Harsy, 1581), pp. 32–9. This text, which presents some flaws, has been compared with the Lyon edition, Apud Iacobum Giunctam, 1544, which in turn contains some deficiencies.

the authority to declare war, and thirdly, a right intention, therefore war can be considered unjust in three ways, either [by a lack of justice in the cause[12]], or by a lack of authority in the leader, or a lack of rightness of intention. If any of these deficiencies occurs, the war is rendered iniquitous. . . .[13]

As a confessor, if you are unable to determine with certainty the cause for a just war, then you can trust those who are worthy of credence.

By the name of "prince" in this context you should understand a perfect commonwealth, for example the Pope, Emperor, King, and free lord,[14] that is, one who has no superior, but is like a prince.

Understand that a bad intention also will render a war unjust, even if it satisfies the other conditions, no less than the just punishment of a robber would be rendered evil if justice were administered with hatred; a sin arises from an evil intention in a just action. Therefore [in such a case] only repentance should be demanded, and not restitution, because the injuring or subduing of a robber is a just injuring and should in no way be condemned as unjust, although the presence of malice in the mind of the person who carries out justice rightly threatens the damnation of his soul.

If a just cause or proper authority is lacking in war, it is not a war at all, but an invasion, murder, and rapine.

In the second place, concerning the participation of soldiers in a war of doubtful legitimacy, it should be said that to participate in a just war is in no way a sin, if it is certainly a just war. If however this is not certain, subordinates of the sovereign declaring war, in obeying their master, are forgiven. . . . Therefore a subordinate is excused, on grounds of his obedience, in a war of which he does not know whether it is just, as an agent of the judge executing a condemned man is excused if no manifest error is involved. The universal principle why obedience in doubtful cases is excusable is that it is not the role of subordinates to challenge the determinations and decrees of their lords, but it ought to be presumed that they are just, unless they contain a manifest iniquity. Those who are not subordinates, however, are not so excused. Nor do I exclude from among subordinates mercenary soldiers who serve under the continuous pay of some king in times of peace as well as in war, for indeed they are subordinates. Similarly, agents of justice need not be subjects by reason of their origin; it is enough that they be hired for the office of justice in order to be excused if they should happen by ignorance to execute an unjust sentence.

As a confessor you therefore should distinguish between foreigners who, on the occurrence of a questionable war, were previously hired for the military exercises

---

[12]   This phrase is missing in the edition of 1581; it has been inserted from the edition of 1544.

[13]   In the omitted material Cajetan cites passages from St. Augustine and Gratian.

[14]   The edition of 1544 reads *dominum liberum . . . quod* (a free dominion that) instead of *dominum liberum . . . qui* as in the edition of 1583, which is being followed here. Both readings make sense, the sentence being somewhat elliptic.

of a monarch in general, and those who were recruited for that occasion. The former are indeed thought to be hired in the service of a just war, and the order of service under which they follow a king determines that it is not their role to examine with precision the exact justness of the war. The latter, however, are like those who would consent to work under a judge of doubtful integrity, and thus know that it is not safe to participate in a venture of dubious justice. Those, however, whether subordinate or not, who hearing of war do not care about the justice of the war but follow the lure of money, are beyond the scruples of conscience; they are clearly in a state of eternal damnation until they repent, just like those who rush to make havoc and collect booty, not caring about justice or injustice.

In the third place, considering the revocation of a war, the question ought to be solved as to whether, after the onset of war, he who has a just war is required to desist from the war, if the iniquitous enemy offers satisfaction. If so, we say, distinguishing three stages of war (i.e. the beginning, the middle, and the near end), that at the beginning of the war (that is, after war has been declared, [troops] assembled, etc., but before hostilities [have started]), the matter of sanction being still pending, the prince is obliged to accept the satisfaction and call off the war. The reason for this is that warring does not depend on will but on necessity, as Augustine declares at [*Decretum Gratiani* II], causa 23, q. 1, [canon] *Noli*.[15] In the case at issue, the necessity for war has ended, since satisfaction has been offered, and the matter is still in its original state. But do understand, dear reader, that I speak of complete satisfaction – not only concerning injuries and properties, but also concerning expenses and damages.

After [the war] has been fought a while, and human casualties have occurred on both sides, he who has a just war is not required to end the war, merely because the enemy now offers satisfaction. The reason for this is that the prosecutor of the just war functions as a judge of criminal proceedings. That he functions as a judge of criminal proceedings is clear from the fact that a just combat is an act of vindicative justice (*actus vindicativae iustitiae*), which is properly within the power of a prince or judge. A private person is not empowered to seek vengeance, for it is written, "Vengeance is mine."[16] That it is a criminal matter is clear from the fact that it leads to the killing and enslavement of persons and the destruction of goods, for all of these things result from a just war – although today slavery is avoided among Christians. It is also clear that he who has a just war is not a party, but becomes, by the very reason that impelled him to make war, the judge of his enemies; for the same reason that a prince can resort to the sword against internal and external disturbers of the commonwealth, that is, owing to the nature of a perfect commonwealth. For it is not a perfect commonwealth if it lacks the ability to exercise vindicative justice, either against

---

[15] Augustinus Hipponensis, *Epistulae*; Epistula 189 (CPL 262) p. 135.
[16] Romans 12:9.

internal disturbers of the commonwealth or external disturbers. If this were not the case, since an equal has no empire (*imperium*) over his equal, all wars would be unjust with the exception of defensive ones. Because he who has a just war embodies a judge of proceedings in vindicative justice against foreign disturbers of the commonwealth, and in the middle of the war has already become the master (*dominus*) of the case, the vindicative proceedings being no longer in their initial state, he can continue the war and enforce vindicative justice with the sword of war (unless he chooses to exercise mercy). It is his enemy's own fault if he reduced himself to that state where foreigners can exercise vindicative justice against him, for it was in his power to offer satisfaction earlier.

And if it be objected against this that in this case the continuation of the war is voluntary, not necessary, since the necessity of waging war has been interrupted by the new offer of satisfaction, we answer that the new offer of satisfaction has not the force of interrupting the necessity of a war already half fought; for it is no longer up to them who wage an unjust war to offer satisfaction (*satisfacere*); their part is to suffer (*satispati*) according to the judgment of him who has a just war. For since they who had an unjust war chose not to offer satisfaction when they could and should have, but instead engaged in war, they have been removed, by the law of right reason, from the order of satisfaction to the order of submitting to a just war; consequently, according to the dictates of right reason, it does not depend on the guilty ones, but on those pursuing vindicative justice, whether vengeance should continue with the sword of war, leading to the subjugation of the enemy and his lands (which amounts to compelling the enemy to "satispassion"[17]), or by way of restitution or satisfaction. Therefore, the war may be continued by the same necessity with which it was begun, if it seems expedient to the prince, because this necessity is not interrupted with respect to the war that has begun against those who refused to offer satisfaction when they were in a position to do so. For although the will of the guilty has changed and they now would be willing to offer satisfaction, because they are no more in a condition where they can offer satisfaction, but instead voluntarily subjected themselves to the condition in which they have to undergo "satispassion" (so to speak), therefore the original necessity and authority of defeating them remains. Similarly, after a master receives a servant in payment of a debt, the power of retaining that servant remains, even though he might wish to repay what he owed.

And hence it is evident that the continuation of the war is all the more at the discretion of the justly warring prince who justly continues the war when the war is near its end, even though the enemies offer satisfaction.

In the fourth place, concerning the harm inflicted by war, four points should be understood. First, that all of the losses resulting from a just war, not only for the

---

[17] This neologism is conceived as an antonym to "satisfaction"; it is derived from Cajetan's *satispati* and *satispassorius*, which are equally neologisms.

soldiers, but also for any member of the commonwealth against which there is a just war are devoid of sin and entail no duty of restitution on the part of those who inflicted them, even if by accident innocents should happen to be injured; for instance, if some city in a just war is given over to plunder, it would be allowed to take the goods of any citizen, although one among them might perhaps be innocent, because the sentence pronouncing the justice of the war need not distinguish whether some part of the enemy state is innocent, since it is presumed to be entirely hostile, the whole of it being considered as enemy, and therefore it is entirely condemned and pillaged. Strictly speaking, one justly receives, even though another innocent person accidentally suffers unjustly, for what happens by accident falls outside of the rules. It would be otherwise if one acted intentionally to harm the innocent. It is on purpose that I have called them members of the commonwealth, because the clergy, who are not part of the people, would not be justly plundered.

Here we should not omit to say, secondly, that certain persons are by canon law exempted from harm brought about by war; you find these in the Decretals, under the title *De pace et treuga*, chapter *Innovamus*, where it is said: "We newly decree that priests, monks, converts, pilgrims, merchants, farmers traveling and returning, and animals with which they plow and carry seed to the field enjoy adequate security." Also, in [*Decretum Gratiani* II, causa] 24, q. 3, chapter *Paternarum*, pilgrims are exempted.[18] I do not know whether these canons, which are reasonable and holy as to what they contain in terms of positive law, have been abolished through frequent violation. By "merchants" I do not mean traders who live there, but those who are merely guests there or who are traveling through; for I do not think that resident merchants have any higher status than laborers.

The third point is that, once an unjust war is under way, everyone is liable for the losses incurred, unless they are excused because of legitimate ignorance. But this does not excuse them from returning stolen items which are in their possession once they learn that the war had been unjust.

The fourth point is that, whether the war be just or unjust,[19] the warriors must follow the rule given them by John the Baptist, namely: "Do violence to no man, neither accuse any falsely, and be content with your wages" (Luke 3:14). Those who oppress farmers and travelers at their discretion, even unto death, as well as all those who commit acts of brigandage, sin mortally. Nor are they to be excused for not being paid their salary, because merely on this account the property of the farmers and citizens is not owed to them. Nor does connivance or authority on the part of the commander or prince provide an excuse, unless this would be

---

[18] The editions of 1544 and 1581 each have *explicantur*, which hardly makes sense (although *explicare* can mean "to extricate somebody from a danger"). Verbs such as *excluduntur*, *excipiuntur*, or *eximuntur* would seem better in place.

[19] The edition of 1544 reads *sive iustum sive iniustum*; the words *iustum sive* are omitted in the edition of 1581, which is obviously a misprint.

inflicted upon the farmers and citizens as a just penalty; because the sovereign ought to pay his soldiers adequately out of the resources which the whole commonwealth (*status*) proportionately contributed, and those private individuals ought not be harassed. For a law which does not burden the people proportionately is formally unjust. However, if by accepted practice it happens that landlords freely supply firewood and straw to the soldiers, I do not censure this, for it is then in a way as by lot[20] that some regions or estates happen to be burdened more than others.[21]

---

[20]   The edition of 1581 reads *fortè* (perhaps) instead of *sorte* (by lot) as does the edition of 1544. The adverb *forte* makes no sense in this context; it probably results from a misreading by the printer of the long *s* which is easily confused with an *f.*

[21]   This chapter concludes with a discussion of "whether it would be a sin to wage war on fast days."

23

Niccolò Machiavelli (1469–1527)

War is Just to Whom it is Necessary

> For injuries must be done all together, so that, tasted less, they offend less; and benefits should be done little by little so that they may be tasted better.
>
> *The Prince*

As with Thucydides earlier in this book, and Thomas Hobbes and Carl von Clausewitz later, Machiavelli might seem an odd candidate for inclusion in an anthology devoted to the ethics of warfare. Like the authors mentioned, he is known as a political realist, whose focus is on winning and consolidating power. In his writings he rarely, if ever, reflects on moral restraints that ought to be imposed upon the use of violent force.

For Machiavelli, more than for these other "realist" authors, such an impression is confirmed rather than denied upon closer inspection. Machiavelli, whether advising a prince or a republic, or simply laying out the best way to wage war, never lets morality play a primary role in his argument, at least if we take morality to mean an other-regarding concern to restrict violence and human suffering

A possible link to ethics could, however, be construed from Machiavelli's recurring use of the concept of virtue (*virtù*), which together with fortune or luck (*fortuna*) is the single element in Machiavelli that explains the difference between successful and unsuccessful political leadership. The good ruler needs his share of good luck, but he also needs *virtue* to know when opportunity knocks. Without the requisite virtue to read the signs of the times, a political leader will inevitably fail.

But Machiavelli is not primarily thinking of *moral* virtue – although he sometimes uses the word *virtù* in that more traditional sense. He mainly draws our attention to a political sort of virtue: the ability to recognize and act on opportunities for acquiring and securing power when they present themselves. We are in reality faced with a combination of cunning and courage, presented under the attractive banner of virtuous disposition and action. Further down the chain of command, Machiavelli's virtue looks more recognizable, extolling a concern for loyalty, discipline, and courage among soldiers and citizens in general. Yet, to call even this *moral* virtue, is misleading – power, not charity or justice, lies at the heart of Machiavelli's argument.

It has nonetheless often been argued that Machiavelli was not as "Machiavellian" – power-centered and cynical – as he is often made out to be, since his preferred regime seems not to have been a one-man principality, but rather a republic or a "mixed regime," where power is much less centralized and personal liberty is valued. While Machiavelli in his famous *The Prince* (1513) gives advice on how to sustain a prince's power, his *Discourses on the First Decade of Livy* (ca. 1519) indeed come across as the work of a true republican. However, this does not lead to a concern for morality in the ordinary sense. Machiavelli never, not even in his defense of liberty, strays from his foremost concern: to describe how power can be secured in cities or states – be they principalities or republics – so that they do not suffer enslavement or destruction.

As a parallel, we can think of someone asking how her house can be guarded effectively. We can imagine advice given along moral lines, stressing the obligation not to defraud or destroy, staying within the boundaries of law, and finding good solutions for defending one's property within those restraints. Or we can construe a totally different line of argument: Get the most from your insurance company, by lying if necessary. Take possession of your neighbor's property, whenever it can be of use to you. If your neighbor protests, use all the force necessary to subdue him. Respect the law and show mercy only when this best secures your own power. Let the tenants of your house have liberty and private property, but only if this makes them more vigorous in defending the house as a whole. Always make sure your tenants know who is in charge. And so on.

Machiavelli uncompromisingly develops the second line of argument, in giving advice to republics as much as to principalities. Indeed, his ostensible defense of republics is not primarily ethical in nature, but rather constitutes (a) an argument from fact – i.e. some political entities are actually republics, and you must deal with them accordingly – and (b) an argument from stability – republics are often more vigorous in their defense of property and power than more authoritarian regimes, and thus more stable.

Underlying Machiavelli's whole line of argument is the idea of *necessity*. We are reminded of the Melian dialogue in Thucydides's *History of the Peloponnesian War*, where the Athenians claim that they must pursue power and glory, simply because that is what the more powerful always do. We find the same idea implicitly expressed in Machiavelli: If you are a prince or a ruling member of a republic your obligation to secure your state's power is not optional. It is your job, and all other concerns are insignificant by comparison. A deeper philosophical reflection, problematizing such a view of power as a goal in itself, is largely absent from Machiavelli's writings.

We should notice that this is a very different understanding of necessity than the one found in Augustine. The latter also stressed that war should be fought out of necessity. Augustine's point, however, is a moral one: War is to be avoided because of its attendant evils, and only overwhelming necessity – situations where one's survival or faith is at stake – can trump the *prima facie* presumption against going to war. In Machiavelli we find no such presumption. The necessity he has in mind is one dictated by the logic of power, not by a desire for peace.

Even if we find few explicitly moral reflections on war in Machiavelli, it is nonetheless fitting to include him among the benchmark contributors to the ethics of war. We need, not least, to remind ourselves of his importance as a writer who has influenced generations of philosophers and politicians faced with the moral quandaries of warfare. Indeed, war and the frequently heard moral arguments against it are never far from Machiavelli's attention. More than anything he urges statesmen to realize that using force in what is normally seen as a brutal and cruel manner is sometimes necessary if one's power is to remain intact. Thus, in one of his few explicit references to just war ideas, he approvingly relates the Roman saying that war is just to whom it is necessary.[1] In *The Prince*, the quote appears in the context of an impassioned plea for the unification and strengthening of the Italian peninsula, which – in Machiavelli's view – was in a state of total disarray and to a worrying extent subject to foreign enslavement.

From *The Prince*, chap. 26[2]

Here [in Italy] there is great justice: "for war is just to whom it is necessary, and arms are pious when there is no hope but in arms" [Livy, *History of Rome*, IX, 1].[3] Here there is very great readiness, and where there is great readiness, there cannot be great difficulty.

In *The Prince*, Machiavelli repeatedly appeals to nature and necessity to justify the ways of securing one's principality and enlarging one's possessions.

[1] Said by Claudius Pontius during the Second Samnite War, according to Titus Livy in bk. IX of his *History of Rome* (quoted by Machiavelli in *The Prince*, chap. 26, and in the *Discourses*, bk. III, chap. 12). In his *Discourses*, Machiavelli uses Livy's *History* as his point of departure. Livy (ca. 64 BC – 17 AD) stands as the most famous Roman historian of the Augustan era. The subject matter of the first ten books of his history, which constitute Machiavelli's main focus of attention, is the beginnings of the Roman republic, up to approximately 300 BC.

[2] From Niccolò Machiavelli, *The Prince*, trans. Harvey C. Mansfield, Jr. (Chicago: University of Chicago Press, 1985), p. 103. We know that a first draft of the work was finished in 1513, so we have given that date. It was, however, revised by its author later, and it never appeared in print during Machiavelli's lifetime.

[3] [*Editor's footnote:*] When this quote appears in the *Discourses*, bk. III, chap. 12, Machiavelli's focus is much more clearly on necessity than justice.

From *The Prince*, chap. 3[4]

And truly it is a very natural and ordinary thing to desire to acquire, and always, when men do it who can, they will be praised or not blamed; but when they cannot, and want to do it anyway, here lie the error and the blame.

From *The Prince*, chap. 5[5]

When those states that are acquired . . . are accustomed to living by their own laws and in liberty, there are three modes for those who want to hold them: first, ruin them; second, go there to live personally; third, let them live by their laws, taking tribute from them and creating within them an oligarchical state which keeps them friendly to you. . . .

As examples there are the Spartans and the Romans. The Spartans held Athens and Thebes by creating oligarchical states there; yet they lost them again. The Romans, in order to hold Capua, Carthage, and Numantia, destroyed them and did not lose them. They wanted to hold Greece much as the Spartans had held it, by making it free and leaving it its own laws. But they did not succeed; so they were compelled to destroy many cities in that province so as to hold it. For in truth there is no secure mode to possess them other than to ruin them. And whoever becomes patron of a city used to living free and does not destroy it, should expect to be destroyed by it; for it always has as a refuge in rebellion the name of liberty and its own ancient orders which are never forgotten either through length of time or because of benefits received. . . . [I]n republics there is greater life, greater hatred, more desire for revenge; the memory of their ancient liberty does not and cannot let them rest, so that the most secure path is to eliminate them or live in them.

There is one place in *The Prince* where Machiavelli singles out and seemingly criticizes principalities acquired through criminal acts. It is a peculiar passage, since so much of what Machiavelli recommends – in *The Prince* and in his *Discourses* – could easily be described as criminal acts. However, Machiavelli seems to have in mind here men who have ruthlessly broken the law of their own land and thereby have risen to the rank of political or military leaders in a way that has threatened and challenged power, rather than secured it. From the point of view of steadfast leadership, such actions can hardly be deemed laudable. However, even if the passage can be thus explained – and even if we balk at Machiavelli's concluding words about "evil well used" – it is noteworthy for its sudden injection of ethical concerns, and for its use of the concept of "virtue" in a more traditional way than can usually be found in this author.

---

[4] *The Prince*, pp. 14–15.
[5] Ibid., pp. 20–1.

From *The Prince*, chap. 8[6]

[O]ne cannot call it virtue to kill one's citizens, betray one's friends, to be without faith, without mercy, without religion; these modes can enable one to acquire empire, but not glory. For, if one considers the virtue of [the Sicilian tyrant] Agathocles in entering into and escaping from dangers, and the greatness of his spirit in enduring and overcoming adversities, one does not see why he has to be judged inferior to any most excellent captain. Nonetheless, his savage cruelty and inhumanity, together with his infinite crimes, do not allow him to be celebrated among the most excellent men. Thus, one cannot attribute to fortune or to virtue what he achieved without either. . . .

Someone could question how it happened that Agathocles and anyone like him, after infinite betrayals and cruelties, could live for a long time secure in his fatherland, defend himself against external enemies, and never be conspired against by his citizens, inasmuch as many others have not been able to maintain their states through cruelty even in peaceful times, not to mention uncertain times of war. I believe that this comes from cruelties badly used or well used. Those can be called well used (if it is permissible to speak well of evil) that are done at a stroke, out of the necessity to secure oneself, and then are not persisted in but are turned to as much utility for the subjects as one can. Those cruelties are badly used which, though few in the beginning, rather grow with time than are eliminated. Those who observe the first mode can have some remedy for their state with God and with men, as had Agathocles; as for the others it is impossible for them to maintain themselves.

Hence it should be noted that in taking hold of a state, he who seizes it should examine all the offenses necessary for him to commit, and do them all at a stroke, so as not to have to renew them every day and, by not renewing them, to secure men and gain them to himself with benefits. Whoever does otherwise, either through timidity or bad counsel, is always under necessity to hold a knife in his hand. . . . For injuries must be done all together, so that, being tasted less, they offend less; and benefits should be done little by little so that they may be tasted better.

From *The Prince*, chap. 15[7]

For a man who wants to make a profession of good in all regards must come to ruin among so many who are not good. Hence it is necessary to a prince, if he wants to maintain himself, to learn to be able not to be good, and to use this and not use it according to necessity.

---

[6]   Ibid., pp. 35, 37–8.
[7]   Ibid., p. 61.

As is the case with *The Prince*, much of Machiavelli's *Discourses* revolves around war, with plentiful advice on how to organize military forces and use them in battle. Machiavelli stresses the need to have good soldiers, who are willing to fight loyally and selflessly. (He is, as could be expected, very critical of mercenaries.) Loyal soldiers are more easily acquired in republics than in principalities, since citizens of a republic will typically be eager to fight for their freedom.

Explicitly *moral* advice on how to use armed force is, however, hardly to be found in the *Discourses*, even when Machiavelli is writing about such an "ethical" theme as defense of republican freedom. His infrequent encouragement to act mercifully is always couched in terms of securing power. Indeed, the following statement is typical: "subject peoples should either be generously treated or wiped out."[8]

The passages below are also quite symptomatic of Machiavelli's approach to the use of violence – in them, he analyzes cruelty and compassion, and thus indirectly weighs the arguments for and against use of violent force to keep order. Here, as is also the case in his discussions about how to treat conquered territories and enemies in war, the debate is cast in terms of efficacy rather than morality.

From *Discourses on the First Decade of Livy* (ca. 1519), bk. III, chap. 19[9]

Though the Roman republic was distraught owing to the hostility between the nobles and the plebs, none the less, when war came, it commissioned Quintius and Appius Claudius to lead the armies forth. Appius, who was a brutal and harsh commander, was so badly obeyed by his troops that he had to quit his province as though he had been defeated. Quintius, who was of a kindly and humane disposition, was obeyed by his troops and returned victorious. It would seem better, therefore, in controlling a large number of men, to be humane rather than arrogant, compassionate rather than cruel. Cornelius Tacitus, however – and many other writers agree with him – arrives at the opposite conclusion, which he expresses in these words: "In ruling the masses punishment is of more avail than considerateness."

With a view to reconciling these two opinions I would point out that either the men you have to rule are in ordinary circumstances your associates, or they have always been your subjects. When they are your associates, you cannot in your dealings with them use penalties, nor yet that severity which Cornelius advocates. Wherefore, since in Rome the plebs had an equal share in the government with

---

[8] From Niccolò Machiavelli, *The Discourses*, ed. Bernard Crick, trans. Leslie J. Walker, SJ (London: Penguin, 1970), p. 349. We can surmise from other sources that Machiavelli stopped working on this book in 1519, so we have given that date. It seems he never completed or revised it. The book never appeared in print during Machiavelli's lifetime.

[9] Ibid., pp. 459–60.

the nobility, neither could, on becoming the ruler for the time being, treat the other brutally and harshly. Very often, too, one sees that Roman generals succeeded better when they made their armies love them and treated them with consideration than did those who made themselves excessively feared, unless such behaviour was accompanied by outstanding virtue. . . . On the other hand, in governing one's subjects, which is what Cornelius has in mind, lest they should become insolent and trample on you should you be too easy with them, it is better to rely on punishment rather than on considerateness. But this also should be used with moderation, so as to avoid cause for hatred; for no ruler benefits by making himself odious. To avoid this he should leave his subjects' property alone; for, except as a cover for pillage, no prince is keen on shedding blood unless he be driven to it, and need for this seldom arises. . . . More praise is due, then, to Quintius than to Appius, and Cornelius's view, under the conditions he supposes but not in those observed in the case of Appius, deserves approbation.

From *Discourses on the First Decade of Livy*, bk. III, chap. 41[10]

For when the safety of one's country wholly depends on the decision to be taken, no attention should be paid either to justice or injustice, to kindness or cruelty, or to its being praiseworthy or ignominious. On the contrary, every other consideration being set aside, that alternative should be wholeheartedly adopted which will save the life and preserve the freedom of one's country.

This last remark shows the difficulty of describing Machiavelli in terms of morality. His stand on defending one's country and one's freedom – the latter being especially pertinent in the case of republics – can be read as a moral one, as can many of his patriotic sentiments in *The Prince* and elsewhere. But Machiavelli himself explicitly warns against making moral concerns decisive in such contexts – these are primarily *political* considerations, not moral ones. In the end, one's judgment on Machiavelli and ethics boils down to one's definition of ethics – what remains within the sphere of moral discourse, and what should rightly be placed outside it. Most readers of Machiavelli will agree that the great Florentine writer as a rule kept politics and morality – and not least war and morality – separate.

We should finally mention that Machiavelli dedicated a whole book to war, in addition to the many comments about armed force in *The Prince* and the comprehensive account of warfare in his *Discourses*. However, Machiavelli's *Art of War* (1521) concentrates on the construction and maintenance of an effective army, and is all but silent on questions about when armed force can be used rightly. Even its thorough treatment of *in bello* issues is not concerned with moral

[10] Ibid., p. 515.

strictures on the actual execution of war, but rather on the more technical character, quality, and arms of those who fight war. It is true that Machiavelli again invokes *virtù* as a required trait for soldiers and officers alike, if they are to be successful. But, as in Machiavelli's other works, political and military rather than moral virtue completely dominates the discussion, and morality is not allowed to tread on to the sacred grass of power, security, and real-life politics.

If this had been an anthology of texts on military strategy and tactics, Machiavelli's *Art of War* would have deserved a prominent place – but in the present context the excerpts we have given from his more famous books give a more fitting impression of Machiavelli's peculiar contribution to the ethics of war.

24

Thomas More
(ca. 1478–1535)

Warfare in Utopia

> Their one and only aim in warfare is to gain the objective which, if they had obtained it beforehand, would have kept them from going to war at all.
>
> *Utopia*

Along with his friend and collaborator Erasmus of Rotterdam, Thomas More epitomizes the spirit of Christian humanism that blossomed between the Renaissance and the Reformation. Yet the fame of his best-known work *Utopia*[1] (1516) is such that it virtually eclipses both its author and the period out of which it grew, embodying a socio-political vision which is in many aspects as timeless as More intended it to be placeless (*utopia* is a constructed term, literally meaning "no-place").

Utopia is presented as a fantastic travelogue, in which its narrator enthusiastically relates the workings of a purportedly ideal society, in the process providing a thinly disguised critique of political practices in Europe at the time. Indeed, parts of the political thrust of *Utopia* seem so radical, and so prescient of themes that would come to occupy the mainstream political discussion only centuries later, that one can scarcely help but wonder whether More himself – a lawyer and Speaker of parliament, eventually beheaded in 1535 for his unbending allegiance to the pope – could really have intended their full recommendation.

In particular, Utopia's abolition of the institution of money and its advocacy of radical redistributive measures touch on issues that still loom large on any agenda for social justice.[2] But more to the tune of this volume's theme, the Utopians also adhere to a remarkably modern theory of war. However, the two issues – economy and warfare – are by no means unconnected: their political judgment not swayed by economic interest, the Utopians have vastly fewer incentives than other people

---

[1] All excerpts and citations are taken from the translation of Clarence H. Miller (New Haven and London: Yale University Press, 2001).
[2] See for instance *Utopia*, Book II, pp. 132–3.

to go to war. Indeed, as we learn in the following excerpt, they are willing to engage militarily only to defend their own territory, to protect the interests of an ally, or to liberate a people from a tyrant. When they do engage, however, they do so with great force and ferocity.

From *Utopia*, bk. II[3]

They [the Utopians] loathe war as positively bestial (though no sort of beast engages in it as constantly as mankind), and unlike almost all nations they consider nothing more inglorious than glory won in warfare. Therefore, though they regularly devote themselves to military training on certain appointed days so that they will not be incapable of fighting when circumstances require it – and not only the men do so but also the women – they are reluctant to go to war and do so only to defend their own territory, or to drive an invading enemy from the territory of their friends, or else, out of compassion and humanity, they use their forces to liberate a oppressed people from tyranny and servitude. When they come to the aid of their friends, it is not always to defend them but sometimes also to requite and avenge injuries inflicted on them. But they do this only if they have been consulted before any steps are taken and if, after they have verified the facts, demanded restitution, and been refused, they themselves declare war. They decide to do this not only when an enemy has invaded and plundered one of their friends, but also, and even more fiercely, when their friends' merchants in any part of the world have been unjustly accused under some pretext of justice, either by using unjust laws speciously or by interpreting good laws perversely.

This was the only reason for the war which the Utopians fought a little before our time on behalf of the Nephelogetes against the Alaopolitans: some Nephelogete merchants among the Alaopolitans had been treated unjustly under some pretext of justice (or so the merchants thought). Certainly, whether the cause was just or unjust, it was avenged by a hideous war, in which the surrounding nations also added their energy and resources to the hostile forces of the major opponents so that some prosperous peoples were ravaged, others were badly shaken. One disaster followed upon another until finally the surrender and enslavement of the Alaopolitans put an end to the war. The Utopians, who sought nothing for themselves, subjected the vanquished to the Nephelogetes – a people hardly to be compared with the Alaopolitans in their heyday.

So fierce are the Utopians even when they are punishing only monetary injuries against their friends; but they are not so when the injury is against themselves. If they should be cheated out of their property, as long as they are subjected to no physical force, they set limits to their anger: they merely refrain from trade with that nation until restitution is made, not because they care less for their own

[3] Ibid., pp. 105–7.

citizens than for their allies but rather they are more offended by their friends' loss of money than by their own because their friends' merchants are severely injured by such a loss, since it comes from their own private possessions. But their own citizens lose nothing but public property, goods which were abundant at home, even superfluous, for otherwise they would not have been exported. So the loss is hardly perceived by anyone. Hence they feel that it would be cruel to punish an injury by killing many people when it causes no inconvenience to any of the Utopians in their lives or livelihood. But if any of their citizens is unjustly disabled or killed, wherever it may be, whether it be done by a public decision or by a private citizen, they send ambassadors to ascertain the facts, and if the malefactors are not handed over to them they cannot be put off but declare war immediately. If the guilty persons are handed over for punishment, they are sentenced to death or servitude.

They are not only grieved by a bloody victory but also ashamed of it, thinking that it is stupid to pay too much for merchandise, however valuable it may be. But if they conquer and crush an enemy by skill and cunning, they glory mightily in the victory, holding public parades to celebrate it and putting up a monument as if for a hard-won victory. For they boast that they have acted with courage and fortitude only when they have won the victory as no other creature but man is able to win it, that is, by the power of his wits. For bears, lions, boars, wolves, dogs, and other animals (they say) fight with the power of their bodies; and though most of them surpass us in strength and ferocity we outdo them all in intelligence and reasoning.

Yet, if the aims of Utopian warfare seem noble enough, their methods prove somewhat more controversial. If drawn into a war, the Utopians will first seek to encourage sedition and even assassinations among enemy ranks by way of the one incentive to which they themselves are immune – economic bribery. Should that strategy prove insufficient, they then turn to mercenaries. These are exclusively recruited from among a people known as the Zapoletes, who know no loyalty but to money and for whose lives the Utopians have little regard. Only in the last instance will Utopian citizens be brought into battle.

From *Utopia*, bk. II[4]

Their one and only aim in warfare is to gain the objective which, if they had obtained it beforehand, would have kept them from going to war at all. Or, if circumstances make that impossible, they seek to punish those they consider culpable so severely that fear will keep them from daring to do such a thing in the

---

[4]   Ibid., pp. 107–9, 110–11, 112.

future. These are the goals they set for their undertaking, and they try to achieve them quickly, but yet in such a way that a concern for avoiding danger takes precedence over winning praise and glory.

And so, immediately after declaring war, they see to it that many notices certified by their official seal are put up secretly and simultaneously in the most conspicuous places in the enemy's territory promising a huge reward to anyone who does away with the enemy's prince; they also assign lesser, but still very substantial, sums for the deaths of those individuals they list in the same notices. These are the persons who, apart from the prince himself, were responsible for plotting against the Utopians. They double the reward assigned to the assassin if he brings them any of the proscribed persons alive; in fact, they offer the same rewards to the proscribed persons themselves, and throw immunity into the bargain, if they turn against their comrades. Thus their enemies quickly suspect all outsiders and even among themselves they are neither trusting nor trustworthy so that they live in a state of utter panic and no less peril. For it has very often turned out (as is well known) that a good number of them, and among them the prince himself, have often been betrayed by those they trusted the most. So easy is it to get someone to commit any crime whatsoever by means of bribes, and for that reason the Utopians set no limits to their bribes. Keeping in mind the great risks they are urging people to take, they take care to balance the magnitude of the danger with the lavishness of the reward; hence they promise not only enormous quantities of gold but also personal and perpetual title to rich estates in the safe and secure territory of their friends, and they faithfully keep their promises.

Other nations condemn this practice of bidding for and buying off an enemy as a barbarous, degenerate crime, but the Utopians think it does them great credit: it shows them to be wise, since in this way they win great wars without fighting at all, and also humane and compassionate, since by killing a few malefactors they spare the lives of many innocent persons who would have fallen in battle, both their own soldiers and those of the enemy; for they pity the rank-and-file of the enemy's soldiers almost as much as their own citizens because they know they do not go to war of their own accord but are driven to it by the madness of princes.

If this procedure is not successful, they sow and cultivate the seeds of dissension by encouraging the brother of the prince or some nobleman to have hopes of gaining the throne. If such internal factions languish, they stir up neighboring peoples and set them against their enemy by digging up some ancient claim such as is never lacking to kings.

When they have promised resources for war, they supply money lavishly, but their citizens very sparingly. They hold their own people so very dear and value each other so highly that they would not be willing to exchange a single one of their own citizens for the enemy's prince. But they are not at all reluctant to pay out gold and silver, since they keep it only for this purpose and would live no less comfortably if they spent all of it. Then too, apart from the wealth they have at home, they also have a limitless treasure abroad, since many nations, as I said before, owe them money. And so they hire mercenaries from everywhere and send them to war, especially the Zapoletes. . . .

These people fight for the Utopians against any mortals whatsoever because they hire their services for more than they can get anywhere else. And just as the Utopians seek good men in order to use them, so too they also enlist these wicked men in order to use them up. When they need to use them, they urge them on with great promises and expose them to the greatest dangers so that most of them do not return to claim what they were promised. To the survivors they faithfully keep their promises so as to make them eager to undertake similar exploits. Nor do they have any qualms about doing away with so many of them, since they believe the human race would owe them a great debt of gratitude if they could purge the whole world of such loathsome and wicked scum.

Apart from the Zapoletes, they use the forces of those for whom they have taken up arms, and after that the auxiliary troops of other friendly nations. As a last resort they add their own citizens, from whom they choose a man of proven valour to command the whole army. Under him they appoint two men who remain private citizens as long as he is safe, but if he is captured or killed, one of the two succeeds him, and in case of a mishap he himself is succeeded by the third, so that if the commander is in danger (and the fortunes of war are quite various) the whole army does not panic.

In each city they choose troops from a list of volunteers. No one is sent out to foreign wars against his will, for they are convinced that if someone is by nature fearful he will not only not fight vigorously himself but he will also inspire fear in his comrades. But if their country is invaded during a war, cowards of this sort, as long as they are physically fit, are dispersed among better troops in the ships or they are spread out here and there on the walls so that they have no place to run away to. Thus shame in the presence of their friends, the confrontation with the enemy, and the absence of any hope of escaping overcome fear, and often they make a virtue out of extreme necessity. . . .

Certainly they take every precaution to avoid having to fight themselves, as long as they can wage war using mercenaries to take their place. But when they can no longer avoid entering the fray, the courage with which they fight matches the prudence with which they avoided fighting as long as they could. They do not give their all in a first furious attack but rather they grow stronger gradually and over a period of time, and they are so resolute that they would rather die than retreat. For one thing, they are certain that everyone at home is provided for, and they do not need to worry about their children (such concern generally breaks the spirits of lofty souls); so their courage is proud and contemptuous of defeat. Moreover, their skill in the arts of war gives them confidence. Finally, sound ideas, instilled in them from childhood on, both by instruction and through the institutions of the commonwealth, give them courage: they hold life neither so cheap as to throw it away recklessly nor so perversely dear as to cling to it greedily and shamefully when honor requires them to give it up.

Once their aims are achieved, however, the Utopians return to moderation. Not having entered the war from economic incentives, they see no reason to ravage their former enemy. They impose no hardships on civilians, and offer amnesty to anyone whose wartime conduct was conducive to the Utopian cause. Finally, even while they reserve the right to demand compensation from the vanquished, our narrator ensures us that "it rarely happens that they demand all of it."

From *Utopia*, bk. II[5]

If they win a victory they do not slaughter the defeated; they would rather capture than kill those they have put to flight. And they never pursue retreating troops without keeping in reserve at least one battalion drawn up under its colors. They do this so regularly that if the rest of their own forces have been defeated and they win the victory with their last battalion, they would rather let the whole enemy army escape than get into the habit of pursuing the fugitives with their own forces in disarray. . . .

When they make a truce with their enemies, they keep it so religiously that they do not violate it even under provocation. They do not lay enemy territory waste or burn their crops; they even do what they can to keep the grain from being trampled by men and horses, for they think it may be of some use to them. They injure no unarmed civilians except for spies. They offer amnesty to cities that surrender and even those taken by siege they do not sack; instead they execute those who prevented the surrender; they enslave the rest of the defenders, but the civilian populace they leave unharmed. If they find persons who urged the town to surrender, they grant them a share in the property of the condemned; they divide up the rest and give it to their auxiliaries, for none of the Utopians takes any of the booty.

When the war is over, they assess the costs not against the friends for whom they incurred them but against the losers; they demand part of it in money; which they reserve for similar use in warfare, and part in estates within enemy territory from which they forever enjoy a not inconsiderable income. They now have revenues of this sort in many nations; it accumulated gradually in various ways and now amounts to 700,000 ducats a year. To take care of it they send out collectors of revenue, who live there in grand style and play the part of great lords. But there is plenty left over to put into the treasury, unless they choose to give credit to the nation that owes it, which they often do until they need it, and even then it rarely happens that they demand all of it. They also bestow some of these estates on those whom they have persuaded to place themselves in great danger, as I mentioned before.

[5] Ibid., pp. 113, 114–15.

25

Martin Luther (1483–1546) and Jean Calvin (1509–1564)

Legitimate War in Reformed Christianity

> What else is war but the punishment of wrong and evil? Why does anyone go to war, except because he desires peace and obedience?
>
> Martin Luther, *Whether Soldiers, Too, Can Be Saved*

The period of the Reformation was dramatic in several ways. Theologically, it sparked a debate that has continued to the present day, about grace, redemption, faith, and works. Politically, it caused an upheaval in Europe that the continent had not witnessed since the times of the Western Roman Empire, if ever. Directly and indirectly, it caused factions and conflicts in church and state, which in turn set off civil wars over much of Europe, culminating in the Thirty Years War from 1618 to 1648, and the English Civil War from 1642 to 1660.

The two most influential reformers, both theologically and politically, were the German miner's son Martin Luther and the French middle-class attorney's son John [Jean] Calvin. They both contributed to forming new churches and helped end the monopoly on administering the Christian faith and sacraments that the Roman church had held in Western Europe throughout the Middle Ages. In temperament and opinion, however, the two differed starkly – and, it should be noted, they were a generation apart and never actually met.

Martin Luther, while very much engaged in social matters, never drafted a detailed political philosophy. He held that worldly and churchly government belonged to two different "regiments" with different obligations, the one looking after the body, the other the soul. He followed the ethos of Paul's words in Romans 13, that good Christians should obey the powers that be, hoping and praying that such authorities would ensure the peace and stability that Christians

– as much as any others – need to lead their daily lives. While his attitude toward the actual rulers of his time would change from hopeful support to downright hostility and back again to a more hopeful stance, he always stuck to his basic and relatively simple political theory of the two domains, the worldly and the spiritual, combined with the belief that the latter should work actively to enlist the defense and support of the former. He did not assume that all worldly power would be morally good – indeed, he was often as pessimistic as his favorite church father Augustine – yet, in most of his remarks on politics he emphasized the duty of Christians to obey the secular powers that be.

Calvin, while echoing Luther in many respects and endorsing the separation of the two domains in principle, became more intent on creating a political society directly inspired by the religious beliefs of his new, reformed church. Indeed, as pastor in the Swiss city-state of Geneva from the late 1530s, Calvin was put in a position to realize his political ambitions in a way that Luther never was, nor would have wished to be.

According to Calvin, the two domains – secular and spiritual – do not rule over entirely separate matters. They should both ensure faithfulness to the true Gospel teaching, only with different means. And while the many strikingly democratic elements in Calvin's views on both ecclesiastical and secular government, as well as his forceful attacks on monarchy and tyranny, came to influence liberal and dissident thinkers in the following centuries, Calvin himself was hardly an advocate of religious toleration or pluralism. Indeed, Calvin ruled Geneva harshly, displaying little if any toleration of dissident views, authorizing a string of imprisonments and executions.

Luther and Calvin were both inspired by St. Augustine's political thought, and on the question of warfare, they did not depart radically from his writings. However, the ever-present regret and moral condemnation that mark Augustine's treatment of the actual results of war are somewhat less visible in the two reformers. While both make it clear that Christians should avoid fighting wars unless strictly necessary, war is also seen as an important tool of the political authorities for avoiding even greater calamities, and its results are not necessarily to be regretted – that is, as long as the war is just. Where representatives of what became known as the "Radical Reformation" of the sixteenth century present us with more extreme views – endorsing pacifism on the one side, or advocating holy war for the spreading of the true Gospel on the other – Luther and Calvin both see the use of military force mainly as a political rather than a religious tool. This owes, no doubt, much to their resistance to the worldly power of the Roman church, and to the way in which pope and empire together had wielded the sword to put down the Protestant "heresies." Against this background, the reformers were naturally skeptical of giving churchly authorities wide-ranging power over military forces. We should remember, however, that for Calvin, if not so much for Luther, the borderline between church and state cannot be unequivocally drawn, since the defense of the faith is ultimately also a political concern. While this is not explicitly borne out in Calvin's relatively sparse comments on war and military matters in his famous *Institutes*, it is a vital backdrop to understanding his thought, as well as the political dimension of Reformation theology in general.

While Calvin's political thought was first laid out in a scholarly, almost scholastic manner, and subsequently adjusted as he gained experience in Geneva, Luther's political thought was from the start directly informed by the tumultuousness of the dramatic events he witnessed. One such incident was the famous Peasants' Rebellion and the ensuing War in 1524–5 in Southern Germany and the surrounding areas. Luther initially supported the peasants, whose radical social program he no doubt also helped inspire. Yet, the bloodiness of the revolt caused him to criticize the peasants harshly and eventually to support the violent retribution of the secular authorities, causing many peasants to turn against him. Luther's stance on the issue is reflected in many of his writings after 1525, for instance in the tract *Whether Soldiers, Too, Can Be Saved*, excerpts from which can be found below.

From Martin Luther, *On Temporal Authority: To What Extent It Should Be Obeyed* (1522)[1]

In short, here one must go by the proverb, "He cannot govern who cannot wink at faults." Let this be his rule: Where wrong cannot be punished without greater wrong, there let him waive his rights, however just they may be. He should not have regard to his own injury, but to the wrong others must suffer in consequence of the penalty he imposes. What have the many women and children done to deserve being made widows and orphans in order that you may avenge yourself on a worthless tongue or an evil hand which has injured you?

Here you will ask: "Is a prince then not to go to war, and are his subjects not to follow him into battle?" Answer: This is a far-reaching question, but let me answer it very briefly. To act here as a Christian, I say, a prince should not go to war against his overlord – king, emperor, or other liege lord – but let him who takes, take. For the governing authority must not be resisted by force, but only by confession of the truth. If it is influenced by this, well and good; if not, you are excused, you suffer wrong for God's sake. If, however, the antagonist is your equal, your inferior, or of a foreign government, you should first offer him justice and peace, as Moses taught the children of Israel. If he refuses, then – mindful of what is best for you – defend yourself against force by force, as Moses so well describes it in Deuteronomy 20[:10–12]. But in doing this you must not consider your personal interests and how you may remain lord, but those of your subjects to whom you owe help and protection, that such action may proceed in love. Since your entire land is in peril you must make the venture, so that with

---

[1] From J. J. Schindel's translation, in *Luther's Works*, vol. 45, ed. Walther I. Brandt (Philadelphia: Fortress Press, 1962), pp. 124–6.

God's help all may not be lost. If you cannot prevent some from becoming widows and orphans as a consequence, you must at least see that not everything goes to ruin until there is nothing left except widows and orphans.

In this matter subjects are in duty bound to follow, and to devote their life and property, for in such a case one must risk his goods and himself for the sake of others. In a war of this sort it is both Christian and an act of love to kill the enemy without hesitation, to plunder and burn and injure him by every method of warfare until he is conquered (except that one must beware of sin, and not violate wives and virgins). And when victory has been achieved, one should offer mercy and peace to those who surrender and humble themselves. In such a case let the proverb apply, "God helps the strongest." This is what Abraham did when he smote the four kings, Genesis 14; he certainly slaughtered many, and showed little mercy until he conquered them. Such a case must be regarded as sent by God as a means to cleanse the land for once and drive out the rascals.

What if a prince is in the wrong? Are his people bound to follow him then too? Answer: No, for it is no one's duty to do wrong; we must obey God (who desires the right) rather than men [Acts 5:29]. What if the subjects do not know whether their prince is in the right or not? Answer: So long as they do not know, and cannot with all possible diligence find out, they may obey him without peril to their souls. For in such a case one must apply the law of Moses in Exodus 21, where he writes that a murderer who has unknowingly and unintentionally killed a man shall through flight to a city of refuge and by judgment of a court be declared acquitted. Whichever side then suffers defeat, whether it be in the right or in the wrong, must accept it as a punishment from God. Whichever side fights and wins in such ignorance, however, must regard its battle as though someone fell from a roof and killed another, and leave the matter to God. It is all the same to God whether he deprives you of life and property by a just or by an unjust lord. You are His creature and He can do with you as He wills, just so your conscience is clear. Thus in Genesis 20[:2–7] God himself excuses Abimelech for taking Abraham's wife; not because he had done right, but because he had not known that she was Abraham's wife.

From Martin Luther, *Whether Soldiers, Too, Can be Saved* (1526)[2]

In the first place, we must distinguish between an occupation and the man who holds it, between a work and the man who does it. An occupation or a work can be good and right in itself and yet be bad and wrong if the man who does the work is evil or wrong or does not do his work properly. The occupation of a

---

[2]   From Charles M. Jacobs's translation, in *Luther's Works*, vol. 46, ed. Robert C. Schulz (Philadelphia: Fortress Press, 1967), pp. 94–6, 105, 121, 123, 125–7, 129–31.

judge is a valuable divine office. This is true both of the office of the trial judge who declares the verdict and the executioner who carries out the sentence. But when the office is assumed by one to whom it has not been committed or when one who holds it rightly uses it to gain riches or popularity, then it is no longer right or good. The married state is also precious and godly, but there are many rascals and scoundrels in it. It is the same way with the profession or work of the soldier; in itself it is right and godly, but we must see to it that the persons who are in this profession and who do the work are the right kind of persons, that is, godly and upright, as we shall hear.

In the second place, I want you to understand that here I am not speaking about the righteousness that makes men good in the sight of God. Only faith in Jesus Christ can do that; and it is granted and given us by the grace of God alone, without any works or merits of our own, as I have written and taught so often and so much in other places. Rather, I am speaking here about external right-eousness which is to be sought in offices and works. In other words, to put it plainly, I am dealing here with such questions as these: whether the Christian faith, by which we are accounted righteous before God, is compatible with being a soldier, going to war, stabbing and killing, robbing and burning, as military law requires us to do to our enemies in wartime. Is this work sinful or unjust? Should it give us a bad conscience before God? Must a Christian only do good and love, and kill no one, nor do anyone any harm? I say that this office or work, even though it is godly and right, can nevertheless become evil and unjust if the person engaged in it is evil and unjust.

In the third place, it is not my intention to explain here at length how the occupation and work of a soldier is in itself right and godly because I have written quite enough about that in my book *Temporal Authority: To What Extent It Should Be Obeyed*. Indeed, I might boast here that not since the time of the apostles have the temporal sword and temporal government been so clearly de-scribed or so highly praised as by me. Even my enemies must admit this, but the reward, honor, and thanks that I have earned by it are to have my doctrine called seditious and condemned as resistance to rulers. God be praised for that! For the very fact that the sword has been instituted by God to punish the evil, protect the good, and preserve peace [Romans 13:1–4; 1 Peter 2:13–14] is powerful and sufficient proof that war and killing along with all the things that accompany wartime and martial law have been instituted by God. What else is war but the punishment of wrong and evil? Why does anyone go to war, except because he desires peace and obedience?

Now slaying and robbing do not seem to be works of love. A simple man therefore does not think it is a Christian thing to do. In truth, however, even this is a work of love. For example, a good doctor sometimes finds so serious and terrible a sickness that he must amputate or destroy a hand, foot, ear, eye, to save the body. Looking at it from the point of view of the organ that he amputates, he appears to be a cruel and merciless man; but looking at it from the point of view of the body, which the doctor wants to save, he is a fine and true man and does a good and Christian work, as far as the work itself is concerned. In the same way, when I think of a soldier fulfilling his office by punishing the wicked, killing the wicked, and creating so much misery, it seems an un-Christian work completely contrary to Christian love. But when I think of how it protects the good and keeps and preserves wife and child, house and farm, property, and honor and peace, then I see how precious and godly this work is; and I observe that it amputates a leg or a hand, so that the whole body may not perish. For if the sword were not on guard to preserve peace, everything in the world would be ruined because of lack of peace. Therefore, such a war is only a very brief lack of peace that prevents an everlasting and immeasurable lack of peace, a small misfortune that prevents a great misfortune.

What men write about war, saying that it is a great plague, is all true. But they should also consider how great the plague is that war prevents. If people were good and wanted to keep peace, war would be the greatest plague on earth. But what are you going to do about the fact that people will not keep the peace, but rob, steal, kill, outrage women and children, and take away property and honor? The small lack of peace called war or the sword must set a limit to this universal, worldwide lack of peace which would destroy everyone. . . .

It is only right that if a prince, king, or lord becomes insane, he should be deposed and put under restraint, for he is not to be considered a man since his reason is gone. "That is true," you say, "and a raving tyrant is also insane; he is to be considered as even worse than an insane man, for he does much more harm." It will be a little difficult for me to respond to that statement, for that argument seems very impressive and seems to be in agreement with justice and equity. Nevertheless, it is my opinion that madmen and tyrants are not the same. A madman can neither do nor tolerate anything reasonable, and there is no hope for him because the light of reason has gone out. A tyrant, however, may do things that are far worse than the insane man does, but he still knows that he is doing wrong. He still has a conscience and his faculties. There is also hope that he may improve and permit someone to talk to him and instruct him and follow this advice. We can never hope that an insane man will do this for he is like a clod or a stone. Furthermore, such conduct has bad results or sets a bad example. If it is considered right to murder or depose tyrants, the practice spreads and it becomes a commonplace thing arbitrarily to call men tyrants who are not tyrants, and even to kill them if the mob takes a notion to do so. The history of the Roman people shows us how this can happen. They killed many a fine emperor simply because they did not like him or he did not do what they wanted, that is, let them be lords and make him their fool. This happened to Galba, Pertinax, Gordian, Alexander, and others. . . .

No war is just, even if it is a war between equals, unless one has such a good reason for fighting and such a good conscience that he can say, "My neighbor compels and forces me to fight though I would rather avoid it." In that case, it can be called not only war, but lawful self-defense, for we must distinguish between wars that someone begins because that is what he wants to do and does before anyone else attacks him, and those wars that are provoked when an attack is made by someone else. The first kind can be called wars of desire; the second, wars of necessity. The first kind are of the devil; God does not give good fortune to the man who wages that kind of war. The second kind are human disasters; God help in them!

Take my advice, dear lords. Stay out of war unless you have to defend and protect yourselves and your office compels you to fight. Then let war come. Be men, and test your armor. Then you will not have to think about war to fight. The situation itself will be serious enough, and the teeth of the wrathful, boasting, proud men who chew nails will be so blunt that they will scarcely be able to bite into fresh butter. . . .

This is the first thing to be said in this matter. The second should be just as carefully observed. Even though you are absolutely certain that you are not starting a war but are being forced into one, you should still fear God and remember him. You should not march out to war saying, "Ah, now I have been forced to fight and have good cause for going to war." You ought not to think that that justifies anything you do and plunge headlong into battle. It is indeed true that you have a really good reason to go to war and to defend yourself, but that does not give you God's guarantee that you will win. Indeed, such confidence may result in your defeat – even though you have a just cause for fighting the war – for God cannot endure such pride and confidence except in a man who humbles himself before him and fears him. He is pleased with the man who fears neither man nor devil and is bold and confident, brave and firm against both, if they began the war and are in the wrong. But there is nothing to the idea that this will produce a victory, as though it were our deeds or power that did it. Rather, God wants to be feared and he wants to hear us sing from our hearts a song like this, "Dear Lord, you see that I have to go to war, though I would rather not. I do not trust, however, in the justice of my cause, but in your grace and mercy, for I know that if I were to rely on the justness of my cause and were confident because of it, you would rightly let me fall as one whose fall was just, because I relied upon my being right and not upon your sheer grace and kindness." . . .

The third question is whether overlords have the right to go to war with their subjects. We have, indeed, heard above that subjects are to be obedient and are even to suffer wrong from their tyrants. Thus, if things go well, the rulers have nothing to do with their subjects except to cultivate fairness, righteousness, and judgment. However, if the subjects rise up and rebel, as the peasants did recently, then it is right and proper to fight against them. That, too, is what a prince should do to his nobles and an emperor to his princes if they are rebellious and start a war. Only it must be done in the fear of God, and too much reliance must not be placed on being in the right, lest God determine that the lords are to be punished by their subjects, even though the subjects are in the wrong. This has often happened, as we have heard above. For to be right and to do right do not always go together. Indeed, they never go together unless God joins them. Therefore, although it is right that subjects patiently suffer everything and do not revolt, nevertheless, it is not for men to decide whether they shall do so. For God has appointed subjects to care for themselves as individuals, has taken the sword from them, and has put it into the hands of another. If they rebel against this, get others to join them and break loose, and take the sword, then before God they are worthy of condemnation and death.

Overlords, on the other hand, are appointed to be persons who exist for the sake of the community, and not for themselves alone. They are to have the support of their subjects and are to bear the sword. Compared to his overlord the emperor, a prince is not a prince, but an individual who owes obedience to the emperor, as do all others, each for himself. But when he is seen in relationship to his own subjects he is as many persons as he has people under him and attached to him. So the emperor, too, when compared with God, is not an emperor, but an individual person like all others; compared with his subjects, however, he is as many times emperor as he has people under him. The same thing can be said of all other rulers. When compared to their overlord, they are not rulers at all and are stripped of all authority. When compared with their subjects, they are adorned with all authority.

Thus, in the end, all authority comes from God, whose alone it is; for he is emperor, prince, count, noble, judge, and all else, and he assigns these offices to his subjects as he wills, and takes them back again for himself. Now no individual ought to set himself against the community or attract the support of the community to himself, for in so doing he is chopping over his head, and the chips will surely fall in his eyes. From this you see that those who resist their rulers resist the ordinance of God, as St. Paul teaches in Romans 13[:2]. In 1 Corinthians 15[:24] Paul also says that God will abolish all authority when he himself shall reign and return all things to himself. . . .

Of course, it is true that if a man serves as a soldier with a heart that neither seeks nor thinks of anything but acquiring wealth, and if temporal wealth is his only reason for doing it, he is not happy when there is peace and not war. Such a man strays from the path and belongs to the devil, even though he fights out of obedience to his lord and at his call. He takes a work that is good in itself and makes it bad for himself by not being very concerned about serving out of obedience and duty, but only about seeking his own profit. For this reason he does not have a good conscience which can say, "Well, for my part, I would like to stay at home, but because my lord calls me and needs me, I come in God's name and know that I am serving God by doing so, and that I will earn or accept the pay that is given me for it." A soldier ought to have the knowledge and confidence that he is doing and must do his duty to be certain that he is serving God and can say, "It is not I that smite, stab, and slay, but God and my prince, for my hand and my body are now their servants." That is the meaning of the watchwords and battle cries, "Emperor!" "France!" "Lüneburg!" "Braunschweig!" This is how the Jews cried against the Midianites, "The sword of God and Gideon!" Judges 7[:20].

Such a greedy man spoils all other good works, too. For example, a man who preaches for the sake of temporal wealth is lost, though Christ says that a preacher shall live from the gospel. It is not wrong to do things for temporal wealth, for income, wages, and pay are also temporal wealth. If it were wrong, no one should work or do anything to support himself on the ground that it is done for temporal wealth. But to be greedy for temporal wealth and to make a Mammon of it is always wrong in every office, position, and occupation. Leave out greed and other evil thoughts, and it is not sin to fight in a war. Take your wages for it, and whatever is given you. This is why I said above that the work, in itself, is just and godly, but that it becomes wrong if the person is unjust or uses it unjustly.

A second question: "Suppose my lord were wrong in going to war." I reply: If you know for sure that he is wrong, then you should fear God rather than men, Acts 4 [5:29], and you should neither fight nor serve, for you cannot have a good conscience before God. "Oh, no," you say, "my lord would force me to do it; he would take away my fief and would not give me my money, pay, and wages. Besides, I would be despised and put to shame as a coward, even worse, as a man who did not keep his word and deserted his lord in need." I answer: You must take that risk and, with God's help, let whatever happens, happen. He can restore it to you a hundredfold, as he promises in the gospel, "Whoever leaves house, farm, wife, and property, will receive a hundredfold," etc. [Matthew 19:29].

In every other occupation we are also exposed to the danger that the rulers will compel us to act wrongly; but since God will have us leave even father and mother for his sake, we must certainly leave lords for his sake. But if you do not know, or cannot find out, whether your lord is wrong, you ought not to weaken certain obedience for the sake of an uncertain justice; rather you should think the best of your lord, as is the way of love, for "love believes all things" and "does not think evil," 1 Corinthians 13[:4–7]. So, then, you are secure and walk well before God. If they put you to shame or call you disloyal, it is better for God to call you loyal and honorable than for the world to call you loyal and honorable. What good would it do you if the world thought of you as a Solomon or a Moses, and in God's judgment you were considered as bad as Saul or Ahab?

The following excerpt deals with one of the most hotly debated political topics of the fifteenth and sixteenth centuries in Europe (aside from the Reformation itself), namely, the successful advance of the Turkish empire following the Turkish victory at Constantinople in 1453. Luther had early on criticized the crusading zeal of the Roman church against the Turks and continued to insist that the church had no business in waging war against the Muslims. He held, however, that the Christian emperor – that is, the *secular* authorities – could and indeed should fight against attacking Muslim forces in self-defense, and also that Christians through prayer and reform should make themselves morally strong so as to resist the advance of the Turks. This is a good example of the more peaceable side of Luther; a trait which, alas, was obscured by his infamous diatribe in *On the Jews and Their Lies* in 1543 – a work that recommended violent measures against Jews if they did not convert. While his anti-Semitic leanings ought to be neither forgotten nor forgiven, we can surmise – based on his general teaching on the two "regiments," and on the negative and indeed surprised reaction of many of his contemporaries and friends to his attack on the Jews[3] – that the warning against using military power for purely religious purposes in the work here quoted, is closer to Luther's core teaching on religion and politics.

From Martin Luther, *On War against the Turk* (1529)[4]

The popes had never seriously intended to wage war against the Turk; instead they used the Turkish war as a cover for their game and robbed Germany of money by means of indulgences whenever they took the notion. The whole world knew it, but now it is forgotten. So they condemned my article not because it opposed the Turkish war, but because it tore away this cloak and blocked the path along which the money went to Rome. If they had seriously wished to fight the Turk, the pope and the cardinals would have had enough from the pallia, annates, and other unmentionable sources of income so that they would not have needed to practice such extortion and robbery in Germany. If there had been a general opinion that a serious war was at hand, I could have polished my article somewhat more and made some distinctions.

Nor did I like it that the Christians and the princes were driven, urged, and irritated into attacking the Turk, and making war on him, before they amended their own ways and lived as true Christians. These two points, or either one by itself, were enough reason to dissuade from war. I shall never advise a heathen or a Turk, let alone a Christian, to attack another or begin war. That is nothing else than advising bloodshed and destruction, and it brings no good fortune in the end, as I have written in the book *Whether Soldiers, Too, Can Be Saved*; and it never does any good when one rascal punishes another without first becoming good himself.

But what motivated me most of all was this: They undertook to fight against the Turk in the name of Christ, and taught and incited men to do this, as though

---

[3] See Franklin Sherman, in the Introduction to *On the Jews and their Lies*, in *Luther's Works*, vol. 47 (Philadelphia: Fortress Press, 1971), pp. 123, 135.

[4] From Charles M. Jacobs's translation, in *Luther's Works*, vol. 46, ed. Robert C. Schulz (Philadelphia: Fortress Press, 1967), pp. 164–6.

our people were an army of Christians against the Turks, who were enemies of Christ. This is absolutely contrary to Christ's doctrine and name. It is against his doctrine because he says that Christians shall not resist evil, fight, or quarrel, nor take revenge or insist on rights [Matthew 5:39]. It is against his name because there are scarcely five Christians in such an army, and perhaps there are worse people in the eyes of God in that army than are the Turks; and yet they all want to bear the name of Christ. This is the greatest of all sins and is one that no Turk commits, for Christ's name is used for sin and shame and thus dishonored. This would be especially so if the pope and the bishops were involved in the war, for they would bring the greatest shame and dishonor to Christ's name because they are called to fight against the devil with the word of God and with prayer, and they would be deserting their calling and office to fight with the sword against flesh and blood. They are not commanded to do this; it is forbidden.

O how gladly Christ would receive me at the Last Judgment if, when summoned to the spiritual office to preach and care for souls, I had left it and busied myself with fighting and with the temporal sword! Why should Christ or his people have anything to do with the sword and going to war, and kill men's bodies, when he declared that he has come to save the world, not to kill people [John 3:17]? His work is to deal with the gospel and to redeem men from sin and death by his Spirit to help them from this world to everlasting life. According to John 6[:15] he fled and would not let himself be made king; before Pilate he confessed, "My kingship is not of this world" [John 18:36]; and in the garden he bade Peter to put up his sword and said, "All who take the sword will perish by the sword" [Matthew 26:52].

I say this not because I would teach that worldly rulers ought not be Christians, or that a Christian cannot bear the sword and serve God in temporal government. Would to God they were all Christians, or that no one could be a prince unless he were a Christian! Things would be better than they now are, and the Turk would not be so powerful. But what I want to do is to keep a distinction between the callings and offices, so that everyone can see to what God has called him and fulfil the duties of his office faithfully and sincerely in the service of God. I have written more than enough about this elsewhere, especially in the books *Whether Soldiers, Too, Can Be Saved* and *Temporal Authority*. In the church, where all should be Christians, Paul will not permit one person to assume another's office, Romans 12[:4] and 1 Corinthians 12[:14–26], but exhorts every member to do his own work so that there be no disorder, rather, that everything be done in an orderly way [1 Corinthians 14:40]. How much less, then, are we to tolerate the disorder that arises when a Christian abandons his office and assumes a temporal office, or when a bishop or pastor gives up his office and assumes the office of a prince or judge; or, on the other hand, when a prince takes up the office of a bishop and gives up his princely office? Even today this shameful disorder rages and rules in the whole papacy, contrary to their own canons and laws.

In the following excerpt from Calvin's monumental *Institutes* we see him echoing many of Luther's concerns, but in a somewhat more organized and scholastic fashion. As does Luther, he sees the waging of war basically as punishment for misdeeds. He stresses that using armed force should always be a last resort, and that organized violence should never be resorted to for personal benefit, but only for the common good.

From John Calvin, *Institutes of the Christian Religion* (1559), bk. IV, chap. 20, 11–12[5]

11. On the Right of the Government to Wage War

But kings and people must sometimes take up arms to execute such public vengeance. On this basis we may judge wars lawful which are so undertaken. For if power has been given them to preserve the tranquillity of their dominion, to restrain the seditious stirrings of restless men, to help those forcibly oppressed, to punish evil deeds – can they use it more opportunely than to check the fury of one who disturbs both the repose of private individuals and the common tranquillity of all, who raises seditious tumults, and by whom violent oppressions and vile misdeeds are perpetrated? If they ought to be the guardians and defenders of the laws, they should also overthrow the efforts of all whose offenses corrupt the discipline of the laws. Indeed, if they rightly punish those robbers whose harmful acts have affected only a few, will they allow a whole country to be afflicted and devastated by robberies with impunity? For it makes no difference whether it be a king or the lowest of the common folk who invades a foreign country in which he has no right, and harries it as an enemy. All such must, equally, be considered as robbers and punished accordingly. Therefore, both natural equity and the nature of the office dictate that princes must be armed not only to restrain the misdeeds of private individuals by judicial punishment, but also to defend by war the dominions entrusted to their safekeeping, if at any time they are under enemy attack. And the Holy Spirit declares such wars to be lawful by many testimonies of Scripture.

12. Restraint and Humanity in War

But if anyone object against me that in the New Testament there exists no testimony or example which teaches that war is a thing lawful for Christians, I answer first that the reason for waging war which existed of old still persists

5 From Ford Lewis Battles's translation, in John Calvin, *Institutes of the Christian Religion*, vol. 2, ed. John T. McNeill (Philadelphia: The Westminster Press, 1960), pp. 1499–1501.

today; and that, on the other hand, there is no reason that bars magistrates from defending their subjects. Secondly, I say that an express declaration of this matter is not to be sought in the writings of the apostles; for their purpose is not to fashion a civil government, but to establish the spiritual Kingdom of Christ. Finally, that it is there shown in passing that Christ by his coming has changed nothing in this respect. For if Christian doctrine (to use Augustine's words) condemned all wars, the soldiers asking counsel concerning salvation should rather have been advised to cast away their weapons and withdraw completely from military service. But they were told: "Strike no man, do no man wrong, be content with your wages" [Luke 3:14 p.]. When he taught them to be content with their wages, he certainly did not forbid them to bear arms.

But it is the duty of all magistrates here to guard particularly against giving vent to their passions even in the slightest degree. Rather, if they have to punish, let them not be carried away with headlong anger, or be seized with hatred, or burn with implacable severity. Let them also (as Augustine says) have pity on the common nature in the one whose special fault they are punishing. Or, if they must arm themselves against the enemy, that is, the armed robber, let them not lightly seek occasion to do so; indeed, let them not accept the occasion when offered, unless they are driven to it by extreme necessity. For if we must perform much more than the heathen philosopher required when he wanted war to seem a seeking of peace,[6] surely everything else ought to be tried before recourse is had to arms. Lastly, in both situations let them not allow themselves to be swayed by any private affection, but be led by concern for the people alone. Otherwise, they very wickedly abuse their power, which has been given them not for their own advantage, but for the benefit and service of others.

Moreover, this same right to wage war furnishes the reason for garrisons, leagues, and other civil defenses. Now, I call "garrisons," those troops which are stationed among the cities to defend the boundaries of a country; "leagues," those pacts which are made by neighboring princes to the end that if any trouble should happen in their lands, they may come to one another's aid, and join forces to put down the common enemies of mankind. I call "civil defenses," things used in the art of war.

---

[6] The reference is to Cicero's *On Duties*, bk. 1, e.g. section 35.

26

The Radical Reformation (Sixteenth Century)

Religious Rationales for Violence and Pacifism

> Now, to knock people such as Moab, Agag, Ahab, and Nero from their thrones is God's highest pleasure. Scripture does not call them servants of God, but instead snakes, dragons, and wolves.
>
> Anonymous, *To the Assembly of the Common Peasantry*

It is common to view the Lutheran and Calvinist Reformation as representing a radical break with medieval Christianity. However, Luther, Calvin, and many of their collaborators were in truth outflanked by a number of considerably more radical theologians and religious activists, who opposed the more famous reformers with charges that the mainstream Reformation movement was neither consistent, nor radical, nor Christian enough. These thinkers and activists often go under the name of the "Radical Reformers."[1]

"Radical," however, is a term to be used with caution. Most Protestant reformers of the sixteenth century, even the most radical, thought of themselves as theological conservatives, who were intent on protecting the "authentic" Christian faith from corruption, idolatry, and the trappings of worldly power. They were certainly not what the nineteenth and twentieth centuries would term "theological liberals." Many of them were Biblical literalists, who staunchly opposed compromise on questions of dogma. Even those who were less rigid in their theological commitments – often called "Spiritualists" as opposed to "Literalists" – saw themselves as conserving the true faith against corruption. Yet, in opposing the existing church

---

[1] The more mainstream reformers, including Luther, Melanchthon, Zwingli, and Calvin, are often referred to as the Magisterial Reformers. Although the term "Radical Reformation" is normally used to denote the movement around the Peasants' Rebellion in the 1520s, it can usefully be applied to a full century's worth of theorizing in Protestant circles.

hierarchies, and in recognizing the faith and conscience of each individual as the ultimate court of appeal in theological questions (in theory, if not always in practice), they did come across as decidedly *radical* in their own day. And with their teaching of legitimate opposition to – even rebellion against – political authority, they laid the groundwork for later political liberalism, even if most of the Radical Reformers themselves were neither liberals nor democrats.

The thorny question of armed force inevitably became part of the Radical Reformers' agenda. The Peasants' Rebellion in Germany (1524–6)[2] became the first manifestation of their radical views. This uprising was justified on grounds that the common people had a right to use armed force in order to defend themselves against corrupt and un-Christian rulers. Support for such a radical outlook waned somewhat after the Peasants' Rebellion was harshly suppressed, with Martin Luther condemning the uprising in the most certain of terms. The outlook nevertheless maintained much of its vigor and survived into the next century, when it was, for instance, taken up by the Puritan cause in the English Civil War. Indeed, the century following the Lutheran Reformation in Europe, from the 1520s until the 1640s (often simply called "the century of religious civil wars") was teeming with radical Protestants, and similarly radical Catholics, whose articulation of religious rationales for war went well beyond mere rhetoric. Interestingly, however, within the same era we also find pacifist calls to non-violence, patience, and tolerance.

To exemplify the kinds of attitudes found among the most radical Protestants of this era, we will excerpt from three texts from the 1520s, as well as a later manifestation of Protestant political theology from the 1550s. Variable, both in form and content, these texts evince the wide range of radical views represented within the sixteenth-century Reformation movement. Portraying these views as representative of one unified doctrine is misleading. But some elements do bind them together:

(1) In contrast to Luther, and to a somewhat lesser extent Calvin, the Radical Reformers did not recognize a clear-cut distinction between church and state, or between a churchly and a secular "regiment," as Luther famously called it. They held that Christian communities as a whole should be governed by the faith-informed actions of individual Christians. Hierarchies, powerful secular rulers, and elites were deemed to be unnecessary and dangerous.

(2) Although they often differed on matters of eschatology (i.e. how to understand the Last Days and Final Judgment of Christ), they shared a decidedly millenarian rhetoric, emphasizing the importance of inward purity, and readiness for the Second Coming of Christ.[3]

---

[2] Also known as the Peasants' Revolt or the Peasants' War.

[3] As Michael G. Baylor points out in his informative discussion of the radical reformers in Baylor (ed. and trans.), *The Radical Reformation* (Cambridge: Cambridge University Press, 1991), p. xix, reformers such as Thomas Müntzer seem not to have believed literally in an imminent end to the world, but they found the language of millenarianism effective in motivating commoners to rally around their movement.

(3) And they shared a strong anti-Catholic sentiment, stronger even than that of Luther.

The Call to Act and the Opposition to Gradual Change

Thomas Müntzer (1490–1525) and Andreas Karlstadt (1486–1541) were among the most influential radicals of the 1520s. Unlike Luther, who argued for gradual social reform, they maintained that injustice should be forcibly and swiftly opposed, and they thus provided inspiration for the Peasants' Rebellion. Müntzer was captured and beheaded in 1525, while Karlstadt survived to become an early proponent of the Pietist movement, which emphasized clean living and spiritual renewal.

For our purposes, their advocacy of radical change and popular rebellion is most crucial. Although they seem to have seen theological reformation and political resistance as, in theory, *defensive* rather than *offensive*, they gave impetus to a movement that sought to achieve swift political change, if necessary through resort to violence.

From Andreas Karlstadt, *Whether One Should Proceed Slowly, and Avoid Offending the Weak in Matters that Pertain to God's Will* (1524)[4]

Now, as I have just proven through scriptural testimony that no one should look around for the other person or wait until others follow him in the knowledge of the truth (John 5[:39–41]),[5] so too when it concerns action, we should obey all of God's commands according to our capacity and not wait until those without understanding, or the weak, follow. For God has always commanded all of us to teach his covenant and to act accordingly. It is always written, "Learn it and keep it so that you act according to it" (Deuteronomy 4[:2], 5[:1]). Action has been commanded of all of us, and each one should do what God commands, even if the whole world hesitates and does not want to follow.

Look, I am asking you whether a son should wait to honor his parents until the weak follow, understand, and want to honor their parents? . . . I am asking whether one should wait to stop coveting the goods of other people until others do [so.] May one steal until the thieves stop stealing? And thus I ask, again and again, in

---

[4]   From Baylor (ed. and trans.), *The Radical Reformation*, pp. 52–3, 54, 58–9.
[5]   Karlstadt has previously referred to, *inter alia*, Luke 15:1f., Isaiah 29:14, Matthew 16:4, 13ff., Deuteronomy 12:8, and Galatians 1:8.

the case of all the commandments, whether it is proper that we wait until others have learned, and have the will to follow us and to do what God wants.

Now, just as I have asked this with respect to the commandments which concern the love of one's neighbor, I also ask it about the works and deeds which directly concern God's honor. Namely, I ask whether I should let the idols stand, which God commands me to remove, until all the weak follow in removing them? Again, may I blaspheme God as long as the others do not stop blaspheming? If you say yes, then the enemies of Christ and God can also say, with the same right, that murderers may murder, thieves may steal, adulterers may commit adultery, and similar rogues may practice every kind of vice until all rogues become pious. For there is one reason and one basis in all commandments. . . .

If one says, "You should preserve brotherly love," this means absolutely nothing, because it is not yet clear whether their brotherly love is not a cloak of Antichrist, which is certainly as wicked and harmful as any invention of the pope. But for now I will leave that undetermined and say that Christ has removed and cut off all brotherly love if it is against his commandment, or diverts the least person away from God. For love fulfills God's commandments, and it is impossible for someone to love Christ and to act against his commandment, or not do what Christ commanded. . . .

. . . [E]ach community and household should pay attention so that it understands God's commandment and acts accordingly. And God wants us so little to wait until others follow and become pious that he has commanded that the godless be punished just as other vices are punished (Deuteronomy 13 and 17). And in addition he has commanded that whole cities that cultivate their idolatry or do not want to turn to the right path be killed and destroyed.

It is astonishing that our scripturally wise and our rulers punish carnal adultery and allow spiritual adultery to go unpunished. They want to defeat spiritual adultery with their breath and to stave off carnal adultery with swords, iron, fire, and the executioner's wheel. But is this not miserable conduct among Christians? Is it not a devilish thing that they have more regard for, and punish more severely, the dishonoring of man than the dishonoring of God? Moses orders that idolatrous people or spiritual adulterers be killed no less than carnal adulterers. If they looked at their Paul correctly, they would certainly find that Paul did not punish the servants of idols less than the servants of whores. Nor does it have to be true because they want to have it thus, to defend their honor and their beautiful reputation.

Among the era's most outspoken works legitimizing violence was the anonymous treatise *To the Assembly of the Common Peasantry*. It addressed representatives of German peasants on the question of just revolt. The author has not been identified, but the ideas put forward in this treatise are closely related to views expressed by Thomas Müntzer.

From Anonymous, *To the Assembly of the Common Peasantry* (1525), chap. 7: "Whether a Community May Depose its Authorities or Not?"[6]

Now to the heart of the matter! God wants it! Now the storm bells will be sounded! . . . Did not that blasphemous animal, the ass, punish the false prophet Baal for his godlessness?[7] . . . Was not godless Cain shot by blind Lamech without any danger to himself? [Genesis 4:23–4]. Here God's miracles can be seen clearly, in that he brings such hard punishment on the godless! But how else will arbitrary power (our harsh Babylonian captivity by the unchristian nature of the criminal authorities) reach its end?

I will speak only briefly about this. All the lords who issue selfish commands stemming from the desires of their hearts and their willful, unjust heads, and who appropriate for themselves – I will remain silent about their plunder – taxes, customs, payments, and what similarly serves the common fund for the protection and maintenance of the common territory, these lords are in truth the real robbers and the declared enemies of their own territory.

Now, to knock people such as Moab, Agag, Ahab, and Nero from their thrones is God's highest pleasure. Scripture does not call them servants of God, but instead snakes, dragons, and wolves. Go to it! . . .

I will prove that a territory or community has the power to depose its pernicious lords . . .[8]

Joshua 1[:7f.] commands the principle that no lord has the power to act according to his own will, but only on the basis of divine law. If he does not, simply get rid of him and leave him far behind. This is most pleasing to God. . . .

[W]e Christians have sufficiently sound and sincere reasons [to depose our lords], and we are also obliged to redeem ourselves from these godless lords out of this Babylonian captivity, as St. Peter says, Acts 5[:29], "We must obey God rather than men." And the earlier divine chancellor, Paul, says in 1 Corinthians 7[:21], "If you are a slave, you can make yourself free, so take the chance." . . .

Also, the fourth divine jurist, St. Mark, writes most clearly for us in chapter 9[:43–7], "If your eye, hand, or foot offends you, cut it off," etc. Both kinds of authority are indicated here, the clerical with the eye and the temporal with the hand. And although some say that this refers to spiritual things, as does Matthew 5[:29f.], I shall say, "No!" For here he deals quite obviously with external, proud, and useless authorities, who rule with frivolous wrath and who give an

---

[6]   From Baylor (ed. and trans.), *The Radical Reformation*, pp. 118, 119, 120–1.

[7]   The reference here is to Numbers 22:25–33.

[8]   The author says he will do this by reference to thirteen sayings from divine law. A selection of these arguments and "sayings" are included in the following.

example of every vice, such as inordinate drunkenness, vomiting, whoring, blaspheming, torturing, making a show of their power and might, etc. It is their "Christian tongue" which daily prays, "Holy be your name," etc. Therefore St. Mark affirms here[9] that it would be better to hang a millstone around the necks of such authorities and throw them into the depths of the sea! . . .

In sum, let them prattle and gossip about whatever they want. Their power derives ultimately either from the spirit or from the flesh. If it derives from the spirit, it is just and most pleasing to God, says Paul to the Romans in chapter 8[:1–8]. But if their authority is derived from the flesh, it is devilish and a most openly declared enemy of God. May God pity us that such fleshly authority should rule over Christian people. And unceasingly they may talk about two kinds of commandments, namely the divine, which concerns the salvation of the soul, and the political, which concerns the common good. Oh God, these commandments cannot be separated from each other. For the political commandments are also divine: truly to further the common good is nothing except truly to maintain brotherly love, which is of the highest merit for blessedness.

Radical Non-resistance

But the Radical Reformation produced not only the calls to violent resistance found above, it also inspired the opposite persuasion: that true Christians should form a peace-loving community in the world, thereby accepting persecution with patience and never resisting it by violent means. According to this point of view, sincere Christians should separate themselves totally from the bloody and brutal dealings of this world. For some of its adherents, this frame of mind must have seemed a natural reaction to the brutality and eventual failure of the Peasants' Rebellion, but their message has remained influential well beyond the confines of the early sixteenth century. Indeed, this non-violent wing of the Reformation movement has continued to inspire much of Christian pacifism up to our own day, as witnessed among such groups as the Mennonites and the Quakers, both of which have their origins in this era.

A good formulation of the idea of non-resisting separation from the world can be found in *The Schleitheim Articles* of 1527, normally attributed to the Swiss Anabaptist leader Michael Sattler (1495–1527).[10]

---

[9] The editor (Michael G. Baylor) assumes that the author actually has Matthew 18:6 or Luke 17:12 in mind.

[10] Anabaptism is used as a designation for that wing of the Reformation which rejected infant baptism, along with several other practices that were deemed without scriptural basis, such as the taking of oaths. (However, several Anabaptists themselves rejected the label.) The Anabaptists were Scriptural literalists, professing a wholehearted return to the practices and teachings of primitive Christianity. The Mennonites are among the most important descendants of the Reformation

From Michael Sattler, *The Schleitheim Articles* (1527)[11]

Concerning the sword we have reached the following agreement. The sword is ordained by God outside the perfection of Christ. It punishes and kills evil people and protects and defends the good. In the law the sword is established to punish and to kill the wicked, and secular authorities are established to use it. But in the perfection of Christ the ban alone will be used to admonish and expel him who has sinned, without putting the flesh to death, and only by using admonition and the command to sin no more.

Now, many who do not recognize what Christ wills for us will ask whether a Christian may also use the sword against evil people for the sake of protecting the good or for the sake of love. Our unanimous answer is as follows: Christ teaches us to learn from him that we should be mild and of humble heart, and in this way we will find rest for our souls. . . .

Secondly, it is asked about the sword, whether a Christian may pass judgment in worldly quarrels and conflicts at law such as unbelievers have with one another. This is the answer: Christ did not want to decide or judge between brother and brother concerning an inheritance, and he refused to do so [Luke 12:13]. Thus, we should do likewise.

Thirdly, it is asked about the sword, whether a Christian may hold a position of governmental authority if he is chosen for it. This is our reply: Christ should have been made a king, but he rejected this [John 6:15] and did not view it as ordained by his father. We should do likewise and follow him. . . .

Lastly, it should be pointed out that it is not fitting for a Christian to be a magistrate for these reasons: the authorities' governance is according to the flesh, but the Christian's is according to the spirit. Their houses and dwellings remain in this world, but the Christian's are in heaven. Their weapons of conflict and war are carnal and only directed against the flesh, but the Christian's weapons are spiritual and directed against the fortifications of the devil. Worldly people are armed with spikes and iron, but Christians are armed with the armor of God – with truth, with justice, with peace, faith, and salvation, and with the word of God.

John Knox and the Call to Rebellion

Inspired partly by theologians and jurists such as Vitoria, Suárez, and Grotius, and partly by the emerging liberalism of the seventeenth century, the idea of religious

Anabaptists. A good and sympathetic overview of the ideas of the Anabaptists and other representatives of what is often called "the Left Wing of the Reformation," can be found in Charles Villa-Vicencio (ed.), *Between Christ and Ceasar* (Grand Rapids: Wm. B. Eerdmans, 1986), pp. 60–85.

[11] From Baylor (ed. and trans.), *The Radical Reformation*, pp. 176–7, 178.

rebellion and holy war would soon be totally discredited within Christendom. But in the sixteenth century, and well into the seventeenth, arguments in favor of holy wars were still alive, not least among the direct and indirect descendants of the Radical Reformation of the 1520s.[12]

Most famous of these later radicals is John Knox (1505–72), a Scottish Calvinist and founder of Scottish Presbyterianism, who became known for his fierce opposition to the rule of Mary Tudor, the Catholic Queen of England. His vitriolic *First Blast of the Trumpet against the Monstrous Regiment of Women* (1558) was written in protest against the reign of Queen Mary.

While some of Knox's writings are notorious for their fierceness and temper, his thinking also bears the stamp of serious theological reflection. He sought to conform his views about rebellion to Biblical teaching, which he read not least in the light of writings by Calvin and other leading thinkers of the Reformation. Knox thus recognized how violent resistance to earthly authorities could not be asserted without contradicting important texts, such as the thirteenth chapter of St. Paul's Letter to the Romans, which urged obedience to temporal powers, Calvin's condemnation of the rebellious spirit, and the practice of several Swiss radicals. Thus, while Knox seems to have viewed himself as a prophet destined to champion true Christianity in Scotland and drive out Catholicism from its territory, for a long time he could *not* bring himself to support violent rebellion.[13]

Knox's solution hinged on re-interpreting the plural term "powers" in St. Paul's text: There are *several* powers in society, not just one, and when some of these powers, even the highest, act against God's express will, the *other* powers of society, such as that represented by the nobility, must act in order to restore order and true religion. In doing this, they are not illegitimately resisting the power of the state, but rather wielding rightful power against usurpers and tyrants.

Once Knox had reached this far, he exhibited little of the caution of John of Salisbury (in the twelfth century) or Thomas Aquinas (in the thirteenth), who had both indicated that a tyrant could rightly be resisted and deposed only in extreme situations. In Knox we find a much less qualified call to rebellion.

While Knox's explicitly religious reasons for using armed force would not be echoed by the British liberal thinkers of the following centuries, his legitimation of

---

[12]   A good summary of holy war ideas in the Radical Reformation and its aftermath (well into the seventeenth century) may be found in James Turner Johnson, *Ideology, Reason, and the Limitation of War* (Princeton, NJ: Princeton University Press, 1975), pp. 81–133. Johnson's overview includes a fascinating discussion of Francis Bacon's advocacy of holy war reasoning and of the radical English Puritans' arguments for holy war during the Thirty Years War and the English Civil War. In Alexander Leighton (1568–1649), an English Puritan and holy war advocate, Johnson finds one of the relatively few explicit references in this tradition to *ius in bello* considerations, although these are inspired mainly by a concern for the prudence and military discipline that ought to exist among the "perfect," holy warriors (see ibid., pp. 126–7). See also James Turner Johnson, *The Holy War Idea in Western and Islamic Traditions* (University Park: Pennsylvania State University Press, 1997).

[13]   This is well described in Roger A. Mason's introduction to John Knox, *On Rebellion* (Cambridge: Cambridge University Press, 1994).

resistance and rebellion are nonetheless important stepping stones on the way to the political liberalism that would inspire many Protestants in the following centuries – including many Calvinists, not least several important architects of the American Revolution.

From John Knox, *The Appellation to the Nobility and the Estates* (1558)[14]

As the Apostle in these words [Romans 13:1–4] most straitly commandeth obedience to be given to lawful powers, pronouncing God's wrath and vengeance against such as shall resist the ordinance of God, so doth he assign to the powers their offices, which be to take vengeance upon evil doers, to maintain the well doers, and so to minister and rule in their office that the subjects by them may have a benefit and be praised in well doing. Now if you be powers ordained by God (and that I hope all men will grant), then by the plain words of the Apostle is the sword given unto you [i.e. the Nobles] by God for maintenance of the innocent and for punishment of malefactors. . . . [B]y the plain doctrine of the Apostle you are bound to maintain us and to punish the other being evidently convict and proved criminal.

Moreover, the former words of the Apostle do teach how far high powers be bound to their subjects: to wit, that because they are God's ministers by Him ordained for the profit and utility of others, most diligently ought they to intend upon the same. For that cause assigneth the Holy Ghost, commanding subjects to obey and to pay tribute, saying: 'For this do you pay tribute and toll.' [Romans 13:6] That is, because they are God's ministers, bearing the sword for your utility. Whereof it is plain that there is no honour without a charge annexed. And this one point I wish your wisdoms deeply to consider: that God hath not placed you above your brethren to reign as tyrants without respect of their profit and commodity. . . .

And therefore, my Lords, to return to you, seeing that God hath armed your hands with the sword of justice, seeing that His law most strictly commandeth idolaters and false prophets to be punished with death, and that you be placed above your subjects to reign as fathers over their children; and further, seeing that not only I, but with me many thousand famous, godly and learned persons, accuse your bishops and the whole rabble of the papistical clergy of idolatry, of murder and of blasphemy against God committed, it appertaineth to your Honours to be vigilant and careful in so weighty a matter. . . .

I am not ignorant that great troubles shall ensue your enterprise. For Satan will not be expelled from the possession of his usurped kingdom without resistance.

---

[14] From John Knox *On Rebellion*, ed. Roger A. Mason (Cambridge: Cambridge University Press, 1994), pp. 84–5, 110, 111.

But if you, as is said, preferring God's glory to your own lives, unfeignedly seek and study to obey His blessed will, then shall your deliverance be such as evidently it shall be known that the angels of the Eternal do watch, make war and fight for those that unfeignedly fear the Lord. But if you refuse this my most reasonable and just petition, what defence that ever you appear to have before men, then shall God (whom in me you contemn) refuse you.

27

Francisco de Vitoria (ca. 1492–1546)

Just War in the Age of Discovery

[W]ar is no argument for the truth of the Christian faith.

De Indis

As we have seen from the preceding selections, there has hardly been a time when war has not cast its shadow over philosophical speculation.[1] Yet not until Francisco de Vitoria wrote the *De Indis* (*On the American Indians*) and its sequel *De iure belli* (*On the Law of War*), did the problem of war between nations become the express theme of a full-fledged work by a philosopher of note. Delivered in 1539, and first published in 1557, the two lectures were destined to enjoy great notoriety. From Molina and Suárez onwards, philosophers and jurists would use Vitoria's writings as an essential point of reference for normative thinking about international relations.

Spain's expansion into the newly discovered territories of the Americas had by Vitoria's time become a subject of heated debate. Reports of indiscriminate killing, forced labor, and confiscation of land, had raised doubts about the fast-growing colonies. Most vexing was the issue of slavery. In the early years of the Spanish conquest it had been thought relatively easy to justify this practice by an appeal either to the Christian faith (the Amerindians were said to be enemies of the one, true religion) or to natural reason, since, in the light of the latter, it was considered manifestly evident that the natives of the Caribbean Islands, who appeared to lack all but the most rudimentary social development, were incapable

---

[1] Some of the passages in this introduction have been reproduced from Gregory M. Reichberg, "Philosophy Meets War: Francisco de Vitoria's *De Indis* and *De jure belli relectiones* (1557)," in *The Classics of Western Philosophy*, ed. J. Gracia, G. Reichberg, and B. Schumacher (Oxford: Blackwell, 2003), pp. 197–204.

of self-government. The views on natural slavery expressed by Aristotle in *Politics*, bk. 1, chaps. 4–7 (see chap. 3, this volume, pp. 39–40), where he argues that some people, due to their inferior intelligence, are fit to be ruled by others with superior mental endowments, were adduced as theoretical justification for the enslavement of local populations.

However, by the early 1530s, with the discovery in the preceding decade of the great empires of Mexico and Peru, it had become increasingly difficult to allege cultural impoverishment as a basis for enslavement. Growing dissatisfaction with the putative reasons justifying enslavement prompted a storm of controversy among Spanish intellectuals over the legitimacy of their country's colonization of the Americas. This controversy provided the setting for Vitoria's two lectures on the "affair of the Indies."

Vitoria was at that time a noted professor of theology at the University of Salamanca. A member of the Dominican religious order, he received his higher education in Paris, where he was schooled in the thought of Thomas Aquinas. There he was also exposed to nominalism, as well as to the new French humanism, which was very much in vogue at the time.

Little of Vitoria's own teaching was published in his lifetime. Apart from several prefaces which were written for works that he edited, his writings have survived mainly in the form of notes taken down by university students, to whom he dictated lectures under two different rubrics. First, there were his lectures on Aquinas's *Summa theologiae*.[2] Second, each academic year Vitoria would speak before the entire university community. Taking as point of departure some passage which had already been covered in the regular course syllabus, this kind of address was accordingly named a *relectio* (a "rereading"). At the beginning of the *De Indis*, Vitoria informs his audience that a question taken from Aquinas's *Summa theologiae* (II–II, q. 10, a. 2), "Whether it is licit to baptize the children of unbelievers against the wishes of their parents," would serve as the springboard for a broad-ranging discussion of Spanish rule in the New World. Since it was by force of arms that his countrymen had come to exercise dominion over the indigenous peoples of the Americas, Vitoria would, in the course of his treatment, assess whether religious motives – for instance a desire to convert the Amerindians to Christianity – could provide moral warrant for the employment of these coercive measures.

Vitoria divided his discussion into two parts, each representing a distinct *relectio*. First, under the heading (affixed by a later editor) *De Indis*, Vitoria critically examines the reasons ("titles") which apologists had put forward to justify "in the forum of conscience" Spain's claim to dominion in the New World. Next, in the companion

---

[2]   An English translation of Vitoria's commentary on *Summa theologiae* II–II, q. 40, may be found in James Brown Scott, *Francisco de Vitoria and his Law of Nations*, trans. Gwladys L. Williams (Oxford: Clarendon Press, 1934; reprint Union, NJ: The Lawbook Exchange, 2000), appendix F, pp. cxv–cxxxi. Presented several years before the *De Indis* and *De jure belli relectiones*, Vitoria's commentary on this *quaestio* of the *Summa* largely parallels his later discussion of war, although between the two accounts there exist some notable differences.

piece *De iure belli*, Vitoria discusses in more abstract terms whether military force can rightly be made to serve aims such as self-defense, sheltering the innocent from harm, regaining stolen property, or punishing evildoers. He also gives ample consideration to the sort of behavior that should be observed in wartime.

In the introductory section of the *De Indis*, Vitoria indicates that the problem to be discussed transcends the whole order of positive civil law. This kind of law he deems inapplicable in the present case, since, on his view, prior to their conquest by the Spaniards, the barbarians of the New World were self-governing. Thus the question of their subjection could not be decided by reference to the laws of the Spanish Crown. Ecclesiastical law, likewise, was of little relevance in settling this question, since Roman Catholic authorities in his opinion had no legitimate temporal jurisdiction over these non-Christians. Moreover, few if any positive international laws had yet been codified to regulate the nascent relations between European states, on the one hand, and the autochthonous peoples of Africa, the Americas, and the Far East, on the other. To determine the normative principles which ought to govern Spain's expansion into the New World, Vitoria accordingly appealed to the precepts of an unwritten code of conduct, which, in the following passage, he refers to as "divine laws" (*leges divinas*). In contrast to the laws enacted by human beings (*leges humanas*) within civil society or the church, these precepts were said to be rooted in a source antecedent to human deliberation and choice, namely God. Yet, insofar as this was a moral instruction that did not inherently depend upon special religious revelation, Vitoria subsequently follows Thomas Aquinas (see *Summa theologiae* I–II, q. 90), in placing these precepts under the heading of "natural law" (*lex naturalis*). And, insofar as these "natural" moral norms are reflected in the customs of diverse peoples, Vitoria likewise refers to them by the ancient Roman name of *ius gentium* (the law of nations): a set of moral requirements which are binding among all nations that have achieved a modicum of social organization. The establishment of a tight conceptual linkage between the moral problem of conquest and war, on the one hand, and the tradition of natural law, on the other, is central to these two *relectiones*. Written on the eve of the sectarian strife that was soon to engulf Europe, Vitoria's emphasis on natural law would have a formative influence on the development of the modern, post-Westphalian conception of the legitimate use of force by sovereign states, wherein the *ius ad bellum* (the right to go to war) is framed in terms of secular rather than religious reasons.

From *On the American Indians* (*De Indis*)[3]

The text to be re-read is "Go ye therefore, and teach all nations, baptizing them in the name of the Father, and of the Son, and of the Holy Ghost" (Matthew

---

[3]   This translation is borrowed from *Francisco de Vitoria: Political Writings*, ed. Anthony Pagden and Jeremy Lawrance (Cambridge: Cambridge University Press, 1991), pp. 233–92. (Most of the editors'

28:19). This raises the following problem: *whether it is lawful to baptize the children of unbelievers against the wishes of their parents?* The problem is discussed by the doctors on Lombard's *Sentences* IV. 4. 9, and by Aquinas in *ST* II–II. 10. 12 and III. 68. 10.

This whole dispute and relection has arisen again because of these barbarians in the New World, commonly called Indians, who came under the power of the Spaniards some forty years ago, having been previously unknown to our world.

My present discussion of these people will be divided into three parts: first, by what right (*ius*) were the barbarians subjected to Spanish rule? Second, what powers has the Spanish monarchy over the Indians in temporal and civil matters? And third, what powers has either the monarchy or the Church with regard to the Indians in spiritual and religious matters? The conclusion to the last question will thus lead back to a solution of the question posed at the outset.

[Introduction: Whether This Dispute is Justified]

As for the first part, it may first of all be objected *that this whole dispute is unprofitable and fatuous*, not only for those like us who have no warrant to question or censure the conduct of government in the Indies irrespective of whether or not it is rightly administered, but even for those whose business it is to frame and administer that government. . . .

[R]eturning to this business of the barbarians, we may reply that the matter is neither so evidently unjust of itself that one may not question whether it is just, nor so evidently just that one may not wonder whether it might be unjust. It seems rather to have arguments on both sides. At first sight, it is true, we may readily suppose that, since the affair is in the hands of men both learned and good, everything has been conducted with rectitude and justice. But when we hear subsequently of bloody massacres and of innocent individuals pillaged of their possessions and dominions, there are grounds for doubting the justice of what has been done. Hence it may be concluded that *disputation is not unprofitable*, and the objection is answered. . . .

But if anyone objects that, even if there was once some doubt about this business, it has long since been discussed and settled by wise men, and matters fully arranged according to their verdict, so that further deliberation is unnecessary, my first reply is: "if so, blessed be the Lord!" My lecture does not seek to imply the contrary, and I have no desire to stir up fresh contentions. And second,

explanatory footnotes and most references to manuscript variants have not been included here.) Latin edition: Francisco de Vitoria, *Relectio de Indis*, ed. L. Pereña and J. M. Pérez Prendes, Corpus Hispanorum de Pace V (Madrid: Consejo Superior de Investigaciones Científicas, 1967).

I say that it is not the province of lawyers, or not of lawyers alone, to pass sentence in this question. Since these barbarians we speak of are not subjects [of the Spanish Crown] by human law (*iure humano*), as I shall show in a moment, their affairs cannot be judged by human statutes (*leges humanae*), but only by divine ones, in which jurists are not sufficiently versed to form an opinion on their own. And as far as I am aware, no theologian of note or worthy of respect in a matter of such importance has ever been called upon to study this question and provide a solution. Yet since this is a case of conscience, it is the business of the priests, that is to say of the Church, to pass sentence upon it. So it is written of the king "that it shall be, when he sitteth upon the throne of his kingdom, that he shall write him a copy of the Law out of that which is before the priests the Levites" (Deuteronomy 17:18). And third, even if the principal question has been sufficiently examined and resolved, in so great a matter there may yet remain particular matters of doubt which merit some clarification.

In conclusion, I should regard it as something not unprofitable and fatuous, but an achievement of considerable worth, if I were to succeed in treating this question with the seriousness which it deserves.

Working from the premise that Spain and the pagan nations of America were common participants in the *ius gentium*, Vitoria divided his *De Indis* treatment of the Spanish occupation into two sets of arguments, one dealing with *illegitimate* titles of conquest and the other with possible *legitimate* titles.

The discussion of these titles is preceded by consideration of the question whether or not the barbarians should be viewed as rational and free human beings, capable of exercising dominion over self or others. If it could be shown that they were incapable of self-rule, the Spanish Crown would then not be obliged to deal with their leaders on an equal footing. By contrast, if they could be shown to possess true dominion, the ensuing analysis of legitimate and illegitimate titles of conquest would have to proceed on the assumption that the Amerindians were bearers of substantive rights that would have to be respected by the European newcomers.

Opting for the latter alternative, Vitoria inveighs against the view that the barbarians' state of unbelief would prevent them from owning property and exercising self-rule. The main thrust of his rebuttal consists in arguing that dominion derives not from profession of the Christian faith (a view he ascribes to some Protestant Reformers) but rather from the natural law. Since non-Christian faith does not cancel out entitlements received from the natural law, nor does it cancel out the capacity for self-rule.

In the passage reproduced below we find Vitoria addressing the argument, advanced in his day by some prominent theologians, that the Amerindians were in a state akin to what Aristotle termed "natural slavery." This view he vigorously rebuts.

From *On the American Indians*[4]

[Question 1, Conclusion]

The conclusion of all that has been said is that the barbarians undoubtedly possessed as true dominion, both public and private, as any Christians. That is to say, they could not be robbed of their property, either as private citizens or as princes, on the grounds that they were not true masters (*ueri domini*). It would be harsh to deny to them, who have never done us any wrong, the rights we concede to Saracens and Jews, who have been continual enemies of the Christian religion. Yet we do not deny the right of ownership (*dominium rerum*) of the latter, unless it be in the case of Christian lands which they have conquered.

To the original objection one may therefore say, as concerns the argument that *these barbarians are insufficiently rational to govern themselves* and so on (1. 1 ad 2):

1 Aristotle certainly did not mean to say that such men thereby belong by nature to others and have no rights of ownership over their own bodies and possessions (*dominium sui et rerum*). Such slavery is a civil and legal condition, to which no man can belong by nature.

2 Nor did Aristotle mean that it is lawful to seize the goods and lands, and enslave and sell the persons, of those who are by nature less intelligent. What he meant to say was that such men have a natural deficiency, because of which they need others to govern and direct them. It is good that such men should be subordinate to others, like children to their parents until they reach adulthood, and like a wife to her husband. That this was Aristotle's true intention is apparent from his parallel statement that some men are "natural masters" by virtue of their superior intelligence. He certainly did not mean by this that such men had a legal right to arrogate power to themselves over others on the grounds of their superior intelligence, but merely that they are fitted by nature to be princes and guides.

Hence, granting that these barbarians are as foolish and slow-witted as people say they are, it is still wrong to use this as grounds to deny their true dominion (*dominium*); nor can they be counted among the slaves. It may be, as I shall show, that these arguments can provide legal grounds for subjecting the Indians, but that is a different matter.

For the moment, the clear conclusion to the first question is therefore *that before arrival of the Spaniards these barbarians possessed true dominion, both in public and private affairs.*

Vitoria now turns to reviewing the titles advanced in his own day to justify the imposition of Spanish rule over the Amerindians. He begins with the "illegitimate titles," of which he lists seven in all. The first two were based on claims of prior

---

[4] Vitoria, *Political Writings*, pp. 250–1.

legal jurisdiction – that the Holy Roman Emperor (then Charles I of Spain) possessed dominion over the whole world, and that the pope had conferred the lands of the New World on the Spanish Crown. In rebuttal, Vitoria argues at some length that neither the emperor nor the pope enjoy secular jurisdiction over the non-Christian world. The question of sovereign rights over America could only be decided on the basis of natural, not positive (civil or ecclesiastical) law. This having been established, Vitoria proceeds to inquire whether Spain's jurisdiction over the New World had devolved to it by right of discovery.

From *On the American Indians*[5]

[Question 2: By What Unjust Titles the Barbarians of the New World Passed under the Rule of the Spaniards]

Accepting, therefore, that they were true masters, it remains to consider by what title we Christians were empowered to take possession of their territory. I shall first list the irrelevant and illegitimate titles which may be offered, and then pass to the legitimate titles by which the barbarians could have been subjected to Christian rule. There are seven irrelevant titles, and seven or perhaps eight just and legitimate ones. . . .

Question 2, Article 3: Third unjust title, that possession of these countries is by right of discovery

This title by right of discovery (*in iure inuentionis*) was the only title alleged in the beginning, and it was with this pretext alone that Columbus of Genoa first set sail. And it seems that this title is valid because:

  1 All things which are unoccupied or deserted become the property of the occupier by natural law and the law of nations, according to the law *Ferae bestiae* (*Institutions* II. 1. 12). Hence it follows that the Spaniards, who were the first to discover and occupy these countries, must by right possess them, just as if they had discovered a hitherto uninhabited desert.

But on the other hand, against this third title, we need not argue long; as I proved above (1. 1–6), the barbarians possessed true public and private dominion. The law of nations, on the other hand, expressly states that goods which belong to no owner pass to the occupier. Since the goods in question here had an

---

[5] Ibid., pp. 251–2, 264–5.

owner, they do not fall under this title. Therefore, although this title may have some validity when taken in conjunction with another (as I shall discuss below), of itself it provides no support for possession of these lands, any more than it would if they had discovered us.

The remaining illegitimate titles (not all of which have been included in the passages reproduced below) postulate that the newly discovered lands had been ceded to Spain as a consequence of the Amerindians' misconduct. Deriding as preposterous the contention that on first encountering representatives of the Spanish Crown the barbarians had recognized this ruler as their rightful ruler – this consent, if ever given, would have been uttered under invalidating circumstances of fear and ignorance – Vitoria instead focused his attention mainly on two sorts of claims: that the Amerindians had refused to accept faith in Christ, and that their culture was rife with violations of the natural law. In rejecting the former claim, Vitoria was one of the first to articulate at length the idea, now widely accepted, that religious belief may not be imposed by force.

From *On the American Indians*[6]

Question 2, Article 4: Fourth unjust title, that they refuse to accept the faith of Christ, although they have been told about it and insistently pressed to accept it

...**2** My second conclusion is that *the barbarians are not bound to believe from the first moment that the Christian faith is announced to them,* in the sense of committing a mortal sin merely by not believing a simple announcement, unaccompanied by miracles or any other kind of proof or persuasion, that the true religion is Christian, and that Christ is the Saviour and Redeemer of the universe.

The proof follows from my discussion of the first proposition. If they were excused before they heard anything about the Christian religion, then again they are not obliged by a simple statement or announcement of this kind. Such an announcement is no argument or reason for believing; indeed, as Cajetan says (in *ST* II–II. 1. 4 ad 2), it is foolhardy and imprudent of anyone to believe a thing without being sure it comes from a trustworthy source, especially in matters to do with salvation. But the barbarians could not be sure of this, since they did not know who or what kind of people they were who preached the new religion to them. This is confirmed by St Thomas, who says that things which are of faith

---

[6] Ibid., pp. 269–70, 271–5.

visibly and clearly belong to the realm of the credible; the faithful man would not believe them unless he could see that they were credible, either by palpable signs or by some other means (*ST* II–II. 1. 4 ad 2, 1. 5 ad 1). Therefore where there are no such signs nor any other persuasive factor, the barbarians are not obliged to believe. . . .

From this proposition it follows that if the faith is proposed to the barbarians only in this way and they do not accept it, the Spaniards cannot use this pretext to attack them or conduct a just war against them. This is obvious, because the barbarians are innocent on this count, and have not done any wrong to the Spaniards.

The corollary is proved by St Thomas' teaching that for the just war a just cause is required; namely, that those who are attacked have deserved attack by some culpable action (*ST* II–II. 40. 1). . . .

If the barbarians have done no wrong, there is no just cause for war; this is the opinion shared by all the doctors, not only theologians but also jurists such as Hostiensis, Innocent IV, and others; Cajetan expounds it eloquently in his commentary on *ST* II–II. 66. 8. I know of no author who opposes it. Therefore this would not be a legitimate title for occupying the lands of the barbarians and despoiling their previous owners of them. . . .

6 My sixth conclusion is that, however probably and sufficiently the faith may have been announced to the barbarians and then rejected by them, *this is still no reason to declare war on them and despoil them of their goods.* This conclusion is expressed by St Thomas in his *ST* II–II. 10. 8, where he says that unbelievers who have never taken up the faith such as the pagans and Jews are by no means to be compelled to believe. And this is the common conclusion of the doctors of both canon and civil law. The proof is that belief is a matter of will, but fear considerably diminishes the freedom of will (Aristotle, *Nicomachean Ethics* $1110^2 1$–12). To come to the mysteries and sacraments of Christ merely out of servile fear would be sacrilege. . . . The proposition is also proved by the use and custom of the Church, since no Christian emperor, with the benefit of the advice of the most holy and wise popes, has ever declared war on unbelievers simply because they refused to accept the Christian religion.

Besides, war is no argument for the truth of the Christian faith. Hence the barbarians cannot be moved by war to believe, but only to pretend that they believe and accept the Christian faith; and this is monstrous and sacrilegious. Duns Scotus says that it is a religious act for princes to compel unbelievers to believe with threats and terror (in *Sentences,* IV. 4. 9); but this can only be understood to refer to unbelievers who are already the subjects of Christian princes. Of such subjects I shall speak later. But the barbarians do not belong to this group, and therefore I do not believe that Scotus would have applied his assertion to these barbarians of ours.

It is therefore clear that this title to the conquest of the lands of the barbarians, too, is neither applicable nor legitimate.

Question 2, Article 5: Fifth unjust title, the sins of the barbarians

This next title is also seriously put forward by those who say that, although the barbarians may not be invaded because of their unbelief or their refusal to accept the Christian faith, war may nevertheless be declared on them for their other mortal sins, which according to the proponents of this argument are manifold, and very serious to boot.

Concerning mortal sins, however, they make a distinction. Some sins, they say, are not against natural law, but only against positive divine law; and for these the barbarians cannot be invaded. But others, such as cannibalism, incest with mothers and sisters, or sodomy, are against nature; and for these sins they may be invaded and compelled to give them up. The reasoning behind this is that in the former category of sins against positive law, it cannot be demonstrated by evidence that they are sinful, whereas in the case of sins against the law of nature the barbarians can be shown that they are committing an offence against God, and may consequently be compelled not to offend Him further. Again, they can be forced to observe a law which they themselves profess; and this is the case with natural law. This is the opinion of St Antonino of Florence (*Summa theologica*, III. 22. 5 §8), following Agostino Trionfo (*De potestate ecclesiastica*, I. 23. 4); and the same opinion is held by Silvestro Mazzolini da Priero (*Summa Syluestrina*, *s.v.* papa §7), and Innocent IV in his commentary on the decretal *Quod super his* (X. 3. 34. 8), where he expressly says: "I believe that if the gentiles break natural law, which is the only law they have, they may be punished by the pope". He adduces to this purpose the fact that the Sodomites were punished by God (Genesis 19); "since God's judgments are examples to us, I do not see why the pope, who is the vicar of Christ, should not be empowered to do the same". So says Innocent; and by this argument, they might also, on the pope's authority, be punished by Christian princes.

But on the other hand I adduce the following proposition: *Christian princes, even on the authority of the pope, may not compel the barbarians to give up their sins against the law of nature, nor punish them for such sins.*

I reply with the following proofs. First of all, our opponents' presupposition that the pope has jurisdiction over the barbarians is false, as I have said above (*On the American Indians*, 2. 2).

Second, they either interpret "sins against the law of nature" in a universal sense, as including theft, fornication, and adultery; or in the special sense of "sins against nature" as defined by St Thomas (*ST* II–II, 154 11–12), that is to say, not only "against natural law" but "against the natural order", or what is described by the word "uncleanness" in 2 Corinthians 12:21, which the *Glossa ordinaria* explains as pederasty, buggery with animals, or lesbianism, which are referred to also in Romans 1:24–7. Now if they interpret the expression exclusively in the second of these two ways, one may argue against them that murder is as serious a sin, or more serious; and therefore it is clear that if it is lawful to punish men for these "sins against nature", it must also be lawful to punish them for murder; and similarly, blasphemy is as serious a sin, and so it is obvious that one may punish them for blasphemy too, and so on. But if they extend their interpretation to include the general sense of "any sin against the law of nature", the reply is that it is not lawful to punish them for fornication, and therefore it is not lawful to punish them for the other sins against natural law. The minor premiss is clear from 1 Corinthians 5:9–13, which says: "I wrote unto you in an epistle not to company with fornicators . . . and not to keep company, if any man *that is called a brother* be a fornicator or an idolater", and then adds: "For what have we to do to judge them also that are without?" St Thomas expounds this as meaning that prelates have received power only over those who have subjected themselves to the faith (in 1 Corinthians 5:12, lect. 3). It is quite clear, then, that Paul means that the judgment of unbelievers, whether they be fornicators or idolaters, is none of his business.

A further argument is that not all sins against natural law can be demonstrated to be so by evidence, at least to the satisfaction of all men. Furthermore, to make this assertion is tantamount to saying that the barbarians may be conquered because of their unbelief, since they are all idolaters. Besides, the pope may not make war on Christians because they are fornicators or robbers, or even because they are sodomites; nor can he confiscate their lands and give them to other princes; if he could, since every country is full of sinners, kingdoms could be exchanged every day. And a further confirmation is that such sins are more serious in Christians, who know them to be sins, than in the barbarians, who do not. Besides, it would be extraordinary that the pope should be able to pronounce judgments and inflict punishments on unbelievers, and yet be prevented from making laws for them.

And there is a further argument, which seems to conclude the matter. Either the barbarians are obliged to suffer the penalties ordained for these sins, or they are not. If they are not, the pope is not empowered to inflict them. If they are, then they are obliged to recognize the pope as their lord and legislator; but if this is the case, then the very fact that they refuse to recognize him as such is a reason for declaring war upon them. But even my opponents deny this conclusion, as I have said above. It would indeed be extraordinary that they should be able to deny the authority and jurisdiction of the pope with impunity, and yet be obliged to suffer his judgments. Again, those who are not Christians cannot accept the judgment of the pope, since the pope cannot condemn or punish them by any right other than that he is the vicar of Christ. But all these opponents, St Antonino and Silvestro Mazzolini da Priero as well as Agostino Trionfo and even Innocent IV himself, admit that unbelievers cannot be punished on the grounds that they have not accepted Christ. Therefore they cannot be punished because they do not accept the judgment of the pope; the latter presupposes the former.

And a confirmation that neither this nor the preceding title is sufficient is that even in the Old Testament, where affairs were conducted by force of arms, the people of Israel never occupied the lands of the unbelievers either on the grounds that they were infidels and idolaters or because they were otherwise sinners against nature, even though they were sinful in many ways, being idolaters and sinners against nature, for instance by sacrificing their sons and daughters to demons. They only conquered such peoples by God's special gift, or because they refused to allow them free passage, or because they had wronged them first.

Besides, what do these opponents mean by "professing" the law of nature? If they mean "knowing what it is", the barbarians do not have complete knowledge of it. But if they mean "being willing to observe the law of nature", I counter by pointing out that, in this case, they must also mean "willing to observe the whole of Christ's law", since if they knew that Christian law was divine law, they would be willing to observe it. In this sense, they no more "profess" divine law than Christian law.

And again, we actually have better proofs to show that Christ's law is true and God-given than to show that fornication is evil or that the other things prohibited by natural law are to be avoided. Therefore, if the barbarians can be forced to keep the law of nature because it can be proved, they can also be forced to keep the law of the Gospels; but this is indeed an incredible deduction.

In the next question, Vitoria advances the first of eight legitimate titles for waging war against the Amerindians, although he nowhere asserts that these precise reasons actually motivated the Spanish military initiatives in the New World. His treatment has two prongs. On the one hand, he articulates a vision of human sociability, which emphasizes the natural ties (reinforced by travel and trade) that bind all human beings together. As participants in a common natural law, we are possessed of certain obligations toward one another that cannot be overridden by our religious, cultural, or ethnic differences. While quite familiar to us now, a universalist vision such as this would have seemed novel in Vitoria's own day. On the other hand, Vitoria is intent on demonstrating the consequences which follow from the Indian's refusal to abide by these obligations. This leads him into a discussion of the rights of war (iura belli), wherein several important points are made: sincere negotiations should precede the resort to armed force; a purely defensive war should not aim at punishing the adversary; a party may wage war for what is (de facto) an unjust cause while nevertheless sincerely believing that justice is on its side, hence special restraint should be shown against such an enemy; war may be initiated for the protection of the innocent; and so forth. Only a partial selection of the list of eight legitimate titles is reproduced below. Each of these is subdivided into "conclusions," some of which have been omitted.

From *On the American Indians*[7]

Question 3: The Just Titles by which the Barbarians of the New World Passed under the Rule of the Spaniards

I shall now discuss the legitimate and relevant titles by which the barbarians could have come under the control of the Spaniards.

Question 3, Article 1: First just title, of natural partnership and communication

My first conclusion on this point will be that *the Spaniards have the right to travel and dwell in those countries, so long as they do no harm to the barbarians, and cannot be prevented by them from doing so.*

The first proof comes from the law of nations (*ius gentium*), which either is or derives from natural law, as defined by the jurist [Gaius]: "What natural reason has established among all nations is called the law of nations" (*Institutions* I. 2. 1). Amongst all nations it is considered inhuman to treat strangers and travellers badly without some special cause, humane and dutiful to behave hospitably to strangers. This would not be the case if travellers were doing something evil by visiting foreign nations. Second, in the beginning of the world, when all things were held in common, everyone was allowed to visit and travel through any land he wished. This right was clearly not taken away by the division of property (*diuisio rerum*); it was never the intention of nations to prevent men's free mutual intercourse with one another by this division. Certainly it would have been thought inhuman to do so in the time of Noah. . . .

. . . Sixth, it is an act of war to bar those considered as enemies from entering a city or country, or to expel them if they are already in it. But since the barbarians have no just war against the Spaniards, assuming they are doing no harm, it is not lawful for them to bar them from their homeland.

An eighth proof is given in the words of Scripture: "Every living creature loveth his like" (Ecclesiasticus 13:15), which show that amity (*amicitia*) between men is part of natural law, and that it is against nature to shun the company of harmless men. . . . And a tenth, the jurist's determination that by natural law running water and the open sea, rivers, and ports are the common property of all, and by the law of nations (*ius gentium*) ships from any country may lawfully put in anywhere (*Institutions* II. 1. 1–4); by this token these things are clearly public property from which no one may lawfully be barred, so that it follows that the

---

[7] Ibid., pp. 277–84, 285–6, 287–8, 289, 290–1.

barbarians would do wrong to the Spaniards if they were to bar them from their lands. . . .

My second proposition is that *the Spaniards may lawfully trade among the barbarians, so long as they do no harm to their homeland.* In other words, they may import the commodities which they lack, and export the gold, silver, or other things which they have in abundance; and their princes cannot prevent their subjects from trading with the Spaniards, nor can the princes of Spain prohibit commerce with the barbarians.

The proof follows from the first proposition. In the first place, the law of nations (*ius gentium*) is clearly that travellers may carry on trade so long as they do no harm to the citizens. . . . Third, their princes are obliged by natural law to love the Spaniards, and therefore cannot prohibit them without due cause from furthering their own interests, so long as this can be done without harm to the barbarians. Fourth, to do so would appear to fly in the face of the old proverb, "do as you would be done by".

In sum, it is certain that the barbarians can no more prohibit Spaniards from carrying on trade with them, than Christians can prohibit other Christians from doing the same. It is clear that if the Spaniards were to prohibit the French from trading with the Spanish kingdoms, not for the good of Spain but to prevent the French from sharing in any profits, this would be an unjust enactment, and contrary to Christian charity. But if this prohibition cannot justly be proscribed in law, neither can it be justly carried out in practice, since an unjust law becomes inequitable precisely when it is carried into execution. And "nature has decreed a certain kinship between all men" (*Digest* I. 1. 3), so that it is against natural law for one man to turn against another without due cause; man is not a "wolf to his fellow man", as Ovid says, but a fellow.

My third proposition is that *if there are any things among the barbarians which are held in common both by their own people and by strangers, it is not lawful for the barbarians to prohibit the Spaniards from sharing and enjoying them.* For example, if travellers are allowed to dig for gold in common land or in rivers or to fish for pearls in the sea or in rivers, the barbarians may not prohibit Spaniards from doing so. But the latter are only allowed to do this kind of thing on the same terms as the former, namely without causing offence to the native inhabitants and citizens.

The proof of this follows from the first and second propositions. If the Spaniards are allowed to travel and trade among the barbarians, they are allowed to make use of the legal privileges and advantages conceded to all travellers.

Secondly, in the law of nations (*ius gentium*) a thing which does not belong to anyone (*res nullius*) becomes the property of the first taker, according to the law *Ferae bestiae* (*Institutions* II. 1. 12); therefore, if gold in the ground or pearls in the sea or anything else in the rivers has not been appropriated, they will belong by the law of nations to the first taker, just like the little fishes of the sea. And there are certainly many things which are clearly to be settled on the basis on the law of nations (*ius gentium*), whose derivation from natural law is manifestly sufficient to enable it to enforce binding rights. But even on the occasions when it is not derived from natural law, the consent of the greater part of the world is enough to make it binding, especially when it is for the common good of all men. If, after the dawn of creation or after the refashioning of the world following the Flood, the majority of men decided that the safety of ambassadors should everywhere be inviolable, that the sea should be common property, that prisoners of war should be enslaved, and likewise that it would be inexpedient to drive strangers out of one's land, then all these things certainly have the force of law, even if a minority disagree.

My fourth proposition is that *if children born in the Indies of a Spanish father wish to become citizens* (cives) *of that community, they cannot be barred from citizenship or from the advantages enjoyed by the native citizens born of parents domiciled in that community*. The proof is that the law of nations (*ius gentium*) clearly defines a "citizen" (*ciues*) as a man born in a community (*ciuitas*) (*Codex* X. 40. 7). The confirmation is that man is a civil animal (*animal ciuile*), but a man born in one community is not a citizen of another community; therefore, if he is not a citizen of the first community, he will not be a citizen of any community, and this would be inequitable by the law of nature and of nations (*ius naturale et gentium*).

Indeed, if anyone were willing to take up domicile in one of these barbarian communities, for example because he had taken a wife there or for one of the other reasons by which denizens customarily acquire citizenship, it does not seem to me he could be prohibited from doing so, any more than the other inhabitants. Consequently, it seems he would enjoy the same privileges as the rest, at least as long as he accepted the same burdens as they. . . .

My fifth proposition is that if the barbarians attempt to deny the Spaniards in these matters which I have described as belonging to the law of nations (*ius gentium*), that is to say from trading and the rest, the Spaniards ought first to remove any cause of provocation by reasoning and persuasion, and demonstrate with every argument at their disposal that they have not come to do harm, but wish to dwell in peace and travel without any inconvenience to the barbarians. And they should demonstrate this not merely in words, but with proof. As the saying goes, "in every endeavour, the seemly course for wise men is to try persuasion first" (Terence, *Eunuchus* 789). But if reasoning fails to win the acquiescence of the barbarians, and they insist on replying with violence, the Spaniards may defend themselves, and do everything needful for their own safety. It is lawful to meet force with force. And not only in this eventuality, but also if there is no other means of remaining safe, they may build forts and defences; and if they have suffered an offence, they may on the authority of their prince seek redress for it in war, and exercise the other rights of war. The proof is that the cause of the just war is to redress and avenge an offence, as said above in the passage quoted from St Thomas (*ST* II–II. 40. 1; see above, 2. 4 §11). But if the barbarians deny the Spaniards what is theirs by the law of nations, they commit an offence against them. Hence, if war is necessary to obtain their rights (*ius suum*), they may lawfully go to war.

But I should remark that these barbarians are by nature cowardly, foolish, and ignorant besides. However much the Spaniards may wish to reassure them and convince them of their peaceful intentions, therefore, the barbarians may still be understandably fearful of men whose customs seem so strange, and who they can see are armed and much stronger than themselves. If this fear moves them to mount an attack to drive the Spaniards away or kill them, it would indeed be lawful for the Spaniards to defend themselves, within the bounds of blameless self-defence; but once victory has been won and safety secured, they may not exercise the other rights of war against the barbarians such as putting them to death or looting and occupying their communities, since in this case what we may suppose were understandable fears made them innocent. So the Spaniards must take care for their own safety, but do so with as little harm to the barbarians as possible since this is a merely defensive war. It is not incompatible with reason, indeed, when there is right on one side and ignorance on the other, that a war may be just on both. For instance, the French hold Burgundy in the mistaken but colourable belief that it belongs to them. Now our emperor Charles V has a certain right to that province and may seek to recover it by war; but the French may defend it. The same may be true of the barbarians. This is a consideration which must be given great weight. The laws of war against really harmful and offensive enemies are quite different from those against innocent or ignorant ones. The provocations of the Pharisees are to be met with quite a different response from the one appropriate to weak and childish foes.

My sixth proposition is that if all other measures to secure safety from the barbarians besides conquering their communities and subjecting them have been exhausted, the Spaniards may even take this measure. The proof is that the aim of war is peace and security, as St Augustine says in his letter to Boniface (*Ep.* 189. 6). Therefore, once it has become lawful for the Spaniards to take up war or even to declare it themselves for the reasons stated above, it becomes lawful for them to do everything necessary to the aim of war, namely to secure peace and safety.

My seventh proposition goes further: once the Spaniards have demonstrated diligently both in word and deed that for their own part they have every intention of letting the barbarians carry on in peaceful and undisturbed enjoyment of their property, if the barbarians nevertheless persist in their wickedness and strive to destroy the Spaniards, they may then treat them no longer as innocent enemies, but as treacherous foes against whom all rights of war can be exercised, including plunder, enslavement, deposition of their former masters, and the institution of new ones. All this must be done with moderation, in proportion to the actual offence. The conclusion is evident enough: if it is lawful to declare war on them, then it is lawful to exercise to the full the rights of war. And is confirmed by the fact that all things are lawful against Christians if they ever fight an unjust war; the barbarians should receive no preferential treatment because they are unbelievers, and therefore can be proceeded against in the same way. It is the general law of nations (*ius gentium*) that everything captured in war belongs to the victor, as stated in the laws *De captiuis* and *Si quid in bello* (*Digest* XLIX. 15. 28 and 24), in the canon *Ius gentium* (*Decretum* D. 1. 9), and more expressly still in the law *Item ea quae ab hostibus* (*Institutions* II. 1. 17), which reads: "in the law of nations, anything taken from the enemy immediately becomes ours, even to the extent that their people become our slaves". Furthermore, as the doctors explain in their discussions of war, the prince who wages a just war becomes *ipso jure* the judge of the enemy, and may punish them judicially and sentence them according to their offence.

The foregoing is confirmed by the fact that ambassadors are inviolable in the law of nations (*ius gentium*). The Spaniards are the ambassadors of Christendom, and hence the barbarians are obliged at least to give them a fair hearing and not expel them.

This, then, is the first title by which the Spaniards could have seized the lands and rule of the barbarians, so long as it was done without trickery or fraud and without inventing excuses to make war on them. But on these grounds, if the barbarians allowed the Spaniards to carry on their business in peace among them, the Spaniards could make out no more just a case for seizing their goods than they could for seizing those of other Christians.

Question 3, Article 2: Second possible title, for the spreading of the Christian religion

My first proposition in support of this is that *Christians have the right to preach and announce the Gospel in the lands of the barbarians*. This conclusion is clear from the passage "Go ye into all the world and preach the gospel to every creature" (Mark 16:15); and "the word of God is not bound" (2 Timothy 2:9). Second, it is clear from the preceding article, since if they have the right to travel and trade among them, then they must be able to teach them the truth if they are willing to listen, especially about matters to do with salvation and beatitude, much more so than about anything to do with any other human subject. Third, if it were not lawful for Christians to visit them to announce the Gospel, the barbarians would exist in a state beyond any salvation. Fourth, brotherly correction is as much part of natural law as brotherly love; and since all those peoples are not merely in a state of sin, but presently in a state beyond salvation, it is the business of Christians to correct and direct them. Indeed, they are clearly obliged to do so. Fifth and finally, they are our neighbours, as I have said above (3. 1 §1 *ad fin.*), "and God gave them commandment, each man concerning his neighbour"

(Ecclesiasticus 17:14). Therefore it is the business of Christians to instruct them in the holy things of which they are ignorant. . . .

My fourth conclusion is that if the barbarians, either in the person of their masters or as a multitude, obstruct the Spaniards in their free propagation of the Gospel, the Spaniards, after first reasoning with them to remove any cause of provocation, *may preach and work for the conversion of that people even against their will*, and may if necessary take up arms and declare war on them, insofar as this provides the safety and opportunity needed to preach the Gospel. And the same holds true if they permit the Spaniards to preach, but do not allow conversions, either by killing or punishing the converts to Christ, or by deterring them by threats or other means. This is obvious, because such actions would constitute a wrong committed by the barbarians against the Spaniards, as I have explained, and the latter therefore have just cause for war. Second, it would be against the interests of the barbarians themselves, which their own princes may not justly harm; so the Spaniards could wage war on behalf of their subjects for the oppression and wrong which they were suffering, especially in such important matters.

From this conclusion it follows that on this count too, if the business of religion cannot otherwise be forwarded, that the Spaniards may lawfully conquer the territories of these people, deposing their old masters and setting up new ones and carrying out all the things which are lawfully permitted in other just wars by the law of war, so long as they always observe reasonable limits and do not go further than necessary. They must always be prepared to forgo some part of their rights rather than risk trespassing on some unlawful thing, and always direct all their plans to the benefit of the barbarians rather than their own profit, bearing constantly in mind the saying of St Paul: "all things are lawful unto me, but all things are not expedient" (1 Corinthians 6:12). Everything that has been said so far is to be understood as valid in itself; but it may happen that the resulting war, with its massacres and pillage, obstructs the conversion of the barbarians instead of encouraging it. The most important consideration is to avoid placing obstructions in the way of the Gospel. If such is the result, this method of evangelization must be abandoned and some other sought. All that I have demonstrated is that this method is lawful *per se*. I myself have no doubt that force and arms were necessary for the Spaniards to continue in those parts; my fear is that the affair may have gone beyond the permissible bounds of justice and religion.

This, then, is the second possible legitimate title by which the barbarians may have fallen under the control of the Spaniards. But we must always keep steadfastly before us what I have just said, lest what is in substance lawful becomes by accident evil. Good comes from a single wholly good cause, whereas evil can come from many circumstances, according to Aristotle (*Nicomachean Ethics* 1106^{b}35) and Dionysius the Pseudo-Areopagite (*Divine Names* 4. 30).

Question 3, Article 5: Fifth just title, in defence of the innocent against tyranny

The next title could be either on account of the personal tyranny of the barbarians' masters towards their subjects, or because of their tyrannical and oppressive laws against the innocent, such as human sacrifice practised on innocent men or the killing of condemned criminals for cannibalism. I assert that *in lawful defence of the innocent from unjust death, even without the pope's authority, the Spaniards may prohibit the barbarians from practising any nefarious custom or rite*. The proof is that God gave commandment to each man concerning his neighbour (Ecclesiasticus 17:14). The barbarians are all our neighbours, and therefore anyone, and especially princes, may defend them from such tyranny and oppression. A further proof is the saying: "deliver them that are drawn unto death, and forbear not to deliver those that are ready to be slain" (Proverbs 24:11). This applies not only to the actual moment when they are being dragged to death; they may also force the barbarians to give up such rites altogether. If they refuse to do so, war may be declared upon them, and the laws of war enforced upon them; and if there is no other means of putting an end to these sacrilegious rites, their masters may be changed and new princes set up. In this case, there is truth in the opinion held by Innocent IV and Antonino of Florence, that sinners against nature may be punished (q. 2, a. 5, above). It makes no difference that all the barbarians consent to these kinds of rites and sacrifices, or that they refuse to accept the Spaniards as their liberators in the matter. This could therefore be the fifth legitimate title. . . .

Question 3, Article 7: Seventh just title, for the sake of allies and friends

A further title may arise whenever the barbarians themselves are engaged in legitimate war with one another, in which case the injured party has the right to wage war, and may call upon the Spaniards to help them, and then share the prizes of victory with them. This is what is said to have happened when the Tlaxcaltecs were fighting the Mexicans; they made a treaty with the Spaniards that they should help them to defeat the Mexicans, and promised them in return whatever they might win by the laws of war. There can be no doubt that fighting on behalf of allies and friends is a just cause of war, as Cajetan declares (in *ST* II–II. 40. 1 §5); equally, a commonwealth may call upon foreigners to punish its enemies and fight external malefactors. The confirmation of this is provided by the Romans, who extended their empire in just this way, by coming to the aid of their friends and allies and profiting from the opportunity to declare just wars, thereby taking possession of new provinces by the laws of war. . . .

This, then, is the seventh and last title by which the barbarians and their lands may or might have come into the possession and dominion (*dominium*) of the Spaniards.

Question 3, [Article 8: An eighth possible title, the mental incapacity of the barbarians]

There is one further title which may be mentioned for the sake of the argument, though certainly not asserted with confidence; it may strike some as legitimate, though I myself do not dare either to affirm or condemn it out of hand. It is this: these barbarians, though not totally mad, as explained before, are nevertheless so close to being mad, that *they are unsuited to setting up or administering a commonwealth both legitimate and ordered in human and civil terms.* Hence they have neither appropriate laws nor magistrates fitted to the task. Indeed, they are unsuited even to governing their own households (*res familiaris*); hence their lack of letters, of arts and crafts (not merely liberal, but even mechanical), of systematic agriculture, of manufacture, and of many other things useful, or rather indispensable, for human use. It might therefore be argued that for their own benefit the princes of Spain might take over their administration, and set up urban officers and governors on their behalf, or even give them new masters, so long as this could be proved to be in their interest.

As I have said, this argument would be persuasive if the barbarians were in fact all mad; in that case, it is beyond doubt that such a course would be not merely lawful, but wholly appropriate, and princes would be bound to take charge of them as if they were simply children. In this respect, there is scant difference between the barbarians and madmen; they are little or no more capable of governing themselves than madmen, or indeed than wild beasts. They feed on food no more civilized and little better than that of beasts. On these grounds, they might be handed over to wiser men to govern. And an apparent confirmation of this argument is if some mischance were to carry off all the adult barbarians, leaving alive only the children and adolescents enjoying to some degree the use of reason but still in the age of boyhood and puberty, it is clear that princes could certainly take them into their care and govern them for as long as they remained children. But if this is admitted, it seems impossible to deny that the same can be done with their barbarian parents, given the supposed stupidity which those who have lived among them report of them, and which they say is much greater than that of children and madmen among other nations. Such an argument could be supported by the requirements of charity, since the barbarians are our neighbours and we are obliged to take care of their goods.

But I say all this, as I have already made clear, merely for the sake of argument; and even then, with the limitation that only applies if everything is done *for the*

benefit and good of the barbarians, and not merely for the profit of the Spaniards.
But it is in this latter restriction that the whole pitfall to souls and salvation is
found to lie.

On the Law of War (*De iure belli*)

Notwithstanding Vitoria's disclaimer that herein he will give only "the briefest
proofs," this *relectio* in fact represents one of the fullest ethical treatments of war
to have appeared up to its day. A modern reader might infer from the title that
this work is concerned solely with enunciating guidelines that should be observed
once war is already under way (*ius in bello*). While the treatise does offer an
extended consideration of this theme, it is equally concerned with questions that
relate to when, by whom, and for what aim, war may rightly be initiated (*ius ad
bellum*).

The work begins with a few words of introduction, followed by a refutation of
Christian pacifism. In arguing for the moral acceptability of a limited resort to
violence, Vitoria introduces two ideas that will be discussed throughout this *relectio*:
the distinction between defensive and offensive war, on the one hand, and the
connection between war and just punishment, on the other. In this first part he
also mentions the idea – alluded to in subsequent passages – that there is a "good
of the whole world" (*bonum totius orbis*), which ought to serve as the horizon for
decision-making about war.

From *On the Law of War*[8]

[Introduction]

Since it emerges finally, after the lengthy discussion in my first relection on the
just and unjust titles of the Spanish claim to the barbarian lands of the so-called
Indians, that possession and occupation of these lands is most defensible in terms
of the laws of war, I have decided to round off the previous relection with a brief
discussion of these laws. Since I shall be prevented by the strict time limit from
dealing with every topic which might be discussed under this head, I have not
given my pen the freedom to rove as broadly and profoundly as the subject
requires, but only so far as the short time at our disposal allows. I shall merely
note here the most salient propositions on the topic, confining myself to the

---

[8] Translation from Vitoria, *Political Writings*, ed. Pagden and Lawrance, pp. 295–8. Latin edition:
Francisco de Vitoria, *Relectio de iure belli; o, Paz dinámica*, ed. L. Pereña, V. Abril, C. Baciero, A.
García, and F. Maseda, Corpus Hispanorum de Pace VI (Madrid: Consejo Superior de Investigaciones
Científicas, 1981).

briefest proofs and ignoring many of the doubts which might arise in the course of a thorough discussion. I shall thus consider four problems:

1   Whether it is lawful for Christians to wage war at all
2   On whose authority war may be declared or waged
3   What may and ought to be the causes of the just war
4   What Christians may lawfully do against enemies, and to what extent.

These, then, will be the problems to be discussed in the first question.

[Question 1, Article 1: Whether it is lawful for Christians to wage war]

Proceeding to the first, it seems that *wars are altogether prohibited for Christians*:

1   Christians are prohibited from defending themselves, according to the passage in Romans which says: "Dearly beloved, defend not yourselves, but rather give place unto wrath" (Romans 12:19). And the Lord said in the Gospels, "whosoever shall smite thee on thy right cheek, turn to him the other also"; and in the same passage, "I say unto you, That ye resist not evil" (Matthew 5:39). Elsewhere He says: "they that take the sword shall perish with the sword" (Matthew 26:52). It is not enough to reply that these words are not precepts, but advice. The objection against warfare would stand, even if wars undertaken by Christians were merely "against the Lord's advice".

But on the other hand the opinion of all the doctors and the accepted custom of the Church are against this conclusion, for they all show that wars are in many cases lawful. . .

I reply . . . with a single proposition:

1   *A Christian may lawfully fight and wage war.* This conclusion is proved by Augustine in several places. . . .

A second proof, this time by reason, is provided by Aquinas (*ST* II–II. 40. 1). According to the passage in Romans, "for he beareth not the sword in vain; for he is the minister of God, a revenger to execute wrath upon him that doeth evil" (Romans 13:4), it is lawful to draw the sword and use weapons against malefactors and seditious subjects within the commonwealth; therefore it must be lawful to use the sword and take up arms against foreign enemies too. So princes are told in the psalm: "Deliver the poor and needy: rid them out of the hand of the wicked" (Psalm 82:4).

Third, war was permitted under the natural law, as shown by Abraham, who fought against the four kings (Genesis 14:14–16); it was also permitted in Mosaic law, as the cases of David and the Maccabees show. But the law of the Gospels does not prohibit anything which is permitted by natural law, which is why it is called the "law of liberty" (James 1:25; 2:12), as Aquinas elegantly shows (*ST* I–II. 108. 1 ad 2; cf. *On Civil Power* 1. 5 ad 6). Therefore anything which is permitted in natural and Mosaic law is by that token permitted in evangelical law. And there can be no doubt about the rights of defensive war, since "it is lawful to resist force with force" (*Vim ui repellere licet*, *Digest* I. 1. 3, and X. 5. 12. 18).

Fourth, the same proof holds true also for offensive war; that is to say, not only war in which property is defended or reclaimed, but also war in which vengeance for an injury is sought. This is proved by the authority of Augustine contained in the canon *Dominus Deus noster* (*Decretum* C.23. 2. 2): "The usual definition of just wars is that they are those which avenge injustices (*iniurias*) in cases where a nation or city is to be scourged for having failed to punish the wrongdoings of its own citizens, or restore property which has been unjustly stolen" (*Quaest. in Heptateuch*. 6. 10).

Fifth, a further proof concerning offensive war is that even defensive war could not conveniently be waged unless there were also vengeance inflicted on the enemy for the injury they have done, or tried to do. Otherwise, without the fear of punishment to deter them from injustice, the enemy would simply grow more bold about invading a second time.

The sixth proof is that the purpose of war is the peace and security of the commonwealth [as Augustine says in *De ciuitate Dei* XIX. 12, and in his *Ep.* 189. 6 to Boniface. But there can be no security for the commonwealth] unless its enemies are prevented from injustice by fear of war. It would be altogether unfair if war could only be waged by a commonwealth to repel unjust invaders from its borders, and never to carry the conflict into the enemies' camp.

A seventh proof is based on the purpose and good of the whole world. Surely it would be impossible for the world to be happy – indeed, it would be the worst of all possible worlds – if tyrants and thieves and robbers were able to injure and oppress the good and the innocent without punishment, whereas the innocent were not allowed to teach the guilty a lesson in return.

The last proof is the authority and example of saints and good men, always the strongest argument in any moral question. Many of them have not only protected their homes and property with defensive war, but also punished the injuries committed or even planned against them by their enemies with offensive war. Take, for example, the case of Jonathan and Simon, who avenged the murder of their brother John on the children of Jambri (1 Maccabees 9:32–42). In the Christian Church the same is true of Constantine the Great, Theodosius the Great, and many other distinguished Christian emperors who waged countless wars of both kinds, though they had saintly and learned bishops as their advisers.

The conclusion, then, is beyond doubt.

Using the distinction between defensive and offensive war as an organizing principle, in this second article Vitoria takes up the question of *legitimate authority*.

While clearly inspired by Aquinas's treatment in *Summa theologiae* (II–II, q. 40, a. 1), Vitoria seems most indebted to Cajetan, whose *Summa* commentary (see chap. 22, this volume) he follows in some detail. Vitoria nevertheless adds some significant nuances of his own, for instance the claim that the legitimate authority to wage war may be transferred from a higher to a lower power, in cases where the former has been derelict in opposing grave wrongdoing.

From *On the Law of War*[9]

Question 1, Article 2: On whose authority may war be declared or waged?

Proceeding to the second, we may answer with these propositions:

1 *Any person, even a private citizen, may declare and wage defensive war.* This is clear from the principle "force may be resisted by force" quoted above from the *Digest*. From this we may gather that any person may wage war without any other person's authority, not only for self-defence but also for the defence of their property and goods.

. . . [N]o one can sin by following the authority of the law, for laws justify in the forum of conscience. Hence, even if natural law did not permit us to kill in defence of our property, civil law appears to have made it permissible. And this, I may say, holds true not only for the laity, but also for the clergy and the religious, so long as there is no hint of provocation.

2 Second, *any commonwealth has the authority to declare and wage war.* For the proof of this proposition, it is to be noted that the difference in this respect between a private person and the commonwealth is that the private person has, as I have said, the right to defend himself and his property, but does not have the right to avenge injury, nor even, indeed, to seize back property which has been taken from him in the past. Self-defence must be a response to immediate danger, made in the heat of the moment or *incontinenti* as the lawyers say. Once the immediate necessity of defence has passed, there is no longer any licence for war. In my opinion, however, a man who has been unjustly struck may strike back immediately, even if the attack would probably have gone no further. For example, to avoid disgrace and humiliation a man who has been struck in the face with the fist may immediately retaliate with his sword, not to avenge himself but (as explained above) to escape dishonour and loss of face. The commonwealth, on the other hand, has the authority not only to defend itself, but also to avenge and punish injuries done to itself and its members. This is proved by Aristotle's dictum that "the commonwealth should be self-sufficient (*sibi sufficiens*)" (*Politics*

---

[9] Ibid., pp. 299–302.

1280^{b}33–5); the commonwealth cannot sufficiently guard the public good and its own stability unless it is able to avenge injuries and teach its enemies a lesson, since wrongdoers become bolder and readier to attack when they can do so without fear of punishment. So it is necessary for the proper administration of human affairs that this authority should be granted to the commonwealth.

3 Third, *in this matter the prince has the same authority as the commonwealth.* This proposition is expressly expressed in Augustine's dictum: "The natural order, being concerned with peace, requires that the authority and decision to undertake war be in the hands of princes" (*Contra Faustum* 22:75). And it is proved by the following argument the prince must be chosen by the commonwealth, therefore he is the authorized representative of the commonwealth. Indeed, where the commonwealth has a legitimate prince, all authority rests in his hands, and no public action can be taken, whether in peace or in war, without him.

But the nub of the problem is to define the commonwealth, and say who is properly its prince. The short answer is that the commonwealth is, properly speaking, a perfect community (*perfecta communitas*); but this too needs clarification. What is a "perfect" community? Let us begin by noting that a "perfect" thing is one in which nothing is lacking, just as an "imperfect" thing is one in which something is lacking: "perfect" means, then, "complete in itself" (*quod totum est, perfectum quid*). A perfect community or commonwealth is therefore one which is complete in itself; that is, one which is not part of another commonwealth, but has its own laws, its own independent policy, and its own magistrates. Such commonwealths are the kingdom of Castile and Aragon, and others of the same kind. It does not matter if various independent kingdoms and commonwealths are subject to a single prince; such commonwealths, or their princes, have the authority to declare war.

But it may fairly be asked whether, if several such commonwealths or princes share a single prince, they can of themselves wage war without the authority of their supreme sovereign? I reply that they undoubtedly can. Thus kings who are subject to the emperor can wage war on each other without waiting for the emperor's leave, since (as I said above) a commonwealth must be self-sufficient, which it cannot be without this ability.

But it clearly follows from the preceding argument that princelings who are not sovereigns of independent commonwealths, but simply rulers of parts of a greater commonwealth, cannot declare or wage war. For example, the lands of the Duke of Alba or the Count of Benavente are parts of the kingdom of Castile, not independent commonwealths.

Despite all this, however, it must be admitted that for the most part these matters are done according to the law of nations or human law; and therefore, custom may establish the right and authority to wage war. If any city or prince has obtained the customary right to wage war on their own account, then this right may not be contested, even if in other respects the commonwealth is not independent.

Furthermore, this licence and authority to wage war may be conferred by necessity. If, for example, one city attacks another in the same kingdom, or if a duke attacks another duke, and if the king fails, through negligence or timidity, to avenge the damage done, then the injured party, city or duke, may not only defend itself, but may also carry the war into its attacker's territory and teach its enemies a lesson, even killing the wrongdoers. Otherwise the injured party would have no adequate self-defence; enemies would not abstain from harming others, if their victims were content only to defend themselves. By the same argument, even a private individual may attack his enemy if there is no other way open to him of defending himself from harm.

This will suffice for the discussion of this article.

In this third article, Vitoria discusses *just cause* (the second of Aquinas's conditions for a just war), outlining the key restrictions that must be placed on this notion. In the process, he rejects some of the rationales for war that had figured prominently in classical Greek and Roman thought, as well as in Christian holy war.

From *On the Law of War*[10]

Question 1, Article 3: What are the permissible reasons and causes of just war?

Proceeding to the third, which brings us closer to the subject of our barbarians, we may reply with the following propositions:

1 First, *difference of religion cannot be a cause of just war.* This proposition was amply proved in the previous relection, where I refuted the fourth title offered to justify the enslavement of the barbarians, namely "that they refuse to receive the Christian faith" (*On the American Indians* 2. 4). This is the opinion of St Thomas (*ST* II–II. 66. 8 ad 2) and of all the other doctors; I know of no one who thinks the contrary.

2 Second, *enlargement of empire cannot be a cause of just war.* This proposition is too well known to require further proof. If it were not so, both parties in a war would have equally just cause to fight, and both would be innocent; from this it would follow that it was unlawful for either side to kill the other; and this would be self-contradictory, for it would mean that the war was just, but the killing was unjust.

3 Third, *the personal glory or convenience of the prince is not a cause of just war.* This proposition is also well established. The prince must order war and peace for

---

10   Ibid., pp. 302–4.

the common good of the commonwealth; he may not appropriate public revenues for his own aggrandisement or convenience, still less expose his subjects to
danger. This is the difference between a legitimate king and a tyrant: the tyrant
orders the government for his own profit and convenience, whereas the king
orders it for the common good, as Aristotle demonstrates (*Politics* 1295^{a}19–21).
The prince has his authority from the commonwealth, and must therefore exercise
it for the good of the commonwealth; and laws must not be framed for the
convenience of any private individual, but for the common utility of the members
of the commonwealth, as stated in the canon *Erit autem lex* (*Decretum* D.4. 2),
citing St Isidore (*Etymologies* V. 1. 21). Therefore the laws of war ought to be
for the common utility, not for the utility of the prince. This is the difference
between free men and slaves, as Aristotle shows in *Politics* 1253^{b}15–1255^{b}40.
Masters use their slaves for their own convenience, without consideration of the
slaves' convenience; free men, on the other hand, do not live for the convenience
of others, but for themselves. For a prince to abuse his position by forcing his
subjects into military service and by imposing taxes on them for the conduct of
wars waged for his convenience rather than the public good, is therefore to make
his subjects slaves.

4 Fourth, *the sole and only just cause for waging war is when harm has been
inflicted*. This is first proved by the authority of Augustine: "The usual definition
of just wars, etc." (*Quaest. in Heptateuch.* 6. 10). It is also the conclusion of
St Thomas (*ST* II–II. 40. 1) and all the doctors. Similarly, offensive war is for the
avenging of injuries and the admonishment of enemies, as we have seen; but
there can be no vengeance where there has not first been a culpable offence; *ergo*,
etc. Likewise, a prince cannot have greater authority over foreigners than he has
over his own subjects; but he may not draw the sword against his own subjects
unless they have done some wrong; therefore he cannot do so against foreigners
except in the same circumstances. The confirmation of this is the passage about
the prince in the epistle of Paul to the Romans, cited above: "For he beareth not
the sword in vain; for he is the minister of God, a revenger to execute wrath upon
him that doeth evil" (Romans 13:4). It follows from this that we may not use the
sword against those who have not harmed us; to kill the innocent is prohibited by
natural law. For the moment I postpone the question of whether God made any
other special teachings in this matter; He is the lord of life and death, and may
dispose differently if He sees fit.

5 Fifth, *not every or any injury gives sufficient grounds for waging war*. The
proof of this proposition is that it is not lawful to inflict cruel punishments such
as death, exile, or confiscation of goods for all crimes indiscriminately, even on
our own common people and native subjects of the realm. Therefore, since all the
effects of war are cruel and horrible – slaughter, fire, devastation – it is not lawful
to persecute those responsible for trivial offences by waging war upon them.
The wicked man "shall be beaten according to his fault, by a certain number"
(Deuteronomy 25:2).

Therefore it is not lawful to start war for every reason or injury. And this is sufficient for this article.

In this fourth article, Vitoria considers what sort of actions may be carried out in a just war. He begins with an assessment of the period immediately following victory. Is it permissible to exact war reparations from a defeated enemy? Can there be justification for taking hostages in order to enforce the terms of a peace agreement? May those who are guilty of having caused the war be punished for their misdeeds? Is it permissible to build fortifications on enemy soil so as to insure against future aggression?

From *On the Law of War*[11]

Question 1, Article 4: what, and how much, may be done in the just war?

Proceeding to the fourth, let us make the following propositions:

1 First, *in the just war one may do everything necessary for the defence of the public good.* This is obvious, since the defence and preservation of the commonwealth is the purpose of war. We have proved that this is lawful in the case of a private individual in his own defence, and therefore it must be all the more so in the case of a commonwealth or its prince.

2 Second, *in the just war it is also lawful to reclaim all losses, or their precise value.* This is too well known to need proof. This is the reason for undertaking war in the first place.

3 Third, *it is lawful to seize the goods of the enemy as indemnity for the costs of war, and for all losses unjustly caused by the enemy.* This is clear, since enemies who have caused injury are bound to make such restitution, and princes may accept and sue for all such things in war. If there was a legitimate arbiter to judge between the two parties to a war, he would have to condemn the unjust aggressor and perpetrator of the damage not only to the restitution of all goods stolen, but also to making good the costs and losses incurred by the war. But a prince who wages a just war acts the part of the judge in the contention which is the cause of war, as I shall shortly show, and therefore he too may demand all these things from his enemy. As I said before, if a private individual when he has no other redress is permitted to seize what he is owed from his debtor, then a prince may do so too.

4 Fourth, *a prince may do everything in a just war which is necessary to secure peace and security from attack*, for instance pulling down fortresses and all other

---

[11]   Ibid., pp. 304–6.

such actions of this kind. The proof of this is that, as I have said above, the purpose of war is peace, and therefore those who wage just war may do everything necessary for security and peace. Tranquillity and peace are counted among the good things which men strive for; without security, all the other good things together cannot make for happiness. When enemies upset the tranquillity of the commonwealth, therefore, it is lawful to take vengeance upon them.

5 Fifth, this is not all that is allowed in the just war, but even after the victory has been won and property restored to its rightful owners, and peace and security are established, *it is lawful to avenge the injury done by the enemy, and to teach the enemy a lesson by punishing them for the damage they have done.* For the proof of this point it should be noted that the prince has the authority not only over his own people but also over foreigners to force them to abstain from harming others; this is his right by the law of nations and the authority of the whole world.[12] Indeed, it seems he has this right by natural law: the world could not exist unless some men had the power and authority to deter the wicked by force from doing harm to the good and the innocent. Yet those things which are necessary for the governance and conservation of the world belong to natural law. What other argument than this can we use to prove that the commonwealth has the authority in natural law to punish those of its own members who are intent on harming it with execution or other penalties? If the commonwealth has these powers against its own members, there can be no doubt that the whole world has the same powers against any harmful and evil men. And these powers can only exist if exercised through the princes of commonwealths. Therefore it is certain that princes have the power to punish enemies who have done harm to the commonwealth; and even after the war has been duly and justly carried to its conclusion, these enemies remain as hateful to the prince as they would be to a proper judge. This is proved and confirmed by the authority of the best men. As demonstrated above in the case of the Maccabees, those who wage war do not do so only to recover their losses but also to avenge injury; and this has also been the practice of most Christian kings. The simple rout of the enemy is not enough to cancel out the shame and dishonour incurred by the commonwealth; this must be done by the imposition of severe penalties and punishments. Amongst other things, a prince is required to defend and preserve the honour and authority of the commonwealth.

In the following passages we find Vitoria engaged with a problem that is now often raised in connection with the ethics of war: the possibility that opposing

---

[12] "Totius orbis auctoritate." This is a famous expression where Vitoria suggests (without developing the idea further) that a just war is akin to an act of policing which is carried out on behalf of the international community. For a treatment of this theme, see Peter Haggenmacher, "La place de Francisco de Vitoria parmi les fondateurs du droit international," in A. Truyol Serra et al., *Actualité de la pensée juridique de Francisco de Vitoria* (Brussels: Bruylant, 1988), pp. 27–80.

parties to an armed conflict will each firmly believe in the rightness of its cause. If this impression were sustainable, it would appear to contradict the very logic of the just war theory, since, in such a case, both belligerents would be innocent and neither would have justification for using armed force against the other. Vitoria's approach was to distinguish *substantive* from *merely ostensible* justice. Substantively, justice cannot reside on both sides at once, at least with respect to the reasons which justify going to war. The impossibility of simultaneous justice is implied by the very notion of just cause, which, as we have seen, may be claimed only by reference to another party's wrongdoing. Vitoria acknowledges, however, that error may induce a belligerent to believe that it is in the right when in fact it is squarely at fault. This gives rise to a situation in which the guilty party (sincerely) believes itself to be innocent. Vitoria divides this erroneous belief into two kinds. On the one hand, it may result from an interplay of factors that are beyond the agent's control. This (borrowing from Aquinas[13]) he terms "invincible ignorance," to underscore how it may not be imputed to the agent as a personal fault. Other errors, by contrast, are "vincible." These result from negligence or even bad will and hence constitute a culpable fault on the agent's part. Agents have a moral responsibility to inquire into the justice of their claims, especially when making assertions about matters so weighty as war. This holds especially true of statesmen, senators, and others in positions of authority. Yet soldiers and even ordinary individuals, too, have an obligation to consider the claims put before them, reserving the right to disagree when the truth seems *manifestly* opposed to the decisions that their leaders have made. Vitoria thus laid the groundwork for what nowadays is termed the "right of conscientious objection."[14]

From *On the Law of War*[15]

[Question 2: Doubts concerning the Justice and Conduct of War]

Now from everything that has been said above there arise a number of doubts.[16] The first concerns the article on "the reasons and causes of just war":

---

[13]   See *Summa theologiae* I–II, q. 76, especially articles 2–3.

[14]   Although in line with much of the earlier scholastic tradition, Vitoria's argumentation is characteristically framed in terms of obligations rather than rights.

[15]   From Vitoria, *Political Writings*, ed. Pagden and Lawrance, pp. 306–9.

[16]   [*Pagden and Lawrance's note:*] "Ex omnibus supradictis": the *dubia* discussed by Vitoria in the remainder of the relection in fact concern only the points raised in Articles 3 and 4 of Question 1. The first five *dubia*, which relate to 1. 3, are arranged as Question 2, and the remaining nine, which relate to 1. 4, as Question 3.

[Question 2,] Article 1: Whether it is enough for the just war that the prince should believe that his cause is just

Proceeding to the first, let us make the following propositions:

1 First, *this is not always enough.* The first proof is that in lesser cases it is not enough, either for the prince or for private subjects, to believe that they are acting justly, as is well known. It is possible that they act in vincible error, or under the influence of some passion. Any man's opinion is not sufficient to make an action good; it must be an opinion formed according to the judgment of a wise man, as is clear from Aristotle's *Nicomachean Ethics* ($1106^{b}36–1107^{a}2$; cf. *On the American Indians* 1. 1). Furthermore, it would otherwise follow that most wars would be just on both sides. It does not usually happen that princes wage war in bad faith; for the most part they believe that their cause is just. In these circumstances, then, all the belligerents would be innocent, and consequently it would not be lawful for either side to kill anyone on the other. Even the wars of Turks and Saracens against Christians would be justified, since these peoples believe that they are serving God by waging them.

2 Second, *for the just war it is necessary to examine the justice and causes of war with great care, and also to listen to the arguments of the opponents, if they are prepared to negotiate genuinely and fairly.* As Terence says, "in every endeavour the seemly course for the wise man is to try persuasion before turning to force" (*Eunuchus* 789). One must consult reliable and wise men who can speak with freedom and without anger or hate or greed. This is obvious.

[Question 2, Article 2: Whether subjects are required to examine the causes of war]

The second doubt is this: *whether subjects are required to examine the cause of war,* or whether they may go to war without any inquiry on this matter, as officers of the law may carry out the commands of a judge without questioning his orders.

In reply let us make the following propositions:

1 First, *if the war seems patently unjust to the subject, he must not fight, even if he is ordered to do so by the prince.* This is obvious, since one may not lawfully kill an innocent man on any authority, and in the case we are speaking of the enemy must be innocent. Therefore it is unlawful to kill them. In this case the prince commits a sin in declaring war; but "they which commit such things [as] are worthy of death, not only do the same, but have pleasure in them that do them" (Romans 1:32). So even soldiers, if they fight in bad faith, are not excused. Furthermore, one may not kill innocent members of the commonwealth at the prince's behest, and therefore one may not kill foreigners either.

And from this flows the corollary that if their conscience tells subjects that the war is unjust, *they must not go to war even if their conscience is wrong*, for "whatsoever is not of faith is sin" (Romans 14:23).

2 Second, all senators and territorial magnates, and in general *all those who are admitted or called or of their own accord attend the public or royal council are in duty bound to examine the cause of just war.* This is obvious, because any person who has the power to prevent his neighbours' danger or loss is obliged to do so, especially when it is a question of danger of death and greater evils, as it is in war. If such men can by examining the causes of hostility with their advice and authority avert a war which is perhaps unjust, then they are obliged to do so. If an unjust war is started because they neglect to do this, then they are taken to have given their consent to it; if a man can prevent something which he ought to prevent, but fails to do so, then the blame rests with him. Besides, the king is not capable of examining the causes of war on his own, and it is likely that he may make mistakes, or rather that he *will* make mistakes, to the detriment and ruin of the many. So war should not be declared on the sole dictates of the prince, nor even on the opinion of the few, but on the opinion of the many, and of the wise and reliable.

3 Third, *lesser subjects who are not invited to be heard in the councils of the prince nor in public council are not required to examine the causes of war, but may lawfully go to war trusting the judgment of their superiors.* This is proved, in the first place, because it would be impossible, and inexpedient, to put the arguments about difficult public business before every member of the common people. Second, men of lower condition and class cannot prevent war even if they consider it to be unjust, since their opinion would not be heard; it would therefore be a waste of time for them to examine the causes of war.

4 Fourth, *there may nevertheless be arguments and proofs of the injustice of war so powerful, that even citizens and subjects of the lower class may not use ignorance as an excuse for serving as soldiers.* It is clear, for example, that such ignorance may be wilful and wicked, deliberately fostered out of hostility. Besides, if it were not so even the infidels would be justified in following their princes to war, and it would not be lawful for Christians to make reprisals against them, for it is certain that they believe they have just cause in their wars. Furthermore, the soldiers who crucified Christ could have used this excuse of ignorance since they were following the orders of Pilate; and so might the Jews, who followed their leaders in shouting "Away with him, away with him, crucify him" (John 19:15). None of these excuses can be accepted; *ergo*, etc.

Vitoria now proceeds to consider debatable cases, where reasons for war are couched in claims that are less than compelling. When confronted by such a circumstance, the prince, he argues, must observe the high standards normally expected of a judge, conscientiously weighing the reasons put forward by the opposing side. Moreover, such a prince has an obligation to engage in forthright negotiations with the opposing party. Attempts to settle such doubtful cases by resort to armed force must accordingly be preceded by sincere efforts at negotiation. The case is different, however, for ordinary soldiers, civilians, and other subordinates. When confronted by such doubtful cases they need not engage in sustained personal reflection about the *casus belli*. In this instance Vitoria discerns little room for conscientious objection. Rather, such subordinates have an obligation to follow the judgment of their legitimate leaders; not to do so would expose the commonwealth to injury from its enemies. The section concludes that, due to invincible ignorance, a war may seem just on the part of subjects who fight in an unjust war. Vitoria suggests, however, that this excuse rarely, if ever, holds for princes, who are in a position to know about the injustice of their cause.

From *On the Law of War*[17]

[Question 2, Article 3: What is to be done when the justice of war is undecided?]

The third doubt is *what is to be done when the justice of a war is debatable*, when both parties seem to have convincing reasons on their side?

In reply let us make the following propositions, beginning with the arguments which concern princes:

1 First, *if one has a legitimate possession, even though some particular doubt remains over his title, another prince may not seek to take it away by force of arms.* For example, if the king of France is in legitimate possession of Burgundy, even though his right to it may be doubtful it does not seem that our Emperor may seize Burgundy by force; on the other hand, the king of France ought not to try to seize it. This is proved by the legal maxim that in cases of doubt possession is nine parts of the law. It is not lawful to rob a man of his property simply on the grounds that one disputes his right to possess it. If the case were to be tried before a duly constituted judge, he would never dispossess the man of his property while the case remained unresolved; therefore, since the prince who seeks justice is himself the judge in the case, he cannot lawfully plunder the possessor as long as some doubt about the title remains. Another argument is that, if it is never lawful to dispossess the legal owner in an unresolved civil or private case, then it cannot be lawful in the disputes of princes, since the laws are the prince's laws. If according to human laws it is not permissible to dispossess a legitimate

---

17   Ibid., pp. 309–13.

owner in an unresolved case, then such action may justly be objected to in the case of princes. Besides, if this principle were not observed, both sides in a war would be just and the war could never be settled.

2 Second, *if a city or province of doubtful title has no legitimate owner* (for instance, if it is left unclaimed by the death of the legitimate owner, and it cannot be established whether the heir is the king of Spain or the king of France), *in law it is apparent that if one of the two claimants is willing to negotiate a division of the territory or compensation for part of it, then the other prince must accept the negotiation, even when he is stronger and has the power to take the whole territory by force of arms.* He would not in this case have just cause for war, as is proved by the fact that the other prince could not be said to be doing him any unjust harm by asking for an equal share in a case where he has an equal claim. In private cases, even disputed ones, it is not lawful for one of the parties to preempt the whole of the disputed property; therefore it cannot be lawful in the disputes of princes either. Finally, in this case too, the war would be just on both sides; the just judge would not give the whole territory to one or the other side, but would divide it between them.

3 Third, even when a prince enjoys peaceful possession, *if he is in doubt about his rightful title he must carefully examine the case and listen peacefully to the reasons of the other side, to see if a clear decision can be reached in favour of himself or the other party.* The proof of this proposition is that if, despite his doubts, he neglected to find out the truth, he would no longer possess the territory in good faith. In matrimonial cases, even a man who has legitimate conjugal rights must unquestionably take steps to verify the matter if he begins to suspect that his wife is married to another man; therefore the same reason must hold true of other cases. Princes are the only judges in their own affairs, since they have no superiors; but it is clear that if anyone raises an objection to another's just title to his property, the judge is bound to examine the case, and therefore princes are similarly bound to examine their own title in cases of doubt.

4 Fourth, *once the case has been examined as long as it reasonable, if the doubt remains unresolved, the legitimate owner is not required to relinquish his territory, but may henceforth own it lawfully.* This is obvious, first of all because a judge is not required in these circumstances to dispossess him of his property, so he himself cannot be required to relinquish it, either wholly or in part. . . .

So much, then, for the propositions concerning princes in an unresolved dispute. But what of their subjects, when in doubt about the justice of war? Hadrian himself in the same passage (*Quodlibets* 2 ad 1) says that a subject who is in doubt about the justice of war may not lawfully go to war at the command of his superior. He proves this assertion by arguing that the subject who does go to war in these circumstances is not acting in good faith, and therefore runs the danger of incurring mortal sin. The same opinion is formulated by Silvestro Mazzolini da Priero in his *Summa Syluestrina, s.v.* bellum 1 §9.

But against this let us make the following proposition:

5 Fifth, *in the first place, there is no doubt that in defensive wars subjects are not merely permitted to follow their prince into battle even where the justice of the case is in doubt, but are indeed bound to do so; and in the second place, that the same is true also of offensive wars.* The first proof of this is that, as has been said already, a prince neither can nor ought always to explain the reasons for war to his subjects; if subjects were unable to fight until they understood the justice of the war, the safety of the commonwealth would be gravely endangered. Second, in cases of doubt the safer course should be followed; but if subjects fail to obey their prince in war from scruples of doubt, they run the risk of betraying the commonwealth into the hands of the enemy, which is much worse than fighting the enemy, doubts notwithstanding; therefore they had better fight. Another clear proof is that an officer of the law must carry out the sentence of a judge even if he doubts its justice; to argue the contrary would be extremely dangerous. . . .

[Question 2, Article 4: War cannot be just on both sides]

The fourth doubt is this: *whether war can be just on both sides.*

In reply let us make the following propositions:

1 First, except in ignorance it is clear *that this cannot happen.* If it is agreed that both parties have right and justice on their side, they cannot lawfully fight each other, either offensively or defensively.

2 Second, where there is provable ignorance either of fact or of law, *the war may be just in itself for the side which has true justice on its side, and also just for the other side, because they wage war in good faith and are hence excused from sin.* Invincible error is a valid excuse in every case. This is often the position of subjects: even if the prince who wages war knows that his cause is unjust, his subjects may nevertheless obey him in good faith, as explained in the previous article. In such situations, the subjects on both sides are justified in fighting, as is well known. . . .

Having discussed the questions of right which arise in connection with just cause, Vitoria now insists that a ruler should take into account prudential considerations when deciding whether or not to exercise a legitimate right to go to war. The focus of this brief discussion (which is taken up again in the next section) are the issues of proportionality and side-effect harm. War results in much evil. Should this evil be excessively great, the ruler must be willing to waive the exercise of his right, in the higher interests of the common good.

From *On the Law of War*[18]

To conclude, the salient point to be considered is that war in itself is just; it is unjust and unlawful only in its accidents. But it is clear that one may have a right to reclaim a city or province, and yet find that right nullified by the danger of provoking greater conflict. As I have said, wars should only be waged for the common good (1. 3 §12); if the recovery of one city is bound to involve the commonwealth in greater damage, for instance the devastation of several cities, heavy casualties, or rivalry between princes and the occasion of further wars, there can be no doubt that the prince should cede his right and abstain from war.

Returning now to the main theme of this section ("what, and how much may be done in the just war") Vitoria provides an extended discussion of non-combatant immunity, treatment of enemy prisoners, seizure of booty, side-effect harm to civilians, the taking of hostages, punishment of offenders, and related matters that now go under the heading of *ius in bello*. "Looking at the problem from the point of view of the 'just' belligerent, Vitoria inquires into the types of harm the latter is authorized to inflict on his – hypothetically 'unjust' – adversary, and within what limits. . . . This leads him virtually to rule out St. Thomas' third condition for just war, namely *recta intentio*, which had been central to the latter's thought, and to replace it with what Suárez and other authors in the sixteenth century were to call *debitus modus*, the right manner of waging war, the limit not to be exceeded. This is then a *ius in bello* conceptually dissociated from the *ius ad bellum* dealt with in the first three parts. Yet despite a superficial similarity, we are still a long way from the 'means of injuring the enemy' set out in Articles 22 and following of the Hague Regulations respecting war on land. For Vitoria's *ius in bello*, in line with the logic of just war, is ultimately no more than a unilateral extension of the *ius ad bellum*."[19]

"It is true that at the heart of Vitoria's considerations lies an idea which appears to herald the modern principle of protection of civilian persons: only the individuals responsible in one capacity or another for the wrongful act and its persistence may be fought, since they alone are the offenders, the *nocentes*; all other subjects of the enemy are by definition *innocentes* and should thus be spared. This principle recurs as a leitmotif throughout the fourth part of the *Relectio*."[20]

---

[18]   Ibid., p. 314.
[19]   Peter Haggenmacher, "Just War and Regular War in Sixteenth Century Spanish Doctrine," *International Revue of the Red Cross*, September–October 1992 (no. 290), pp. 440–1.
[20]   Ibid., p. 141.

From *On the Law of War*[21]

Question 3: What may be Done in a Just War

About the other question there also arise a number of doubts; I mean the fourth article (1. 4), which was "what, and how much, may be done in the just war?". The first doubt – and a strong one too – is this:

Question 3, Article 1: Whether one may kill innocent people in a just war

Proceeding to the first, it seems that one may:

1 We read in Joshua 6:21 that the children of Israel killed the children in Jericho, and Saul slew the children and young women of Amalek (1 Samuel 15:3, 8), both on the authority and command of the Lord. "Whatsoever things were written aforetime were written for our learning" (Romans 15:4); therefore it must still be true today that it is lawful to kill the innocent if the war is just.

But on the other hand let us make the following propositions:

1 First, *it is never lawful in itself intentionally to kill innocent persons.* This is proved, in the first place, by Exodus 23:7, where it says "the innocent and righteous slay thou not". Second, the foundation of the just war is the injury inflicted upon one by the enemy, as shown above (1. 3 §13); but an innocent person has done you no harm. *Ergo*, etc. Third, within the commonwealth it is not permissible to punish the innocent for the crimes of the evil, and therefore it is not permissible to kill innocent members of the enemy population for the injury done by the wicked among them. Fourth, the war would otherwise become just on both sides, since it is clear that the innocent would also have the right to defend themselves. All this is confirmed by Deuteronomy 20:10–20, where the children of Israel are commanded, when they have captured a city, to smite every male thereof with the edge of the sword, but to spare the women and the little ones.

It follows that even in wars against the Turks we may not kill children, who are obviously innocent, nor women, who are to be presumed innocent at least as far as the war is concerned (unless, that is, it can be proved of a particular woman that she was implicated in guilt). It follows also that one may not lawfully kill travellers or visitors who happen to be in the enemy's territory, who are presumed innocent. And the same is true of clergy and monks, unless there is evidence to the contrary or they are found actually fighting in the war. I think there can be no doubt about this.

---

[21]   Vitoria, *Political Writings*, ed. Pagden and Lawrance, pp. 314–17, 318–22, 323–4, 325–7.

2 Second, *it is occasionally lawful to kill the innocent not by mistake, but with full knowledge of what one is doing, if this is an accidental effect*: for example, during the justified storming of a fortress or city, where one knows there are many innocent people, but where it is impossible to fire artillery and other projectiles or set fire to buildings without crushing or burning the innocent along with the combatants. This is proven, since it would otherwise be impossible to wage war against the guilty, thereby preventing the just side from fighting. Nevertheless, we must remember the point made a moment ago (2. 5, conclusion): that care must be taken to ensure that the evil effects of the war do not outweigh the possible benefits sought by waging it. If the storming of a fortress or town garrisoned by the enemy but full of innocent inhabitants is not of great importance for eventual victory in the war, it does not seem to me permissible to kill a large number of innocent people by indiscriminate bombardment in order to defeat a small number of enemy combatants. Finally, it is never lawful to kill innocent people, even accidentally and unintentionally, except when it advances a just war which cannot be won in any other way. In the words of the parable: "Let the tares grow until the harvest, lest while ye gather up the tares, ye root up also the wheat with them" (Matthew 13:24–30).

Against this, one may ask whether it is lawful to kill people who are innocent, but may yet pose a threat in the future. For example, the sons of Saracens are harmless, but it is reasonable to fear that when they reach manhood they will fight against Christendom. And according to the previous argument adult enemy civilians are also presumed innocent, but they too could later take up arms and fight. The question is whether it is lawful to kill such people; and the answer would seem to be yes, since one is permitted to kill other innocent people too, as an accidental effect. When, in Deuteronomy 20:10–20, the children of Israel are commanded, when they have captured a city, to smite every adult male thereof with the edge of the sword, it is not to be supposed that every one of them is a combatant.

In reply, however, I say this: it is perhaps possible to make a defence of this kind of for killing innocent people in such cases, but I nevertheless believe that it is utterly wrong. It is never right to commit evil, even to avoid greater evils. It is quite unacceptable that a person should be killed for a sin he has yet to commit. In the first place, there are many other measures for preventing future harm from such people, such as captivity, exile, etc. It is not lawful to execute one of our fellow members of the commonwealth for future sins, and therefore it cannot be lawful with foreign subjects either; I have no doubts on this score. It follows that, either after the battle has been won or even in the midst of hostilities, if a man's innocence is proved and the soldiers are able to set him free, they must do so. As for the authorities adduced to prove the contrary, we may reply that the passages in question refer to a special command of God, who was angry with the peoples in question and wished to destroy them utterly, just as he rained fire on Sodom and Gomorrah which devoured both guilty and innocent together. But he is the

Lord of all, and did not intend this to be a general rule. The same reply holds true for the passage from Deuteronomy 20: though what is said there is intended as a general law of war for all time, what the Lord seems to have meant was that in reality all the adult men in an enemy city are to be thought of as enemies, since the innocent cannot be distinguished from the guilty, and therefore they may all be killed.

[Question 3, Article 2: Whether one may plunder innocent people in a just war]

Another valid doubt is *whether one may nevertheless plunder the innocent in the just war.*

In answer to this let us make the following propositions:

1 First, it is certain *that we may plunder them of the goods and property which have been used against us by the enemy.* This is clear, because otherwise we cannot gain victory against them. Indeed, we may take the money of the innocent, or burn and ravage their crops or kill their livestock; all these things are necessary to weaken the enemies' resources. There can be no argument about this.

From this there flows the corollary that if the state of war is permanent, it is lawful to plunder the enemy indiscriminately, both innocent and guilty, since the enemy rely upon the resources of its people to sustain an unjust war, and their strength is therefore weakened if their subjects are plundered.

2 Second, if the war can be satisfactorily waged without plundering farmers or other non-combatants, *it is not lawful to plunder them. . . .*

3 Third, if the enemy refuse to restore the property they have unjustly seized, and the injured party is unable to recover his property in any other way, then *he may seek redress in any way he chooses, from the innocent or the guilty.* For example, if French bandits plunder Spanish territory and the king of France refuses to compel them to make restitution, though able to do so, then the Spaniards may, with their prince's permission, plunder French merchants or farmers, however innocent they may be; though the French commonwealth or king may not initially have been to blame, by their refusal to punish the injustice done by their own subjects they put themselves in the wrong, as Augustine says (*Quaest. in Heptateuch.* 6. 10), and the injured prince can therefore seek satisfaction from any or all the members of the offending commonwealth. Hence the letters-of-marque or *reprisals* granted by princes in these cases are not in themselves altogether unjust;[22] because of the negligence and injustice of another prince, the prince gives to one of his subjects the right to recover his property even from

---

[22] [*Pagden and Lawrence's note:*] The reference is to the official patents or *cartas de represalia* given by various crowns to privateers or *corsairs*, as they were known in Spain, to plunder the ships of other nations for their own profit.

innocent victims. Such grants are nevertheless dangerous, as they give an excuse for mere piracy.

[Question 3, Article 3: Whether one may enslave the innocent in a just war]

A third doubt, given that one may not lawfully kill children and innocent non-combatants, is *whether one may nevertheless enslave them.*

In answer to this let us make the following proposition:

1 That *one may lawfully enslave the innocent under just the same conditions as one may plunder them.* Freedom and slavery are counted as goods of fortune; therefore, when the war is such that it is lawful to plunder all the enemy population indiscriminately and seize all their goods, it must also be lawful to enslave them all, guilty and innocent alike. Hence, since our war against the pagans is of this kind, being permanent because they can never sufficiently pay for the injuries and losses inflicted, it is not to be doubted that we may lawfully enslave the women and children of the Saracens. But since it seems to be accepted in the law of nations that Christians cannot enslave one another, it is not lawful to enslave fellow-Christians, at any rate during the course of the war. If necessary, when the war is over one may take prisoners, even innocent women and children, but not to enslave them, only to hold them to ransom; and this must not be allowed to go beyond the limits which the necessities of warfare demand, and the legitimate customs of war permit.

[Question 3, Article 4: Whether one may execute hostages]

A fourth doubt is *whether one may execute enemy hostages, either received during a truce or taken in war, if the enemy break their promises?*

In answer to this let us make the following single proposition:

1 That *if the hostages would otherwise be combatants,* for instance if they have already borne arms against us, *they may be executed*; but *if they are non-combatants,* it is clear from what has been said that *they may not.* There is no arguing against this.

[Question 3, Article 5: Whether one may execute all the enemy combatants]

The fifth doubt is *whether one may execute all the enemy combatants in a just war?*

In answering this let us remember the following points: that war is waged, in the first place, for our own defence and the defence of our property; then, for the recovery of property that has been seized; third, in revenge for an injury received; and lastly, to establish peace and security. With these premises in mind, let us make the following proposition:

1 In the actual conflict of battle, or during the storming or defence of a city, in short so long as matters hang dangerously in the balance, *it is lawful to kill indiscriminately all those who fight against us.* It is clear that the combatants cannot very well wage war without eliminating their opponents. But the whole point of this doubt is, rather, *whether we may lawfully kill all the enemy combatants after victory has been gained,* when there is no longer any danger from them. And the answer to this would seem to be that we may. . . .

But on the other hand let us make the following further propositions:

2 *After victory has been gained and the matter is beyond danger, we may lawfully kill all the enemy combatants.* The proof of this is that war is not only ordained for the recovery of lost possessions, but also for the avenging of injury, and therefore one may lawfully execute those responsible for the injury inflicted. Furthermore, we have the same right against our fellow members of the commonwealth when they commit crimes, and therefore we must have this right against foreigners, since (as discussed above) by the laws of war the prince has the same authority over the enemy as a judge or legitimate prince. And last, although there may be no present danger from the enemy, there can be no future guarantee of our security from their attack.

3 However, *it is not always lawful to execute all the combatants for the sole purpose of avenging injury.* The proof of this is that, when dealing with our fellow members of the commonwealth, if the crime is the responsibility of an entire city or province, it is not lawful to kill all the delinquents; in a popular rebellion, it would not be permissible to execute and destroy the entire populace. It was for just such an act that Theodosius was excommunicated by Ambrose.[23] Such action would be against the public good, which is the purpose of war and peace. And if this is so, then it cannot be lawful to kill all enemy combatants either. We must take account of the scale of the injury inflicted by the enemy, of our losses, and of their other crimes, and base the scale of our revenge on this calculation, without cruelty or inhumanity. In this connexion, Cicero remarks that we should punish wrongdoers only so far as justice and humanity permit (*De officiis* II. 5. 18). Sallust also says that "our ancestors, the most God-fearing and righteous of men, never took anything from the vanquished except the licence to do harm" (*Coniuratio Catilinae* 12. 3–4).

---

[23] [Pagden and Lawrance's note:] The reference is to the massacre of Thessalonica in 390 AD, to St Ambrose's subsequent excommunication of Theodosius I, and to the emperor's penitent submission.

4 *It is sometimes lawful and expedient to kill all the enemy combatants.* The proof runs as follows: war is waged to produce peace, but sometimes security cannot be obtained without the wholesale destruction of the enemy. This is particularly the case in wars against the infidel, from whom peace can never be hoped for on any terms; therefore the only remedy is to eliminate all of them who are capable of bearing arms against us, given that they are already guilty. This is how the precept given in Deuteronomy 20 should be understood. In other cases, however, in wars against fellow-Christians I do not believe that it is permissible. The necessary result would be to provoke further offences and wars between princes (Matthew 18:7): therefore, if the victor were always to put to death all his adversaries, great harm would result for humankind. It is better that the punishment be fitted to the crime, and the wicked man beaten according to his fault, by a certain number of stripes (Deuteronomy 25:2–3). And in this connexion it must be taken into consideration that subjects neither must nor ought to examine the causes of war, but may follow their prince into war, content with the authority of their prince and public council; so that in general, even though the war may be unjust on one side or the other, the soldiers on each side who come to fight in battle or to defend a city are all equally innocent. Once they are defeated and pose no further threat, it is my opinion that not so much as a single one of them should be killed, so long as the presumption is that they fought in good faith.

[Question 3, Article 6: Whether one may execute those who have surrendered or been taken prisoner]

The sixth doubt is *whether one may execute those who have surrendered or been taken prisoner, supposing that they too were enemy combatants?*

I reply that, in itself, there is no reason why prisoners taken in a just war or those who have surrendered, if they were combatants, should not be killed, so long as common equity is observed. But as many practices in war are based on the law of nations, it appears to be established by custom that prisoners taken after a victory, when the danger is past, should not be killed unless they turn out to be deserters and fugitives. This law of nations should be respected, as it is by all good men. As for those who surrender, however, I have neither read nor heard of such a custom of leniency.

[Question 3, Article 7: Whether all the booty taken in war belongs to the captors]

The seventh doubt is *whether all the booty taken in war belongs to those who capture it?*

In answer to this let us make the following proposition:

1 There is no doubt that *all booty taken in a just war up to a value sufficient to recompense the property unjustly seized by the enemy, and also including reparation of the costs of the war, become the property of the captors.* No proof of this conclusion is needed, since this is the very purpose of war. . . .

But this conclusion leads to a further doubt: whether it is lawful to allow our soldiers to sack a city? Let us therefore make a further proposition:

3 Third, *this is not of itself unlawful if it is necessary to the conduct of the war*, whether to strike terror into the enemy or to inflame the passions of the soldiers. . . . It is likewise permissible to set fire to a city when there are reasonable grounds for doing so. But this sort of argument licenses the barbarians among the soldiery to commit every kind of inhuman savagery and cruelty, murdering and torturing the innocent, deflowering young girls, raping women, and pillaging churches. In these circumstances, it is undoubtedly unjust to destroy a Christian city except in the most pressing necessity and with the gravest of causes; but if necessity decrees, it is not unlawful, even if the probability is that the soldiery will commit crimes of this kind. Their officers, however, have a duty to give orders against it.

4 Fourth, notwithstanding all this, *soldiers may not plunder or burn without the authority of their prince or commander.* The soldiers are not the judges, but simply the executors; if they behave otherwise, they must make restitution.

But the question of immovable property is more difficult. In this connexion, let us state these further propositions:

5 Fifth, there is no doubt that *it is lawful to occupy and keep land and forts*, to the extent necessary for compensation of losses. There is certainly no reason in divine or natural law why this dispensation should be more applicable to movable goods than to immovables.

6 Sixth, to protect life and safety where there is danger from the enemy, *it is lawful to occupy and hold any enemy fort or city which is necessary for our defence.*

7 Seventh, for an injury received *it is also lawful to deprive the enemy of part of his land in the name of punishment*, that is, in revenge and according to the scale of the injury. By this token, it is sometimes lawful to occupy a fort or town, but the governing factor in this case must be moderation, not armed might. If necessity and the requirements of war demand that the greater part of enemy territory or a large number of cities be occupied in this way, they ought to be returned once the war is over and peace has been made, only keeping so much as may be considered fair in equity and humanity for the reparation of losses and expenses and the punishment of injustice. Punishment should fit the crime; it would be intolerable if we were allowed to occupy the whole kingdom of France because they had plundered a few cattle or burnt a single village. But the fact that we may occupy a part of enemy territory or an enemy city on these grounds is quite clear from the passage already cited from Deuteronomy 20 where the Lord

gives permission to occupy a city which has refused to surrender peacefully in war. Likewise, we are allowed to punish our own domestic malefactors by depriving them of a fortress or house, according to their crime, and therefore we must have the same right against our external enemies. Similarly, a legitimate judge of a higher court may fine the perpetrator of a crime by confiscating a city or fort belonging to him; so a prince who has been offended may do the same, since the law of war effectively makes him judge. . . .

[Question 3, Article 8: Whether one may impose tribute on a defeated enemy]

The eighth doubt is *whether one may impose tribute on a defeated enemy?*

I reply that *it is certainly lawful to do so*, not only for the compensation of losses, but also as punishment and revenge. I have already said enough above to prove this point, and the passage cited from Deuteronomy 20 leaves no room for doubt.

[Question 3, Article 9: Whether one may depose the enemy's princes and set up new ones]

The ninth doubt is *whether we may depose the enemy' princes and set up new ones in their place, or take over the government ourselves?*

In answer to this let us make the following propositions:

1 *It is not lawful to do this in every case, or for any cause of just war.* This is clear from what has been said: punishment should not exceed the crime. On the contrary, punishments should be diminished in favour of mercy. This is a rule not only of human law, but also of natural and divine law. Therefore, although the harm done by the enemy may be a sufficient cause of war, it will not always be sufficient to justify the extermination of the enemy's kingdom and deposition of its legitimate native princes; this would be altogether too savage and inhumane.

2 However, it cannot be denied that there may sometimes be legitimate reasons for supplanting princes, or for taking over the government. This may be because of the number or atrocity of the injuries and harm done by the enemy, and especially when security and peace cannot otherwise be ensured, when failure to do so would cause a dangerous threat to the commonwealth. This is clear enough; if it is lawful to occupy a city for this reason, as explained above, then it must be lawful to remove its princes.

But it is to be noted, with reference to articles 6, 7, 8, and 9, that sometimes, and indeed often, not only the princes themselves but also their subjects, though in fact they have no just cause, nevertheless wage war in good faith – and in such good faith, I emphasize, that they are to be excused from any guilt. Take, for example, the case of a war waged, after careful examination, on the advice of judgment of the wisest men: in this event, no person who is not directly responsible should be punished, and though the victor may lawfully recover the property which was seized from him, and perhaps even his war expenses, he may not kill anyone after victory has been won, nor exact just retribution, nor demand satisfaction from the temporal property of the vanquished, since all these things can only be done in the name of punishment; manifestly, punishment should not fall upon the innocent.

[Conclusion: Three rules of war]

From all this we may deduce a few rules and canons of warfare:

1 First Canon: since princes have the authority to wage war, *they should strive above all to avoid all provocations and causes of war.* If it be possible, the prince should seek as much as lieth in him to live peaceably with all men, according to Paul's words in Romans 12:18. He should remember that other men are his neighbours, whom we are all enjoined to love as ourselves (Matthew 22:39); and that we all have a single Lord, before whose tribunal we must each render account for our actions on the day of judgment. It is a mark of utter monstrousness to seek out and rejoice in causes which lead to nothing but death and persecution of our fellow-men, whom God created, and for whom Christ suffered death. The prince should only accede to the necessity of war when he is dragged reluctantly but inevitably into it.

2 Second Canon: once war has been declared for just causes, the prince should press his campaign not for the destruction of his opponents, but *for the pursuit of the justice for which he fights and the defence of his homeland,* so that by fighting he may eventually establish peace and security.

3 Third Canon: once the war has been fought and victory won, he must use his victory with moderation and Christian humility. The victor must think of himself as a judge sitting in judgment between two commonwealths, one the injured party and the other the offender; he must not pass sentence as the prosecutor, but as a judge. He must give satisfaction to the injured, but as far as possible without causing the utter ruination of the guilty commonwealth. Let him remember above all that for the most part, and especially in wars between Christian commonwealths, it is the princes themselves who are completely to blame; for subjects usually fight in good faith for their princes.

And so I end this whole disputation about the Indians, which I have undertaken for the glory of God and the utility of my fellow-men.

28

Luis de Molina
(1535–1600)

Distinguishing War from Punishment

[I]t is sometimes sufficient for a just war that there be a material injury, which involves no sin.

De iustitia et iure

The Spanish Jesuit Luis de Molina was instrumental in reformulating the notion of just cause so that it no longer presupposed personal guilt on the part of the adversary. Echoing the work of his predecessor Vitoria, Molina argued that one party could injure another without necessarily incurring moral guilt for its offense. This he termed "material injury." Such an injury would arise if the offender carried out a wrongful act while in a state of "invincible ignorance."[1] If the injury was of sufficient gravity, the offended party could have just cause to seek redress through resort to armed force. This resort would count as an instance of offensive war, yet, since it was not predicated on the culpability of the adversary, it could not be waged in view of punishment. In this manner, Molina severed the tight connection which Cajetan had earlier established between offensive war and vindicative justice. Whereas Cajetan viewed all offensive war as having a retributive dimension, Molina maintained that offensive war could also be legitimately undertaken for non-punitive ends, such as the recovery of land wrongly occupied.

By explicitly distinguishing several possible modes of offensive war, Molina made an important contribution to the development of just war thinking. No longer would punishment be viewed as the proximate goal of waging war. Military acts were henceforth conceived as directed first and foremost to the defeat of the enemy.[2] This proximate goal would itself be sought by reference to several possible

---

[1] On the meaning of this expression, see chap. 27, this volume, p. 317.
[2] This line of thinking was further developed by Wolff and Vattel (see chaps 37 and 40, this volume).

final goals: defense, recovery of property, or punishment of wrongdoing. And even in this last case, the punishment in question would be meted out not during the war, but only afterwards, once the enemy was defeated. In other words, war should never be conducted as though it were itself a form of punishment. In this fashion, Molina established one of the central premises on which the modern notion of the *ius in bello* came to be built.[3]

From: *De iustitia et iure* (*On Justice and Law*) [written ca. 1593], tract II, disputation 102: A common just cause of war, comprising all of the others[4]

[1 What the second condition for a just war is]

Next should be discussed the second condition required in order that a war be just and licit, namely, it must have a sufficient cause. Before we proceed to discuss certain particular causes that are sufficient, a general cause has to be considered that comprises all of the others.

Vitoria, in *De iure belli*, n. 13,[5] asserts that this [general cause] consists in an injury. You should understand [this as meaning an injury which is] to be hindered, redressed, or avenged. Augustine speaks in agreement in [*Decretum Gratiani*, II, causa] 23, question 2, canon *Dominus*, when he says: "A just war is defined as one that avenges wrongs, when a nation or state has to be punished for refusing to make amends for the wrongs inflicted by its subjects, or to restore what has been taken away unjustly." And St. Thomas [Aquinas] in [*Summa theologiae* II–II, q. 40 a. 1, when he quotes those words of Augustine, says that for an offensive war to have a just cause it is necessary that those who are attacked should deserve the attack on account of some fault.

[2 Sometimes a material injury suffices for a just war; this is shown by example]

Notice, however, that it is sometimes sufficient for a just war that there be injury [committed] materially (*iniuria materialiter*),[6] which involves no sin. For owing to the very fact that God granted the lands of the Canaanites and the Amorites to the children of Israel [Deuteronomy 1:7], they had the right to expel by war those peoples who resisted them, in order to occupy the land that God

---

[3] See Robert Regout, *La doctrine de la guerre juste de saint Augustin à nos jours d'après les théologiens et les canonistes catholiques* (Paris: A. Pedone, 1935), pp. 25–36, 140–6, and 182–5; also Peter Haggenmacher, *Grotius et la doctrine de la guerre juste* (Paris: Presses Universitaires de France, 1983), pp. 421–6.

[4] Ludovicus Molina, *De iustitia et iure opera omnia* (Geneva: M. M. Bousquet, 1733), pp. 227–9. Translated by Robert Andrews and Peter Haggenmacher.

[5] See chap. 27, this volume, p. 314.

[6] The adjective "material" is not to be understood in the sense of "serious" or "grave," but by reference to the Aristotelian concepts of "matter" and "form."

had given to them – even if those peoples were ignorant of God's gift, and were thereby without blame in resisting and trying to retain these lands; and therefore they inflicted only a material injury upon the children of Israel. For this reason Abulensis,[7] on Joshua 11, asserts that this war was just on both sides: materially and formally on the side of the children of Israel, but only formally on the side of those peoples, inasmuch as they defended themselves and their property without sin, being invincibly ignorant of God's donation and will.

Note however that the children of Israel not only had the right (*ius*) to undertake that war – otherwise they would surely have been behaving impiously in killing all those peoples who had committed no sin against them; and therefore they were only allowed under this title to do those things which were absolutely necessary to wrest from those peoples' power what God had given them, and nothing more. But beyond that title, they had another one, because on account of the idolatry and other grave sins that those peoples had committed against God, God had ordered the children of Israel to kill and destroy them. And this is the reason why they punished their sins, as God's executioners, with the authority and command of God, killing these men and occupying their lands and goods. Yet because those peoples were likewise [in]vincibly[8] ignorant of all this, they were without sin in defending themselves and fighting against the invaders.

[**3** The different kinds of material injury, and the one which best suffices for a just war]

I said a bit earlier that sometimes an injury [committed] materially is sufficient for a just war, because there are two kinds of material injury (*materialis iniuria*). One kind, whereby what is in fact owed the other party is withheld without sin on account of invincible ignorance, so that the obligation to hand it over arises from the thing itself (*ex parte ipsius rei*), while invincible ignorance excuses from any guilt. There is another kind [of material injury], where, on account of the same ignorance, and hence without guilt, damage or injury is inflicted, but he who inflicts the injury becomes no richer; and so there arises no obligation to make restitution either because of an illegitimate enrichment (*ex parte rei acceptae*) or because of a wrongful act (*ex parte iniustae acceptionis*),[9] since ignorance

---

[7] Alfonso de Madrigal (1400–55) was bishop of Avila, whence his usual appellation as "Abulensis" (he was also nicknamed "Tostado", literally "toasted", on account of his dark skin). His commentary on Joshua and other books of the Old Testament is part of an extensive theological work. Concerning the passage mentioned, see Haggenmacher, *Grotius et la doctrine*, pp. 207–8.

[8] The text says *vincibiliter*, which is obviously a misprint for *invincibiliter*. In fact there are quite a few other misprints, which have been tacitly corrected in our translation.

[9] The verb *accipere* (and the corresponding substantive *acceptio*) has a special meaning in canon law and scholastic legal theory: rather than "accepting," it means "holding," "detaining" something illegally (as a result of having "received" or "taken" it), which entailed a corresponding duty of restitution. See Günther Nufer, *Ueber die Restitutionslehre der spanischen Spätscholastiker und ihre Ausstrahlung auf die Folgezeit* (Munich: Dissertationsdruck Schön, 1969), in particular pp. 12–15.

absolves him from blame. Materially considered, the first sort of injury suffices for a just war. The other sort of injury does not, for neither can it be justly declared by way of punishment, nor for the recovery of what is due to him who declares the war, since nothing belonging to him is detained by him against whom the war is declared.

[4 Two kinds of offensive war. The first kind is declared in order to avenge an inflicted injury]

According to what has been said, we can distinguish two kinds of offensive war. The first kind is to avenge an inflicted injury, whether or not we intend at the same time to recover our property and to claim damages owed to us. In order for this sort of war to be just, there must first be guilt on the part of the enemy; this seems to be what Augustine, St. Thomas, and Vitoria mean in the cited passages when they say that the culpability of the enemy is a prerequisite for the justice of this sort of war. Notice however that, although a just cause for this sort of war is not only determined by the guilt of the enemy, but also by the value of the property which is owed to us and has been withheld, nonetheless the amount of punishment and vengeance to be inflicted upon the enemy, above and beyond the recovery of property owed to us, ought to be proportionate to the amount of guilt which they incurred in committing the injury, for punishment, if it is to be just and legitimate, should always correspond only to the crime committed.

[5 The second kind [of offensive war] is to recover property, when it is held because of unavoidable ignorance]

The second kind of just [offensive] war is to recover property which is due us, when it is held because of invincible ignorance, and there is no other way for us to recover it. For this sort of war no preexisting guilt is required, but it is enough that a material injury has occurred, as was explained a bit earlier. For just as a prince upholds the law for his subjects not only in the case of someone's formally unjust detention of something that belongs to another, but also when his unjust detention of it is merely material and the prince orders it to be removed with force from the one who possesses it in good faith, even if the latter considers himself wronged in this matter; thus also he has a like right over those foreigners who similarly withhold in good faith what belongs to him or his subjects, when there is no other way of recovering it; for then he assumes with respect to them the role of judge and bailiff.

[6 Who should bear the costs in this sort of war, since there is no guilt on the part of the enemy]

In this second kind of just war, since there is no guilt on the part of the enemy, it is only permitted to use against them the force necessary to wrest from their power what they have unjustly withheld materially, even if this may extend so far as to their death and destruction. Nevertheless, this should be carried out with the least possible damage to them. If more [force] than necessary is used, this is an unjust act for which one is obliged to make restitution. At any rate, nothing more may be done to them in the way of punishment, so that not even the expenses of the war that were necessary to rescue the things can be demanded of them – because they owe nothing more, neither by way of unjust enrichment, nor on account of a wrongful act (since it is without any guilt that they were the cause or occasion of these expenses). It is indeed the same as when two plaintiffs contend in court over some property: he who loses the case is never sentenced to pay the expenses that the other party incurred in recovering the property; nor is it just that he be so sentenced, unless he was put into the wrong by refusing to return the property to his adversary without trial. Likewise, the costs of a war are never charged to the adversary unless he incurred actual guilt in fighting, so that the war was unjust on his part, not only materially, but also formally. Note, however, that if, before the war is declared, those points are observed which are to be set out in the following disputation,[10] it will rarely happen that guilt will not be at least presumed on the part of the adversary, and that therefore he will not be liable to punishment, nor that the expenses for the war may not be demanded by the side who formally and materially declared the war justly.

[7 Not every injury, either material or formal, is sufficient for declaring a just war]

It should be noted, together with Vitoria in the work cited above [*De iure belli*], n. 14,[11] and others, that not any injury [whatsoever], whether material or also formal, is sufficient to declare a war justly; it has to be serious, according to an expert assessment, and such as to justify the terrible evil that is war. The reason for this is that just as it is not permitted to inflict for any sort of crime serious punishments, such as death, dismemberment, and flogging, upon criminal citizens, so likewise it is not permitted for just any sort of injury caused by external enemies to declare war, which brings with it death, plundering, arson, destruction, and other terrible evils. Indeed, punishment ought to be proportionate to the crime. Thus the response to minor injuries and grounds usually consists in granting reprisals,[12] as they call it, which will be dealt with later.

---

[10]   Disputation 103 deals with "the degree to which the cause of war has to be inquired into; and whether war may be declared in doubtful cases; and what is the procedure to be followed before war breaks out."

[11]   See chap. 27, this volume, pp. 314–15.

[12]   Letters of reprisal (or letters of marque) were granted by the sovereign authority of a state at the request of one of its subjects who had tried and failed to obtain redress in a foreign state for a wrong suffered from one of its citizens. The letter authorized him to seek adequate compensation for the denial of justice at the expense of any member of the guilty commonwealth. He thereby "took back" the equivalent of his loss: this is what is meant by the term "reprisal," which derives from the Italian verb *riprendere* through medieval Latin *represaliae*. Reprisals were considered during the Middle Ages as a kind of limited war. Our modern acceptation of reprisals only appears during the eighteenth century, when the function of medieval reprisals was assumed by diplomatic protection.

[**8** A prince, in waging war, can be equally unjust against his own commonwealth as against foreigners]

This too should be noted: a prince may be equally unjust to his own commonwealth in waging war as he can be to the other commonwealth against which he is preparing to fight. Therefore he should not only consider whether he has a just cause of war against the other commonwealth, but also whether he is not being unjust against his own commonwealth by undertaking such a war. Indeed, if prudent judgment shows that such a war will lead to the greatest harm of his commonwealth, either because his forces are not enough to win, or because, with but little benefit for his commonwealth and the common good, he will expose his subjects to the greatest perils and harm, use up public revenues in the venture, saddle his commonwealth with new taxes and levies, and so on – it would indeed be a deadly sin against the justice due his own commonwealth to declare such a war if he could easily refrain from doing so. For a commonwealth does not exist because of its king, but the king because of his commonwealth, so as to defend, administer, and govern it not for his own whims, vanity, and benefit, but for the common good of the state. To this end the assembled peoples set above themselves kings and princes, so that they might exercise the law and the power which was given to them. Thus Aristotle rightly says in *Politics*, bk. IV, chap. 10, that the distinction between a king and a tyrant is that a tyrant administers the commonwealth for his own profit and benefit, but a king rules for its common and public good.

29

Francisco Suárez (1548–1617)

Justice, Charity, and War

The right to make war is detrimental to others, and the punishment inflicted through war is of the severest kind; therefore, that punishment ought to be inflicted with the utmost restraint.

De bello

Francisco Suárez was among the most systematic of the scholastic thinkers. In comparison to Vitoria, who made reference to the social and political events of his day, the Jesuit Suárez favored a more abstract and speculative style. This was exemplified by his most famous work, the *Metaphysical Disputations* (1597), which had a significant impact on the development of modern philosophy. While showing a detailed knowledge of earlier philosophical and theological thought, Suárez always sought to maintain his independence as a thinker. Thus even though he viewed himself as a disciple of both Thomas Aquinas and his compatriot Vitoria, and like them articulated an ethics of war and peace based on a theory of natural law, Suárez did not hesitate to strike out in new directions, sometimes distancing himself from their views.

An early Christian theorist of democratic governance, he may be credited with other important contributions to scholastic thought: a theory of rights, which he applied to a range of issues (including jurisdiction for declaring war and self-defense), a treatment of non-combatant immunity, and an emphasis on arbitration as an alternative to war.

Suárez's disputation *De bello* is part of a larger work on the theological virtues of faith, hope, and charity (*De triplici virtute theologica*). He follows Aquinas in placing the discussion of war within a part of this work ("De charitate"), which is devoted to the context of the last-mentioned virtue. Yet, in so doing, he took care to situate problems associated with war also in relation to the virtue of justice. Upon distinguishing the exigencies of justice from those of charity, Suárez articulated a concept of vindicative justice, in which one commonwealth comes to have jurisdiction over another by reason of the latter's fault.

After a short preface, which defines the subject matter to be investigated, Suárez proceeds in the first section to explain how Christian moral life allows for (and sometimes even requires) participation in war. Suárez underscores how this applies to both defensive and offensive war. Defensive war is a reaction to armed attack that is under way, whereas offensive war seeks redress for an injustice that has already been committed and is now past.

From Disputation XIII: On War (*De bello*)[1]

An external combat (*pugna*)[2] which is incompatible with external peace is properly called war when it takes place between two princes or two commonwealths; but when it takes place between a prince and his commonwealth, or between the citizens and the commonwealth, it is termed sedition; when it is between private individuals it is called a brawl or a duel. The difference between these [various kinds of combat] appears to be material rather than formal, and we shall discuss them all, as did St. Thomas (*Summa theologiae*, II–II, qq. 40–2) and others who will be mentioned below.

Section I: Is War Intrinsically Evil?[3]

1 The first heresy [in connexion with this subject] consists in the assertion that it is intrinsically evil and contrary to charity to wage war. Such is the heretical belief attributed by Augustine to the Manichaeans. . . . The second error is the assertion that war is specifically forbidden to Christians, and especially, war against Christians. So Eck maintains (*Enchiridion locorum communium*, chap. 22); and other persons of our own time, who are heretics, advance the same contention. They distinguish, however, two kinds of war, defensive and offensive, which we shall discuss in sub-section 6 of this section. The conclusions that follow will elucidate the matter.

2 Our *first conclusion* is that war, absolutely speaking, is not intrinsically evil, nor is it forbidden to Christians. This conclusion is a matter of faith and is laid

---

[1]   These passages represent an emended version of the English translation by Gwladys L. Williams et al. of *Selections from Three Works of Francisco Suárez, SJ*, The Classics of International Law, no. 20, vol. 2 (Oxford: Clarendon Press, 1944), pp. 800–9, 815–41, 843–55. Latin text in Franciscus Suárez, *Opera omnia*, vol. 12 (Paris: Vivès, 1858).

[2]   "External combat" contrasts with the "internal combat" of the soul, described by St. Augustine (*De civitate Dei*, bk. XIX, chap. 4) in terms of the "war internal to our ourselves." Human activity in this world, he says, is an "unceasing warfare with vices, and those not external vices but internal, not other people's vices but quite clearly our very own."

[3]   Williams et al. (trans.), *Selections*, pp. 800–5.

down in the Scriptures. . . .[4] The same principle is confirmed by further testimony, that of the Fathers quoted by Gratian (*Decretum*, pt. II, causa 23, qq. 1–2), and also that of Ambrose (*On Duties*, various chapters). . . .

[Yet to this last point it may be objected[5] that] war ordinarily brings with it innumerable sins; and a given course of action is considered in itself evil and forbidden, if it is nearly always accompanied by unseemly circumstances and harm to one's neighbours. [In support of this] one may add that war is opposed to peace, to the love of one's enemies, and to the forgiveness of injuries. . . .

To [this last objection], Augustine replies (*On the City of God*, bk. XIX, last chapter [chap. vii]) that he deems it advisable to avoid war in so far as is possible, and to undertake it only in cases of extreme necessity, when no alternative remains; but he also holds that war is not entirely evil, since the fact that evils follow upon war is incidental (*per accidens*), and since greater evils would result if war were never allowed.

Against the supporting claim that war is opposed to an honourable peace, it must rather be said that it is opposed to an unjust peace. War is a means of attaining a peace that is true and secure. Similarly, war is not opposed to the love of one's enemies; for whoever wages war honourably hates, not individuals, but actions, which are justly punished. And the same reasoning is true of the forgiveness of injuries, especially since this forgiveness is not enjoined under every circumstance, for vengeance may sometimes be exacted by legitimate means, without injustice.

4 *Second conclusion*: I hold that defensive war not only is permitted, sometimes it is even prescribed. The first part of this proposition follows from the first conclusion, which even the Doctors cited above accept; and it holds true not only for public magistrates, but also for private individuals, since all laws allow the repelling of force with force. . . . The reason supporting it is that the right of self-defence is natural and necessary. Whence the second part of our second proposition is easily proved. For self-defence is sometimes prescribed, at least in accordance with the order of charity. . . . The same is true of the defence of the commonwealth, especially if such defense is an official duty. On this, see Ambrose, *On Duties*, bk. I, chap. 7.

5 *Third conclusion*: even when war is offensive, it is not an evil in itself, but may be right and necessary. This is clear from the passages of Scripture cited above, which make no distinction [between offensive and defensive wars]. The same fact is evidenced by the custom of the Church, one that has quite frequently been approved by the Fathers and the popes. . . .

The reason supporting our third conclusion is that such a war is often necessary to a commonwealth, in order to repel injuries and to hold enemies in check. Nor

---

[4] In the body of the text Suárez refers to several passages from the Bible, including Genesis 14:19–20 and Epistle to the Hebrews 9:33.

[5] This is the last of four objections listed by Suárez.

would it be possible, without these wars, for commonwealths to be maintained in peace. Hence, this kind of warfare is allowed by natural law; and even by the law of the Gospel, which derogates in no way from natural law, and contains no new divine commands save those regarding faith and the sacraments. . . .

6 It remains for us to explain what constitutes an offensive war (*bellum aggressivum*),[6] and what, on the other hand, constitutes a defensive war; for sometimes that which is merely defence may present the appearance of an offensive. Thus, for example, if enemies seize houses or property belonging to others, and are attacked as a consequence, this is not an offensive attack, rather it is a defence. To this extent, civil laws . . . are justified in conscience when they provide that if any one tries to dispossess me of my property, it is permissible for me to repel force with force. For such an act is not offensive, but is defence, and may be lawfully undertaken even on one's own authority. . . .

Consequently, we have to consider whether the injustice is, morally speaking, in progress (*in fieri*); or whether it has already occurred (*facta iam sit*), such that satisfaction is sought through war. In this latter case, the war is offensive. In the former case, war has the character of self-defence, provided it is waged with a moderation of defence that is blameless. Now the injury is considered as *in progress*, either when the injurious action has actually begun, even physically, as when a man has not yet been entirely deprived of a possession that is his by right; or when he has already been so deprived, but immediately (*in continenti*) – that is, without notable delay – attempts to protect himself and to reinstate himself in possession. The reason for this is as follows: When morally speaking a person is actually resisting, and is attempting – in so far as possible – to protect his right, he is not considered as having already suffered injury, in an absolute sense, nor as having been deprived of his possession. This is the common opinion of the Doctors. . . .

7 *Fourth conclusion*: for a war to be honourable, a number of conditions must be observed, which may be grouped under three heads. First, the war must be undertaken by a legitimate power; second, it must have a just cause and title; and third, it must be carried out in a proper manner (*debitus modus*), with due proportion observed at its beginning, during its prosecution, and at victory. All of this will be made clear in the following sections. The underlying principle of this general conclusion, indeed, is that, while war is not in itself evil, nevertheless, on account of the many misfortunes which it brings in its train, it is one of those undertakings that are often carried out badly; consequently, in order to be honourable, numerous circumstances must be met.

---

[6]   In Suárez's lexicon, *bellum aggressivum* refers to a first use of armed force. It is equivalent to Vitoria's term *bellum offensivum*. Unlike the morally pejorative connotation of the English term "aggressive war" (which, in the aftermath of the post-World War II Nuremberg trials, has come to designate a crime), on Suárez's understanding *bellum aggressivum* is not necessarily unjust. We have thus translated it by the more neutral term "offensive war."

Section II is devoted to the question of legitimate authority for waging war. Suárez makes clear at the outset that the requirement of legitimate authority applies especially to offensive war. Hence this kind of war constitutes the main focus of the present section. Suárez offers a tripartite definition of legitimate war-making authority (the "power to declare war" in his terminology). It is (i) a power of jurisdiction, (ii) a power for exercising vindicative justice; which is to say that it is (iii) the prerogative of a sovereign commonwealth and/or its prince. The third idea in particular gives rise to a number of difficulties, which are formulated by reference to the writings of earlier authors (e.g. Cajetan and Vitoria). Can subordinate princes rightly declare war if this power has been accorded to them by a very ancient custom? Can such princes declare war without the consent of their superior prince, when the latter has been negligent in avenging a wrong? What, in this regard, is the status of superior princes who are members of a federation ("under one king")? And do Christian princes have an obligation to obtain an authorization from the pope before declaring war? The section concludes with a comment on the obligation of restitution that arises when a war has been waged with just cause, yet without the requisite authority.

From Disputation XIII. Section II: Who Has the Legitimate Power of Declaring War?[7]

1 Our question relates to offensive war; for the power of defending oneself against an unjust attacker is conceded to all.

In the *first* place, I hold that a supreme prince (*supremus princeps*) who has no superior in temporal affairs, or a commonwealth that has retained for itself a like jurisdiction, has by natural law (*iure naturae*) legitimate power to declare war. . . .

A reason in support of this conclusion is, first, that this sort of war is at times permitted by natural law, as we have demonstrated; hence, the power of declaring such a war must rest with someone; and therefore it must rest, most of all, with the possessor of supreme power, for it is particularly his function to protect the commonwealth, and to command inferior authorities.

A second reason is that the power of declaring war is (so to speak) a power of jurisdiction, the exercise of which pertains to vindicative justice, which is especially necessary to a commonwealth for the purpose of constraining evildoers. Hence, just as the supreme prince may punish his own subjects when they harm others, so may he avenge himself on another prince or commonwealth, that, by reason of some offence, has become subject to him. This vengeance cannot be sought at the hands of another judge, because the prince of whom we are speaking has no superior in temporal affairs; therefore, if the offender is not prepared to give satisfaction, he may be compelled to do so by war.

---

[7] Williams et al. (trans.), *Selections*, pp. 805–9.

In this first conclusion, I used the words, 'or a commonwealth', in order that I might include every kind of regime; for the same reasoning holds true for all of them. Nevertheless, of a monarchical regime it must be noted that after a commonwealth has transferred its power to a single individual, it is not allowed to declare war against his will, since it no longer enjoys supremacy (*non est suprema*); unless perchance the prince should be so negligent in avenging or defending the commonwealth as to cause public and very grave harm to that commonwealth. In such a case the commonwealth as a whole may take vengeance on the prince, depriving him of his authority, for the commonwealth is always regarded as retaining this power within itself, if the prince fails in his duty.

2 *Secondly,* I hold that an inferior prince, or an incomplete commonwealth, or whosoever in temporal affairs is under a superior, cannot justly declare war without the authorization of that superior. A reason for the conclusion is, first, that a prince of this kind can claim his right from his superior, and therefore has not the right to declare war; since, in this respect, he has the character of a private person. For it is because of the reason stated that private persons cannot declare war. A second reason in support of this same conclusion is that such a declaration of war is opposed to the right of the supreme prince, to whom that power has been especially entrusted; for without such power he could not govern peacefully and suitably.

Victoria [*De iure belli*, q. 1, a. 2, prop. 3, no. 9; see chap. 27, this volume, pp. 312–13], however, sets certain limitations to what has been here stated, as do Cajetan and others.

The first limitation to this second conclusion is this: [subordinate princes cannot justly declare war] provided no contrary practice shall have been observed by very ancient custom. This provision applies when a war has been declared against parties who are not subjects of the king who governs the declarer of war. But if on the other hand the war is declared against another part of the same realm, the custom in question would certainly appear to be contrary to the natural law; for when there exists a tribunal and a power superior to both parties, it is contrary to the law of nature to demand one's right by force, acting as it were on one's own proper authority. [When carried out by] private persons such an attempt would no doubt be contrary to natural law. Likewise, in the case at hand, these two parts of the same commonwealth, although they may be of more importance [than single individuals], are nevertheless both in the position of private persons.

To the same conclusion, Vitoria sets a second limitation, namely: unless the supreme king is negligent in avenging an injury, for in this case an inferior prince may avenge himself. Nevertheless this course of action is not [entirely] commendable, especially when the conflict occurs between two parts of the same commonwealth. For, although a private person, when he cannot obtain his right through a public tribunal, may secretly and without scandal protect himself, nevertheless he may not do so by force and through war; and still less may he avenge himself if he is not able to obtain this through the judge. For to avenge oneself, on one's own private authority, is intrinsically evil, and tumults and wars might easily be stirred up within a commonwealth on this pretext. The right of vengeance as possessed by a part of the commonwealth, or by a mere private person, is only incomplete, and on its account these inconveniences mostly arise. Therefore, [an inferior prince] is not to be granted this licence [to exact vengeance], save only within the limits of just defence.

3 But it must be added, first, that when a matter is pressing, and recourse [to the prince] is not immediately possible, it is sometimes sufficient to interpret his will, particularly if the war is to be undertaken against foreigners, and above all if these foreigners are on other grounds overt enemies of the prince.

Second, I must also note that if at any time enemies of this kind are seized within the boundaries of some incomplete commonwealth, not only is it permitted to undertake a just defense against them, but attack, vengeance, and punishment [are allowed] as well; for, by reason of the crime committed in the territory of that commonwealth, they have made themselves its subjects.

Finally, it should be added that more things are allowable to a given city or commonwealth with regard to its own defence than to a private person; because the good defended in the former case is common to many, and is of a higher grade, and also because the power of a commonwealth is by its very nature public and common; therefore, it is not strange that more things are permissible to a commonwealth than to an individual.

4 But it may be asked, what is a complete commonwealth (*respublica perfecta*); or, who is a supreme prince? The reply is, first, that all kings are in this respect supreme. . . . Many counts also claim this supreme power. Hence, certain of the canonists are mistaken in saying that only the emperor is supreme in this fashion. Consequently, the issue depends on the mode of jurisdiction exercised by each particular prince, or commonwealth; and it is the mark of supreme jurisdiction when, under such a prince or such a commonwealth, there exists a tribunal before which all cases of litigation in that realm are decided, and from which there is no appeal to any superior tribunal.

But when there is room for an appeal, which is the mark of an incomplete commonwealth, since an appeal is the act of an inferior towards a superior. Hence it must be noted, first, that not all commonwealths that are subject to one and the same king are necessarily incomplete. For it may happen that such a union has been established accidentally, a fact indicated by a diversity in laws, taxes, and so forth [from one commonwealth to another under the same king]. And this distinction between a complete and incomplete commonwealth, although it bears no great importance to the power of which we now treat, since the latter is already vested in the king, has, nevertheless, an important relation to the power which such a commonwealth may possess in opposition to its own king, if he lapses into tyranny. For if the commonwealth is complete, it has power against its own king, even when the latter rules also over other kingdoms. But the case is otherwise when the commonwealth is incomplete, and a part of one kingdom; for then nothing can be done without the consent of the whole. All of the foregoing statements, since they are founded upon natural law, are applicable to both Christians and unbelievers.

5 In the case of Christian kings, however, a second point must be noted, namely, that the supreme pontiff, although he has no direct power in temporal affairs outside of his own domain, nevertheless does possess such power indirectly, as is indicated in certain passages of the *Decretals* (bk. I, tit. vi, chap. xxxiv). Therefore, under this title, he has a right to require that a cause of war be referred to him, and the power to give a judgment thereon, which the parties in question are bound to obey, unless his decision is manifestly unjust. For such [authority on the part of the Pope] is certainly necessary for the spiritual welfare of the Church and for the avoidance of almost infinite evils. Accordingly, Soto said (on Romans 12:18), that war between Christian princes is rarely just, since they have at hand another ready means of settling their mutual disputes.

But sometimes the pope does not interpose his authority, lest perchance greater evils result. In that event, to be sure, supreme princes are not bound to secure any authorization from the pope, and may enforce their own right as long as they are not forbidden to do so. Nevertheless, they should take care lest they themselves be a cause of the fact that the pope dares not intervene; for in that case they will not be free from fault.

6 *Thirdly*, in connection with the preceding conclusion, I hold that when a war is declared without legitimate authority, it is contrary not only to charity, but also to justice, even if a legitimate cause for it exists. The reason supporting this conclusion is that such an act is performed without legitimate jurisdiction, consequently it is illegitimate. Therefore, it follows that a war of this kind gives rise to an obligation of making restitution for all ensuing damages.

Therefore, it is indeed true that if someone merely recovers his own property in such a war, he will not be bound to restore that property; but he will be held liable for all injuries and losses inflicted upon others. The reason for such a distinction is that in the latter case he has done an injustice, since there was no just cause for all that damage; whereas, in recovering his own property, he has not, strictly speaking, committed an injustice – save possibly in the means used (*in modo*) – from which, in a strict sense, there arises no obligation to make restitution.

Whence follows the conclusion noted by Sylvester (word *bellum*, pt. I, q. 10 [q. 11, no. 4]), that he who makes war without the authorization in question, even if he has, in other respects, a just title for so doing, nevertheless incurs the sanctions imposed on those who wage war unjustly; so that if, for example, he be an incendiary, he will incur the excommunication promulgated against incendiaries. . . .[8]

---

[8] After elaborating on the special case of a Christian prince who wages war in defiance of papal prohibition (§7), Suárez proceeds to discuss in section 3 (omitted) whether clerics are permitted to declare or otherwise participate in war.

In the next section, under the heading of "just title for war," Suárez takes up the traditional problematic of just cause, in which he analyzes the right and wrong reasons for going to war. The reasons in question are knowable on the basis of "natural reason," and hence are applicable to all human beings regardless of their particular religious convictions. (The question whether or not religious revelation can provide special reasons for going to war is taken up in section V). Again emphasizing that his main theoretical concern is with offensive war, Suárez concentrates his attention on the idea of injury, with an eye toward determining what sort of injuries can warrant resort to armed force. While the notion of just title is framed in terms of the broad category of "seeking redress" (this might include retaking stolen property or land, or regaining a right such as freedom of transit over highways), Suárez seems most intent on explaining how, through war, commonwealths may punish wrongs for which no satisfaction has been offered. On this score, he adds several nuances to the account previously given by Vitoria and sometimes voices strong disagreement with his eminent predecessor (again without mentioning him by name). For instance, the idea that "supreme kings have the power of avenging injuries throughout the whole world"[9] is denounced by Suárez as "entirely false."

This section also includes an important discussion of the difference between private and public vengeance, wherein Suárez explains how a wronged commonwealth can serve as a judge in its own case. Finally, after renewed consideration of the contrasting exigencies of justice and charity, Suárez concludes the section with a reflection on reasonable hope of success: before undertaking an offensive war, a leader must have a probable expectation of victory.

From Disputation XIII. Section IV: What is a Just Title for War, on the Basis of Natural Reason?[10]

There was an old error current among the Gentiles, who held that the rights of kingdoms were based on arms, and that it was permissible to make war solely to acquire prestige and wealth; a belief which, even from the standpoint of natural reason, is most absurd.

1 Therefore I hold, *first* that there can be no just war without an underlying legitimate and necessary cause. The truth of this conclusion is indubitable and clearly evident. Now, that just and sufficient reason for war is the infliction of a grave injury that cannot be avenged or repaired in any other way. This is taught by all of the theologians. . . .

---

[9]   This view, which Suárez attributes to "some writers," seems to be an allusion to Vitoria's *De iure bello*, q. 1, a. 4, prop. 5; see chap. 27, this volume, p. 316.
[10]   Williams et al. (trans.), *Selections*, pp. 815–20, 821–3.

First reason in support of this conclusion: war is permissible in order that the commonwealth may protect itself from harm; for in other respects, war is opposed to the good of the human race on account of the slaughter, material losses, and other misfortunes which it involves; and therefore, if the cause in question should cease to exist, the justice of war would also cease to exist.

Secondly, in war, men are despoiled of their property, their liberty, and their lives. To do such things without just cause is absolutely iniquitous; otherwise men could kill one another without cause.

Third, the concern of the present discussion [about just cause] is chiefly with offensive war. This is ordinarily waged against non-subjects. Consequently, it is necessary that they shall have committed some wrong on account of which they render themselves subjects [of the commonwealth that they have offended]. Otherwise, by what title would they merit punishment or be subject to a foreign jurisdiction?

Furthermore, if the grounds or purposes which the Gentiles had in view (for example, ambition, avarice, and even vainglory or a display of fierce courage) were legitimate and sufficient, any commonwealth whatsoever could aspire to these ends; and hence, a war would be just on both sides, essentially and apart from ignorance. This supposition is entirely absurd; for two opposing rights cannot both be just.

2 But in order that this matter may be explained more clearly, there are several points that should be noted.

First, not any cause whatsoever is sufficient to justify war, but only causes that are very serious and proportionate to the ravages of the war. For it would be contrary to reason to inflict the most serious damage because of a slight injury. In like manner, a judge can punish, not all offences whatsoever, but only those that militate against the general peace and to the good of the commonwealth. In this connection, however, we must remember that not infrequently a wrong which appears to be slight is in fact serious, if all the aspects are weighed, or if other and similar wrongs are permitted [as a consequence], since thereby great harm may gradually ensue. Thus, for example, to seize even the smallest town, or to make raids, etc., may sometimes constitute a grave injury, especially when the prince who has caused the injury treats with scorn the protest that is made.

3 Secondly, it must be noted that different kinds of injuries can cause a just war. These may be grouped under three heads. One of the heads would be the seizure by a prince of another's property, and his refusal to restore it. Another head would be his denial, without reasonable cause, of the common rights of nations, such as the right of transit over highways, trading in common, etc. The third would be any grave injury to one's reputation or honour. It should be added that it is a sufficient cause for war if an injury of this kind is inflicted either upon a prince himself or upon his subjects; for the prince is guardian of his commonwealth and also of his subjects. Furthermore, the cause is sufficient if the wrong is inflicted upon any one who has placed himself under the protection of a prince, or even if it is inflicted upon allies or friends, as may be seen in the case of Abraham (Genesis 14), and in that of David (1 Kings 28). For "a friend is a second self," says Aristotle (*Nicomachean Ethics*, bk. IX, chaps. 4 and 9). This must be understood with the proviso that the friend himself has a right to [undertake] such a war, and wills to do so, either expressly or by implication. The reason for this proviso is that a wrong done to another does not give me the right, to avenge him, unless he would be justified in avenging himself and actually proposes to do so. Assuming, however, that these conditions exist, my aid to him is an act of co-operation in a good and just deed; but if [the injured party] does not entertain such a wish, no one else may intervene, since he who committed the wrong has made himself subject not to every one indiscriminately, but only to the person who has been wronged. Wherefore, the assertion made by some writers, that supreme kings have the power of avenging injuries throughout the whole world (*totius orbis*), is entirely false, and throws into confusion all the orderly distinctions of jurisdiction; for such power was not [expressly] granted by God and its existence is not to be inferred by any process of reasoning.

4 Thirdly, we must note that, in regard to an injury inflicted, two arguments may be alleged [to justify a declaration of war]. The first is [that such a declaration is justifiable] in order that restitution for the losses suffered should be made to the injured party. For this cause, indeed, it is not to be questioned that war may legitimately be declared; for if this declaration is to be permitted because of an injury [already done], then it is in the highest degree permissible when the object is that each one may secure himself against loss. Many examples illustrating this point are to be found in the Scriptures (Genesis 14, and similar passages). The other argument is [that war should be declared] in order that the offender may be duly punished; a contention which presents its own difficulty.

5 In the *second* place, then, I hold that a war may also be justified on the ground that he who has inflicted an injury should be justly punished, if he refuses to give just satisfaction for that injury, without resort to war. This conclusion is commonly accepted. In connection with it, and with the preceding conclusion, we must assume that the opposing party is not ready to make restitution, or to give satisfaction; for if he were so disposed, waging offensive war [against him] would become unjust, as we shall demonstrate in the following sections.

The conclusion is proved, first, by certain Scriptural passages (Numbers 25; 2 Kings 10–11), according to which, unconditional punishment for offences was carried into execution, by the command of God.

The reason in support of this same conclusion is that, just as within a commonwealth some legitimate power to punish crimes is necessary to the preservation of domestic peace; so in the world, in order that diverse commonwealths may dwell in peace, there must exist some power for punishing injuries inflicted by one upon another. Such a power is not to be found in any superior, for we assume that these commonwealths have no commonly acknowledged superior; therefore, the power in question must reside in the supreme prince of the injured commonwealth, to whom, by reason of that injury, the opposing prince is made subject. Consequently, war of this kind [offensive war] has been instituted in place of a tribunal administering just punishment.

6 But, on the other hand, one may object in the first place that to fight in this manner seems opposed to the admonitions in the Epistle to the Romans (12:17–19): "'To no man rendering evil for evil," and "Not avenging yourselves." The reply to the objection is that the passages quoted refer to acts performed by private authority and with the intention of doing evil for its own sake, to another. But if the acts in question be done under legitimate and public power, with the intention of holding an enemy to his duty and of reducing to its due order that which was disorderly, then they are not only not prohibited but even necessary. Hence, in that same Epistle (Romans 13:4), we find this additional passage: "For he beareth not the sword in vain. For he is God's minister: to work vengeance upon evildoers."

Secondly, it is objected that [if our second general conclusion be true,] then, as a consequence, the same party in one and the same case is both plaintiff and judge, a situation which is contrary to the natural law. The truth of the conclusion is evident, since the prince who has been wronged assumes the role of judge through his attack.

The objection is confirmed, in the first place, by the fact that for this reason private individuals are not allowed to take vengeance into their own hands. This is denied them because they would nearly always exceed the bounds of justice. And yet the same danger exists in the case of a prince who avenges himself.

A second confirmation of the same objection is that, by a like reasoning, any private person who might be unable to avenge himself through a judge could assume this right, executing it upon his own authority – since this privilege is granted to princes on the sole ground that there exists no other way of securing a just vengeance.

7 In response, it cannot be denied that in this matter [of public vengeance], one and the same person assumes, in a sense, the role of plaintiff and judge; even as we understand that God, to whom there is some analogy in the public authority, likewise assumes this double role. But the reason for this is simply that the act of vindicative justice has been indispensable to mankind, and that no more fitting method for its performance could, in the order of nature and humanly speaking, be found. This is especially true given the fact that prior to the war, the offending party has shown obstinacy in not wanting to give satisfaction; if he thereby finds himself in subjection to the offended party, he may impute this [misfortune] to himself.

Nor is this case analogous to that of a private individual. For in the first place, such an individual is directed by private judgment, and therefore he will easily exceed the limits of vengeance; whereas the public power is guided by public counsel, to which heed must be paid, and consequently authority of this sort may more easily avoid the disadvantages arising from personal inclination. Secondly, this vindicative power has for its essential purpose not private but public good, and hence it has been entrusted to a public and not private person. Therefore, if the former is unable or unwilling to mete out vengeance [on behalf of a private person], such an individual should patiently endure his loss. From the foregoing remarks, then, our reply to the first confirmation of the objection is evident.

As to the second confirmation, it has been said by some persons that in the situation referred to, a private person is allowed to avenge himself secretly; and in the *Code* [III, xxvii] there is a title, *Quando liceat sine judice se vindicare* [When it is permitted to avenge oneself without recourse to a judge]. But this must be understood as referring to restitution for losses suffered; if referred to the punishment of an offence, it is an inadmissible error. Indeed, the act of vindicative justice falls within a jurisdiction that private individuals do not possess, and cannot obtain by reason of an offence committed by another. For if they could possess it, there would be no need to employ the public power of jurisdiction; or, alternatively, since this power of jurisdiction [could be said to] flow from human beings themselves, each one would have had the power to refrain from transferring it to a magistrate, retaining it, on the contrary, for himself; a conclusion which would be opposed to the natural law, and to the good governance of the human race.

Therefore, we deny the consequent involved in the second confirmation. For laws regard those things which are necessary by themselves; yet private individuals considered in themselves may effectively obtain vengeance for offences through the public authority. If sometimes it happens that they fail to obtain it, this is accidental and has therefore necessarily to be endured, as we have said. But, between two supreme powers, the necessity [of punishing offenses] exists by itself. . . .

8 *Thirdly*, I hold that whoever initiates a war without just cause, sins not only against charity, but also against justice; and hence he is bound to make reparation for all the harm that results. The truth of this conclusion is manifest. . . .[11]

Finally, turning to the second case mentioned, if one prince begins a war upon another, even with just cause, while exposing his own realm to disproportionate loss and peril, then he will be sinning not only against charity, but also against the justice due to his own commonwealth. The reason for this assertion is as follows: a prince is bound in justice to have greater regard for the common good of his commonwealth than for his own good; otherwise, he will become a tyrant. So a judge who condemns to hanging a criminal deserving of execution but very necessary to the commonwealth, would act in a manner opposed to his official obligations, and, consequently, to justice. Similarly, a physician would sin against the justice required by his profession if he should give medicine which would heal a present disease but would cause more serious diseases to ensue.

---

[11] In the omitted passage, Suárez considers whether "there may sometimes exist a cause for war which absolves one from the charge of injustice, but not from the charge of sinning against charity."

9 However, with respect to this last point, we must take into consideration the fact that a single king who rules over several kingdoms, can often make war for the sake of one of these to the detriment of another. For though the various kingdoms may be distinct from one another, nevertheless, inasmuch as they are subject to one head, they can and should be of mutual aid, since the defence of one contributes to the benefit of another and in this way, the principle of equality is preserved. For in its own emergency, one kingdom might require the aid of another. In addition to all these considerations, the mere fact that their [common] prince is rendered more powerful, is in itself extremely advantageous to each of the kingdoms involved. In short, greater peace, and other advantages, may perhaps accrue to a commonwealth so supported; and many other [similar] points can easily be perceived upon reflection. There are, then, numerous considerations which may oblige a prince to abandon his right to make war lest his realm suffer loss.

10 Furthermore, we should call attention to the conclusion, drawn from these primary considerations by Cajetan (commenting on *Summa theologiae*, II–II, q. 96, a. 4) namely, that for a war to be just, the prince ought to be so sure of the degree of his power, that he is morally certain of victory. The first reason for this conclusion is the fact that otherwise the prince would incur the evident peril of inflicting upon his commonwealth losses greater than the advantages involved. In the same way, says Cajetan, a judge would do wrong in attempting the arrest of a criminal without a force that, to his certain knowledge, could not be overpowered. Second, whoever begins a war assumes an active role; and the one who assumes such a role must always be the stronger, in order to vanquish the one who plays a passive part.

But this condition [of certitude] does not appear to me to be absolutely essential. First, because, from a human standpoint, it is almost impossible of realization. Second because it is often to the common interest of the commonwealth not to await such a degree of certitude, but rather to test its ability to conquer the enemy, even when that ability is somewhat doubtful. Third, because if the conclusion were true, a weaker sovereign could never declare war upon a stronger, since he is unable to attain the certitude which Cajetan demands.

Therefore, the following rules should be laid down. A prince [who declares war] is indeed bound to attain the maximum certitude possible regarding victory. Furthermore, he ought to balance the expectation of victory against the risk of loss, and ascertain whether, all things being carefully considered, the expectation [of victory] is preponderant. If so great a degree of certitude is impossible of attainment, he ought at least to have either a more probable expectation of victory, or one equally balanced as to the chances of victory or defeat, and that, in proportion to the need of the commonwealth and the communal welfare. But if the expectation of victory is less apt to be realized than the chance of defeat, and if the war is offensive in character, then in almost every case that war should be avoided. If [on the other hand,] the war is defensive, it should be attempted;

for in that case it is a matter of necessity, whereas the offensive war is a matter of choice. All of these conclusions are sufficiently clear in the light of the principles of conscience and justice. . . .

In this next section Suárez argues that religious teachings (revelation) can provide no special grounds for waging war. Similar in this regard to his predecessor Vitoria, Suárez seems intent on distancing the just war idea from the related notion of holy war, warning princes against taking it upon themselves to avenge sins against God, since "he can easily avenge himself, if he so wills." Suárez does, however, note one possible exception to this rule: If a people subject to a non-Christian ruler wish to accept the faith of Christ, and their ruler prevents them from doing so, then Christian princes may resort to force in defense of this people. This line of reasoning would not, however, be available to Muslims and other non-Christians, since on Suárez's view, Christianity represents the one true religion. Thus, should a people wish to embrace Islam against the wishes of their ruler, Muslim princes would not have license to intervene on its behalf. Suárez tempers this conclusion somewhat, when he asserts toward the end of this section that his overall argument is founded on natural reason. Hence he concludes that even individuals who have never heard of Christ and the Christian religion, yet who sincerely wish to worship God and observe the law of nature, have a right to practice their religion. Significantly, this section represents one of Suárez's most extended discussions on the use of force in defense of the innocent ("humanitarian intervention" in today's parlance).

From Disputation XIII. Section V: Can Christian Princes Have any Just Title for War beyond that which Natural Reason Dictates[12]

1 . . . The first title is that of simple unbelief [on the part of the enemy], that is, a refusal to accept the true religion. But this is a false ground, a point with which we deal in the treatise *De fide*.

The second title is that God may be avenged for injuries that are done to Him by sins against nature, and by idolatry . . . . But this opinion is also false, and it is so first of all, even if we speak of "vengeance," in the strict sense. For God did not give to all men the power to avenge the injuries they do to him, since he can easily avenge himself, if he so wills. Moreover, it would not have been well for the human race had men received this power from God, for the greatest disorder would thereby have resulted. The same argument holds true with respect to the plea of defending [the majesty of God]; since the sins against Him would thus

---

[12] Williams et al. (trans.), *Selections*, pp. 823–7.

be multiplied rather than prevented. On this same ground, moreover, Christian princes could declare war even upon one another, for many of these princes also offend God. Likewise, since such a title for initiating war could never be sufficiently established, those who were so attacked could justly defend themselves, and the war would thus become just for both sides. . . .

3 It must be noticed, however, that the second title mentioned has been virtually accepted by a number of authorities, with respect to cases in which it happens that a state worshipping the one God inclines toward idolatry through the wickedness of its prince; these authorities claim that it is allowable to initiate war against such a prince. Their contention would be valid if the prince forcibly compelled his subjects to practice idolatry; but under any other circumstances, [such a title] would not be a sufficient cause for war, unless the whole commonwealth should demand assistance against its prince. For where compulsion does not intervene, defense has no place.

This position is supported, first, by the fact that, if the reasoning in question were valid, it would always be permissible to declare such a war on the ground of protecting innocent children. Secondly, on the basis of that same reasoning, Christian princes would always be permitted to wage war among themselves, upon their own authority. Finally, by whatever arguments this title for war may be justified, [the title urged] is not confined to Christians alone, but is possessed in common with all unbelievers who worship only the one God; and accordingly; these unbelievers could rightfully defend those who wished to worship the same God, and who were forced by others into idolatry.

4 A third title for war is advanced, namely, the supreme temporal dominion [of Christians]. That is to say, the authorities mentioned above maintain either that unbelievers are not true owners of their possessions; or else that the Christian Emperor, or – at least – the supreme Pontiff, has direct temporal dominion over the whole world.

But all such claims are vain inventions, a point which we discuss elsewhere, on the subject of dominion and laws. In the second place, even if we grant that such a title does indeed exist, still it would be impossible either to demonstrate its existence to the satisfaction of infidels, or to force them to believe in the existence of such dominion; and therefore, they could not be forced to obey. Finally, on that same ground, the pope or the emperor could make war [even] upon all Christian princes. Wherefore, it must be observed that although the pope has indirectly supreme power in temporal affairs, nevertheless, the existence of such temporal power is always based, essentially, upon the assumption of direct power in spiritual matters; and therefore, this indirect power does not essentially extend to unbelievers, over whom no direct spiritual dominion exists even in the pope himself. But I use the term, 'essentially', because 'incidentally' the case may be otherwise, as I shall presently show.

5 A fourth title urged is that unbelievers are barbarians and incapable of governing themselves properly; and that the order of nature demands that men of this condition should be governed by those who are more wise, as Aristotle (*Politics*, bk. I, chap. 1) has taught, saying that (ibid., chap[s]. 5[–8][13]) a war is by nature just, when it is waged against men born to be under obedience but who are unwilling to accept that condition. . . .

In the first place, however, such a contention cannot have a general application; for it is evident that there are many unbelievers more gifted by nature than are the faithful, and better adapted to political life. Second, in order that the title in question may be valid, it is not enough to judge that a given people are of inferior natural talents; for they must also be so wretched as to live in general more like wild beasts than like men, as those persons are said to live who have no human polity, and who go about entirely naked, eat human flesh, etc. If there are any such, they may be brought into subjection by war, not with the purpose of destroying them, but rather that they may be organized in human fashion, and justly governed. However, this title for war should rarely or never be approved, except in circumstances in which the slaughter of innocent people, and similar wrongs take place; and therefore, the title in question is more properly included under defensive than under offensive wars.

Finally, Aristotle, in the passage cited above, declares that a war of this sort is permissible only when those men who are subdued in order that they may be governed, are as different from the rest of mankind as is the body from the soul. From this proposition one must conclude, however, that the said title for war, if it really exists, is valid not only for Christians, but also for every prince who wishes to defend the law of nature, which, when understood narrowly, gives rise to that title.

6 Therefore, the assertion must be made that there is no title for war so exclusively reserved to Christian princes that it has not some basis in, or at least some due relation to, natural law, being therefore also applicable to princes who are unbelievers.

By way of explaining this assertion, I conclude, *first*, that a Christian prince may not declare war save either by reason of some injury inflicted or for the defence of the innocent. We have, already given sufficient proof of this fact, by rejecting all the invalid titles for war, [advanced above]. The arguments we have adduced are a proof of this same fact; for the law of grace has not destroyed, but on the contrary completes the natural law.

7 *Secondly*, I must say that the defence of the innocent is permissible in a special sense to Christian princes, and that the same proposition holds true, proportionately, with respect to avenging injuries. For if a commonwealth subject to an infidel prince wishes to accept the law of Christ and the unbelieving king prohibits that acceptance, then Christian princes have the right to defend that innocent people. But if the same commonwealth wishes to submit to the law of

---

[13] For the relevant passages in Aristotle, see chap. 3, this volume.

unbelievers – for example, to the Mohammedan [law] – and its prince is opposed to this submission, then an infidel Turkish prince would not have a similar right of war against that other prince. The reason for this distinction is that to prevent the acceptance of the law of Christ does indeed involve grievous injustice and harm, whereas there is no injury at all in prohibiting the acceptance of another law. Likewise, if [a given people] are willing to listen [to the Gospel], they may be convinced through reason that this is the more credible faith and that it ought to be believed; and therefore, it is just to assist them, under these circumstances. . . .

8 I hold, *thirdly*, that all of the foregoing considerations are so founded on natural reason that they may, to a certain extent and in due proportion, be applied to unbelievers. The explanation of this conclusion is that if any commonwealth wishes to worship the one God and observe the law of nature, or to listen to preachers who teach these things, and if the prince of that state forcibly prevents [that commonwealth] from doing so, there would spring up in consequence a just title for war to be waged by some other prince. This holds even if the latter should be an unbeliever, and is guided solely by natural reason, because such a war would be a just defence of innocent persons.

Likewise, if any nation should worship the one God and observe the laws of nature, while another nation practised idolatry and lived contrary to natural reason, then the former state would have the right to send missionaries to instruct [the citizens of the latter state], and to free them from their errors. And if this action were forcibly prevented, then war could justly follow. This holds first, because such a right is entirely in keeping with nature; secondly, because the defence of the innocent would be involved in that procedure, since it is only reasonable to think that, there would not fail to be some who wished to be taught the natural truths necessary for an upright and virtuous life, and who would be wickedly impeded in the attainment of this wish. . . .

The next section continues the earlier investigation into the concept of just cause. The focus is now on private conscience. What degree of certitude must a person have before going to war? What should one do when the justice of one's cause is in doubt, or when there seem to be equally probable arguments for war on the opposing side? The answer to these questions hinges in large measure on one's place in the political–military hierarchy. Political leaders, statesmen, and leading military officers, have a greater responsibility for investigating the causes of war than do ordinary soldiers and citizens. This section also emphasizes the importance of arbitration. In a famous passage (§5), Suárez asserts that human beings are not condemned to settle their disputes by war since God has provided us with other means – including arbitration – for resolving controversies between commonwealths.

From Disputation XIII. Section VI: What Certitude as to the Just Cause of War is Required in order that War may be Just?[14]

Three kinds of persons must here be distinguished, to wit: the supreme king and prince, the leading men and commanders (*duces*), and the common soldiers (*milites*). It is to be assumed that practical certitude is required of all these persons, a certitude which may be expressed in the statement: 'It is permissible for me to make war.' The whole doubt [to be discussed here] revolves around [the issue of] theoretical certitude. This may be expressed as follows: 'This cause of war is just in itself', or, 'This thing which I seek through war is rightfully mine'.

1 I hold, *first*, that the supreme king is bound to make a diligent examination of the cause and its justice, and that after making this examination, he ought to act in accordance with the knowledge thus obtained.

The basis of the first part of this conclusion is that war is a matter of the gravest character; and reason demands that in any matter whatsoever, deliberation and diligence should be applied, commensurate with its importance. Furthermore, a judge, in order to pass judgment in a private matter, ought to make diligent investigation; hence, the necessity for such diligence exists in due proportion in a public cause of war. Finally, if the prince were not bound to make this investigation, the rashness of princes would easily result in universal disturbance. With regard to the first part of this assertion, then, there is no difficulty.

2 The explanation of the second part of the conclusion is as follows. Let us suppose that the ground for a war is the fact that a certain king claims a certain city as belonging to him, or as falling newly to him by hereditary right. Now if, when the matter has been carefully examined, the truth of that claim is clearly established, what I have asserted is obviously true. But when the case of each side contains [an element of] probability, then the king ought to act as a just judge.

Therefore, if he finds that the opinion favouring his own side is the more probably true, he may, even justly, prosecute his own right; because, so I believe, the more probable opinion should always be preferred in passing judgment. For that is an act of distributive justice, in which the more worthy party is to receive the preference; and he is the more worthy party who enjoys the more probable right, as we shall explain below at greater length. For the same reason, however, if the more probable opinion favors the opposing side, the prince in question may on no account proceed to war.

3 If, finally, after diligent investigation, the probabilities on both sides are found to be equal, or if, at least, equal uncertainty exists – whatever the ground of the uncertainty – then, if the opposing party is in possession, he ought to have the preference, because even in a judicial process, that party is favoured, inasmuch

---

[14] Williams et al. (trans.), *Selections*, pp. 828–32.

as he has the greater right. On this account, the party who is not in possession cannot proceed to war against the possessor; while the latter, on the other hand, is secure [in his conscience] and may justly defend himself. . . .

4 Another aspect of the question regards the situation in which no one is in possession and the doubts and probabilities balance each other. The more common opinion seems to be that either party has the right to seize first the thing in dispute. In accordance with this opinion, the war would become just on both sides; but this point is of no importance, when ignorance intervenes. The reason, indeed, which is offered in support of this opinion is that in a similar case a judge could award the property by his own decision to either one of the parties to the litigation, as he might choose.

However, I am unable to persuade myself that a judge may act thus in the case supposed. For certainly, under those circumstances, the judge is merely a distributor of property over which he personally has no right; consequently, if the rights of the parties in question are at all times entirely equal, there is no reason which would allow him to allot the whole property to either party; and therefore, the judge is bound to divide the property. Or, if this cannot be advantageously done, it will be necessary to satisfy both sides, in some fashion. Hence, in a question involving war, the princes shall be bound to this same attitude. Accordingly, they must either divide between them the thing in dispute, or cast lots for it, or settle the matter in some other way. But if one party should attempt to seize the whole possession to the exclusion of the other party, by that very act he would be doing the other an injury which the latter might justly repel, thus seizing, on this just ground of war, the entire disputed possession.

5 But the question may be asked whether, in cases of this kind, supreme princes are bound to submit the matter to the decision of good men. This question, moreover, arises from the standpoint of natural law only, so that, in our discussion, we shall not include the authority of the pope, of which we have already spoken.

Indeed, I am of the opinion that the affirmative answer to this question is, in all probability, correct. For the said princes are bound to avoid war in so far as is possible, and by upright means. Therefore, if no danger of injustice is to be feared, the above-mentioned [arbitration] is plainly the best means of decision, and consequently resort should be had to it.

This opinion is confirmed as follows: it is impossible that the Author of nature should have left human affairs, governed as they are by conjecture more frequently than by any sure reason, in such a critical condition that all controversies between supreme princes and commonwealths should be settled only by war; for such a condition would be contrary to wisdom and the common good of the human race; and therefore it would be contrary to justice. Furthermore, if this condition prevailed, those persons would as a rule possess the greater right who were the more powerful, and [this right] would have to be measured by arms, which is manifestly a barbarous and absurd supposition.

6 In this connection, however, we must observe, first, that a supreme prince is not bound by the judgment of those whom he himself has not appointed to render judgment. Therefore, it would be necessary for the arbitrators to be chosen with the consent of both sides. Resort to this method, indeed, is a most rare occurrence, inasmuch as [these princes] seldom favour it; for very frequently one or other of the princes holds the external judges in suspicion.

Secondly, it should be noted that a supreme prince, if he is acting in good faith, should assess what is his right by [seeking the council] of prudent and learned men; then he may follow their judgment, if by [this consultation] his right is made clear to him. Under these circumstances he will not be bound to abide by the decision of an outside judge. The reason in support of this statement is that the right in question must be judicially ascertained, after the fashion of a just legal process. In [rendering] a just decision, two things are intended. One involves [both] an examination of the grievance and an acquaintance with the right of each side. In this process, knowledge and prudence are necessary, not jurisdiction. For since such a judgment is not sought through war, but, on the contrary, as a substitute for war, there is no need to call in an arbitrator. The other involves enforcing the right, after it has been made clear. For this, jurisdiction is indeed required; but such jurisdiction is inherent in a supreme prince when in other respects he is sufficiently certain of his right. In that case, then, there is no reason binding him to await the judgment of an outside arbitrator, although he ought to accept just settlements if they are offered to him.

7 In the *second* place, I hold that generals and other princes of the kingdom, whenever they are summoned for consultation to give their opinion on beginning a war, are bound to inquire diligently into the truth of the matter; but if they are not called, they are under no greater obligation to do so than others who are common soldiers. The first part of this conclusion is clearly true because these generals, having been summoned, are bound in justice to give a just opinion, for if they did not do so, any injustice that there might be in the war will be laid to their charge. The proof of the second part of the conclusion is the fact that, when they are not summoned [to give advice], their part in the affair becomes simply that of private soldiers, since they are merely set in action by others, but do not control action; while it is only incidental that they are wealthy or of noble birth. . . .

8 I hold *thirdly*, that: common soldiers, as subjects of princes, are in no wise bound to make diligent investigation, but rather may go to war when summoned to do so, provided it is not clear to them that the war is unjust.[15]

In the next section, Suárez engages in a reflection that ranges across what now goes under the headings of *ius ad bellum* and *ius in bello*. Although he rarely uses

---

[15]   In these passages Suárez considers some objections about the responsibility of individual soldiers, and then takes on a detailed discussion of mercenaries.

the term explicitly, the idea of "right intention," the last of the three conditions for just war mentioned by Thomas Aquinas in *Summa theologiae,* II–II, q. 40, a. 1, is what gives unity to the different topics taken up in the present section. After some preliminary comments on the three main classes of individuals participating in war (princes, intermediate commanders, and ordinary soldiers), Suárez proceeds to explain how the prince has obligations, not only toward his own subordinates, but toward the enemy commonwealth as well. Before declaring war he must first make his grievances known to the enemy commonwealth, affording it an opportunity to avoid war by offering restitution for the wrong done. After dealing with the question of restitution, Suárez moves into the problem of civilian immunity. In one of the first systematic treatments of this theme, he argues that those not engaged in the fighting ("innocents") may not be directly targeted. Yet, they may indirectly be visited with side-effect (now termed "collateral") harm. This, he cautions, should not be done lightly, but only in proportion to the gravity of the cause at stake. Suárez elucidates this idea of civilian side-effect harm by reference to the principle of double effect.

From Disputation XIII. Section VII: What is the Proper Mode (*Debitus Modus*) of Conducting War?[16]

1 Three periods must be distinguished: the beginning of war; its prosecution, before victory is gained; and the period after victory. The three classes of persons already mentioned, must also be distinguished, namely: the supreme prince; the intermediate commanders; and the soldiers of the rank and file.

All of these persons may be considered in certain specific relationships. First, with respect to the enemy, that is to say: how may these classes justly conduct themselves toward the enemy? Secondly, with respect to their mutual relations: how should the king conduct himself toward his soldiers? Thirdly, [and again in connection with their mutual relations,] how should the soldiers conduct themselves toward their kings? Fourthly, how should they conduct themselves toward other persons, for example, those persons in whose houses the soldiers are quartered during the march?

At present, we are dealing in the main with the first question; but we shall also treat briefly of the others.

2 With respect to the fourth relationship, then, we may repeat briefly the admonition of John the Baptist (Luke 3:14): "Do violence to no man . . . and be content with your pay." Hence, none of these soldiers may take anything from his hosts, beyond that which has been determined by the king; otherwise, he sins

---

[16] Williams et al. (trans.), *Selections,* pp. 836–41, 843, 845–6, 847–8, 849, 850–1, 852–3. The editors of the present volume are indebted to Professor Peter Haggenmacher, who assisted us in revising the translation of this section of the *De bello.*

against justice and is bound to make restitution. The same is true if he does any other damage to houses, fields, etc. To be sure, the intermediate commanders and the princes are bound, by virtue of their office, to prevent such acts in so far as they are able. If they fail to do so, the whole duty of making restitution falls upon them, in default of the soldiers.

Concerning the third head, just as the kings are under an obligation to give pay to the soldiers, so the latter are bound to discharge all the duties pertaining to their office. Hence, justice requires of them brave conduct, even to such a degree that they shall not take to flight, nor desert their stations or fortifications; a matter concerning which there are many laws (in *Digest*, 49, 16). Cajetan, also, should be consulted in his brief treatise on the subject (*Opusculum*, bk. 4, penultimate question [bk. 3, treatise 9: *De vinculo obedientiae*]); for he holds that commanders of forts are under an obligation not to surrender through any fear of death or starvation, since they have made a contract with the prince not to do so, and since they receive their payment because of this contract, whence there arises an obligation binding them in justice. . . .

Only the first head, then, still remains for discussion.

3 I hold, *first*, that before a war is begun the [attacking] prince must present the opposing commonwealth with the just cause of war, and demand adequate restitution. If the other commonwealth offers such restitution, he is bound to accept it, and desist from war; if he does not do so, the war will be unjust. If, on the other hand, the opposing prince refuses to give satisfaction, he may initiate war. . . .

4 But Cajetan[17] limits this conclusion by the following proviso: namely, that the satisfaction shall be offered before the encounter in war [has occurred]. After the hostilities have begun, the [future] victor is not bound to accept such satisfaction, because in war he is like a judge, and once it has begun, he becomes master of the case. He has acquired the right to proceed to the very end; so that the vanquished party has only himself to blame, in that he did not offer to make restitution at the proper time.

But, I ask, what does Cajetan mean by *actual encounter in war?* If he is referring to actually the final struggle in which the whole war will find its conclusion, there is no doubt that, if the affair has already been entered into and victory is beginning to favour the side of the just belligerent, the latter is not bound, under such circumstances, to accept satisfaction short of complete victory; for morally speaking such victory does not seem far off, nay, to treat of peace at that juncture can hardly be expected in moral terms.

If, on the other hand, by *actual encounter*, Cajetan means a war in which several fights have [already] occurred, I do not see how it may be asserted with any solid assurance that [the just belligerent] is more judge of the proceedings at that time than [he was] before the war had begun; for previously, he had

---

17 In his *Summula*, "When war should be called just or unjust, licit or illicit" (see chap. 22, this volume).

the same right to begin the war that he now has to proceed with it. The sole difference is that the injury has grown greater, and that consequently an increased right to a greater satisfaction has arisen. Moreover, the arguments set forth above apply equally to both of the situations in question, for the continuance no less than the beginning of the war ought to be dictated by necessity. The more so as [in both cases] similar damages arise to the common good, which should be avoided while preserving one's own right; this however is preserved when satisfaction is offered, since nothing more can be claimed after victory has been achieved, a point which we shall discuss below. In short, the right to make war is detrimental to others, and the punishment inflicted through war is of the severest kind; therefore, that punishment ought to be inflicted with the utmost restraint.

5 Therefore, the contrary opinion to Cajetan's appears to be in every respect nearer the truth; with the sole proviso that complete satisfaction shall include first, that all things unjustly withheld shall be restored; second, that reimbursement must be made for all expenses due to injuries inflicted by the enemy, so that, once the war has been begun, a claim may justly be made for all its costs, to date; third, something may be demanded as a penalty for the injury inflicted, for in war regard must be had not only for commutative justice, but also for vindicative justice; finally, a demand may justly be made for whatever will seem necessary for the maintenance and safeguard of peace in the future, since the chief end of war is to establish such a future peace. It should also be added that this condition of war flows from justice; consequently, if war is made contrary to justice, there will arise an obligation to make restitution.

6 I hold, *secondly*, that after war has been begun, and during the whole period thereof up to the attainment of victory, it is just to visit upon the enemy all losses which may seem necessary either for obtaining satisfaction or for securing victory, provided that these losses do not involve direct intrinsic injury to innocent persons, which would be intrinsically evil, of which we shall treat below, in the sixth conclusion. The reason in support of this conclusion is as follows: if the end is permissible, the means necessary to that end are also permissible; and hence it follows that in the whole course, or duration, of the war hardly anything done against the enemy involves injustice, except the slaying of the innocent. For all other damages are usually held to be necessary for attaining the end to which the war is directed.

7 In the *third* place, I hold that after victory has been achieved, a prince is allowed to inflict upon the conquered commonwealth such losses as are sufficient for a just punishment, satisfaction, and reparation for all losses suffered. The conclusion is commonly accepted and undoubtedly true, both because this is the object of war, and also because in a regular judgment this likewise is permissible. It should however be observed that in computing the sum required for this satisfaction, all the losses endured by the commonwealth in question during the course of the war (i.e. the deaths of men, conflagrations, etc.) must be taken into account. Yet we do not disagree, first, with the additional comment made by

Sylvester (word *bellum*, pt. I, qu. 9 [qu. 10]) and by Vitoria (*De iure belli*, no. 51), namely, that movable goods captured by soldiers during the war are not to be reckoned by the prince as part of the restitution. For this rule has become a part of the *ius gentium*, through common custom. The reason underlying it is that, since the soldiers' lives are exposed to dangers so numerous and so grave, they should be allowed something; and the same is true of their prince.

Secondly, it is to be observed with regard both to this and the previous conclusion, that soldiers are not allowed to seize anything on their own authority, whether after or even before the victory is won, because by themselves they have no power, but possess it solely through their prince, as his agents; therefore they may not justly take anything without his express or implied authorization.

Thirdly, it follows from this conclusion that, if all the aforementioned penalties seem insufficient in view of the gravity of the wrong done, then, after the war has entirely ended, some of those among the enemy who are guilty may also, with justice, be put to death, although the killing of a great multitude should not be done without the most urgent cause; also such slaughter may be allowed in order to provoke terror in the rest, as is indicated in the following passage from Deuteronomy (20:13–14): "When the Lord thy God shall deliver the city into thy hands, thou shalt slay all that are therein of the male sex, with the edge of the sword, excepting women and children," etc. Whence it follows that those among the vanquished who are guilty may with much more reason be reduced to captivity and have all their property seized.

Fourthly, it is to be noted that one should interpret in accord with this conclusion the civil laws which assert that, through the *ius gentium*, it has been established that all the property of the enemy, both movable and immovable, passes to the victors. . . . But all of these passages must be interpreted in conformity with the rule previously laid down, equality of justice being preserved, and regard must be had for the future peace, as we shall show below. For in war the same equality as in a just judgment has to be preserved and in [such a judgment] the offender cannot be visited with every sort of punishment nor deprived of all his property without any restriction, but only in proportion to his fault. . . .[18]

10 But another doubt remains, namely: whether it is equally allowable to inflict penalties of this kind upon all those who are numbered among the enemy. In answering this question we must note that some of these persons are guilty, and others are innocent. By a kind of natural law the innocent include children, women, and all unable to bear arms; by *ius gentium* [the innocent include] diplomats; and by the positive law applicable among Christians [the innocent

---

[18]   In the omitted passage (§§ 7–8), Suárez considers whether, in the interests of restitution, it is allowable to seize goods from a vanquished enemy, when the enemy is not their rightful owner. In arguing against this practice, Suárez notes how even provisions of positive law alleged to be part of *ius gentium* can sometimes spring from unjust customs, specifically "from the unjust manner in which wars were at that time carried on."

include] members of religious order, priests, etc. (*Decretals*, bk. I, tit. xxxiv, chap. ii). . . . All other persons are considered guilty; for in human judgment those who are presumed to be able to take up arms [are viewed] as if they have actually done so. Now, the opposing commonwealth is composed of both classes of persons [innocent and guilty], and therefore, all these persons are held to be enemies (*Digest*, XLIX. xv. 24). In this respect, strangers and foreigners, since they form no part of the commonwealth and therefore are not reckoned among the enemy unless they are allies in the war, differ from the persons above mentioned.

11 Assuming that the foregoing is true, I hold, *fourthly*, that if the penalties inflicted upon the guilty are sufficient for restitution and satisfaction, they cannot justly be extended to affect the innocent. This fact is self-evident as a result of what has already been said, for one may not demand greater satisfaction than that which is just. The only question that might arise is whether or not victorious soldiers are always bound to observe this order in their procedure, taking vengeance upon the guilty and their property, rather than upon the innocent. The reply is briefly that, other things being equal, and within the limits of the same class of property, they are so bound. For the principle of equity clearly imposes this rule, a fact which will become more evident from what follows.

12 *Fifthly*, I hold that if such a course of action is essential to complete satisfaction, it is permissible to deprive the innocent of their goods, even of their liberty. The reason is that the innocent form a part of one iniquitous commonwealth; and on account of the fault of the whole, this part may be punished even though it does not of itself share in the fault. . . .

15 *Sixthly*, I hold that the innocent as such (*per se*) may under no condition be killed, even if the punishment inflicted upon their commonwealth would, otherwise, be deemed inadequate; but incidentally (*per accidens*) they may be slain, when such an act is necessary in order to secure victory.

The reason supporting this conclusion is that the killing of innocent persons is intrinsically evil. However, one may object that this is true with respect to killing upon private authority and without just cause, but that the case in question involves both public authority and a just cause. Nevertheless, such a plea must be rejected when the killing is not necessary for victory (a condition which we have already assumed to exist), and when the innocent can be distinguished [from the guilty].

The conclusion is confirmed by the difference existing between life and other possessions. For the latter fall under human dominion, and the commonwealth as a whole has a greater right to them than do individual persons. Hence, such persons may be deprived of [their] property because of the fault of the whole commonwealth. But life does not fall under human dominion, and therefore, no one may be deprived of his life save by reason of his own fault. . . .

But one may ask, who actually are the innocent, with respect to this issue? My reply is that they include not only the persons enumerated above [§10], but also those who are able to bear arms, if it is evident that, in other respects, they have not shared in the crime nor in the unjust war. The natural law demands that, generally speaking, no one who is actually known to be free from fault, may be killed. But what shall we say, if certain persons are not known to have participated either [in the crime or in the unjust war], and if there exists only the presumption that they were able to bear arms? On this point, I shall speak shortly.

16 ... These arguments prove beyond a doubt that, after victory has been attained, only those who are known to be guilty may be slain. . . . [T]he slaughter of all those whose innocence is not clearly evident by reason of age or sex is, in general, permitted, as long as the actual combat continues; but the case will be otherwise after the cessation of combat, and the attainment of victory.

17 The latter part of the [sixth] conclusion is also commonly accepted, and is clearly true in the case of certain means essential to victory, which, however, necessarily involve the death of the innocent, as in the burning of cities and the destruction of fortresses. For, strictly speaking, whoever has the right to attain the end sought by a war, has the right to use the means to that end. Moreover, in such a case, the death of the innocent is not directly intended, it follows rather as an incidental consequence. Hence, it is not considered voluntary, rather it is permitted by one who exercises his right in a time of necessity. A confirmation of this argument lies in the fact that it would [otherwise] be impossible to conclude the war. In like manner, a pregnant woman may use medicine necessary to preserve her own life, even if she knows that this will result in the death of her unborn child. From these arguments it is to be inferred that, save out of necessity, the means in question are not permissible.

18 On the other hand, one may argue, first: that in the case described, one really cooperates, as a positive factor, in bringing about the death of an innocent person; hence, one cannot be excused from sin.

In the second place: it may be alleged that to kill an innocent person is as intrinsically evil as to kill oneself; and to kill oneself in this manner, even incidentally, is evil; as, for example, when soldiers demolish a citadel and a wall, although they know with certainty that they will be crushed at the moment [when the fortifications fall]. An indication of this fact is that Samson, who committed such an act [of self-destruction], is exonerated by the Fathers, St. Augustine (*On the City of God*, bk. I, chaps. 21 and 26), St. Bernard (*De praecepto et dispensatione* [chap. 3]), St. Thomas (*ST* II–II, q. 64, a. 5, ad 4) only because he acted at the prompting of the Holy Spirit.

In the third place: evil may not be done that good may ensue. . . .

Fifthly: the innocent persons in question would be justified in defending themselves if they were able to do so; hence the attack on them is unjust. . . .

19 The reply to the first of the foregoing arguments is as follows: if the matter be considered physically, the victor does not really kill, for he is an incidental but not an essential cause (*non est causa per se sed per accidens*); morally he is not responsible for homicide, because he is exercising his own right, nor is he bound to avoid to [his own] great detriment, the resulting harm to his neighbour.

As for the second argument, I deny that [the act in question] is intrinsically evil, basing my denial on that same ground, namely, that the person described does not in fact kill himself, but merely permits his own death. The question of whether or not this may be allowed under such circumstances must be considered in the light of the order of charity; that is to say, one must consider whether the good at stake in the case is to such an extent the common good, that there is an obligation to expose oneself in its defense to a peril so great. There are some who think that Samson's action may be excused from this point of view; but such a reason would not seem to serve as a sufficient excuse for that action, because, if the matter is looked at from a purely human standpoint, the punishment of one's enemies would not seem to be a good so great as to justify Samson in killing himself, even though his death would be only incidental [to the attainment of his end].[19]

With respect to the third argument, it is true that morally evil deeds may not be performed that good may ensue, but it is permissible to inflict the evils of punishment [for that purpose]; though, [in point of fact,] in the present case, the evils in question are not so much brought about [with deliberation], as they are allowed to follow [incidentally]. . . .

To the fifth argument, some persons reply that, under such circumstances, the war may incidentally be just for both sides. Excluding cases of ignorance, however, this seems impossible. Accordingly, my reply is that these innocent individuals[20] may indeed defend themselves in a purely defensive manner: by preventing the burning of the city, for example, or the destruction of the citadel, etc. Such actions involve solely the protection of their own lives, and this they are allowed to do. I maintain, however, that they may not defend themselves offensively so to speak by fighting against those who are justly fighting, for at bottom they [the non-combatants] do not undergo injury from them [the just enemy combatants]. But these innocent persons may fight against those who are responsible for the war, since from them they truly suffer injury. . . .

20 *Seventhly*, I hold that, in addition to all the losses which have previously been enumerated and which may be claimed as necessary to satisfaction, a prince who has obtained a just victory may do everything with the property of the enemy that is essential to the preservation of an undisturbed peace in the future,

---

[19] Vitoria (in his commentary on *Summa theologiae*, II–II, q. 64), likewise discusses Samson's action by reference to the principle of double effect, although he finds more justification for it than does Suárez (see John P. Doyle [trans.], *On Homicide & Commentary on Summa theologiae II–II, q. 64* [Milwaukee: Marquette University Press, 1997], pp. 181–3). The case of Samson has provided a Biblical point of reference for contemporary discussions of suicide missions (see Diego Gambetta [ed.], *Making Sense of Suicide Missions* [Oxford: Oxford University Press, 2005], p. 279).

[20] Suárez is here speaking of individuals who are in the category of non-combatants. If their nation is engaged in an unjust war, and they find themselves under attack (say in a siege), they may legitimately defend themselves in the manner described.

provided that he spare the lives of the enemy. Therefore, if it is necessary, he may on this ground seize cities, provinces, etc.

That is the doctrine supported by all, and the rational basis thereof is derived from the very purpose of an honorable war; since war is permissible especially for this reason, namely, as a way (so to speak) to an upright peace.

This reasoning is confirmed by the fact that within the commonwealth itself, wrongdoing is punished in accordance with what is necessary for the public peace with the result that, frequently, some person is ordered into exile, or visited with a similar punishment, etc. From this example it may be inferred that, if a [precautionary] measure of this sort is taken, and at the same time it has the character of a penalty, this measure should be taken for both of these reasons [and not just one of them]; nor is it permissible to multiply without cause the harm inflicted upon the enemy.

21 *Finally,* I hold that a war will not be unjust, if all the precautions that we have enumerated are observed in it, and if at the same time the other general conditions of justice are fulfilled. Nevertheless such a war may still contain some evil element opposed to charity or to some other virtue. . . .[21]

23 A second doubt, according to St. Thomas (*ST* II–II, q. 40, a. 3), is whether stratagems are permissible in war. To this we must briefly reply, in agreement with him, that they are permissible in so far as relates to the prudent concealment of one's plans; but not with respect to the telling of lies. Regarding this point, what we have said elsewhere (Disp. XIV, section IV) on the concealment of one's religious faith should be consulted.

From the foregoing, another doubt is resolved *a fortiori,* the doubt as to whether it is permissible in war to break faith pledged with the enemy. For we must say that, generally speaking, this is not permissible, since it involves patent injustice; and consequently, if the enemy suffers loss for this reason, full restitution should be made. However, all this is true only provided that the promise shall have been made from the beginning [of the war], by a just and mutual agreement (as it were) in such a way as to be binding; and it is also necessary that this promise shall have remained and persisted in full vigor and force, since, if one side has perchance broken faith, the other side will be entirely freed from its own obligation. For the equity of law demands that this condition be understood to

---

[21]   Here Suárez explains how a war that is opposed to charity (although not to justice) has implications for the question of restitution. One such case concerns a situation where the two parties "voluntarily engage in war, without just cause" as a mutually agreed upon method of settling their dispute. This would be developed by later thinkers into the idea that war is analogous to a contract between two sovereigns, in which they agree to let the settlement be determined by the outcome of battle. This view would later be adopted by Immanuel Kant, when he wrote that "[i]f one wishes to find any rights in wartime, one must assume the existence of something analogous to a contract; in other words, one must assume that the other party has *accepted* the declaration of war and that both parties therefore wish to prosecute their rights in this manner"; *Metaphysics of Morals,* §56 (in *Kant: Political Writings,* 2nd edn. [Cambridge: Cambridge University Press, 1991], p. 167).

exist. The same holds true if any change in circumstances has occurred, such that the promises in question cannot be kept without grave loss. In that event, the opposing side must be warned that it is not possible to keep the promise made to it; and, after [either side] has issued this declaration, it is freed from the pledge. However, such a declaration is seldom to be permitted. . . .[22]

"Sedition" was the heading under which Scholastic thinkers took up the problem of civil war. Suárez builds his argument around Aquinas's earlier treatment of this theme (especially as interpreted by Cajetan in his commentary on the *Summa theologiae*). Suárez makes an original contribution to this discussion when he explains how a commonwealth may have moral license to rise up in war against a tyrant. His explanation is based on a transmission theory of political authority.[23] The authority to rule resides primarily in the political community as a whole. It is the first bearer of civil authority and from there (the body politic) authority is transferred to king. Hence, if the king does not govern as he should, the whole people may remove this authority from him. Arguing along these lines, Suárez elucidated the medieval notion of just revolt by reference to the emerging ideal of democratic governance.[24]

From Disputation XIII. Section VIII: Is Sedition Intrinsically Evil?[25]

1 Sedition is the term used to designate general warfare carried on within a single commonwealth, and waged either between two parts thereof or between the prince and the commonwealth. I hold, *first*, that sedition involving two factions of the commonwealth is always evil on the part of the attacker, but just on the defensive side. The truth of the latter statement is self-evident. The truth of the former is proved by the fact that no legitimate authority to declare war is discernible in such a situation, for this authority, as we have seen (section II), resides in the supreme prince.

The objection will be made that, sometimes, a prince will be able to delegate this authority, if urgent public necessity demands that he do so. In such a case, however, the prince himself, and not a part of the commonwealth, is held to be

---

[22]   In the omitted section Suárez deals with specialized questions relating to Christians: whether they may fight on feast days; whether Christian princes may call infidel princes to their aid, and so forth.
[23]   On this, see Yves R. Simon, *Philosophy of Democratic Government* (Chicago: University of Chicago Press, 1951), pp. 158–76.
[24]   Suárez offered a more detailed account of this theme in his polemical work *Defensio fidae catholicae*, which was written against King James I of England.
[25]   Williams et al. (trans.), *Selections*, pp. 854–5.

the attacker; so that no sedition will exist in the sense in which we are using the term. But what if one part of the commonwealth actually suffers injury from another part, and is unable to secure its right through the prince? My reply is that this injured part may do nothing beyond that which a private individual may do, as can easily be gathered from what we have said above.

2 I hold, *secondly,* that a war of the commonwealth against the prince, even if it be offensive, is not intrinsically evil; but that the conditions necessary for a war that is in other respects just must nevertheless be present in order that this sort of war may be honorable. This conclusion holds true only when the prince is a tyrant, a situation which may occur in one of two ways, as Cajetan notes (on II–II, q. 64, a. 1, ad 3 [a. 3]). In the first place, the prince may be a tyrant with respect to [the way in which he has assumed] dominion and power; secondly, he may be so merely in regard to [the manner in which he] has governed.

When the first kind of tyranny occurs, the whole commonwealth, or any portion thereof, has the right [to revolt] against the prince. Hence, it follows that any person whatsoever may avenge himself and the commonwealth against [such] tyranny. The reason supporting these statements is that the tyrant in question is the attacker, and is iniquitously waging war against the commonwealth and its separate parts. By consequence, all those parts have the right of defense. Such is the opinion expressed by Cajetan (*loc. cit.*); and this conclusion may also be derived from a passage in St. Thomas's works (on the *Sentences,* bk. II, dist. 44, q. 2, a. 2).[26]

John Huss upheld the same doctrine with respect to the second kind of tyrant, and, indeed, with respect to every unjust superior. But this teaching was condemned at the Council of Constance (sessions VIII and XV). Consequently, it is most certain that no private person, nor any incomplete power, may justly initiate an offensive war against this kind of tyrant, and that such a war would be sedition in the strict sense of the term.

The proof of these assertions is as follows: the prince in question is, we assume, the true ruler (*dominus*); and inferiors have not the right of declaring war, but only that of defending themselves, a right which does not apply in connection with this sort of tyrant; for the latter does not always do wrong to individuals, and in any attack which [these individuals] might make, they would be obliged to confine themselves to what suffices for self-defense. The commonwealth as a whole, however, may rise in war against such a tyrant; and this uprising would not be a case of sedition in the strict sense, since the word is commonly employed with a connotation of evil. The reason for this distinction is that under the circumstances described the commonwealth, as a whole, is superior to the prince, for the commonwealth, when it granted him his power, is held to have granted it upon these conditions: that he should govern politically, and not tyrannically; and that, if he did not govern thus, he might be deposed.

---

[26] See chap, 16, this volume, pp. 194–5.

However, [in order that such an uprising may justly occur] the situation must be one in which it is observed that the king does really and manifestly behave in a tyrannical manner; and the other conditions laid down for a just war must concurrently be present. . . .

3 I hold, *thirdly*, that a war of the commonwealth against a king who is tyrannical in neither of these two ways, is sedition in the truest sense and intrinsically evil. This is certainly true, as is evident from the fact that, in such a case, both a just cause and a [rightful] authority are lacking. From this, conversely, it is also evident that the war of a prince against a commonwealth subject to himself, may be just, from the standpoint of rightful authority, if all the other required conditions be present, but that, in the absence of those conditions, that same war is entirely unjust.[27]

---

[27]   The last section (omitted) of this disputation consists in an ethical assessment of the practice of dueling.

30

Alberico Gentili
(1552–1608)

The Advantages of
Preventive War

No one ought to expose himself to danger. No one ought to wait to be struck, unless he is a fool. One ought to provide not only against an offence which is being committed, but also against one which may possibly be committed. Force must be repelled and kept aloof by force.

De iure belli libri tres

An Italian Protestant whose family had fled their homeland in order to avoid persecution, Alberico Gentili spent much of his professional life at Oxford University, where he was recognized as one of the leading jurists of the day. Schooled in civil law at the University of Perugia, he followed in the tradition of Bartolus (1313–57), whose disciple Baldus (1327–1406) he often quotes, and like them his works draw heavily from Roman legal sources. Author of numerous works – legal briefs, commentaries, and treatises – Gentili is most famous for his *De iure belli libri tres* (On the Law of War in Three Books). First published as a single text in 1598,[1] this work combined a keen attention to historical detail – scholarly writings, ancient and modern military practice, actual events – with a systematic treatment of the normative dimensions of war. His discussion of just cause (bk. I, chaps. VII–XXV) in particular was very extensive. The divisions that he introduced into this topic would later serve as a key point of reference for the work of Hugo Grotius.

The selections that follow open with Gentili's definition of war as "a just and public contest of arms." In line with the ancient Roman jurists, he takes war to be a formal contest between sovereign equals (bk. I, chap. III). And drawing on the

---

[1] The three books of this work were published separately in 1588–9 under the title *De iure belli commentatio.*

work of the legal humanists Raphaël Fulgosius[2] and Andreas Alciatus,[3] Gentili likens this contest to a legal process in which the two litigants are presumed to have entered the proceedings in good faith. Since in war (as in litigation) it usually remains doubtful which of the opposing sides is possessed of the just cause, it is incumbent on the belligerents to observe the same code of honor in their conduct toward each other. On a theoretical plane, the difference between just and unjust causes of war can be determined with adequate clarity. Nevertheless, the application of this knowledge to concrete cases will nearly always be fraught with difficulty. Recognition of this practical difficulty appears to have been the central factor that induced Gentili to argue that "war may be waged justly on both sides" (bk. I, chap. VI). He was thus an early proponent of what Vattel would later term "war in due form" or "regular war."

Also included below are three additional selections from Gentili's treatment of just cause. In the first, he explains why it is never just to wage war for the sake of religion (bk. I, chap. IX). In the second, he maintains that the causes of war are not due to nature (bk. I, chap. XII), while in the third he argues for preventive attack as a legitimate mode of self-defense (bk. I, chap. XIV).

From *On the Law of War*, book I[4]

Chapter II: The Definition of War[5]

War is a just and public contest of arms.[6] In fact, war is nothing if not a contest, and it is a contest of arms, because to wage war in one's mind and not with arms is surely cowardice, and not war. . . .

. . . And although much is accomplished in war without the use of arms, yet there is never a war without the preparation of arms, and there is nothing in war which does not resort to the protection of arms and is not referred to arms.

Furthermore, the contention must be public; for war is not a broil, a fight, the hostility of private individuals. And the arms on both sides should be public, for *bellum*, 'war', derives its name from the fact that there is a contest

---

[2] See chap. 20, this volume.

[3] Andreas Alciatus (1492–1550) was an Italian legal humanist, author of *inter alia* the *Paradoxurum iuris civilis*, who did much to give credit to the idea that a war could be "just on both sides" due to uncertainty surrounding the rights and wrongs of the case. On this see Peter Haggenmacher, *Grotius et la doctrine de la guerre juste* (Paris: Presses Universitaires de France, 1983), pp. 204–6, 211–12.

[4] The English translation is taken (with alterations) from *De iure belli libri tres*, vol. 2, trans. John C. Rolfe, The Classics of International Law (Oxford: Clarendon Press, 1933). Volume 1 reproduces the Latin text of 1612 (Hanover: G. Antonius).

[5] Gentili, *De iure belli libri tres* (trans. Rolfe) pp. 12–13.

[6] "Bellum est publicorum armorum iusta contentio."

for victory between two equal parties, and for that reason it was at first called *duellum*, 'a contest of two'. . . . The term *hostis* [enemy] was applied to a foreigner who had equal rights with the Romans. In fact, *hostire* means 'to make equal'. . . . Therefore *hostis* is a person with whom war is waged and who is the equal of his opponent. . . .

Therefore that definition . . . , 'war is armed force against a foreign prince or people', is shown to be incorrect by the fact that it applies the term 'war' also to the violence of private individuals and of brigands. It is further faulty in making no mention of justice. . . .

I said 'a just contention'; for I maintain that the war must be just and that all the acts of the war must be just. In this sense one speaks of a just and righteous war and of just and righteous arms. Therefore all our research will be directed towards this point. But we must also in this connection exclude raids and plundering expeditions, such, namely, as do not have a just and full equipment of arms and cannot rightly be termed war; for *iustum*, 'just', signifies not only what is according to law (*a iure*), but also what is complete in all its parts. . . .

Chapter III: War is Waged by Princes[7]

'The enemy are those who have officially declared war upon us, or upon whom we have officially declared war; all others are brigands or pirates', says Pomponius (*Digest*, L. xvi. 118; XLIX. xv. 24). . . . That is to say, the war on both sides must be public and official and there must be princes on both sides to direct the war.[8] This is the view both of Augustine (*Against Faustus*, XXII. lxxi) and of the other theologians, and reason shows that war has its origin in necessity; and this necessity arises because there cannot be judicial processes between supreme princes or free peoples unless they themselves consent, since they acknowledge no judge or superior. Consequently, they are only supreme and they alone merit the title of public, while all others are inferior and are rated as private individuals. The prince has no earthly judge, for one over whom another holds a superior position is not a prince. And in fact princes act in accordance with this principle, as that best of these, the emperor Marcus Aurelius, declared. . . .

But I am speaking here only of a real and actual necessity. For whereas there are two modes of contention, one by argument and the other by force, one should not resort to the latter if it is possible to use the former. The necessity which justifies war, says Baldus (*Consilia*, V), arises when one is driven to arms as the last resort. . . .

---

[7] Ibid., p. 15.

[8] In chap. IV (omitted), Gentili explains why it cannot rightly be said that "brigands (*latrones*) wage war."

Chapter VI: That War May Be Waged Justly on Both Sides[9]

But may a war be waged with justice on both sides? . . . Among our jurists Fulgosius maintained the affirmative against the opinion of others. Alciatus has followed Fulgosius in more than one place. I too follow him, but with the proviso that there may be probable doubt as to the justice of the cause. This same point has been made by other jurists and by our theologians, who declare that there is justice on one side in reality, but on the other and on both through a justifiable ignorance (*ignorantiam iustam*). . . .

It is the nature of wars for both sides to maintain that they are supporting a just cause. In general, it may be true in nearly every kind of dispute, that neither of the two disputants is unjust. Aristotle makes an exception only when the inquiry is 'whether the act took place'. And indeed in the case of one's own act our jurists are not in the habit of admitting ignorance as a defence. But they do admit it in the case of another's act, because that happens under different conditions. We are driven to this distinction by the weakness of our human nature, because of which we see everything dimly, and are not cognizant of that purest and truest form of justice, which cannot conceive of both parties to a dispute being in the right. For why, says Maximus of Tyre (*Sermones*, xiv) in this connection, should those whose purposes are just engage in strife with one another? And in fact it is either the unjust who fight with one another or the unjust with the just.

But we for the most part are unacquainted with that truth. Therefore we aim at justice as it appears from man's standpoint. In this way we avoid the objection of Baldus (*On Digest*, I. i. 5), that when war arises among contending parties, it is absolutely inevitable that one side or the other is in the wrong. Accordingly we say that if it is evident that one party is contending without any adequate reason, that party is surely practising brigandage and not waging war. All agree on this point, and rightly. And it is quite true that the cause of the party which is in the right receives additional justification from that fact. . . .

But if it is doubtful on which side justice is, and if each side aims at justice, neither can be called unjust. Thus Baldus (*Consilia*, I. cccxxvi) himself maintains that war between kings is just, whenever the aim on both sides is to retain majesty and justice. . . .

. . . Of all our laws, however, that one seems to me the clearest which grants the rights of war (*belli iura*) to both contestants, makes what is taken on each side the property of the captors, and regards the prisoners of both parties as slaves. While others are endeavouring to evade this law, in opposition to Fulgosius, they are unquestionably indulging in a pleasurable madness; as was demonstrated

---

[9] Ibid., pp. 31–3.

by Alciatus, who also insists on that equality among enemies of which we made note before.

But although it may sometimes happen (it will not occur very often, as you will learn forthwith) that injustice is clearly evident on one of the two sides, nevertheless this ought not to affect the general principle, and prevent the rights of war from applying to both parties. . . . For laws are not based upon rare instances and adapted to them; that is to say, on events which are rare in their own class, and which take place only occasionally, contrary to the general nature of the case. . . .

Perhaps you may console yourself by saying with the theologians and the philosophers that there is no sin without retribution, since every wicked deed is its own punishment. . . . Besides, there is ill repute in the eyes of others and remorse in one's own heart, as the philosophers have made clear. There is also Hell, of which the philosophers have told us by induction, and the theologians from knowledge. . . .

Chapter IX: Whether it is Just to Wage War for the Sake of Religion[10]

Now if religion is of such a nature that it ought to be forced upon no one against his will, and if a propaganda which exacts faith by blows is called a strange and unheard-of thing, it follows that force in connection with religion is unjust. . . .

. . . What ever is contrary to the nature of a thing does not tend to establish that thing, but rather to destroy it. To attempt by force what cannot be done by force is madness. A thing which is a matter of choice should not be made a necessity. . . .

Religion is a matter of the mind and of the will, which is always accompanied by freedom, as was brilliantly demonstrated, both by philosophers and by others, and by Bernard in his book *On Free Will*. Our mind and whatever belongs to our mind are not affected by any external power or potentate, and the soul has no master save God only, who alone can destroy the soul. Do you understand? Yet hear still one more thing. Religion ought to be free. Religion is a kind of marriage of God with man. And so, as liberty of the flesh is resolutely maintained in the other wedlock, so in this one freedom of the spirit is granted. . . .

Chapter XII: Whether there are Natural Causes for Making War[11]

. . . If the causes for war were really due to nature, every war arising from them would also be just. But the causes are not of that kind. Men are not foes of one

[10]   Ibid., pp. 38–9.
[11]   Ibid., pp. 55–7.

another by nature. But our acts and our customs, whether these be like or unlike, cause harmony or discord among us. They say that men are not friends by nature, a statement which I do not accept. Therefore the Spaniards were not just in giving that pretext or the pretext of religion as the reason for their war with the Indians; nor the barbarians with reference to the Greeks, nor the Greeks to the barbarians. Except perhaps that the Greeks and barbarians were trained to be enemies one of the other. That is a different reason, and perhaps it is not very far, from being a natural one, for it is the result of education, which is a second nature. . . .

War is not waged on account of religion, and war is not natural either with others or even with the Turks. But we have war with the Turks because they act as our enemies, plot against us, and threaten us. With the greatest treachery they always seize our possessions, whenever they can. Thus we constantly have a legitimate reason for war against the Turks. We ought not to break with them; no! We ought not to make war upon them when they are quiet and keeping the peace, and have no designs upon us; no! But when do the Turks act thus? Let the theologians keep silence about a matter which is outside of their province. . . .

Chapter XIV: Of Defence on Grounds of Utility[12]

I call it a useful defence (*utilem defensionem*), when we make war through fear that we may ourselves be attacked. No one is more quickly laid low than one who has no fear, and a sense of security is the most common cause of disaster. This is to begin with. Then, we ought not to wait for violence to be offered us, if it is safer to meet it halfway. . . . Therefore . . . those who desire to live without danger ought to meet impending evils and anticipate them.

One ought not to delay, or wait to avenge at one's peril an injury which one has received, if one may at once strike at the root of the growing plant and check the attempts of an adversary who is meditating evil. . . .

No one ought to expose himself to danger. No one ought to wait to be struck, unless he is a fool. One ought to provide not only against an offence which is being committed, but also against one which may possibly be committed. Force must be repelled and kept aloof by force. Therefore one should not wait for it to come; for in this waiting there are the undoubted disadvantages which have been enumerated above and also the considerations which are mentioned in the suits of private individuals: that we may not fall by submitting to the first blow, and that we may not give ground in flight, and be overwhelmed when prostrate. But to flee is not to defend oneself. This may be understood from the testimony of learned men and also from the facts themselves; and this our jurists also tell us.

---

[12]   Ibid., pp. 61–2, 64–6.

These things are clear and well established and thoroughly adapted to a treatise on war.

What follows is more doubtful, namely, the question when a matter may be said to have reached the point where it is necessary to resort to that useful defence. A just cause for fear is demanded; suspicion is not enough. Now a just fear is defined as the fear of a greater evil, a fear which might properly be felt even by a man of great courage. Yet in the case of great empires I cannot readily accept that definition, which applies to private affairs. For if a private citizen commit some offence against a fellow citizen, reparation may be secured through the authority of a magistrate. But what a prince has done to a prince, no one will make good. . . .

But since there is more than one justifiable cause for fear, and no general rule can be laid down with regard to the matter, we will merely say this, which has always been a powerful argument and must be considered so to-day and hereafter: namely, that we should oppose powerful and ambitious chiefs. For they are content with no bounds, and end by attacking the fortunes of all. . . .

We must therefore oppose them; and it is better to provide that men should not acquire too great power, than to be obliged to seek a remedy later, when they have already become too powerful. . . .

But to conclude, a defence is just which anticipates dangers that are already meditated and prepared, and also those which are not mediated, but are probable (*verisimilia*) and possible (*possibilia*). This last word, however, is not to be taken literally, for in that case my statement would be that it is just to resort to a war of this kind as soon as someone becomes too powerful, which I do not maintain. For what if a prince should have his power increased by successions and elections? Will you assail him in war because his power may possibly be dangerous to you? Some other reason must be added for justice's sake. We will add this reason to others which have some justice. Give ear.

31

Johannes Althusius
(1557–1638)

Defending the Commonwealth

But before undertaking war a magistrate should first check his own judgment
and reasoning, and offer prayers to God to arouse and direct the spirit and
mind of his subjects and himself.

Politica

Although rarely mentioned in textbooks of political philosophy, many legal scholars
have come to consider the German lawyer and politician Johannes Althusius a
benchmark figure in early modern political thought. Unlike his more famous French
counterpart Jean Bodin (1530–96), who argued that political sovereignty belongs
to one absolute ruling power, Althusius insisted that this pertained to the whole
people (*populus*). The *populus*, on his view, was an organic assemblage of various
capacities: families, guilds, corporations, cities, provinces, and commonwealths.
This conception of popular sovereignty did not, however, arise out of a social
contract theory based on individual rights – such as the theory proposed by John
Locke nearly a decade later. Instead, Althusian politics comes across as a bridge
between a medieval, collectivist, and organic perspective on society on the one
hand, and a modern, more democratic approach on the other.

Althusius was a Calvinist who spent the last 34 years of his life managing public
affairs in the German city of Emden in much the same way as Calvin had in
Geneva. Yet, he appears to have been less dogmatic than Calvin, which is obvious
from his relatively tolerant description of the ecclesiastical affairs of the city.

In his writings, Althusius draws on a wide range of sources, including both
secular and Catholic writers, in addition to writings by the reformers. His foremost
aim was to show how a community may live as a harmonious and secure whole,
securing the needs of all its parts. He builds up his argument in logical – some
would say tedious – fashion, delineating both ecclesiastical and secular matters in
considerable detail.

Military affairs are, as one might expect, subsumed under secular government. In this discussion, Althusius provides a truly useful summary of what seems to have been a widespread consensus on *ius ad bellum* criteria among most academic Christians of the early seventeenth century. He also debates *ius in bello*, based on conventions and widespread opinions of his day (building on, among others, Gentili, see chap. 30, this volume). In doing so, Althusius does not come across as a representative of the emerging seventeenth-century school of individual natural rights (or, as we would say today, human rights). With the advent of rights teachings, the debate on war would come to stress the claims of individuals against interference in their lives in a new and different way (see, for instance, Locke, chap. 36, this volume). Thus, the debate on *ius in bello* would no longer be a matter merely of the virtue, honor, and compassion of the fighters; it also looked to define the rights of the opposing party (both combatants and civilians). Such a rights-oriented perspective does not fit naturally with the task that Althusius set for himself in the *Politica*.

We should note that the fifth and sixth just causes for waging war in chapter XVI below are concerned with internal (civil) and not external war. The fifth discusses the right of a ruler to put down rebellious subjects, while the sixth considers the right of internal rebellion against tyrants, a topic Althusius returns to later in his work. Both cases are subsumed under the heading of war (*bellum*), which means that Althusius does not reserve that label for external war only. Significantly, the seventh and last just cause allows for intervention on behalf of third parties who are suffering under tyranny; this is the only *causa belli* in Althusius's list that is not directly justified by reference to the interests of the commonwealth that employs armed force. His discussion – lodged in a treatise almost exclusively concerned about one's own interests as a commonwealth – thus prefigures the humanitarian intervention debate in our own day.

From *Politica* (1614), chap. XVI[1]

XVI We have thus far spoken of the first part of special right of sovereignty, namely, the right established to procure the material necessities of life. We turn now to the second part, which pertains to the protection of the universal association[2] and symbiosis. By this right everything necessary for avoiding or removing all difficulties, impediments, and obstacles to the universal association, and for avoiding any troubles, dangers, evils, and injuries to any distressed or needy

---

[1]   From Johannes Althusius, *Politica*, trans. and ed. Frederick S. Carney, foreword by Daniel J. Elazar (Indianapolis: Liberty Fund, 1995), pp. 88–9. Carney's translation was originally published in 1964 (Boston: Beacon Press). The full title of the original work is *Politica methodice digesta*. It was first published in 1603. This translation is based on the third revised and enlarged edition of 1614.

[2]   Althusius uses the term "universal association" to denote the commonwealth, the most encompassing political community, which in turn can be divided into provinces and cities or villages, and further down into corporations, guilds, and families.

member of the universal association, is offered with mutual feeling and concern by each and all members thereof. This second and latter right, therefore, is principally concerned with the arrangement established for protection and defense.

This right of protection consists in (1) aid and (2) counsel. Aid is the assistance and prompt support provided by the communication of things and services to a distressed and needy member of this universal association. It consists, first, in defense and, then, in the care of goods belonging to the universal association. . . .

Defense is threefold. It is the safeguarding of the associated individual members when one of them – a province, city, village, or town – suffers violence and injury, or requires the commonwealth's support for its basic interests and needs. It is, furthermore, the guaranty of free passage and public security against those who disturb, plunder, or restrict commercial activity in the territory of the associated bode. It is, finally, the conduct of war. . . . Just cause for waging war occurs when all other remedies have first been exhausted and peace or justice cannot otherwise be obtained. There are seven just causes for declaring and waging war. The first cause is the recovery of things taken away through violence by another people. The second cause is the defense against violence inflicted by another, and the repulsion of it. The third cause is the necessity for preserving liberty, privileges, rights, peace, and tranquillity, and for defending true religion. The fourth cause occurs when a foreign people deny peaceful transit through its province without good reason. The fifth cause occurs when subjects rise up against their prince and lord, do not fulfill their pledged word, and are not willing to obey him, although they have been admonished many times. The sixth reason is contumacy, which occurs when any prince, lord, or city has so contemptuously and repeatedly scorned the decisions of courts that justice cannot otherwise be administered and defended. The seventh just cause of war occurs when agreements are not implemented by the other party, when he does not keep his promises, and when tyranny is practiced upon subjects.

From *Politica*, chaps. XXXIV–XXXVI[3]

XXXIV The care of arms is the process by which the supreme magistrate keeps his forces always prepared and ready so that if an unexpected emergency should arise, or a hostile force should suddenly attack, he can defend the commonwealth and realm from harm and destruction.

The care and handling of arms is twofold. One function of it is exercised in time of peace, and the other in time of war. The care and handling of arms in time of peace is the program by which the citizens are trained in the arts of war at a time when there is no war, or by which the science of waging war is demonstrated to subjects and they are given practice in military exercises. . . .

---

[3] Althusius, *Politica* (trans. and ed. Carney), pp. 186–9.

XXXV We turn now to the care and handling of arms in time of war. War is a hostile action legitimately undertaken and administered by the magistrate for the sake of preserving or seeking peace, and for deterring injury or defending the commonwealth against its enemies by force and arms. . . . War is therefore a general state of strife, and a proceeding in which two conflicting peoples who submit to no common magistrate settle their controversy by force and arms.

The conduct of war contains two parts, namely, the undertaking and the waging of war. The undertaking of war is the process by which the just principles and foundations of war are laid out and examined. Such are the just cause of war and the necessary preparation for war. A just cause of war is considered to be one that depends upon both right and the authority of the supreme magistrate. The causes of war that rely upon right are (1) defense of the liberty and of one's rights, and repulsion of a launched attack, (2) defense of pure religion, (3) recovery of properties unjustly seized, (4) denial of justice, and (5) conspiracy with an enemy, and rebellion. . . .[4] But these causes can easily be reduced to two, the first of which is defense and the other vindication. The former repulses and the latter vindicates injury launched against God, the commonwealth, its subjects, or the church. I understand defense to be either of your own nation or of another. . . . Vindication is a legitimate cause for war when a judgment and recovery of what has been seized has not yet taken place. . . .

The authority of the supreme magistrate in undertaking war, and the agreement of the orders of the realm, are so necessary for the waging of war that without them a war is said to be unjustly and unlawfully undertaken. This authority to undertake war ought not to be employed by the magistrate unless all other remedies have failed, and there is no other way to repel an attack upon his subjects, to avoid and vindicate injustice to them, or to obtain peace and tranquillity in the realm. . . .

There are two cases in which even an inferior magistrate without consulting his superior can undertake war. The first is when he is assaulted unjustly by another force and defends himself and his subjects against violent invasion. The second is when the superior magistrate does not do his duty, or exercises tyranny over his subjects.

But before undertaking war a magistrate should first check his own judgment and reasoning, and offer prayers to God to arouse and direct the spirit and mind of his subjects and himself to the well-being, utility, and necessity of the church and community, and to avoid all rashness and injustice. . . .

The necessary preparation for war is the procurement of all that is required for the prosecution of war, together with a declaration of war. . . .

XXXVI The waging of war is the execution by military actions of that which has been legitimately undertaken. It can be called the conduct or administration of

---

[4]   At this point, Althusius refers back in a footnote to what he wrote on the matter in chap. XVI, and enlists a number of other writers as well as Biblical passages in support.

war. Military or warlike actions are those that are used to break the forces and strength of the enemy and to attain victory. These are the establishment of military discipline, and the inflicting of wartime losses upon the enemy and the avoidance of the same to oneself. Military discipline is the training of the soldier to a hardy and brave life, as established by the leader of the war. . . . The other action of war is the inflicting of losses by soldiers. These losses result from the pillaging of enemy lands, the siege of places and towns belonging to the enemy, combat, fire and demolition of villages and fortified places, deaths, captivities, and other similar war-inflicted disasters, miseries, and injuries.[5]

Tyrannicide was a hotly contested topic in the Middle Ages, and continued to be so in Althusius's time. Writing in the twelfth century, John of Salisbury, although ambiguous and cautious on the subject, is often considered the first openly to have legitimized killing a tyrant, thus opening up (even if reluctantly) a category of "just internal war" (or "just civil war").[6]

It is important, as we also pointed out in our discussion of John of Salisbury (see chap. 11, this volume), to distinguish between the tyrant by usurpation (Althusius: "tyrant without title") and the tyrant by oppression (Althusius: "tyrant by practice").[7] The former has illegitimately taken the place of a legitimate ruler, either through invasion or sedition, and may, as such, be subject to punishment by death. Aside from the question whether any *private* individual could lawfully execute that punishment – medieval writers indeed disagreed on this point – the usurping tyrant nevertheless represented less of a philosophical quandary than the oppressive tyrant. (It may be, of course, that the former has become a usurper because his rival had developed into the latter, but we will leave that question aside here.)

On the thornier problem of whether there could be any justification for killing a legitimate ruler (i.e. one who acceded to power in a lawful way) whose actions gravely endangered the common good of the realm – i.e. a "tyrant by oppression" – most Christian writers followed John of Salisbury, who had expressed strong caution in this regard. They advised a policy of restraint and non-violence, in line with the principle of the lesser evil: Deposing and killing a tyrant could endanger stability and thus result in the loss of many more lives than would the tyranny itself. It could also endanger obedience to authority in general and set a precedent for private resort to violence of a sort that would be highly detrimental to peace and the common good. Still, most medieval writers admitted the possibility

---

[5] Althusius goes on from here to discussing a relatively wide range of *ius in bello* issues (albeit, admittedly, not in any great detail), including the order of military forces, the taking of captives, the prohibitions against rapine and theft, and the end of peace, using mostly examples from the Bible, but also drawing on, among others, Cicero, Jean Bodin, and Gentili.

[6] Medieval writers typically did not use specialized names to distinguish internal from external war; see chaps. 13, 15 and 16, this volume, on Innocent, Hostiensis and Aquinas, for more on this problem.

[7] Althusius's terms are known from Bartolus: *tyrannus absque titulo* and *tyrannus exercitio*; see Daniel J. Elazar's introduction to Carney's translation of *Politica*, p. xxiii.

that under extreme circumstances it could indeed be morally right to depose an oppressive tyrant. The Reformers were somewhat more permissive as regards tyrannicide, but followed the same logic of restraint.

Althusius, here as on other questions, gives us a useful summary of a moderate stance, ending up – as he often does – with the sovereignty of the commonwealth as a whole and the interests of morality and religion trumping the sovereignty and rights of the supreme magistrate. We should note also that he advocates a right of secession from a commonwealth in cases of severe oppression.

From *Politica*, chap. XXXVIII[8]

XXXVIII [T]he manner of resisting one who has entered upon tyranny is by defensive, not offensive means. . . . The tyrant is to be resisted, I say, by words and deeds: by words when he by words only violates the worship of God and assaults the rights and foundations of the commonwealth: by force and arms when by military might and outward force he exercises tyranny, or has so progressed in it that without armed force such tyranny cannot be restrained, confined, or driven out. In the latter event, it is permitted to enlist an army from among the inhabitants, confederates, friends, and others, just as against an enemy of the fatherland and realm. . . .

What, then, is to be decided about private subjects from among the people? For the position we have thus far taken about the ephors [who may legitimately resist a tyrant] applies only to public persons. It plainly does not apply to private persons when the magistrate is a tyrant by practice because they do not have the use and right of the sword, nor may they employ this right. . . . This is to be understood, however, in such a manner that these private persons are not forced to be servants of tyranny, or to do anything that is contrary to God. Under these circumstances they should flee to another place so that they avoid obedience not by resisting, but by fleeing. Nevertheless, when manifest force is applied by the magistrate to private persons, then in case of the need to defend their lives resistance is permitted to them. For in this case private persons are armed against the magistrate who lays violent hands upon them by the natural law and the arrangements constituting kings.

Accordingly, such private persons may do nothing by their private authority against their supreme magistrate, but rather shall await the command of one of the optimates before they come forth with support and arms to correct a tyrant by practice.[9] But when a tyrant without title invades the realm, each and every

---

8   Ibid., pp. 195, 196–7, 199.

9   "Optimates" is another word for Althusius's "ephors," the office-holders immediately under the supreme magistrate, with authority, on the people's behalf, to rule in the supreme magistrate's absence, appoint a new supreme magistrate when necessary, and depose him in cases of emergency. See Daniel J. Elazar's introduction to Carney's translation of *Politica*, pp. xxi–xxiii.

optimate and private person who loves his fatherland can and should resist, even by his private authority without awaiting the command of another. . . .

One of the estates, or one part of the realm, can abandon the remaining body to which it belonged and choose for itself a separate ruler or a new form of commonwealth when the public and manifest welfare of this entire part altogether requires it, or when fundamental laws of the country are not observed by the magistrate but are obstinately and outrageously violated, or when the true worship and disclosed commands of God clearly require and demand that this be done. And then this part of the realm can defend by force and arms its new form and status against the other parts of the realm from which it withdrew. . . .

[W]e do not say that a tyrannical prince is immediately to be killed, but that resistance is to be made against his force and injury. In one instance only can he justly be killed, namely, when his tyranny has been publicly acknowledged and is incurable: when he madly scorns all laws, brings about the ruin and destruction of the realm, overthrows civil society among men so far as he is able, and rages violently: and when there are no other remedies available.

32

Hugo Grotius (1583–1645)

The Theory of Just War Systematized

> [T]he sources from which wars arise are as numerous as those from which lawsuits spring; for where judicial means fail, war begins.
>
> *De iure belli ac pacis*

Few names are as associated with the idea of just war as that of the Dutch Protestant Hugo Grotius. A jurist by profession, but also very much a philosopher and classicist, Grotius wrote two major works on the normative foundations of war. The first, *De iure praedae* (On the Law of Prize and Booty)[1] was written as a legal brief during the years 1604–6 and was never published in his lifetime.[2] It was occasioned by an internal crisis which arose when a Dutch admiral of the East India Company seized a Portuguese vessel in prize during the United Provinces' protracted war of liberation against the Spanish Crown. In order to justify this prize case vis-à-vis a group of shareholders of the company who had objected to it on moral grounds, Grotius sought to map out the full set of formal and substantive conditions by which an employment of armed force might be deemed legitimate. This general theory of war and prize clearly foreshadowed his main work *De iure belli ac pacis* (On the Law of War and Peace), on which his fame principally rests. It is from this work, published in 1625, that we reproduce the extracts below.

Often presented as the founding treatise of the new discipline of international law, the *De iure belli ac pacis* would more accurately be described as a summation

---

[1]   English translation: *Commentary on the Law of Prize and Booty*, trans. Gwladys L. Williams, The Classics of International Law (Oxford: Clarendon Press, 1950).

[2]   Except for the twelfth chapter, which appeared in 1609 under the title *Mare liberum* (Freedom of the Seas).

of the earlier tradition of just war. Drawing from an impressive body of biblical, classical (Greek and Roman), and scholastic literature, Grotius's stated aim was to provide a complete account of all issues pertinent to the normative assessment of war. While recognizing that his predecessors had covered portions of this field, he nevertheless claimed to be the first to have "treated it in a comprehensive and systematic manner." The work is indeed vast, totaling over eight hundred pages in the English translation. Discreetly underlying its three books is the theory of just war that Grotius had earlier set out in *De iure praedae*: book I of the mature work considers how different sorts of agents may be empowered to wage war; book II – by far the largest – analyzes the grounds on which war may be undertaken; while book III discusses what conduct is permissible in war and how to restore peace.

The three books are preceded by the famous *Prolegomena*, a monumental preface which discloses Grotius's basic approach, intent, and method. He begins by taking a firm stand against political "realists" who, from Thrasymachus to Machiavelli, denied the existence of a natural legal order which would encompass the community of humankind and of nations; if indeed everything at this level boiled down to a mere play of power, deceit, and utility, his reflections would have no basis and point. Against this realism, personified by the Greek philosopher Carneades, Grotius accordingly asserts that "there is a common law among nations, which applies both to war and in war." This is the law of war and peace that he proposes to establish irrefutably on the philosophical foundations which he discerns in human nature and society. By the same token, he makes clear that he intends to make a contribution to the discipline of "jurisprudence"; his treatise therefore contains a general theory of law which would in turn be further developed by his successors (especially Pufendorf and Wolff) who formed the "School of the Law of Nature and Nations." In the remainder of the *Prolegomena*, Grotius outlines the sources that he will invoke to elucidate his system: philosophers and historians, poets and orators, Holy Writ and synodal canons, church fathers and scholastic theologians, Roman lawyers ancient, medieval, and modern.[3] This whole array of authorities would have little weight in our current legal thinking; yet the very success of Grotius's *magnum opus* shows how much credit they enjoyed in the eyes of his contemporaries.[4]

---

[3] To exhibit these sources, Grotius intersperses his discourse with many quotes, some quite lengthy. For purposes of economy, we have set aside most of these citations in the selections that follow. Nor have we included Grotius's annotations (reproduced as footnotes in the English translation), in which he engages in (sometimes lengthy) discussion of classical and biblical texts.

[4] See Peter Haggenmacher, *Grotius et la doctrine de la guerre juste* (Paris: Presses Universitaires de France, 1983), pp. 615–29, for a discussion of the main differences between Grotius's project in the *De iure belli ac pacis* and the modern discipline of international law. For a running commentary on the *De iure belli ac pacis*, see Yasuaki Onuma (ed.), *A Normative Approach to War: Peace, War, and Justice in Hugo Grotius* (Oxford: Clarendon Press, 1993).

From *De iure belli ac pacis*
(On the Law of War and Peace)[5]

Prolegomena[6]

<1>[7] The civil law of Rome or of other states has been treated by many, who have undertaken to elucidate it by means of commentaries or to reduce it to a convenient digest. That body of law (*ius*), however, which is concerned with the relations between different peoples or between leaders of peoples, whether it be derived from nature, or established by divine ordinances, or as having its origin in custom and tacit agreement, few have touched upon. Up to the present time no one has treated it in a comprehensive and systematic manner; yet the welfare of humankind demands that this task be accomplished. <2> It is indeed rightly that Cicero characterized as of surpassing worth this knowledge of alliances, conventions, and understandings of peoples, kings and foreign nations; a knowledge, in short, of the whole law of war and peace. . . .

<3> Such a work is all the more necessary because in our day, as in former times, there is no lack of men who view this branch of law with contempt as having no reality outside of an empty name. Almost everybody echoes the saying of Euphemus, quoted by Thucydides (bk. VI),[8] that for a king or a sovereign state nothing is unjust which is expedient. Of like implication is the statement that for those whom fortune favours might makes right, and that the administration of a commonwealth (*rempublicam*) cannot be carried on without injustice. Furthermore, the controversies which arise between peoples or kings generally have Mars as their arbiter. That war is irreconcilable with all law is a view held not alone by an ignorant people; expressions are often let slip by well-informed and thoughtful men which lend countenance to such a view. Nothing is more common than the assertion of antagonism between law and arms. . . .

---

[5] These passages from *De iure belli ac pacis* represent a much emended version of the English translation by Francis W. Kelsey, in The Classics of International Law, no. 3, vol. 2 (Oxford: Clarendon Press, 1925); volume 1 reproduces the Latin text of the 1646 Amsterdam edition. The editors of the present volume are indebted to Professor Peter Haggenmacher, who provided invaluable assistance in revising the Kelsey translation.

[6] *De iure belli ac pacis* (trans. Kelsey), pp. 9–13, 15–22.

[7] The Arabic paragraph numbers that appear in most editions (including the Kelsey translation) are not from Grotius's own hand and often are misleading. They have nevertheless been retained here in order to assist the reader in referring the present text to the complete Kelsey translation. These numbers are enclosed in angle brackets as in the *Editio maior* of 1939.

[8] This and all the other textual references are given as they appear in the 1646 Amsterdam edition (reproduced in the margins of the Kelsey translation, which, in brackets, supplies additional information on Grotius's sources).

<5> Since our discussion concerning law will have been undertaken in vain if there is no law, in order to open the way for a favourable reception of our work and at the same time to fortify it against attacks, this very serious error must be briefly refuted. In order that we may not be obliged to deal with a crowd of opponents, let us assign to them a pleader. And whom should we choose in preference to Carneades?[9] For he had attained to so perfect a mastery of the peculiar tenet of his Academy that he was able to devote the power of his eloquence to the service of falsehood not less readily than to that of truth.

Carneades, then, having undertaken to hold a brief against justice, in particular against that kind of justice with which we are here concerned, was able to muster no argument stronger than this, that, for reasons of utility, men imposed upon themselves laws, which vary according to customs, and among the same peoples often undergo changes as times change; moreover that there is no law of nature, because all creatures, men as well as animals, are impelled by nature toward ends advantageous to themselves; that, consequently, there is no justice, or, if such there be it is supreme folly, since he does violence to his own interests who consults the advantage of others.

<6> What the philosopher here says, and the poet reaffirms in verse "And just from unjust Nature cannot know" must not for one moment be admitted. Man is, to be sure, an animal, but an animal of a superior kind, much farther removed from all other animals than the different kinds of animals are from one another; evidence on this point may be found in the many traits peculiar to the human species. But among the traits characteristic of man is an impelling desire for society, that is, for community, not of any and every sort, but peaceful, and organized according to the measure of his intelligence, with those who are of his own kind, which the Stoics called *oikeiosis*. Stated as a universal truth, therefore, the assertion that every animal is impelled by nature to seek only its own good cannot be conceded. . . .

<8> This maintenance of the social order, which we have roughly sketched, and which is consonant with human intelligence, is the source of law properly so called. To this sphere of law belong the abstaining from that which is another's, the restoration to another of anything of his which we may have, together with any gain which we may have received from it; the obligation to fulfil promises, the making good of a loss incurred through our fault, and the inflicting of penalties upon men according to their deserts. . . .

---

[9]   Carneades (214/213–129/128 BC) was a leader of the ancient Greek school of Academic Skeptics. He was reputed to be unbeatable in philosophical argument. Around 156 BC, he delivered two orations in Rome, "one praising justice and proving that its foundations are in natural law, the other, with equal persuasiveness, praising injustice and reducing the notion of justice to utility" (Philip P. Hallie, "Carneades," in *The Encyclopedia of Philosophy*, vol. 2 [New York: Macmillan, 1967], p. 33). Grotius is here referring to the second of these two orations.

<11> What we have been saying would have a degree of validity even if we should concede that which cannot be conceded without the utmost wickedness – that there is no God or that the affairs of men are of no concern to Him. The very opposite of this view has been implanted in us partly by reason, partly by unbroken tradition, and confirmed in many proofs as well as by miracles attested by all ages. Hence it follows that we must without exception render obedience to God our Creator, to Whom we owe all that we are and have; especially since, in manifold ways, He has shown himself supremely good and supremely powerful, so that to those who obey Him He is able to give supremely great rewards, even rewards that are eternal, since He Himself is eternal. We ought, moreover, to believe that He has willed to give rewards, and all the more should we cherish such a belief if He has so promised in plain words; that he has done this, we Christians believe, convinced by the indubitable assurance of testimonies. . . .

<16> What is said, therefore in accordance with the view not only of Carneades but also of others, that "Utility is, as it were, the mother of what is just and fair," is not true, if we wish to speak accurately. For the very nature of man, which even if we had no lack of anything would lead us into the mutual relations of society, is the mother of the law of nature. But the mother of civil law is that obligation which arises from mutual consent; and since this obligation derives its force from the law of nature, nature may be considered, so to say, the great-grandmother of civil law. The law of nature nevertheless has the reinforcement of utility (*utilitas*); for the Author of nature willed that as individuals we should be weak, and should lack many things needed in order to live properly, to the end that we might be the more constrained to cultivate the social life. Utility, however, also gave rise to civil law, since that kind of association or subjection [to authority], of which we have spoken, has its roots in utility. . . . <17> But just as the laws of each state (*civitatis*) have in view the advantage of that state, so certain laws could, and obviously did, originate between all or most states (*inter civitates*) by mutual consent, aiming at the advantage, not of individual nations, but of this great global community (*universitatis*). And this is what is called the law of nations (*ius gentium*), whenever we distinguish that term from the law of nature (*iure naturali*). . . .

<18> Wrongly, however, does Carneades ridicule justice as folly. For since, by his own admission, the citizen who in his own country obeys its laws is not foolish, even though, out of regard for that law, he may be obliged to forgo certain things advantageous for himself, so that nation is not foolish which does not press its own advantage to the point of disregarding the laws common to nations. The reason in either case is the same. For just as the citizen who violates the law of his country in order to obtain an immediate advantage breaks down that by which the advantages of himself and his posterity are for all future time assured, likewise, the people which transgresses the laws of nature and of nations cuts away also the bulwarks which safeguard its own future peace. . . .

<21> Many hold, in fact, that the standard of justice which they insist upon in the case of individuals within the state is inapplicable to a nation or the ruler of a nation. The reason for the error lies in this, first of all, that in respect to law they have in view nothing except the advantage which accrues from it, such advantage being apparent in the case of citizens who, taken singly, are powerless to protect themselves. But great states, since they seem to contain in themselves all things required for the adequate protection of life, seem not to have need of that virtue which looks toward the outside, and is called justice.

<22> But, not to repeat what I have said, that law is not founded on utility alone, there is no state so powerful that it may not some time need the help of others outside itself, either for purposes of trade, or even to ward off the forces of many foreign nations united against it. In consequence we see that even the most powerful peoples and sovereigns seek alliances, which are quite devoid of significance according to the point of view of those who confine law within the boundaries of states. Most true is the saying, that all things are uncertain the moment men depart from law.

<23> If no community can be maintained without law, which Aristotle proved by the memorable example of brigands, surely also that community which binds together the human race, or a number of nations, has need of law. . . .

<25> Least of all should that be admitted which some people imagine, that in war all laws are in abeyance. On the contrary war ought not to be undertaken except in pursuit of what is right and, when once undertaken, it should be conducted only within the bounds of law (*iuris*) and good faith. Demosthenes well said that war is directed against those who cannot be held in check by judicial means. For judgments are efficacious against those who feel that they are too weak to resist; against those who are equally strong, or think they are, wars are undertaken. But in order that wars may be justified, they must be carried on with not less scrupulousness than judicial processes are wont to be.

<26> Let the laws be silent, then, in the midst of arms, but only the laws of the state (*civiles leges*), those which the courts are concerned with, which are adapted to peacetime; not those other laws which are of perpetual validity and suited to all times. It was exceedingly well said by Dio of Prusa, that between enemies written laws, that is, laws of particular states, are not in force, but that unwritten laws (*iura non scripta*) are in force, that is, those which nature prescribes, or the agreement of nations has established. . . .

<28> Fully convinced, by the considerations which I have advanced, that there is a common law among nations (*inter populos ius commune*), which applies both to war (*ad bella*) and in war (*in bellis*), I have had many and weighty reasons for undertaking to write upon this subject. Throughout the Christian world I observed a lack of restraint in relation to war, such as even barbarous races should be ashamed of. Men rush to arms for slight causes, or no cause at all, and when

arms have once been taken up there is no longer any respect for law, divine or human, as if, in accordance with a general decree, frenzy had openly been let loose for the committing of all crimes. . . .

<30> At the same time I have endeavoured through devotion to study in private life – as the only course now open to me, undeservedly forced out from my native land,[10] which had been graced by so many of my labours – to contribute somewhat to jurisprudence, which previously, in public service, I practised with the utmost degree of integrity of which I was capable. Many heretofore have purposed to give to this subject a well-ordered presentation; no one has succeeded. And in fact such a result cannot be accomplished unless – a point which until now has not been sufficiently kept in view – elements which come from positive law are properly separated from those which arise from nature. For the principles of the law of nature, since they are always the same, can easily be brought into a systematic form; but the elements of positive law, since they often undergo change and are different in different places, are outside the domain of systematic treatment, just as other notions of particular things are. . . .

<32> What method we think should be followed we have shown by deed rather than by words in this work which treats by far the noblest part of jurisprudence.

<33> In the first book, having by way of introduction spoken of the origin of law (*iuris origine*), we have examined the general question, whether there is any such thing as a just war; then, in order to determine the differences between public and private war, we had to explain the nature of supreme governing power (*summi imperii*); which nations (*populi*) and kings possess it completely, which possess it only in part, which possess it with right of alienation, or otherwise; then it was necessary to speak also concerning the duty of subjects to their superiors.

<34> The second book, having for its object to set forth all the causes from which war can arise, undertakes to explain fully what things are held in common, what may be owned individually; what right some persons have over other persons, what obligation arises from ownership; what is the rule governing royal successions; what right is established by a pact or a contract; what is the force of treaties of alliance; what of an oath private or public, and how it is necessary to interpret these; what is due in reparation for damage done; in what the inviolability of ambassadors consists; what law controls the burial of the dead, and what is the nature of punishments.

<35> The third book having for its subject, first, what is permissible in war (*in bello licet*), distinguishes what is done with impunity or is even defended as lawful

---

[10] In 1621 Grotius fled Holland for France after having become embroiled in a political crisis which had resulted in his being sentenced to perpetual detention. It was in France that he wrote *De iure belli ac pacis*.

among foreign peoples, from that which actually is free from fault, and then proceeds to the different kinds of peace and all compacts relating to war.

<36> The undertaking seemed to me all the more worthwhile because, as I have said, no one has dealt with the subject-matter as a whole, and those who have treated portions of it have done so in a way to leave much to the labours of others.

Book I of *De iure belli ac pacis* opens with an introductory chapter which defines the two main concepts involved: war (*bellum*) and law (*ius*). The latter permits of three basic meanings: first, in a general sense *ius* signifies that which is just in relation to the rational beings who together form human society; secondly, in a more specific sense, it signifies a right vesting in a person; and thirdly, it functions as a synonym of "law," that is, an objective rule of conduct. All three meanings are operative in Grotius's treatise. The first appears nearly everywhere; in practice it replaces the more stringent definition of natural law which he gives apropos of the third meaning. There Grotius distinguishes between natural and "volitional" law: while the former is grounded in human nature, the latter depends on a legislative will, divine or human.[11] The "law of war and peace" which is expounded in this work consists of both natural law and a special kind of human "volitional" law – the law of nations. As to the second meaning of *ius* – a right or legal claim – it is central to book II, which is entirely built on the axiom that there can be no just cause of war without a prior rightful claim.

Regarding Grotius's concept of war, it is defined quite broadly in chapter I as "the state of those contending by force"; this includes any resort to force, whether by public authorities (at all levels), or by private individuals. Depending on the nature of the belligerents involved, war could therefore be "public," "private," or "mixed." Grotius was thus at variance with a steadily growing trend among jurists and theologians who restricted war to a relationship between sovereign powers. He too would of course see this as the most important case, and hence he developed a theory of sovereignty in chapter III of this book. Private war, which is discussed at the beginning of this chapter, appears in practice as licit only in exceptional circumstances. As to mixed war, it comprises various types of conflict between public powers on the one hand, and private individuals on the other; Grotius nevertheless discusses at length only the case of subjects fighting against their rulers (the theme of chapter IV). Chapter V concludes with a short discussion of the different kinds of agents who can take part in warfare: the belligerent proper, his possible allies as co-belligerents, and his subjects as mere "instruments." As to chapter II, it presents a lengthy disquisition on the basic legitimacy of recourse to war, a theme that Grotius discusses in light of the teaching of various church fathers and medieval scholastics.

---

[11]   The difference between natural and volitional law is explained in bk. I, chap. I, sections IX–XVII.

From *De iure belli ac pacis,* bk. I[12]

Chapter I: What is War, What is Law?[13]

I. Scope of the treatise

Controversies among those who are not held together by a common bond of civil law are related either to times of war or to times of peace. Such controversies may arise for instance among those who have not yet united to form a nation or who belong to different nations. They may arise between private persons, kings, or those whose entitlement is similar to that of kings, whether they be members of a ruling aristocracy or free peoples. But since war is undertaken in order to secure peace, and as there is no controversy which may not give rise to war, we will treat such controversies, of whatever kind, as are wont to arise in dealing with the law of war; war itself will then lead us over to peace as its ultimate goal.

II. Definition of war, and origin of the word

<1> As we set out to treat the law of war, then, we ought to see what is war, which we are treating, and what is the law which forms the subject of our investigation. Cicero defined war as a "contention by force." A usage has obtained, however, which designates by the word not an action but a state (*non actio sed status*); thus war is the state of those contending by force, viewed simply as such. This general definition includes all the classes of wars which it will hereafter be necessary to discuss. For I do not exclude private war, since in fact it is more ancient than public war and has, incontestably, the same nature as public war; wherefore both should be designated by one and the same term. <2> The origin of the word, moreover, is not inconsistent with this use. For *bellum*, 'war', comes from the old word *duellum*. . . . <3> Nor does usage reject this broader meaning of the word. If, to be sure, the term 'war' is at times limited to public war, this implies no objection to our view, since it is quite certain that the name of a genus is often applied in a particular way to a species, especially a species that is more prominent.

I do not include justice in my definition since the very point of our investigation is to assess whether there can be a just war, and what kind of a war is just. Indeed, a subject which is under investigation ought to be distinguished from the object towards which the investigation is directed. . . .

---

[12] *De iure belli ac pacis* (trans. Kelsey), pp. 33–4, 51–4, 91–2, 97–103, 138–9, 164–6.

[13] *Ius* is here translated as "law," although the English term is too specific to render the richness of its Latin counterpart. Grotius's observations on *ius*, which take up the bulk of this chapter, have been omitted.

Chapter II: Whether it is Ever Just to Wage War

I. That war is not in conflict with the law of nature is proved by several considerations

<1> Having seen what the sources of law (*iuris*) are,[14] let us come to the first and most general question, which is this: whether any war is just (*iustum*), in other words, whether it is ever permissible to wage war. This question, as also the others which will follow, must first be taken up from the point of view of the law of nature. Marcus Tullius Cicero, both in the third book of his treatise *On Ends* and in other places, following Stoic writings learnedly argues that there are certain first principles of nature – "first according to nature," as the Greeks phrased it – and certain other principles that are later manifest but which are to have preference over those first principles. . . .

<4> In the first principles of nature there is nothing which is opposed to war; rather, all points are in its favour. The end and aim of war being the preservation of life and limb, and the keeping or acquiring of things useful to life, war is in perfect accord with those first principles of nature. If in order to achieve these ends it is necessary to use force, no inconsistency with the first principles of nature is involved, since nature has given to each animal strength sufficient for self-defence and self-assistance. . . .

<5> As to right reason and the nature of society, which must be studied in the second place and are of even greater importance, they do not prohibit all use of force, but only that use of force which is repugnant to society, that is, which infringes upon another's right. For society has in view this object, that through community of resource and effort each individual be safeguarded in the possession of what belongs to him. . . . <6> It is not, then, contrary to the nature of society to look out for oneself and advance one's own interests, provided the right of another is not infringed; and consequently the use of force which does not violate the right of others is not unjust. . . .

Chapter III: Distinction between Public and Private War; Explanation of Supreme Governing Power

I. Division of war into public and private

<1> The first and most essential division of war is that into public war, private war, and mixed war.

---

[14]   Bk. I, chap. I, sections III–XVII (passages not included in this anthology).

A public war is that which is waged by him who has jurisdiction; a private war, that which is waged by one who has none; and a mixed war is that which is on one side public, on the other side private. Let us deal first with private war, as the more ancient.

<2> That private wars in some cases may be waged lawfully, so far as the law of nature is concerned, is, I think, sufficiently clear from what was said above, when we showed that the use of force to ward off injury is not in conflict with the law of nature. But possibly some may think that after public tribunals had been established private wars were not permissible. For although public tribunals are the creation not of nature but of man, it is, nevertheless, much more consistent with moral standards, and more conducive to the peace of individuals, that a matter be judicially investigated by one who has no personal interest in it, than that individuals, too often having only their own interests in view, should seek by their own hands to obtain that which they consider right; wherefore equity and reason given to us by nature declare that so praiseworthy an institution should have the fullest support. . . .

II. The proposition, that according to the law of nature not all private war is impermissible since the establishment of courts, is defended, illustrations being added

<1> It is surely beyond doubt that the licence which was prevalent before the establishment of courts (*iudicia*) has been greatly restricted. Nevertheless there are circumstances under which such licence even now holds good, that is, undoubtedly, where judicial procedure ceases to be available. For the law which forbids a man to seek to recover his own otherwise than through judicial process is ordinarily understood as applicable only where judicial process has been possible.

Now, judicial procedure ceases to be available either temporarily or continuously. It ceases to be available temporarily when one cannot wait to refer a matter to a judge without certain danger or loss. It ceases to be available continuously either in law or in fact: in law, if someone finds himself in places without inhabitants, as on the sea, in a wilderness, or on vacant islands, or in any other places where there is no state; in fact, if those who are subject to jurisdiction do not heed the judge, or if the judge has openly refused to take cognizance of the matter. . . .

IV. Division of public war into formal and less formal

<1> Public war is either formal under the law of nations, or non-formal. The word 'formal' (*solenne*) I use here as equivalent to 'just' (*iustum*) in the sense in which we speak of a just will as distinguished from codicils. . . . This does not mean that it is not permissible for any one to make codicils who may desire to do so, . . . but it does mean that from the point of view of the civil law the formal

will . . . has certain peculiar effects. It is useful to note this distinction; for many, having a wrong understanding of the word 'just' in such a connection think that all wars, to which the adjective 'just' (*iusta*)[15] is inapplicable, are to be blamed as iniquitous or illicit.

In order for a war to be formal under the law of nations, two conditions are requisite: first, that on both sides it be waged under the authority (*auctore*) of the one who holds the supreme power (*summam potestatem*) within the state; second, that certain formalities be observed, which we shall discuss later in the proper connection. Since both conditions are conjointly requisite, one without the other does not suffice.

<2> A non-formal public war may lack the formalities referred to, and may be waged against private persons, and on the authority of any civil ruler (*magistratum*). And surely if the matter be viewed without reference to the laws of particular states, it would seem that every subordinate ruler has the right to wage war for the protection of the people entrusted to his charge, and also in order to maintain his jurisdiction if assailed by force. But because the whole state is endangered by war, provision has been made by the laws of almost every state that war may be waged only under the authority of him who holds the supreme power in the state. . . .

V. Whether there may be a public war waged by the authority of a ruler not having supreme power, and when

<1> The jurists are by no means agreed, however, whether, in the cases where it is certain that subordinate rulers (*magistratibus minoribus*) have the right to take up arms, such a war should be called a public war. The affirmative view is held by some, the negative by others. Truly if we use the word 'public' as including whatever is done under the jurisdiction of a ruler (*fit iure magistratus*), there is no doubt that such wars are public, and consequently those who under conditions of this sort oppose rulers expose themselves to the punishment awaiting men that stubbornly resist their superiors. But if the word 'public' is understood in a higher sense as characterizing that which is done with due formality, as beyond question this word often is, such wars are not public, for the reason that both the decision of the supreme authority and other conditions are necessary for the fulfilment of the legal requirements involved. . . .

<2> This situation, moreover, may arise, whereby in an empire (*imperio*) having a wide extent of territory, subordinate authorities may have a delegated power of beginning war. If such a situation does arise, we are to consider that the war is

---

[15]   Grotius is here referring to Roman authors who used the adjective *iustum* ("just") as an equivalent for "legal" or "regular." On this meaning only wars that are formally declared may be deemed "just." As Grotius indicates in this passage, *iustum* has additional meanings, so that it can legitimately be applied to other (non-formally declared) wars as well.

actually being waged by virtue of the supreme authority; for he who vests another with the right (*ius*) to do anything is himself regarded as doer (*auctor*) of it.

<3> A more controverted question is whether, in case such an authorization has not been given, the presumption that such an authorization is intended will be sufficient. The affirmative view should not, I think, be conceded. For it is not enough to consider what under such conditions would be acceptable to him who holds the supreme power if he could be consulted; the real point to be considered is, what he would wish to be done without being consulted, when the matter allows for delay, or is fraught with doubt, if a general law covering the case were to be passed. . . .

<7> Since, then, it has been said that a public war ought not to be waged except by the authority of him who holds the supreme power, for the under-standing both of this subject and of questions relating to formal war, and con-sequently for the understanding of many other questions, it will be necessary to understand what this supreme power (*summa illa potestas*) is, and who holds it; this inquiry is all the more necessary because learned men of our own age, treating the matter from the point of view of present opportunity rather than from that of the truth, have added greatly to the complexity of the subject, which in itself was far from simple. . . .

VII. What is the supreme power?

<1> That power is called 'supreme' whose actions are not under the authority (*iuri*) of another, so that they cannot be rendered void by the operation of another human will. When I say 'of another', I exclude from consideration him who exercises the supreme power, who has the right to change his determinations; I exclude also his successor, who enjoys the same right, and therefore has the same power, not a different power. Let us, then, see who is the subject of this supreme power.

The subject of a power is either common (*commune*) or proper (*proprium*). Just as the body is the common subject, the eye the proper subject of the power of sight, so the state (*civitas*), which we have defined above as a perfect associ-ation, is the common subject of the supreme power.

<2> We exclude from consideration, therefore, the peoples who have passed under the sway of another people, such as the provinces of the Romans, for such peoples are not in themselves a state, in the sense in which we are now using the term, but the inferior members of a great state, just as slaves are members of a household. Again, it happens that several peoples may have the same head, while nevertheless each of them in itself forms a perfect association. Indeed, while in the case of the natural body there cannot be one head belonging to several bodies, this does not hold also in the case of a moral body, for here the same person, viewed in different relations, may be the head of several distinct bodies. A clear proof of this may be found in the fact that on the extinction of the reigning

house, the right of government reverts to each people (*populum*) separately. It may also happen that several states are bound together by a very narrow alliance, and form a kind of 'system', as Strabo in more than one passage calls it, while nevertheless the different members do not cease in each case to retain the status of a perfect state. This fact was noted by other writers, and by Aristotle also in more than one passage.

<3> It may be granted, then, that the common subject of supreme power is the state, understood as we have already indicated. The proper subject consists in one or more persons, according to the laws and customs of each nation. . . .

Chapter IV: War of Subjects against Superiors

I. State of the question

<1> War may be waged by private persons against private persons, as by a travel-ler against a highwayman; by those who have supreme governing power (*summum imperium*) against those who possess like power, as by David against the King of the Ammonites; by private persons against those who have sovereign governing power, but not over themselves, as by Abraham against the King of Babylon and his neighbours; and by those who have sovereign governing power against private persons who are either their subjects, as in the war waged by David against the party of Ishbosheth, or are not their subjects, as in the war waged by the Romans against the pirates. <2> The only question to be considered here is whether it is permissible for either private or official persons to wage war against those under whose power (*imperio*) they are, whether this power be supreme or subordinate. First of all, the point is settled beyond controversy, that arms may be taken up against subordinates by those who are armed with the authority of the supreme power. . . . Our question, then, is to determine what action is permissible against the supreme power, or against inferior officials acting under the authority of the supreme power. <3> Among all good men one principle at any rate is established beyond controversy, that if the authorities issue any order that is contrary to the law of nature or to the commandments of God, it should not be carried out. . . . If, however, from any such cause, or otherwise because such is the pleasure of him who holds the supreme governing power, unjust treatment be inflicted on us, we ought to endure it rather than resist by force.

II. That as a general rule war against one's superiors is not permitted by the law of nature

<1> By nature all men have a right of resistance (*ius resistendi*) against injury, as we have said above. But as civil society was instituted in order to maintain public

tranquillity, the state forthwith acquires over us and our possessions a kind of greater right, to the extent necessary to accomplish this end. The state, therefore, in the interest of public peace and order, can exclude that common right of resistance. That such was the purpose of the state we cannot doubt, since it could not in any other way achieve its end. If indeed that common right of resistance should subsist, there will no longer be a state, but only an incoherent multitude. . . .[16]

Chapter V: Who May Permissibly Wage War

I. The efficient causes of war are on the one hand those who wage war on their own account, as principals

As in other matters, so also in acts originating in the will, there are ordinarily three kinds of efficient causes – principal agents, auxiliary agents, and instruments. In war the principal efficient cause is generally the person whose interest is at stake – in private war, the individual; in public war, the public power, above all the supreme power. Whether war can be made by one on behalf of others who do not make war on their own account, we shall see elsewhere. Meanwhile we shall hold to this principle, that by nature it falls to each to vindicate his right (*sui iuris esse vindicem*); that is why hands were given to us.

II. Or those who wage war on another's account, as auxiliaries

<1> But to render service to another, so far as we can, is not only permissible, it is also honourable. Those who have written on the subject of duties rightly say that nothing is more useful to a man than another man. There are, however, various ties which bind men together and summon them to mutual aid. Thus those who are related by kinship unite to assist one another. Neighbours, too, and those who belong to the same state, call on one another for help. . . .

III. On the other hand those who wage war as instruments, such as servants and subjects

When we use the word 'instruments' in this connection we do not mean 'weapons' and similar things; we mean persons whose acts of will are dependent on the will

---

[16] In subsequent sections (VIII–XX) of chapter IV (omitted here), Grotius considers possible exceptions to the rule prohibiting rebellion against rulers. This can include resistance against a king who has sought to transfer his kingdom to an alien power, who attempts to possess a part of the kingdom that does not belong to him, or who openly has shown himself to be an enemy of the whole people. He argues too that force may also be used against an individual who has usurped power from the rightful sovereign.

of another. An instrument, as we use the term here, is a son in relation to his father, viewed by nature as a part, so to speak, of the father; such an instrument also is a slave in relation to his master, a part, as it were, in a legal sense. For just as a part is part of the whole not only in the same relation that the whole sustains to the part, but also the very thing which constitutes a part pertains to the whole, so a possession becomes something of the possessor. . . . What a slave is to the household, a subject is in the state, an instrument, accordingly, of the ruler.

IV. By the law of nature no one is enjoined from waging war

There is no doubt that by nature all subjects may be used for purposes of war; but certain classes are exempted by special enactment, as formerly slaves at Rome, now men in holy orders generally. Nevertheless a special enactment of this kind, as such laws generally, must be understood as subject to exception in cases of extreme necessity. . . .

Book II of *De iure belli ac pacis* focuses on the question of what constitutes a just cause for war. Grotius takes the standard line (already enunciated by Aquinas, Vitoria, and others) that war will be permissible only when it is a "reaction to a wrong that the responsible party refuses to repair. Just war is thus primarily a sanction aimed at restoring the law which has been violated. . . . Central to this conception is therefore the wrong committed: for the injured party it represents the just cause, and hence the basis for the material claim it is pressing by means of its just war."[17] On this basis Grotius argues (chap. I, section II, 2) that a just war may be undertaken for four different reasons (each of which he explores in great detail): defence of self or property against unjust attack, recovery of things wrongly taken, exaction of outstanding debts, and punishment of wrongdoing. In what follows, we have retained much of his discussion of self-defence (chap. I), some paragraphs on the relation between war and punishment (chap. XX), and the chapters on unjust and doubtful causes of war (XXII–XXIII). Also included is some material from the concluding chapters (XXIV–XXVI), where Grotius warns against undertaking war rashly (even for a just cause), and then discusses the conditions under which war may be waged to assist others, and, finally, whether soldiers may refuse to serve in an unjust war. By contrast, the very elaborate chapters on ownership, promises, contracts, oaths, treaties, liability for wrongs, rights of legation, etc. (II–XIX) have not been retained in this anthology. It should be noted, however, that these chapters represent much more than a lengthy digression on

[17] Peter Haggenmacher, "Just War and Regular War in Sixteenth Century Spanish Doctrine," *International Review of the Red Cross* (September–October 1992), pp. 434–45 (on p. 435).

topics alien to the problem of war. Grotius's aim in introducing these considerations was to enumerate, as exhaustively as possible, all of the rights (*iura*) whose violation could justify resort to armed force. Historically this was very significant, since it represents the first attempt at organizing the *ius ad bellum* around a system of subjective rights.[18] Clearly, if not unparadoxically, it is also one of the roots of modern human rights doctrine.

From *De iure belli ac pacis,* bk. II[19]

Chapter I: The Causes of War: First, Defence of Self and Property

I. What causes of war may be called justifying

<1> Let us proceed to the causes of war – I mean justifying (*iustificae*) causes; for there are also other causes which influence men through regard for what is useful and differ from those that influence men through regard for what is just. . . .

<4> No other just cause for undertaking war can there be except injury received. 'The iniquity of the opposing side occasions just wars,' said . . . Augustine (*On the City of God*, IV), using 'iniquity' (*iniquitas*) when he meant 'injury' (*iniuria*). . . . In the formula used by the Roman fetial are the words, "I call you to witness that that people is unjust (*iniustum*) and does not pay its due."

II. These justifying causes arise from defence, the exaction of what belongs to us or is owed to us, or punishment

<1> It is evident that the sources from which wars arise are as numerous as those from which lawsuits spring; for where judicial means (*iudicia*) fail, war begins. Legal actions, furthermore, are directed against injuries not yet committed or committed. In the former case, a guarantee is sought to forestall an offence, or likewise to prevent imminent harm, and other injunctions so that violence will not be done. In the latter case, the injury is either to be repaired or to be punished. . . .

---

[18] On the connection established by Grotius between just war and subjective rights, see Peter Haggenmacher, "Droits subjectifs et système juridique chez Grotius," in Luc Foisneau (ed.), *Politique, droit et théologie chez Bodin, Grotius et Hobbes* (Paris: Éditions Kimé, 1997), pp. 73–130.
[19] *De iure belli ac pacis*, trans. Kelsey, pp. 169–74, 176, 179, 184–5, 462, 502–8, 546–52, 556–7, 559–60, 565–8, 574–6, 578–93, 595.

<2> Most authors assign three just causes to wars: defence, recovery of property, and punishment. . . . Missing from this enumeration is the obtaining of what is owed to us.

<3> . . . The first cause of a just war, then, is an injury not yet committed (*iniuria nondum facta*), which menaces either one's body or one's property.

III. War for the defence of life is permissible

If an attack by violence is made on one's body, endangering life, and no other way of escape is open, then war is permissible, even though it involve the slaying of the assailant; we said this above when we showed, through this generally acknowledged case, that some private war may be just. This right of defence (*ius defensionis*), it should be observed, has its origin directly and chiefly in the fact that nature commits to each his own protection, not in the injustice or sin of the other. Wherefore, even if the assailant be blameless, as for instance a soldier acting in good faith, or one who mistakes me for someone else, or one who is rendered irresponsible by madness or by sleeplessness – this, we read, has actually happened to some – the right to protect oneself (*ius se tuendi*) is not thereby taken away; it is enough that I am not under obligation to suffer what such an assailant attempts, any more than I should be if attacked by an animal belonging to another.

IV. War in defence of life is permissible
only against an actual assailant

<1> It is a disputed question whether innocent persons can be cut down or trampled upon when by getting in the way they hinder the defence or flight by which alone death can be averted. That this is permissible, is maintained even by some theologians. And certainly, if we look to nature alone, there is much less regard for society than concern for the preservation of the individual. But the law of love, especially as set forth in the Gospel, which puts consideration for others on a level with consideration for ourselves, clearly does not permit this.

<2> It has been well said by Thomas [Aquinas][20] – if he is rightly understood – that if a man in true self-defence kills his assailant the slaying is not intentional (*ex intentione*); not that, if reason supplies no other means of saving oneself, it is not sometimes permissible to do with set purpose (*destinato*) that which will result in the death of the assailant; rather it is that in such a case his death is not chosen as something primarily intended, as in a judicial punishment, but is the only resource available at the time. Even under such circumstances the person

---

[20] This is a reference to Aquinas's famous discussion of lethal self-defense, in *Summa theologiae*, II–II, q. 64, a. 7, reproduced above (chap. 16, pp. 190–1).

who is attacked ought to prefer to do anything possible to frighten away or weaken the assailant, rather than cause his death.

V. War in defence of life is permissible only when the danger is immediate and certain, not when it is merely assumed

<1> The danger, again, must be immediate (*praesens*) and on the spot as it were (*quasi in puncto*). I admit, to be sure, that if the assailant seizes weapons in such a way that his intent to kill is manifest the crime can be forestalled; for in morals as in material things a point is not to be found which does not have a certain breadth; but those who accept fear of any sort as justifying anticipatory slaying are themselves greatly deceived, and deceive others. Cicero said truly, in book I of *On Duties*, that most injuries have their origin in fear, since he who plans to do harm to another fears that otherwise he may himself suffer harm. In Xenophon, Clearchus says: 'I have known men who, becoming afraid of one another, in consequence of calumny or suspicion, and purposing to inflict injury before receiving injury, have done the most dreadful wrongs to those who had had no such intention, and had not even thought of such a thing. . . . 'In the effort to guard against fear,' says Livy (bk. III), 'men cause themselves to be feared, and we inflict upon others the injury which has been warded off from ourselves, as if it were necessary either to do or to suffer wrong.' To such men the query of Vibius Crispus, which Quintilian praised, is quite applicable: 'Who has permitted you to harbour so great fear?' According to Dio (bk. IV), Livia said that they do not escape disgrace who are first to do the deed that they fear.

<2> Further, if a man is not planning an immediate attack, but it has been ascertained that he has formed a plot, or is laying an ambush, or preparing a poison, making ready a false accusation and false evidence, corrupting the judicial procedure, I maintain that he cannot rightly (*iure*) be killed, either if the danger can in any other way be avoided, or if it is not altogether certain that the danger cannot be otherwise avoided. Usually, in fact, the delay that will intervene affords opportunity to apply many remedies and to take advantage of many accidental occurrences. . . . There are, it is true, theologians and jurists who would extend their indulgence somewhat further; but the opinion stated, which is better and safer, does not lack the support of authors. . . .

VIII. Not to take advantage of the right of defence is permissible

We said above, that while it is permissible to kill him who is making ready to kill, yet the man is more worthy of praise who prefers to be killed rather than to kill; this, however, is by some conceded in such a way that an exception is made in the case of a person whose life is useful to many. But I should deem it unsafe to extend this rule, which is inconsistent with patience, to all those whose lives are necessary for others. And so I should think that the exception ought to be restricted to those whose duty it is to ward off violence from others, such as members of an escort on a journey, who were hired with that purpose in view, and public officials. . . .

XI. By the law of nature it is permissible to kill in defence of property

Let us now come to injuries that are attempted upon our property. If we have in view commutative justice (*iustitia expletrix*) only, I shall not deny that in order to preserve property a robber can even be killed, in case of necessity; for the disparity between property and life is offset by the favourable position of the innocent party and the odious role of the robber, as we have said above. From this it follows, that if we have in view this right only, a thief fleeing with stolen property can be felled with a missile, if the property cannot otherwise be recovered. . . . Nor does any hindrance arise to this from charity, by way of precept, apart from divine and human law, unless the stolen property is of extremely slight value and consequently worthy of no consideration, an exception rightly added by some. . . .

XVI. Concerning defence in public war

What has been said by us up to this point, concerning the right to defend oneself and one's possessions, applies chiefly, of course, to private war; yet it may be made applicable also to public war, if the difference in conditions be taken into account. In private war this right is, so to say, momentary; it ceases as soon as circumstances permit an approach to a judge. But since public wars do not arise except where there are no courts, or where courts cease to function, they are prolonged, and are continually augmented by the increment of fresh losses and injuries. Besides, in private war, self-defence is generally the only consideration; but public powers have not only the right of defence but also the right to exact punishment. Hence for them it is permissible to forestall (*praevenire*) an act of violence which is not immediate, but which is seen to be threatening (*imminere*) from a distance; not directly – for that, as we have shown,[21] would work injustice – but indirectly, by inflicting punishment for a crime commenced but not yet carried through: this point there will be an opportunity to take up later.[22]

---

[21]   Bk. II, chap. II, section V, 1–2.
[22]   Bk. II, chap. XX, section XXXIX, 4.

XVII. A public war is not admitted to be defensive which has as its only purpose to weaken the power of a neighbour

Quite untenable is the position, which has been maintained by some,[23] that according to the law of nations it is right to take up arms in order to weaken a growing power which may do harm, should it become too great. That this consideration does enter into deliberations regarding war, I admit, but only on grounds of utility, not of justice. Thus if a war be justifiable for other reasons, for this reason also it might be deemed far-sighted to undertake it; that is the gist of the argument which the writers cited on this point present. But that the possibility of being attacked confers the right to attack is abhorrent to every principle of equity. Human life exists under such conditions that complete security is never guaranteed to us. For protection against uncertain fears we must rely on divine providence, and on a wariness free from reproach, not on force.

XVIII. A public war is not admitted to be defensive on the part of him who has himself given just cause for war

<1> Not less unacceptable is the doctrine of those who hold that defence is justifiable on the part of those who have deserved that war be made upon them; the reason they allege is, that few are satisfied with exacting vengeance in proportion to the injury suffered. But fear of an uncertainty cannot confer the right to resort to force (*ius ad vim*); hence a man charged with a crime, because he fears that his punishment may be greater than he deserves, does not, on that account, have the right to resist by force the representatives of public authority who desire to take him. <2> He who has done injury to another ought first to offer satisfaction to him whom he has injured, through the arbitration of a fair-minded man; if such an offer of satisfaction is rejected, then his taking up of arms will be beyond reproach. . . .

Chapter XX: On Punishments

I. Definition and origin of punishment

<1> Above, when we began to speak of the reasons for which wars are undertaken,[24] we said that [wrongful] deeds are considered in two categories, according

---

[23] This is a reference to Gentili's endorsement of preventive attack, as articulated in *De iure belli*, bk. I, chap. 14; reproduced in chap. 30, this volume, pp. 376–7.

[24] This refers to bk. II, chap. I, section II, 1, where, upon noting that actions of war can be directed "against injuries not yet committed, or committed," Grotius divided the latter category into wars "undertaken so that the injury is either repaired or punished."

as they can be repaired or punished. The former class we have already discussed.[25] There remains the latter, which concerns punishments: this we must consider all the more carefully because the lack of a clear understanding as to the origin and nature of punishment has given rise to many mistaken opinions. Now punishment in general means *an evil of suffering which is inflicted because of an evil of action.* . . . <2> But among those things which nature itself declares are permissible and not iniquitous is this, that he who does evil shall suffer evil; this the philosophers call the most ancient law, and law of Rhadamanthus, as we have said elsewhere. . . .

XXXVIII. On war waged to inflict punishment

We have previously shown, and histories here and there teach, that wars are usually begun for the purpose of exacting punishment. Most of the time, however, this cause is joined with a second, the desire to make good a loss, when the same act was both wicked and involved loss; and from these two characteristics two separate obligations arise.

Yet, it is quite clear that wars should not be undertaken for any sort of delinquency. For even the vengeance of the laws, which is exercised in safety and only harms the guilty, does not follow upon every wrong. As we have just said, Sopater rightly declares that delinquencies which are of little importance and common should be passed over and not avenged. . . .

XXXIX. By distinguishing various cases, it is explained whether a war waged to punish incipient crimes (*delicta inchoata*) is just

. . . <2> But, on the other hand, not every wicked intention which has been revealed by some fact gives an occasion for punishment. For if not all wrongs that have been perpetrated are punished, much less are to be punished those wrongs that have only been planned and initiated. . . .

<4> Crimes that have only just begun are therefore not to be punished by armed force, unless the matter is serious, and has reached a point where a certain damage has already followed from such action, even if it is not yet that which was aimed at; or at least great danger has ensued, so that the punishment is joined either with a precaution against future harm (about which we spoke above in the chapter on defence[26]), or protects injured dignity, or checks a dangerous example.

---

[25]   The theme of reparation was earlier discussed in bk. II, chap. II ff., which began with the words "Next in the order of the causes of war is an injury actually received; and first, an injury to our property".

[26]   Bk. II, chap. I, section II, 1.

XL. A discussion whether kings and peoples may rightly wage war on account of things done contrary to the law of nature, although not against them or their subjects; with a refutation of the view that the law of nature requires a right of jurisdiction for the exaction of punishment

<1> The fact must also be recognized that kings, and those who possess rights on a par with kings, have the right of demanding punishments not only on account of injuries committed against themselves or their subjects, but also on account of injuries which do not directly affect them but grossly violate the law of nature or of nations (*ius naturae aut gentium*) in regard to any persons whatsoever. For liberty to serve the interests of human society through punishments, which originally, as we have said, rested with individuals, now after the organization of states and courts of law is in the hands of the highest authorities, not, properly speaking, in so far as they rule over others but in so far as they are themselves subject to no one. For subjection has taken this right away from others. Truly it is more honourable to avenge wrongs done to others than done to oneself, since in the case of wrongs done to oneself it is more to be feared that through a sense of personal suffering one may exceed the proper limit or at least prejudice one's mind.

<2> And for this cause Hercules was famed by the ancients because he freed from Antaeus, Busiris, Diomedes and like tyrants the lands which, as Seneca says (*On Benefits*, I. xiv) he traversed, not from a desire to acquire but to protect, becoming, as Lysias points out, the bestower of the greatest benefits upon men through his punishment of the unjust. . . . Aristides in his *Panathenaic Oration* declares that Hercules deserved to be elevated among the gods because of his espousal of the common interest of the human race. . . . <3> So we do not doubt that wars are justly waged against those who act with impiety towards their ancestors, like the Sogdianians before Alexander taught them to abandon this form of barbarity; against those who feed on human flesh, from which custom, according to Diodorus, Hercules compelled the ancient Gauls to abstain; and against those who practise piracy. . . . Regarding such barbarians, wild beasts rather than men, one may rightly say what Aristotle wrongly said of the Persians, who were in no way worse than the Greeks, that war against them was sanctioned by nature; and what Isocrates said, in his *Panathenaic Oration*, that the most just war is against savage beasts, the next against men who are like beasts.

<4> Thus far we follow the opinion of Innocent [IV] (*On Decr.*, III. xxxiv. 8), and others who say that war may be waged upon those who sin against nature. The contrary view is held by Vitoria (*Relectiones de Indis*, I, no. 40),[27] Vázquez

---

[27] This corresponds to q. 2, a. 5, nn. 21–2 (fifth unjust title; reproduced in chap. 27, this volume, pp. 297–9).

(*Contr. Ill.*, I. xxv), Azor, Molina, and others, who in justification of war seem to demand that he who undertakes it should have suffered injury either in his person or his commonwealth, or that he should have jurisdiction over him who is attacked. For they claim that the power of punishing is the proper effect of civil jurisdiction, while we hold that it also is derived from natural law; this point we discussed at the beginning of the first book.[28] And in truth, if we accept the view of those from whom we differ, no enemy will have the right to punish (*puniendi ius*) another, even after a war that has been undertaken for a non-punitive reason.[29] Nevertheless many persons admit this right, which is confirmed also by the usage of all nations, not only after the conclusion of a war but also while the war is still going on; and not on the basis of any civil jurisdiction, but by that law of nature which existed before states were instituted, and is even now enforced, in places where men live in family groups and not in states.

XLI. The law of nature must be distinguished from widely current national customs

But at this point certain precautions need to be stated. First, national customs are not to be taken for a law of nature, although they have been received on reasonable grounds among many peoples. Of this type chiefly were the things which distinguished the Persians from the Greeks, to which you may rightly apply the saying of Plutarch: 'To wish to impose civilization upon barbarous peoples is a pretext which may serve to conceal greed for what is another's.'

XLII. The law of nature must be distinguished also from the voluntary divine law that is not recognized by all

Second, we should not hastily class with the things forbidden by nature those with regard to which this point is not sufficiently clear, and which are rather prohibited by the law of the divine will: in this class we may perhaps place unions not classed as marriages and those which are called incestuous, as well as usury.

---

[28] Grotius gives no exact reference to the passage in question. It may be an allusion to bk. I, chap. II, section V, 5 (not reproduced in this anthology), where, apropos of a biblical passage (Genesis 4:24) he observes that the right to administer punishment was originally not restricted to judges alone, but could pertain even to ordinary individuals. See Peter Haggenmacher, "Sur un passage obscur de Grotius: Essai de réponse à Cornelis van Vollenhoven," *Legal History Review*, 51 (1983), pp. 295–315.

[29] "Etiam post susceptum bellum ex causa non punitiva." Read in the context of the entire sentence, this phrase makes little sense. For an analysis of the semantic problems involved, see Haggenmacher, "Sur un passage," pp. 306–11.

XLIII. In the law of nature we must distinguish between what is evident and what is not evident

<1> Third, we should carefully distinguish between general principles, as, for example, that one must live honourably, that is, according to reason, and certain principles akin to these, but so evident that they do not admit of doubt, as that one must not seize what belongs to another, and inferences, which in some cases easily gain recognition, as that, for example, accepting marriage we cannot admit adultery, but in other cases are not so easily accepted, as the inference that vengeance which is satisfied with the pain of another is wicked. Here we have almost the same thing as in mathematics, where there are certain primary notions (*notitiae*), or notions akin to these, and certain proofs (*demonstrationes*) which are at once recognized and admitted, while certain others are true indeed but not evident to all. <2> Therefore, just as in the case of civil laws we excuse those who lack knowledge or understanding of the laws, so also with regard to the laws of nature it is right to pardon those who are hampered by weakness of their powers of reasoning or deficient education. . . .

<3> Let me finally add, once and for all, that wars which are undertaken to inflict punishment are under suspicion of being unjust, unless the crimes are very atrocious and most evident, or there is some other coincident reason. . . .[30]

Chapter XXII: On Unjust Causes [of War]

I. The distinction between justifying and persuasive causes is explained

<1> We said above, when we set out to treat the causes [of wars], that some are justifying (*iustificas*) and others persuasive (*suasorias*). Polybius (bk. II. i), who was the first to observe this distinction, calls the former 'pretexts', because they are wont to be openly alleged (Livy sometimes employs the term 'title'), and the latter by the generic name, 'causes'. <2> Thus in the war of Alexander against Darius the 'pretext' was the avenging of the injuries which the Persians had inflicted upon the Greeks, while the 'cause' was the desire for renown, empire, and riches, to which was added a great expectation of an easy victory arising from the expeditions of Xenophon and Agesilaus. The 'pretext' of the Second Punic War was the dispute over Saguntum, but the cause was the anger of the Carthaginians at the agreements which the Romans had extorted from them in

---

[30] The remaining paragraphs in this chapter (omitted here) discuss whether or not violations against true religion may be punished by acts of war. Chapter XXI (also omitted) considers whether persons (or even groups) who indirectly participate in a crime (by aiding and abetting, praising, or even failing to prevent it) should also share in the punishment.

times of adversity, and the encouragement which they derived from their successes in Spain, as was observed by Polybius (bk. I). Likewise Thucydides thinks that the true cause of the Peloponnesian War was the power of Athens, which was on the increase and was regarded with suspicion by the Lacedaemonians, but that the pretext was the dispute over Corcyra, that over Potidaea, and other points of difference; in this, however, he confuses the terms 'cause' and 'pretext'. . . .

II. Wars which lack causes of either sort are wars of savages

There are some who rush into war without a cause of either sort, led, as Tacitus says, by the desire of incurring danger for its own sake. The vice of these men exceeds what is ordinarily found among human beings; Aristotle calls it 'the savagery of wild beasts'. . . .

III. Wars which have persuasive but not justifying causes are wars of robbers

<1> In most cases, however, those who go to war have persuasive causes, sometimes with justifying causes, sometimes without. There are some indeed who clearly ignore justifying causes; to these we may apply the dictum uttered by the Roman jurists, that the man is a robber who, when asked the origin of his possession, adduces none other than the fact of possession. . . .

IV. There are certain causes which present a false appearance of justice

Others allege quasi-justifying causes which, when examined in the light of right reason, are found to be unjust. In such cases, as Livy says, it is clear that a decision is sought not on the basis of right, but of force. Most kings, says Plutarch, make use of the two terms, peace and war, as if they were coins, to obtain not what is right but what is advantageous. Now, which causes are unjust may, up to a certain point, be recognized from the foregoing discussion of just causes. What is straight is in fact a guide to what is crooked. For the sake of clearness, however, we proceed to mention the principal kinds of unjust causes.

V. Among these causes is the fear of something uncertain

<1> We have said above that fear with respect to a neighbouring power is not a sufficient cause. For in order that defence may be lawful it must be necessary; and

it is not necessary unless we are certain, not only regarding the power of our neighbour, but also regarding his intention (*animo*), the degree of certainty required being that which is accepted in moral matters. <2> Wherefore we can in no wise approve the view of those who declare that it is a just cause of war when a neighbour who is restrained by no agreement builds a fortress on his own soil, or some other fortification which may some day cause us harm. Against the fears which arise from such actions we must resort to counter-fortifications on our own land and other similar remedies, but not to force of arms. . . .

VIII. As well as the desire for richer land

Nor does the desire to change abode any more [afford a just cause for war], in order that by abandoning swamps and wildernesses a more fruitful soil may be acquired, which had been a cause of warfare among the ancient Germans, according to Tacitus (*Histories*, iv).

IX. And also the discovery of things previously taken over by others

Equally dishonest is it to claim for oneself by right of discovery what is held by another, even though the occupant may be wicked, may hold wrong views about God, or may be dull of wit. For discovery applies to those things which belong to no one. . . .

XI. An unjust cause is also the desire for freedom among a subject people

Freedom (*libertas*), whether of individuals or of states, that is 'autonomy', cannot give the right to war, as if by nature and at all times [the condition of] freedom was adapted to all persons. . . .

XII. And the desire to rule others against their will on the pretext that it is for their good

Not less iniquitous is it to desire by arms to subdue other men, as if they deserved to be slaves, and were such as the philosophers at times call slaves by nature. For even if something is advantageous for any one, the right is not forthwith conferred upon me to impose this upon him by force. For those who have the use of their reason ought to have the free choice of what is advantageous or not advantageous, unless another has acquired a certain right over them. . . .

XIII. As well as the title to universal empire which some give to the Emperor, and which is shown to be inapplicable

<1> I should hardly trouble to add that the title which certain persons give to the Roman Emperor is absurd, as if he had the right of ruling over even the most distant and hitherto unknown peoples, were it not that Bartolus (*On Digest*, XLIX. xv. 24), long considered first among jurists, had dared to pronounce him a heretic who denies to the Emperor this title. His ground, forsooth, is that the Emperor at times calls himself lord of the world, and that in the sacred writings that empire, which later writers call 'Romania', is called 'the whole world'. . . . Nor should any one be influenced by the arguments of Dante, by which he strives to prove that such a right belongs to the Emperor because it is expedient for the human race. The advantages which it brings are in fact offset by its disadvantages. For as a ship may attain to such a size that it cannot be steered, so also the number of inhabitants and the distance between places may be so great as not to tolerate a single government. <2> But even if we should grant that this be expedient, the right to rule by no means follows, since it cannot come into existence except by consent or by punishment. . . .

XVII. The difference between a war the cause of which is unjust and a war in which there is a wrong of another kind; and the different effects of each

<1> It is also to be observed that this often happens, that a just cause for a war may in fact exist, but that in making war a wrong may arise from the intent of the party who engages in hostilities. This may come about either because some other thing, not in itself illicit, in a greater degree and more effectively influences his purpose than the right itself, as, for example, an eager desire for honour, or some advantage, whether private or public, which is expected from the war considered apart from its justifying cause; or because there may be present a manifestly illicit desire, such as the delight of him who has pleasure in another's ill, without regard to what is good. . . . <3> However, while these things do indeed convict of wrong the party that makes war, yet when a justifiable cause is not lacking, they do not render the war itself properly unjust; hence no restitution is due as a result of a war undertaken under such conditions.

Chapter XXIII: On Doubtful Causes [of War]

I. On the source of the causes of doubt in moral questions

What Aristotle (*Nicomachean Ethics*, I. i) wrote is perfectly true, that certainty is not to be found in moral questions in the same degree as in the mathematical sciences. . . . Thus it comes about that between what should be done and what it is wrong to do there is a mean, that which is permissible; and this is now closer to the former, now to the latter. Hence there often comes a moment of doubt, just as when day passes into night, or when cold water slowly becomes warm. This is what Aristotle means when he says: 'Oftentimes it is hard to decide what is to be preferred.' Andronicus of Rhodes states the matter thus: 'It is hard to distinguish what is truly just from that which appears to be so.' . . .

V. If in a weighty matter there is doubt on both sides, and one of two courses must be chosen, that which is the safer is to be adopted

<1> In many controversies it may happen that strong arguments are forthcoming in support of both sides, whether drawn from the facts in the case or supported by the authority of others. When this occurs, if the matters which are in question are of slight moment the choice may evidently be free from harm, no matter on which side it may fall. But if the question is one of great importance, such as the infliction of capital punishment, in that case, because of the great difference between the courses to be chosen, the safer is to be preferred. . . .

VI. Whence it follows that in case of doubt we must refrain from war

Now war is of the utmost importance, seeing that in consequence of war most sufferings usually fall also upon innocent persons. Therefore in the midst of divergent opinions we must lean towards peace. . . .

XIII. The question whether a war may be just on both sides is discussed, with many qualifications

<1> From what we have said it is possible to reach a decision regarding the question, which has been discussed by many, whether, if we take into consideration the principal movers, a war can be just on both sides. We must distinguish various interpretations of the word 'just'.[31] Now a thing is called just either from its

---

[31] So Gratian, after *Decretum*, II. xi. 3. 65, distinguished a 'justice of cause, of sequence, of mind'.

cause, or because of its effects; and again, if from its cause, either in the particular sense of justice, or in the general sense in which all right conduct comes under this name. . . .

<2> In the particular sense and with reference to the thing itself, a war cannot be just on both sides, just as a legal claim cannot. . . . Yet it may actually happen that neither of the warring parties does wrong. No one acts unjustly without knowing that he is doing an unjust thing, but in this respect many are ignorant.

<3> In the general sense that is usually called just which is free from all blame on the part of the doer. However, many things are done without right and yet without guilt, because of unavoidable ignorance. . . .

<5> If, however, we interpret the word 'just' in relation to certain legal effects, in this sense surely a war may be just for both sides, as will appear from what we shall have to say later regarding a formal public war. . . .

Chapter XXIV: Warnings not to Undertake War Rashly, Even for Just Causes

I. Often a right should be set aside in order to avoid war

<1> Although it does not seem properly to be a part of a work on the law of war to inquire what other virtues enjoin or admonish with regard to war, nevertheless we must proceed to correct an error, in order to prevent any one from thinking that, where a right has been adequately established, either war should be waged forthwith, or even that war is permissible in all cases. On the contrary it frequently happens that it is more upright and just to abandon one's right. That we may honourably neglect the care of our own lives in order that, to the best of our ability, we may safeguard the life and eternal salvation of another, has been stated above in its proper place. Such conduct is above all becoming for Christians. . . .

II. Especially the right to inflict punishments

. . . <3> At times the circumstances of the case are such that to refrain from the exercise of one's right is not merely praiseworthy but even due, by reason of the love which we owe even to men who are our enemies, whether this be viewed in itself or as the most sacred law of the Gospel demands. . . .

VII. He who is not much the stronger ought to refrain from exacting penalties

In exacting penalties, moreover, this must be observed particularly, that war is not to be waged on this ground against him whose forces are equal to our own.

For, as in the case of a civil judge, he who wishes to avenge crimes by armed force ought to be much more powerful than the other party. Not merely prudence, in truth, or love of one's own people, ordinarily demands that we refrain from a dangerous war, but oftentimes justice also requires it; that is, rectorial justice, which from the very nature of government binds the superior to care for his inferiors no less than it binds the inferiors to obedience. From this follows the view rightly handed down by the theologians, that the king who undertakes a war for trivial reasons, or to exact unnecessary penalties involving great dangers, is responsible to his subjects for making good the losses which arise therefrom. . . .

IX. Again, war is not to be undertaken save from a most weighty cause at a most opportune time

Another occasion to engage in war is when, after inquiring into the matter as one ought, the right, one of highest moment to be sure, is at the same time matched by strength. This is what Augustus used to say, that war ought not to be undertaken save when the hope of gain was shown to be greater than the fear of loss. . . . Such an opportunity will be found particularly when there is hope that the matter may be settled by inspiring fear and on the strength of reputation, with little or no risk. . . .

Chapter XXV: On the Causes of Undertaking War on behalf of Others

I. War may rightfully be undertaken on behalf of subjects

<1> In the earlier part of this work, when we dealt with those who wage war, we asserted and showed that by the law of nature each individual was justified in enforcing not merely his own right but also that of another. The causes, therefore, which are just in relation to the person whose interest is at stake are just also in relation to those who give assistance to others. . . .

II. Yet war is not always to be undertaken on behalf of subjects

Nevertheless, wars are not always to be waged on behalf of subjects even though the just cause of some subject places the rulers under obligation to undertake them; but only inasmuch as this can be done without loss to all the subjects, or to the majority of them. The duty of the ruler concerns the whole rather than parts; and the greater a part is, the more nearly it approaches the character of the whole.

III. Whether an innocent subject may be surrendered to an enemy, in order that danger may be avoided

<1> Thus if one citizen, although innocent, is demanded by an enemy, to be made away with, there is no doubt that he may be abandoned to them if it appears that the state is by no means a match for the power of the enemy. . . .

IV. Wars may rightfully be undertaken also on behalf of allies of equal or unequal standing

Next to subjects, and indeed on an equal footing with them in this respect, that they ought to be defended, are allies, in whose treaty of alliance this obligation is embraced, whether they have surrendered themselves to the guardianship and good faith of others, or have agreed to give and receive mutual assistance. 'He who does not protect an ally from wrong, when he can do so, is at fault, just as he who does the wrong,' says Ambrose (*On Duties*, I. xxxvi). We have said elsewhere, however, that such agreements cannot be stretched to include wars for which no just cause exists. . . . We may now add this principle, that not even under such conditions is an ally bound to render aid if there is no hope of a successful issue. For an alliance is formed for the sake of good, and not of ill. . . .

V. And on behalf of friends

The third cause for undertaking wars on behalf of others is obligation to friends, to whom aid has not been promised, to be sure, but yet is owed under a certain principle of friendship, if it can be rendered easily and without loss. . . .

VI. And even on behalf of any persons whatsoever

The final and most wide-reaching cause for undertaking wars on behalf of others is the mutual tie of kinship among men, which of itself affords sufficient ground for rendering assistance. . . .

VII. Nevertheless the obligation to undertake war may be disregarded without wrong, if one fears for oneself, or even for the life of the aggressor

<1> At this point the question arises, whether a man is bound to defend a man, or one people another people, from wrong. Plato (*Laws*, IV) thinks that he who does not defend another from violence should be punished; and this was provided

for even in the laws of the Egyptians. But first, if danger is evident, it is certain that a man is not so bound; for he may prefer his own life and interests to those of others. . . . <2> Nor should this statement of Seneca be scorned: 'I shall come to the aid of the perishing, but in such a way that I myself may not perish, unless I am to be the price of a great man or a great cause.' But not even in this case will a man be obliged to render aid if the person oppressed cannot be delivered save by the death of the aggressor. For if the person who is attacked can put the life of the aggressor above his own, as we have said elsewhere,[32] he will not do wrong who either believes or desires that the person attacked may prefer this also; especially when in the case of the aggressor there is the greater danger of irreparable and eternal loss.

VIII. The question whether a war for the defence of subjects of another power is rightful is explained by a distinction

<1> This too is a matter of controversy, whether there may be a just cause for undertaking war on behalf of the subjects of another ruler, in order to protect them from wrong at his hands. Now it is certain that, from the time when political associations were formed, each of their rulers has sought to assert some particular right over his own subjects. . . . The purpose no doubt is, as Ambrose (*On Duties*, I) correctly explains, 'to prevent men from provoking wars by usurping the care for things under the control of others'. . . .

<2> If, however, the wrong is obvious . . . the exercise of the right vested in human society is not precluded. . . .

<3> Nay, though it be granted that even in extreme need subjects cannot justifiably take up arms . . . , it would still not follow that others may not take up arms on their behalf. For whenever the check imposed upon some action arises from the person and not from the matter concerned, then what is refused to one may be permitted to another on his behalf, provided that the matter is such that the one may therein be of service to the other. . . . The restriction, in fact, which prevents a subject from resisting, does not arise from a cause which is identical in the case of a subject and of one who is not a subject, but from the personal condition which is not transferred to others.

<4> Hence, Seneca thinks that I may make war upon one who is not one of my people but oppresses his own, as we said when dealing with the infliction of punishment; a procedure which is often connected with the protection of innocent persons. We know, it is true, from both ancient and modern history, that the desire for what is another's seeks such pretexts as this for its own ends; but a right does not at once cease to exist in case it is to some extent abused by evil men. . . .

---

[32] Bk. II, chap. I, section VIII.

IX. Military alliances and mercenary service without discrimination regarding the causes of war are unjust

<1> Again, just as military alliances, which were entered into with the intention that aid should be rendered for any sort of war without distinction of cause, are not permissible, as we have said, so no manner of life is more wicked than that of those who serve as soldiers for hire without regard to the cause of hostilities. . . .

<2> It would in truth matter little that mercenaries sell their own lives, if they did not sell also the lives of others, who are often innocent; in this respect they are much more abominable than an executioner in the degree that it is worse to slay without cause than with cause. . . .

<3> War has no place among the useful arts. Nay, rather, it is so horrible that only the utmost necessity, or true charity, can render it honourable. How this is possible may be gathered from what we have said in the last of the preceding chapters. In the opinion of Augustine (*On the Words of the Lord according to Matthew*, cited in [Gratian, *Decretum*,] causa XXIII) 'to serve as a soldier is no crime: but to do so for the sake of plunder is a sin.'

X. It is also particularly wrong to take service merely for the sake of plunder or pay. . . .

Chapter XXVI: On Just Causes for War Waged by Those who are under the Command of Another

I. Who may be said to be under the command of another

We have dealt with those who are their own masters (*sunt sui iuris*); there are others in a condition which requires them to render obedience, as sons in a household, slaves, subjects, also individual citizens considered in relation to the body politic of their state.

II. What those under the command of another should do if they are summoned to share in deliberation, or have a free choice of action

If those under the command of another are admitted to a deliberation, or there is given to them a free choice of going to war or remaining at peace, they should be governed by the same rules as those who, at their own discretion, take up arms for themselves or on behalf of others.

III. If those under the command of another should be ordered to go to war, and should believe the cause of the war to be unjust, they ought not to serve

\<1\> If those under the command of another are ordered to take the field, as often occurs, they should altogether refrain from so doing if it is clear to them that the cause of the war is unjust. That God must be obeyed, rather than men, was said not only by the Apostles, but also by Socrates; and among the learned men of the Jews is found an opinion indicating that one must no longer obey a king who issues commands contrary to the law of God. . . .

IV. What they who are under the rule of another, and are ordered to go to war, should do if they are in doubt

\<1\> Now if one who is under the rule of another is in doubt whether a thing is permissible or not, is he to remain inactive, or obey? Very many think that he should obey; and further, that he is not hindered by the famous maxim, 'What you question, do not do,' because he who doubts as a matter of reflection does not doubt in a decision involving action, for he can believe that in a matter of doubt he must obey his superior. It cannot in truth be denied that this distinction of a double judgment applies in many actions. The civil law, not only of Rome but of other nations as well, under such circumstances not only grants impunity to those who obey, but also refuses to admit a civil action against them. He does the injury, they say, who orders that it be done; there is then no guilt on the part of him who has to obey. The constraint of authority excuses; and like arguments. . . .

\<4\> This view, however, is not free from inherent difficulty. Our countryman Adrian, who was the last pope of Rome from north of the Alps, supports the contrary opinion, and this may be established, not exactly by the reason which he adduces, but by the more pressing one that whoever hesitates, when reflecting, in his decision to act ought to choose the safer course. The safer course, however, is to refrain from war. . . .

\<5\> It is no objection that on the other side there is danger of disobedience. For when either course is uncertain, that which is the lesser of two evils is free from sin (for if a war is unjust there is no disobedience in avoiding it). Disobedience in things of this kind, by its very nature, is a lesser evil than manslaughter, especially than the slaughter of many innocent men. . . . Nor is it of great weight as some adduce, that if this principle should be admitted the state would in many cases perish, because oftentimes it is not expedient that the reasons for policies should be made public. Although this may be true of persuasive causes, it is not true of justifying causes, which ought to be clear and open and, further, should be such as may and ought to be openly set forth. . . . \<7\> Declarations of war in fact, as we shall shortly be saying, were wont to be made publicly, with a statement of the cause, in order that the whole human race as it were might judge of the justness of it. Clearly prudence is the virtue characteristic of the ruler, as it seemed to Aristotle also; but justice is the virtue characteristic of a man, in so far as he is a man.

<8> At any rate, the view which we said was that of Adrian seems absolutely to be followed if a subject not only hesitates, but, led by more convincing arguments, leans rather to the view that the war is unjust; especially if it is a question of attacking others, not of defending oneself. . . .

VI. When it may be just for subjects to bear arms in a war that is unjust

<1> I think however that there may be a just defence of subjects in a war that is not merely doubtful but obviously unjust. For since an enemy, although waging a just war, does not have the true and perfect right of killing innocent subjects who are not responsible for the war, unless either as a necessary defensive measure or by way of consequence and apart from his purpose (for these are not liable to punishment), it follows that, if it is certain that the enemy comes with such a spirit that he absolutely refuses to spare the lives of hostile subjects when he can, these subjects may defend themselves by the law of nature, of which they are not deprived by the law of nations. <2> Nor would we then say that the war is just on both sides; for it is not a question of the war, but of a certain and definite act. This act, although done by him who in other respects has a right to make war, is unjust, and hence is justly resisted.

Book III of *De iure belli ac pacis* concentrates on the sort of issues that now go under the heading of *ius in bello* or proper conduct in war. This is what earlier authors such as Suárez referred to as *debitus modus*: the limits that ought to be observed by belligerents in a just war. Grotius works from the presupposition – central to the classical just war tradition – that the rights of war may be exercised only by the party that possesses a just cause. The opposing party, whose cause is by definition unjust, has no right to use armed force, not even in self-defense. The limits to be observed in war are thus in large measure dependent on the nature of the just cause. The just belligerent may do whatever is necessary to rectify the violated order of justice, although he may not go beyond this limit. Hence, unlike the later tradition of international law, which sought to separate the *ius in bello* from considerations of material justice, Grotius views the question of right conduct in war against the normative background of the *ius ad bellum*. There is in principle no postulation of legal equality between opposing belligerents. Hence when Grotius sets out the principles of moderation that ought to be observed in war (chaps. XI and ff.), these are addressed first and foremost to the just belligerent.

Grotius does, however, leave an opening for the modern idea of bilateral justice in war. This appears in his conception of formally declared public war between sovereign powers (chaps. III and ff.). Referring to the practice of the ancient Romans, Grotius notes that under the law of nations, the parties to a public war may with impunity carry out deeds which normally would be considered unlawful under natural law. This bilateral regime founded on a tacit agreement among nations applies regardless of the belligerents' standing vis-à-vis the just cause. Grotius justifies this by an appeal to the principle of the lesser evil. Neutral powers would inevitably get drawn into a conflict (by, for example, being pressured to make determinations about which side should possess a particular territory at the close of the fighting) unless it was mutually recognized that certain legal effects should accompany the state of war. Grotius provides an extended treatment of these legal effects, only a small part of which is included below. Some of these effects would seem repugnant to us today (for example, enslaving or killing prisoners of war) yet these were the sort of deeds that were considered acceptable practice among the peoples (Romans especially) documented by Grotius. In book III he accordingly provides us with two very different outlines of what may be deemed permissible in war. Chapters IV–IX proceed from the point of view of what Grotius termed "external justice" (here identified with a special kind of *ius gentium*), while chapters X–XVI detail what may be done according to the requirements of "internal justice" (i.e. that which is inherently right, in conformity with *ius naturae* and some complementary virtues such as charity).

Book III closes with a discussion of peace. Chapters XIX–XXV consider what sort of acts are apt to restore the peace that has been disrupted by war.

From *De iure belli ac pacis*, bk. III[33]

Chapter I: General Rules from the Law of Nature regarding what is Permissible in War

I. The order of treatment in the discussion which follows

We have considered both those who wage war and on what grounds war may be waged. It follows that we should determine what is permissible in war, also to what extent, and in what ways, it is permissible. What is permissible in war is viewed either absolutely or in relation to a previous promise. It is viewed absolutely, first from the standpoint of the law of nature, and then from that of the law of nations. Let us see, then, what is permissible by nature.

---

[33] Grotius, *De iure belli ac pacis* (trans. Kelsey), pp. 599–601, 630–3, 639, 641–50, 656–7, 716, 718–19, 722–3, 729–44, 746–8, 751–2, 804, 814, 817, 860–2.

II. The first rule: in war things which are necessary to attain the end in view are permissible. This is explained

<1> First, as we have previously said on several occasions, in a moral question things which lead to an end receive their intrinsic value from the end itself. In consequence we are understood to have a right to those things which are necessary for the purpose of securing a right, the necessity being understood not in terms of physical exactitude but in a moral sense. By right I mean that which is strictly so called, denoting the power of acting in respect to society only. . . .

III. The second rule: a right is to be viewed as arising not only from the origin of the war but also from causes which subsequently develop

In the second place the fact must be recognized that our right to wage war is to be regarded as arising not merely from the origin of the war but also from causes which subsequently develop; just as in lawsuits a new right is often acquired by one party after suit has been brought. Thus those who associate themselves with him who assails me, either as allies or subjects, confer upon me the right to protect myself against them also. In like manner those who join in a war that is unjust, especially if they can or ought to know that it is unjust, obligate themselves to make good the expenses and losses incurred, because through their guilt they cause the loss. Similarly, those who join in a war that has been undertaken without a cause worthy of approval draw upon themselves the desert of punishment, in a degree proportionate to the injustice which lies in their action. . . .

IV. The third rule: some things, which are not permissible according to the purpose of a war, may follow therefrom without wrong; a precaution is added

<1> In the third place, it must be observed that in addition to the right of action many things follow indirectly, and beyond the purpose of the doer, for which in and of themselves a right would not exist. We have explained elsewhere how this may occur in a case of self-defence. Thus in order to obtain what is ours, if we cannot get that by itself, we have the right to accept more, subject to the obligation, nevertheless, of restoring the value of the excess. Similarly we may bombard a ship full of pirates, or a house full of brigands, even if there are within the same ship or house a few infants, women, or other innocent persons who are thereby endangered. Says Augustine: 'A man is not guilty of homicide if he has built a wall about his property and another is killed by the fall of it when trying to make use of it.'

<2> But, as we have admonished upon many occasions previously, what accords with right strictly considered is not always, or in all respects, permitted. Often, in fact, love for our neighbour prevents us from pressing our right to the utmost limit. Wherefore we must also beware of what happens, and what we foresee may happen, beyond our purpose, unless the good which our action has in view is much greater than the evil which is feared, or, unless the good and the evil balance, the hope of the good is much greater than the fear of the evil; the decision in such matters must be left to a prudent judgment, but in such a way that, when in doubt, we should favour that course, as the more safe, which has regard for the interest of another rather than our own. . . .

Chapter III: On War that is Just or Public according to the Law of Nations; and Therein, on the Declaration of War

I. A public war according to the law of nations is a war between distinct peoples

<1> In a previous passage[34] we began to say that by authors of repute a war is often called just not from the cause from which it arises, nor, as is done in other cases, from the importance of its operations, but because of certain particular legal effects (*iuris effectus*). Of what sort such a war is, however, will best be perceived from the definition of enemies given by the Roman jurists: 'Enemies are those who in the name of the state declare war upon us, or upon whom we in the name of the state declare war; others are brigands and robbers', says Pomponius (*Dig.*, L. xvi. 118). . . .

II. The distinction between a people, although acting unjustly, and pirates or brigands

<1> Moreover, a commonwealth (*respublica*) or state (*civitas*) does not immediately cease to be such if it commits an injustice, even as a body (*communiter*); and a gathering of pirates and brigands is not a state, even if they do perhaps mutually maintain a sort of equality, without which no association can exist. The reason is that pirates and brigands are banded together for crime; the members of a state, even if at times they are not free from wrongdoing, nevertheless have been united for enjoying the rule of law (*iuris fruendi causa*), and they do render justice to foreigners, if not in all respects according to the law of nature, which, as we have showed elsewhere, has become partly obscured among many peoples, at

---

[34] Bk. I, chap. III, section IV.

least according to agreements entered into with each state or in accordance with customs. . . .

IV. It is essential to the nature of a public war that it should have the supreme power as its author; in what way this is to be understood

What persons have the supreme governing power, we have already stated. Hence it may be understood that if any possess this power in part, they may to that extent wage a lawful war. This principle applies with even greater force to those who are not subjects, but are allied on an unequal footing. So we learn from history that all formalities of lawful war were observed between the Romans and their allies, the Volsci, Latins, Spaniards, and Carthaginians, although these had an inferior status in the alliance.

V. A declaration of war is also requisite

That a war may be lawful in the sense indicated, it is not enough that it be waged by the supreme powers on each side. It is also necessary, as we have said, that it should be publicly declared, and indeed proclaimed publicly in such manner that the notification of this declaration be made by one of the parties to the other. . . .

XI. The reason why a declaration is required in order to secure certain effects

Furthermore the reason why nations required a declaration for the kind of war which we have called just according to the law of nations was not that which some adduce, with the purpose that nothing should be done secretly or deceitfully. . . . The purpose was, rather, that the fact might be established with certainty that war was being waged not by private initiative but by the will of each of the two peoples or of their heads. Hence indeed arise the peculiar effects which do not develop in a war against brigands, nor in a war which a king wages against his subjects. . . .

XII. The effects referred to are not found in other wars

What certain writers point out and teach by citing examples, to the effect that even in such wars what is seized belongs to those who take it, is indeed true, but only for one side, and by the law of nature, not by the voluntary law of nations, since this concerns nations only, not persons who form no nation or form a part of a nation. The writers in question err in this also, that they think that a war

undertaken for the defence of one's person or property does not require a declaration. Such a war does require a declaration, not indeed of itself, but for the sake
of those effects of which we have begun to speak, and which we shall shortly
explain. . . .

Chapter IV: On the Right of Killing Enemies in a Public War, and on Other Violence against the Person

I. The effects of a public war are explained in general terms

On the verse of Virgil,

> Then to strive in hatred, then to plunder,
> Will be permitted,

Servius Honoratus, after tracing the fetial law from Ancus Martius, and more
remotely from the Aequicoli, makes this comment:

> If at any time it happened that either men or cattle had been carried off from the
> territory of the Roman people by any nation, the *pater patratus*, with the fetials, that
> is, the priests who preside over the conclusion of treaties, would set out, and
> standing before the frontier would state the cause of war in a loud voice; if they
> refused to restore the things that had been carried off, or to surrender the wrongdoers,
> he would hurl a spear toward them. This constituted the beginning of hostilities,
> and then it was permissible to pillage in accordance with the usage of war.

. . . From this we learn that a war declared between two peoples, or the heads of
two peoples, has certain particular effects which do not arise from the nature of
war itself. . . .

II. A distinction is made between the word 'permissible' as referring to that which is done with impunity, although not without moral wrong, and to that which is free from moral wrong even if virtue would enjoin not to do it; with examples

<1> But let us see the import of the 'will be permitted' (*licebit*) in Virgil's line.
For sometimes that is said to be permissible (*licere*) which is right (*rectum*) from
every point of view and is free from reproach, even if there is something else which
might more honourably be done. . . . <2> In another sense, however, something

is said to be permissible, not because it can be done without prejudice to piety and rules of duty, but because among men it is not liable to punishment. In this sense fornication is permitted among many peoples; among the Lacedaemonians and Egyptians even thieving was permissible. . . . This, however, is a less proper meaning of the expression 'it is permitted'. . . . <3> In this sense we often see 'what is permitted' (*licet*) contrasted with 'what should be done' (*oportet*). . . .

III. The effects of a public war in general are concerned with permission that grants impunity

In this way, accordingly, it is permitted to harm an enemy, both in his person and in his property; that is, it is permissible for either side indiscriminately and not merely for him who wages war for a just cause, and who injures within that limit, a permission which we said at the beginning of this book was granted by the law of nature. . . .

IV. Why such effects have been introduced

The reason why such effects met with the approval of nations was this. To undertake to decide regarding the justice of a war between two peoples had been dangerous for other peoples, who were on this account involved in a foreign war; just so the Massilians said, in relation to the struggle between Caesar and Pompey, that it was not within the province of their judgment or their power to determine which party had the more just cause. Furthermore, even in a just war, from external indications it can hardly be adequately known what is the just limit of self-defence, of recovering what is one's own, or of inflicting punishments; in consequence it has seemed altogether preferable to leave decisions in regard to such matters to the scruples of the belligerents rather than to have recourse to the judgements of others. . . .

V. Testimony regarding these effects

<1> Now, that licence to injure, which we have just begun to consider, extends in the first place to persons; in regard to it there are many evidences in writers of authority. There is a Greek proverb from a tragedy of Euripides:

> Pure are all they who shed the blood of foes.

According to an ancient custom of the Greeks it was not permitted (*fas*) to bathe, to eat or drink, and much less to perform sacred rites, in company with those who had slain a man in time of peace; but to do so with those who had killed in war was allowed. And often killing is called the right of war (*ius belli*). . . .

<2> However, it is clear from other passages that when these writers say 'by right of war' we must not understand such a right as would free what is done from all blame, but only impunity, as is apparent from what I have already said. . . .

VI. By virtue of this right all who are in the territory of the enemy may be killed or injured

Furthermore, this right of doing what is permissible has a wide application. In the first place it extends not only to those who actually bear arms, or are subjects of him that stirs up the war, but in addition to all persons who are in the enemy's territory. . . . The reason is that injury may be feared from such persons also; and this is sufficient, in a prolonged and general war, to give rise to the right which we are discussing. . . . At any rate what I have said applies beyond doubt to foreigners who enter hostile territory after a war has commenced and are aware of it.

VII. What of foreigners having entered a country before the outbreak of war?

As to foreigners who have gone there in a period prior to the war, they are apparently to be regarded as enemies according to the law of nations, after the lapse of a moderate time, in which they could have departed. . . .

VIII. Enemy subjects may be injured anywhere, unless the law of the foreign territory prevents it

<1> Now those who are truly subjects of the enemy, that is to say from a permanent cause, may in respect to their persons be lawfully injured in any place whatsoever, according to this law of nations. For when war is declared upon any one it is at the same time declared upon the men of his people. . . . <2> Such persons therefore may be slain with impunity in their own land, in the land of an enemy, on land under the jurisdiction of no one, or on the sea. The fact that it is not permissible to slay or injure such persons in neutral (*pacato*) territory is based on a right derived not from their persons but from the right of him who exercises governing power (*imperium*) there. . . .

IX. This right to inflict injury extends even over infants and women

<1> But to return to the point under consideration: How far this permission (*licentia*) to inflict injury extends may be perceived from the fact that the slaughter

even of infants and of women is made with impunity, and that this is included in the right of war. . . .

X. And even over captives, and without limitation of time

<1> Not even captives are exempt from this permission to inflict injury. In Seneca Pyrrhus says, in accordance with the accepted custom of the time,

No law the captive spares or punishment restrains. . . .

XI. And even over those who wish to surrender, but whose surrender is not accepted

Furthermore we meet with frequent examples of the slaughter of suppliants, as by Achilles in Homer, and in Virgil the cases of Mago and Turnus. These instances of the killing of suppliants, we see, are related in such a way that they are defended by the right of war of which I have spoken. In fact, Augustine also, when praising the Goths, who had spared suppliants and those that had taken refuge in temples, says: 'What would have been permissible by the law of war they judged was not permissible for them.' . . .

XII. And even over those who have surrendered unconditionally

But you may read also that captives, whose unconditional surrender was accepted, have been put to death. . . . There was indeed almost a permanent custom among the Romans with respect to the commanders of the enemy, whether captured or received by surrender, that they should be put to death on the day of the Roman triumph. . . .

XIX. Whether rape is contrary to the law of nations

<1> You may read in many places that the raping of women in time of war is permissible, and in many others that it is not permissible. Those who sanction rape have taken into account only the injury done to the person of another, and have judged that it is not inconsistent with the law of war that everything which belongs to the enemy should be at the disposition of the victor. A better conclusion has been reached by others, who have taken into consideration not only the injury but the unrestrained lust of the act; also, the fact that such acts do not contribute to safety or to punishment, and should consequently not go unpunished in war any more than in peace. The latter view is the law not of all nations, but

of the better ones. . . . <2> Among Christians it is right that the view just presented shall be enforced, not only as a part of military discipline, but also as a part of the law of nations; that is, whoever forcibly violates chastity, even in war, should everywhere be subject to punishment. . . .

Chapter X: Cautions in regard to Things which are Done in an Unlawful War

I. In what sense a feeling of honour may be said to forbid what the law permits

<1> I must retrace my steps, and must deprive those who wage war of nearly all that I may have seemed to grant, yet did not grant to them. For when I first set out to explain this part of the law of nations I bore witness that many things are said to be 'lawful' or 'permissible' for the reason that they are done with impunity, in part also because coactive tribunals lend to them their authority; things which, nevertheless, either deviate from the rule of right (whether this has its basis in law strictly so called, or in the admonitions of other virtues), or at any rate may be omitted on higher grounds and with greater praise among good men. <2> In the *Trojan Women* of Seneca, when Pyrrhus says:

No law the captive spares, nor punishment restrains,

Agamemnon makes answer:

What law permits, this sense of shame forbids to do.

In this passage the sense of shame signifies not so much a regard for men and reputation as a regard for what is just and good, or at any rate for that which is more just and better. . . .

III. What is done by reason of an unjust war is unjust from the point of view of internal injustice

In the first place, then, we say that if the cause of a war should be unjust, even if the war should have been undertaken in a lawful way, all acts which arise therefrom are unjust from the point of view of internal injustice (*interna iniustitia*). In consequence the persons who knowingly perform such acts, or cooperate in them, are to be considered of the number of those who cannot reach the Kingdom of Heaven without repentance. True repentance, again, if time and means are adequate, absolutely requires that he who inflicted the wrong, whether by killing, by destroying property, or by taking booty, should make good the wrong done. . . .

IV. Who are bound to make restitution,
and to what extent

Furthermore, according to the principles which in general terms we have elsewhere set forth, those are bound to make restitution who have brought about the war, either by the exercise of their power, or through their advice. Their accountability concerns all those things, of course, which ordinarily follow in the train of war; and even unusual things, if they have ordered or advised any such thing, or have failed to prevent it when they might have done so. Thus also generals are responsible for the things which have been done while they were in command; and all the soldiers that have participated in some common act, as the burning of a city, are responsible for the total damage. In the case of separate acts each is responsible for the loss of which he was the sole cause, or at any rate was one of the causes. . . .

Chapter XI: Moderation with respect to the Right of Killing in a Just War

II. Who may be killed in accordance
with internal justice

When it is just to kill – for this must be our starting point – in a just war in accordance with internal justice (*iustitia interna*) and when it is not just to do so, may be understood from the explanations which were given by us in the first chapter of this book. Now a person is killed either intentionally or unintentionally. No one can justly be killed intentionally, except as a just penalty or in case we are able in no other way to protect our life and property; although the killing of a man on account of transitory things, even if it is not at variance with justice in a strict sense, nevertheless is not in harmony with the law of love. However, that punishment may be just, it is necessary that he who is killed shall himself have done wrong, and in a matter punishable with the penalty of death on the decision of a fair judge. But we shall here say less on this point, because we think that what needs to be known has been sufficiently set forth in the chapter on punishments. . . .

V. Those who are responsible for a war
are to be distinguished from those
who follow them

The counsel of Themistius, who warns us that we must distinguish between those who were responsible for a war and those who followed the leadership of others, is supported by numerous historical examples. Herodotus (bk. IX) relates that the Greeks exacted punishment from those who instigated the Thebans to desert to the Medes. . . . The Athenians, according to Thucydides (bk. III), repented of their decree against the inhabitants of Mitylene, 'that they should put to death the whole city rather than merely the instigators of the revolt'. . . .

VI. With regard to those who are responsible for a war we must distinguish between causes which may be and those which may not he approved

<1> Further, in considering those who are responsible for a war, we must distinguish between the causes of their action; for there are some causes which are not indeed just, but still are such that they may deceive persons who are by no means wicked. . . . <2> In his first book *On Duties* Cicero says that we must spare those who were not cruel, not inhuman, in war; then, that wars in which the prize is glory of empire, should be waged with less bitterness. . . . <3> Often there occurs what we find stated in Cicero regarding the war between Caesar and Pompey: 'There was some uncertainty; there was a contest between the most eminent generals; many were in doubt as to what it would be best to do.' The same author says elsewhere: 'Even if we are guilty of some fault arising from human error, we are certainly guiltless of crime.' Evidently, as in Thucydides, those acts are said to deserve pardon which are done, 'not from wickedness, but rather from an error of judgment'. . . .

VII. Punishment may often be remitted justly even to enemies who have deserved death

<1> Even where justice does not demand this, it is nevertheless often in conformity with goodness, with moderation, with highmindedness. . . .

VIII. One must take care, so far as is possible, to prevent the death of innocent persons, even when done unintentionally

Again, with regard to the death of those who are killed by accident and without intent, we must hold fast to the principle which we mentioned above: it is the bidding of mercy, if not of justice, that, except for reasons that are weighty and will affect the safety of many, no action should be attempted whereby innocent persons may be threatened with destruction. . . .

IX. Children should always be spared; women,
unless they have been guilty of an extremely
serious offence; and old men . . .

X. Those also should be spared whose occupations
are solely religious or concerned with letters . . .

XI. As well as farmers should be spared . . .

XII. As well as merchants and like persons . . .

XIII. As well as prisoners of war . . .

XIV. The surrender of those who wish to yield
upon fair terms should be accepted . . .

XV. Those also who have surrendered unconditionally
should be spared . . .

XVI. What has been stated is true, provided that no
serious crime has preceded; how this is to be understood

<1> Against these precepts of justice and the law of nature frequently exceptions
are offered, which are by no means just; as, for example, if retaliation is required,
if there is need of inspiring terror, if too determined a resistance has been offered.
Yet he who recalls what has previously been said in regard to valid reasons for
putting to death will easily perceive that such exceptions do not afford just
grounds for an execution. There is no danger from prisoners and those who have
surrendered or desire to do so; therefore in order to warrant their execution it
is necessary that a crime shall have been previously committed, such a crime,
moreover, as a just judge would hold punishable by death. Yet we sometimes see
anger vented upon prisoners or upon those who have surrendered, or a surrender
upon guarantee of life refused, if any who were convinced of the injustice of a war
have still remained in arms; if they have injured the good name of their enemies
with monstrous slanders; if they have violated their pledged word, or another
right of nations, such as that of ambassadors; if they were deserters.

<2> But nature does not sanction retaliation except against those who have
done wrong. It is not sufficient that by a sort of fiction the enemy may be
conceived as forming a single body; this may be understood from our foregoing
discussion on participation in punishments.[35] . . .

---

[35]   This topic is discussed at length in bk. II, chap. XXI (*De poenarum communicatione*), not included
in this anthology.

<3> Even the advantage, which is anticipated in the future from terror, does not suffice to give the right to kill; but if the right already exists it may be among the reasons for not waiving the right.

<4> Furthermore a quite obstinate devotion to one's own party, provided only that the cause is not altogether dishonourable, does not deserve punishment. . . . Or, if such devotion is punished in any way, the penalty should not be carried so far as death; for no just judge would so decide. . . .

XVII. It is right to spare those who are guilty, if their number is very great . . .

XVIII. Hostages should not be put to death unless they have themselves done wrong

XIX. All useless fighting should be avoided

This remains to be added, that all engagements, which are of no use for obtaining a right or putting an end to a war, but have as their purpose a mere display of strength, that is, as the Greeks say (*Arrian*, V), 'an exhibition of strength rather than a combat against the enemy', are incompatible both with the duty of a Christian and with humanity itself. Consequently rulers, who must render account of the useless shedding of blood to Him in Whose name they bear the sword, should strictly forbid such combats. . . .

Chapter XII: Moderation in Laying Waste and Similar Things

I. What devastation may be just and to what degree

. . . <3> That kind of devastation at least must be tolerated which compels the enemy to sue for peace in a short time. . . . Yet, if you examine the matter aright you will find that such havoc is ordinarily committed from motives of hatred rather than from considerations of prudence. It usually happens either that those conditions which justify devastation are lacking, or that there are other more cogent reasons which advise against it.

II. Devastation should be refrained from if the area is profitable for us and out of the power of the enemy

<1> This will happen, first, if our occupation of fruitful ground is such that it cannot yield produce for the enemy. That is the particular point of the divine law,

which ordains that wild trees be employed in making walls and military structures, but that fruit-bearing trees be preserved for purposes of food, with the explanation that trees, unlike men, cannot rise up against us in battle. . . .

<2> Furthermore, in describing the customs of the Jews, in the fourth book of his work *On Abstaining from Animal Food*, Porphyry extends this rule (interpreted, as I think, in the light of custom) even to living things employed in agricultural work. He says that Moses commanded that these too should be spared in war; the writings of the Talmud and the Hebrew interpreters add that this law is to be extended to anything whatever which may be destroyed without cause, as touching the burning of buildings, or the destruction of supplies which can be eaten or drunk. . . .

<3> Still more will this restriction apply after a complete victory. Cicero (*On Duties*, I) disapproved of the destruction of Corinth, even though Roman ambassadors had been shamefully treated there; and he also characterizes as horrible, criminal, and steeped in the depths of hatred, a war which is waged against walls, roofs, columns, and doors. . . .

V. Devastation should be refrained from if the thing itself is of no use in furnishing resources for war

In the fourth place, it happens that certain things are of such a nature that they are of no value for making or waging war: such things reason also bids us to spare while the war is going on. . . . Polybius (bk. V) says it is a sign of an infuriated mind to destroy those things which, if destroyed, do not weaken the enemy, nor bring gain to the one who destroys them; such things are temples, colonnades, statues, and the like. . . .

VI. The principle stated is particularly applicable to things that are sacred or connected with things that are sacred

<1> While what has been said holds true of other things of artistic value, for the reason which we have already given, there is a particular reason in the case of those things which have been devoted to sacred uses. Although such things also, as we have said elsewhere, are public in their own way, and so, according to the law of nations, are violated with impunity, nevertheless, if there is no danger from them, reverence for divine things urges that such buildings and their furnishings be preserved, particularly among those who worship the same God, in accordance with the same law, even if perhaps they disagree in respect to certain doctrines or points of ritual. . . .

Chapter XX: On the Good Faith of Public Powers, by which War is Ended; also on the Working of Peace Treaties, on Decision by Lot, on Combat by Agreement; on Arbitration, Surrender, Hostages, and Pledges

. . . XXVII. Distinctions are drawn between furnishing a new cause for war and breaking a treaty of peace

Of daily occurrence is the discussion of the question, when should a treaty of peace be considered broken? This the Greeks call a 'breach of faith'. It is, in fact, not the same thing to furnish a new cause for war and to break a treaty; but there is a great difference as regards both the penalty incurred by the one at fault and the relieving of the innocent party from his pledge in other matters. A treaty of peace is broken in three ways: by acting either contrary to what is involved in every peace, or against what was expressly stated in the treaty of peace, or against what ought to be understood from the nature of each kind of peace.

XXVIII. How a treaty of peace may be broken by acting contrary to what is contained in every peace

A violation of what is involved in every peace will take place if a warlike attack is made, that is, when no new cause occurs. If it can be alleged with probability, it is better to believe that the wrong was committed without faithlessness than with it. This statement of Thucydides hardly needs mention: 'Not those who ward off force with force break the peace, but those who are the first to make the attack.' Having established this point, we must see by whom, and against whom, the armed attack which breaks the peace is made. . . .

XXXIV. How a treaty of peace may be broken by acting contrary to what has been stated in the peace terms

As I have said, a treaty of peace is broken also by acting contrary to what has been stated in the peace terms. Under action, moreover, is included the failure to do what one should, and when one should. . . .

Chapter XXV: Conclusion, with Admonitions on behalf of Good Faith and Peace

I. Admonitions to preserve peace

<1> ... [B]efore I dismiss the reader I shall add a few admonitions which may be of value in war, and after war, for the preservation of good faith and of peace; just as in treating of the commencement of war I added certain admonitions regarding the avoidance of wars, so far as this can be accomplished. And good faith should be preserved, not only for other reasons but also in order that the hope of peace may not be done away with. For not only is every state sustained by good faith, as Cicero declares, but also that greater society of states. Aristotle (*Rhetoric*, I, xv) truly says that, if good faith has been taken away, 'all intercourse among men ceases to exist'....

II. In war peace should always be kept in view ...

III. And peace should also be accepted even at a loss, especially by Christians ...

IV. The consideration stated is useful to the conquered

This one consideration ought to be sufficient. However, human advantage also often draws in the same direction, first, those who are weaker, because a long contest with a stronger opponent is dangerous, and, just as on a ship, a greater misfortune must be avoided at some loss, with complete disregard of anger and hope which, as Livy has rightly said, are deceitful advisers. The thought is expressed by Aristotle thus: 'It is better to relinquish something of one's possessions to those who are stronger, than to be conquered in war and perish with the property.'

V. The consideration stated is also useful to the conqueror

Again, human advantage draws in the same direction also the stronger. The reason is, as the same Livy no less truly says, that peace is bounteous and creditable to those who grant it while their affairs are prosperous; and it is better and safer than a victory that is hoped for....

VI. The consideration stated is useful likewise to those whose fortunes are in doubt

But, if both sides seem to be equal to each other, this in truth, as Caesar (*Civil War*, I) says, is the best time to treat of peace, while each has confidence in himself.

VII. Peace, when made, must be kept with the utmost scruple

Moreover peace, whatever the terms on which it is made, ought to be preserved absolutely, on account of the sacredness of good faith, which I have mentioned; and not only should treachery be anxiously avoided, but everything else that may arouse anger. What Cicero said about private friendships you may apply to public friendships no less correctly: not only should all friendships be safeguarded with the greatest devotion and good faith, but especially those which have been restored to goodwill after enmity.

VIII. A prayer, and the end of the work

May God, who alone hath the power, inscribe these teachings on the hearts of those who hold sway over the Christian world. May He grant to them a mind possessing knowledge of divine and human law, and having ever before it the reflection that it hath been chosen as a servant for the rule of man, the living being most dear to God.

Part IV
Modern

33

Thomas Hobbes (1588–1679)

Solving the Problem of Civil War

> One may easily see how incompatible perpetual *War* is with the preservation of the human race or of individual men.
>
> *De cive*

Thomas Hobbes, widely regarded as one of the foremost political philosophers of the modern era, seemingly paid scant attention to the morality of warfare – whether its initiation or its conduct. Yet, he made a benchmark contribution to normative reflection on war. Indeed, it is not unreasonable to call Hobbes's philosophy a "philosophy of war" – not in the sense that he idealized war, but in the sense that he made its presence his philosophical point of departure.

Hobbes's political thought takes as its starting point the regrettable naturalness of civil war and proposes a remedy to its ubiquity. This remedy is described in terms of right, law, and contract, and is no doubt seen by its author as an *ethical* project. Thus – even if not explicitly – Hobbes sees the presence of war as a moral problem, requiring a moral solution. Indeed, Hobbes spent much of his career as a writer and thinker arguing forcefully that society must be organized so that civil war becomes obsolete.

Hobbes is one of several theorists in the seventeenth century to employ the concept of a *state of nature* as an important building block for political thought. The idea implies a consideration of human beings as they are naturally (apart from civil society), with the aim of erecting a theory about civil society and legitimate sovereignty.

Hobbes, influenced by events in his own time as well as elements of Augustinian and Protestant theology, argues that the state of nature is by definition a *state of war*. Against that background it is no exaggeration to say that he presents us with a bleak view of human nature and what it is capable of. The natural state of humankind is one of war, period.

For our purposes, there are several points to notice in the selections that follow from *The Elements of Law* (1640), *De cive* (1642), and *Leviathan* (1651).

A state of nature exists because there is no common sovereign. This means that between sovereign nations, a state of war *always* exists. Hobbes does not foresee or even discuss the possibility of an international body, along the lines of a "League of Nations," adjudicating disputes between sovereign states.

Hobbes's writings thus deal with the possibility of preventing war on the *domestic* level, not between states. According to Hobbes, each individual in the state of nature has a "right of nature" (or a "human right," as we would say today) to do what is necessary for the preservation of his or her life. The problem is that there is no sovereign to decide when one's preservation has actually been threatened. In the absence of a common standard or universal arbiter, fear leads individuals to preempt the actions of their fellows. This is why the state of nature degenerates into a state of war. Hence, Hobbes's right of nature is not a "human right" in the sense of a rightful claim with legal and/or moral force; it is simply the liberty human beings have in a condition where no legal or moral powers exist. Only by *giving up* this right or liberty, and by contracting to leave the state of nature through erecting a common sovereign, can the problem of civil war be solved.

The rules for setting up the envisaged contract (and for creating the ensuing sovereign power), Hobbes names "the laws of nature." The departure from the medieval, Catholic conception of natural law (known from Thomas Aquinas) – which had influenced early modern formulations of international law (as expressed by Vitoria, Suárez, and Grotius) – should be noted. Rejecting the medieval understanding of natural law, which held that natural law tells us what is right or wrong in light of man's highest good, Hobbes declares that, "there is no such *Finis ultimus* (utmost ayme) or *Summum Bonum* (greatest good) as is spoken of in the books of the old Morall Philosophers" (*Leviathan*, chap. 11, p. 70).[1] Instead, the law of nature is nothing more than a "Precept or generall Rule, found out by Reason" (*Leviathan*, chap. 14, p. 91), by which a man discerns what is apt to preserve his life and what may destroy it.

Hobbes thus claims to solve the problem of civil war. However, his solution was very much debated from the start. It seems to lend itself to brutal authoritarianism, which enraged Hobbes's liberal critics. On the other hand, his theory is radically centered on the rights or liberties of each individual (cf. the concept of the "right of nature"). This led many of his less liberal contemporaries to fear that the state of civil war can never actually be left behind, because even in the state of civil society each individual has a *right* to resist if he deems his life to be in danger. Hobbes was thus attacked from both sides of the political spectrum.

Importantly, and as already noted, while Hobbes "solves" the problem of civil war, he has no remedy for inter-state war. Indeed, he gives us a powerful realist explanation for its unavoidable existence: War is fueled by self-interest, and in the

---

[1] The page references here are to Richard Tuck's edition of *Leviathan* from 1991 (see note 5 below for details).

case of inter-state war, there is no authority to quell it. Therefore, as a matter of right, each sovereign state may wage war for its survival. Ethical concerns *per se*, restraining war, will merely be prudential rules for the preservation of one's own existence. Any deeper common ground or rationale for what we today call the "ethics of war" cannot be discerned in Hobbes's powerful and influential portrayal of international war.

However, one is left wondering why, in principle, the erection of an international sovereign is not possible. If the problem of civil war is solved by the monopolization of political power, why cannot a world government, or at least regional alliances, do something of the same work on the international level? Hobbes's answer is that since self-interest drives war, only an even more powerful entity can keep war in check and possibly abolish it. On the domestic level, such an entity can be erected, building on the natural fear of every human being in the state of nature, thus leading everyone to create a social contract. On the international level, Hobbes discerns no such mechanism. However, we should note that Hobbes does not view international anarchy as such an acute problem: Civil wars destroy community and peace among human beings, making the lives of human beings truly miserable. Wars between states, on the other hand, do not endanger civil society in the same way; they may even strengthen the feeling of community among human beings within the same state. Furthermore, the erection of alliances can render each state more secure both from and in war.[2] It is thus clear that, from the point of view of Hobbes's political philosophy, civil war is a much more problematic occurrence than international war.

The reader should notice in the following excerpts that war is portrayed equally much as a state of mind as the actual incidence of violent conflict. Being in a state of war does not imply being in constant conflict, but rather having to be in constant readiness for actual, physical war. Thus, Hobbes's philosophy of war and peace is very much a psychological teaching. However, given his pervasive materialism – encompassing even God and the human mind – the solution is formulated more as a set of mechanistic laws than as a traditional program of moral education.[3]

From *De Cive* (1642), chap. I, sections 2, 13–15[4]

2 The majority of previous writers on public Affairs either assume or seek to prove or simply assert that Man is an animal born fit for Society, – in the Greek phrase, *zoon politikon*. On this foundation they erect a structure of civil doctrine,

---

[2] See *De cive*, chap. I, section 13; and *Leviathan*, chap. XXV.

[3] We should point out that Thomas Hobbes is considered one of philosophy's best writers, expressing his thoughts in an engaging and often dramatic style. To convey a real sense of authenticity, the selections from *Leviathan* below use Hobbes's own spelling, capitalization, and punctuation – and the other selections also preserve much of Hobbes's original, inimitable style.

[4] From Thomas Hobbes, *On the Citizen*, trans. and ed. Richard Tuck and Michael Silverthorne (Cambridge: Cambridge University Press, 1998), pp. 21–2, 23–4, 30–1.

as if no more were necessary for the preservation of peace and the governance of the whole human race than for men to give their consent to certain agreements and conditions which, without further thought, these writers call laws. This Axiom, though very widely accepted, is nevertheless false; the error proceeds from a superficial view of human nature. Closer observation of the causes why men seek each other's company and enjoy associating with each other, will easily reach the conclusion that it does not happen because by nature it could not be otherwise, but by chance. For if man naturally loved his fellow man, loved him, I mean, as his fellow man, there is no reason why everyone would not love every-one equally as equally men; or why every man would rather seek the company of men whose society is more prestigious and useful to him than to others. By nature, then, we are not looking for friends but for honour or advantage (*commodum*) from them. . . . So clear is it from experience to anyone who gives any serious attention to human behaviour, that every voluntary encounter is a product either of mutual need or of the pursuit of glory; hence when people meet, what they are anxious to get is either an advantage for themselves or what is called [in Greek] *eudokimein*, which is reputation and honour among their companions. Reason reaches the same conclusions from the actual definitions of *Will, Good, Honour* and *Interest* (*Utilis*). For since a society is a voluntary arrangement, what is sought in every society is an Object of will, i.e. something which seems to each one of the members to be Good for himself. Whatever seems Good is pleasant, and affects either the organs (of the body) or the mind. Every pleasure of the mind is either glory (or a good opinion of oneself), or ultimately relates to glory; the others are sensual or lead to something sensual, and can all be comprised under the name of advantages. All society, therefore, exists for the sake either of advantage or of glory, i.e. it is a product of love of self, not of love of friends. However, no large or lasting society can be based upon the passion for glory. The reason is that glorying, like honour, is nothing if everybody has it, since it consists in comparison and preeminence; nor does association (*societas*) with others increase one's reason for glorying in oneself, since a man is worth as much as he can do without relying on anyone else. It is true that the advantages of this life can be increased with other people's help. But this is much more effectively achieved by Dominion over others than by their help. Hence no one should doubt that, in the absence of fear, men would be more avidly attracted to domination than to society. One must therefore lay it down that the origin of large and lasting societies lay not in mutual human benevolence but in men's mutual fear. . . .

13 One may easily see how incompatible perpetual *War* is with the preserva-tion of the human race or of individual men. Yet a war which cannot be brought to an end by victory because of the equality of the contestants is by its nature perpetual; for the victors themselves are so constantly threatened by danger that it must be regarded as a miracle if even the strongest survives to die of years and old age. The present century presents an example of this in the Americans. Past centuries show us nations, now civilized and flourishing, whose inhabitants then were few, savage, short lived, poor and mean, and lacked all the comforts and amenities of life which *peace* and society afford. Anyone who believes that one should remain in that state, in which all is allowed to all, is contradicting himself; for by natural necessity every man seeks his own good, but no one believes that the *war* of all against all which naturally belongs to such a state, is good for him. And so it comes about that we are driven by mutual fear to believe that we must emerge from such a state and seek allies (*socii*); so that if we must have *war*, it will not be a war against all men nor without aid.

14 Allies are acquired either by force or by consent: by force when the victor in a conflict compels the vanquished to serve him by fear of death, or by taking him prisoner; by consent, when an association (*societas*) for mutual assistance is made with the consent of both parties, without violence. And the victor may *rightly* compel the vanquished (as a strong and healthy person may compel the sick or an adult an infant) to give a guarantee of future obedience, unless he prefers to die. For since the *right* of protecting ourselves at our own discretion proceeds from our danger, and the danger arises from equality, it is more rational and gives more assurance of our preservation if we make use of our present advantage to build the security we seek for ourselves by taking a guarantee, than to attempt to recover it later with all the risks of conflict when the enemy has grown in numbers and strength and escaped from our power. And from the other side it is the height of absurdity, when you have him in your power in feeble condition, to make him strong again as well as hostile by letting him go. From this another corollary follows, that in the natural state of men, *sure and irresistible power gives the right of ruling and commanding those who cannot resist*; so that the right to do anything whatsoever is an essential and direct attribute of omnipotence.

15 However, because of their natural equality of strength and of the other human faculties, men in the state of nature, i.e. men who live in a state of war, cannot expect long preservation. *Therefore, to seek peace when some hope of having peace exists, and to seek aid for war when peace cannot be had, is a dictate of right reason*, i.e. *a law of Nature*.

From *Leviathan* (1651), chaps. 13 and 14[5]

13 . . . Whatsoever therefore is consequent to a time of Warre, where every man is Enemy to every man; the same is consequent to the time, wherein men live without other security, than what their own strength, and their own invention shall furnish them withall. In such condition, there is no place for Industry;

---

[5] From Thomas Hobbes, *Leviathan*, ed. Richard Tuck (Cambridge: Cambridge University Press, 1991), pp. 89–91. *Leviathan* was originally written and published in English, as was *The Elements of Law*, while *De cive* was originally written and published in Latin.

because the fruit thereof is uncertain: and consequently no Culture of the Earth; no Navigation, nor use of the commodities that may be imported by Sea; no commodious Building; no Instruments of moving, and removing such things as require much force; no Knowledge of the face of the Earth; no account of Time; no Arts; no Letters; no Society; and which is worst of all, continuall feare, and danger of violent death; And the life of man, solitary, poore, nasty, brutish, and short.

It may seem strange, to some man that has not well weighed these things, that Nature should thus dissociate, and render men apt to invade, and destroy one another: and he may, therefore, not trusting to this Inference, made from the Passions, desire perhaps to have the same confirmed by Experience. Let him therefore consider with himselfe, when taking a journey, he armes himselfe, and seeks to go well accompanied; when going to sleep, he locks his dores; when even in his house he locks his chests; and this when he knowes there bee Lawes, and publike Officers, armed, to revenge all injuries shall bee done him; what opinion he has of his fellow subjects, when he rides armed; of his fellow Citizens, when he locks his dores; and of his children, and servants, when he locks his chests. Does he not there as much accuse mankind by his actions, as I do by my words? But neither of us accuse mans nature in it. The Desires, and other Passions of man, are in themselves no Sin. No more are the Actions, that proceed from those Passions, till they know a Law that forbids them: which till Lawes be made they cannot know: nor can any Law be made, till they have agreed upon the Person that shall make it.

It may peradventure be thought, there was never such a time, nor condition of warre as this; and I believe it was never generally so, over all the world: but there are many places, where they live so now. For the savage people in many places of *America*, except the government of small Families, the concord whereof dependeth on naturall lust, have no government at all; and live at this day in that brutish manner, as I said before. Howsoever, it may be perceived what manner of life there would be, where there were no common Power to feare; by the manner of life, which men that have formerly lived under a peacefull government, use to degenerate into, in a civill Warre.

But though there had never been any time, wherein particular men were in a condition of warre one against another; yet in all times, Kings, and Persons of Soveraigne authority, because of their Independency, are in continuall jealousies, and in the state and posture of Gladiators; having their weapons pointing, and their eyes fixed on one another; that is, their Forts, Garrisons, and Guns upon the Frontiers of their Kingdomes; and continuall Spyes upon their neighbours, which is a posture of War. But because they uphold thereby, the Industry of their Subjects; there does not follow from it, that misery, which accompanies the Liberty of particular men.

To this warre of every man against every man this also is consequent; that nothing can be Unjust. The notions of Right and Wrong, Justice and Injustice have there no place. Where there is no common Power, there is no Law: where no Law, no Injustice. Force, and Fraud, are in warre the two Cardinall vertues. Justice, and Injustice are none of the Faculties neither of the Body, nor Mind. If they were, they might be in a man that were alone in the world, as well as his Senses, and Passions. They are Qualities, that relate to men in Society, not in Solitude. It is consequent also to the same condition, that there be no Propriety, no Dominion, no *Mine* and *Thine* distinct; but onely that to be every mans, that he can get; and for so long, as he can keep it. And thus much for the ill condition, which man by meer Nature is actually placed in; though with a possibility to come out of it, consisting partly in the Passions, partly in his Reason.

The Passions that encline men to Peace, are Feare of Death; Desire of such things as are necessary to commodious living; and a Hope by their Industry to obtain them. And Reason suggesteth convenient Articles of Peace, upon which men may be drawn to agreement. These Articles, are they, which otherwise are called the Lawes of Nature: whereof I shall speak more particularly, in the two following Chapters.

14 The RIGHT OF NATURE, which Writers commonly call *Jus Naturale*, is the Liberty each man hath, to use his own power, as he will himselfe, for the preservation of his own Nature; that is to say, of his own Life; and consequently, of doing any thing, which in his own Judgement, and Reason, hee shall conceive to be the aptest means thereunto.

By LIBERTY, is understood, according to the proper signification of the word, the absence of externall Impediments: which Impediments, may oft take away part of a mans power to do what hee would; but cannot hinder him from using the power left him, according as his judgement, and reason shall dictate to him.

A LAW OF NATURE, (*Lex Naturalis*,) is a Precept, or generall Rule, found out by Reason, by which a man is forbidden to do, that, which is destructive of his life, or taketh away the means of preserving the same; and to omit, that, by which he thinketh it may be best preserved. For though they that speak of this subject, use to confound *Jus*, and *Lex*, *Right* and *Law*; yet they ought to be distinguished; because RIGHT, consisteth in liberty to do, or to forbeare; Whereas LAW, determineth, and bindeth to one of them: so that Law, and Right, differ as much, as Obligation, and Liberty; which in one and the same matter are inconsistent.

The actual conduct of war may seem to fall under the general description of the state of nature, namely, a condition in which there is no right or wrong. Yet, in his "Review and Conclusion" to *Leviathan*, Hobbes does outline the obligation of soldiers, describing it as a "law of nature." This obligation to one's sovereign lasts only as long, however, as the sovereign can reasonably be said to be a protector. For soldiers, that obligation must be understood to last longer than for other men; yet, it has its limits.

Hobbes adds an interesting warning about glorifying the origins – i.e. the mode of acquisition – of one's commonwealth, since such origins in most cases would legitimize any new rebellion. The justification of political authority should instead come from its ability to protect and keep the peace within a territory, not from its military prowess in winning that territory.

From *Leviathan,* "Review & Conclusion"[6]

To the Laws of Nature, declared in the 15. Chapter, I would have this added, *That every man is bound by Nature, as much as in him lieth, to protect in Warre, the Authority, by which he is himself protected in time of peace.* For he that pretendeth a Right of Nature to preserve his owne body, cannot pretend a Right of Nature to destroy him, by whose strength he is preserved: It is a manifest contradiction of himselfe. And though this Law may bee drawn by consequence, from some of those that are there already mentioned; yet the Times require to have it inculcated, and remembered.

And because I find by divers English Books lately printed, that the Civill warres have not yet sufficiently taught men, in what point of time it is, that a Subject becomes obliged to the Conquerour; nor what is Conquest; nor how it comes about, that it obliges men to obey his Laws: Therefore for farther satisfaction on men therein, I say, the point of time, wherein a man becomes subject to a Conquerour, is that point, wherein having liberty to submit to him, he consenteth, either by expresse words, or by other sufficient sign, to be his Subject. When it is that a man hath the liberty to submit, I have shewed before . . . namely, that for him that hath no obligation to his former Soveraign but that of an ordinary Subject, it is then, when the means of his life is within the Guards and Garrisons of the Enemy; for it is then, that he hath no longer Protection from him, but is protected by the adverse party for his Contribution. Seeing therefore such contribution is every where, as a thing inevitable, (not withstanding it be an assistance to the Enemy), esteemed lawfull; a totall submission, which is but an assistance to the Enemy, cannot be esteemed unlawful. Besides, if a man consider that they who submit, assist the Enemy but with part of their estates, whereas they that refuse, assist him with the whole, there is no reason to call their Submission, or Composition an Assistance; but rather a Detriment to the Enemy. But if a man, besides the obligation of a Subject, hath taken upon him a new obligation of a Souldier, then he hath not the liberty to submit to a new Power, as long as the old one keeps the field, and giveth him means of subsistence, either in his Armies, or Garrisons: for in this case, he cannot complain of want of Protection, and means to live as a Souldier: But when that also failes, a Souldier

---

[6]   Ibid., pp. 484–5, 486.

also may seek his Protection wheresoever he has most hope to have it; and may lawfully submit himself to his new Master. . . .

. . . [T]hey will all of them justifie the War, by which their Power was at first gotten, and whereon (as they think) their Right dependeth, and not on the Possession. As if, for example, the Right of the Kings of England did depend on the goodnesse of the cause of William the Conqueror, and upon their lineall, and directest Descent from him; by which means, there would perhaps be no tie of the Subjects obedience to their Soveraign at this day in all the world: wherein whilest they needlessly think to justifie themselves, they justifie all the successefull Rebellions that Ambition shall at any time after raise against them, and their Successors. Therefore I put down for one of the most effectuall seeds of the Death of any State, that the Conquerors require not onely a Submission of mens actions to them for the future, but also an Approbation of all their actions past; when there is scarce a Common-wealth in the world, whose beginnings can in conscience be justified.

Finally, Hobbes in an earlier work describes the rudiments of a *ius in bello* based on ideas of honor and dishonor. In war, the press of necessity and individual judgment as to the defense of one's life and person are decisive. Yet, in actually securing one's life, violent and brutal behavior is often counterproductive, as Hobbes also claims is true of civil society when he lays out the "laws of nature" in both *De cive* and *Leviathan*. When it comes to war, men who wish to come across as courageous or magnanimous often restrain their brutality, since they do not want to display their fear – that animating passion which may lead men to peace (cf. *De cive* and *Leviathan*), but which also causes men to be violent and brutal in a state of war.

From *The Elements of Law* (1640), pt. I, chap. XIX, sections 1–2[7]

1 . . . [I]t hath been shewed, that the opinions men have of the rewards and punishments which are to follow their actions, are the causes that make and govern the will to those actions. In this estate of man therefore, wherein all men are equal, and every man allowed to be his own judge, the fears they have one of another are equal, and every man's hopes consist in his own sleight and strength; and consequently when any man by his natural passion, is provoked to break these laws of nature, there is no security in any other man of his own defence but

---

[7] From Thomas Hobbes, *The Elements of Law National and Politic: Human Nature and De Corpore Politico*, ed. J. C. A. Gaskin (Oxford: Oxford University Press, 1994), pp. 103–4. "Human Nature" and "De corpore politico" are the two constituent parts of *The Elements of Law* – the excerpts here are from the first of those two parts.

anticipation. And for this cause, every man's right (howsoever he be inclined to peace) of doing whatsoever seemeth good in his own eyes, remaineth with him still, as the necessary means of his preservation. And therefore till there be security amongst men for the keeping of the law of nature one towards another, men are still in the estate of war, and nothing is unlawful to any man that tendeth to his own safety or commodity; and this safety and commodity consisteth in the mutual aid and help one of another, whereby also followeth the mutual fear of one another.

2 It is a proverbial saying, *inter arma silent leges*. There is little therefore to be said concerning the laws that men are to observe one towards another in time of war, wherein every man's being and well-being is the rule of his actions. Yet thus much the law of nature commandeth in war: that men satiate not the cruelty of their present passions, whereby in their own conscience they foresee no benefit to come. For that betrayeth not a necessity, but a disposition of the mind to war, which is against the law of nature. And in old time we read that rapine was a trade of life, wherein nevertheless many of them that used it, did not only spare the lives of those they invaded, but left them also such things, as were necessary to preserve that life which they had given them; as namely their oxen and instruments for tillage, though they carried away all their other cattle and substance. And as the rapine itself was warranted in the law of nature, by the want of security otherwise to maintain themselves; so the exercise of cruelty was forbidden by the same law of nature, unless fear suggested anything to the contrary. For nothing but fear can justify the taking away of another's life. And because fear can hardly be made manifest, but by some action dishonorable, that bewrayeth [i.e. betrays] the conscience of one's own weakness; all men in whom the passion of courage or magnanimity have been predominated, have abstained from cruelty, insomuch that though there be in war no law, the breach whereof is injury, yet there are those laws, the breach whereof is dishonour. In one word, therefore, the only law of actions in war is honour; and the right of war providence.

34

Baruch Spinoza (1632–1677)

The Virtue of Peace

[P]eace is not just the absence of war, but a virtue which comes from strength of mind.

Political Treatise

Spinoza's views on the ethics of war and peace can be inferred first and foremost from his political writings. His last and unfinished work, the *Political Treatise* (*Tractatus Politicus*, 1677), from which the extract below is taken, elucidates the political implications of his more famous works, the *Ethics* and the *Theological-Political Treatise*. In its subtitle, the *Political Treatise* announces that the work will show "how a community . . . should be organized if it is not to degenerate into a Tyranny, and if the Peace and Freedom of its citizens is to remain inviolate."[1] Living in a society torn by civil unrest, Spinoza, much like his contemporary Thomas Hobbes, aimed to show how political philosophy could chart a path toward domestic peace and security. Yet, in contrast to Hobbes, Spinoza emphasized how this goal would have to be achieved in ways compatible with human freedom and sociability. Peace can never be secured by political power or military prowess alone.

In the passage below, we find Spinoza combining three themes that run through his political philosophy: the importance of good laws and institutions, the indispensability of reason and virtue, and respect for human freedom. Moreover, in line with much of modern philosophy (and in contradistinction to what had gone before) Spinoza maintained that the challenge of peace involves first and foremost the establishment of a sound social and political organization, rather than the inculcation of morality or religious piety on an individual level.

In his own day, Spinoza, like Hobbes, was often criticized for holding atheistic and subversive views. In Spinoza's case, the stigmatization was even more effective

---

[1] *Spinoza, Complete Works*, trans. Samuel Shirley, ed. Michael Morgan (Indianapolis: Hackett Publishing, 2002). The editors are grateful to Kristoffer Lidén, who, as our research assistant, helped to prepare this chapter.

than with Hobbes, and he ended up having little influence on his contemporaries and indeed for a significant time after his death. Over the last century, however, Spinoza has been eagerly studied, and his ideas about power and freedom have fascinated many.

From *Political Treatise*, chap. 5, sections 1–6[2]

[1] [A] man is most completely in control of his own right when he is most guided by reason, and consequently . . . a commonwealth is most powerful and most completely in control of its own right if it is founded on and guided by reason. Now since the best method of ensuring that one preserves oneself as far as possible is to live in the way that reason prescribes, it follows that those actions are the best which are done by a man or commonwealth when it is most completely in control of its own right. We are not asserting that everything that is done by right is also done in the best way; it is one thing to till a field by right, another thing to till it in the best way. It is one thing, I say, to defend oneself, to preserve oneself, to give judgment, etc., by right, another thing to defend and preserve oneself in the best way and to give the best judgment. Consequently, it is one thing to rule and to take charge of public affairs by right, another thing to rule in the best way and to direct public affairs in the best way. . . .

[2] The best way to organise a state is easily discovered by considering the purpose of civil order, which is nothing other than peace and security of life. Therefore the best state is one where men live together in harmony and where the laws are preserved unbroken. For it is certain that rebellions, wars, and contempt for or violation of the laws are to be attributed not so much to the wickedness of subjects as to the faulty organisation of the state. Men are not born to be citizens, but are made so. Furthermore, men's natural passions are everywhere the same; so if wickedness is more prevalent and wrongdoing more frequent in one commonwealth than in another, one can be sure that this is because the former has not done enough to promote harmony and has not framed its laws with sufficient forethought, and thus it has not attained the full right of a commonwealth. For a civil order that has not removed the causes of rebellion and where the threat of war is never absent and the laws are frequently broken is little different from a state of Nature, where every man lives as he pleases with his life at risk.

[3] But just as the vices of subjects and their excessive license and willfulness are to be laid at the door of the commonwealth, so on the other hand their virtue and steadfast obedience to the laws must be attributed chiefly to the virtue and the absolute right of the commonwealth. . . . Hence it is deservedly regarded as a remarkable virtue in Hannibal that there was never a mutiny in his army.

---

[2] Ibid., pp. 698–700.

[4] A commonwealth whose subjects are deterred from taking up arms only through fear should be said to be not at war rather than to be enjoying peace. For peace is not just the absence of war, but a virtue which comes from strength of mind; for obedience is the steadfast will to carry out orders enjoined by the general decree of the commonwealth. Anyway, a commonwealth whose peace depends on the sluggish spirit of its subjects who are led like sheep to learn simply to be slaves can more properly be called a desert than a commonwealth.

[5] So when we say that the best state is one where men pass their lives in harmony, I am speaking of human life, which is characterised not just by the circulation of the blood and other features common to all animals, but especially by reason, the true virtue and life of the mind.

[6] But be it noted that in speaking of the state as being established to this end, I meant one established by a free people, not dominion over a people acquired by right of war. For a free people is led more by hope than by fear, while a subjugated people is led more by fear than by hope; the former seeks to engage in living, the latter simply to avoid death. The former, I say, seeks to live for itself, the latter is forced to belong to a conqueror; hence we say that the latter is a slave, the former is free. So the aim of a state that has been acquired by right of war is to dominate and to have slaves rather than subjects. And although, if we have regard to their right in a general way, there is no essential difference between a state created by a free people and one acquired by right of war, their aims, as we have just shown, are very different, and so too are the means by which each must be preserved.

35

Samuel von Pufendorf (1632–1694)

War in an Emerging System of States

> We have to regard any man who is not our fellow-citizen, or with whom we live in a state of nature, not indeed as our enemy, but as a friend we cannot wholly rely on.
>
> *On the Duty of Man and Citizen*

Samuel Freiherr von Pufendorf is one of the first – and quickly became one of the most influential – post-Westphalian writers to address the question of ethics and war. He shows confidence in the emerging state system's ability to create order and stability, and he thus comes across as more optimistic than Thomas Hobbes, who put little faith in the ability of states to live peacefully with each other.

Pufendorf's seeming optimism comes from his belief in a God-willed natural law, which commands men to be "sociable" (*sociabilis*) and other-regarding. This is, however, not something human beings do naturally or automatically. As fallen beings – Pufendorf was a Lutheran and strongly believed in the deleterious effects of the fall – we are given to the pursuit of self-interest.

In order to make it possible for human beings to live "sociably" nonetheless, God has decreed certain duties (*officii*), known as "natural law," that take their content from the basic fact of our common humanity. These duties must be submitted to if we are to live in peace and security. Pufendorf sets out to explain what these duties are, and he emphasizes that they include rules of war. While similar to Hobbes's laws of nature in being rules devised to secure life in peace, they have more clearly a *moral* content, and they are more explicitly presented as the work of a good God.

Pufendorf's idea of human "sociability" leads to a strong emphasis not only on formal duties, but on the virtues needed to fulfill those duties. Pufendorf thus stresses the character traits that should be fostered, even in war, and he reminds us of the limits we ought to respect in order not to "lose our humanity" (see *On the Duty of Man and Citizen*, bk. II, chap. 16, section 6). Pufendorf likewise claims that there are virtues not only of individuals but of institutions as well. The formal function of a state is to preserve sociability and peacefulness among its citizens and inhabitants – and as far as possible in relation to other states. As such, the state and its institutions are morally legitimate entities with rights and duties.

In order to preserve itself and its people, and in order to punish wrongdoers, the state can authorize actions that no individual in the condition of civil society has any right to perform. This is what keeps the system of states in balance: the right to use armed force against each other, and to punish and if necessary destroy evildoers.[1] This is an absolute right of the state, and in marked contrast to St. Augustine's oft-quoted assertion that states are nothing but bands of robbers, Pufendorf forcefully defends the state's *moral* right to use violent force (see *The Law of Nature and Nations*, bk. VIII, chap. 6, section 9). However, even in dealing with evildoers and enemies, promises must be kept, and the procurement of goods such as reparation after a war should preferably be secured by agreement, so that the other side will not be able justly to take their property back by force at a later date (see *On the Duty of Man and Citizen*, bk. II, chap. 16, section 13).

This double emphasis on sociability and humanity on the one hand, and the moral and political legitimacy of the state on the other, leads to a relative lack of attention to the requirements of *ius in bello*. When another state has acted in a way that makes it liable to be attacked, there are, strictly speaking, no legal or moral limits to what may be done to avenge the injury. Pufendorf does think, however, that there are *prudential* limits to what one should do in war. These arise from the need to preserve one's own humanity, and from the fact that the other side will be more likely to seek revenge if one acts in a violent and unrestrained way. One should therefore limit the acts of violence to those that are actually necessary. Beyond this, Pufendorf gives us no detailed provisions for such concerns as the defense of non-combatants or the treatment of prisoners of war, beyond references (with approval) to what Grotius had written. The latter is of course not insignificant; yet, it should be noted that Pufendorf feels little need personally to enlarge on these themes. Individual virtue and political necessity provide the most important restraints that are needed.

Pufendorf distinguishes between declared and undeclared wars without denouncing all wars within the latter category as necessarily unjust (cf. *On the Duty of Man and Citizen*, bk. II, chap. 16, section 7). However, his legalistic approach to politics and institutions suggests that a formal declaration of war is always to be preferred; yet, there may be cases where a party acts firmly within the just causes for going

---

[1] Seven decades later, in his *Spirit of the Laws* (bk. XIII, chap. 17) Montesquieu would challenge this assertion by pointing to the arms race as a logical and lamentable side effect of the system of independent sovereign states. See chap. 38, this volume, on Montesquieu; see also James Tully's introduction to Pufendorf's *On the Duty of Man and Citizen* (Cambridge: Cambridge University Press, 1991), p. xxxvii.

to war (see ibid., section 2), while not being *able* to declare the war formally. Although Pufendorf does not clearly say so, we can surmise that the latter can be the case in civil wars, where one party may have a fully just cause for resorting to armed force without possessing the formal authority to do so.

Finally, Pufendorf emphasizes that rulers have a duty to prevent their subjects from engaging in criminal acts of violence against foreigners (see ibid., section 9). Such acts, if sufficiently grave, may legitimately be countered by a declaration of war, even if the ruler in the state that the evildoers operate from, or its state apparatus, did not order the evildoing. This is the same line of argument recently adopted by the administration of George W. Bush in countering terrorism: States that knowingly harbor or aid terrorists, even without taking part in terrorist attacks themselves, must be considered enemies and are thus liable to be attacked.

From *On the Duty of Man and Citizen* (1673), bk. II, chap. 1, "On Man's Natural State"[2]

9 ... To put the matter in a few words, in the state of nature each is protected only by his own strength; in the state by the strength of all. There no one may be sure of the fruit of his industry; here all may be. There is the reign of the passions, there there is war, fear, poverty, nastiness, solitude, barbarity, ignorance, savagery; here is the reign of reason, here there is peace, security, wealth, splendour, society, taste, knowledge, benevolence.

10 In the natural state, if one does not do for another what is due by agreement, or does him wrong, or if a dispute arises in other ways, there is no one who can by authority compel the offender to perform his part of the agreement or make restitution, as is possible in states, where one may implore the aid of a common judge. But as nature does not allow one to plunge into war on the slightest provocation, even when one is fully convinced of the justice of his cause, an attempt must first be made to settle the matter by gentler means, namely, by friendly discussion between the parties and an absolute (not conditional) mutual promise or by appeal to the decision of arbitrators.

Such arbitrators must be fair to both sides and not show prejudice or favour in giving their verdict; they must look only at the merits of the case. For the same reason a man is not appointed as arbitrator in a case in which he has greater expectation of benefit or glory from the victory of one of the parties than from the other, and so has an interest in one party winning the case no matter how. So there must be no agreement or promise between the arbitrator and the parties, to oblige him to pronounce in favour of one rather than the other. . . .

---

[2]   From Samuel Pufendorf, *On the Duty of Man and Citizen According to Natural Law*, ed. James Tully, trans. Michael Silverthorne (Cambridge: Cambridge University Press, 1991), pp. 118, 119. The full title of the original is *De officio hominis et civis iuxta legem naturalem libri duo*.

11 Nature herself has willed that there should be a kind of kinship among men, by force of which it is wrong to harm another man and indeed right for everyone to work for the benefit of others. However, kinship usually has a rather weak force among those who live in natural liberty with each other. Consequently, we have to regard any man who is not our fellow-citizen, or with whom we live in a state of nature, not indeed as our enemy, but as a friend we cannot wholly rely on. The reason is that men not only can do each other very great harm, but do very often wish to do so for various reasons. Some are driven to injure others by their wickedness of character, or by lust for power and superfluous wealth. Others, though men of moderation, take up arms to preserve themselves and not to be forestalled by others. Many find themselves in conflict because they are competing for the same object, others through rivalry of talents. Hence in the natural state there is a lively and all but perpetual play of suspicion, distrust, eagerness to subvert the strength of others, and desire to get ahead of them or to augment one's own strength by their ruin. Therefore as a good man should be content with his own and not trouble others or covet their goods, so a cautious man who loves his own security will believe all men his friends but liable at any time to become enemies; he will keep peace with all, knowing that it may soon be exchanged for war. This is the reason why that country is considered happy which even in peace contemplates war.

From *On the Duty of Man and Citizen,* bk. II, chap. 16, "On War and Peace"[3]

1 It is most agreeable to natural law that men should live in peace with each other by doing of their own accord what their duty requires; indeed peace itself is a state peculiar to man, insofar as he is distinct from the beasts. Nevertheless, for man too war is sometimes permitted, and occasionally necessary, namely when by the ill will of another we cannot preserve our property or obtain our right without the use of force. In this situation, however, good sense and humanity counsel us not to resort to arms when more evil than good is likely to overtake us and ours by the prosecution of our wrongs.

2 The just causes of engaging in war come down to the preservation and protection of our lives and property against unjust attack, or the collection of what is due to us from others but has been denied, or the procurement of reparations for wrong inflicted and of assurance for the future. Wars waged for the first of these causes are said to be defensive, for the other causes, offensive.

3 One should not have immediate recourse to arms as soon as one thinks oneself wronged, particularly so long as there remains some doubt about right or fact. One should explore the possibility of amicable settlement of the matter by

---

[3]   Ibid., pp. 168–72.

various means, for example by initiating dialogue between the parties, by appealing to an arbitrator, or by submitting the question to lot. The claimant particularly is obliged to try this method, since there is in any case a predisposition to favour possession with some title.

4 Unjust causes of war are either openly such or have some plausible pretext, however weak. Open causes come down to two main types: avarice and ambition, namely lust for wealth and lust for power. Those covered by pretexts are various: they include fear of the wealth and power of a neighbour, unjustified aggrandizement, desire for better territory, refusal of something which is simply and straightforwardly owed, stupidity on the part of a possessor, a desire to extinguish another's legitimately acquired right which the aggressor finds rather inconvenient, and others of this kind.

5 The most proper forms of action in war are force and terror. But one has equal right to use fraud and deceit against an enemy, provided one does not violate one's pledged faith. Hence one may deceive an enemy by false statements or fictitious stories, but never by promises or agreements.

6 As for force used in war against an enemy and his property, one must distinguish between what an enemy may suffer without wrong and what we ourselves may inflict without loss of humanity. When a man has declared himself my enemy, he has by that fact made known his intention to inflict the last degree of suffering on me, and by that same fact he grants me, so far as he can, an unlimited right against himself. Humanity however requires that so far as the momentum of warfare permits, we should inflict no more suffering on an enemy than defence or vindication of our right and its future assurance requires.

7 War is normally divided into two forms: declared and undeclared. There are two necessary conditions of a declared war: first that it be waged by the authority of the sovereigns on both sides, and secondly that it be preceded by a declaration. Undeclared war is either war waged without formal declaration or war against private citizens. Civil wars also are in this category.

8 The right of initiating war in a state lies with the sovereign. It is beyond the capacity of an official to exercise that right without the authority delegated to him by the sovereign to do so, even in a situation in which he infers that the sovereign, if consulted, would decide upon immediate war. However, all who have charge of a province or fortified place with military forces under their command are understood to be obliged by the nature of their office to repel an invading enemy from the area entrusted to them by whatever means they can. But they should not without grave cause move the war on to the enemy's territory.

9 Whereas one who lives in natural liberty may be pursued in war only for wrongs he has committed himself, in civil society the ruler of a state or the state as a whole is often attacked, even though he or it was not the source of the wrong. But for this to be justified, it is essential that the wrong pass in some way to the ruler. And in fact rulers of states do share in wrongs committed by their long-settled citizens or by those who have recently taken refuge with them, if the rulers allowed the commission of the wrongs or provide refuge. For such allowance to be culpable, there must be a knowledge of the crime and ability to prevent it. Rulers are presumed to be aware of the open and habitual actions of their citizens, and there is always a presumption of their ability to prevent them, unless there is obvious evidence of its absence. However, the right to make war upon a ruler who accepts and protects a delinquent, who is seeking refuge with him solely to escape punishment, arises more from particular agreements between neighbours and allies than from any common obligation. This is not the case, however, if the refugee while with us is planning hostilities against the state he has left.

10 It is also accepted among nations that the goods of private citizens may be held for a debt which is properly the state's or for something which the state confiscated without observing the requirements of justice, so that foreigners to whom the debt is due may impound any goods of citizens from the debtor state which they find on their own territories. In such cases, however, the citizens whose goods have been taken in this way should obtain restitution from the actual debtors. Such exactions are known as reprisals and are frequently preludes to war.

11 One may wage war on another's behalf as well as for oneself. This is justified where the party for whom one is going to war has a just cause, and where the party coming to aid has a reasonable ground for conducting hostilities on his behalf against the third party.

The first among those for whom we not only may but should take up arms are our subjects both as a whole and as individuals, provided that the state would not evidently be involved in greater suffering as a result. Then come allies who have a treaty which includes this provision. However, they yield precedence to our own citizens, if the latter need our help at the same moment; and it is assumed that they have a just cause of war and that they are showing some prudence in undertaking it. Next in order are friends, even if no such specific promise has been given them. And finally, where no other ground exists, kinship alone may suffice for us to go to the defence of an oppressed party who makes a plea for assistance, so far as we conveniently may.

12 The extent of licence in war is such that, however far one may have gone beyond the bounds of humanity in slaughter or in wasting and plundering property, the opinion of nations does not hold one in infamy nor as deserving of being shunned by honest men. However, the more civilized nations condemn certain ways of inflicting harm on an enemy: for instance, the use of poison or bribing the citizens or soldiers of other rulers to assassinate them.

13 Movable property is considered to be captured from the moment that it is beyond enemy pursuit, immovable property when we hold it so effectively as to have the ability to keep the enemy off it. However, the condition of the absolute extinction of the former owner's right of recovery is his renunciation by subsequent agreement of all claim to it. Otherwise what is ours by force may be taken back by force.

As soldiers fight by the authority of the state, so what they take from the enemy is acquired for the state, not for themselves. However, it is a universal practice that movable property, especially if of no great value, is tacitly left to the soldiers who took it, either as a reward, or sometimes in lieu of pay, or to give incentive to men to put their lives on the line without compulsion.

When captured property is taken back from an enemy, immovable property returns to its former owners. So too should movable property, but among most peoples it is left to the soldiers as booty.

14 Rule over conquered peoples as over individuals is also won by war. For it to be legitimate and binding upon the consciences of subjects, the conquered must swear loyalty to the conquerors and the conquerors give up their state of enmity and hostile intention towards the conquered.

15 Acts of war are suspended by a truce, which is an agreement to refrain from acts of war for a period of time, without ending the state of war or settling the dispute from which the war started. When the period of the truce has expired, there is a return to a state of war without a new declaration, unless peace has been made in the meantime.

16 Truces may be divided into those which are made with the armies remaining in the field and fighting readiness maintained on both sides (the period of such truces is fairly short), and truces in which fighting readiness is disbanded on both sides. The latter may be made for quite long periods of time and normally are; they have the appearance of complete peace, and sometimes are even termed peace with the specification of a fixed period of time. For otherwise every peace is assumed to be perpetual and to lay permanently to rest the disputes from which the war broke out. The arrangements normally called tacit truces impose no obligation; in such cases the parties remain quiet on both sides at their discretion and may resume acts of war whenever they so please.

17 A war is definitively ended only when peace is ratified by the sovereigns on both sides. Both the parties to the agreement must define its terms and conditions, and have equally the obligation to put them into effect at the agreed time, and to observe them faithfully. To assure this, an oath is normally included and hostages given, and often other parties, particularly those who take part in the peacemaking, accept the duty of ensuring compliance by promising aid to the party which is injured by the other contrary to the terms of the peace.

From *The Law of Nature and Nations* (1672), bk. VIII, chap. 6[4]

7 ... [N]ot only may I use force against an enemy until I have warded off the peril with which he threatened me, or have received or extorted from him what

---

[4]   From Samuel Pufendorf, *De jure naturae et gentium libri octo*, vol. 2, trans. C. H. and W. A. Oldfather (Oxford: Clarendon Press, 1934), pp. 1298–9, 1301. This is Pufendorf's longest and most elaborate work on natural and international law.

he had unjustly robbed me of, or refused to furnish, but I can also proceed so far as to secure guarantees for the future. And if he allows that to be forced from him, he shows clearly enough that he still intends to injure me again in the future. Nor is it in fact always unjust to return a greater evil for a less, for the objection made by some that retribution should be rendered in proportion to the injury, is true only of civil tribunals, where punishments are meted out by superiors. But the evils inflicted by right of war have properly no relation to punishments, since they neither proceed from a superior as such, nor have as their direct object the reform of the guilty party or others, but the defence and assertion of my safety, my property, and my rights. To secure such ends it is permissible to use whatever means I think will best prevail against such a person, who, by the injury done me, has made it impossible for me to do him an injury, however I may treat him, until we have come to a new agreement to refrain from injuries for the future.

But now the law of humanity would not only have one consider how much an enemy can suffer without injury, but also what should be the deeds of a humane and, above all, a generous victor. Therefore, we should take care that, so far as it is possible, and as our defence and future security allow, we suit the evils inflicted upon an enemy to the process usually observed by a civil court in meting out justice in offences and other quarrels. This proportion and measure is treated in detail by Grotius [in *De iure belli ac pacis*, bk. III, chaps. 11–16]. . . .

9 . . . [A] state should not be considered as no better than a band of robbers, merely because it has officially, in a way, been guilty of unjust practices, nor should a band of robbers receive the dignity of a state, even though they treat their members with some show of justice.

36

John Locke
(1632–1704)

The Rights of Man and the Limits of Just Warfare

> Over those, then, that joined with him in the war, and over those of the subdued country that opposed him not, and the posterity even of those that did, the conqueror, even in a just war, hath, by his conquest, no right of dominion.
>
> *Second Treatise of Government*

The English philosopher John Locke is famous for his defense of the sovereignty of the people and their right to depose their rulers. This was based on his conviction that a policy of individual rights ensures a more just and peaceful society than any other political regime. In his *Two Treatises of Government*, Locke sought to give a theoretical foundation for this liberal political theory by showing how the "true original" of government is the consent of the people. In so doing, he employed the popular seventeenth-century concept of a "state of nature" – the natural, pre-political condition of humankind, where there is no sovereign authority to pass judgment in cases of disagreement between individuals. Unlike Thomas Hobbes, who famously used the same image in several of his works, Locke did not equate the condition of nature with a state of war. For Hobbes, the natural state was so disastrous that only a complete renouncement of the natural rights of man can ever secure peace. Locke, by contrast, insisted that the state of nature is potentially peaceful, governed, as it is, by a law of nature, and he thus insists that the departure from that condition requires no complete loss of rights. Indeed, quite the opposite is the case in Locke: political society is instituted not so that people can give away their rights of nature, but so that they can defend them more effectively and forcefully.

What relevance does this have for the ethics of war? First, by insisting that the state of war is not the original condition of mankind, Locke tells us that it is not natural for human beings to solve conflicts through the use of armed force.

Second, he reminds us that the state of nature that still exists in the world, namely, between the different polities in the international arena, is not a condition of pure license, but a state governed by a law of nature. Thus, there *do* exist rules even when there is no common sovereign. This also means that "law of nature" means something slightly different for Locke than it does for Hobbes. Hobbes defines the law of nature as a set of prudential rules for erecting civil society. Locke, by contrast, comes closer to the traditional scholastic understanding of the term, where the law of nature is a guide to a meaningful, peaceful, and ethical life. The ethical part is admittedly toned down in Locke's political thought – he is remarkably silent on questions of virtue and individual morality in the *Two Treatises* – yet the overall tenor of his natural law philosophy comes very close to the traditional idea that the law of nature is not merely a set of prudential rules of thumb, but a true law calling human beings to live in peace and harmony with each other.

There is a heated debate whether Locke succeeds in giving a plausible argument for this "law of nature."[1] Locke himself equates the law of nature sometimes with "the light of reason," at other times with a reasonable, undogmatic interpretation of New Testament ethics. Most of the time, however, he skips the question of the origin and justification of the law of nature completely. Being highly skeptical of the ability of human beings to grasp this law by the aid of reason alone, we may at least say that he comes closer to the Lutheran views of Pufendorf than the more rationalist belief in a law of nations expressed by Grotius.

But, whether or not we hold Locke's grounding of the law of nature to be philosophically (or theologically) persuasive, there is little doubt that he gives us a heartfelt and effective argument for equal rights for all human beings, and a parallel argument – based on his idea of natural rights – for a certain restraint in connection with war.

However, Locke does not take the full step towards a *ius in bello*. His remarks on actual conduct in war are sparse. But he does impose severe restraints on the rights of the conqueror *after* a war, restraints which have relevance even for conduct *in bello*, since they deal with the rights of all those who do (or did) not actively support the war, as well as the descendants of those who do (or did). The rights to life and property of these people are not to be violated. Thus, strict duties are imposed on the conqueror – even the conqueror who has fought a just war.

There is a contrast to Pufendorf here, although it is not very sharp: Where Pufendorf imposes no legal or moral limits on the actual conduct of a just war, save those limits dictated by prudence, Locke at least indirectly argues for restraint and legal limits, especially towards civilians, based on the idea of a binding law of nature.

---

[1]   See, for instance, Leo Strauss, *Natural Right and History* (Chicago: University of Chicago Press, 1953); A. John Simmons, *The Lockean Theory of Rights* (Princeton, NJ: Princeton University Press, 1992); and James Tully, *An Approach to Political Philosophy: Locke in Contexts* (Cambridge: Cambridge University Press, 1993).

In the following excerpts we first find Locke's description of the natural state of humankind and what characterizes a state of war, thereafter his treatment of the limited rights of conquest, and finally a short excerpt from his defense of the right to rebellion against an unjust ruler, one of Locke's most lasting legacies.

Note that Locke's expression "appeal to Heaven," in chap. 3, section 20, and again in chap. 16, section 176, means the right all human beings have of utilizing force, when there is no other way to secure one's rights. When no judge or politician can help, one must appeal to God and throw oneself into a state of war. It is clear, however, that Locke believed that his doctrine of popular sovereignty and a law of nature that governs relations between human beings (and between states) would lead to fewer rather than more wars. The possibility of "appealing to heaven," and the right of the individual to oppose tyranny, are safeguards *against* war, in Locke's view, rather than a permissive doctrine opening the floodgates to conflict and violence.

From *Second Treatise of Government* (1690)[2]

Chapter 2: Of the State of Nature[3]

4 To understand political power aright, and derive it from its original, we must consider what estate all men are naturally in, and that is, a state of perfect freedom to order their actions, and dispose of their possessions and persons as they think fit, within the bounds of the law of Nature, without asking leave or depending upon the will of any other man. . . .

6 But though this be a state of liberty, yet it is not a state of licence; though man in that state have an uncontrollable liberty to dispose of his person or possessions, yet he has not liberty to destroy himself, or so much as any creature in his possession, but where some nobler use than its bare preservation calls for it. The state of Nature has a law of Nature to govern it, which obliges every one, and reason, which is that law, teaches all mankind who will but consult it, that being all equal and independent, no one ought to harm another in his life, health, liberty or possessions; for men being all the workmanship of one omnipotent and infinitely wise Maker; all the servants of one sovereign Master, sent into the world by His order and about His business; they are His property, whose workmanship they are made to last during His, not one another's pleasure. . . .

---

[2] From John Locke, *Two Treatises of Government* (London: Everyman's Library, 1924). Note that Locke's sections are numbered consecutively through each of his two treatises, so that each new chapter does not start with "section 1," but rather continues its section numbering from where the previous chapter ended.

[3] Ibid., pp. 118, 119–20, 124.

14 It is often asked as a mighty objection, where are, or ever were, there any men in such a state of Nature? To which it may suffice as an answer at present, that since all princes and rulers of "independent" governments all through the world are in a state of Nature, it is plain that the world never was, nor never will be, without numbers of men in that state.

Chapter 3: On the State of War[4]

16 The state of war is a state of enmity and destruction; and therefore declaring by word or action, not a passionate and hasty, but sedate, settled design upon another man's life puts him in a state of war with him against whom he has declared such an intention, and so has exposed his life to the other's power to be taken away by him, or any one that joins with him in his defence, and espouses his quarrel; it being reasonable and just I should have a right to destroy that which threatens me with destruction; for by the fundamental law of Nature, man being to be preserved as much as possible, when all cannot be preserved, the safety of the innocent is to be preferred, and one may destroy a man who makes war upon him, or has discovered an enmity to his being, for the same reason that he may kill a wolf or a lion, because they are not under the ties of the common law of reason, have no other rule but that of force and violence, and so may be treated as a beast of prey, those dangerous and noxious creatures that will be sure to destroy him whenever he falls into their power. . . .

19 And here we have the plain difference between the state of Nature and the state of war, which however some men have confounded, are as far distant as a state of peace, goodwill, mutual assistance, and preservation; and a state of enmity, malice, violence and mutual destruction are one from another. Men living together according to reason without a common superior on earth, with authority to judge between them, is properly the state of Nature. But force, or a declared design of force upon the person of another, where there is no common superior on earth to appeal to for relief, is the state of war; and it is the want of such an appeal [that] gives a man the right of war even against an aggressor, though he be in society and a fellow-subject. . . . Want of a common judge with authority puts all men in a state of Nature; force without right upon a man's person makes a state of war both where there is, and is not, a common judge.

---

[4]   Ibid., pp. 125, 126–7. Note that the argument in section 16 implies a right to preemptive strikes, when it is said that one may destroy those that *threaten* with destruction or have a *settled design* to kill, not only those that have already killed or used violent force. This point is well made by James Turner Johnson in *Ideology, Reason, and the Limitation of War* (Princeton: Princeton University Press, 1975), p. 234. Johnson's full discussion of Locke (ibid., pp. 232–40) constitutes a strong claim for Locke's importance and originality as a just war thinker, as he argues against Richard Cox's contention in *Locke on War and Peace* (Oxford: Clarendon Press, 1960) that Locke's distinction between justice and injustice in war eventually falls apart and is not consistently maintained by Locke himself.

20 But when the actual force is over, the state of war ceases between those that are in society and are equally on both sides subject to the judge; and, therefore, in such controversies, where the question is put, "Who shall be judge?" it cannot be meant who shall decide the controversy; every one knows what Jephtha here tells us, that "the Lord the Judge" shall judge. Where there is no judge on earth the appeal lies to God in Heaven. That question then cannot mean who shall judge, whether another hath put himself in a state of war with me, and whether I may, as Jephtha did, appeal to Heaven in it? Of that I myself can only judge in my own conscience, as I will answer it at the great day to the Supreme Judge of all men.

Chapter 16: Of Conquest[5]

175 Though governments can originally have no other rise than that before mentioned, nor polities be founded on anything but the consent of the people, yet such have been the disorders ambition has filled the world with, that in the noise of war, which makes so great a part of the history of mankind, this consent is little taken notice of; and, therefore, many have mistaken the force of arms for the consent of the people, and reckon conquest as one of the originals of government. But conquest is as far from setting up any government as demolishing a house is from building a new one in the place. Indeed, it often makes way for a new frame of a commonwealth by destroying the former; but, without the consent of the people, can never erect a new one.

176 That the aggressor, who puts himself into the state of war with another, and unjustly invades another man's right, can, by such an unjust war, never come to have a right over the conquered, will be easily agreed by all men, who will not think that robbers and pirates have a right of empire over whomsoever they have force enough to master, or that men are bound by promises which unlawful force extorts from them. Should a robber break into my house, and, with a dagger at my throat, make me seal deeds to convey my estate to him, would this give him any title? . . .

177 But supposing victory favours the right side, let us consider a conqueror in a lawful war, and see what power he gets, and over whom.

First, it is plain he gets no power by his conquest over those that conquered with him. They that fought on his side cannot suffer by the conquest, but must, at least, be as much free men as they were before. . . .

178 But supposing, which seldom happens, that the conquerors and conquered never incorporate into one people under the same laws and freedom; let us see next what power a lawful conqueror has over the subdued, and that I say is purely despotical. He has an absolute power over the lives of those who, by an

---

[5]   Locke, *Two Treatises*, pp. 206–7, 208, 209, 210–12, 213.

unjust war, have forfeited them, but not over the lives or fortunes of those who engaged not in the war, nor over the possessions even of those who were actually engaged in it.

179 Secondly, I say, then, the conqueror gets no power but only over those who have actually assisted, concurred, or consented to that unjust force that is used against him. For the people having given to their governors no power to do an unjust thing, such as is to make an unjust war (for they never had such a power in themselves), they ought not to be charged as guilty of the violence and injustice that is committed in an unjust war any farther than they actually abet it, no more than they are to be thought guilty of any violence or oppression their governors should use upon the people themselves or any part of their fellow-subjects, they having empowered them no more to the one than to the other. Conquerors, it is true, seldom trouble themselves to make the distinction, but they willingly permit the confusion of war to sweep all together; but yet this alters not the right; for the conqueror's power over the lives of the conquered being only because they have used force to do or maintain an injustice, he can have that power only over those who have concurred in that force; all the rest are innocent, and he has no more title over the people of that country who have done him no injury, and so have made no forfeiture of their lives, than he has over any other who, without any injuries or provocations, have lived upon fair terms with him.

180 Thirdly, the power a conqueror gets over those he overcomes in a just war is perfectly despotical; he has an absolute power over the lives of those who, by putting themselves in a state of war, have forfeited them, but he has not thereby a right and title to their possessions. This I doubt not but at first sight will seem a strange doctrine, it being so quite contrary to the practice of the world. . . .

182 But because the miscarriages of the father are no faults of the children, who may be rational and peaceable, notwithstanding the brutishness and injustice of the father, the father, by his miscarriages and violence, can forfeit but his own life, and involves not his children in his guilt or destruction. His goods which Nature, that willeth the preservation of all mankind as much as is possible, hath made to belong to the children to keep them from perishing, do still continue to belong to his children. For supposing them not to have joined in the war either through infancy or choice, they have done nothing to forfeit them, nor has the conqueror any right to take them away by the bare right of having subdued him that by force attempted his destruction, though, perhaps, he may have some right to them to repair the damages he has sustained by the war, and the defence of his own right, which how far it reaches to the possessions of the conquered we shall see by-and-by; so that he that by conquest has a right over a man's person, to destroy him if he pleases, has not thereby a right over his estate to possess and enjoy it. . . .

183 Let the conqueror have as much justice on his side as could be supposed, he has no right to seize more than the vanquished could forfeit; his life is at the victor's mercy, and his service and goods he may appropriate to make himself reparation; but he cannot take the goods of his wife and children, they too had a title to the goods he enjoyed, and their shares in the estate he possessed. . . . Here then is the case: The conqueror has a title to reparation for damages received, and the children have a title to their father's estate for their subsistence. For as to the wife's share, whether her own labour or compact gave her a title to it, it is plain her husband could not forfeit what was hers. What must be done in the case? I answer: The fundamental law of Nature being that all, as much as may be, should be preserved, it follows that if there be not enough fully to satisfy both – viz., for the conqueror's losses and children's maintenance, he that hath and to spare must remit something of his full satisfaction, and give way to the pressing and prefer-able title of those who are in danger to perish without it. . . .

185 Over those, then, that joined with him in the war, and over those of the subdued country that opposed him not, and the posterity even of those that did, the conqueror, even in a just war, hath, by his conquest, no right of dominion. They are free from any subjection to him, and if their former government be dissolved, they are at liberty to begin and erect another to themselves.

Chapter 19: Of the Dissolution of Government[6]

228 But if they who say [that this doctrine of popular sovereignty] lays a founda-tion for rebellion mean that it may occasion civil wars or intestine broils to tell the people they are absolved from obedience when illegal attempts are made upon their liberties or properties, and may oppose the unlawful violence of those who were their magistrates when they invade their properties, contrary to the trust put in them, and that, therefore, this doctrine is not to be allowed, being so destructive to the peace of the world; they may as well say, upon the same ground, that honest men may not oppose robbers or pirates, because this may occasion disorder or bloodshed. If any mischief come in such cases, it is not to be charged upon him who defends his own right, but on him that invades his neighbour's. If the innocent honest man must quietly quit all he has for peace sake to him who will lay violent hands upon it, I desire it may be considered what a kind of peace there will be in the world which consists only in violence and rapine, and which is to be maintained only for the benefit of robbers and oppressors. . . .

229 The end of government is the good of mankind; and which is best for mankind, that the people should be always exposed to the boundless will of tyranny, or that the rulers should be sometimes liable to be opposed when they grow exorbitant in the use of their power, and employ it for the destruction, and not the preservation, of the properties of their people?

---

[6]   Ibid., pp. 232–3.

37

Christian von Wolff (1679–1754)

Bilateral Rights of War

[N]o nation can assume for itself the functions of a judge.

Wolff, *The Law of Nations Treated according to a Scientific Method*

An extremely prolific thinker, whose writings covered all of the major areas of philosophy, Christian von Wolff played a decisive role in the development of the modern conception of laws of war. Although much of his terminology was taken from earlier authors in the natural law tradition, Wolff infused this terminology with new meaning. The "law of nations" (*ius gentium*) now came to designate a sphere of rules that regulated solely the mutual relations of independent states.

Wolff still speaks in terms of just and unjust belligerents. However, unlike some of his predecessors (Pufendorf especially, but also possibly Gentili) he maintained that a just belligerent does not enjoy an unlimited right of war against his unjust adversary. On the contrary, Wolff argued that every action of war must be measured, not only by what is necessary to recover one's violated right, but first and foremost by the proximate goal of defeating the enemy's armed resistance. He thereby provided one of the first modern formulations of what is now termed "military necessity," the principle that only "so much is allowable in a just war against the person of the enemy as is sufficient to ward from us and our property the force used by him" (§791). Although this principle is here articulated as a unilateral right that the just belligerent can bring to bear against his unjust opponent, Wolff in fact organized his system so that the norm of "military necessity" would apply simultaneously to all belligerents, regardless of the justice or injustice of their cause. And he was particularly insistent that the civilian population should be protected from direct military action (§792).

Within the sphere of public, international justice (the "voluntary law of nations"), Wolff maintained that no one nation can stand as judge over any other. As a consequence, each is free to decide on the substantive justice of its own course of action (§888). War thus introduces a normative condition in which each side has an equal right to use force against the other. Once this "state of war" is in effect, both sides must conduct themselves in conformity with the same set of rules. Wolff conceived of this arrangement as a kind of lesser evil. If belligerents were allowed to regulate their conduct solely by reference to the justice of their cause, the savagery of war would only increase, since each naturally believes that it is possessed of a just cause.

The selections below are taken from the first of two treatises that Wolff wrote on the *ius gentium*. The initial group of passages (§§577–9, 636–9) present his conception of the relationship between war and punishment, wherein he shows an affinity for the views earlier expressed by Vitoria and Molina. As is indicated by its title, the work is written in a "scientific" style that is meant to mirror a treatise in geometry. The concatenation of syllogisms makes for difficult reading, and, for this reason, the work has not achieved the broad readership that it otherwise deserves.[1]

From *The Law of Nations Treated according to a Scientific Method* (1749)[2]

§577. Of the Right of Retaliation between Nations

Retaliation (*talio*) is not allowable between nations, nor does a right of retaliation exist in the voluntary law of nations; but if retaliation has been introduced by custom, this must be attributed to the unjust customary law of nations. For retaliation has been forbidden by the law of nature, consequently it is illicit. Therefore, since nations use natural law in their relations with each other, consequently that cannot be licit between them which is by nature illicit. Retaliation, therefore, cannot be allowed between nations. . . .

§578. Whether Irreparable Injury Makes a Place for It

Since retaliation is not allowed by nature even among nations, and, moreover, since retaliation consists in this, that one should suffer as much wrong as he has

---

[1]   For a summary of Wolff's main contribution to the just war tradition, and a comparison with his predecessors (Grotius and Pufendorf especially), see Peter Haggenmacher, *Grotius et la doctrine de la guerre juste* (Paris: Presses Universitaires de France, 1983), pp. 605–12.

[2]   The English translation is taken (with alterations) from *Ius gentium methodo scientifica pertractatum*, vol. 2, The Classics of International Law, trans. Joseph H. Drake (Oxford: Clarendon Press, 1934), pp. 295–6, 325–8, 403, 408–12, 454–5. Volume 1 reproduces the Latin text of 1764 (Frankfurt and Leipzig: Rengerius). Full Latin title: *Ius gentium methodo scientifica pertractatum, in quo ius gentium naturale ab eo, quod voluntarii, pactitii et consuetudinarii est, accurate distinguitur* (The Law of Nations Treated according to a Scientific Method, in which the Natural Law of Nations is Carefully Distinguished from that which is Voluntary, Stipulative and Customary).

inflicted, if irreparable injury has been done to any nation by another nation, or there is no hope that this injury can be repaired, it is not allowable to do to that other nation what it itself has done. . . .

§579. When Retaliation Becomes even more Illicit

Since retaliation is not allowable, it will be much more illicit if it consists in an act disgraceful by nature.

> For example, let us suppose that soldiers have been promised that they may publicly rape honourable women; since rape of that sort is by nature disgraceful, however much the right of retaliation may have been introduced by the custom of certain nations, it will not be allowable to permit it to their soldiers in turn; and if, nevertheless, it should be done, such retaliation would be much more illicit than that which consists in some physical harm which is not considered illicit in itself.

§636. When a Punitive War is Legal

Punitive war (*bellum punitivum*) is not licit except for one who has received irreparable injury, and when he cannot obtain satisfaction for it in any other way. For no one has a right of war except one to whom a wrong has been done. Therefore, since a penalty is exacted from another in a punitive war, and since we must combat to exact a penalty so that we may compel the offender not to injure us again in the future, we must accordingly be on guard, lest we, following his example, or he himself, may dare to injure others. A punitive war can be legal only in the case of one who has received irreparable injury. But a punitive war is an offensive war. Therefore, since an offensive war is licit on the occasion of an irreparable injury only if satisfaction cannot be obtained for it otherwise than by force of arms, a punitive war is not legal except for one who has received irreparable injury, and when he cannot obtain satisfaction for it otherwise. . . .

§637. Whether One Nation Can be Punished by Another Nation for Crimes and an Offence towards God

Since a punitive war is not licit except for one who has received irreparable injury from another, a punitive war is not allowed against a nation for the reason that it is very wicked, or violates dreadfully the law of nature, or offends against God. . . .

§638. Whether Atheism, Deism, and Idolatry are a Just Cause for a Punitive War

In like manner, since a punitive war is legal only for one who has received irreparable injury, punitive war is legal for no nation against another because it professes atheism, or deism, or is idolatrous. . . .

§639. When a War is at the Same Time Vindicative and Punitive

If any one seeks by force of arms that which has been taken from him unjustly by force; his offensive war is at the same time vindicative (*vindicativum*) and punitive (*punitivum*). The same is to be said of a war which is prosecuted in order that a loss caused by a wrong should be repaired. For if what is his own has been taken away from any one unjustly by force, he who does the wrong is a robber. But an owner not only has the right to compel a robber by force to restore the property taken from him, but he has also the right to punish him. Therefore, if he makes war upon him to recover his property by force of arms, since that is a vindicative war in which we strive to gain what is our own, but [likewise] a punitive war is one in which a penalty is exacted from one against whom the war is brought; the war, which is obviously an offensive war, is at the same time both a vindicative and a punitive war. Which was the first point.

But if war should be made with the purpose that a loss caused should be repaired, the one making it does so that he may acquire what is due to him. Therefore, since that is a vindicative war by which we strive to gain that which is due to us, an offensive war is in this respect vindicative. But since, indeed, the loss is caused by a wrong, and by hypothesis the right belongs by nature to a man, consequently also to a nation, to punish one who has done him wrong, and a punitive war is one by which a penalty is exacted from another; in that respect, a war which is made with the purpose that a loss caused by a wrong should be repaired is a punitive war. Therefore it is plain that if the war is made with the purpose that a loss caused by a wrong should be repaired, that war is at the same time both vindicative and punitive. Which was the second point.

> Just as by one act property has been taken from its owner and also irreparable injury done him, in so far as the deed cannot be undone; so also, by one act of war, his property is regained and also he who did the injury is punished. But it is of importance that an offensive war, in which there are at the same time vindicative and punitive elements, should be distinguished from that which belongs to only one category. For more is allowable in the former than in the latter, as will be plain from what follows. The same is true in the other case in which loss is caused by wrong.

§781. Concerning [One's] Right in a Just War

That is licit in war, for one who is waging a just war, without which he cannot acquire his right (*ius suum*) from the other party; that is not allowable which does not help to attain this end. For by the law of nature a right in war exists only to do that without which one cannot attain one's right, for the sake of which the war is waged. Therefore, since nations and their rulers use natural law in their relations with each other, that is allowable in war, for one who is waging a just war, without which he cannot acquire his right from the other party; but that is not allowable, which does not help to attain this end. . . .

§790. Concerning a Right against Persons in a Just War

A right against persons (*ius in personas*) arises in a just war from defence of oneself and one's property. For since in hostilities force is used against both persons and things, he who wages an unjust war, either in fact assails with illicit force, or at least attempts to assail our body or our property. Therefore, because by nature every one has the right to defend both himself and his property, consequently to ward off force by force, a right against persons arises in a just war from defence of oneself and his property. . . .

§791. How That Is to be Determined

Since a right against persons arises in a just war from defence of oneself and one's property, and since he defends himself who resists one intending or attempting to injure him, in order that the other may not injure him, or that he may avoid injury as far as possible, the right against persons in a just war is to be determined from that which is necessary to resist the violence which an enemy is attempting or intending to use against us or our property, or to repel him from us and from our property. Consequently so much is allowable in a just war against the person of an enemy as is sufficient to ward from us and our property the force used by him. . . .

§792. Of the Right against the Person of the Subjects of Belligerents

Because a right against persons arises in a just war from defense of oneself and one's property, and therefore is to be determined from that which is necessary to resist an enemy by force or to repel him from us and from our property; the subjects of the one who is engaging in unjust war, although they are considered in the number of the enemy, as long as they refrain from all violence, and do not show an intention to use force, may not be killed nor may violence be inflicted in any way upon their persons, nor may they be treated badly; consequently it is never allowable to kill children, boys, girls, those weakened by age, the sick, those who are weak, bodily or mentally, and those who have already surrendered themselves, or wish to do so. . . .

§795. When One Ceases to be an Enemy

As soon as an enemy is in my power, he ceases to be an enemy. For those are enemies who are at war with each other. But since he who is in my power can no longer in any way resist me in the prosecution of my right, as soon as he is in my power I can have no further war with him; consequently he ceases to be an enemy. . . .

§888. What War is to be Considered Just by the Voluntary Law of Nations

With respect to its effects, by the voluntary law of nations, war should be considered just on either side. For all nations are free by nature (*naturaliter liberae*), consequently by nature no nation has any control over the actions of another, and by virtue of liberty each must be allowed to follow its own judgment in determining its actions, as long as it does nothing contrary to the right of another, nor has any nation the right to demand that another should give to it a reason for its actions. Therefore, since no nation can assume for itself the functions of a judge, and consequently cannot pronounce upon the justice of the war, although by natural law a war cannot be just on both sides, since nevertheless each of the belligerents claims that it has just cause of war, each must be allowed to follow its own opinion. Consequently, by the voluntary law of nations the war must be considered as just on either side, not indeed in itself . . . , but as regards the effects of the war (*effectus belli*).

38

Montesquieu (1689–1755)

National Self-preservation and the Balance of Power

> A new disease has spread across Europe; it has afflicted our princes and made them keep an inordinate number of troops.
>
> Montesquieu, *The Spirit of the Laws*

The Spirit of the Laws (*De l'esprit des lois*) from 1748, by Charles Louis de Secondat, Baron de la Brède et Montesquieu (1689–1755), stands as one of the eighteenth century's most influential works on laws, ethics, and politics. Applying his vast learning and wide reading to an analysis of the different regimes, ways of life, and laws of humankind, Montesquieu made crucial contributions both to the empirical understanding of various cultures, and to normative ideas about how the emerging liberal societies of Europe ought to be organized. Most famous among his normative (but, simultaneously, empirically based) contributions is, of course, his celebrated theory of the separation of powers.

For our purposes, he is worth remembering as one of the first major thinkers to warn against the dangers of mass rearmament in a world of sovereign states. We have already discussed (in chapter 35, this volume) Samuel von Pufendorf's apparent confidence that the system of sovereign states constituted a condition of "armed peace,"[1] much superior to the instability and lack of predictable rules that had created the previous century of religious civil war. Montesquieu was less sanguine about such prospects and saw the only viable bulwark against the threat of increasing violence in a world rich in arms in the close cooperation between liberal states, preferably in federative arrangements. This idea would later be developed further by Immanuel Kant.

---

[1] James Tully, in Samuel Pufendorf, *On the Duty of Man and Citizen* (Cambridge: Cambridge University Press, 1991), p. xxxvii.

Also significant is the way in which Montesquieu unequivocally bases the right to use armed force on the right to self-preservation. In this sense, he clearly belongs to the state-centered liberal school that Pufendorf had helped inaugurate. The state is not an arbitrary collection of people, with its right of existence based merely on convenience or tradition. The state is also a moral entity which, in its ideal form, preserves peace both internally and externally by securing liberty and making it possible to achieve material well-being through production and trade. Even in his theory of war, Montesquieu comes across as a defender of this emerging liberal theory of international affairs, based on the strict (procedural and moral) justice of the sovereign state. Based on this premise, we see that Montesquieu accepts preemptive – maybe even preventive – attacks as sometimes justified.

From *The Spirit of the Laws* (1748), bk. I: On Laws in General[2]

Chapter 3: On Positive Laws

As soon as men are in society, they lose their feeling of weakness; the equality that was among them ceases, and the state of war begins.

Each particular society comes to feel its strength, producing a state of war among nations. The individuals within each society begin to feel their strength; they seek to turn [to] their favor the principal advantages of this society, which brings about a state of war among them.

These two sorts of states of war bring about the establishment of laws among men. . . .

The *right of nations* is by nature founded on the principle that the various nations should do to one another in times of peace the most good possible, and in times of war the least ill possible, without harming their true interests.

The object of war is victory; of victory, conquest; of conquest, preservation. All the laws that form the *right of nations*, should derive from this principle and the preceding one.

All nations have a right of nations; and even the Iroquois, who eat their prisoners, have one. They send and receive embassies; they know rights of war and peace: the trouble is that their right of nations is not founded on true principles.

---

[2] From *The Spirit of the Laws*, ed. and trans. Anne M. Cohler, Basia Carolyn Miller and Harold Samuel Stone (Cambridge: Cambridge University Press, 1989), pp. 7–8.

From *The Spirit of the Laws,* bk. X: On Laws in their Relation with Offensive Force[3]

Chapter 2: On War

The life of states is like that of men. Men have the right to kill in the case of natural defense; states have the right to wage war for their own preservation.

In the case of natural defense, I have the right to kill, because my life is mine, as the life of the one who attacks me is his; likewise a state wages war because its preservation is just, as is any other preservation.

Among citizens, the right to natural defense does not carry with it a necessity to attack. Instead of attacking they have the recourse of the tribunals. Therefore, they can exercise that right of defense only in cases that occur so suddenly that one would be lost if one waited for the aid of the laws. But among societies, the right of natural defense sometimes carries with it a necessity to attack, when one people sees that a longer peace would put another people in a position to destroy it and that an attack at this moment is the only way to prevent such destruction.

Hence small societies more frequently have the right to wage wars than large ones, because they are more frequently in a position to fear being destroyed.

Therefore, the right of war derives from necessity and from a strict justice. If those who direct the conscience or the councils of princes do not hold to these, all is lost; and, when that right is based on arbitrary principles of glory, of propriety, of utility, tides of blood will inundate the earth.

Above all, let one not speak of the prince's glory; his glory is his arrogance; it is a passion and not a legitimate right.

It is true that his reputation for power could increase the forces of his state, but his reputation for justice would increase them in any case.

Chapter 3: On the Right of Conquest

From the right of war derives that of conquest, which is its consequence; therefore, it should follow the spirit of the former.

When a people is conquered, the right of the conqueror follows four sorts of laws: the law of nature, which makes everything tend toward the preservation of species; the law of natural enlightenment (Fr. *lumières*), which wants us to do to others what we would want to have done to us; the law that forms political societies, which are such that nature has not limited their duration; lastly, the law drawn from the thing itself. Conquest is an acquisition; the spirit of acquisition carries with it the spirit of preservation and use, and not that of destruction.

[3] Ibid., pp. 138–40.

One state that has conquered another treats it in one of these four ways: the state continues to govern its conquest according to its own laws and takes for itself only the exercise of the political and civil government; or it gives its conquest a new political and civil government; or it destroys the society and scatters it into others; or, finally, it exterminates all the citizens.

The first way conforms to the right of nations we follow at present; the fourth is more in conformity with the right of nations among the Romans; on this point, I leave others to judge how much better we have become. Here homage must be paid to our modern times, to contemporary reasoning, to the religion of the present day, to our philosophy, and to our mores.

When the authors of our public right, for whom ancient histories provided the foundation, have no longer followed cases strictly, they have fallen into great errors. They have moved toward the arbitrary; they have assumed among conquerors a right, I do not know which one, of killing; this has made them draw consequences as terrible as this principle and establish maxims that the conquerors themselves, when they had the slightest sense, never adopted. It is clear that, once the conquest is made, the conqueror no longer has the right to kill, because it is no longer for him a case of natural defense and of his own preservation.

What has made them think in this way is that they have believed the conqueror had the right to destroy the society; thus they have concluded that he had the right to destroy the men composing it, which is a consequence wrongly drawn from a wrong principle. For, from the annihilation of the society, it would not follow that the men forming that society should also be annihilated. The society is the union of men and not the men themselves; the citizen may perish and the man remain.

From the right to kill during conquest, political men have drawn the right to reduce to servitude, but the consequence is as ill founded as the principle.

From *The Spirit of the Laws*, bk. XIII: On the Relations that the Levy of Taxes and the Size of the Public Revenues have with Liberty[4]

Chapter 17: On the Increase in Troops

A new disease has spread across Europe; it has afflicted our princes and made them keep an inordinate number of troops. It redoubles in strength and necessarily becomes contagious; for, as soon as one state increases what it calls its troops, the others suddenly increase theirs, so that nothing is gained thereby but the common ruin. Each monarch keeps ready all the armies he would have if his peoples were in danger of being exterminated; and this state in which all strain

---

[4]   Ibid., pp. 224–5.

against all is called peace.[5] Thus Europe is so ruined that if individuals were in the situation of the three most opulent powers in this part of the world, they would have nothing to live on. We are poor with the wealth and commerce of the whole universe, and soon, as a result of these soldiers, we shall have nothing but soldiers and we shall be like Tartars.[6]

The great princes, not content to buy troops from smaller ones, seek everywhere to buy alliances, that is, almost always to lose their silver.

The consequence of such a situation is the permanent increase in taxes; and that which prevents all remedies in the future is that one no longer counts on the revenues, but makes war with one's capital. It is not unheard of for states to mortgage their lands even during peace and to ruin themselves by means they call extraordinary, which are so highly extraordinary that the most deranged son of a family could scarcely imagine them.

[5] [*Author's note:*] It is true that it is this state of effort which principally maintains the balance, because it exhausts the great powers.

[6] [*Author's note:*] For this, one must make use of the new invention of the militia established in almost the whole of Europe and push them to the same excess as the regular troops.

39

Jean-Jacques Rousseau (1712–1778)

Supranational Government and Peace

[F]ar from the state of war being natural to man, war is born out of peace, or at least out of the precautions men have taken to ensure themselves of peace.

Rousseau, *The State of War*

The name of Jean-Jacques Rousseau is almost invariably invoked in connection with the Enlightenment – the eighteenth-century intellectual revolution that would also inspire countless major and minor political ones. Yet even the most cursory glance at his writings will reveal a thinker in curious tension with his times. For Rousseau – the Enlightenment hero, and author of immensely popular works such as *Discourse on the Origin and Foundations of Inequality among Men* (1755), *The Social Contract* (1762), *Émile* (1762), as well as the best-selling novel *Julie, or the New Heloise* (1761) – was also the *salon* dissident, possessed of an almost pathological penchant for sparking controversies with his contemporary intellectual luminaries – notably Voltaire and Diderot.

In this chapter we will be excerpting from three of Rousseau's lesser-known works: the unfinished *The State of War*, as well as his *Summary* and *Critique* of the Abbé de Saint-Pierre's *Project for Perpetual Peace*.[1] Between them, these three manuscripts perfectly portray Rousseau's ambivalence toward the philosophical and political temper of his times. Virtually brimming with radical political implications, in these works we still find him battling in the grips of hesitancy – revolutionary as his proposals may be, he does not seem sure that he would like to see them pushed through. In the process, Rousseau casts long shadows of doubt over one of the most central tenets of Enlightenment philosophy – namely the notion of progress in human affairs. Foreshadowing the advent of the Romantic movement,

---

[1] We use the translations of Grace G. Roosevelt, whose *Reading Rousseau in the Nuclear Age* (Philadelphia, PA: Temple University Press, 1990), includes all three works as appendices.

Rousseau takes issue with the widespread image of the state of nature as one riveted by chaos and conflict. Content with satisfying his basic needs, he argues, natural man exists in a state of peaceful bliss. By contrast, it is civilized man that is decadent, wretched and war-torn. The advent of civilization is the story of man's fall from grace, so to speak. Can a revolution return us to the innocence of natural man? Rousseau is doubtful, as his writings clearly reveal.

The State of War

In *The State of War* this reversal of the orthodox way of narrating social and political history is brought out with great acuity. Rousseau drafted the manuscript in the mid-1750s, thus prior to some of his most famous works, but never finished it for publication. The work opens with a passionate prologue lamenting the evils of the modern world, the first paragraph of which is well worth quoting in its entirety:

From *The State of War*[2]

I open my books about rights and morals, I listen to scholars and legal experts, and inspired by their suggestive discourses, I deplore the miseries of nature, admire the peace and justice established by the civil order, bless the wisdom of public institutions, and find consolation for being a man by seeing myself as a citizen. Well instructed as to my duties and my happiness, I close the books, leave the lecture room, and look around me. There I see a miserable people groaning under an iron yoke, the whole human race crushed by a handful of oppressors, and an enraged mob overwhelmed by pain and hunger whose blood and tears the rich drink in peace. And everywhere the strong are armed against the weak with the formidable power of the law.

The work's argument proper takes its cues from Thomas Hobbes's *Leviathan*. Like Hobbes, Rousseau notes the discrepancy between the orderly reign we enjoy in civil society and the anarchical character of international relations, commenting that "living simultaneously in the social order and in the state of nature, we are subjected to the evils of both without gaining the security of either" (*The State of War*, p. 186). However, it is not obvious that it is this residual element of the state of nature that threatens to wreak havoc upon us. "[T]he error of Hobbes and the *philosophes*," Rousseau claims, "is to confuse natural man with the man that they have before their eyes, and to transport into one system a being which could only exist in another" (p. 187). Rousseau then expands on his notion that war is not

---

[2] Ibid., p. 185.

natural to man, and hence cannot be thought of as a feature of the state of nature. On the contrary, he avers, coining the influential slogan "surplus awakens greed" (p. 187), war can only arise within a certain framework, one that presupposes the so-called civilized order. As he influentially put it in his later work *The Social Contract*:

> War is . . . not a relationship between one man and another, but a relationship between one State and another, in which individuals are enemies only by accident, not as men, nor even as citizens, but as soldiers; not as members of the fatherland, but as its defenders. Finally, any State can only have other States, and not men, as enemies, inasmuch as it is impossible to fix a true relation between things of different natures.[3]

But why, we may ask, does the relation of state to state invite such prolonged and systematic hostilities, if no comparable misfortune characterizes the relations of individual to individual in the state of nature? The reason, Rousseau argues, is that unlike "natural bodies," "artificial bodies" (as exemplified by the state) know no natural boundaries – they could in principle continue to expand indefinitely. In the absence of such natural boundaries, the inevitably competitive comparison between state and state is the only available measure.

From *The State of War*[4]

When I reflect upon the condition of the human race, the first thing that I notice is a manifest contradiction in its constitution. As individuals we live in a civil state and are subject to laws, but as nations each enjoys the liberty of nature. The resulting continual vacillation makes our situation worse than if these distinctions were unknown. For living simultaneously in the social order and in the state of nature, we are subjected to the evils of both without gaining the security of either. The perfection of the social order consists, it is true, in the conjunction of force and law. But for this it is necessary that law direct force. According to the notion that princes must be absolutely independent, however, force alone, which appears as law to its own citizens and "raison d'état" to foreigners, deprives the latter of the power and the former of the will to resist, so that in the end the vain name of justice serves only to safeguard violence.

As for what is called the law of nations, it is clear that without any real sanction these laws are only illusions that are more tenuous even than the notion of natural law. The latter at least addresses itself to the heart of individuals, whereas decisions based on the law of nations, having no other guarantee than the utility of the one who submits to them, are respected only as long as those decisions

---

[3] J.-J. Rousseau, *The Social Contract*, bk. I, chap. 4, §9, in *The Social Contract and other Later Political Writings*, ed. and trans. Victor Gourevitch (Cambridge: Cambridge University Press, 1997), pp. 46–7.

[4] Roosevelt, *Reading Rousseau*, pp. 186–9, 190, 191.

confirm one's own self-interest. In the double condition in which we find ourselves, by doing too much or too little for whichever of the two systems we happen to prefer, we in fact have done nothing at all, and thereby have put ourselves in the worst possible position. This, it seems to me, is the true origin of public calamities.

For a moment let us put these ideas in opposition to the horrible system of Hobbes. We will find, contrary to his absurd doctrine, that far from the state of war being natural to man, war is born out of peace, or at least out of the precautions men have taken to assure themselves of peace. . . .

I have said before and cannot repeat too often that the error of Hobbes and the *philosophes* is to confuse natural man with the man that they have before their eyes, and to transport into one system a being which could only exist in another. Man wishes for his own well-being and for all that can contribute to it – this is incontestable. But by nature the well-being of man is limited to physical necessity. For when he has a healthy soul and his body is not in pain, what does his natural constitution lack to make him happy? He who has nothing desires few things; he who commands no one has few ambitions. But surplus awakens greed: The more one accumulates, the more one desires. Those who have much want to have all, and the mad passion for universal monarchy has only tormented the hearts of great kings. This is in the nature of things – this is how the passions expand. A superficial philosopher observes souls that are endlessly kneaded and allowed to ferment in the yeast of society and believes he has observed man. But in order to know man well, he must know how to separate out the natural growth of the sentiments. And it is not among city dwellers that he must search to find nature's first imprint on the human heart. . . .

But even if it were true that this unlimited and uncontrollable greed had developed in every man to the extent that Hobbes presumes, still it would not bring on that state of universal war of each against all that he has described in such odious terms. For the frenzied desire to appropriate everything for oneself is incompatible with the desire to destroy one's fellow men. The victor in such a war would face the world alone, and having gained everything he would enjoy nothing. What good are riches if they cannot be exchanged? What good would it be to possess the whole universe if one were its only survivor? Can one man's belly devour all the earth's fruit? Who would harvest for him all the world's crops? Who would carry the word of his empire to the vast wastelands where he himself could never live? What would he do with his treasures, who would consume his commodities, before whose eyes would he display his power? I know: Instead of massacring everyone, he would put them all in chains and then he at least would own some slaves. And this of course would immediately change things, for as soon as destruction itself is no longer the issue, the state of war as such disappears. May the reader here suspend his judgment; I will return to this point.

Man is naturally peaceful and shy; at the slightest danger his first movement is to flee. He only becomes emboldened by force of habit and experience. Honor, self-interest, prejudice, vengeance – all the passions that can make him brave the perils of death – are far from him in the state of nature. It is only after having associated with one man that he determines to kill another. He only becomes soldier after having been citizen. It is not in natural man that one finds the great propensities for war. But I need not dwell on a system that is as revolting as it is absurd, and that has been refuted a thousand times.

In the state of nature there is thus no general war of every man against every man; the human race was not created simply to destroy itself. But it still remains for us to consider those accidental and specific wars that might arise between two or several individuals.

If natural law were inscribed only on human reason, it would hardly be capable of directing most of our actions. But it is also indelibly engraved in the human heart. It is from the heart that natural law speaks to man more powerfully than all the precepts of philosophers. It is from there that it cries out to him that he may not sacrifice the life of his fellow man except to save his own, and that even when he sees himself obliged to do so, he cannot but feel a sense of horror at the idea of killing in cold blood.

I can imagine that in the unmediated quarrels that sometimes arise in the state of nature an irritated man might happen to kill another, either openly or by surprise. But think what a strange position this same man would be in were he to find himself in a real war where he could not save his own life except at the expense of another's – and by virtue of an agreement established between them that one must die so that the other might live. War is a continual state, but the constant relationships that the state of war presupposes can rarely be found between man and man. Everything among individuals is in a continual flux which incessantly alters their interests and ties. The subject of a dispute thus appears and disappears in almost an instant, a quarrel begins and ends in a day, and while there may be conflicts and killings there is never, or at least very rarely, long-standing enmity or general war.

Nor does the state of war exist between individuals in the civil state. For there the life of all the citizens is within the power of the sovereign, and each one has no more right to dispose of another's life than he has to dispose of his own. As for duels, threats, rivalries, or individual challenges, except for those times when a military constitution is illegitimately and barbarously abused, what has ensued is not an actual state of war but rather a single conflict which was settled at a specific time and place – so that a second battle required a new call to arms. (One exception to this was the private wars suspended by daily truces – called the "Peace of God" – which received official sanction during the reign of Louis IX. But this example is unique in history.) . . .

Concerning Civil Society

We now enter into a new order of things where we see men united by an artificial accord coming together to cut one another's throats, and where all the horrors of war arise from the efforts that were taken to prevent it. But first of all it is important to formulate more exact notions than we have up until now about the essence of this body politic. Here the reader must realize that it will be less a matter of history and facts than of right and justice, and that I examine things by their nature rather than by our prejudices.

From the first formed society the formation of all the others necessarily follows. These must either become part of the first or unite to resist it; they must imitate it or be swallowed up by it.

Thus the whole face of the earth is changed. Everywhere nature has disappeared and human art has taken its place, independence and natural liberty have given way to laws and to slavery, and there no longer exists a free being. The philosopher searches for man and does not find him.

But it would be vain to think that we had crushed nature completely, for nature has broken loose and can be found where least expected. The independence that was wrenched from man has sought refuge in civil societies; and these great bodies, left to their own impulses, produce shocks whose terror is proportional to their mass.

But, one may ask, if each one of these political bodies has a stable base, why must they come into conflict? Should their own constitutions not keep them in peace? Must states, like men, search outside themselves to provide for their needs? Can political bodies not be self-sufficient? Are competition and trade an inevitable source of discord? And is not the fact that in all the countries of the world inhabitants existed before commerce the invincible proof that they could subsist without it?

Natural man, after all, has no necessary ties to his fellow men; he can survive in good health without their assistance. Indeed, he needs the attentions of men less than he needs the fruit of the earth, and the earth produces more than enough to feed all of its inhabitants. Add to this that the extent of man's strength and size has been fixed by nature: No matter how he imagines himself, his faculties are limited. His life is short, his years are numbered, fortune cannot stretch his stomach, his passions multiply in vain, his pleasures have their measure, his heart too its natural confines, his capacity for enjoyment is always the same. His ideas may convince him of his grandeur, but in his life he is always small.

The state, in contrast, since it is an artificial body, has no fixed measure and is never sure of its proper size. It can always expand, and yet it always feels weak as long as there are other states that are stronger than itself. Its security, its defense, demand that it try to appear more powerful than its neighbors; and it can only grow, feed itself, and test its strength at their expense. Even if it does not actually need to seek its subsistence beyond its own borders, it is ceaselessly on the lookout for new members who might give it a more stable base. For the inequality of men has limits put in place by the hands of nature, but the inequalities of states can grow incessantly, until one alone absorbs all the others.

Its power thus being purely relative, the political body is forced ceaselessly to compare itself in order to know itself. It depends on its surroundings, and must take an interest in all that happens there. For in vain might it wish simply to keep to itself without risking gain or loss; whether a state becomes small or great, weak or strong, depends on whether its neighbor expands or pulls back, adds to its forces or reduces them. Finally even political stability, insofar as it results in a more systematic foreign policy, can give an added forcefulness to a state's actions and thus make its conflicts more severe.

Thus, Rousseau claims, war is not natural to man, but presupposes the framework provided by the civilized order of sovereign states. While random bursts of violence can most certainly arise also in the state of nature, such hostilities do not yet constitute war. For war, according to Rousseau, "consists in the constant, reflected, and manifest will to destroy one's enemy" (*The State of War*, p. 195). Thus, war presupposes a stability and longevity in relationships that cannot be had in the state of nature.

As we shall see, moreover, once this framework is in place, no mere ceasing of battle will return us to a state of peace. For a *state of war* persists even in the absence of any actual *waging of war*, and continues so to persist for as long as neither party possesses any comprehensive assurance that the other party will not re-ignite its hostility at the first opportune moment. Anticipating his later writings on the perpetual peace ideal, Rousseau surmises that such assurance will be forth-coming only through a fundamental recasting of the international political order. Rousseau's explanation of the occurrence of war is to a large degree a structural one, and the problem of war therefore also requires a structural solution.

In the following paragraphs of *The State of War*, Rousseau anticipates one of his most famous works, *The Social Contract*. War, the will to destroy one's enemy, is not merely directed toward securing external strategic advantages, but constitutes an attack on a nation's social contract. This can be witnessed, claims Rousseau, in the widespread practice on the part of conquerors of altering the constitution of the conquered countries.

From *The State of War*[5]

The General Idea of War between State and State

The life principle of the body politic, and, if I may say so, the heart of the state, is the social pact, which, if harmed in any way, immediately dies, falls apart, and dissolves. But this pact is not a charter made out of parchment that can simply be

---

[5]   Ibid., pp. 193, 194–6, 197.

torn apart into shreds. It is written into the general will, where it is not at all easy to get rid of.

Unable at first to be broken up all at once, the social pact can be attacked part by part. If the body is invulnerable, its separate members can be struck at one by one. If its life cannot be taken, at least its health can be altered. If the source of its life cannot be reached, that which maintains it – the government, laws, customs, holdings, possessions, men – can still be destroyed. When everything that preserves it is annihilated, the state will finally die.

All these means are used or can be used in a war of one power against another, and they are also often the conditions imposed by the conquerors as a way further to harm a disarmed and defeated state. For the objective of all the harm inflicted on one's enemy at war is to force him to accept those things that he will have to suffer even more from when at peace. . . .

That the purpose and the effect of war may only be to alter the constitution of the enemy state is also not difficult to justify. The Greek republics attacked one another less in order to take away one another's liberty than to change the form of their governments, and they changed the government of those who were defeated only to hold them in a more servile dependence. The Macedonians and all the conquerors of Sparta always gave great importance to abolishing the laws of Lycurgus, and the Romans believed that there was no greater sign of their clemency toward a subjected people than to leave them their own laws. . . .

What the State of War Is

Although these two words *war* and *peace* appear to be exactly correlative, the second contains a broader significance, since peace can be troubled or interrupted in many different ways without leading to war. . . .

The constitution of this universe does not permit all the sensible beings that compose it to concur at the same time in their mutual happiness. Instead, the happiness of one is the misfortune of another, and thus according to the law of nature each gives himself preference, both when he works to his own advantage and when he works to the disadvantage of others. As soon as peace is upset on the side of the one who suffers, then not only is it natural to rebuff the hurt that is directed at us, but, in cases when an intelligent being sees that this hurt comes from the ill will of someone else, it is natural to get angry and seek to counter it. From this arise discord, quarrels, sometimes conflicts, but still not war.

Finally, when things have arrived at the point where a rational being is convinced that the care for its own preservation is incompatible not only with the well-being of another but with that other's existence, then this being takes up arms and seeks to destroy the other with the same ardor with which it seeks to preserve itself, and for the same reason. The one that is attacked, sensing that the security of its existence is incompatible with the existence of the aggressor, attacks in turn with all its strength the life of the one who is after him. This manifest will to destroy each other and all the actions that it gives rise to produce between the two enemies a relation that is called war.

From the above it follows that war does not consist of one or a few unpremeditated conflicts, or even of homicide or murder as long as they are committed in a brief fit of anger. Instead, war consists in the constant, reflected, and manifest will to destroy one's enemy. For in order to judge that the existence of this enemy is incompatible with our well-being, one needs coolness and reason – both of which produce a lasting resolve; and in order for the relationship to be mutual, the enemy in turn, knowing that its life is in jeopardy, must have the intention to defend its own life at the risk of ours. All these ideas are contained in the word war.

The public effects of this will reduced into acts are called hostilities. But whether or not there are hostilities, the relation of war, once established, can only cease by means of a formal peace. Otherwise, each of the two enemies, having no proof that the other has ceased resenting its existence, cannot or should not cease defending its own life at the cost of the other's.

These differences lead to a certain distinction in terminology. When both sides continue to engage in acts of hostility, there is what is properly called the *waging of war*. On the other hand, when two self-declared enemies remain stationary and take no offensive actions against each other, the relationship has not in any way changed, but so long as there are no actual effects there is what is called only *a state of war*. Long wars that people get tired of but that they cannot end ordinarily produce this state. Sometimes, far from being lulled into inaction, the animosity needs only to wait for a favorable moment to surprise the enemy, and then often the state of war that produces this release is more dangerous than war itself.

It has been argued whether a truce, a suspension of arms, a "Peace of God" are a state of war or peace. It is clear from the preceding notions that they all constitute a modified state of war in which the two enemies tie their own hands without losing or disguising the will to harm each other. They make preparations, pile up weapons and materials for a siege, and all the nonspecified military operations continue apace. This is enough to show that intentions have not changed. It is also the same when two enemies meet in neutral territory without attacking each other. . . .

I thus define *war* between one power and another the effect of a mutual, constant, and manifest intention to destroy the enemy state, or at least to weaken it by all possible means. This intention carried into action is *war* properly so called; but as long as it does not come into effect it is only the *state of war*. . . .

Fundamental Distinctions

. . . If there has never been, and never could be, an actual war between private individuals, whom therefore does it take place between? Who can really be called enemies? To this I answer that war takes place between public persons. And what is a public person? To this I answer that it is an artificial being that one calls sovereign, which is brought into existence by the social pact, and whose collective will carries the name of law. Applying the preceding distinctions here, we thus can say that in the effects of war it is the sovereign that inflicts the harm but the state that receives it. . . .

As an artificial being, the body politic is essentially only a creature of reason. Remove public convention, and at that instant the state is destroyed without the slightest alteration in all that comprises it; and never will all the conventions of men be able to change this physical nature of things.

What is it then to make war on a sovereign? It is to attack public convention and everything that results from it, for the essence of the state consists only in that. If the social pact could be broken apart in one blow, at that instant there would no longer be war; and by this one blow the state would be killed without a single man having died.

Summary of the Abbé de Saint-Pierre's Project for Perpetual Peace

We now turn to Rousseau's *Summary* of the Abbé de Saint-Pierre's *Project for Perpetual Peace*. The Abbé de Saint-Pierre (1658–1743) is a curious figure in the history of political thought. He was an enthusiastic amateur, whose admittedly naïve works have had to withstand scorn from his contemporaries and successors alike, but who nonetheless baptized, and provided the rough outlines for, one of the most significant traditions in international political thought. Although there are no doubt important historical precedents for his perpetual peace project (see for instance chapter 17, this volume, on Dante), Saint-Pierre brought to the project an unprecedented sense of political immediacy in the form of apparently simple step-by-step procedures to instigate such a peace, at least among the powers of Europe.

Saint-Pierre's plan for a perpetual peace among the European powers first saw the light of day in short form in 1712. The following year, he published a two-volume work detailing the plan, to which a third volume was added in 1717. It is in the form of Rousseau's *Summary*, however, that the work gained respectable philosophical form, and to be frank, readability. Rousseau was entrusted with Saint-Pierre's life work by one of the latter's relatives in the 1750s, hence about the time that he was working on *The State of War*, and in 1761 he published the *Summary* from which we are excerpting here. Although purportedly Saint-Pierre's own work rendered in popular form by an editor, Rousseau's abridgment is not without critical bite toward the original. Rousseau was eventually also to clarify his own stance toward the project in a separate *Critique*, but already in the *Summary* his doubts regarding the feasibility of the entire plan are plain to see.

Spelling out the need of a confederate, supranational government, through which alone perpetual peace can be achieved, the work opens with an echo of

Rousseau's own *The State of War*, highlighting the disastrous consequences of the discrepancy between the civil order in which we live as citizens of nations and the state of nature in which we live as citizens of the world.

From *Summary of the Abbé de Saint-Pierre's Project for Perpetual Peace*[6]

[I]f our social order were, as it is claimed to be, the work of reason rather than of the passions, would we have taken so long to see that as far as our well-being is concerned we have accomplished either too much or too little; that each one of us being both in the civil state with his fellow citizens and in the state of nature with the whole rest of the world, we have prevented private wars only so as to set off public wars, which are a thousand times worse; and that by uniting with a few men we have really become the enemies of mankind?

If there is any means of removing these dangerous contradictions it can only be by a form of confederative government, which, by uniting nations with ties similar to those which unite individuals, submits each of them equally to the authority of laws. This form of government, moreover, appears preferable to any other in that it combines at the same time the advantages of both large and small states. It is externally secure because of its power, internally sound because of its laws, and it is the only form which is able to include subjects, leaders, and foreigners on an equal basis.

Although this form of government seems new in certain respects and has only been well understood in modern times, the ancients were not ignorant of the concept. The Greeks had their Amphictyons, the Etruscans their Iucumonies, the Romans their *feriae*, the Gauls their *cités*, and Greece's last moments were made even more illustrious by the Achaean League. But none of these confederations approach the wisdom of the union of German states, or the Helvetian League, or the Estates-General. If these political bodies are still small in number and far from realizing their full potential, it is because what is best does not always work the way we think it should, and because in politics as in morals the reach of our knowledge rarely proves anything except the extent of our wrongs. . . .

When we see, on the other hand, the endless conflicts, violence, usurpations, revolts, wars, and murders that daily lay waste to this respectable abode of the wise, this brilliant haven for the sciences and the arts; . . . then we hardly know how to reconcile such strange contradictions, and the so-called fraternity of the peoples of Europe seems nothing more than a name of derision to express with irony their mutual hate.

In all this, however, things are only following their natural course. Any society without leaders or without laws, its union formed or maintained by chance, must

---

[6]   Ibid., pp. 200–1, 203–4.

necessarily degenerate into quarrels or dissension at the first change in circumstance. The ancient union of the peoples of Europe has complicated their interests and their rights in a thousand ways; they overlap at so many points that the slightest movement of some cannot help but trouble the others; their divisions are all the more deadly as their ties are more intimate; and their frequent quarrels have almost the same cruelty as civil wars.

Let us agree then that the relative state of the powers of Europe is properly speaking a state of war, and that all the partial treaties among certain of these powers are but temporary truces rather than true states of peace – either because such treaties commonly have no other guarantee than the contracting parties themselves or because the rights of each of them are never determined in any fundamental way – and thus that these half-stifled rights (or the claims substituted for them between powers that recognize no superior) will infallibly become the source of new wars as soon as different circumstances have given new strengths to the claimants.

International public law, moreover, having never been established or authorized in concert, having no general principles, and varying incessantly according to time and place, is full of contradictory rules that can only be tested by the right of the strongest. With reason having no definite guide and in questionable matters always leaning toward personal self-interest, war thus becomes inevitable even when each side would like to be just. With all good intentions, all that can be done is to settle these kinds of problems by means of arms, or to assuage them by temporary treaties. Soon, however, to the occasions that rekindle the same quarrels are added others that modify them. Then everything gets more confused, everything gets more complicated, no one sees clearly, usurpation passes for right and weakness for injustice, and in the midst of this continual disorder each party gradually becomes so unsettled that if it were possible to return to basic original rights there would be few sovereigns in Europe who would not be obliged to give up everything they now possess. . . .

But once the causes of an evil are known, they are sufficient to indicate a remedy, if one exists. Everyone can see that society is formed by common interests; that discord arises out of opposing ones; that since a thousand fortuitous events can change and modify these interests, then once there is a society it is necessary to have a coercive force to organize and coordinate the movements of its members so that the common interests and reciprocal ties are given the solidity they would not be able to have by themselves.

It would be a great error, however, to hope that the violent state of things could ever change simply by the force of circumstances and without the help of art.

Turning now to the perspective of the princes of Europe, why should they wish to enter such a union rather than aim to usurp complete power into their own hands? Saint-Pierre has little but ridicule for the princes whose vain thirst for glory and power still remains undiminished after so many failed attempts; failures whose consequences both they and not least their subjects have had to endure in the most terrible manner.

From *Summary of the Abbé de Saint-Pierre's Project for Perpetual Peace*[7]

For how could one envisage such a plan for one moment without immediately perceiving its folly? How can anyone avoid seeing that there is no power in Europe superior enough ever to become its master? Conquerors who have succeeded in overthrowing states have always appeared with unexpected military forces or with strangely armed foreign troops before peoples who were either disarmed or divided or completely lacking in discipline. But where could a European prince, aiming to overthrow all the others, find such an unprecedented force, since the most powerful state is still such a small part of the whole and since the others would be on their guard against such an attack? . . .

But if the present system is unshakable, it is by the same token all the more violent, for there is among the European powers an action and reaction which, while not dislodging them completely, hold them in a continual agitation. Such efforts are always futile and always recurring, like the currents of the sea that ceaselessly agitate the surface without ever changing its level, and the people are incessantly devastated, without any visible rewards for the sovereigns.

It would be easy for me to deduce the same truth from the individual interests of all the courts of Europe, for I could easily show that these interests coincide in a way that could hold all their forces in mutual respect, except that the ideas of commerce and money have produced a kind of political fanaticism that makes the apparent interests of princes change every day. Since everything now depends on the rather bizarre economic theories that happen to pass through the heads of ministers, it has become impossible to form any firm convictions about princes' true interests. Nevertheless, commerce does tend on a daily basis to move toward an equilibrium: By depriving certain powers of the exclusive advantage that they might gain from it, commerce deprives them at the same time of one of the great means that they have to make others obey them.

If I have insisted on the equal distribution of power that results in Europe from its present situation, it was to point to a consequence that is important for the establishment of any more general association. For, in order to form a solid and durable confederation, it would be necessary to put all the members in such a mutual dependence not only that no one singly would be in a condition to resist all the others, but also that particular associations that might be harmful to the whole would meet in it obstacles sufficient to prevent their execution. Without

[7]   Ibid., pp. 205, 206–7.

such mutual dependence the confederation would be useless, and each one while appearing to be subjected, would really remain independent. Now, if these obstacles are such as I have described them above, when at present all the powers are in complete liberty to form leagues and offensive treaties with each other, just imagine what they might be if there were a great armed league, always ready to intervene against those who would like to start to destroy it or resist it. This suffices to show that such an association would not consist simply of futile deliberations that each participant could ignore at will; instead, it would give rise to an effective power capable of forcing ambitious men to keep within the limits of the general treaty.

At this point, Saint-Pierre's decidedly utopian project acquires an oddly realist flavor, setting it apart from most later writings within the perpetual peace tradition, which can be witnessed in its insistence on the union's coercive power to keep "ambitious men" in check. Does this also mean that the federation must be instituted by force? This, apparently, remains one of Rousseau's most significant worries about the project. If coercive power is needed to hold the federation together, why would not, contrary to the Abbé's pacific assurances, coercive power also be required to institute it in the first place?

In the next excerpt, Rousseau elaborates constructive proposals that would lend practical feasibility to Saint-Pierre's plan. The substance of the proposals is contained in five articles apparently meant to be ready for signing by the princes of Europe. After that, he considers some possible objections to the plan.

From *Summary of the Abbé de Saint-Pierre's Project for Perpetual Peace*[8]

Now let us see how this great work, begun by chance, could be achieved by reason, and how, by taking on the force and the solidity of a true body politic, the free and voluntary society that unites all the European states could change into a real Confederation. By giving to this association the perfection it now lacks, it is clear that such an institution would destroy its present abuses, extend its advantages, and force all its members to cooperate for the common good. But for that it is necessary that this Confederation be so general that no considerable power could refuse it; that it have a judiciary tribunal to establish laws and regulations that would be binding on its members; that it have a compulsory and coercive force to constrain each state to submit to the common deliberations, whether by taking action or abstaining from action; finally, that it be firm and durable, to prevent members from seceding from it at will the moment they believe their particular interests to be contrary to the general interest. These are

[8] Ibid., pp. 208–9.

the sure signs that will show whether or not the institution is wise, useful, and sound. . . .

By the first Article the contracting sovereigns would establish among themselves a perpetual and irrevocable alliance and would name delegates to hold, in a designated place, an assembly or a permanent congress, in which all the differences between the contracting parties would be regulated and settled by means of arbitration or judgment.

The second Article would specify the number of sovereigns whose voices the delegates would represent in the assembly, those who would be invited to comply with the treaty, the order, the time, and the manner in which the presidency would pass from one to another by equal intervals, and finally the relative quota of contributions and the manner of levying them to provide for common expenses.

The third Article of the Confederation would guarantee to each of its members the possession and the government of all the states that it at present possesses; likewise its elective or hereditary succession according to how it is established by the fundamental laws of each country; and, in order to suppress all at once the source of contentions that incessantly arise, it would be agreed to take the current possession and the most recent treaties as the basis for all mutual rights of the contracting powers, renouncing forever and reciprocally any prior pretensions. Any future contentious successions and other devolving rights would all be regulated by the arbitration of the assembly, without its being permitted to exact reparation by violent means, or to take up arms against each other under any pretext whatsoever.

The fourth Article would specify the cases in which any ally who infringes on the treaty would be put under a ban by the rest of Europe and proscribed as a public enemy, that is to say, if it refused to execute the judgments of the great alliance – whether by making preparations for war, negotiating treaties contrary to the confederation, or taking up arms either to resist it or to attack anyone of the allies.

It would also be agreed by the same Article that the Confederation would be armed and would act offensively and at common expense against any banned state until the latter had put down its arms, executed the judgments and the rules of the assembly, repaired its wrongs, paid back its costs, and made reparation for the preparations for a war that was contrary to the treaty.

Finally, the fifth Article would give the delegates of the European body the power to form in the assembly – with a plurality of votes needed for adoption and a three-quarters majority needed for ratification five years after, according to instructions from their sovereigns – rules that they might judge important to procure all possible advantages for the European Republic and for each of its members. But no part of these five fundamental Articles could be changed without the unanimous consent of the confederees.

Then, in order better to assess to what extent such a confederation could actually fulfill its intentions, we are given a very interesting treatment of "the motives that cause princes to take up arms." These motives are six in kind, none of which could plausibly arise within the framework set by the Confederation.

From *Summary of the Abbé de Saint-Pierre's Project for Perpetual Peace*[9]

[L]et us consider the motives that cause princes to take up arms. These motives are either to make conquests, or to defend oneself from an invasion, or to weaken a too-powerful neighbor, or to uphold one's rights when those rights have been infringed upon, or to settle a difference that cannot be settled amicably, or, finally, to fulfill the responsibilities of a treaty. There has never been a cause or pretext for war that does not fall under one of these six headings. Now, it is evident that not one of these six motives could exist in the proposed new state of things.

First, any form of invasion would have to be renounced because of the impossibility of its success. Any invader would be sure to be stopped in his tracks by forces much greater than those he could muster alone, and by risking all, he would be powerless to gain anything. An ambitious prince who wishes to gain power in Europe usually does two things. He begins by fortifying himself with good alliances, and then, he tries to take his enemy by surprise. But individual alliances will serve no purpose against a more powerful and permanent alliance; and without any real reason for being armed, no prince would be able to do so without being noticed, warned, and punished by the Confederation, which would always be in a state of preparedness.

The same reason that deprives each prince of all hope of invasion relieves him at the same time of all fear of being attacked. And not only would his states be guaranteed by the whole of Europe and made as secure to him as the personal possessions of citizens in a well-regulated nation are, but as much more so than if he were their sole and only protector as Europe as a whole is stronger than he alone.

There is no reason to want to weaken a neighbor from whom one no longer has anything to fear, and there is not even a temptation to do so when one has no hope of succeeding.

Regarding the protection of one's rights, it is first of all necessary to say that an infinite number of quibbles and obscure pretensions and quarrels would be eliminated by the third Article of the Confederation, which regulates definitively all the reciprocal rights of the allied sovereigns on the basis of their present possessions. Thus all the demands and possible pretensions would become clear

---

[9] Ibid., pp. 211–13.

in the future and would be judged in the assembly as they might arise. In addition, if anyone infringes on my rights, I must uphold them by the same means. But, within the terms of the Confederation, no one could infringe on my rights by force without incurring the ban of the assembly. Thus, it would no longer be by force that I now should defend those rights. The same can be said of insults, damages, reparations, and all the different unforeseen events that can arise between two sovereigns. The same power that must defend their rights must also settle their grievances.

As for the last motive for going to war, the solution offered by the Confederation is right before our eyes. First we can see that, no longer having any aggressor to fear, there would be no longer any need for defensive treaties, and that since one could not devise a treaty that was more solid and more secure than the great Confederation, any others would be useless, illegitimate, and consequently nil.

It would thus be impossible that the Confederation, once established, could let fall a single seed of war between the Confederees, and that the objective of perpetual peace could not be perfectly fulfilled by carrying out the proposed system.

We then turn to the advantages that the contracting princes may expect from entering into this Confederation. Here, interestingly, Rousseau claims to part ways with Saint-Pierre, at least as regards the choice of persuasion strategy. As Rousseau sees it, the Abbé holds altogether too lofty a view of what constitutes the real motivation of princes, and that this, ironically, is what has brought his proposals scorn in the corridors of power. Instead, Rousseau claims to think only in terms of the self-interest of princes. For Saint-Pierre's project, he notes, amounts to depriving "the sovereigns' right to determine justice for themselves." He asks with acrid scorn: "How will they be compensated for such cruel deprivations?" (*Summary*, p. 213). Behind Rousseau's sarcasm, however, looms a very real worry, one that threatens to overshadow the entire project, however laudable it may be in theory. For while the gains for contracting princes, once the system has been instituted, are plain for all to see, it is not clear how, from the present situation, we could move toward such an institution. This worry is brought out more clearly in Rousseau's separate critique, which we shall look at later.

From *Summary of the Abbé de Saint-Pierre's Project for Perpetual Peace*[10]

It now remains for us to examine the other question, which has to do with the advantages for the contracting parties, for it is obvious that it would be futile to speak of the public self-interest to the detriment of private self-interest. Proving

---

[10]   Ibid., pp. 213–15.

that peace is in general preferable to war says nothing to someone who believes that he has reasons to prefer war over peace; indeed, showing him the means of establishing a durable peace is only going to arouse his opposition. . . .

All the powers of Europe have rights or claims relative to one another. However, these rights are inherently unable to be elucidated in any absolute way, both because there is no common or constant rule with which to judge them and because they are often founded on ambivalent or uncertain facts. Nor can the conflicts that they cause ever be completely settled in any permanent way – as much because of the lack of any competent arbiter as because each prince will heedlessly take any chance he can get to revoke the concessions that were forced upon him, either by treaties made by the more powerful or by his defeat in a bitter war.

It is therefore an error to think only about one's own claims upon others and to forget the claims that others have upon us, for there is no means on either side to make these reciprocal claims valid. Once it becomes clear that these things all depend on chance, then simple common sense forbids us to risk our present possessions for a future gain, even when the odds for success are even. Certainly everyone blames a well-to-do man who, in the hope of doubling his holdings, dares risk them all with a throw of the dice. But we have made it clear that, in plans for expansion, each one, even in the present system, would find a resistance superior to his effort. It follows from this that, since the more powerful have no reason to play the game and the weak have no hope of profiting from it, it would be a benefit for all to renounce what they desire in the interests of guaranteeing what they have.

Let us consider the expenditure of men, of money, of force of all kinds, the impoverishment into which even the most propitious war throws any state, and let us compare this damage to the advantages that might be drawn from it. We will find that the victor often has lost when he thinks he has won, and that, being always weaker after the war than he was before, his only consolation is to see the defeated suffering even more than himself. But even this advantage is more apparent than real, because whatever superiority one might have gained over one's adversary is at the same time lost in respect to the neutral states, which, without changing their status, fortify themselves in direct relation to what the combatants have lost.

If every king has not yet renounced the lust for conquest, it seems that the wiser of them are at least beginning to see that wars cost more than they are worth. In this regard, without entering into a thousand distinctions that would lead us too far afield, we can say in general that a prince who, to extend his frontiers, loses as many former subjects as he acquires new ones, thus becomes weaker through his desire to grow. With a greater territory to defend, he no longer has any defenders. Moreover, we cannot ignore that, in the manner in which war is waged today, it is not in the armies that the greatest fatalities occur. It is there that we may find the most apparent and obvious losses, but at the same time throughout the state the increase in the number of those who will never be

born, the rise in taxes, the interruption of commerce, the desertion of the countryside, and the abandonment of agriculture all cause a more serious and irreparable harm than the loss of men who die. Such evils, while perhaps not immediately
evident, make themselves known painfully later on, and it is then that people are
surprised at being so weak after supposedly making themselves so strong. . . .

It would be useless to object here that I am proving too much and that if
things were really the way I represent them and each sovereign had a true
common interest in maintaining peace, then peace would be established by itself
and would last forever without any confederation. This would be to engage in
very poor reasoning in the present situation. For although it would be much
better for everyone always to be at peace, the common lack of security in this
respect makes it so that each one, lacking any assurance of being able to avoid
war, tries at least to begin it with an advantage in case the occasion presents itself,
and to anticipate his neighbor – who in turn does not miss any favorable occasion
to anticipate him. Hence many wars, even offensive wars, result less from the
desire to usurp the interests of others than from the unjust precautions that each
side takes to make its own interests secure. However worthy a commitment to
the public good might be in general, given the objectives that are followed in
politics and even in morality, it is certain that these commitments become dangerous
to anyone who persists in practicing them with others when no one else practices
them with him.

Having registered this unease, Rousseau seems again to take on the cloak of Saint-
Pierre, so to speak, and turns to the interesting question of where these plans
leave individual states with regard to their sovereignty. His answer is that such a
federation by no means infringes on a state's rightful claim to sovereignty – quite
the contrary: "they would only assure themselves of their real rights and renounce
those that they do not have" (*Summary*, p. 216). However, it is only as an appended
thought here, an "added bonus" of the system, so to speak, that the contemporary reader will locate the Achilles' heel of the project. "[T]he tribunal would make
the rights of sovereignty even more assured than they are now," writes Rousseau,
"by guaranteeing to each not only his security against any foreign invasion but
also his authority in respect to any internal rebellion. Consequently princes would
not be less absolute, and their crown would be even more secure" (ibid.). This
observation would seem simply to bypass, or indeed fall squarely and unreflectively
to one side of, the dilemma that today faces anyone who wishes to take seriously
the notion of humanitarian intervention. Today, a consensus seems to be emerging that human rights place constraints on the legitimate exercise of sovereignty,
even if controversies persist as to exactly what these constraints are and how
we may enforce their observance. It might perhaps seem paradoxical that while
supranational adjudicatory institutions such as that proposed by Saint-Pierre may
be our greatest chance of enforcing such constraints, the very prospect of having

to countenance such constraints may, tragically, be the greatest obstacle to seeing such institutions into existence.

Finally, Rousseau summarizes the many advantages he sees as flowing from Saint-Pierre's proposal, were it to be adopted.

From *Summary of the Abbé de Saint-Pierre's Project for Perpetual Peace*[11]

1   Complete assurance that their present and future conflicts would always be terminated without any war – an assurance incomparably more useful for sovereigns than a similar assurance of never having to engage in lawsuits would be for individuals.
2   The removal or at least the reduction to a minor role of the causes of conflict by the erasure of all prior claims – an act which will compensate for what they give up and secure what they possess.
3   Complete and perpetual security both for the person of the prince and for that of his family, and for his states, and for the order of succession fixed by the laws of each country – as much against the ambition of unjust and power-hungry pretenders as against the revolts of rebel subjects.
4   Perfect security for the administration of all reciprocal agreements between one prince and another to be guaranteed by the European Republic.
5   Liberty and perfect and perpetual security in regard to commerce, both between state and state and for each state in distant regions.
6   Total and perpetual cutting back of prodigious military expenditures on land and at sea in times of war and a considerable lowering of ordinary expenditures in times of peace.
7   Evident progress in agriculture and in population growth, in the wealth of the state, and in the revenues of the prince.
8   Greater ease in establishing projects that could add to the glory and authority of the sovereign, the resources of the public, and the happiness of the people.

As I have said before, I will leave to the judgment of my readers both the examination of all these articles and the comparison of the state of peace that would result from the Confederation with the state of war that results from European anarchy.

If we have reasoned well in the exposition of this project, it is demonstrated, first, that the establishment of perpetual peace depends solely on the consent of sovereigns and presents no difficulty other than their resistance; second, that this establishment would be useful to them in every way and that there is no comparison even for them between its inconveniences and its advantages; third, that it is

---

[11]   Ibid., pp. 219–20.

reasonable to suppose that their will accords with their self-interest; finally, that this establishment, once it is developed according to the proposed plan, would be solid and durable and would fulfill its objective perfectly. Doubtless this is not to say that sovereigns will adopt this project (who can speak for the reasoning of others?) but only that if they were to adopt it, they would be acting with respect to their own true interests. For it must be observed that we have not been considering men such as they ought to be – good, generous, disinterested, and loving the public well-being from a humanitarian standpoint – but such as they are – unjust, greedy, and looking to their own self-interest above all else. The only thing that we have assumed about them is that they are both rational enough to perceive what is useful to them and courageous enough to work toward their own happiness. If, despite all this, the project remains unfulfilled, it is not therefore because it is too idealistic; rather, it is because men are insane and because it is a sort of folly to remain wise in the midst of those who are mad.

Critique of the Abbé de Saint-Pierre's Project for Perpetual Peace

The last of Rousseau's works from which we will be excerpting here is his *Critique* of Saint-Pierre's perpetual peace project. The *Critique* was first published in 1782, six years after Rousseau's death, having been held back by the author for fear of controversy. The work opens with praise for Saint-Pierre's bold and visionary peace plan, but soon enough its critical intent shines through. For while it would be true that the European Republic, could it first be brought about, would have the effects envisioned by Saint-Pierre, the problem remains that, if we follow his proposals, it will never come into existence. As such, while it is "a solid and sensible book", Rousseau worries that, in its present form, its proposals may be "ineffectual for producing peace and superfluous for maintaining it" (*Critique*, pp. 221–2).

As Rousseau sees it, Saint-Pierre takes a much too charitable view of the motivation of sovereigns, assuming that they can be persuaded by way of reason, rather than merely appealed to by way of passions. Accordingly, if there is to be a future to Saint-Pierre's peace proposal, it must be recast in a form that speaks to the base sentiments of rulers.

From *Critique of the Abbé de Saint-Pierre's Project for Perpetual Peace*[12]

We must distinguish, then, in politics as well as in morality, real interest from apparent interest. The first is to be found in perpetual peace – that has been

---

[12]   Ibid., pp. 222–3, 224–5.

demonstrated in the *Project*. The second can be found in the condition of absolute independence that draws sovereigns away from the rule of law in order to submit them to the rule of chance – like a mad sailor who, to show off his knowledge and intimidate his crew, would prefer to drift dangerously among the reefs during a storm than to secure his ship with an anchor.

The whole preoccupation of kings, or of those to whom they delegate their duties, centers on two sole objectives – to extend their domination outside their borders and to make it more absolute within. Any other purpose either relates to one of these two or else only serves as a pretext for them. Examples of such pretexts are the notions of "public well-being," the "happiness of the people," and the "glory of the nation."

Judge, on the basis of these two fundamental principles, how princes might receive a proposal that strikes directly at the first and is hardly favorable to the second. For it is clear that with the European Assembly the government of each state would be just as clearly defined as its borders, that princes could not be guaranteed their security from the revolts of their subjects without at the same time guaranteeing their subjects security from the tyranny of princes, and that otherwise the institution could not survive. Now, I ask if there is in the whole world even one sovereign who, limited thus for ever in his most cherished projects, would support without indignation the idea of seeing himself forced to be just, not only toward foreigners but even toward his own subjects. . . .

A prince who places his survival on the chances of war is not unaware that he runs certain risks, but he pays less attention to the risks than to the advantages that he anticipates. For he fears fortune far less than he hopes to profit from his own skill. If he is powerful, he counts on his own forces; if he is weak, he counts on his allies. Furthermore, war can be useful to him internally as a way of getting rid of domestic complaints, of weakening subjects who are unruly, even of suffering reversals – for the clever politician knows how to take advantage of his own defeats. . . .

. . . Always to evaluate a sovereign's gains and losses in monetary terms makes for a very faulty form of calculation, for the extent of one's actual power cannot be measured by how many millions one possesses. The schemes of a prince form a never-ending upward spiral. He wants to have more power in order to increase his wealth and to increase his wealth in order to have more power. He will sacrifice each in turn to acquire that which is lacking. . . .

We must add, in considering the great commercial advantages that would result from a general and perpetual peace, that while they are obviously in themselves certain and incontestable, being common to all they would not be relative advantages to anyone. Since advantage is usually only sensed by virtue of difference, to add to one's relative power one must seek out only exclusive gains. . . .

Nor is it possible to believe along with the Abbé de Saint-Pierre that, even with the good will which neither princes nor ministers will ever have, it would be easy to find a favorable moment to set this system in motion. For that it would be necessary that the sum of individual interests would not outweigh the common interest, and that each one would believe that he had found in the good of all the greatest good that he could hope for for himself. Now this would require a convergence of wisdom among so many different minds and a convergence of aims among so many different interests that one could hardly hope to get the happy agreement of all these necessary circumstances simply by chance. The only way to make up for the failure of this agreement to come about by chance would be to make it come about by force. Then it would no longer be a question of persuading but of compelling, and then what would be needed is not to write books but to levy troops.

Thus, although the project was very wise, the means of putting it into effect reflect the naiveté of the author. He innocently imagined that all you would need to do is to assemble a committee, propose his articles, have everyone sign them, and that would be it. We must conclude that, as with all the projects of this good man, he could envision quite well the effect of things after they had been established, but he judged with too little sophistication the methods for getting them established in the first place.

Rousseau then takes issue with one of the Abbé's favored examples, one which he frequently cited as the inspiration for his own thoughts on the matter, namely the peace plan that Sully drafted on behalf of Henri IV. Sully's "Grand Design" to create a peaceful Europe through cooperative effort was cut short by the assassination of the king in 1610. However, Rousseau does not dismiss the relevance of the example: rather he uses it for his own critical purposes, subtly turning the tables on Saint-Pierre. For the way in which Sully and Henri IV schemed to bring the federation into existence was not the way proposed by Saint-Pierre. Instead it spoke directly to the strategic interests of the princes, addressing their wish to counteract the ascendancy of the House of Habsburg. The end may have been peace, but the means were anything but pacific.

From *Critique of the Abbé de Saint-Pierre's Project for Perpetual Peace*[13]

Everyone concurred with the great aim without really being able to say what that aim was – like workers who labor separately at parts of a new machine without knowing either its form or its function.

What helped this general movement along? Was it a perpetual peace, which no one foresaw and few even cared about? Was it public concern, which is never any private person's concern? The Abbé de Saint-Pierre might have thought so! But

---

[13]   Ibid., pp. 227, 228–9.

in fact each one worked only with regard to his own individual self-interest, which Henri had the ingenuity to show them all in a very attractive guise. . . .

Without knowing his views, Europe watched his extensive preparations attentively, and, with a certain amount of trepidation, waited to see what would happen. A minor pretext was to set off this great upheaval – a war that would end all wars was to make way for immortal peace – when an event, which was made even more shocking by the mystery surrounding it, came to banish forever this last hope of the world. The same blow that ended the days of this good king plunged Europe back into eternal wars that she can scarcely hope to see come to an end. Nevertheless, those were the elements that Henri IV brought together to form the same enterprise that the Abbé de Saint-Pierre claimed to create with a book.

We may not say, therefore, that if his system has not been adopted, it is because it was not good; on the contrary, we must say that it was too good to be adopted. For evil and abuse, which so many men profit from, happen by themselves, but whatever is useful to the public must be brought by force-seeing as special interests are almost always opposed to it. Doubtless perpetual peace is at present a project that seems absurd; but were we to be given a Henri IV and a Sully, perpetual peace might become a project that once again would seem reasonable. Instead, let us admire such a fine plan, but be consoled that we will never see it come about, for that can only happen by means that humanity might find violent and fearful.

We will not see federative leagues establishing themselves except by revolution, and, on this principle, who would dare to say whether this European league is to be desired or to be feared? It would perhaps cause more harm in one moment than it could prevent for centuries to come.

Thus, Rousseau's *Critique*, and by that token, his writings on war and peace, end on a note of uncertainty. While there is no disputing the ideal of a perpetual peace, the means by which such a peace could be brought into existence may cause more harm than good. Moreover, being fatefully dependent on "great men" – the warlords and princes of Europe – for its feasibility, who is to say that behind the plan there may not lurk the intention to strike at the least expected time?

Still, while Rousseau himself could not give the perpetual peace ideal his full and unqualified approval, his writings on war and peace, including his *Summary of Saint-Pierre's Project*, would wield an enormous influence. Not long after, the perpetual peace tradition would find its arguably most sophisticated spokesman in Immanuel Kant, whose *Perpetual Peace* in many ways marks the tradition's coming of age. Moreover, with Kant's cosmopolitan ambitions, the plans for a pacific federation would no longer just encompass Europe, but would in principle stretch worldwide.

40

Emer de Vattel (1714–1767)

War in Due Form

Thus, considered externally and in the sight of men, the rights founded on the state of war . . . in no way depend on the justice of the cause. They depend rather on the legitimacy of the means, that is to say, on the presence of the elements constituting a war in due form.

The Law of Nations

The Law of Nations (*Le droit des gens*), by the Swiss diplomat Emer de Vattel, stands at the crossroads between the centuries' old tradition of just war and the newly emergent discipline of international law. The work's treatment of the *ius ad bellum* is framed in traditional categories. Vattel's main innovation in this domain was to provide a set of arguments justifying resort to preventive war. It was, however, in his articulation of the *ius in bello* that Vattel broke decisively with the idea, shared by all classical just war theorists, that the rights of war pertain unilaterally to the just belligerent.[1] In close conformity with the thought of Christian von Wolff (whose conception of the law of nations he sought to popularize), Vattel contended that the depredations of war would greatly be reduced if sovereigns could be persuaded to observe general rules of warfare.[2] From Wolff he took the idea that the rules of "war in due form" or "regular war" were to be reciprocally binding upon all states, regardless of the justice (or injustice) of their cause. Likewise, the legal effects of war (impunity for killing enemy soldiers, the right to seize and

---

[1] For an account of Vattel's break with the earlier just war tradition, and his relation to Grotius, Pufendorf, Wolff, and other leading figures in the development of classical international law, see Emmanuelle Jouannet, *Emer de Vattel et l'émergence doctrinale du droit international classique* (Paris: A. Pedone, 1998), especially, partie I, titre II, chap. 2: "Mise en oeuvre du droit des gens volontaire: De l'unilatéralisme au bilatéralisme des règles du droit des gens," pp. 221–50.

[2] Wolff and Vattel both maintained that these "external" rules of conduct in some measure depend on the common consent of nations, hence, following Grotius's terminology, they pertain to the *voluntary law of nations* (*ius gentium voluntarium*).

acquire enemy property, and so forth) were to apply bilaterally to all belligerents, provided that they had the status of sovereign states. One belligerent could not allege the justice of his cause as a ground for excluding these prerogatives from his opponent.

On this account, concrete decision-making about the resort to armed force was taken to be the exclusive privilege of individual states. Each state was free to choose the course of action that seemed best suited to its interests. And although a sovereign could inwardly sin by going to war for unjustifiable reasons (thus violating the *ius ad bellum* dictates of the natural law), he could not be held publicly accountable by the community of states for such wrongdoing. Public accountability was confined to violations of the laws of war. These laws were now conceptualized as an autonomous sphere of norms regulating the conduct of independent nations within the juridical "state of war." Vattel discussed these rules of war in considerable detail. First published in 1758, *The Law of Nations* circulated widely, and exercised a broad influence on both sides of the Atlantic. It served as a basic handbook for diplomats up until World War I, and articulated the main presuppositions which underlie the later codification of humanitarian law in the Hague and Geneva Conventions.

The selections that follow offer a cross-section of Vattel's basic ideas on the law of war. They begin with some lines (taken from the Introduction to the *Law of Nations*) on the independence and juridical equality of sovereign states. Vattel makes clear from the outset that he will study the special rights and duties that exist between independent nations. He and Wolff were among the very first authors to make the *ius inter gentes* a deliberate object of study. Previous authors (Grotius and Zouche,[3] in particular) had already developed theories about the international legal order, and had sought to explain what rules might regulate disputes between distinct "jurisdictions" or "sovereignties," i.e. between those individuals and communities who have "no common judge." Wolff and Vattel broke new ground, however, when they discarded individuals from the scene, and thereby conceived of "peoples" (or, better, "nations") as compact entities confronting each other within a distinct sphere of action.[4]

Vattel's vision of sovereign states, juridically equal, each bound by a fundamental obligation of self-preservation, set the stage for his re-appraisal of preventive war, a practice that had been defended by Gentili, but rejected by Grotius. Vattel situates his treatment within the context of eighteenth-century balance-of-power politics. In this respect he brings to the question of preventive war (discussed in bk. III, chap. III on just causes of defensive and offensive war) a perspective quite different from that of his predecessor Gentili.

[3]   The English jurist Richard Zouche (1590–1661) was an key figure in the development of international law. In 1650, he published the first textbook on *ius inter gentes*, as indicated by its subtitle: *Iuris et iudicii fecialis, sive iuris inter gentes, et quaestionum de eodem explicatio.*

[4]   See Peter P. Remec, *The Position of the Individual in International Law according to Grotius and Vattel* (The Hague: Martinus Nijhoff, 1960).

The remaining selections focus on Vattel's conception of right conduct in war (bk. III, chaps. VIII, IX, and XII), both the general principles of "war in due form," as well as their application to specific cases (for instance, whether enemy soldiers who have surrendered may be killed, or whether buildings of cultural significance may be destroyed). The selections conclude with some passages where Vattel explains how the bilateral laws of war extend even to civil wars, despite the fact that one of the two belligerents does not have the formal status of a sovereign.

From *The Law Of Nations*[5]

Introduction: Idea and General Principles of the Law of Nations[6]

1 Nations or States are political bodies, societies of men who have united together and combined their forces, in order to procure their mutual welfare and security.

2 Such a society has its own affairs and interests; it deliberates and takes resolutions in common, and it thus becomes a moral person having an understanding and a will peculiar to itself, and susceptible at once of obligations and of rights.

3 The object of this work is to establish on a firm basis the obligations and the rights of Nations. The *Law of Nations* is *the science of the law* (la science du droit) *which exists between Nations or States, and of the obligations which follow from this law*.

It will be seen from this treatise how States, as such, ought to regulate all of their actions. . . . A Nation must therefore understand the nature of its obligations, not only to avoid acting contrary to its duty, but also to obtain there from a clear knowledge of its rights, of what it can legitimately exact from other Nations. . . .

18 Since men are by nature equal, and their individual rights and obligations the same, as coming equally from nature, Nations, which are composed of men and may be regarded as so many free persons living together in a state of nature, are by nature equal and hold from nature the same obligations and the same rights. Strength or weakness, in this case, counts for nothing. A dwarf is as much a man as a giant is; a small Republic is no less a sovereign State than the most powerful Kingdom.

---

[5]   Full title: *The Law of Nations or the Principles of Natural Law, Applied to the Conduct and to the Affairs of Nations and of Sovereigns*. The passages reproduced below are taken (with some amendments) from the English translation by Charles G. Fenwick, in The Classics of International Law (Washington, DC: Carnegie Institution, 1916). Volumes I and II of this edition reproduce the original text of 1758 (Neuchâtel).

[6]   Ibid., pp. 6–7.

19 From this equality it necessarily follows that what is permitted or prohibited for one Nation is equally permitted or prohibited for every other Nation. . . .

21 Since Nations are free, independent, and equal, and since each has the right to decide in its conscience what it must do to fulfill its duties, the effect of this is to produce, before the world at least, a perfect equality of rights among Nations in the conduct of their affairs and in the pursuit of their policies. The intrinsic justice of their conduct is another matter which it is not for others to make a definitive judgment upon; so that what one may do another may do, and they must be regarded in the society of mankind as having equal rights (*un droit égal*).

Book I. Chapter II: General Principles of the Duties of a Nation towards Itself[7]

13 If the rights of a Nation are derived from its obligations (section 3), they are chiefly derived from those which the Nation owes to itself. We shall likewise see that its duties toward others mainly depend on, and should be regulated and measured by, its duties toward itself. Hence in treating of the obligations and rights of Nations we shall begin, for the sake of order, by setting forth what each Nation owes to itself. . . .

16 When men, by the act of associating together, form a State or Nation, each individual agrees to procure the common good of all, and all together agree to assist each in obtaining the means of providing for his needs and to protect and defend him. It is clear that these reciprocal agreements can only be fulfilled by maintaining the political association. The whole Nation is therefore bound to maintain it; and since its maintenance constitutes the self-preservation of a Nation, it follows that every Nation is bound to preserve its corporate existence. . . .

17 If a Nation is bound to preserve its existence it is not less bound to preserve carefully the lives of its members. It owes this duty to itself; for the loss of any one of its members would weaken it and in so far attack its corporate existence. It owes the same duty to its individual members by reason of the very act of association by which they united for their mutual defense and welfare. No one may be deprived of the benefits of that union so long as he fulfills his part of the agreement.

The body of a Nation, therefore, may not abandon a province, a town, or even an individual belonging to it, unless necessity should constrain it to do so, or urgent reasons of public safety make the act lawful.

18 The right of self-preservation carries with it the right to whatever is necessary for that purpose, for the natural law gives us the right to all those things without which we cannot satisfy our obligations; otherwise it would oblige us to do what is impossible, or rather it would contradict itself, by prescribing a duty

---

[7] Ibid., pp. 13–14.

and at the same time refusing us the sole means of fulfilling it. However, it is clear that these means must not be unjust in themselves, or such as the natural law absolutely prohibits. As the use of such means would never be allowed, a general obligation, which could be satisfied on a given occasion in no other way, would be regarded as impossible of fulfillment, and consequently void.

19 It clearly follows from what has been said that that a Nation should avoid carefully and so far as possible whatever might bring about its destruction, or that of the State, for the two are identical.

20 A Nation or State has the right to whatever can assist it in warding off a threatening danger, or in keeping at a distance things that might bring about its ruin. The same reasons hold good here as for the right to whatever is necessary for self-preservation. . . .

Book III. Chapter I: War; the Various Kinds of War; the Right to Make War[8]

1 *War is that state in which one prosecutes one's right by force.* The word is also taken to mean the act itself or the manner of prosecuting one's right by force. But it is more in accord with usage, and more suitable in a treatise on the law of war, to take the term in the sense we have given it.

2 *Public war* is that which takes place between Nations or sovereigns, which is carried on in the name of the public power and by its order. It is public war of which we are to treat here. *Private war*, which takes place between individuals, belongs to the field of the natural law in its strict sense. . . .

4 . . . It is the sovereign power alone, therefore, which is entitled to make war. But as the various rights constituting that power, which ultimately resides in the body of the Nation, can be separated or limited, according to the will of the Nation (bk. I, sections 31 and 45), it is in the individual constitution of each State that we must look to find where is located the power to make war in the name of the State. The Kings of England, whose power is in other respects so limited, have the right to declare war, and to make peace. The Kings of Sweden have lost it. . . .

5 War is either *defensive* or *offensive*. A State which takes up arms to repel the attack of an enemy carries on a *defensive* war. A State which is the first to take up arms, and which attacks a Nation living at peace with it, carries on an *offensive* war. The purpose of defensive war is simple, namely, self-defense; the purpose of offensive war varies according to the different affairs of each Nation, but in general it relates either to the prosecution of certain rights or to their protection. A sovereign attacks a Nation, either to obtain something to which he lays claim or to punish the Nation for an injury he has received from it or to forestall an

---

[8]   Ibid., pp. 235–6, 243, 248–53, 279–80, 293–4, 304–6, 336, 338–40.

injury which it is about to inflict upon him, and avert a danger which seems to threaten him. . . .

Chapter III: The Just Causes of War

. . . **25** If men were always reasonable they would settle their quarrels by an appeal to reason; justice and equity would be their rule of decision, their judge. Forcible means (*voies de la force*) are a sad and unfortunate expedient to be used against those who despise justice and refuse to listen to reason; but, after all, these means must be adopted when all others fail. A wise and just Nation, a good ruler, will only use it as a last resort (*à l'extrémité*). . . .

42 We are here presented with a celebrated question which is of the greatest importance. It is asked whether the aggrandizement of a neighboring State, in consequence of which a Nation fears that it will one day be oppressed, is a sufficient ground for making war upon it; whether a Nation can with justice take up arms to resist the growing power of that State, or to weaken the State, with the sole object of protecting itself from the dangers with which weak States are almost always threatened from an overpowerful one. The question presents no difficulties to the majority of statesmen; it is more perplexing for those who seek at all times to unite justice with prudence.

On the one hand, a State which increases its power by all the efforts of a good government does nothing but what is praiseworthy; it fulfills its duties towards itself and does not violate those which it owes to other Nations. The sovereign who by inheritance, by a free election, or by any other just and proper means, unites new provinces or entire kingdoms to his States, is merely acting on his right, and wrongs no one. How would it be right to attack a State which increases its power by legitimate means? A Nation must have received an injury, or be clearly threatened with one before it is authorized to take up arms as having a just ground for war (sections 26, 27). On the other hand, we know only too well from sad and constant experience that predominant States rarely fail to trouble their neighbors, to oppress them, and even to subjugate them completely, when they have an opportunity of doing so with impunity. Europe was on the point of being enslaved for lack of timely opposition to the growing power of Charles V. Must we await the danger? Must we let the storm gather strength when it might be scattered at its rising? Must we suffer a neighboring State to grow in power and await quietly until it is ready to enslave us? Will it be time to defend ourselves when we are no longer able to? Prudence is a duty incumbent upon all men, and particularly upon the rulers of Nations, who are appointed to watch over the welfare of an entire people. Let us try to solve this important question conformably to the sacred principles of the Law of Nature and of Nations. It will be seen that they do not lead to weak scruples, and that it is always true to say that justice is inseparable from sound statesmanship.

43 First of all, let us observe that prudence, which is certainly a virtue very necessary in sovereigns, can never counsel the use of illegitimate means in order to obtain a just and praiseworthy end. Do not object here that the welfare of the people is the supreme law of the State; for the welfare of the people, the common welfare of Nations, forbids the use of means that are contrary to justice and honor. Why are certain means illegitimate? If we look at the matter closely, if we go back to first principles, we shall see that it is precisely because the introduction of such means would be hurtful to human society, a source of evil to all Nations. Note in particular what we said in treating of the observance of justice (bk. II, chap. V). It is, therefore, to the interest and even to the welfare of all Nations that we must hold as a sacred principle that the end does not justify the means. And since war is only permissible in order to redress an injury received, or to secure oneself against an injury which threatens (section 26), it is a sacred rule of the Law of Nations that the aggrandizement of a State can not alone and of itself give any one the right to take up arms to resist it.

44 Supposing, then, that no injury has been received from that State, we must have reason to think ourselves threatened with one before we may legitimately take up arms. Now, power alone does not constitute a threat of injury; the will to injure must accompany the power. It is unfortunate for the human race that the will to oppress can almost always be believed to exist where there is found the power to do so with impunity. But the two are not necessarily inseparable; and the only right which results from the fact that they ordinarily or frequently go together is that first appearances may be taken as a sufficient proof. As soon as a State has given evidence of injustice, greed, pride, ambition, or a desire of domineering over its neighbors, it becomes an object of suspicion which they must guard against. They may hold it up at the moment it is about to receive a formidable addition to its power, and demand securities of it; and if it hesitates to give these, they may impede (*prévenir*) its designs by force of arms. The interests of Nations have an importance quite different from the interests of individuals; the sovereign can not be indolent in his guardianship over them; he can not put aside his suspicions out of magnanimity and generosity. A Nation's whole existence is at stake when it has a neighbor that is at once powerful and ambitious. Since it is the lot of men to be guided in most cases by probabilities, these probabilities deserve their attention in proportion to the importance of the subject-matter; and, if I may borrow a geometrical expression, one is justified in forestalling a danger in direct ratio to the degree of probability attending it, and to the seriousness of the evil with which one is threatened. If the evil in question be endurable, if the loss be of small account, prompt action need not be taken; there is no great danger in delaying measures of self-protection until we are certain that there is actual danger of the evil. But suppose the safety of the State is endangered; our foresight can not extend too far. Are we to delay averting our destruction until it has become inevitable? . . .

If an unknown man takes aim at me in the middle of a forest I am not yet certain that he wishes to kill me; must I allow him time to fire in order to be sure of his intent? Is there any reasonable casuist who would deny me the right to forestall the act? But presumption becomes almost equal to certitude if the Prince who is about to acquire enormous power has already given evidence of an unbridled pride and ambition. . . .

45 It is still easier to prove that if this formidable sovereign should betray unjust and ambitious dispositions by doing the smallest wrong to another State, all Nations may profit by the opportunity, and together join forces with the injured State in order to put down the ambitious Prince and disable him from so easily oppressing his neighbors, or from giving them constant cause for fear. For a State which has received an injury has the right to provide for its future security by depriving the offender of the means of doing harm; and it is permissible, and even praiseworthy, to assist those who are oppressed or unjustly attacked. . . .

46 But suppose that this powerful State is both just and prudent in its conduct and gives no ground of complaint; are we to regard its progress with an indifferent eye? Are we idly to look upon its rapid increase of power and imprudently lay ourselves open to the designs which its power may inspire in it? Certainly not. Careless indifference would be unpardonable in a matter of such great importance. . . . But force of arms is not the only means of guarding against a formidable State. There are gentler means, which are always legitimate. The most efficacious of these is an alliance of other less powerful sovereigns, who, by uniting their forces, are enabled to counterbalance the sovereign who excites their alarm. Let them be faithful and steadfast in their alliance, and their union will insure the safety of each.

They have also the right mutually to favor one another, to the exclusion of the sovereign whom they fear; and by the privileges of every sort, and especially by the commercial privileges which they will mutually grant to one another's subjects, and which they will refuse to the subjects of that dangerous sovereign, they will add to their strength, and at the same time lessen his, without giving him reason for complaint, since every one may dispose freely of his favors. . . .

48 . . . It is simpler, easier, and more just to have recourse to the method just referred to, of forming alliances in order to make a stand against a very powerful sovereign and prevent him from dominating. This is the plan followed by the sovereigns of Europe at the present day. They look upon the two principal powers, who for that very reason are naturally rivals, as destined to act as a mutual check upon each other, and they unite with the weaker of the two, thereby acting as so much weight thrown into the lighter scale in order to make the balance even. . . .

49 . . . Finally, there is no question but that if that formidable prince is clearly entertaining designs of oppression and conquest, if he betrays his plans by preparations or other advances, other Nations have the right to check him; and if the fortune of war be favorable to them, they may profit by the favorable opportunity

to weaken and reduce his strength, which upsets the balance of power and constitutes a menace to the common liberty of all.

This right on the part of Nations is still more evident as against a sovereign
who is always ready to take to arms without cause and without plausible pretext,
and who is thus a constant disturber of the public peace.

50 . . . We have now said enough on the general principles by which the
justice of a war may be estimated. Those who understand well the principles, and
who have just ideas of the various rights of Nations, will easily apply the rules to
particular cases. . . .

Chapter VIII: The Law of Nations in Time of War; First, What it is Justifiable and What it is Permissible to Do to the Person of the Enemy in a Just War[9]

136 What we have said thus far relates to the right to make war. Let us now
proceed to the law which should govern the war itself, to the rules which Nations
should mutually observe, even when they have taken up arms for the settlement
of their disputes. Let us begin by setting forth the rights of the sovereign who
is waging a just war; let us see what it is permitted for him to do to his enemy.
His whole conduct may be deduced from a single principle – namely, from the
aim (*but*) of a just war; for when the end is legitimate he who has a right to
pursue that end has, naturally, a right to make use of all the means necessary
to attain it. . . .

137 A legitimate end confers a right only to those means which are necessary
to attain that end. Whatever is done in excess of such measures is contrary to the
natural law, and must be condemned as despicable before the tribunal of conscience. Hence it follows that certain acts of hostility may be justifiable or not,
according to circumstances. What is perfectly innocent and just in one war, owing
to peculiar conditions, is not always so on other occasions; right keeps pace with
need, with the demands of the situation; it never goes beyond those limits.

But as it is very difficult always to form a just estimate of what the actual
situation demands, and, moreover, as it is for each Nation to determine what its
particular circumstances warrant it in doing (Introduction, section 16), it becomes
absolutely necessary that Nations should mutually conform to certain general

---

[9]   In this and the following readings we provide only some short excerpts from Vattel's very lengthy
treatment of issues relating to proper conduct in war. He covers a wide variety of topics, including an
assessment of practices such as assassination, the use of poisoned weapons, enslavement of prisoners,
spying, seduction of enemy subjects as an inducement to treason, devastation of enemy property, and
so forth.

rules on this subject. Thus, when it is clear and well recognized that such a measure, such an act of hostility, is, in general necessary for overcoming the resistance of the enemy and achieving the goal of a legitimate war, that measure, viewed thus in the abstract, is regarded by the Law of Nations as legitimate and proper in war, although the belligerent who makes use of it without necessity, when less severe measures would have answered his purpose, would not be guiltless before God and in his own conscience. This is what constitutes the difference between what is just, proper, and irreprehensible in war, and what is merely permissible and may be done by Nations with impunity. . . .

139 The enemy who unjustly attacks me gives me an unquestionable right to repel his attack; and he who takes up arms against me, when I am demanding only what is due to me, becomes himself the real aggressor by his unjust resistance; he is the original author of the war, since he obliges me to use force in order to protect myself from the wrong he wishes to do me either in my person or in my property. If the use of this force be carried so far as to take away his life, he alone is responsible for that unfortunate result; for if I were obliged to submit to the wrong rather than hurt him, the good would soon become the prey of the wicked. Such is the source of the right to kill our enemies in a just war. . . .

140 But the very argument for the right to kill our enemies points out the limits of that right. As soon as an enemy submits and hands over his arms we are no longer entitled to take away his life. Hence we must give quarter to those who lay down their arms, and when besieging a town we must never refuse to spare the lives of a garrison which offers to surrender. . . .

141 There is one case, however, in which we may refuse to give quarter to enemies who surrender, or to accept any terms of capitulation from a locale reduced to extremities. This is when the enemy have rendered themselves guilty of some grave violation of the Law of Nations, and especially when they have violated the laws of war. Such a refusal to spare their lives is not a natural consequence of the war, but a punishment of their crime, a punishment which the injured party has a right to inflict. But in order that the punishment may be just, it must fall upon those who are guilty. When a sovereign is at war with a savage Nation which observes no rules and never thinks of giving quarter he may punish the Nation in the person of those whom he captures (for they are among the guilty), and by such severity endeavor to make them observe the laws of humanity; but in all cases where severity is not absolutely necessary mercy should be shown. . . . No matter how just the grounds one may have for punishing a sovereign with whom one is at war, one will always be accused of cruelty if this punishment is inflicted upon his innocent subjects. There are other means of punishing the sovereign; he may be deprived of some of his rights, or certain of his towns and provinces may be taken away. The evil which his whole Nation suffers in this last case is an unavoidable result of the common destiny shared by those who unite in civil society. . . .

Chapter IX: The Law of War with respect to the Property of the Enemy

168 . . . For whatever cause a country be devastated those buildings should be spared which are an honor to the human race and which do not add to the strength of the enemy, such as temples, tombs, public buildings, and all edifices of remarkable beauty. What is gained by destroying them? It is the act of a declared enemy of the human race thus wantonly to deprive men of these monuments of art and models of architecture. . . .

However, if in order to carry on the operations of the war, or to push forward the plans of a siege, it is necessary to destroy buildings of that character, we have an undoubted right to do so. The sovereign of the country, or his general, does not scruple to destroy them when the needs or the policy of war call for such a step. The governor of a besieged town burns the suburbs to prevent the besiegers from encamping in them. No one thinks of blaming a general for devastating gardens, vineyards, and orchards, in order to locate his camp on the spot and throw up an entrenchment. If he thereby destroys some work of art it is an accident, an unfortunate consequence of the war; and he will not be blamed except on those occasions when he could have camped elsewhere without any inconvenience. . . .

172 What we have said is sufficient to give a general idea of the moderation with which, in the most just war, a belligerent should use the right to pillage and devastate the enemy's country. Apart from the case in which there is question of punishing an enemy, the whole may be summed up in this general rule: All acts of hostility which injure the enemy without necessity, or which do not tend to procure victory and bring about the end of war, are unjustifiable, and as such condemned by the natural law. . . .

Chapter XII: The Voluntary Law of Nations with respect to the Effects of War in Due Form, Independently of the Justice of the Cause

188 . . . It belongs to every free and sovereign State to decide in its own conscience what its duties require of it, and what it may or may not do with justice (Introduction, section 16). If others undertake to judge of its conduct, they encroach upon its liberty and infringe upon its most valuable rights (Introduction, section 15). Moreover, since each Nation claims to have justice on its side, it will arrogate to itself all the rights of war and claim that its enemy has none, that his hostilities are but deeds of robbery, acts in violation of the Law of Nations, and deserving of punishment by all Nations. A rightful determination (*la décision du droit*) of the controversy will not be advanced thereby, and the contest will become more cruel, more disastrous in its effects, and more difficult of termination. Further still, neutral Nations themselves will be drawn into the dispute and implicated in the quarrel. . . .

189 Let us, therefore, leave to the conscience of sovereigns the observance of the natural and necessary law in all its strictness; and indeed it is never permitted for them to depart from it. But as regards the external effects of that law in human society, we must necessarily have recourse to certain rules of more certain and easy application, and this in the interest of the safety and welfare of the great society of the human race. These rules are those of the *voluntary* Law of Nations (Introduction, section 21). . . .

190 The first rule of that law, with respect to the subject under consideration, is that *war in due form, as regards its effects, must be accounted just on both sides*. This principle, as we have just shown, is absolutely necessary if some sort of procedure (*ordre*) or regulation (*règle*) is to be introduced into a method of redress as violent as that of war, if any bounds are to be set to the disasters it occasions, and if a door is to be left at all times open for the return of peace. Moreover, any other rule would be impracticable as between Nation and Nation, since they recognize no common judge.

Thus, considered externally and in the sight of men, the rights founded on the state of war and the legitimacy of its effects, in no way depend on the justice of the cause. They depend rather on the legitimacy of the means, that is to say, upon the presence of the elements constituting a war in due form. If the enemy observes all the rules proper to war in due form (see chap. IV of this Book[10]), we are not to be heard in complaint of him as a violator of the Law of Nations; he has the same right as we to assert a just cause; and our entire hope lies in victory or in a settlement (*un accomodement*).

191 Second rule: Since two enemies are regarded as having an equally just cause; *whatever is permitted to one because of the state of war is also permitted to the other*. In fact, no Nation, on the ground of having justice on its side, ever complains of the hostilities of its enemy, so long as they remain within the bounds prescribed by the common laws of war. . . .

192 Thirdly, it must never be forgotten that *this voluntary Law of Nations*, established from necessity and for the avoidance of greater evils (sections 188, 189), *does not confer upon him whose cause is unjust any true right capable of justifying his conduct and appeasing his conscience, but merely provides an external legality* (l'effet extérieur du droit), *and exempts him from human punishment* (l'impunité parmi les hommes). This is sufficiently clear from the principles on which the voluntary Law of Nations is based. Consequently, the sovereign who has no just cause in authorization of his hostilities is not less unjust, or less guilty of violating the sacred Law of Nature, merely because that same natural law, in

---

[10] Vattel here noted (section 66) that "a war in due form (*la guerre en forme*) may also be called a regular war (*guerre réglée*), because it is carried on subject to certain rules either prescribed by natural law or sanctioned by custom."

the effort not to increase the evils of human society while seeking to prevent them, requires that he be conceded the same legal rights as more justly belong to his enemy. . . .

. . . In this work we are laying down the natural principles of the Law of Nations; we deduce them from Nature itself; and what we call the voluntary Law of Nations consists in the rules of conduct, of external law, to which the natural law obliges Nations to consent; so that we rightly presume their consent, without seeking any record of it; for even if they had not given their consent, the Law of Nature supplies it, and gives it for them. Nations are not free in this matter to consent or not; the Nation which would refuse to consent would violate the common rights of all Nations. (See Introduction, section 21.) . . .

Chapter XVIII: Civil War

287 It is a hotly debated question whether the sovereign must observe the ordinary laws of war in dealing with rebellious subjects who have openly taken up arms against him. . . .

292 When a party is formed within the State which ceases to obey the sovereign and is strong enough to make a stand against him, or when a Republic is divided into two opposite factions, and both sides take up arms, there exists a *civil* war. . . .

293 . . . Civil war breaks the bonds of society and of government, or at least suspends the force and effect of them; it gives rise, within the Nation, to two independent parties, who regard each other as enemies and acknowledge no common judge. Of necessity, therefore, these two parties must be regarded as forming thenceforth, for a time at least, two separate bodies politic, two distinct peoples. Although one of the two parties may have been wrong in breaking up the unity of the State and in resisting the legitimate authority, still they are none the less divided in fact. Moreover, who is to judge them, and to decide which side is in the wrong and which in the right? They have no common superior upon earth. They are therefore in the situation of two Nations which enter into a dispute and, being unable to agree, have recourse to arms.

294 That being so, it is perfectly clear that the common laws of war, those principles of humanity, forbearance, truthfulness, and honor, which we have earlier laid down, should be observed by both sides in a civil war. The same reasons which make those laws of obligation between State and State render them equally necessary, and even more so, in the unfortunate event when two determined parties struggle for the possession of their common fatherland. If the sovereign believes himself justified in hanging the prisoners as rebels, the opposite party will retaliate; if he does not strictly observe the terms of surrender and all the agreements made with his enemies, they will cease to trust his word; if he burns and lays waste the country they will do the same; and the war will become cruel, terrible, and daily more disastrous to the Nation. . . .

295 When, without ceasing to acknowledge the authority of the sovereign, subjects take up arms merely to obtain redress for grievances, there are two reasons for observing in their regard the customary laws of war: (1) the fear of rendering the civil war more cruel and destructive, from the fact, as we have already observed, that the insurgents will retaliate upon the severities of the prince; (2) the danger of committing great injustice as a result of too great haste in punishing those we are regarding as rebels. The heat of passion attending civil strife is not favorable to the administration of pure and sacred justice; a time of greater tranquility must be awaited. The prince will act wisely in keeping the rebels prisoners until, having restored tranquility to the country, he is in a position to have them judged according to the laws. . . .

But when the Nation is divided into two absolutely independent parties, who acknowledge no common superior, the State is broken up and the war between the two parties falls, in all respects, into the class of a public war between two different Nations. If a Republic is split up into two factions, each of which claims to form the body of the State, or if a Kingdom is divided between two claimants to the throne, the contending parties which thus sever the Nation will mutually regard each other as rebels. Here, then, we have two bodies which claim to be absolutely independent and which have no judge to decide between them (section 293). They settle their dispute by having recourse to arms, just as two distinct Nations would do. The obligation upon the two parties to observe towards each other the customary laws of war is therefore absolute and indispensable, and the same which the natural law imposes upon all Nations in contests between State and State.

296 Foreign Nations must not interfere in the domestic affairs of an independent State (bk. II, section 54 and foll.). It is not their part to decide between citizens whom civil discord has driven to take up arms, nor between the sovereign and his subjects. The two parties are equally alien to them, and equally independent of their authority. It only remains for them to interpose their good offices for the re-establishment of peace, and this they are called upon to do by the natural law (see bk. II, chap. I). But if their efforts are without avail, those Nations which are not bound by treaty obligations may, in order to determine upon their own conduct, decide for themselves the merits of the case, and assist the party which seems to have justice on its side, should that party ask for their help or accept the offer of it; they may do so, I say, just as they are at liberty to take up the quarrel of one Nation with another if they find it a just one.

41

Immanuel Kant
(1724–1804)

Cosmopolitan Rights, Human Progress, and Perpetual Peace

Peace means an end to all hostilities, and to attach the adjective 'perpetual' to it is already suspiciously close to pleonasm.

Immanuel Kant, *Perpetual Peace*

It is difficult to overestimate the importance of Immanuel Kant for the course of modern philosophy. He perceptively diagnosed the impasse at which the new philosophy with its various competing schools had arrived and proposed a novel approach to philosophical problems, an approach he would expound through the systematic synthesis he dubbed his *critical philosophy*. The breadth and depth of his system is best gauged in a formidable trio of works, *Critique of Pure Reason* (1781, revised edition 1787), *Critique of Practical Reason* (1788), and *Critique of Judgment* (1790), which continues to exercise a decisive influence in practically all fields of philosophy.

But alongside these uncompromisingly theoretical works, Kant was also the source of a prolific output of commentary on the political issues of his day, among which the most famous pieces include *What is Enlightenment?* (1784), *Idea for a Universal History with Cosmopolitan Intent* (1784), and *Perpetual Peace* (1795). This last text will provide our main focus here, along with a short excerpt from another of his important theoretical works, *The Metaphysics of Morals* (1797).[1]

---

[1] For both works, we will be using, with minor modifications, the translation of H. B. Nisbet, included in Hans Reiss (ed.), *Kant: Political Writings*, 2nd edn. (Cambridge: Cambridge University Press, 1991).

Perpetual Peace: A Philosophical Sketch

Although Kant elsewhere acknowledged his intellectual debt to the political theories of Rousseau, he did not do so in his text on the ideal of perpetual peace. For although Rousseau (and Saint-Pierre) are clearly intellectual ancestors to the thesis he sets out here, Kant's contribution is deeply embedded within his own philosophical system. Of central importance to this system is the distinction between *morality* and *political prudence*. In cases where the two come into conflict, Kant argues that we must abstain from casuistry and let prudence yield to the demands of morality. Also novel to *Perpetual Peace* is the universalist ambition of the work. Whereas earlier efforts had confined their horizon to the central powers of Europe, Kant makes clear that the republican ideal that stands at the foundation of his vision of peace extends, in principle, to all nations of the earth. This gives the work a distinctive appeal and makes it a natural starting point for contemporary discussions of the subject.

Indeed, since the publication of Michael Doyle's two-part article "Kant, Liberal Legacies, and Foreign Affairs"[2] in 1983, Kant's text has enjoyed a remarkable renaissance, mostly cited in support of the so-called "democratic peace" – the thesis that democratic regimes rarely wage war on each other. And, certainly, Kant does claim that "constitutional republics"[3] are naturally less bellicose than their despotic counterparts. Moreover, he also holds that history will prove the thesis right, and thus that the spread of representative democracy will eventually promote peace worldwide. However, and as Kant's general philosophical orientation would lead one to expect, it is not empirical claims and predictions such as these which capture his interest, but precisely their moral foundation.

The work starts by listing the following six "Preliminary Articles of a Perpetual Peace between Nations."[4] Admirably clear and concise, these formulate ways of removing incentives to war and establishing a climate of mutual trust among states, thereby setting the stage for an enduring peace.

---

[2] Michael Doyle, "Kant, Liberal Legacies, and Foreign Affairs," *Philosophy and Public Affairs*, 12 (1983), pp. 205–35, 323–53. For a recent critical analysis of Doyle's argument, consult Georg Cavallar, "Kantian Perspectives on Democratic Peace: Alternatives to Doyle," *Review of International Studies*, 27 (2001), pp. 229–48.

[3] Kant distinguishes republicanism, marked by the separation of executive and legislative power, from direct democracy, which he derides as despotic, thereby anticipating the fear articulated by Tocqueville and Mill of a "tyranny of the majority." It seems clear, however, that by republicanism Kant means what we today would call a representative democracy. On this, see *Perpetual Peace*, pp. 100–2.

[4] For an analysis of Kant's distinction between Preliminary and Definitive articles of Perpetual Peace, see Jörg Fisch, "When Will Kant's Perpetual Peace be Definitve?" *Journal of the History of International Law*, 2 (2000), pp. 125–47, sections II–V.

1. 'No conclusion of peace shall be considered valid as such if it was made with a secret reservation of the material for a future war.' (*Perpetual Peace*, p. 93)

Here Kant draws a distinction between a mere truce and peace proper, adding that "[p]eace means an end to all hostilities, and to attach the adjective 'perpetual' to it is already suspiciously close to pleonasm" (ibid.). Any arrangement worthy of the name peace must seek to remove the very conditions that lead to hostility and war.

2. 'No independently existing state, whether it be large or small, may be acquired by another state by inheritance, exchange, purchase or gift.' (*Perpetual Peace*, p. 94)

For this would amount to turning societies into commodities, thereby "contradict[ing] the idea of the original contract, without which no rights over a people are thinkable" (ibid.). However, Kant's point may not be quite as liberal as it sounds: he adds later in the text that "the prohibition relates only to the *mode of acquisition*, which is to be forbidden hereforth, but not to the present *state of political possessions*. For although this present state is not backed up by the requisite legal authority, it was considered lawful in the public opinion of every state at the time of the putative acquisition" (p. 97). In other words, the onset of a perpetual peace will not provide occasion to seek redress on long-standing territorial controversies between nations. Kant's point appears to be pragmatic in intent: although certainly not without moral warrant, the prospect of such claims will likely prevent any onset of peace in the first place.

3. 'Standing armies (*miles perpetuus*) will gradually be abolished altogether.' (*Perpetual Peace*, p. 94)

In Kant's words: "For they constantly threaten other states with war by the very fact that they are always prepared for it" (ibid.).

4. 'No national debt shall be contracted in connection with the external affairs of the state.' (*Perpetual Peace*, p. 95)

Such loans are one way in which states seek to keep up with the spiraling expenditures of the military sector. An effective prohibition on such financing would therefore, we might surmise, contribute massively toward realizing Article 3 above.

5. 'No state shall forcibly interfere in the constitution and government of another state.' (*Perpetual Peace*, p. 96)

This is the famous principle of non-intervention, which is much discussed today in the context of so-called "humanitarian interventions" (e.g. NATO's 1999 air campaign in Kosovo). Like many commentators today, Kant worries that overriding this principle would set a dangerous precedent that would lead to an increased frequency of war: "Such interference would be an active offence and would make the autonomy of all other states insecure" (*Perpetual Peace*, p. 96). Whether Kant in fact held to an absolute principle of non-intervention is difficult to ascertain from the text, and largely hinges on how narrowly we construe the notion of "the constitution and government of another state." Kant's clarificatory comments provide only the roughest map of the territory:

> [I]t would be a different matter if a state, through internal discord, were to split into two parts, each of which set itself up as a separate state and claimed authority over the whole. For it could not be reckoned as interference in another state's constitution if an external state were to lend support to one of them, because their condition is one of anarchy. But as long as this internal conflict is not yet decided (*noch nicht entscheiden ist*), the interference of external powers would be a violation of the rights of an independent people who are merely struggling with its internal ills. Such interference would be an active offence and would make the autonomy of all other states insecure. (*Perpetual Peace*, p. 96)

And finally:

> 6. 'No state at war with another shall permit such acts of hostility as would make mutual confidence impossible during a future time of peace. Such acts would include the employment of *assassins* (*percussores*) *or poisoners* (*venefici*), *breach of capitulation, the instigation of treason* (*perduellio*) within the enemy state, etc.' (*Perpetual Peace*, p. 96)

In this Article, Kant articulates certain restraints on warfare that are necessary for preserving a minimal level of trust between warring parties (e.g. bans on espionage and assassinations). Only if this trust is maintained can the parties hope to achieve a stable peace at war's end. Kant develops this point further in the *Metaphysics of Morals*, where he concludes that "[i]n short, a state must not use such treacherous methods as would destroy that confidence which is required for the future establishment of a lasting peace" (pt. I, §57, p. 168).[5]

However, this Article also considers the idea of punishment as a rationale for waging war and rejects this as untenable so long as there is no public authority to adjudicate disputes between states. Kant thereby questions the idea, central to the just war tradition, that individual states have the competence to make binding determinations about justice, based either on natural law or *ius gentium*.[6]

---

[5] This connects with the idea of war as analogous to a contractual relation, which Kant touches on in *The Metaphysics of Morals* (pt. I, §56, p. 167: "[I]f one wishes to find any rights in wartime, one must assume the existence of something analogous to a contract; in other words, one must assume that the other party has *accepted* the declaration of war and that both parties therefore wish to prosecute their rights in this manner."

[6] See Peter Haggenmacher, "Kant et la tradition du droit des gens," in Laberge, Lafrance, and Dumas (eds.), *L'Année 1795 – Kant. Essai sur la Paix* (Paris: Libraire Philosophique J. Vrin, 1997), pp. 122–39.

[W]ar is only a regrettable expedient for asserting one's rights by force within a state of nature, where no court of justice is available to judge with legal authority. In such cases, neither party can be declared an unjust enemy, for this would already presuppose a judge's decision; only the outcome of the conflict, as in the case of a so-called 'judgement of God', can decide who is in the right. A war of punishment (*bellum punitivum*) between states is inconceivable, since there can be no relationship of superior to inferior among them. It thus follows that a war of extermination, in which both parties and right itself might all be simultaneously annihilated, would allow perpetual peace only on the vast graveyard of the human race. A war of this kind and the employment of all means which might bring it about must thus be absolutely prohibited. But the means listed above would inevitably lead to such a war, because these diabolical arts, besides being intrinsically despicable, would not long be confined to war alone if they were brought into use. This applies, for example, to the employment of spies (*uti exploratoribus*), for it exploits only the dishonesty of others (which can never be completely eliminated). Such practices will be carried over into peacetime and will thus completely vitiate its purpose. (*Perpetual Peace*, pp. 96–7)

We now move to the three Definitive Articles of a Perpetual Peace. Kant starts with a short preamble again emphasizing the distinction between genuine peace and a mere suspension of hostilities.

In this passage, the influence of the social-contract tradition on Kant's thought is evident, especially in its stipulation of a close connection between a civil constitution and the possibility of peace.

From *Perpetual Peace*[7]

Second Section: Which Contains the Definitive Articles of a Perpetual Peace between States

A state of peace among men living together is not the same as the state of nature, which is rather a state of war. For even if it does not involve active hostilities, it involves a constant threat of their breaking out. Thus the state of peace must be *formally instituted*, for a suspension of hostilities is not in itself a guarantee of peace. And unless one neighbour gives a guarantee to the other at his request (which can happen only in a *lawful* state), the latter may treat him as an enemy. [*Added footnote.*[8] It is usually assumed that one cannot take hostile action against anyone unless one has already been actively *injured* by them. This is perfectly correct if both parties are living in a *legal civil state*. For the fact that the one has entered such a state gives the required guarantee to the other, since both are

---

[7]   *Kant: Political Writings* (ed. Reiss), pp. 98–9.
[8]   Kant added this long footnote to the second edition of *Perpetual Peace*.

subject to the same authority. But man (or an individual people) in a mere state of nature robs me of any such security and injures me by virtue of this very state in which he coexists with me. He may not have injured me actively (*facto*), but he does injure me by the very lawlessness of his state (*statu iniusto*), for he is a permanent threat to me, and I can compel him (*ihn nötigen*) either to enter into a common lawful state along with me or to move away from my vicinity. Thus the postulate on which all the following articles are based is that all men who can at all influence one another must adhere to some kind of civil constitution. But any legal constitution, as far as the persons who live under it are concerned, will conform to one of the three following types:

1 a constitution based on the *civil right* of individuals within a nation (*ius civitatis*).
2 a constitution based on the *international right* of states in their relationship with one another (*ius gentium*).
3 a constitution based on *cosmopolitan right*, in so far as individuals and states, coexisting in an external relationship of mutual influences, may be regarded as citizens of a universal state of mankind (*ius cosmopoliticum*). This classification, with respect to the idea of a perpetual peace, is not arbitrary, but necessary. For even if one of the parties were able to influence the others physically and yet itself remained in a state of nature, there would be a risk of war, which it is precisely the aim of the above articles to prevent.]

In the first Definitive Article, Kant argues more specifically for a close connection between the perpetual peace ideal and the republican form of government.[9] Republics, he says, are naturally less prone to war than despotisms for the simple reason that those who would be adversely affected by the decision to wage war – namely common citizens – are also those whose decision it is.

From *Perpetual Peace*[10]

First Definitive Article of a Perpetual Peace: The Civil Constitution of Every State shall be Republican

A *republican constitution* is founded upon three principles: firstly, the principle of *freedom* for all members of a society (as human beings); secondly, the principle of

---

[9] See footnote 3 for more on the relationship between Kantian republicanism and modern representative democracy.
[10] *Kant: Political Writings* (ed. Reiss), pp. 99–100.

the *dependence* of everyone upon a single common legislation (as subjects); and thirdly, the principle of legal *equality* for everyone (as citizens). It is the only constitution which can be derived from the idea of an original contract, upon which all rightful legislation of a people must be founded. Thus as far as right is concerned, republicanism is in itself the original basis of every kind of civil constitution, and it only remains to ask whether it is the only constitution which can lead to a perpetual peace.

The republican constitution is not only pure in its origin (since it springs from the pure concept of right); it also offers a prospect of attaining the desired result, i.e. a perpetual peace, and the reason for this is as follows. – If, as is inevitably the case under this constitution, the consent of the citizens is required to decide whether or not war is to be declared, it is very natural that they will have great hesitation in embarking on so dangerous an enterprise. For this would mean calling down on themselves all the miseries of war, such as doing the fighting themselves, supplying the costs of the war from their own resources, painfully making good the ensuing devastation, and, as the crowning evil, having to take upon themselves a burden of debt which will embitter peace itself and which can never be paid off on account of the constant threat of new wars. But under a constitution where the subject is not a citizen, and which is therefore not republican, it is the simplest thing in the world to go to war.

In the second Definitive Article, Kant makes clear that he is not proposing a world state. For in contrast to a world state, his pacific federation would not strive for separate power, but only serve to remove, by its bare existence, obstacles to peace as well as diplomatically intervening in nascent conflicts. The insistence that peace shall not be instituted through the coercive power of an international body signals Kant's most decisive departure from Saint-Pierre and Rousseau. This federation will thus be a union of free and independent nations.[11] The only "right" these nations will be forced to forswear is the delusional right to wage war on its neighbors. Indeed, it is only with the advent of such a federation that the language of rights will find any real application to the international sphere at all. Kant rebukes as "sorry comforters" his philosophical predecessors who naively spoke of the rights of nations even in the absence of an effective legal code, thereby unwittingly providing justification for war-prone national leaders.

---

[11]   This theme is taken up again in *The Metaphysics of Morals*, pt. I (§61, p. 171), where Kant seems to highlight the practical difficulties of governing such a vast territory as one of the main points against a world republic.

From *Perpetual Peace*[12]

Second Definitive Article of a Perpetual Peace: The Right of Nations shall be Based on a Federalism between Free States

Peoples, as states, may be judged in the same way as individual men living in a state of nature, independent of external laws; for they are a standing offence to one another by the very fact that they are neighbours. Each nation, for the sake of its own security, can and ought to demand of the others that they should enter along with it into a constitution, similar to the civil one, within which the rights of each could be secured. This would mean establishing a *federation of peoples* (*Völkerbund*). But a federation of this sort would not be the same thing as an international state (*Völkerstaat*). For the idea of an international state is contradictory, since every state involves a relationship between a superior (the legislator) and an inferior (the people obeying the laws), whereas a number of nations forming one state would constitute a single nation. And this contradicts our initial assumption, as we are here considering the right of nations in relation to one another in so far as they are a group of separate states which are not to be welded together as a unit. . . .

Although it is largely concealed by governmental constraints in law-governed civil society, the depravity of human nature is displayed without disguise in the unrestricted relations which obtain between the various nations. It is therefore to be wondered at that the word *right* has not been completely banished from war politics as superfluous pedantry, and that no state has been bold enough to declare itself publicly in favour of doing so. For Hugo Grotius, Pufendorf, Vattel and the rest (sorry comforters as they are) are still dutifully quoted in *justification* of military aggression, although their philosophically or diplomatically formulated codes do not and cannot have the slightest *legal* force, since states as such are not subject to a common external constraint. Yet there is no instance of a state ever having been moved to desist from its purpose by arguments supported by the testimonies of such notable men. This homage which every state pays (in words at least) to the concept of right nevertheless proves that man possesses a greater moral capacity (*Anlage*), though dormant at present, eventually to gain control over the evil principle within him (for he cannot deny that it exists), and to hope that others will do likewise. Otherwise the word *right* would never be used by states which intend to make war on one another, unless in a derisory sense, as when a certain Gallic prince declared: 'Nature has given to the strong the prerogative of making the weak obey them.'

---

[12] *Kant: Political Writings* (ed. Reiss), pp. 102, 103–5.

The way in which states seek their rights can only be by war, since there is no external tribunal to put their claims to trial. But rights cannot be decided by military victory, and a *peace treaty* may put an end to the current war, but not to that general warlike condition within which pretexts can always be found for a new war. And indeed, such a state of affairs cannot be pronounced completely unjust, since it allows each party to act as judge in its own cause. Yet while natural right allows us to say of men living in a lawless condition that they ought to abandon it, the right of nations does not allow us to say the same of states. For as states, they already have a lawful internal constitution, and have thus outgrown the coercive right of others to subject them to a wider legal constitution in accordance with their conception of right. On the other hand, reason, as the highest legislative moral power, absolutely condemns war as a test of rights and sets up peace as an immediate duty. But peace can neither be inaugurated nor secured without a general agreement between the nations; thus a particular kind of league, which we might call a *pacific federation* (*foedus pacificum*), is required. It would differ from a *peace treaty* (*pactum pacis*) in that the latter terminates *one* war, whereas the former would seek to end *all* wars for good. This federation does not aim to acquire any power like that of a state, but merely to preserve and secure the *freedom* of each state in itself, along with that of the other confederated states, although this does not mean that they need to submit to public laws and to a coercive power which enforces them, as do men in a state of nature. It can be shown that this idea of *federalism*, extending gradually to encompass all states and thus leading to perpetual peace, is practicable and has objective reality. For if by good fortune one powerful and enlightened nation can form a republic (which is by its nature inclined to seek perpetual peace), this will provide a focal point for federal association among other states. These will join up with the first one, thus securing the freedom of each state in accordance with the idea of international right, and the whole will gradually spread further and further by a series of alliances of this kind.

It would be understandable for a people to say: 'There shall be no war among us; for we will form ourselves into a state, appointing for ourselves a supreme legislative, executive and juridical power to resolve our conflicts by peaceful means.' But if this state says: 'There shall be no war between myself and other states, although I do not recognise any supreme legislative power which could secure my rights and whose rights I should in turn secure', it is impossible to understand what justification I can have for placing any confidence in my rights, unless I can rely on some substitute for the union of civil society, i.e. on a free federation. If the concept of international right is to retain any meaning at all, reason must necessarily couple it with a federation of this kind.

The concept of international right is unintelligible if interpreted as a right to go to war. For this would make it a right to determine what is lawful not by means of universally valid external laws, constraining the freedom of each, but by means of one-sided maxims backed up by physical force. It would in that case have to be taken to mean that it is perfectly just for men to destroy one another, and thus to find perpetual peace in the vast grave where all the horrors of violence and those responsible for them would be buried. There is only one rational way in which states coexisting with other states can emerge from the lawless condition of pure warfare. Just like individual men, they must renounce their savage and lawless freedom, adapt themselves to public coercive laws, and thus form an *international state* (*civitas gentium*), which would continue to grow until it embraced all the peoples of the earth. But since this is not the will of the nations, according to their present conception of international right (so that they reject *in hypothesi* what is true *in thesi*), the positive idea of a *world republic* cannot be realised. If all is not to be lost, this can at best find a negative substitute in the shape of an enduring and gradually expanding *federation* likely to prevent war. The latter may check the current of man's inclination to defy the law and antagonise his fellows, although there will always be a risk of it bursting forth anew.

The third Definitive Article concerns the rights of civilians (predominantly merchants), ambassadors, and missionaries, traveling in foreign countries. This had also been a central issue for earlier writers, notably Vitoria. Although Kant was optimistic about the cosmopolitan prospects of the human race, he is in this passage mostly concerned to limit this to what he terms "the right of resort." While articulating this right, Kant also provides a scathing indictment of the practices of European nations in remote parts of the world.

From *Perpetual Peace*[13]

Third Definitive Article of a Perpetual Peace: Cosmopolitan Right shall be Limited to Conditions of Universal Hospitality

As in the foregoing articles, we are here concerned not with philanthropy, but with *right*. In this context, *hospitality* means the right of a stranger not to be treated with hostility when he arrives on someone else's territory. He can indeed be turned away, if this can be done without causing his death, but he must not be treated with hostility, so long as he behaves in a peaceable manner in the place he happens to be in. The stranger cannot claim the *right of a guest* (*Gastrecht*) to be entertained, for this would require a special friendly agreement whereby he might become a member of the native household for a certain time. He may only claim a *right of resort* (*Besuchsrecht*), for all men are entitled to present themselves in the

---

[13] Ibid., pp. 105–8.

society of others by virtue of their right to communal possession of the earth's surface. . . . But this natural right of hospitality, i.e. the right of strangers, does not extend beyond those conditions which make it possible for them to *attempt* to enter into relations with the native inhabitants. In this way, continents distant from each other can enter into peaceful mutual relations which may eventually be regulated by public laws, thus bringing the human race nearer and nearer to a cosmopolitan constitution.

If we compare with this end the *inhospitable* conduct of the civilised states of our continent, especially the commercial states, the injustice which they display in *visiting* foreign countries and peoples (which in their case is the same as conquering them) seems appallingly great. America, the negro countries, the Spice Islands, the Cape, etc. were looked upon at the time of their discovery as ownerless territories; for the native inhabitants were counted as nothing. In East India (Hindustan), foreign troops were brought in under the pretext of merely setting up trading posts. This led to oppression of the natives, incitement of the various Indian states to widespread wars, famine, insurrection, treachery and the whole litany of evils which can afflict the human race.

China and Japan (Nippon), having had experience of such guests, have wisely placed restrictions on them. China permits contact with her territories, but not entrance into them, while Japan only allows contact with a single European people, the Dutch, although they are still segregated from the native community like prisoners. The worst (or from the point of view of moral judgements, the best) thing about all this is that the commercial states do not even benefit by their violence, for all their trading companies are on the point of collapse. The Sugar Islands, that stronghold of the cruellest and most calculated slavery, do not yield any real profit; they serve only the indirect (and not entirely laudable) purpose of training sailors for warships, thereby aiding the prosecution of wars in Europe. And all this is the work of powers who make endless ado about their piety, and who wish to be considered as chosen believers while they live on the fruits of iniquity.

The peoples of the earth have thus entered in varying degrees into a universal community, and it has developed to the point where a violation of rights in *one* part of the world is felt *everywhere*. The idea of a cosmopolitan right is therefore not fantastic and overstrained; it is a necessary complement to the unwritten code of political and international right, transforming it into a universal right of humanity. Only under this condition can we flatter ourselves that we are continually advancing towards a perpetual peace.

To these three articles Kant adds two supplements, only the first of which is reproduced below. Here Kant's argument concentrates more specifically on the interplay between morality and politics. Against skeptics who would scorn the perpetual peace ideal as vain utopianism, Kant points out that through the development of trade and the dispersal of populations all over the globe, even the *self-interest* of peoples and nations should naturally incline them toward peace. But this insight raises what Kant calls "the essential question": how does this natural drift toward peace relate to man's moral duties, as dictated by reason? In this selection, it appears that Kant argues that the problem of peace is primarily a problem of *good governance*, and only secondarily involves the *moral improvement* of man. As he famously puts it: "As hard as it may sound, the problem of setting up a state can be solved even by a nation of devils (so long as they possess understanding)" (*Perpetual Peace*, p. 112). Still, although Kant does not think that setting up the antecedent conditions for a civil society (and thus a pacific federation) *presupposes* the moral improvement of man, we can discern in him the distinct hope that once these conditions are set up, such improvement will follow suit. Thus: "we cannot expect their moral attitudes to produce a good political constitution; on the contrary, it is only through the latter that the people can be expected to attain a good level of moral culture" (p. 113).

From *Perpetual Peace*[14]

First Supplement: On the Guarantee of a Perpetual Peace

We now come to the essential question regarding the aim of perpetual peace. What does nature do in relation to the end which man's own reason prescribes to him as a duty, i.e. how does nature help to promote his *moral purpose*? And how does nature guarantee that what man *ought* to do by the laws of his freedom (but does not do) will in fact be done through nature's compulsion without prejudice to the free agency of man? This question arises, moreover, in all three areas of public right – in *political, international* and *cosmopolitan* right. For if I say that nature *wills* that this or that should happen, this does not mean that nature imposes on us a *duty* to do it, for duties can only be imposed by practical reason, acting without any external constraint. On the contrary, nature does it herself, whether we are willing or not: *fata volentem ducunt, nolentem trahunt*.[15]

1 Even if people were not compelled by internal dissent to submit to the coercion of public laws, war would produce the same effect from outside. For in accordance with the natural arrangement described above, each people would find itself confronted by another neighbouring people pressing in upon it, thus forcing it to form itself internally into a *state* in order to encounter the other as an

---

[14] Ibid., pp. 112–13, 114.

[15] [*Translator's footnote:*] Kant's quotation is in incorrect word order. It should run: *Ducunt volentem fata, nolentem trahunt* ("The fates lead him who is willing, but drag him who is unwilling"); Seneca, *Epistle* 107, 11.

armed *power*. Now the *republican* constitution is the only one which does complete justice to the rights of man. But it is also the most difficult to establish, and even more so to preserve, so that many maintain that it would only be possible within a state of *angels*, since men, with their self-seeking inclinations, would be incapable of adhering to a constitution of so sublime a nature. But in fact, nature comes to the aid of the universal and rational human will, so admirable in itself but so impotent in practice, and makes use of precisely those self-seeking inclinations in order to do so. It only remains for men to create a good organisation for the state, a task which is well within their capability, and to arrange it in such a way that their self-seeking energies are opposed to one another, each thereby neutralising or eliminating the destructive effects of the rest. And as far as reason is concerned, the result is the same as if man's selfish tendencies were non-existent, so that man, even if he is not morally good in himself, is nevertheless compelled to be a good citizen. As hard as it may sound, the problem of setting up a state can be solved even by a nation of devils (so long as they possess understanding). It may be stated as follows: 'In order to organise a group of rational beings who together require universal laws for their survival, but of whom each separate individual is secretly inclined to exempt himself from them, the constitution must be so designed that, although the citizens are opposed to one another in their private attitudes, these opposing views may inhibit one another in such a way that the public conduct of the citizens will be the same as if they did not have such evil attitudes.' A problem of this kind must be soluble. For such a task does not involve the moral improvement of man; it only means finding out how the mechanism of nature can be applied to men in such a manner that the antagonism of their hostile attitudes will make them compel one another to submit to coercive laws, thereby producing a condition of peace within which the laws can be enforced. We can even see this principle at work among the actually existing (although as yet very imperfectly organised) states. For in their external relations, they have already approached what the idea of right prescribes, although the reason for this is certainly not their internal moral attitudes. In the same way, we cannot expect their moral attitudes to produce a good political constitution; on the contrary, it is only through the latter that the people can be expected to attain a good level of moral culture. Thus that mechanism of nature by which selfish inclinations are naturally opposed to one another in their external relations can be used by reason to facilitate the attainment of its own end, the reign of established right. Internal and external peace are thereby furthered and assured, so far as it lies within the power of the state itself to do so. We may therefore say that nature *irresistibly wills* that right should eventually gain the upper hand. What men have neglected to do will ultimately happen of its own accord, albeit with much inconvenience. As Bouterwek puts it: 'If the reed is bent too far, it breaks; and he who wills too much wills nothing.' . . .

3 Thus nature wisely separates the nations, although the will of each individual state, even basing its arguments on international right, would gladly unite them under its own sway by force or by cunning. On the other hand, nature also unites nations which the concept of cosmopolitan right would not have protected from violence and war, and does so by means of their mutual self-interest. For the *spirit of commerce* sooner or later takes hold of every people, and it cannot exist side by side with war. And of all the powers (or means) at the disposal of the power of the state, *financial power* can probably be relied on most. Thus states find themselves compelled to promote the noble cause of peace, though not exactly from motives of morality. And wherever in the world there is a threat of war breaking out, they will try to prevent it by mediation, just as if they had entered into a permanent league for this purpose; for by the very nature of things, large military alliances can only rarely be formed, and will even more rarely be successful.

In this way, nature guarantees perpetual peace by the actual mechanism of human inclinations. And while the likelihood of its being attained is not sufficient to enable us to *prophesy* the future theoretically, it is enough for practical purposes. It makes it our duty to work our way towards this goal, which is more than an empty chimera.

Finally, in a lengthy appendix added to the second edition of the work,[16] Kant returns to the question of politics and morality. Owing to its tacked-on character and its apparent, if inexplicit, contradiction of central claims in the main text, this appendix has vexed even his most sympathetic interpreters – indeed, one commentator's frustration has led him to curse it as "among the most badly organized and over-abstract précis of philosophical argument that [Kant] ever perpetrated."[17]

Nonetheless, Kant obviously thought it necessary to clarify and expand on his original remarks on morality and politics, as well as to situate them in relation to the larger structure of his moral philosophy. Constructed around the idea of the categorical imperative – "Act in such a way that you can wish your maxim to become a universal law"[18] – Kant's theory radically abjures the relevance of consequentialistic considerations for moral decision-making, in favor of a focus on the concept of an absolute duty. He makes the distinction vivid in terms of a contrast between the *moral politician* and the *political moralist*. The former subordinates political means to moral ends, while the latter shapes his political ends

---

[16] The appendix is in two parts, but the second strays too far from the topic of war and peace to merit inclusion here.

[17] W. B. Gallie, *Philosophers of Peace and War* (Cambridge: Cambridge University Press, 1978), p. 11.

[18] *Perpetual Peace*, p. 122. The same basic idea is given a somewhat more political spin in *The Metaphysics of Morals*, pt. I. Under the heading "The Universal Principle of Right" (§C, p. 133), Kant here offers the following dictum: "Every action which by itself or by its maxim enables the freedom of each individual's will to co-exist with the freedom of everyone else in accordance with a universal law is *right*."

according to the availability of expedient means. While the foregoing passage at first blush appears to claim that good governance is first and foremost a technical task, the appendix emphatically demands that politics be subjected to the dictates of morality. The apparent contradiction is really no more than apparent – for while the moral politician may indeed "work with nature" in order to instill virtuous behavior among his citizens, he will all the while have the proper moral end in view: that of fashioning a free and dignified society, respectful of the rights of man, and at peace with its neighbors.

From *Perpetual Peace*[19]

Appendix I: On the Disagreement between Morals and Politics in Relation to Perpetual Peace

Morality, as a collection of absolutely binding laws by which our actions *ought* to be governed, belongs essentially, in an objective sense, to the practical sphere. And if we have once acknowledged the authority of this concept of duty, it is patently absurd to say that we *cannot* act as the moral laws require. For if this were the case, the concept of duty would automatically be dropped from morals (*ultra posse nemo obligatur*).[20] Hence there can be no conflict between politics, as an applied branch of right, and morality, as a theoretical branch of right (i.e. between theory and practice); for such a conflict could occur only if morality were taken to mean a general doctrine of expediency, i.e. a theory of the maxims by which one might select the most useful means of furthering one's own advantage – and this would be tantamount to denying that morality exists. . . .

But the man of practice, to whom morality is pure theory, coldly repudiates our well-intentioned hopes, even if he does concede that we *can* do what we *ought* to do. He bases his argument on the claim that we can tell in advance from human nature that man will never *want* to do what is necessary in order to attain the goal of eternal peace. It is perfectly true that the will of all *individual* men to live in accordance with principles of freedom within a lawful constitution (i.e. the *distributive* unity of the will of all) is not sufficient for this purpose. Before so difficult a problem can be solved, all men *together* (i.e. the *collective* unity of the combined will) must desire to attain this goal; only then can civil society exist as a single whole. Since an additional unifying cause must therefore overrule the differences in the particular wishes of all individuals before a common will can arise, and since no single individual can create it, the only conceivable way

---

[19]   *Kant: Political Writings* (ed. Reiss), pp. 116–19, 121–5.
[20]   [*Translator's footnote:*] "No one is obliged to do anything he is incapable of doing."

of executing the original idea *in practice*, and hence of inaugurating a state of right, is by *force*. On its coercive authority, public right will subsequently be based.

We can certainly expect in advance that there will be considerable deviations in actual experience from the original theoretical idea. For we cannot assume that the moral attitude of the legislator will be such that, after the disorderly mass has been united into a people, he will leave them to create a lawful constitution by their own common will.

It might thus be said that, once a person has the power in his own hands, he will not let the people prescribe laws for him. Similarly, a state which is self-governing and free from all external laws will not let itself become dependent on the judgement of other states in seeking to uphold its rights against them. And even a whole continent, if it feels itself in a superior position to another one, will not hesitate to plunder it or actually to extend its rule over it, irrespective of whether the other is in its way or not. In this way, all the plans which theory lays for political, international or cosmopolitan right dissolve into empty and impracticable ideals; but a practice which is based on empirical principles of human nature, and which does not consider it beneath its dignity to shape its maxims according to the way of the world, can alone hope to find a solid foundation for its system of political prudence.

If, of course, there is neither freedom nor any moral law based on freedom, but only a state in which everything that happens or can happen simply obeys the mechanical workings of nature, politics would mean the art of utilising nature for the government of men, and this would constitute the whole of practical wisdom; the concept of right would then be only an empty idea. But if we consider it absolutely necessary to couple the concept of right with politics, or even to make it a limiting condition of politics, it must be conceded that the two are compatible. And I can indeed imagine a *moral politician*, i.e. someone who conceives of the principles of political expediency in such a way that they can co-exist with morality, but I cannot imagine a *political moralist*, i.e. one who fashions his morality to suit his own advantage as a statesman.

The moral politician will make it a principle that, if any faults which could not have been prevented are discovered in the political constitution or in the relations between states, it is a duty, especially for heads of state, to see to it that they are corrected as soon as possible; it should be ensured that these political institutions are made to conform to natural right, which stands before us as a model in the idea of practical reason, and this should be done even if selfish interests have to be sacrificed. It would be contrary to all political expediency, which in this case agrees with morality, to destroy any of the existing bonds of political or cosmopolitan union before a better constitution has been prepared to take their place. And while it would be absurd to demand that their faults be repaired at once and by violent measures, it can still be required of the individual in power that he should be intimately aware of the maxim that changes for the better are necessary, in order that the constitution may constantly approach the optimum end prescribed by laws of right. A state may well *govern* itself in a republican way, even if its existing constitution provides for a despotic *ruling power*, and it will gradually come to the stage where the people can be influenced by the mere idea of the law's authority, just as if it were backed up by physical force, so that they will be able to create for themselves a legislation ultimately founded on right. Even if a more lawful constitution were attained by unlawful means, i.e. by a violent *revolution* resulting from a previous bad constitution, it would then no longer be permissible to lead the people back to the original one, even although everyone who had interfered with the old constitution by violence or conspiracy would rightly have been subject to the penalties of rebellion during the revolution itself. But as for the external relationship between states, no state can be required to relinquish its constitution, even if the latter is despotic (and hence stronger in relation to external enemies), so long as this state is in danger of being engulfed at any moment by other states; hence while plans must be made for political improvement, it must be permissible to delay their execution until a better opportunity arises.

It may well be the case that despotic moralists, i.e. those who err in practice, frequently act contrary to political prudence by adopting or recommending premature measures, yet experience must gradually bring them out of their opposition to nature and make them adopt better ways. But moralising politicians, for what they are worth, try to cover up political principles which are contrary to right, under the pretext that human nature is *incapable* of attaining the good which reason prescribes as an idea. They thereby make progress *impossible*, and eternalise the violation of right. . . .

Armed with concepts such as these, they proceed to take up political and international law as prescribed by reason. But they cannot take this step except in a spirit of chicanery, for they will follow their usual procedure of applying despotically formulated coercive laws in a mechanical manner, even in a sphere where the concepts of reason only allow for lawful coercion, in keeping with the principles of freedom, which alone makes possible a rightfully established political constitution. The supposed practitioner believes he can solve this problem empirically, ignoring the idea of reason and drawing on experience of how the (largely unlawful) constitutions which have hitherto survived best were organised. . . .

In order to end this sophistry (if not the actual injustice which it covers over) and to make the false representatives of those who wield power on earth confess that they are advocating might instead of right (adopting as they do the tone of persons entitled to give orders), it will be well to discover the ultimate principle from which the end of perpetual peace is derived, and thus to destroy the illusions with which men deceive themselves and others. It must likewise be demonstrated that all the evil which stands in the way of perpetual peace results from the fact that the political moralist starts out from the very point at which the moral politician rightly stops; he thus makes his principles subordinate to his end (i.e.

puts the cart before the horse), thereby defeating his own purpose of reconciling politics with morality.

To ensure that practical philosophy is at one with itself, it is first necessary to resolve the question of whether, in problems of practical reason, we should begin with its *material* principle, i.e. its *end*, as an object of the will, or with its *formal* principle, i.e. the principle which rests on man's freedom in his external relations and which states: 'Act in such a way that you can wish your maxim to become a universal law (irrespective of what the end in view may be).'

The latter principle must undoubtedly take precedence. For as a principle of right, it has absolute necessity, whereas the former is necessary only if the empirical conditions which permit the proposed end to be realised can be assumed to exist. And if this end were also a duty, as with the end of perpetual peace, it would itself have to be deduced from the formal principle of the maxims governing external action. Now the former (i.e. material) principle is that of the *political moralist*, and it treats the problems of political, international and cosmopolitan right as mere *technical tasks*; but the latter (i.e. formal) principle is that of the *moral politician*, for whom it is a *moral task*, totally different in its execution from technical problems, to bring about perpetual peace, which is desirable not just as a physical good, but also as a state of affairs which must arise out of recognising one's duty.

For the solution of the first problem (that of political expediency), much knowledge of nature is required, so that one can use its mechanism to promote the intended end. Nevertheless, all this is uncertain so far as its repercussions on perpetual peace are concerned, no matter which of the three departments of public right one considers. For it is uncertain whether the obedience and prosperity of the people can be better maintained over a long period by strict discipline or by appeals to their vanity, by conferring supreme power upon a single individual or upon several united leaders, or perhaps merely by means of an aristocracy of office or by popular internal government. History offers examples of the opposite effect being produced by all forms of government, with the single exception of genuine republicanism, which, however, could be the object only of a moral politician. And it is even more uncertain in the case of an *international right* supposedly based on statutes worked out by ministers, for it is in fact a mere word with nothing behind it, since it depends upon treaties which contain in the very act of their conclusion the secret reservation that they may be violated. On the other hand, the solution of the second problem, that of *political wisdom*, presents itself as it were automatically; it is obvious to everyone, it defeats all artifices, and leads straight to its goal, so long as we prudently remember that it cannot be realised by violent and precipitate means, but must be steadily approached as favourable opportunities present themselves.

We may therefore offer the following advice: 'Seek ye first the kingdom of pure practical reason and its justice, and your object (the blessing of perpetual peace) will be added unto you.' For morality, with regard to its principles of public right (hence in relation to a political code which can be known *a priori*), has the peculiar feature that the less it makes its conduct depend upon the end it envisages (whether this be a physical or moral advantage), the more it will in general harmonise with this end. And the reason for this is that it is precisely the general will as it is given *a priori*, within a single people or in the mutual relationships of various peoples, which alone determines what is right among men. But this union of the will of all, if only it is put into practice in a consistent way, can also, within the mechanism of nature, be the cause which leads to the intended result and gives effect to the concept of right. For example, it is a principle of moral politics that a people should combine to form a state in accordance with freedom and equality as its sole concepts of right, and this principle is based not on expediency, but on duty. Political moralists, on the other hand, do not deserve a hearing, however much they argue about the natural mechanism of a mass of people who enter into society, or claim that this mechanism would invalidate the above principles and frustrate their fulfilment, or try to prove their assertions by citing examples of badly organised constitutions of ancient and modern times (e.g. of democracies without a system of representation). Such theories are particularly damaging, because they may themselves produce the very evil they predict. For they put man into the same class as other living machines, which only need to realise consciously that they are not free beings for them to become in their own eyes the most wretched of all earthly creatures.

The proverbial saying *fiat iustitia, pereat mundus* (i.e. let justice reign, even if all the rogues in the world must perish) may sound somewhat inflated, but it is nonetheless true. It is a sound principle of right, which blocks up all the devious paths followed by cunning or violence. But it must not be misunderstood, or taken, for example, as a permit to apply one's own rights with the utmost rigour (which would conflict with ethical duty), but should be seen as an obligation of those in power not to deny or detract from the rights of anyone out of disfavour or sympathy for others. And this requires above all that the state should have an internal constitution organised in accordance with pure principles of right, and also that it unite with other neighbouring or even distant states to arrive at a lawful settlement of their differences by forming something analogous to a universal state. This proposition simply means that whatever the physical consequences may be, the political maxims adopted must not be influenced by the prospect of any benefit or happiness which might accrue to the state if it followed them, i.e. by the end which each state takes as the object of its will (*Wollen*) (as the highest *empirical* principle of political wisdom); they should be influenced only by the pure concept of rightful duty (*Sollen*), i.e. by an obligation whose principle is given *a priori* by pure reason. The world will certainly not come to an end if there are fewer bad men. Moral evil has by nature the inherent quality of being self-destructive and self-contradictory in its aims (especially in relations between persons of a like mind), so that it makes way for the moral principle of goodness, even if such progress is slow.

Thus in *objective* or theoretical terms, there is no conflict whatsoever between morality and politics. In a *subjective* sense, however (i.e. in relation to the selfish disposition of man, which, since it is not based on maxims of reason, cannot however be called practice), this conflict will and ought to remain active, since it serves as a whetstone of virtue. The true courage of virtue, according to the principle *tu ne cede malis, sed contra audentior ito,*[21] does not so much consist, in the present case, in resolutely standing up to the evils and sacrifices which must be encountered, as in facing the evil principle within ourselves and overcoming its wiles. For this principle is far more dangerous, since it is deceitful, treacherous, and liable to exploit the weakness of human nature in order to justify any violation of justice.

The political moralist may indeed say that the ruler and people, or one people and another people, do no injustice to *each other* if they enter into mutual conflict through violence or cunning, although they act completely unjustly in refusing to respect the concept of right, which would alone be capable of establishing perpetual peace. For if one party violates his duty towards another who is just as lawlessly disposed towards him, that which actually *happens* to them in wearing each other out is perfectly just, and enough of their kind will always survive to keep this process going without interruption into the most distant future, so that later generations may take them as a warning example. Providence is justified in disposing the course of world events in this way; for the moral principle in man is never extinguished, and reason, which is pragmatically capable of applying the ideas of right according to this principle, constantly increases with the continuous progress of culture, while the guilt attending violations of right increases proportionately. If we suppose that mankind never can and will be in a better condition, it seems impossible to justify by any kind of theodicy the mere fact that such a race of corrupt beings could have been created on earth at all. But this kind of judgement is far too exalted for us; we cannot theoretically attribute our conception of wisdom to the supreme power whose nature is beyond our understanding.

Such are the desperate conclusions to which we are inevitably driven if we do not assume that the pure principles of right have an objective reality, i.e. that they can be applied in practice. And whatever empirical politics may say to the contrary, the people within the state, as well as the states in their relations with one another, must act accordingly. A true system of politics cannot therefore take a single step without first paying tribute to morality. And although politics in itself is a difficult art, no art is required to combine it with morality. For as soon as the two come into conflict, morality can cut through the knot which politics cannot untie.

The rights of man must be held sacred, however great a sacrifice the ruling power may have to make. There can be no half measures here; it is no use devising

---

[21] [*Translator's footnote:*] "You for your part must not give way to troubles, but confront them the more boldly" (Virgil, *Aeneid*, VI, 95).

hybrid solutions such as a pragmatically conditioned right halfway between right and utility. For all politics must bend the knee before right, although politics may hope in return to arrive, however slowly, at a stage of lasting brilliance.

Thus, while no doubt indebted to the writings of Saint-Pierre and Rousseau, Kant's text makes a very distinctive contribution of its own, in the process providing the perpetual peace ideal with its modern shape and focus. Neither as naively utopian as Saint-Pierre nor as darkly pessimistic as Rousseau, Kant believes unlike both that perpetual peace can be achieved through the gradual expansion of a pacific federation, wherein states will not be required to relinquish their sovereignty. Thus, although the process might be time-consuming (possibly endless), the virtues of good governance will spread and consolidate themselves once they have first gained a foothold. Kant thereby evades the problem that troubled Rousseau: the potentially violent overthrow of the current order through which such a federation would first see the light of day. Indeed, as the appendix makes clear, Kant prefers reform to revolution.[22] He thereby seems to counsel us to take sides on one of the most contested issues of our time: whether liberal democracies should actively advocate violent overthrow of despotic regimes or seek other ways to set them on the right path.

The Metaphysics of Morals: International Right

We round off our selections from Immanuel Kant with an important passage from part I of The Metaphysics of Morals. Kant here treats of international right, which he defines as being "concerned partly with the right to make war, partly with the right of war itself, and partly with questions of right after a war, i.e. with the right of states to compel each other to abandon their warlike condition and to create a constitution which will establish an enduring peace" (pt. I, §53, p. 164). The first two of these we will readily recognize as pertaining to issues of ius ad bellum and ius in bello respectively. The latter signals, according to commentator Brian Orend, a novelty with Kant's approach, namely the distinctive concern with what is termed

---

[22]   See, for instance, The Metaphysics of Morals (pt. I, p. 175) where he appears to offer as an argument against revolution that any interim arrangement will mark a return to the state of nature, thereby jeopardizing whatever positive steps toward peace and governance that have after all been achieved. On the whole, though, Kant's attitude toward revolution is complex. He is generally held to be an avid supporter of the ideals that inspired the French revolution (cf. What is Enlightenment?), but writing in 1797, shortly after the Reign of Terror, his attitude has changed quite dramatically: "There can . . . be no rightful resistance on the part of the people to the legislative head of state." Sedition and rebellion "may be punished with nothing less than death" (The Metaphysics of Morals, pt. I, §A, p. 144).

the problem of *ius post bellum*.[23] Whether the claim to novelty is completely justified need not bother us here, for it is certainly true that Kant's writings on war are uniquely informed by just such considerations – war must always be waged with an outlook to a lasting peace. As he says in §57 (p. 168) of this work, "[t]he most problematic task in international right is that of determining rights in wartime. For it is very difficult to form any conception at all of such rights and to imagine any law whatsoever in this lawless state without involving oneself in contradictions (*inter arma silent leges*).[24] The only possible solution would be to conduct the war in accordance with principles which would still leave the states with the possibility of abandoning the state of nature in their external relations and of entering a state of right." Thereby both *ius ad bellum* and *ius in bello* are fundamentally constrained by a vision of what shall happen after the war, the *ius post bellum*.

Based very much on his rejection of punishment as a valid ground for war,[25] the following passage finds Kant arguing persuasively for a set of very humane constraints on the post-war treatment of the defeated party. Here Kant's perpetual peace ideal is set to work in a highly favorable light. Since war is a state of lawlessness, a victorious campaign does not confer a new set of rights on the victor. Rather than look back at past grievances, we are beckoned to look forward to constructive and peaceful future relations. Kant's arguments in these sections certainly throw a critical light on many actual post-war treaties, and his point appears to have been confirmed on several occasions: imposing draconian measures on a vanquished state is not likely to produce a stable peace.

From *The Metaphysics of Morals*, pt. I[26]

§58

The right which applies *after* a war, i.e. with regard to the peace treaty at the time of its conclusion and also to its later consequences, consists of the following elements. The victor sets out the conditions, and these are drawn up in a *treaty* on which agreement is reached with the defeated party in order that peace may be concluded. A treaty of this kind is not determined by any pretended right which the victor possesses over his opponent because of an alleged injury the latter has done him; the victor should not concern himself with such questions, but should

---

[23] See chap. 7 of his *War and International Justice: A Kantian Perspective* (Waterloo, Ontario: Wilfrid Laurier University Press, 2000) and "Kant's Ethics of War and Peace," *Journal of Military Ethics*, 3, 2 (2004), pp. 161–77. Orend credits Thomas Pogge with the coinage.

[24] [*Translator's footnote:*] "The laws are silent in times of war." Cicero, *Pro Milone*, 4, 10.

[25] See pp. 521–2, above.

[26] *Kant: Political Writings* (ed. Reiss), pp. 169–70.

rely only on his own power for support. Thus he cannot claim compensation for the costs of the war, for he would then have to pronounce his opponent unjust in waging it. And even if this argument should occur to him, he could not make use of it, or else he would have to maintain that the war was a punitive one, which would in turn mean that he had committed an offence in waging it himself. A peace treaty should also provide for the exchange of prisoners without ransom, whether the numbers on both sides are equal or not.

The vanquished state and its subjects cannot forfeit their civil freedom through the conquest of the country. Consequently, the former cannot be degraded to the rank of a colony or the latter to the rank of bondsmen. Otherwise, the war would have been a punitive one, which is self-contradictory.

A *colony* or province is a nation which has its own constitution, legislation and territory, and all members of any other state are no more than foreigners on its soil, even if the state to which they belong has supreme executive power over the colonial nation. The state with executive power is called the *mother state*. The daughter state is *ruled* by it, although it governs itself through its own parliament, which in turn functions under the presidency of a viceroy (*civitas hybrida*). The relationship of Athens to various islands was of this kind, as is that of Great Britain towards Ireland at the present moment.

It is even less possible to infer the rightful existence of *slavery* from the military conquest of a people, for one would then have to assume that the war had been a punitive one. Least of all would this justify hereditary slavery, which is completely absurd, for the guilt of a person's crime cannot be inherited.

It is implicit in the very concept of a peace treaty that it includes an *amnesty*. . . .

§60

The rights of a state against an *unjust enemy* are unlimited in quantity or degree, although they do have limits in relation to quality. In other words, while the threatened state may not employ *every* means to assert its own rights, it may employ any intrinsically permissible means to whatever degree its own strength allows. But what can the expression 'an unjust enemy' mean in relation to the concepts of international right, which requires that every state should act as judge of its own cause just as it would do in a state of nature? It must mean someone whose publicly expressed will, whether expressed in word or in deed, displays a maxim which would make peace among nations impossible and would lead to a perpetual state of nature if it were made into a general rule. Under this heading would come violations of public contracts, which can be assumed to affect the interests of all nations. For they are a threat to their freedom, and a challenge to them to unite against such misconduct and to deprive the culprit of the power to act in a similar way again. But this does *not* entitle them *to divide up the offending state among themselves* and to make it disappear, as it were, from the face of the earth. For this would be an injustice against the people, who cannot lose their original right to unite into a commonwealth. They can only be made to accept a new constitution of a nature that is unlikely to encourage their warlike inclinations.

Besides, the expression 'an unjust enemy' is a *pleonasm* if applied to any situation in a state of nature, for this state is itself one of injustice. A just enemy would be one whom I could not resist without injustice. But if this were so, he would not be my enemy in any case.

42

G. W. F. Hegel (1770–1831)

War and the Spirit of the Nation-state

> The fact that states reciprocally recognize each other as states remains, even in war . . . a bond wherein each counts to the rest as something absolute. Hence in war, war itself is characterized as something which ought to pass away.
>
> G. W. F. Hegel, *Philosophy of Right*

As famous for his dialectical philosophy of history as he is infamous for his abstruse and convoluted style of writing, Georg Wilhelm Friedrich Hegel ranks among the defining contributors to modern philosophy. The creator of a complex yet systematic framework of philosophical speculation, Hegel's philosophical legacy rests mainly on a remarkable quartet of works: *Phenomenology of Spirit* (1807), *Science of Logic* (1812–16), *Encyclopaedia of the Philosophical Sciences* (1817), and, finally, *Philosophy of Right* (1821), from which the present selection is culled.[1]

While all of Hegel's major works make for difficult reading, the challenge of the closing sections of *Philosophy of Right* (which will be our focus here) is not so much that of digging through layers of philosophical arcana in order to uncover the work's "real meaning," but rather that of placing the most obvious routes of interpretation in proper perspective. Hegel's political views were controversial from the start, and since then virulent disputes have raged about how to characterize his politics – was he a conservative apologist for Prussian nationalism or a visionary theorist of the modern constitutional state? Or was he, as a more recent reading would have it (chiefly following Karl Popper's influential *The Open Society and its Enemies*[2]), a fascist forerunner; a glorifier of war and violence, and a spokesman for totalitarianism?

---

[1] We will be using, with minor modifications, the translation of T. M. Knox, *Hegel's Philosophy of Right* (Oxford: Clarendon Press, 1967).

[2] Karl R. Popper, *The Open Society and Its Enemies*, vol. II (London: Routledge and Kegan Paul, 1945, and subsequent editions). For a critical exposition of Popper's reading of Hegel, see Walter

It is not our task here to pit against each other these diverging interpretations of Hegel's writings. Still, while much of what Hegel writes on politics in general – and war in particular – no doubt makes for a disturbing read, it is clear that Hegel also brings to the discussion a remarkable diversity of philosophical considerations. Any attempt to understand Hegel must struggle to come to grips with his complex relationship to the politico-philosophical climate of his times, and specifically with the ambivalent influence of his predecessor Immanuel Kant. While no doubt appreciative of many of its central tenets, Hegel was scathing of Enlightenment philosophy for its inability to see the nation-state as an essential moment in the unfolding of human history, and not merely as a collection of individuals. In contradistinction to this, Hegel developed a notion of the state as a distinctive "ethical substance" (*Philosophy of Right*, section 337); a substance which encompasses and simultaneously transcends the worth and dignity of the individuals comprising it. In this sense, Hegel is one of the few philosophers of the modern era to take seriously the notion of collective identity, thus providing us with a possible framework in which to understand, if not yet justify, the contemporary resurgence of the concept of "identity conflicts."

Philosophy of Right

In this first excerpt from the *Philosophy of Right*, Hegel probes the concept of sovereignty, and elaborates on the relationship of the individual to the state and, not least, of states to other states. Here Hegel clearly marks his opposition to the individualism that had been the hallmark of political theory since the Enlightenment. Hegel claims that this individualism, insofar as it asserts the authority of individuals over the community, is subjectivity only in its "most external form" (section 320). By contrast, the "true actuality [of subjectivity] is attained . . . in the subjectivity identical with the substantial will of the state" (ibid.). This is where subjectivity passes from mere *actuality* to true *ideality*.

From *Philosophy of Right*, sections 321–2[3]

2. Sovereignty *vis-à-vis* Foreign States

321 Sovereignty at home . . . is this ideality in the sense that the moments of Spirit and its actuality, the state, have become developed in their necessity and subsist as the organs of the state. Spirit in its freedom is an infinitely negative

Kaufmann, "The Hegel Myth and its Methods," in Walter Kaufmann (ed.), *Hegel's Political Philosophy* (New York: Atherton Press, 1970), pp. 137–71.

[3] *Hegel's Philosophy of Right* (trans. Knox), p. 208.

relation to itself and hence its essential character from its own point of view is its singleness, a singleness which has incorporated these subsistent differences into itself and so is a unit, exclusive of other units. So characterized, the state has individuality, and individuality is in essence an individual, and in the sovereign an actual, immediate individual. . . .

322 Individuality is awareness of one's existence as a unit in sharp distinction from others. It manifests itself here in the state as a relation to other states, each of which is autonomous *vis-à-vis* the others. This autonomy embodies Spirit's actual awareness of itself as a unit and hence it is the most fundamental freedom which a people possesses as well as its highest dignity.

Those who talk of the 'wishes' of a collection of people constituting a more or less autonomous state with its own centre, of its 'wishes' to renounce this centre and its autonomy in order to unite with others to form a new whole, have very little knowledge of the nature of a collection or of the feeling of selfhood which a nation possesses in its independence.

In the following paragraphs, Hegel elaborates on the consequences of this view for the bonds of duty between individual and state. The substance of this bond comes out clearly in the case of war, where the interests of the individual are wholly eclipsed by the interests of the state. Hence, the rationale for waging war is not, as is commonly thought, the protection of individual life and property: quite the contrary, it is the *sacrifice* of these – of "property and life, as well as of opinion and everything else naturally comprised in the compass of life" (*Philosophy of Right*, section 324) – in protection of the ethical substance of the state, that marks out the duty of the citizen. Several Hegel scholars have been eager to qualify this idea, by pointing out that this applies *only* in times of war, and perhaps even only during total war.[4] Hence the special interest of war, from the point of view of Hegelian dialectics, is that here, and only here, will the interest of the individual and the interest of the state be no longer distinguishable.

In the following passage, Hegel also makes a first reference to the Enlightenment ideal of *perpetual peace*, as advocated by Rousseau and Kant. Several themes motivate Hegel's rejection of this ideal. In the first place, there is a disagreement about exactly what kind of phenomenon war is, and hence about what kind of philosophical account (if any) would suffice to provide an adequate treatment of it. Whatever else it may be, war, on Hegel's account, is an important catalyst in the dialectical development and fulfilment of history. Hence war cannot be explained, as the tradition culminating with Kant would seem to attempt, in merely negative terms. In this sense, war represents more than merely an irrational deviation from the norm, a deviation that could be remedied once and for all if only state leaders

---

[4]   See, for instance, Allen W. Wood, *Hegel's Ethical Thought* (Cambridge: Cambridge University Press, 1990), p. 28.

could come to realize and follow the dictates of rationality. Rather, war is a *positive* phenomenon that drives history forward (which is not, however, equivalent to providing a moral justification for any specific war).

Secondly, war also serves as a *memento mori*,[5] reminding people (and peoples) of "the vanity of temporal goods and concerns" (section 324), thereby forcing them to set these aside and unite in defense of the higher principle, the state. Against this background, Hegel warns of the "foulness [and] corruption in nations [that] would be the result of prolonged, let alone 'perpetual,' peace" (ibid.). Thus, to conclude that war is "an absolute evil and . . . a purely external contingency" (ibid.) is altogether too shallow.

From *Philosophy of Right*, sections 324–5[6]

324 War is the state of affairs which deals in earnest with the vanity of temporal goods and concerns – a vanity at other times a common theme of edifying sermonizing. This is what makes it the moment in which the ideality of the particular attains its right and is actualized. War has the higher significance that through it, as I have remarked elsewhere, 'the ethical health of peoples is preserved in their indifference to the stabilization of finite institutions; just as the blowing of the winds preserves the sea from the foulness which would be the result of a prolonged calm, so also corruption in nations would be the product of prolonged, let alone 'perpetual', peace.' This, however, is said to be only a philosophic idea, or, to use another common expression, a 'justification of Providence', and it is maintained that actual wars require some other justification. On this point, see below.

The ideality which is in evidence in war, i.e. in a contingent relation of a state to a foreign state, is the same as the ideality in accordance with which the domestic powers of the state are organic moments in a whole. This fact appears in history in various forms, e.g. successful wars have checked domestic unrest and consolidated the power of the state at home. Other phenomena illustrate the same point: e.g. peoples unwilling or afraid to tolerate sovereignty at home have been subjugated from abroad, and they have struggled for their independence with the less glory and success the less they have been able previously to organize the powers of the state in home affairs – their freedom has died from the fear of dying; states whose autonomy has been guaranteed not by their armed forces but in other ways (e.g. by their disproportionate smallness in comparison with their neighbours) have been able to subsist with a constitution of their own which by itself would not have assured peace in either home or foreign affairs.

[5] This notion is developed by Shlomo Avineri, in "The Problem of War in Hegel's Thought," in *Journal of the History of Ideas*, 22, 4 (1961), p. 466, and *Hegel's Theory of the Modern State* (Cambridge: Cambridge University Press, 1972), p. 197.

[6] *Hegel's Philosophy of Right* (trans. Knox), pp. 209–10, 295.

Addition:[7] In peace civil life continually expands; all its departments wall themselves in, and in the long run men stagnate. Their idiosyncrasies become continually more fixed and ossified. But for health the unity of the body is required, and if its parts harden themselves into exclusiveness, that is death. Perpetual peace is often advocated as an ideal towards which humanity should strive. With that end in view, Kant proposed a league of monarchs to adjust differences between states, and the Holy Alliance was meant to be a league of much the same kind. But the state is an individual, and individuality essentially implies negation. Hence even if a number of states make themselves into a family, this group as an individual must engender an opposite and create an enemy. As a result of war, nations are strengthened, but peoples involved in civil strife also acquire peace at home through making wars abroad. To be sure, war produces insecurity of property, but this insecurity of things is nothing but their transience – which is inevitable. We hear plenty of sermons from the pulpit about the insecurity, vanity, and instability of temporal things, but everyone thinks, however much he is moved by what he hears, that he at least will be able to retain his own. But if this insecurity now comes on the scene in the form of hussars with shining sabres and they actualize in real earnest what the preachers have said, then the moving and edifying discourses which foretold all these events turn into curses against the invader. Be that as it may, the fact remains that wars occur when the necessity of the case requires. The seeds burgeon once more, and harangues are silenced by the solemn cycles of history.

325 Sacrifice on behalf of the individuality of the state is the substantial tie between the state and all its members and so is a universal duty. Since this tie is a *single* aspect of the ideality, as contrasted with the reality, of subsistent particulars, it becomes at the same time a *particular* tie, and those who are in it form a class of their own with the characteristic of courage.

Under normal circumstances, Hegel thus contends, the interests of the state are best served by such a distinct "class" – a professional army. However, "if the state as such, if its autonomy, is in jeopardy, all its citizens are in duty bound to answer the summons to its defence" (*Philosophy of Right*, section 326).

In the following sections of the *Philosophy of Right*, Hegel addresses a central theme in the perpetual peace tradition, namely the absence of a Praetor – a supreme judge – to adjudicate international conflicts. The perpetual peace tradition took this absence to be the immediate cause of war, and interestingly, Hegel seems to agree with this diagnosis, even to the point of asserting that "if states disagree and their particular wills cannot be harmonized, the matter can only be

---

[7] These "Additions" contain valuable material from Hegel's lecture notes, and were inserted into the text by Eduard Gans, who edited *Philosophy of Right* for its publication as volume VIII of Hegel's *Sämtliche Werke* (Berlin, 1833).

settled by war" (section 334). However, his thoughts on what follows from this diagnosis could scarcely be more different. Elaborating on the theme developed by Hobbes (against whom, in large measure, many modern perpetual peace theorists were reacting in the first place), Hegel maintains that this lack of supranational adjudication is just a logical upshot of the concept of sovereignty itself. The domestic analogy – that of a number of individual entities joined together under a single jurisdiction – simply has no application to the international sphere. Consequently, the proposed solution of Rousseau and Kant is no solution at all. Binding international law in the requisite sense would not amount to the joining together of *sovereign states* in a pacific federation; rather it would signal an end to sovereignty itself. To the extent that states are to remain sovereign we must see them as "above" any treaty or contract they may enter into. International treaties, being products of the wills of individual sovereigns, must forever remain subordinate to those same wills. Thus, their consent can, by that same token, also be retracted at will. With this in mind, Hegel claims that international law can never transcend the "ought" and attain the status of a categorical imperative.

Instead, Hegel traces the consequences of the complex relations of *mutual recognition* that mark out the relation of state to state.[8] A state is a state only contingent on its giving and receiving recognition as such from other states. From these patterns of mutual recognition emerges a rather different framework for understanding international interaction than the one which places codified international law at its heart.

From *Philosophy of Right,* sections 329–31, 333–5, 337[9]

329 The state's tendency to look abroad lies in the fact that it is an individual subject. Its relation to other states therefore falls to the power of the crown. Hence it directly devolves on the monarch, and on him alone, to command the armed forces, to conduct foreign affairs through ambassadors, etc., to make war and peace, and to conclude treaties of all kinds. . . .

B. International Law

330 International law springs from the relations between autonomous states. It is for this reason that what is absolute in it retains the form of an ought-to-be, since its actuality depends on different wills each of which is sovereign.

---

[8]   The theme of mutual recognition appears frequently in Hegel's writings, most famously in the *Phenomenology of Spirit*'s so-called "Master–Slave dialectic." See *Phenomenology of Spirit*, trans. A. V. Miller (Oxford: Oxford University Press, 1977), pp. 111–19.
[9]   *Hegel's Philosophy of Right* (trans. Knox), pp. 212–15, 297.

Addition: States are not private persons but completely autonomous totalities in themselves, and so the relation between them differs from a moral relation and a relation involving private rights. Attempts have often been made to regard the state as a person with the rights of persons and as a moral entity. But the position with private persons is that they are under the jurisdiction of a court which gives effect to what is right in principle. Now a relation between states ought also to be right in principle, but in mundane affairs a principle ought also to have power. Now since there is no power in existence which decides in face of the state what is right in principle and actualizes this decision, it follows that so far as international relations are concerned we can never get beyond an 'ought'. The relation between states is a relation between autonomous entities which make mutual stipulations but which at the same time are superior to these stipulations.

331 The nation state is Spirit in its substantive rationality and immediate actuality and is therefore the absolute power on earth. It follows that every state is sovereign and autonomous against its neighbours. It is entitled in the first place and without qualification to be sovereign from their point of view, i.e. to be recognized by them as sovereign. At the same time, however, this title is purely formal, and the demand for this recognition of the state, merely on the ground that it is a state, is abstract. Whether a state is in fact something absolute depends on its content, i.e. on its constitution and general situation; and recognition, implying as it does an identity of both form and content, is conditional on the neighbouring state's judgement and will.

A state is as little an actual individual without relations to other states (see section 322) as an individual is actually a person without *rapport* with other persons. . . . The legitimate authority of a state and, more particularly, so far as its foreign relations are concerned, of its monarch also, is partly a purely domestic matter (one state should not meddle with the domestic affairs of another). On the other hand, however, it is no less essential that this authority should receive its full and final legitimation through its recognition by other states, although this recognition requires to be safeguarded by the proviso that where a state is to be recognized by others, it shall likewise recognize them, i.e. respect their autonomy; and so it comes about that they cannot be indifferent to each other's domestic affairs. . . .

333 The fundamental proposition of international law (i.e. the universal law which ought to be absolutely valid between states, as distinguished from the particular content of positive treaties) is that treaties, as the ground of obligations between states, ought to be kept. But since the sovereignty of a state is the principle of its relations to others, states are to that extent in a state of nature in relation to each other. Their rights are actualized only in their particular wills and not in a universal will with constitutional powers over them. This universal proviso of international law therefore does not go beyond an ought-to-be, and what really happens is that international relations in accordance with treaty alternate with the severance of these relations.

There is no Praetor to judge between states; at best there may be an arbitrator or a mediator, and even he exercises his functions contingently only, i.e. in dependence on the particular wills of the disputants. Kant had an idea for securing 'perpetual peace' by a League of Nations to adjust every dispute. It was to be a power recognized by each individual state, and was to arbitrate in all cases of dissension in order to make it impossible for disputants to resort to war in order to settle them. This idea presupposes an accord between states; this would rest on moral or religious or other grounds and considerations, but in any case would always depend ultimately on a particular sovereign will and for that reason would remain infected with contingency.

334 It follows that if states disagree and their particular wills cannot be harmonized, the matter can only be settled by war. A state through its subjects has widespread connexions and many-sided interests, and these may be readily and considerably injured; but it remains inherently indeterminable which of these injuries is to be regarded as a specific breach of treaty or as an injury to the honour and autonomy of the state. The reason for this is that a state may regard its infinity and honour as at stake in each of its concerns, however minute, and it is all the more inclined to susceptibility to injury the more its strong individuality is impelled as a result of long domestic peace to seek and create a sphere of activity abroad.

335 Apart from this, the state is in essence Spirit and therefore cannot be prepared to stop at just taking notice of an injury *after* it has actually occurred. On the contrary, there arises in addition as a cause of strife the *idea* of such an injury as the idea of a danger *threatening* from another state, together with calculations of degrees of probability on this side and that, guessing at intentions, etc., etc. . . . .

337 . . . At one time the opposition between morals and politics, and the demand that the latter should conform to the former, were much canvassed. On this point only a general remark is required here. The welfare of a state has claims to recognition totally different from those of the welfare of the individual. The ethical substance, the state, has its determinate being, i.e. its right, directly embodied in something existent, something not abstract but concrete, and the principle of its conduct and behaviour can only be this concrete existent and not one of the many universal thoughts supposed to be moral commands. When politics is alleged to clash with morals and so to be always wrong, the doctrine propounded rests on superficial ideas about morality, the nature of the state and the state's relation to the moral point of view.

It may come as something of a surprise that Hegel, after seemingly dismissing the viability of any comprehensive framework for the articulation of a *ius ad bellum* (let alone for the complete and systematic eradication of war), proceeds in the following paragraphs to draw up what very much resembles a rudimentary list of *ius in bello* requirements. We should remember, however, that this dovetails nicely with Hegel's characteristic favoring of the historically evolved, informal customs of peoples over the voluntaristic legalism predominant in international relations; in other words, his favoring of *Sittlichkeit* (ethics, custom) over *Moralität* (morality). Although war can never be completely eradicated, Hegel's concept of mutual recognition implies that total war – war of extinction – is a self-defeating enterprise, since states only exist as recognized by other states. Hence, we would do well to look into the actual wartime practices of states, as outlined below, in order to understand how war can be limited in its destruction without binding international law.

From *Philosophy of Right*, sections 338–9[10]

338 The fact that states reciprocally recognize each other as states remains, even in war – the state of affairs when rights disappear and force and chance hold sway – a bond wherein each counts to the rest as something absolute. Hence in war, war itself is characterized as something which ought to pass away. It implies therefore the proviso of the *ius gentium* that the possibility of peace be retained (and so, for example, that envoys must be respected), and, in general, that war be not waged against domestic institutions, against the peace of family and private life, or against persons in their private capacity.

Addition: Modern wars are therefore humanely waged, and person is not set over against person in hatred. At most, personal enmities appear in the vanguard, but in the main body of the army hostility is something vague and gives place to each side's respect for the duty of the other.

339 Apart from this, relations between states (e.g. in war-time, reciprocal agreements about taking prisoners; in peace-time, concessions of rights to subjects of other states for the purpose of private trade and intercourse, etc.) depend principally upon the customs of nations, custom being the inner universality of behaviour maintained in all circumstances.

Addition: The European peoples form a family in accordance with the universal principle underlying their legal codes, their customs, and their civilization. This principle has modified their international conduct accordingly in a state of affairs [i.e. war] otherwise dominated by the mutual infliction of evils. The relations of state to state are uncertain, and there is no Praetor available to adjust them. The only higher judge is the universal absolute Spirit, the world Spirit.

This last line brings us back to the challenge of understanding how Hegel's account of war is tied in with his general philosophy of history. As we noted at the outset,

---

[10]   Ibid., pp. 215, 297.

Hegel's theory is geared towards clearing conceptual space for an understanding of the *positive* attributes of war, in the sense that war must be understood as a catalyst, a moment in the sequence of historical progress. To use one of his own expressions, Hegel's account is thus to a large extent intended as a *phenomenology* of war, purporting to transcend the is–ought distinction that in his judgment had hindered the efforts of so many of his philosophical predecessors.

In these final paragraphs of our selection, Hegel seeks to assure us that "world history is not the verdict of mere might" (*Philosophy of Right*, section 342). Beyond all the seemingly pointless and arbitrary suffering a hidden logic emerges through a dialectical movement. This logic marks out a *narrative of freedom*,[11] a form of freedom of which the modern constitutional state is the pivotal embodiment.

From *Philosophy of Right*, sections 345, 349, 351[12]

C. World History

345 Justice and virtue, wrongdoing, power and vice, talents and their achievements, passions strong and weak, guilt and innocence, grandeur in individual and national life, autonomy, fortune and misfortune of states and individuals, all these have their specific significance and worth in the field of known actuality; therein they are judged and therein they have their partial, though only partial justification. World-history, however, is above the point of view from which these things matter. Each of its stages is the presence of a necessary moment in the Idea of the world Spirit, and that moment attains its absolute right in that stage. The nation whose life embodies this moment secures its good fortune and fame, and its deeds are brought to fruition. . . .

349 A nation does not begin by being a state. The transition from a family, a horde, a clan, a multitude, etc., to political conditions is the realization of the Idea in the form of that nation. Without this form, a nation, as an ethical substance – which is what it is implicitly, lacks the objectivity of possessing in its own eyes and in the eyes of others, a universal and universally valid embodiment in laws, i.e. in determinate thoughts, and as a result it fails to secure recognition from others. So long as it lacks objective law and an explicitly established rational constitution, its autonomy is formal only and is not sovereignty. . . .

351 The same consideration justifies civilized nations in regarding and treating as barbarians those who lag behind them in institutions which are the essential moments of the state. Thus a pastoral people may treat hunters as barbarians, and

[11]   The Hegelian insight that the road to freedom follows a dialectical course, and hence can be reconstructed as a road of *learning*, has been widely influential, for instance on Marxism.
[12]   *Hegel's Philosophy of Right* (trans. Knox), pp. 217, 218–19.

both of these are barbarians from the point of view of agriculturists, etc. The civilized nation is conscious that the rights of barbarians are unequal to its own and treats their autonomy as only a formality.

When wars and disputes arise in such circumstances, the trait which gives them a significance for world history is the fact that they are struggles for recognition in connexion with something of specific intrinsic worth.

These last words provide a fitting closure to our selections from Hegel's *Philosophy of Right*. The concept of a *struggle for recognition* has come to be endowed with a specific form of dignity in our age.[13] Still, as can be gleaned from the above passage, it is not obvious that Hegel's meaning of the term here is one that people involved in such struggles would want to appeal to. Even so, it remains the case that Hegel developed a powerful and pregnant vocabulary with potential applications far beyond anything he himself might have imagined.

In the end, then, a number of vexing questions arise from reading Hegel's complex and enigmatic text. Commentators sympathetic to his overall project have attempted to salvage his thoughts on war by invoking the distinction between *ideality* and *actuality*. Hegel's approach, it is claimed, eschews traditional normative approaches and instead attempts to tackle the problem of war head on. This, as we have noted, amounts to an attempt at providing us with something like a *phenomenology of war*: rather than resorting to a wholesale moral condemnation of war (a condemnation whose terms, to paraphrase Kant, would be bound to come across as a sorry comfort), Hegel seeks to understand the phenomenon by providing a description of its anatomy and function.[14]

---

[13] See, for instance, Charles Taylor, "The Politics of Recognition," in Amy Gutmann (ed.), *Multiculturalism: Examining the Politics of Recognition* (Princeton, NJ: Princeton University Press, 1994), pp. 25–74, and Axel Honneth, *The Struggle for Recognition: The Moral Grammar of Social Conflicts* (Cambridge: Polity Press, 1995).

[14] For elaborations on such a reading, consult D. P. Verene, "Hegel's Account of War," in Z. A. Pelczynski, *Hegel's Political Philosophy* (London: Cambridge University Press, 1971), p. 170, and Avineri, "The Problem of War," p. 465.

43

Carl von Clausewitz (1780–1831)

Ethics and Military Strategy

War is no pastime; it is no mere joy in daring and winning, no place for irresponsible enthusiasts. It is a serious means to a serious end.

Carl von Clausewitz, *On War*

Few books in the field of military strategy can rival Carl van Clausewitz's *Vom Kriege* (*On War*). Published in 1832, a year after the author's death, it eschewed a detailed study of troop formations, armaments, and so forth, in order to focus on the principles most essential to the conduct of war. Famous for its treatment of armed conflict as a distinctive sphere of human endeavor, the work is often classed with Machiavelli's *The Prince* as a quintessential expression of amoral political realism. It is true that ethics is rarely mentioned in *Vom Kriege*. Some statements even seem to imply that moral concerns have no place within the military strategist's art. Indeed, very early in the work, Clausewitz asserts that "war is such a dangerous business that the mistakes which come from kindness are the very worst."[1]

There are, however, indications that Clausewitz intended *On War* to have an ethical dimension. This becomes apparent when he writes that "[m]ilitary activity is never directed against material forces alone; it is always aimed simultaneously at the moral forces which give it life, and the two cannot be separated."[2] He accordingly urged commanders to cultivate the military virtues – courage especially – which can enable them to perform well on the battlefield. In this respect, there is a close affinity between Aristotle's treatment of courage in the *Nicomachean Ethics*, and Clausewitz's penetrating analysis of "strength of character" in *On War* (discussed below in the section on "Military Genius"). For both thinkers, virtue (of the intellect and the emotions) is deemed indispensable if there is to be right action in a world marked by indeterminacy and chance.

---

[1]   *On War*, bk. 1, chap. 1, section 3 (p. 75).
[2]   *On War*, bk. 2, chap. 2, section (p. 137), entitled "Moral Values Cannot be Ignored in War."

Similarly, Clausewitz's insistence on the subordination of war to politics creates a framework for reflection on the relation of military force to justice. Unlike Machiavelli, who reduced war-making to the unitary goal of political survival ("a just war is a necessary war"[3]), in Clausewitz's more nuanced account war can serve a multitude of different political objectives. And since he acknowledges that the state is the embodiment of the highest values of the community, his system is constructed in such a fashion that war-making must be directed and constrained by these values. Echoing Aristotle's famous distinction between means and ends, Clausewitz's dictum that war is "the continuation of policy by other means," can be read as an explicit rejection of militarism (the view that war has an inherent nobility). Some have even argued that there is a fundamental complementarity between Clausewitz's approach to military strategy and professional military ethics as it has been developed in the just war tradition.[4]

From *On War*, bk. I[5]

Chapter One: What Is War?

2: Definition

I shall not begin by expounding a pedantic, literary definition of war, but go straight to the heart of the matter, to the duel. War is nothing but a duel on a larger scale. Countless duels go to make up war, but a picture of it as a whole can be formed by imagining a pair of wrestlers. Each tries through physical force to compel the other to do his will; his *immediate* aim is to *throw* his opponent in order to make him incapable of further resistance.

War is thus an act of force to compel our enemy to do our will.

Force, to counter opposing force, equips itself with the inventions of art and science. Attached to force are certain self-imposed, imperceptible limitations hardly worth mentioning, known as international law and custom, but they scarcely weaken it. Force – that is, physical force, for moral force has no existence save as expressed in the state and the law – is thus the *means* of war; to impose our will on the enemy is its *object*. To secure that object we must render the enemy powerless; and that, in theory, is the true aim of warfare. That aim takes the place of the object, discarding it as something not actually part of war itself.

---

[3] "Iustum enim est bellum quibus necessarium," an ancient Roman adage that Machiavelli cites (approvingly) in chap. 26 of *The Prince*.

[4] See Paul Cornish, "Clausewitz and the Ethics of Armed Force: Five Propositions," *Journal of Military Ethics*, 2, 3 (2003), pp. 213–26.

[5] English translation, *On War*, by Michael Howard and Peter Paret (Princeton, NJ: Princeton University Press, 1976), pp. 75–6, 86–7, 101–4, 105–6, 107–8. Original German text: *Vom Kriege*, ed. Werner Hahlweg (Bonn: Dümmlers Verlag, 1980).

3: The maximum use of force

Kind-hearted people might of course think there was some ingenious way to disarm or defeat an enemy without too much bloodshed, and might imagine this is the true goal of the art of war. Pleasant as it sounds, it is a fallacy that must be exposed: war is such a dangerous business that the mistakes which come from kindness are the very worst. The maximum use of force is in no way incompatible with the simultaneous use of the intellect. If one side uses force without compunction, undeterred by the bloodshed it involves, while the other side refrains, the first will gain the upper hand. That side will force the other to follow suit; each will drive its opponent toward extremes, and the only limiting factors are the counterpoises inherent in war.

This is how the matter must be seen. It would be futile – even wrong – to try and shut one's eyes to what war really is from sheer distress at its brutality.

If wars between civilized nations are far less cruel and destructive than wars between savages, the reason lies in the social conditions of the states themselves and in their relationships to one another. These are the forces that give rise to war; the same forces circumscribe and moderate it. They themselves however are not part of war; they already exist before fighting starts. To introduce the principle of moderation into the theory of war itself would always lead to logical absurdity. . . .

23: But war is nevertheless a serious means to a serious end: a more precise definition of war

Such is war, such is the commander who directs it, and such the theory that governs it. War is no pastime; it is no mere joy in daring and winning, no place for irresponsible enthusiasts. It is a serious means to a serious end, and all its colorful resemblance to a game of chance, all the vicissitudes of passion, courage, imagination, and enthusiasm it includes are merely its special characteristics.

When whole communities go to war – whole peoples, and especially *civilized* peoples – the reason always lies in some political situation, and the occasion is always due to some political object. War, therefore, is an act of policy. Were it a complete, untrammeled, absolute manifestation of violence (as the pure concept would require), war would of its own independent will usurp the place of policy the moment policy had brought it into being; it would then drive policy out of office and rule by the laws of its own nature, very much like a mine that can explode only in the manner or direction predetermined by the setting. This, in fact, is the view that has been taken of the matter whenever some discord between policy and the conduct of war has stimulated theoretical distinctions of this kind. But in reality things are different, and this view is thoroughly mistaken. In reality war, as has been shown, is not like that. Its violence is not of the kind that explodes in a single discharge, but is the effect of forces that do not always develop in exactly the same manner or to the same degree. At times they will expand sufficiently to overcome the resistance of inertia or friction; at others they are too weak to have any effect. War is a pulsation of violence, variable in strength and therefore variable in the speed with which it explodes and discharges its energy. War moves on its goal with varying speeds; but it always lasts long enough for influence to be exerted on the goal and for its own course to be changed in one way or another – long enough, in other words, to remain subject to the action of a superior intelligence. If we keep in mind that war springs from some political purpose, it is natural that the prime cause of its existence will remain the supreme consideration in conducting it. That, however, does not imply that the political aim is a tyrant. It must adapt itself to its chosen means, a process which can radically change it; yet the political aim remains the first consideration. Policy, then, will permeate all military operations, and, in so far as their violent nature will admit, it will have a continuous influence on them.

24: War is merely the continuation
of policy by other means

We see, therefore, that war is not merely an act of policy but a true political instrument, a continuation of political intercourse, carried on with other means. What remains peculiar to war is simply the peculiar nature of its means. War in general, and the commander in any specific instance, is entitled to require that the trend and designs of policy shall not be inconsistent with these means. That, of course, is no small demand; but however much it may affect political aims in a given case, it will never do more than modify them. The political object is the goal, war is the means of reaching it, and means can never be considered in isolation from their purpose. . . .

Chapter Three: On Military Genius[6]

. . . War is the realm of danger; therefore *courage* is the soldier's first requirement.

---

[6] The theme of military virtue was first introduced in chap. 1, section 22 (ibid., p. 86): "The art of war deals with living and with moral forces. Consequently, it cannot attain the absolute, or certainty; it must always leave a margin for uncertainty, in the greatest things as much as in the smallest. With uncertainty in one scale, courage and self-confidence must be thrown into the other to correct the balance. The greater they are, the greater the margin that can be left for accidents. Thus courage and self-confidence are essential in war, and theory should propose only rules that give ample scope to these finest and least dispensable of military virtues, in all their degrees and variations. Even in daring there can be method and caution; but here they are measured by a different standard."

Courage is of two kinds: courage in the face of personal danger, and courage to accept responsibility, either before the tribunal of some outside power or before the court of one's own conscience. Only the first kind will be discussed here.

Courage in face of personal danger is also of two kinds. It may be indifference to danger, which could be due to the individual's constitution, or to his holding life cheap, or to habit. In any case, it must be regarded as a permanent *condition*. Alternatively, courage may result from such positive motives as ambition, patriotism, or enthusiasm of any kind. In that case courage is a feeling, an emotion, not a permanent state.

These two kinds of courage act in different ways. The first is the more dependable; having become second nature, it will never fail. The other will often achieve more. There is more reliability in the first kind, more boldness in the second. The first leaves the mind calmer; the second tends to stimulate, but it can also blind. *The highest kind of courage is a compound of both.*

War is the realm of physical exertion and suffering. These will destroy us unless we can make ourselves indifferent to them, and for this birth or training must provide us with a certain strength of body and soul. If we do possess those qualities, then even if we have nothing but common sense to guide them we shall be well equipped for war: it is exactly these qualities that primitive and semicivilized peoples usually possess.

If we pursue the demands that war makes on those who practice it, we come to the region dominated by the *powers of intellect*. War is the realm of uncertainty; three quarters of the factors on which action in war is based are wrapped in a fog of greater or lesser uncertainty. A sensitive and discriminating judgment is called for; a skilled intelligence to scent out the truth.

Average intelligence may recognize the truth occasionally, and exceptional courage may now and then retrieve a blunder; but usually intellectual inadequacy will be shown up by indifferent achievement.

War is the realm of chance. No other human activity gives it greater scope: no other has such incessant and varied dealings with this intruder. Chance makes everything more uncertain and interferes with the whole course of events.

Since all information and assumptions are open to doubt, and with chance at work everywhere, the commander continually finds that things are not as he expected. This is bound to influence his plans, or at least the assumptions underlying them. If this influence is sufficiently powerful to cause a change in his plans, be must usually work out new ones; but for these the necessary information may not be immediately available. During an operation decisions have usually to be made at once: there may be no time to review the situation or even to think it through. Usually, of course, new information and reevaluation are not enough to make us give up our intentions: they only call them in question. We now know more, but this makes us more, not less uncertain. The latest reports do not arrive all at once: they merely trickle in. They continually impinge on our decisions, and our mind must be permanently armed, so to speak, to deal with them.

If the mind is to emerge unscathed from this relentless struggle with the unforeseen, two qualities are indispensable: *first, an intellect that, even in the darkest hour, retains some glimmerings of the inner light which leads to truth; and second, the courage to follow this faint light wherever it may lead*. The first of these qualities is described by the French term, *coup d'oeil*; the second is *determination*.

. . . *Coup d'oeil* therefore refers not alone to the physical but, more commonly, to the inward eye. The expression, like the quality itself, has certainly always been more applicable to tactics, but it must also have its place in strategy, since here as well quick decisions are often needed. Stripped of metaphor and of the restrictions imposed on it by the phrase, the concept merely refers to the quick recognition of a truth that the mind would ordinarily miss or would perceive only after long study and reflection.

Determination in a single instance is an expression of courage; if it becomes characteristic, a mental habit. But here we are referring not to physical courage but to the courage to accept responsibility, courage in the face of a moral danger. This has often been called *courage d'esprit*, because it is created by the intellect. That, however, does not make it an act of the intellect: it is an act of temperament. Intelligence alone is not courage; we often see that the most intelligent people are irresolute. Since in the rush of events a man is governed by feelings rather than by thought, the intellect needs to arouse the quality of courage, which then supports and sustains it in action.

Looked at in this way, the role of determination is to limit the agonies of doubt and the peril of hesitation when the motives for action are inadequate. Colloquially, to be sure the term "determination" also applies to a propensity for daring, pugnacity, boldness, or temerity. But when a man has adequate grounds for action – whether subjective or objective, valid or false – he cannot properly be called "determined." This would amount to putting oneself in his position and weighting the scale with a doubt that he never felt. In such a case it is only a question of strength or weakness. I am not such a pedant as to quarrel with common usage over a slight misuse of a word; the only purpose of these remarks is to preclude misunderstandings.

Determination, which dispells doubt, is a quality that can be aroused only by the intellect, and by a specific cast of mind at that. More is required to create determination than a mere conjunction of superior insight with the appropriate emotions. Some may bring the keenest brains to the most formidable problems, and may possess the courage to accept serious responsibilities; but when faced with a difficult situation they still find themselves unable to reach a decision. Their courage and their intellect work in separate compartments, not together; determination, therefore, does not result. It is engendered only by a *mental act*; the mind tells man that boldness is required, and thus gives direction to his will. This particular cast of mind, which employs the fear of *wavering* and *hesitating* to suppress all other fears, is the force that makes strong men determined. Men of low intelligence, therefore, cannot possess determination in the sense in which we use the word. They may act without hesitation in a crisis, but if they do, they act *without reflection*; and a man who acts without reflection cannot, of course, be torn by doubt. From time to time action of this type may even be appropriate; but, as I have said before, it is the *average result* that indicates the existence of military genius. The statement may surprise the reader who knows some determined cavalry officers who are little given to deep thought: but he must remember that we are talking about a special kind of intelligence, not about great powers of meditation.

In short, we believe that determination proceeds from a special type of mind, from a strong rather than a brilliant one. We can give further proof of this interpretation by pointing to the many examples of men who show great determination as junior officers, but lose it as they rise in rank. Conscious of the need to be decisive, they also recognize the risks entailed by a *wrong* decision; since they are unfamiliar with the problems now facing them, their mind loses its former incisiveness. The more used they had been to instant action, the more their timidity increases as they realize the dangers of the vacillation that ensnares them.

Having discussed *coup d'oeil* and determination it is natural to pass to a related subject: *presence of mind*. This must play a great role in war, the domain of the unexpected, since it is nothing but an increased capacity of dealing with the unexpected. We admire presence of mind in an apt repartee, as we admire quick thinking in the face of danger. Neither needs to be exceptional, so long as it meets the situation. A reaction following long and deep reflection may seem quite commonplace; as an immediate response, it may give keen pleasure. The expression "presence of mind" precisely conveys the speed and immediacy of the help provided by the intellect.

Whether this splendid quality is due to a special cast of mind or to steady nerves depends on the nature of the incident, but neither can ever be entirely lacking. A quick retort shows wit; resourcefulness in sudden danger calls, above all, for steady nerve.

Four elements make up the climate of war: danger, exertion, uncertainty, and chance. If we consider them together, it becomes evident how much fortitude of mind and character are needed to make progress in these impeding elements with safety and success. According to circumstance, reporters and historians of war use such terms as *energy, firmness, staunchness, emotional balance,* and *strength of character*. These products of a heroic nature could almost be treated as one and the same force – strength of will – which adjusts itself to circumstances: but though closely linked, they are not identical. . . .

Of all the passions that inspire man in battle, none, we have to admit, is so powerful and so constant as the longing for honor and renown. The German language unjustly tarnishes this by associating it with two ignoble meanings in the terms "greed for honor" (*Ehrgeiz*) and "hankering after glory" (*Ruhmsucht*). The abuse of these noble ambitions has certainly inflicted the most disgusting outrages on the human race; nevertheless their origins entitle them to be ranked among the most elevated in human nature. In war they act as the essential breath of life that animates the inert mass. Other emotions may be more common and more venerated – patriotism, idealism, vengeance, enthusiasm of every kind – but they are no substitute for a thirst for fame and honor. They may, indeed, rouse the mass to action and inspire it, but they cannot give the commander the ambition to strive higher than the rest, as he must if he is to distinguish himself. They cannot give him, as can ambition, a personal, almost proprietary interest in every aspect of fighting, so that he turns each opportunity to best advantage – plowing with vigor, sowing with care, in the hope of reaping with abundance. It is primarily this spirit of endeavor on the part of commanders at all levels, this inventiveness, energy and competitive enthusiasm, which vitalizes an army and makes it victorious. And so far as the commander-in-chief is concerned, we may well ask whether history has ever known a great general who was not ambitious; whether, indeed, such a figure is conceivable.

Staunchness indicates the will's resistance to a single blow; *endurance* refers to prolonged resistance.

Though the two terms are similar and are often used interchangeably, the difference between them is significant and unmistakable. Staunchness in face of a single blow may result from strong emotion, whereas intelligence helps sustain endurance. The longer an action lasts, the more deliberate endurance becomes, and this is one of its sources of strength.

We now turn to *strength of mind*, or of *character*, and must first ask what we mean by these terms.

Not, obviously, vehement display of feeling, or passionate temperament: that would strain the meaning of the phrase. We mean the ability to keep one's head at times of exceptional stress and violent emotion. Could strength of intellect alone account for such a faculty? We doubt it. Of course the opposite does not flow from the fact that some men of outstanding intellect do lose their self-control; it could be argued that a powerful rather than a capacious mind is what is needed. But it might be closer to the truth to assume that the faculty known as *self-control* – the gift of keeping calm even under the greatest stress – is rooted in temperament. It is itself an emotion which serves to balance the passionate feelings in strong characters without destroying them, and it is this balance alone that assures the dominance of the intellect. The counterweight we mean is simply the sense of human dignity, the noblest pride and deepest need of all: the urge *to act rationally at all times*. Therefore we would argue that a strong character is one *that will not be unbalanced by the most powerful emotions*. . . .

We say a man has strength of character, or simply has character, if he sticks to his convictions, whether these derive from his own opinions or someone else's, whether they represent principles, attitudes, sudden insights, or any other mental force. Such *firmness* cannot show itself, of course, if a man keeps changing his mind. This need not be the consequence of external influence; the cause may be the workings of his own intelligence, but this would suggest a peculiarly insecure mind. Obviously a man whose opinions are constantly changing, even though this is in response to his own reflections, would not be called a *man of character*. The term is applied only to men whose views are *stable and constant*. This may be because they are well thought-out, clear, and scarcely open to revision; or, in the case of indolent men, because such people are not in the habit of mental effort and therefore have no reason for altering their views; and finally, because a firm decision, based on fundamental principle derived from reflection, is relatively immune to changes of opinion.

With its mass of vivid impressions and the doubts which characterize all information and opinion, there is no activity like war to rob men of confidence in themselves and in others, and to divert them from their original course of action.

In the dreadful presence of suffering and danger, emotion can easily overwhelm intellectual conviction, and in this psychological fog it is so hard to form clear and complete insights that changes of view become more understandable and excusable. Action can never be based on anything firmer than instinct, a sensing of the truth. Nowhere, in consequence, are differences of opinion so acute as in war, and fresh opinions never cease to batter at one's convictions. No degree of calm can provide enough protection: new impressions are too powerful, too vivid, and always assault the emotions as well as the intellect.

Only those general principles and attitudes that result from clear and deep understanding can provide a *comprehensive* guide to action. It is to these that opinions on specific problems should he anchored. The difficulty is to hold fast to these results of contemplation in the torrent of events and new opinions. Often there is a gap between principles and actual events that cannot always be bridged by a succession of logical deductions. Then a measure of self-confidence is needed, and a degree of skepticism is also salutary. Frequently nothing short of an imperative principle will suffice, which is not part of the immediate thought-process, but dominates it: that principle is in all doubtful cases *to stick to one's first opinion and to refuse to change unless forced to do so by a clear conviction*. A strong faith in the overriding truth of tested principles is needed; the *vividness* of transient impressions must not make us forget that such truth as they contain is of a lesser stamp. By giving precedence, in case of doubt, to our earlier con-victions, by holding to them stubbornly, our actions acquire that quality of steadiness and consistency which is termed strength of character.

44

Daniel Webster
(1782–1852)

The *Caroline* Incident
(1837)

It will be for that Government to show a necessity of self-defence, instant,
overwhelming, leaving no choice of means, and no moment for deliberation.

Daniel Webster, letter to the British Ambassador

In December of 1837, a band of Canadian rebels seized an island in the Niagara
River (near Buffalo, New York State) which was then a possession of the British
Crown. An American vessel, the *Caroline*, was subsequently used to transport
armaments and other supplies to the rebel forces on the island. On the night of
December 29, while the boat was still moored on the American side of the river,
British troops attacked it, with "the double purpose of preventing further
reinforcements and supplies from reaching the island, and depriving the rebels of
their means of access to the mainland of Canada."[1] After a scuffle on board, which
resulted in a loss of life, the boat was "set on fire, cut loose from the dock, was
towed into the current of the river, there abandoned, and soon after descended
the Niagara falls."[2] The government of the United States quickly lodged a diplomatic protest against the British action. In response, British diplomats argued that
the seizure and destruction of the *Caroline* was justified in light of the traditional
doctrine of self-defense.

---

[1] R. Y. Jennings, "The *Caroline* and McLeod Cases," *American Journal of International Law*, 32, 1
(1938), pp. 82–99, on pp. 83–4. For an expanded and updated account of the *Caroline* incident,
see Kenneth R. Stevens, *Border Diplomacy: The Caroline and McLeod Affairs in Anglo-American-
Canadian Relations, 1837–1842* (Tuscaloosa: University of Alabama Press), 1989.

[2] From the deposition of the master of the *Caroline*, quoted in Jennings, "The *Caroline*," p. 84.

Three years later the controversy was further enflamed when New York State arrested a British subject, Alexander McLeod,[3] on a charge of murder, for allegedly participating in the destruction of the *Caroline*. The British Envoy in Washington, Henry S. Fox, issued a sharp protest against McLeod's arrest, and demanded his immediate release, on grounds that the action in which he had allegedly participated was undertaken in the service of Her Majesty's Government, and not at his private initiative. A new round of diplomatic exchanges ensued. Finally, in April 1841, the new US Secretary of State, Daniel Webster, wrote a letter to Henry Fox in which he sought to clarify the key issues at stake in the controversy.

Conceding that the British action against the *Caroline* was indeed "an act of public force," Webster nevertheless argued that it was unwarranted. Against the British claim that the *Caroline* was a "piratical vessel," which had been pressed into service by a band of common criminals, the American Secretary of State retorted that the rebels were certainly not "pirates"; rather, they were combatants engaged in what "they regarded as a civil war." Next he argued that the British violation of American soil could not be justified on grounds that the United States had not been exercising proper jurisdiction over its own territory. On the contrary, he maintained that the US had been enforcing the relevant laws which prohibited activities in support of a foreign rebellion. Finally, Webster took up the central claim in the British case, namely, that the destruction of the *Caroline* was undertaken as an act of legitimate self-defense, in conformity with the "laws of nations." He challenged the British to show how their violation of US neutrality could meet the very high standard of what might count as properly *defensive* action. In a formulation that has since become famous (and is frequently quoted in legal arguments and textbooks), Webster proceeded to spell out the key criteria – necessity, proportionality, discrimination – which circumscribe the right of self-defense. It is from this part of the letter that we reproduce the lines below.

From a letter of American Secretary of State Daniel Webster to British Ambassador Henry Fox, dated April 24, 1841[4]

The Undersigned has now to signify to Mr. Fox that the Government of the United States has not changed the opinion which it has heretofore expressed to Her Majesty's Government of the character of the act of destroying the *Caroline*.

---

[3] Public opinion on both sides of the Atlantic was greatly agitated by the arrest of Alexander McLeod. The matter might very well have provoked war between the two nations had McLeod been found guilty of murder and executed. But in 1841 he was acquitted and the *Caroline* controversy quickly subsided.

[4] In *British and Foreign State Papers, 1840–1841*, vol. XXIX (London: James Ridgway and Sons, 1857), pp. 1132–3, and 1137–8.

It does not think that that transaction can be justified by any reasonable application or construction of the right of self-defence under the laws of nations. It is admitted that a just right of self-defence attaches always to nations as well as to individuals, and is equally necessary for the preservation of both. But the extent of this right is a question to be judged of by the circumstances of each particular case, and when its alleged exercise has led to the commission of hostile acts within the territory of a Power at peace, nothing less than a clear and absolute necessity can afford ground of justification. . . .

Under these circumstances . . . , it will be for Her Majesty's Government to show upon what state of facts, and what rules of national law, the destruction of the Caroline is to be defended. It will be for that Government to show a necessity of self-defence, instant, overwhelming, leaving no choice of means, and no moment for deliberation. It will be for it to show, also, that the local authorities of Canada, even supposing the necessity of the moment authorized them to enter the territories of The United States at all, did nothing unreasonable or excessive; since the act, justified by the necessity of self-defence, must be limited by that necessity, and kept clearly within it. It must be shown that admonition or remonstrance to the persons on board the *Caroline* was impracticable, or would have been unavailing; it must be shown that day-light could not be waited for; that there could be no attempt at discrimination between the innocent and the guilty; that it would not have been enough to seize and detain the vessel; but that there was a necessity, present and inevitable, for attacking her in the darkness of the night, while moored to the shore, and while unarmed men were asleep on board, killing some and wounding others, and then drawing her into the current, above the cataract, setting her on fire, and, careless to know whether there might not be in her the innocent with the guilty, or the living with the dead, committing her to a fate which fills the imagination with horror. A necessity for all this, the Government of The United States cannot believe to have existed.

All will see that if such things be allowed to occur, they must lead to bloody and exasperated war.

45

Francis Lieber
(1800–1872)

Devising a Military Code
of Conduct

Modern times are distinguished from earlier ages by the existence, at one and
the same time, of many nations and great governments related to one another
in close intercourse. Peace is their normal condition; war is the exception. The
ultimate object of all modern war is a renewed state of peace.

General Orders No. 100

The second half of the nineteenth century and the first decades of the twentieth
produced important and ambitious juridical contributions to the question of rightful
and wrongful warfare. Some of the most notable came from liberal political thinkers
and activists in the United States, who on *ad bellum* as well as *in bello* issues
wanted to inculcate new ways of thinking, aiming to avoid war when possible,
and civilize it when necessary.

Francis Lieber stands as one of the most important and famous of these figures.
He was the author of General Orders No. 100, the first set of organized rules of
military conduct for the US armed forces, enacted during the American Civil War.
Elihu Root (1845–1937), whose comments on Lieber we include below, continued
in Lieber's footsteps. Alongside Lieber, he is widely regarded as one of the most
resourceful American lawyers and politicians to influence international law and
the ethics of war.

General Orders No. 100

During the first years of the American Civil War, norms restraining the use of
armed force were generally unknown among the men who were commanding
and serving on either side. When General Henry W. Halleck – himself knowledgeable about international law – was made supreme commander of the Union army

in 1862, he called on the already renowned lawyer Francis Lieber to help him in what he saw as a much-needed codification of the rules of war. Lieber was soon thereafter appointed to lead a board to draw up a complete set of rules and articles for the regulation of war, and the fruits of his work were promulgated by Abraham Lincoln in April 1863 as General Orders No. 100.

Since we can only include selected sections from Lieber's code in what follows, we start by reproducing the table of contents, to allow the reader to appreciate the scope of the code. In tenor and content, the orders absorb many lessons from Grotius, Wolff, and Vattel. Yet it is not in terms of their philosophical cogency, but as standing orders applicable in the field, that they prove their mettle. Their wide influence in the decades following their first proclamation testifies to their success in this respect.

As one might expect, the orders are mostly concerned with *in bello* issues, having been designed for use in the field by Lincoln's commanders, officers, and soldiers. It should be noted, nonetheless, that the orders several times touch on *ad bellum* issues, albeit only indirectly; for instance, in their emphasis on the principle of "belligerent equality" – i.e. the moral and legal equality of soldiers on both sides of a war – and by indicating (in arts. 29 and 30) that war can legitimately be fought not only in self-defense, but also for other reasons of state, as long as these are truly important.

From "Instructions for the Government of Armies of the United States in the Field, General Orders No. 100," Promulgated as General Orders No. 100 by President Lincoln, April 24, 1863; Prepared by Francis Lieber, LL.D[1]

Table of Contents[2]

---

[1] Originally issued as General Orders No. 100 by the Adjutant General's Office, 1863; this text is based on the 1898 edition published by the Government Printing Office in Washington, DC; accessed from The Avalon Project at Yale University Law School (http://www.yale.edu/lawweb/avalon/lieber.htm) in May 2004.

[2] Article nos. in parentheses.

Art. 1

A place, district, or country occupied by an enemy stands, in consequence of the
occupation, under the Martial Law of the invading or occupying army, whether
any proclamation declaring Martial Law, or any public warning to the inhabitants, has been issued or not. Martial Law is the immediate and direct effect and
consequence of occupation or conquest.

The presence of a hostile army proclaims its Martial Law.

Art. 2

Martial Law does not cease during the hostile occupation, except by special
proclamation, ordered by the commander in chief; or by special mention in the
treaty of peace concluding the war, when the occupation of a place or territory
continues beyond the conclusion of peace as one of the conditions of the same.

Art. 3

Martial Law in a hostile country consists in the suspension, by the occupying
military authority, of the criminal and civil law, and of the domestic administration and government in the occupied place or territory, and in the substitution of
military rule and force for the same, as well as in the dictation of general laws, as
far as military necessity requires this suspension, substitution, or dictation.

The commander of the forces may proclaim that the administration of all civil
and penal law shall continue either wholly or in part, as in times of peace, unless
otherwise ordered by the military authority.

Art. 4

Martial Law is simply military authority exercised in accordance with the laws and
usages of war. Military oppression is not Martial Law: it is the abuse of the power

which that law confers. As Martial Law is executed by military force, it is incumbent upon those who administer it to be strictly guided by the principles of justice, honor, and humanity – virtues adorning a soldier even more than other men, for the very reason that he possesses the power of his arms against the unarmed.

Art. 5

Martial Law should be less stringent in places and countries fully occupied and fairly conquered. Much greater severity may be exercised in places or regions where actual hostilities exist, or are expected and must be prepared for. Its most complete sway is allowed – even in the commander's own country – when face to face with the enemy, because of the absolute necessities of the case, and of the paramount duty to defend the country against invasion.

To save the country is paramount to all other considerations.

Art. 11

The law of war does not only disclaim all cruelty and bad faith concerning engagements concluded with the enemy during the war, but also the breaking of stipulations solemnly contracted by the belligerents in time of peace, and avowedly intended to remain in force in case of war between the contracting powers.

It disclaims all extortions and other transactions for individual gain; all acts of private revenge, or connivance at such acts.

Offenses to the contrary shall be severely punished, and especially so if committed by officers.

Art. 15

Military necessity admits of all direct destruction of life or limb of armed enemies, and of other persons whose destruction is incidentally unavoidable in the armed contests of the war; it allows of the capturing of every armed enemy, and every enemy of importance to the hostile government, or of peculiar danger to the captor; it allows of all destruction of property, and obstruction of the ways and channels of traffic, travel, or communication, and of all withholding of sustenance or means of life from the enemy; of the appropriation of whatever an enemy's country affords necessary for the subsistence and safety of the army, and of such deception as does not involve the breaking of good faith either positively pledged, regarding agreements entered into during the war, or supposed by the modern law of war to exist. Men who take up arms against one another in public war do not cease on this account to be moral beings, responsible to one another and to God.

Art. 16

Military necessity does not admit of cruelty – that is, the infliction of suffering for the sake of suffering or for revenge, nor of maiming or wounding except in fight, nor of torture to extort confessions. It does not admit of the use of poison in any way, nor of the wanton devastation of a district. It admits of deception, but disclaims acts of perfidy; and, in general, military necessity does not include any act of hostility which makes the return to peace unnecessarily difficult.

Art. 29

Modern times are distinguished from earlier ages by the existence, at one and the same time, of many nations and great governments related to one another in close intercourse.

Peace is their normal condition; war is the exception. The ultimate object of all modern war is a renewed state of peace.

The more vigorously wars are pursued, the better it is for humanity. Sharp wars are brief.

Art. 30

Ever since the formation and coexistence of modern nations, and ever since wars have become great national wars, war has come to be acknowledged not to be its own end, but the means to obtain great ends of state, or to consist in defense against wrong; and no conventional restriction of the modes adopted to injure the enemy is any longer admitted; but the law of war imposes many limitations and restrictions on principles of justice, faith, and honor.

Art. 40

There exists no law or body of authoritative rules of action between hostile armies, except that branch of the law of nature and nations which is called the law and usages of war on land.

Art. 41

All municipal law of the ground on which the armies stand, or of the countries to which they belong, is silent and of no effect between armies in the field.

Art. 42

Slavery, complicating and confounding the ideas of property, (that is of a thing,) and of personality, (that is of humanity,) exists according to municipal or local law only. The law of nature and nations has never acknowledged it. The digest of the Roman law enacts the early dictum of the pagan jurist, that "so far as the law of nature is concerned, all men are equal." Fugitives escaping from a country in which they were slaves, villains, or serfs, into another country, have, for centuries past, been held free and acknowledged free by judicial decisions of European countries, even though the municipal law of the country in which the slave had taken refuge acknowledged slavery within its own dominions.

Art. 43

Therefore, in a war between the United States and a belligerent which admits of slavery, if a person held in bondage by that belligerent be captured by or come as a fugitive under the protection of the military forces of the United States, such person is immediately entitled to the rights and privileges of a freeman. To return such person into slavery would amount to enslaving a free person, and neither the United States nor any officer under their authority can enslave any human being. Moreover, a person so made free by the law of war is under the shield of the law of nations. . . .

Art. 44

All wanton violence committed against persons in the invaded country, all destruction of property not commanded by the authorized officer, all robbery, all pillage or sacking, even after taking a place by main force, all rape, wounding, maiming, or killing of such inhabitants, are prohibited under the penalty of death, or such other severe punishment as may seem adequate for the gravity of the offense.

A soldier, officer or private, in the act of committing such violence, and disobeying a superior ordering him to abstain from it, may be lawfully killed on the spot by such superior.

Art. 56

A prisoner of war is subject to no punishment for being a public enemy, nor is any revenge wreaked upon him by the intentional infliction of any suffering, or disgrace, by cruel imprisonment, want of food, by mutilation, death, or any other barbarity.

Art. 57

So soon as a man is armed by a sovereign government and takes the soldier's oath of fidelity, he is a belligerent; his killing, wounding, or other warlike acts are not individual crimes or offenses. No belligerent has a right to declare that enemies of a certain class, color, or condition, when properly organized as soldiers, will not be treated by him as public enemies.

Art. 67

The law of nations allows every sovereign government to make war upon another sovereign state, and, therefore, admits of no rules or laws different from those of regular warfare, regarding the treatment of prisoners of war, although they may belong to the army of a government which the captor may consider as a wanton and unjust assailant.

Art. 68

Modern wars are not internecine wars, in which the killing of the enemy is the object. The destruction of the enemy in modern war, and, indeed, modern war itself, are means to obtain that object of the belligerent which lies beyond the war.
   Unnecessary or revengeful destruction of life is not lawful.

Art. 80

Honorable men, when captured, will abstain from giving to the enemy information concerning their own army, and the modern law of war permits no longer the use of any violence against prisoners in order to extort the desired information or to punish them for having given false information.

Elihu Root on Lieber and International Peace

Elihu Root received the Nobel Peace Prize for 1912 (awarded in 1913) for his endeavors on behalf of peace and international diplomacy. A scholar and politician, he had been Secretary of War under President William McKinley and both Secretary of War and Secretary of State under President Theodore Roosevelt. Widely known as someone who strove for – and several times succeeded in concluding – negotiated settlements of international conflicts, he campaigned actively (and successfully) to make the International Court in The Hague permanent, in addition to serving on the court himself. He was also named the first president of the

Carnegie Endowment for International Peace. While he would later oppose the creation of the League of Nations, fearing it would gain too much authority and harm the interests of the US and other nations, he continued to champion for more vigorous international arbitration procedures and a forceful role for the International Court in The Hague.

We include the following selections from Root here since they succinctly sum up his and Lieber's common belief in the possibility of creating mutually accepted rules to govern the conduct of war. The first remarks were made to the American Society of International Law in Washington, DC, in 1913, on the fiftieth anniversary of the proclamation of General Orders No. 100, while the last paragraph is from Root's opening address to the National Arbitration and Peace Congress in New York, April 1907. The latter does not touch as directly on Lieber's concerns, but may be seen as a useful bridge to a later chapter in this anthology: the one on Woodrow Wilson (see chap. 48).

From Elihu Root's Presidential Address at the Seventh Annual Meeting of the American Society of International Law, Washington, April 24, 1913[3]

The first service which Lieber rendered was the preparation in 1862 of a statement or essay upon *Guerrilla Parties Considered with Reference to the Laws and Usages of War*. One cannot read this paper now, with its definite and lucid statements based upon grounds of reason and supported by historical reference, without feeling that it must have been a real satisfaction to the burdened and harassed Union authorities at Washington to have such a guide in dealing with the multitude of cases continually arising in that debatable land which intervenes between disciplined and responsible warfare on the one hand and simple robbery and murder on the other.

On the seventeenth of December, 1862, by order of Secretary Stanton, a board was created "to propose amendments or changes in the rules and articles of war and a code of regulations for the government of armies in the field as authorized by the laws and usages of war," and this board was made up of Francis Lieber, LL.D., and four volunteer officers. . . . That part of the board's work which consisted of preparing the code of regulations appears to have been commited to Dr. Lieber. . . .

Lieber's estimate of the work and of the occasion for it is shown in a letter from him to General Halleck of May 20, 1863:

---

[3] From Elihu Root, *Addresses on International Subjects*, ed. Robert Bacon and James Brown Scott (Freeport: Books for Libraries Press, [1916]1969), pp. 90, 91, 93, 95.

. . . As the order now stands, I think that No. 100 will do honor to our country. . . . I believe it is now time for you to issue a *strong* order, directing attention to those paragraphs in the Code which prohibit devastation, demolition of private property, etc. I know by letters from the West and the South, written by men on our side, that the wanton destruction of property by our men is alarming. It does incalculable injury. It demoralizes our troops; it annihilates wealth irrecoverably, and makes a return to a state of peace more and more difficult. Your order, though impressive and even sharp, might be written with reference to the Code, and pointing out the disastrous consequences of reckless devastation, in such a manner as not to furnish our reckless enemy with new arguments for his savagery.

. . . Although [General Orders No. 100] were prepared for use in a civil war, a great part of them were of general application, and they were adopted by the German Government for the conduct of its armies in the field in the war of 1870 with France. . . . The sanction of two powerful governments for these rules and their successful employment in two of the greatest wars of modern times gave to them an authority never before acquired by any codification or statement of any considerable number of rules intended for international application. . . .

When we recall the frightful cruelties upon combatants, upon prisoners, upon citizens, the overturning of all human rights to life and liberty and property, the fiendish malignity of oppression by brutal force, which have characterized the history of war, we cannot fail to set a high estimate upon the service of the man who gave form and direction and effectiveness to the civilizing movement by which man at his best, through the concurrence of nations, imposes the restraint of rules of right conduct, upon man at his worst, in the extreme exercise of force.

From Elihu Root's Address in Opening the National Arbitration and Peace Congress in the City of New York, April 15, 1907[4]

Arbitrations and mediations, treaties and conventions, peace resolutions, declarations of principle, speeches and writings, are as naught unless they truly represent and find a response in the hearts and minds of the multitude of the men who make up the nations of the earth, whose desires and impulses determine the issues of peace and war. The end toward which this assemblage strives – the peace of the world – will be attained just as rapidly as the millions of the earth's peoples learn to love peace and abhor war; to love justice and hate wrongdoing; to be considerate in judgment and kindly in feeling toward aliens as toward their own friends and neighbors; and to desire that their own countries shall regard the rights of others rather than be grasping and overreaching. The path to universal peace is not through reason or intellectual appreciation, but through the development of peace-loving and peace-keeping character among men. . . .

[4] From Root, *Addresses on International Subjects*, p. 144.

46

John Stuart Mill (1806–1873)

Foreign Intervention and National Autonomy

[W]ar, in a good cause, is not the greatest evil which a nation can suffer. . . . [T]he decayed and degraded state of moral and patriotic feeling which thinks nothing *worth* a war, is worse.

"The Contest in America"

John Stuart Mill's unassailable position as one of the most influential moral-political philosophers of the modern era is largely based upon four works written over a remarkably short period of time: *On Liberty* (1859), *Considerations on Representative Government* (1861), *Utilitarianism* (1861), and *The Subjection of Women* (written in 1861, published in 1869). These works, among the most cherished, most debated books in modern moral theory, all deal with different aspects of what we might term civic justice – i.e. the foundations of freedom, equality, rights, and obligations *within* a nation or community. Less read by far are his contributions, dating from the same period, to debates on international justice, particularly with regard to questions of war, colonialism, and intervention, yet these are what we will focus on here.

In this chapter we present two texts by Mill: "A Few Words on Non-intervention" and "The Contest in America." Neither is, in any strict sense, a scholarly article; instead, they should be read as "opinion pieces," contributions to ongoing debates on current events. Of the two, "A Few Words on Non-intervention" is the more widely known, but even this was hardly read in the years between its first publication and 1968, when its inclusion in the first volume of Richard Falk's *The Vietnam War and International Law*[1] brought it back into

---

[1] Richard A. Falk (ed.), *The Vietnam War and International Law*, vol. I (Princeton, NJ: Princeton University Press, 1968).

discussion. Since then, Michael Walzer has used it as the theoretical foundation of one chapter of his 1977 book *Just and Unjust Wars*,[2] henceforth securing its place as a standard text on the principle of non-intervention, i.e. the principle that states should not interfere in the internal affairs of other states. "The Contest in America," a text arising out of an incident that brought England to the verge of a new war with the United States, contains Mill's highly interesting reflections on the American Civil War and the issue of slavery.

"A Few Words on Non-intervention"[3]

This article was written in 1859 and originally published in *Fraser's Magazine*, an important monthly review that would also publish other texts by Mill, among them *Utilitarianism*. The argument of the article resists easy summary, in part because it is neither very systematic nor exhaustive (and, in all likelihood, was not intended to be so) and in part because Mill does not seem to be arguing toward a single decisive conclusion. Instead, he aims to give us a rundown on some of the considerations that inform – or ought to inform – our thinking about international relations in general, and sovereignty and the struggle for freedom in particular.

Mill begins by considering England's practice of not interfering with the internal affairs of other countries. He considers this to be an honorable principle and "a novelty in the world" ("A Few Words," p. 154). Nonetheless, he notes, England has received a lot of criticism for its non-involvement, as being "the type of egoism and selfishness" (ibid.). Mill traces this indictment directly back to English politicians and their "sins of speech," in particular the "shabby *refrain*" that "We ought not to interfere where no English interest is concerned" (p. 158). Against this background Mill argues that we must rethink the foundations of the non-intervention principle. The critical question is: what distinguishes a genuinely *moral* principle of non-intervention from the merely pragmatic resolve, as professed by English statesmen, not to interfere where no English interest is directly involved?

From "A Few Words on Non-intervention"[4]

There is much to be said for the doctrine that a nation should be willing to assist its neighbours in throwing off oppression and gaining free institutions. Much also

[2] Michael Walzer, *Just and Unjust Wars* (New York: Basic Books, 1977), chap. 6: "Interventions," pp. 86–108. Walzer's reading of Mill is explored in detail in Endre Begby, "Liberty, Statehood, and Sovereignty: Walzer on Mill on Non-Intervention," *Journal of Military Ethics*, 2, 1 (2003), pp. 46–62, from which the present chapter draws in part.

[3] John Stuart Mill, "A Few Words on Non-Intervention" [1859]. Reprinted in *Dissertations and Discussions: Political, Philosophical, and Historical*, vol. 3 (London: Longman, Green, Reader and Dyer, 1867).

[4] Ibid., pp. 158–9.

may be said by those who maintain that one nation is incompetent to judge and act for another, and that each should be left to help itself, and seek advantage or submit to disadvantage as it can and will. But of all attitudes which a nation can take up on the subject of intervention, the meanest and worst is to profess that it interferes only when it can serve its own objects by it. Every other nation is entitled to say, 'It seems, then, that non-interference is not a matter of principle with you. When you abstain from interference, it is not because you think it wrong. You have no objection to interfere, only it must not be for the sake of those you interfere with; they must not suppose that you have any regard for their good. The good of others is not one of the things you care for; but you are willing to meddle, if by meddling you can gain anything for yourselves.' Such is the obvious interpretation of the language used.

This, claims Mill, cannot be what the English really have in mind when addressing foreign affairs. What they mean – or what they should mean – is not that English *interest* per se is the foundation of her non-involvement, but English *security*: "This is no more than what all nations, sufficiently powerful for their own protection, do, and no one questions their right to do. It is the common right of self-defence" ("A Few Words," p. 159).

Security is certainly an English *interest* (quite likely her most important interest, even), but unlike, say, her economic interest, the interest in security is not specific to England. Quite the contrary, the interest in security is one which all nations share, for sovereignty is the cornerstone of the international order. For a nation categorically to separate particular and general interest on this score is as absurd as it is immoral, amounting to a declaration that "its interest and that of mankind are incompatible" (p. 164).

Mill now moves into the core of the argument. With a prescience that seems almost uncanny following the many controversies over the intervention issue in recent decades, he underlines the importance of nations in time establishing rules and principles to guide the practice of (or abstention from) intervention.

From "A Few Words on Non-intervention"[5]

There seems to be no little need that the whole doctrine of non-interference with foreign nations should be reconsidered, if it can be said to have as yet been considered as a really moral question at all. We have heard something lately about being willing to go to war for an idea. To go to war for an idea, if the war is aggressive, not defensive, is as criminal as to go to war for territory or revenue; for it is as little justifiable to force our ideas on other people, as to compel them

---

[5]   Ibid., pp. 166–7.

to submit to our will in any other respect. But there assuredly are cases in which it is allowable to go to war, without having been ourselves attacked or threatened with attack; and it is very important that nations should make up their minds in time, as to what these cases are. There are few questions which more require to be taken in hand by ethical and political philosophers, with a view to establish some rule or criterion whereby the justifiableness of intervening in the affairs of other countries, and (what is sometimes fully as questionable) the justifiableness of refraining from intervention, may be brought to a definite and rational test. Whoever attempts this, will be led to recognise more than one fundamental distinction, not yet by any means familiar to the public mind, and in general quite lost sight of by those who write in strains of indignant morality on the subject.

Unfortunately, though, among the "fundamental distinctions" that Mill has in mind here is one that so often characterizes his work, namely that between civilized and barbaric peoples.[6] Although Mill was hardly alone among mid-nineteenth-century intellectuals in professing such views, the following passage is not happy reading for those who are otherwise impressed and encouraged by his general concern for freedom and equality. Still, we must note in Mill's defense his insistence that while barbarians may not have rights as *nations*, they certainly have rights as *human beings*. Belonging to an "inferior" level of civilization does not detract from or in any way influence the individual's status as a rights-bearing human being and partner in the universal fellowship of mankind. Quite the contrary, it is precisely in recognition of such rights that intervention or colonization may be legitimate.

From "A Few Words on Non-intervention"[7]

There is a great difference (for example) between the case in which the nations concerned are of the same, or something like the same, degree of civilization, and that in which one of the parties to the situation is of a high, and the other of a very low, grade of social improvement. To suppose that the same international customs, and the same rules of international morality, can obtain between one civilized nation and another, and between civilized nations and barbarians, is a grave error, and one which no statesman can fall into, however it may be with those who, from a safe and unresponsible position, criticise statesmen. Among many reasons why the same rules cannot be applicable to situations so different, the two following are among the most important. In the first place, the rules of

[6] Most famously, perhaps, in the Introductory chapter of *On Liberty*. "Despotism is a legitimate mode of government in dealing with barbarians, provided the end be their improvement, and the means justified by actually effecting that end" (J. S. Mill, *On Liberty*, Harmondsworth: Penguin, 1974, p. 69).
[7] Mill, "A Few Words," pp. 167–8.

ordinary international morality imply reciprocity. But barbarians will not reciprocate. They cannot be depended on for observing any rules. Their minds are not capable of so great an effort, nor their will sufficiently under the influence of distant motives. In the next place, nations which are still barbarous have not got beyond the period during which it is likely to be for their benefit that they should be conquered and held in subjection by foreigners. Independence and nationality, so essential to the due growth and development of a people further advanced in improvement, are generally impediments to theirs. The sacred duties which civilized nations owe to the independence and nationality of each other, are not binding towards those to whom nationality and independence are either a certain evil, or at best a questionable good. The Romans were not the most clean-handed of conquerors, yet would it have been better for Gaul and Spain, Numidia and Dacia, never to have formed part of the Roman Empire? To characterize any conduct whatever towards a barbarous people as a violation of the law of nations, only shows that he who so speaks has never considered the subject. A violation of great principles of morality it may easily be; but barbarians have no rights as a *nation*, except a right to such treatment as may, at the earliest possible period, fit them for becoming one. The only moral laws for the relation between a civilized and a barbarous government, are the universal rules of morality between man and man.

Not surprisingly, what Mill has immediately in mind here is the English experience with colonization. A central brick in his argument is the contention that if a country intervenes to overthrow a tyrant in another country, and there is no popular base in that country to replace the tyrant with a tolerable rule, then the intervening country has automatically taken on the responsibility to provide such a government. We may or may not agree with Mill's point, but it is important to take notice of it anyway, for it is essential to the remainder of the argument.

From "A Few Words on Non-intervention"[8]

The criticisms, therefore, which are so often made upon the conduct of the French in Algeria, or of the English in India, proceed, it would seem, mostly on a wrong principle. The true standard by which to judge their proceedings never having been laid down, they escape such comment and censure as might really have an improving effect, while they are tried by a standard which can have no influence on those practically engaged in such transactions, knowing as they do that it cannot, and if it could, ought not to be observed, because no human being would be the better, and many much the worse, for its observance. A civilized

[8]   Ibid., pp. 168–70.

government cannot help having barbarous neighbours: when it has, it cannot always content itself with a defensive position, one of mere resistance to aggression. After a longer or shorter interval of forbearance, it either finds itself obliged to conquer them, or to assert so much authority over them, and so break their spirit, that they gradually sink into a state of dependence upon itself: and when that time arrives, they are indeed no longer formidable to it, but it has had so much to do with setting up and pulling down their governments, and they have grown so accustomed to lean on it, that it has become morally responsible for all evil it allows them to do. This is the history of the relations of the British Government with the native States of India. It never was secure in its own Indian possessions until it had reduced the military power of those States to a nullity. But a despotic government only exists by its military power. When we had taken away theirs we were forced, by the necessity of the case, to offer them ours instead of it. To enable them to dispense with large armies of their own, we bound ourselves to place at their disposal, and they bound themselves to receive, such an amount of military force as made us in fact masters of the country. We engaged that this force should fulfil the purposes of a force, by defending the prince against all foreign and internal enemies. But being thus assured of the protection of a civilized power, and freed from the fear of internal rebellion or foreign conquest, the only checks which either restrain the passions or keep any vigour in the character of an Asiatic despot, the native Governments either became so oppressive and extortionate as to desolate the country, or fell into such a state of nerveless imbecility, that everyone, subject to their will, who had not the means of defending himself by his own armed followers, was the prey of anybody who had a band of ruffians in his pay. The British Government felt this deplorable state of things to be its own work; being the direct consequence of the position in which, for its own security, it had placed itself towards the native governments. Had it permitted this to go on indefinitely, it would have deserved to be accounted among the worst political malefactors. In some cases (unhappily not in all) it had endeavoured to take precaution against these mischiefs by a special article in the treaty, binding the prince to reform his administration, and in future to govern in conformity to the advice of the British Government. Among the treaties in which a provision of this sort had been inserted, was that with Oude. For fifty years and more did the British Government allow this engagement to be treated with entire disregard; not without frequent remonstrances, and occasionally threats, but without ever carrying into effect what it threatened. During this period of half a century, England was morally accountable for a mixture of tyranny and anarchy, the picture of which, by men who knew it well, is appalling to all who read it. The act by which the Government of British India at last set aside treaties which had been so pertinaciously violated, and assumed the power of fulfilling the obligation it had so long before incurred, of giving to the people of Oude a tolerable government, far from being the political crime it is so often ignorantly called, was a criminally tardy discharge of an imperative duty.

We now move on to the part of Mill's article which is most immediately relevant to our topic, and which most commentators (among them Michael Walzer) have seized upon. Among civilized nations, Mill contends, even among democracies and tyrannies, there is a presumption in favor of non-intervention. This, however, is not primarily because such interventions would always be morally wrong. The main reason is that freedom cannot be gifted by a third party; rather freedom must be the fruit of the people's own struggle. Much of this is no doubt Mill's famous moral psychology of *On Liberty* writ large. Less immediately, but also less dubiously from a contemporary standpoint, it follows from the argument of the previous section. A country cannot depose the regime of another country – even should this be the wish of its people – without simultaneously incurring the obligation to provide that country with a government, i.e. without, in effect, colonizing it. Exceptions to this general ban on intervention include cases where the regime is of foreign origin (or is materially dependent on foreign support to uphold its tyranny), cases where the intervening country legitimately sees the regime of the other country as a threat to its own security, and cases where the ruling regime upholds its reign by "severities repugnant to humanity" ("A Few Words," p.172).

From "A Few Words on Non-intervention"[9]

But among civilized peoples, members of an equal community of nations, like Christian Europe, the question assumes another aspect, and must be decided on totally different principles. It would be an affront to the reader to discuss the immorality of wars of conquest, or of conquest even as the consequence of lawful war; the annexation of any civilized people to the dominion of another, unless by their own spontaneous election. Up to this point, there is no difference of opinion among honest people; nor on the wickedness of commencing an aggressive war for any interest of our own, except when necessary to avert from ourselves an obviously impending wrong. The disputed question is that of interfering in the regulation of another country's internal concerns; the question whether a nation is justified in taking part, on either side, in the civil wars or party contests of another; and chiefly, whether it may justifiably aid the people of another country in struggling for liberty; or may impose on a country any particular government or institutions, either as being best for the country itself, or as necessary for the security of its neighbours.

Of these cases, that of a people in arms for liberty is the only one of any nicety, which, theoretically at least, is likely to present conflicting moral considerations. The other cases which have been mentioned hardly admit of discussion. Assistance to the government of a country in keeping down the people, unhappily by far the

9   Ibid., pp. 171–2, 173–4, 175–7.

most frequent case of foreign intervention, no one writing in a free country needs take the trouble of stigmatizing. A government which needs foreign support to enforce obedience from its own citizens, is one which ought not to exist; and the assistance given to it by foreigners is hardly ever anything but the sympathy of one despotism with another. A case requiring consideration is that of a protracted civil war, in which the contending parties are so equally balanced that there is no probability of a speedy issue; or if there is, the victorious side cannot hope to keep down the vanquished but by severities repugnant to humanity, and injurious to the permanent welfare of the country. In this exceptional case it seems now to be an admitted doctrine, that the neighbouring nations, or one powerful neighbour with the acquiescence of the rest, are warranted in demanding that the contest shall cease, and a reconciliation take place on equitable terms of compromise. Intervention of this description has been repeatedly practised during the present generation, with such general approval, that its legitimacy may be considered to have passed into a maxim of what is called international law. . . .

With respect to the question, whether one country is justified in helping the people of another in a struggle against their government for free institutions, the answer will be different, according as the yoke which the people are attempting to throw off is that of a purely native government, or of foreigners; considering as one of foreigners, every government which maintains itself by foreign support. When the contest is only with native rulers, and with such native strength as those rulers can enlist in their defence, the answer I should give to the question of the legitimacy of intervention is, as a general rule, No. The reason is, that there can seldom be anything approaching to assurance that intervention, even if successful, would be for the good of the people themselves. The only test possessing any real value, of a people's having become fit for popular institutions, is that they, or a sufficient portion of them to prevail in the contest, are willing to brave labour and danger for their liberation. I know all that may be said. I know it may be urged that the virtues of freemen cannot be learnt in the school of slavery, and that if a people are not fit for freedom, to have any chance of becoming so they must first be free. And this would be conclusive, if the intervention recommended would really give them freedom. But the evil is, that if they have not sufficient love of liberty to be able to wrest it from merely domestic oppressors, the liberty which is bestowed on them by other hands than their own, will have nothing real, nothing permanent. No people ever was and remained free, but because it was determined to be so; because neither its rulers nor any other party in the nation could compel it to be otherwise. If a people – especially one whose freedom has not yet become prescriptive – does not value it sufficiently to fight for it, and maintain it against any force which can be mustered *within* the country, even by those who have the command of the public revenue, it is only a question in how few years or months that people will be enslaved. . . .

It can seldom, therefore – I will not go so far as to say never – be either judicious or right, in a country which has a free government, to assist, otherwise than by the moral support of its opinion, the endeavours of another to extort the same blessing from its native rulers. We must except, of course, any case in which such assistance is a measure of legitimate self-defence. If (a contingency by no means unlikely to occur) this country, on account of its freedom, which is a standing reproach to despotism everywhere, and an encouragement to throw it off, should find itself menaced with attack by a coalition of Continental despots, it ought to consider the popular party in every nation of the Continent as its natural ally: the Liberals should be to it, what the Protestants of Europe were to the Government of Queen Elizabeth. So, again, when a nation, in her own defence, has gone to war with a despot, and has had the rare good fortune not only to succeed in her resistance, but to hold the conditions of peace in her own hands, she is entitled to say that she will make no treaty, unless with some other ruler than the one whose existence as such may be a perpetual menace to her safety and freedom. These exceptions do but set in a clearer light the reasons of the rule; because they do not depend on any failure of those reasons, but on considerations paramount to them, and coming under a different principle.

But the case of a people struggling against a foreign yoke, or against a native tyranny upheld by foreign arms, illustrates the reasons for non-intervention in an opposite way; for in this case the reasons themselves do not exist. A people the most attached to freedom, the most capable of defending and of making a good use of *free* institutions, may be unable to contend successfully for them against the military strength of another nation much more powerful. To assist a people thus kept down, is not to disturb the balance of forces on which the permanent maintenance of freedom in a country depends, but to redress that balance when it is already unfairly and violently disturbed. The doctrine of non-intervention, to be a legitimate principle of morality, must be accepted by all governments. The despots must consent to be bound by it as well as the free States. Unless they do, the profession of it by free countries comes but to this miserable issue, that the wrong side may help the wrong, but the right must not help the right. Intervention to enforce non-intervention is always rightful, always moral, if not always prudent. Though it be a mistake to *give* freedom to a people who do not value the boon, it cannot but be right to insist that if they do value it, they shall not be hindered from the pursuit of it by foreign coercion.

In summary, it seems fair to say that Mill does not write, as many commentators seem to assume, with the aim of providing us with a comprehensive doctrine of non-intervention. Rather, he writes in criticism of two opposed, yet equally immoral sentiments: (i) that a country should keep out of another country's internal affairs come what may, unless its own interest is directly involved, and (ii) that it is somehow the proper assignment of one country to educate others on the issue of internal rule. In other words, "making the world safe for democracy," say, is not a valid pretext for intervention, whereas preventing a ruling majority from tyrannizing or slaughtering a minority most likely is. Mill's distinction between morality and prudence is useful, for it allows us to frame with some force the conclusion that it is not, as such, that the former kinds of pretexts are *always immoral*, but rather that acting on them is *hardly ever prudent*.

What is striking about Mill's argument is the way in which he is able to turn the question of intervention into one of morality as much as of law or politics. Although he argues for a strong presumption against intervention, what is shown to underlie this presumption are precisely moral considerations. Moreover, the same moral considerations which give the principle of non-intervention its general credibility will sometimes force us to break with it. Mill's argument, then, is not meant to dispense with, but precisely to underline, the crucial need for moral reflection in times of war and duress.

"The Contest in America"[10]

Published in 1862, "The Contest in America" offers us something of a case study of Mill's thoughts on morality in international affairs. The immediate backdrop for the article is the so-called "Trent incident," which saw the United States seize a British ship carrying two confederate commissioners. The British saw this, probably rightly so, as a blatant violation of the freedom of the seas, and promptly backed their demands for apology and restoration with the threat of armed attack. Mill wrote this piece as the situation had just been peacefully resolved and with the explicit aim of soothing the tempers of his countrymen. The question is, whether it would have been morally right of the British to wage war against America (irrespective of its legal defensibility), when America was at civil war over the issue of slavery, and any attack by the British would almost certainly have shifted the balance of power in favor of the rebel South. The answer, according to Mill, must be a resounding "No." The institution of slavery involves such gross violations of human rights, claims Mill, that no rightful cause of war on the British side would have excused such an intrusion, albeit indirect, into the American Civil War.

Mill then poses the principled question of whether it would be proper to treat the Rebel case as an instance of "the sacred right of insurrection," so that "the North, in resisting it, are committing the same error and wrong which England committed in opposing the original separation of the thirteen colonies" ("The Contest in America," p. 195). Mill pleads with us that he has "sympathized more or less ardently with most of the rebellions, successful and unsuccessful, which have taken place in my time" (p. 196). But the case of the confederate South is different.

---

[10] John Stuart Mill, "The Contest in America" [1862]. Reprinted in *Dissertations and Discussions*, vol. 3 (London: Longman, Green, Reader and Dyer, 1867).

From "The Contest in America"[11]

I certainly never conceived that there was a sufficient title to my sympathy in the mere fact of being a rebel; that the act of taking arms against one's fellow citizens was so meritorious in itself, was so completely its own justification, that no question need be asked concerning the motive. It seems to me a strange doctrine that the most serious and responsible of all human acts imposes no obligation on those who do it, of showing that they have a real grievance; that those who rebel for the power of oppressing others, exercise as sacred a right as those who do the same thing to resist oppression practised upon themselves. Neither rebellion, nor any other act which affects the interests of others, is sufficiently legitimated by the mere will to do it. Secession may be laudable, and so may any other kind of insurrection; but it may also be an enormous crime. It is the one or the other according to the object and the provocation. And if there ever was an object which, by its bare announcement, stamped rebels against a particular community as enemies of mankind, it is the one professed by the South. Their right to separate is the right which Cartouche or Turpin would have had to secede from their respective countries, because the laws of those countries would not suffer them to rob and murder on the highway.

Not only is slavery a moral abomination of the worst sort, claims Mill; it is also by its very nature an expansive one. In other words, we simply cannot take an indifferent attitude toward countries with slave-driven economies, for sooner or later we will have to face up to them.

From "The Contest in America"[12]

Suppose that the North should stoop to recognise the new Confederation on its own terms, leaving it half the Territories, and that it is acknowledged by Europe, and takes its place as an admitted member of the community of nations. It will be desirable to take thought beforehand what are to be our own future relations with a new Power professing the principles of Attila and Genghis Khan as the foundation of its Constitution. Are we to see with indifference its victorious army let loose to propagate their national faith at the rifle's mouth through Mexico and Central America? Shall we submit to see fire and sword carried over Cuba and Porto Rico, and Hayti and Liberia conquered and brought back to slavery?

[11] Ibid., pp. 196–7.
[12] Ibid., pp. 202–3.

In a passionate final section, Mill pleads with his readers not to encourage a compromise with the rebel South on the issue of slavery.

From "The Contest in America"[13]

For these reasons I cannot join with those who cry Peace, peace. I cannot wish that this war should not have been engaged in by the North, or that being engaged in, it should be terminated on any conditions but such as would retain the whole of the Territories as free soil. I am not blind to the possibility that it may require a long war to lower the arrogance and tame the aggressive ambition of the slave-owners, to the point of either returning to the Union, or consenting to remain out of it with their present limits. But war, in a good cause, is not the greatest evil which a nation can suffer. War is an ugly thing, but not the ugliest of things: the decayed and degraded state of moral and patriotic feeling which thinks nothing *worth* a war, is worse. When a people are used as mere human instruments for firing cannon or thrusting bayonets, in the service and for the selfish purposes of a master, such war degrades a people. A war to protect other human beings against tyrannical injustice; a war to give victory to their own ideas of right and good, and which is their own war, carried on for an honest purpose by their free choice is often the means of their regeneration. A man who has nothing which he is willing to fight for, nothing which he cares more about than he does about his personal safety, is a miserable creature who has no chance of being free, unless made and kept so by the exertions of better men than himself. As long as justice and injustice have not terminated *their* ever renewing fight for ascendancy in the affairs of mankind, human beings must be willing, when need is, to do battle for the one against the other.

---

[13]   Ibid., pp. 204–5.

47

Karl Marx (1818–1883) and Friedrich Engels (1820–1895)

War as an Instrument of Emancipation

[N]ot only has the bourgeoisie forged the weapons that bring death to itself; it has also called into existence the men who are to wield those weapons – the modern working class – the proletarians.

Marx and Engels, *The Communist Manifesto*

It is hard to think of an authorship in intellectual history rivaling in political impact that of Karl Marx and Friedrich Engels, which stretched from the mid-1840s to Marx's death and even beyond – for Engels continued to edit and oversee translations of Marx's work for the remainder of his days. The body of work they produced, including co-authored works such as *The German Ideology* (1845) and *The Communist Manifesto* (1848), as well as Marx's famous *Capital* (3 volumes, 1867–94), was astoundingly successful in its stated aim: that of creating a will and consciousness among the working class to bring about revolution and instigate a new social order. Together they managed, like few other intellectuals before or after, to transform people's sense of society and social justice. For that reason, we also include them here. For while the vast corpus of their writings provide little by way of a systematic doctrine on the ethics of war as such, they did craft a powerful teaching about violence in the service of political change – a teaching that would come to have a decisive and violent impact on normative ideas about the use of force in the twentieth century.

Defining their philosophical stance in ardent opposition to the Hegelian temper of their times, the writings of Marx and Engels nonetheless retain several key Hegelian elements, and many philosophy textbooks continue to introduce Marxism (as the doctrine came to be called) simply as "Hegelianism stood on its head."[1] "Hegelianism," in this context, refers to a specific view of history, the "standing on its head" to a distinctive emphasis on *material* rather than *ideational* factors shaping the course of history. The central thesis of Marxist historiography is that modes of production at all times determine the social structure; more specifically, that each mode of production comes with its own opposed pair of classes, the *haves* and the *have-nots*. History, then, is the history of *Klassenkampf* – class struggle – and each period in history ends with the overthrow of the haves by the have-nots and the inception of a new era with a different mode of production, the former have-nots now playing the role of the haves. But even with the shift from an idealist to a materialist conception of history, Marx and Engels retain a distinctly Hegelian notion of *teleology*. For history is not without aim, but rather moves steadily toward its own consummation. And it is arguably in their vision of what this consummation comes to, and how it will be brought about, that we find one of Marx and Engels's most significant contributions and also, perhaps, their most decisive break with Hegel. For while Hegel placed the *nation state* at the summit of history, the teleology sketched out by Marx and Engels culminates at the hands of what is very much an *international* movement, namely the working classes of all industrialized societies. Although revolution begins at home, the liberation of the working class *by* the working class will simultaneously mark the end of the nation state and the inception of the *classless society*. It is, in this sense, the war to end all wars, and thereby also to end history.

The Marxist view of history, and the role played in it by the proletariat, is nicely summarized in the following passage from *The German Ideology*,[2] the book that is generally heralded as the starting point of their distinctive form of philosophy.

From Marx and Engels, *The German Ideology*[3]

[F]rom the conception of history we have sketched we obtain these further conclusions: (1) In the development of productive forces there comes a stage when productive forces and means of intercourse are brought into being, which, under the existing relationships, only cause mischief, and are no longer productive but destructive forces (machinery and money); and connected with this a class is called forth, which has to bear all the burdens of society without enjoying its advantages, which, ousted from society, is forced into the most decided antagonism to all other classes; a class which forms the majority of all members of society, and from which emanates the consciousness of the necessity of a fundamental revolution,

---

[1] Incidentally, that coinage is derived from a characterization made by Marx himself in the Afterword to the second German edition of *Capital*.
[2] Karl Marx and Friedrich Engels, *The German Ideology*, ed. C. J. Arthur (London: Lawrence and Wishart, 1970). The excerpted passage is translated by W. Lough.
[3] Ibid., pp. 94–5.

the communist consciousness, which may, of course, arise among the other classes too through the contemplation of the situation of this class. (2) The conditions under which definite productive forces can be applied are the conditions of the rule of a definite class of society, whose social power, deriving from its property, has its *practical*-idealistic expression in each case in the form of the State; and, therefore, every revolutionary struggle is directed against a class, which till then has been in power. (3) In all revolutions up till now the mode of activity always remained unscathed and it was only a question of a different distribution of this activity, a new distribution of labour to other persons, whilst the communist revolution is directed against the preceding *mode* of activity, does away with *labour*, and abolishes the rule of all classes with the classes themselves, because it is carried through by the class which no longer counts as a class in society, is not recognised as a class, and is in itself the expression of the dissolution of all classes, nationalities, etc. within present society; and (4) Both for the production on a mass scale of this communist consciousness, and for the success of the cause itself, the alteration of men on a mass scale is necessary, an alteration which can only take place in a practical movement, a *revolution*; this revolution is necessary, therefore, not only because the *ruling* class cannot be overthrown in any other way, but also because the class *overthrowing* it can only in a revolution succeed in ridding itself of the muck of ages and become fitted to found society anew.

The notion that true liberation can only be achieved by the oppressed people themselves would find an echo also among liberal writers, as can be witnessed for instance in our selections from the work of John Stuart Mill (see chap. 46, this volume).

The specific situation of the working class and the necessity of revolution are further addressed in these passages from *The Communist Manifesto*.[4]

From Marx and Engels, *The Communist Manifesto*[5]

The weapons with which the bourgeoisie felled feudalism to the ground are now turned against the bourgeoisie itself.

But not only has the bourgeoisie forged the weapons that bring death to itself; it has also called into existence the men who are to wield those weapons – the modern working class – the proletarians.

---

[4]   Karl Marx and Friedrich Engels, *Manifesto of the Communist Party* (in *Marx & Engels: Selected Works*, vol. I, Moscow: Foreign Languages Publishing House, 1955, translator unacknowledged).
[5]   Ibid., p. 40.

From Marx and Engels, *The Communist Manifesto*[6]

All previous historical movements were movements of minorities, or in the interest of minorities. The proletarian movement is the self-conscious, independent movement of the immense majority, in the interest of the immense majority. The proletariat, the lowest stratum of our present society, cannot stir, cannot raise itself up, without the whole superincumbent strata of official society being sprung into the air.

Though not in substance, yet in form, the struggle of the proletariat with the bourgeoisie is at first a national struggle. The proletariat of each country must, of course, first of all settle matters with its own bourgeoisie.

In depicting the most general phases of the development of the proletariat, we traced the more or less veiled civil war, raging within existing society, up to the point where that war breaks out into open revolution, and where the violent overthrow of the bourgeoisie lays the foundation for the sway of the proletariat.

The thought that the classless society must be instituted by violent means was not universally shared among the members of the socialist movement. In the following passage, culled from the short text *On Authority*,[7] Friedrich Engels takes issue with these "anti-authoritarians," arguing strongly for the use of force to further the revolutionary cause.

From Engels, *On Authority*[8]

All Socialists are agreed that the political state, and with it political authority, will disappear as a result of the coming social revolution, that is, that public functions will lose their political character and will be transformed into the simple administrative functions of watching over the true interests of society. But the anti-authoritarians demand that the political state be abolished at one stroke, even before the social conditions that gave birth to it have been destroyed. They demand that the first act of the social revolution shall be the abolition of authority. Have these gentlemen ever seen a revolution? A revolution is certainly the most authoritarian thing there is; it is the act whereby one part of the population imposes its will upon the other part by means of rifles, bayonets and cannon – authoritarian means, if such there be at all; and if the victorious party does not

---

[6]   Ibid., pp. 44–5.
[7]   Friedrich Engels, *On Authority* (in *Marx & Engels: Selected Works*, vol. I, Moscow: Foreign Languages Publishing House, 1955, translator unacknowledged).
[8]   Ibid., p. 638.

want to have fought in vain, it must maintain this rule by means of the terror which its arms inspire in the reactionists. Would the Paris Commune have lasted a single day if it had not made use of this authority of the armed people against the bourgeois? Should we not, on the contrary, reproach it for not having used it freely enough?

Finally, in a work popularly known as *Anti-Dühring*,[9] Engels targets the work of his German contemporary Eugen Dühring. Dühring held that the economic factors emphasized by Marxism were but higher-order manifestations of the more basic phenomenon of *force*. As an example, Dühring cites the enslavement of Friday by Robinson Crusoe: it is from such an original "act of force," and not from modes of production, that springs the master–servant dialectic which drives history forward. In the following passage, Engels counters by reminding the reader that even the original enslavement must have come about through one side's possessing more efficient weaponry. The supposedly primitive act of force must, then, after all be seen in terms of "the *material* means which force has at its disposal" (*Anti-Dühring*, p. 184).

From Engels, *Anti-Dühring*[10]

[L]et us look a little more closely at this omnipotent "force" of Herr Dühring's. Crusoe enslaved Friday "sword in hand." Where did he get the sword from? Even on the imaginary islands of Crusoe stories, swords have not, up to now, grown on trees, and Herr Dühring gives us no answer whatever to this question. Just as Crusoe could procure a sword for himself, we are equally entitled to assume that one fine morning Friday might appear with a loaded revolver in his hand, and then the whole "force" relationship is inverted. Friday commands, and it is Crusoe who has to drudge. . . . So, then, the revolver triumphs over the sword; and this will probably make even the most childish axiomatician comprehend that force is no mere act of the will, but requires very real preliminary conditions before it can come into operation, that is to say, *instruments*, the more perfect of which vanquish the less perfect; moreover, that these instruments have to be produced, which also implies that the producer of more perfect instruments of force, *vulgo* arms, vanquishes the producer of the less perfect instrument, and that, in a word, the triumph of force is based on the production of arms, and this in turn on production in general – therefore, on "economic power," on the "economic order," on the *material* means which force has at its disposal.

---

[9]   Friedrich Engels, *Herr Eugen Dühring's Revolution in Science (Anti-Dühring)*, trans. Emile Burns (New York: International Publishers, 1939).
[10]   Ibid., p. 184.

Engels then turns to launching an attack on the ideology of militarism, which in his view was casting longer and longer shadows over Europe at the time. In this ever more engulfing arms race, however, he does see a glimpse of hope and prophesies that its latest stage – universal conscription – will also be its last. For once the people have been taught in the ways of violence, it can only be a question of time before this knowledge is used to overthrow the state itself.

From Engels, *Anti-Dühring*[11]

The army has become the main purpose of the state, and an end in itself; the peoples are only there in addition in order to provide and feed the soldiers. Militarism dominates and is swallowing Europe. But this militarism also carries in itself the seed of its own destruction. Competition of the individual states with each other forces them, on the one hand, to spend more money each year on the army and navy, artillery, etc., thus more and more hastening financial catastrophe; and on the other hand, to take universal compulsory military service more and more seriously, thus in the long run making the whole people familiar with the use of arms; and therefore making the people more and more able at a given moment to make its will prevail in opposition to the commanding military lords. And this moment comes as soon as the mass of the people – town and country workers and peasants – *has* a will. At this point the armies of princes become transformed into armies of the people; the machine refuses to work, and militarism collapses by the dialectic of its own evolution. What the bourgeois democracy of 1848 could not accomplish, just because it was *bourgeois* and not proletarian, namely, to give the labouring masses a will whose content was in accord with their class position – socialism will infallibly secure. And this will mean the bursting asunder of militarism *from within*, and with it of all standing armies.

[11]   Ibid., p. 189.

Part V
Twentieth Century

48

Woodrow Wilson (1856–1924)

The Dream of a League of Nations

> A general association of nations must be formed under specific covenants for the purpose of affording mutual guarantees of political independence and territorial integrity to great and small states alike.
>
> Address to Congress, January 8, 1918

Woodrow Wilson contributed to the forming of the League of Nations – and indirectly to the United Nations – through his forcefully formulated liberal internationalism. Wilson followed in the footsteps of such international lawyers as Francis Lieber and Elihu Root (see chap. 45, this volume). All three held that mankind should strive to frame internationally acceptable norms of fair human conduct, and that these should be implemented not only within each nation, but also between states; and not only in times of peace, but also during armed conflict. The aim is clear: such norms will bring humankind closer to a common understanding and lasting peace.

Just a few months after winning re-election for president in 1916 – in large part because he kept America out of the war – Woodrow Wilson asked Congress to declare war on Germany, and thus to have the United States enter that horrendous armed contest which we today know as World War I.

A wartime president, he is nonetheless mainly remembered as the president who helped end the war, and not least as the man who pressed for the creation of a League of Nations, which the United States – to Wilson's disappointment and embarrassment – declined to join.

In the concluding stages of the war, and in the period immediately after its end, Wilson spoke extensively on the need for armed force to be used against aggression, combined with the message that the world should now be made safe for democratic and peace-loving nations. This kind of internationalism, based on his conviction that the time of war and authoritarian rule was coming to an end – and spurred on by a combination of optimism and activism – has subsequently become known simply as Wilsonianism, one of the most celebrated, yet hotly debated ideologies within international relations. An important part of it, as becomes clear in Wilson's speeches, is the institutionalization of the political and moral will to peace, which in Wilson's view ought to replace the military and nationalist enthusiasm for war.

From an Address to Congress, January 8, 1918[1]

We entered this war because violations of right had occurred which touched us to the quick and made the life of our own people impossible unless they were corrected and the world secured once for all against their recurrence. What we demand in this war, therefore, is nothing peculiar to ourselves. It is that the world be made fit and safe to live in; and particularly that it be made safe for every peace-loving nation which, like our own, wishes to live its own life, determine its own institutions, be assured of justice and fair dealing by the other peoples of the world as against force and selfish aggression. All the peoples of the world are in effect partners in this interest, and for our own part we see very clearly that unless justice be done to others it will not be done to us. The program of the world's peace, therefore, is our program, and that program, the only possible program, as we see it, is this: . . .

Here follow Wilson's famous "14 points," concentrating on open and mutually agreed-upon covenants of peace, freedom of navigation, and economic exchange, impartial adjustment of colonial claims, fair resolution of European territorial disagreements, and finally – and most famously – in point 14:

From an Address to Congress, January 8, 1918[2]

XIV. A general association of nations must be formed under specific covenants for the purpose of affording mutual guarantees of political independence and territorial integrity to great and small states alike. . . .

For such arrangements and covenants we are willing to fight and continue to fight until they are achieved; but only because we wish the right to prevail and

---

[1] From *The Politics of Woodrow Wilson*, ed. August Heckscher (New York: Harper and Brothers, 1956), p. 302.
[2] Ibid., pp. 304, 305.

desire a just and stable peace such as can be secured only by removing the chief provocations to war, which this program does remove.

From an address at Baltimore, April 6, 1918[3]

We have ourselves proposed no injustice, no aggression. We are ready, whenever the final reckoning is made, to be just to the German people, deal fairly with the German power, as with all others. . . .

It has been with this thought that I have sought to learn from those who spoke for Germany whether it was justice or dominion and the execution of their own will upon the other nations of the world that the German leaders were seeking. They have answered, answered in unmistakable terms. They have avowed that it was not justice but dominion and the unhindered execution of their own will.

The avowal has not come from Germany's statesmen. It has come from her military leaders, who are her real rulers. Her statesmen have said that they wished peace, and were ready to discuss its terms whenever their opponents were willing to sit down at the conference table with them. . . . At Brest-Litovsk [in March 1918, where peace with Russia was secured] her civilian delegates spoke in similar terms; professed their desire to conclude a fair peace and accord to the peoples with whose fortunes they were dealing the right to choose their own allegiances. But action accompanied and followed the profession. Their military masters, the men who act for Germany and exhibit her purpose in execution, proclaimed a very different conclusion. We cannot mistake what they have done – in Russia, in Finland, in the Ukraine, in Rumania. The real test of their justice and fair play has come. From this we may judge the rest.

From an Address to Congress, on Armistice Day, November 11, 1918[4]

The present and all that it holds belongs to the nations and the peoples who preserve their self-control and the orderly processes of their governments; the future to those who prove themselves the true friends of mankind. To conquer with arms is to make only a temporary conquest; to conquer the world by earning its esteem is to make permanent conquest. I am confident that the nations that have learned the discipline of freedom and that have settled with self-possession to its ordered practice are now about to make conquest of the world by the sheer power of example and of friendly helpfulness.

[3]   Ibid., pp. 307–8.
[4]   Ibid., p. 317.

From the President's Annual Message
to Congress, December 2, 1918[5]

The peace settlements which are now to be agreed upon are of transcendent importance both to us and to the rest of the world, and I know of no business or interest which should take precedence of them. The gallant men of our armed forces on land and sea have consciously fought for the ideals which they knew to be the ideals of their country; I have sought to express those ideals; they have accepted my statements of them as the substance of their own thought and purpose, as the associated Governments have accepted them. . . . It is now my duty to play my full part in making good what they offered their life's blood to obtain. I can think of no call to service which could transcend this.

From an address at the University
of Paris, December 21, 1918[6]

There is a great wind of moral force moving through the world, and every man who opposes himself to that wind will go down in disgrace. . . .

My conception of the League of Nations is just this, that it shall operate as the organized moral force of men throughout the world, and that whenever or wherever wrong and aggression are planned or contemplated, this searching light of conscience will be turned upon them and men everywhere will ask, "What are the purposes that you hold in your heart against the fortunes of the world?" Just a little exposure will settle most questions. If the Central powers had dared to discuss the purposes of this war for a single fortnight, it never would have happened, and if, as should be, they were forced to discuss it for a year, war would have been inconceivable.

From an address at the Guildhall,
London, December 28, 1918[7]

[T]he small and the weak could never live free in the world unless the strong and the great always put their power and strength in the service of right. That is the afterthought – the thought that something must be done now not only to make the just settlements, that of course, but to see that the settlements remained and were observed and that honor and justice prevailed in the world. And as I have conversed with the soldiers, I have been more and more aware that they fought

[5] Ibid., pp. 322–3.
[6] Ibid., p. 326.
[7] Ibid., pp. 329–30.

for something that not all of them had defined, but which all of them recognized the moment you stated it to them.

They fought to do away with an old order and to establish a new one, and the center and characteristic of the old order was that unstable thing which we used to call the "balance of power" – a thing in which the balance was determined by the sword which was thrown in the one side or the other; a balance which was determined by the unstable equilibrium of competitive interests; a balance which was maintained by jealous watchfulness and an antagonism of interests which, though it was generally latent, was always deep-seated. The men who have fought in this war have been the men from free nations who were determined that that sort of thing should end now and forever.

49

Bertrand Russell
(1872–1970)

Pacifism and Modern War

> A large-scale nuclear war would be an utter disaster, not only to the belligerents,
> but to mankind, and would achieve no result that any sane man could desire.
> *Common Sense and Nuclear Warfare*

Bertrand Russell is widely regarded as a benchmark contributor to twentieth-century theoretical philosophy. But Russell was also a public intellectual, in the true sense of the term: he was a tireless champion of social reform, battling against what he considered an outdated and oppressive conception of morality, against intolerance, and, not least, against war. His commitment to these causes was greeted with public and professional ostracism and even, on two occasions, jail sentences (the second time, Russell was sentenced for civil disobedience at the age of 89).

Russell's writings on war and peace stretch over many decades, from the start of World War I until his death in 1970. As is to be expected, his approach to the problem would undergo significant development over the years; yet throughout, his stance revolved around a single, firm commitment: that the particular horrors of modern warfare, resulting not least from the way in which civilian populations have come to be considered as legitimate strategic targets, render war obsolete as an instrument of policy. At both the personal and the national level, Russell thus advocates *pacifism*, which he defines in his book *Which Way to Peace?*[1] as "not . . . a principle, to be deduced from Christ's teaching or from the categorical imperative" but "a course of action recommended, in certain circumstances, by considerations of practical common sense" (*Which Way to Peace?* p. 134).

Writing in 1936, Russell argued that such "considerations of practical common sense" applied even to the encounter with an aggressive regime such as Hitler's Germany in the years leading up to World War II. While Russell later came to

[1] Bertrand Russell, *Which Way to Peace?* (London: Michael Joseph, 1936).

temper his stance on this particular case,[2] his original argument nonetheless merits attention. In particular, it is worth noting that at no point does Russell argue that war is necessarily unjust. His claim is rather that the specific destructiveness and indiscriminateness of its modern manifestation make questions of justice seem beside the point. Even faced with a threat of the magnitude of that presented by Germany, Russell considers that nations are better off disarming than meeting force with force. As an example, he cites Denmark: despite their opposition to Nazism, it seemed clear that the Danes neither could nor would offer resistance to a German invasion. Yet precisely owing to its non-resistance, Russell surmises, Denmark would likely suffer less during the coming war than would Great Britain. In particular, he speculates that Denmark would probably not be subjected to air raids over its population centers – a modern military tactic that for Russell epitomizes the very hideousness of war. In this way, he claims, nations such as Denmark are "defended by their very defencelessness" (p. 137).

Meeting objections to the effect that such pacifism is dangerously defeatist, if not to say morally and politically irresponsible, Russell argues that political malevolence of the kind evinced by the German regime typically results from previous war-related grievances (in this case, the Treaty of Versailles in 1919). This claim resonates with another theme that survives throughout Russell's many writings on war: that the causes of war are in large measure psychological, hence that the solution to war must be psychological as well. On his view, the German population gave its support to the regime in part because of what they perceived as past or present military provocations from other countries. If, instead, pacifism were advocated at a national and individual level, the German regime would gradually lose its support and would either collapse or radically alter its policies. Russell elaborates:

> What we dislike about the Nazis is, psychologically, an outcome of war, and we shall become like them if we fight them. Conversely, if we boldly refuse the method of war, the motives for a swash-buckling mentality on the part of our potential enemies are diminished. . . . War is brutal and horrible, but seems to be ennobled by the fact that the warrior risks his life. If no one resists, the heroism is gone; if the brutality survives, it can no longer command admiration, while all the fine talk becomes laughable.
> (*Which Way to Peace?* pp. 141–2)

If hindsight makes Russell's views seem somewhat naïve, it is nonetheless important to stress that they do raise vital principled issues that no contemporary effort to articulate a theory of just war can afford to evade.

---

[2] See, for instance, his letters to the editor of the *New York Times*, January 27 and February 16, 1941. Here he recants his anti-war stance of 1936 in light of Germany's subsequent behavior in continental Europe, while still defending the form of reasoning that had led him to assume that stance in the first place.

Common Sense and Nuclear Warfare[3]

With this in mind, we turn to our selections from Russell's much-read book *Common Sense and Nuclear Warfare*, first published in 1959. Here attention has shifted from the threat posed by a single nation to the threat posed by two opposing blocs of nations: the strategy of nuclear deterrence adopted by both sides to the Cold War. As in his earlier work, Russell takes care to emphasize the psychological aspects of the politics of war, and in a trenchant critique, he condemns as madness the then current policy of "brinkmanship." But he highlights one positive side effect of this stockpiling of nuclear arsenals: it ensures that no strategic victory could ever be won by military means. The threat of "mutually assured destruction" (known, fittingly perhaps, as "MAD") defines in a wholly new way what is now very much a *shared* interest – namely survival. Interestingly, Russell's concluding lines echo almost to the word the line of thinking that was typically taken to *support* the policy of mutually assured destruction, namely, the idea that it represented the only possible way to make the two superpowers realize that survival is actually at stake, thus ensuring the non-use of these immensely destructive weapons.

From *Common Sense and Nuclear Warfare*, chap. 3[4]

Methods of Settling Disputes in the Nuclear Age

I shall assume the following three propositions conceded:

1 A large-scale nuclear war would be an utter disaster, not only to the belligerents, but to mankind, and would achieve no result that any sane man could desire.
2 When a small war occurs, there is a considerable risk that it may turn into a great war; and in the course of many small wars the risk would ultimately become almost a certainty.
3 If all existing nuclear weapons had been destroyed and there were an agreement that no new ones should be manufactured, any serious war would, nevertheless, become a nuclear war as soon as the belligerents had time to manufacture the forbidden weapons.

From these three theses, it follows that, if we are to escape unimaginable catastrophes, we must find a way of avoiding all wars, whether great or small and whether intentionally nuclear or not.

---

[3]   Bertrand Russell, *Common Sense and Nuclear Warfare* (London: George Allen and Unwin, 1959).
[4]   Ibid., pp. 18–21.

I think that, in a more or less undecided fashion, this conclusion is admitted by most of those who have studied the subject. But statesmen, both in the East and the West, have not arrived at any possible programme for implementing the prevention of war. Since the nuclear stalemate became apparent, the Governments of East and West have adopted the policy which Mr. Dulles[5] calls 'brinkmanship'. This is a policy adapted from a sport which, I am told, is practised by the sons of very rich Americans. This sport is called 'Chicken!' . . . As played by youthful plutocrats, this game is considered decadent and immoral, though only the lives of the players are risked. But when the game is played by eminent statesmen, who risk not only their own lives but those of many hundreds of millions of human beings, it is thought on both sides that the statesmen on one side are displaying a high degree of wisdom and courage, and only the statesmen on the other side are reprehensible. This, of course, is absurd. Both are to blame for playing such an incredibly dangerous game. The game may be played without misfortune a few times, but sooner or later it will come to be felt that loss of face is more dreadful than nuclear annihilation. The moment will come when neither side can face the derisive cry of 'Chicken!' from the other side. When that moment is come, the statesmen of both sides will plunge the world into destruction.

Practical politicians may admit all this, but they argue that there is no alternative. If one side is unwilling to risk global war, while the other side is willing to risk it, the side which is willing to run the risk will be victorious in all negotiations and will ultimately reduce the other side to complete impotence. . . .

This view has governed policy on both sides in recent years. I cannot admit that brinkmanship and surrender are the only alternatives. What the situation requires is a quite different line of conduct, no longer governed by the motives of the contest for power, but by motives appealing to the common welfare and the common interests of the rival parties. What needs to be done is, first of all, psychological. There must be a change of mood and a change of aim, and this must occur on both sides if it is to achieve its purpose. Possibly the initiative, in so far as it is governmental, may have to come from uncommitted nations; but the general attitude to be desired is one which, in the committed nations of East and West, will have to be first advocated by individuals and groups capable of commanding respect.

The argument to be addressed to East and West alike will have to be something on the following lines. Each side has vital interests which it is not prepared to sacrifice. Neither side can defeat the other except by defeating itself at the same time. The interests in which the two sides conflict are immeasurably less important than those in which they are at one. The first and most important of their common interests is survival. This has become a *common* interest owing to the nature of nuclear weapons.

---

[5]   John Foster Dulles (1888–1959) was President Eisenhower's Secretary of State.

It might be possible for Americans, or some of them, to desire a world containing no Russians; and it might be possible for Russians, or some of them, to desire a world containing no Americans; but neither Americans nor Russians would desire a world in which both nations had been wiped out. Since it must be assumed that a war between Russia and America would exterminate both, the two countries have a common interest in the preservation of peace. Their common survival should, therefore, be the supreme aim of policy on both sides.

50

Hans Kelsen
(1881–1973)

Bellum Iustum in
International Law

> A reasonable interpretation of the Kellogg Pact, one not attempting to make of
> it a useless and futile instrument, is that war is not forbidden as . . . an instru-
> ment for the maintenance and realization of international law. This is exactly
> the idea of the *bellum iustum* theory.
>
> *General Theory of Law and State*

An Austrian legal philosopher[1] well known for his theoretical work on the foundations of positive law, Hans Kelsen also wrote extensively on issues in international
law. He maintained that modern attempts at prohibiting international aggression (e.g. the Treaty of Versailles, the Covenant of the League of Nations, and the
Kellogg-Briand Pact) presuppose the classical just war theory. This theory holds
that the resort to force will be legitimate only when it is exercised as a reaction
to prior wrongdoing. Kelsen argued that once the international community has
established norms prohibiting international aggression, a violation of these norms
will have the character of a delict (a legally designated wrong). "Counter war,"
the armed response to such a delict, will consequently have the character of a
sanction. On this basis, Kelsen held that the principle of non-intervention[2] can
indeed be overridden, but only when a state oversteps determinate legal boundaries. Kelsen thus advocated a conception of just war theory the main goal of which
was the enforcement of international law. He did not, however, equate violations

---

[1] Kelsen was also an influential legal practitioner. During World War I he acted as legal advisor to
the Austrian war minister. Later, in 1919, he was entrusted with drafting the new Austrian Constitution, major parts of which are still in effect today.

[2] For a classic statement of the non-intervention principle, see John Stuart Mill, "A Few Words on
Non-intervention," reproduced in chap. 46, this volume.

of international law purely and simply with territorial aggression. For instance, the breach of treaty could, if serious enough, warrant the application of an armed sanction.[3]

Kelsen recognized that this conceptualization was not without its difficulties (outlined below in a section entitled "Arguments against the *bellum iustum* theory"). He held, however, that the evolution of international law, from its initial condition as "primitive law,"[4] toward a generally accepted system of legal norms, indicates, if not conclusively establishes, the plausibility of just war as a legal idea.

From *General Theory of Law and State*[5]

Reprisals and War

If all the material known under the name of international law be investigated, there appear two different kinds of forcible interference in the sphere of interests of a State, normally protected by international law. The distinction rests upon the degree of interference; whether this interference is in principle limited or unlimited; whether the action undertaken against a State is aimed solely at the violation of certain interests of this State, or is directed toward its complete submission or total annihilation.

As to the characterization of limited interference in the sphere of interests of one State by another, a generally accepted opinion prevails: Such an interference is considered either as a delict, in the sense of international law, or as a reprisal. It is permitted as a reprisal, however, only insofar as it takes place as a reaction against a delict. The idea that a reprisal, a limited interference in the normally protected sphere of interests of another State, is only admissible as a reaction against a wrong committed by this State, has been universally accepted and forms an undisputed part of positive international law. It is not essential that interference in the sphere of interests of a State, undertaken as a reprisal, be accompanied by the use of force, but the use of force in a resort to reprisal is permissible, especially if resistance makes it necessary. Similarly, the sanctions of national law, punishment, and civil sanction, are executed by force only in the case of resistance.

---

[3] For this reason, Kelsen's legal conception of just war does not fall under what Michael Walzer later termed the "legalist paradigm," which states that "[n]othing but aggression can justify war" (Michael Walzer, *Just and Unjust Wars* [New York: Basic Books, 1977], pp. 61–3, at p. 62). It seems clear from Walzer's rendition of the idea that it is *territorial aggression* that is in question.

[4] Corresponding, we might presume, to his understanding of the international community as a "primitive society."

[5] Trans. Anders Wedberg (New York: Russell and Russell, 1945), pp. 330–4, 336–9, 341. Parts of this book appeared in earlier German works by Kelsen; other parts were newly written by the author.

There is nothing to prevent our calling a reprisal a sanction of international law. Whether this is true also as to unlimited interference in the sphere of interests of another State remains to be seen. Such an interference is usually called war because it is an action executed by armed forces, the army, the navy, the air force. Our problem leads, therefore, to the question: what is the meaning of war according to international law? Is it possible to interpret war, like the limited interference in the sphere of interests of another State, as either a delict or a reaction against a delict, a sanction? In other words, is it possible to say that according to international law war is permitted only as a sanction, and any war which does not have the character of a sanction is forbidden by international law, is a delict?

The Two Interpretations of War

Two diametrically opposed views exist as to the interpretation of war. According to one opinion war is neither a delict nor a sanction. Any State that is not expressly bound by special treaty to refrain from warring upon another State, or is bound to resort to war only under certain definite conditions, may proceed to war against any other State on any ground without violating international law. According to this opinion, therefore, war can never constitute a delict. For the behavior of a State which is called war is not forbidden by general international law; hence, to this extent, it is permitted. But war cannot constitute a sanction either. For according to this opinion there is in international law no special provision which authorizes the State to resort to war. War is not set up by general international law as a sanction against illegal conduct of a State.

The opposite opinion, however, holds that according to general international law war is forbidden in principle. It is permitted only as a reaction against an illegal act, a delict, and only when directed against the State responsible for this delict. As with reprisals, war has to be a sanction if it is not to be characterized as a delict. This is the theory of *bellum iustum*.

It would be naïve to ask which of these two opinions is the correct one. For each is sponsored by outstanding authorities and defended with weighty arguments. This fact in itself makes any clear decision, any definite choice between the two theories extremely difficult.

By what arguments can the thesis be attacked or defended that according to general international law no war is permissible save as a reaction against a wrong suffered, against a delict? The mere statement of the problem in this form suggests that the position of those who represent the theory of *bellum iustum* is more difficult to maintain; for the burden of proof is theirs, while the opposite view limits itself to a denial of this thesis, and, as is well known, *negantis maior potestas*.

The Doctrine of *Bellum Iustum*

1. International public opinion

If it be asked how it is possible to prove the thesis of the *bellum iustum* theory, that general international law forbids war in principle, the first difficulty is encountered. According to strict juristic thinking, an act is prohibited within a certain legal system when a specific sanction is attached to this act. The only possible reaction that can be provided by general international law against an unpermitted war is war itself, a kind of "counter war" against the State which resorted to war in disregard of international law. No other sanction is possible according to the present technical condition of general international law. But this implies that *war*, or, to be more exact, *counter war*, must be *presupposed* as a sanction, in order to interpret war as a delict. Such a view, however, obviously begs the question, and is, therefore, logically inadmissible as proof of the thesis of the *bellum iustum* theory.

There is, however, another way to go about this: by examining the historical manifestations of the will of the States, diplomatic documents, especially declarations of war and treaties between *States*; all these *show* quite clearly that the different States, i.e., the statesmen representing them, consider war as an illegal act, in principle forbidden by general international law, permitted only as a *reaction* against a wrong suffered. That proves the existence of a legal conviction that corresponds to the thesis of the *bellum iustum* theory. This conviction manifests itself in the fact that the governments of States resorting to war always try to justify this to their own people as well as to the world at large. There is hardly an instance on record in which a State has not tried to proclaim its own cause just and righteous. . . .

2. The idea of *bellum iustum* in positive international law

It is generally admitted that intervention is, as a rule, forbidden by international law. Intervention is the dictatorial interference by a State in the affairs of another State. Dictatorial interference means interference implying the use or threat of force. The duty of non-intervention in the external and internal affairs of another State is considered to be the consequence of the fact that international law protects the internal and external independence of the States. This principle is incompatible with the doctrine that the State, by virtue of its sovereignty, can resort to war for any reason against any other State, without violating general international law. War is an unlimited interference in the affairs of another State implying the use of force; it is an intervention which possibly leads to the complete destruction of another State's external and internal independence. The generally accepted principle of non-intervention presupposes the *bellum iustum* doctrine.

An analysis of the circumstances under which – according to the traditional opinion – a State, exceptionally, has the right of intervention shows that dictatorial interference in the affairs of another State is allowed only as a reaction against a violation of international law on the part of the State against which the intervention takes place. The violation may consist in the fact that this State does not comply with a treaty restricting its external or internal independence, such as intervention on the basis of a treaty of protectorate, or on the basis of a treaty guaranteeing the form of government of another State, or intervention in a State's external affair which, by an international treaty, is at the same time an affair of the intervening State. The violation may consist in noncompliance with a rule of general international law, such as the principle of the freedom of the open sea, or the rule obliging the State to treat foreigners in a certain way. Some writers maintain that intervention is not illegal if performed in the interest of self-preservation; but self-preservation is only a moral-political excuse for a violation of international law, not a right of the State. Some writers maintain also that intervention in the interest of the balance of power is admissible. But this, too, is a political rather than a legal principle. Intervention is legally allowed only if exercised as a reaction against a violation of international law; a rule which confirms the *bellum iustum* doctrine.

It is easy to prove that the theory of *bellum iustum* forms the basis of a number of highly important documents in positive international law, namely, the Peace Treaty of Versailles, the Covenant of the League of Nations, and the Kellogg Pact.

Article 231 of the Treaty of Versailles which establishes the war guilt of Germany justifies the reparation imposed on Germany by maintaining that she and her allies are responsible for an act of aggression. This means that Article 231 characterizes this aggression as an illegal act, as a delict, which would have been impossible if the authors of the Peace Treaty had shared the opinion that every State had a right to resort to war for any reason against any other State. If the aggression which Germany was forced to admit had not been considered "illegal," then it could not have been relied on to justify Germany's obligation to make reparation for the loss and damage caused by the aggression. The Treaty of Versailles did not impose upon Germany a "war-indemnity" but the duty to make "reparation" for illegally caused damages. The aggression of Germany and her allies was considered illegal because the war to which they resorted in 1914 was considered to have been a war "imposed" upon the Allied and Associated Governments. This can mean only that Germany and her allies resorted to war without sufficient reason, that is, without having been wronged by the Allied and Associated Powers, or by any one of them. Only on the basis of the *bellum iustum* doctrine is the idea of "war guilt" possible.

Article 15, paragraph 6, of the Covenant of the League of Nations permits members of the League, under certain conditions, to proceed to war against other League members, but only "for the maintenance of right and justice." Only a just war is permitted.

The Kellogg Pact forbids war, but only as an instrument of national policy. This is a very important qualification of the prohibition. A reasonable interpretation of the Kellogg Pact, one not attempting to make of it a useless and futile instrument, is that war is not forbidden as a means of international policy, especially not as a reaction against a violation of international law, as an instrument for the maintenance and realization of international law. This is exactly the idea of the *bellum iustum* theory. Since, however, the Peace Treaty of Versailles, the Covenant of the League of Nations and the Kellogg Pact are instances of particular international law valid only for the contracting parties, these statements dealing with the "illegality" of war may be considered merely indications of the actual existence of a commonly accepted international legal conviction.

Arguments against the *Bellum Iustum* Theory

The different arguments against the theory that according to general international law war is in principle forbidden, being permissible only as a reaction against a violation of international law, are of varying importance. Certainly the weakest of them, current during the nineteenth century, is that which was most frequently and most successfully relied upon during that period, namely, that it would be inconsistent with the sovereignty of a State to limit its right to resort to war. According to this view, it is especially in war that the sovereignty of a State manifests itself, and sovereignty is the true essence of the State.

Undoubtedly, any norm which forbids a State to resort to war against another State save as a reaction against a wrong suffered by it is contrary to the idea of the sovereignty of the State. This argument is directed not so much against the theory of *bellum iustum*, however, as against international law in general, against every normative legal ordering of the conduct of States. For any legal order obligating States to behave in a certain manner can be conceived only as an authority above the State, and is, therefore, incompatible with the idea of their sovereignty. For to attribute sovereignty to a State means that it is itself the highest authority, above and beyond which there can be no higher authority regulating and determining its conduct. This particular argument does not really constitute a conception of international law opposed to the theory of "just war." It does not afford a different answer to the question of the content of positive international law. It rather denies international law *in toto* as a legal order obligating and authorizing States. Any discussion of the legal importance of war, however, presupposes the existence of a legal order obligating and authorizing States. . . .

Particularly serious is the objection that war of one State against another could never be set up as a sanction because for technical reasons no war can function as a sanction. War never guarantees that the wrongdoer alone will be hit by the evil which a sanction is supposed to mete out. In war not he who is in the "right" is victorious, but he who is the strongest. For this reason, war cannot be a reaction against a wrong, if the party which suffered this wrong is the weaker of the two. There can be no question of a sanction unless there exists an organization to carry out the act of coercion with powers so superior to the power of the wrongdoer that no serious resistance is possible.

The weightiest objection to the theory of just war, however, is the one which claims that according to general international law war cannot be interpreted either as a sanction or as a delict. Who is to decide the disputed issue as to whether one State actually has violated a right of another State? General international law has no tribunal to decide this question. It can only be decided, therefore, through mutual agreement between the parties. But this would be the exception, inasmuch as a State would hardly admit having violated the rights of another State. If no agreement can be reached between the parties to the conflict, the questions of whether or not international law has actually been violated and who is responsible for the violation cannot be uniformly decided, and certainly not – as is now and then believed – by the science of law. Not the science of law, not jurists, but only and exclusively the governments of the States in conflict are authorized to decide this question; and they may decide the question in different ways. If there is no uniform answer to the question whether in a given case there has or has not been a delict, then there is no uniform answer to the question whether the war waged as a reaction is or is not actually a "just war"; whether the character of this war is that of a sanction or of a delict. Thus the distinction between war as a sanction and war as a delict would become highly problematic. Moreover, there would seem to be no difference between the theory which holds that the State has a right to resort to war whenever and against whomever it pleases, and the theory according to which war is permitted only as a reaction against a delict, any other war being itself a delict, but which has to admit that within general international law it is almost impossible to apply these principles satisfactorily in any concrete instance.

The Primitive Legal Order

The attempt to meet all these objections is by no means intended to veil the theoretical difficulties of the enterprise. The objections raised against the theory of "just war" (and therefore against the legal character of international law in general) are grounded primarily in the technical insufficiency of general international law.

In its technical aspects, general international law is a primitive law, as is evidenced among other ways by its complete lack of a particular organ charged with the application of legal norms to a concrete instance. In primitive law, the individual whose legally protected interests have been violated is himself authorized by the legal order to proceed against the wrongdoer with all the coercive means provided by the legal order. This is called self-help. Every individual takes the law into his own hands. Blood revenge is the most characteristic form of this primitive legal technique. Neither the establishment of the delict nor the execution of the sanction is conferred upon an authority distinct from the parties involved or interested. In both these aspects the legal order is entirely decentralized. There is neither a court nor a centralized executive power. The relatives of the murdered person, the bereaved, must themselves decide whether an avenging action should be undertaken, and if so, against whom they should proceed.

Nevertheless, in a primitive community the man avenging the murder of his father upon one whom he considers to be the murderer is himself regarded not as a murderer but as an organ of the community. For by this very act he executes a legal duty, a norm of the social order constituting the community. It is this norm which empowers him, and him only, under certain circumstances, and under these circumstances only, to kill the suspected murderer. This same man would not be acting as an organ or instrument of his community but merely as a murderer himself should this same action on his part be promoted by circumstances other than those provided by the legal order of his community, should he not be acting merely as an avenger. The distinction between murder, as a delict, and homicide, as a fulfillment of a duty to avenge, is of the greatest importance for primitive society. It means that killing is only permitted if the killer acts as an organ of his community, if his action is undertaken in execution of the legal order. The coercive act is reserved to the community, and is, in consequence, a monopoly of this community. The decentralization of the application of the law does not prevent the coercive act as such from being strictly monopolized. This is the way such events are interpreted in primitive society; and this interpretation is one of the most important ideological foundations of primitive society, although it may well be doubted in a concrete instance whether the killing constitutes merely an avenging, a sanction, or should itself be regarded as a delict, and despite the fact that blood revenge is hardly a suitable means for protecting the weak against the strong.

A social order which has not progressed beyond the principle of self-help may produce a state of affairs leaving much to be desired. Nevertheless it is possible to consider this state a legal state, and this decentralized order a legal order. For this order can be interpreted as an order according to which the coercive act is a monopoly of the community, and it is permissible to interpret the primitive social order in this way because the individuals subjected to this order themselves interpret it in this way. History teaches that evolution everywhere proceeds from blood revenge toward the institution of courts and the development of a centralized executive power, that is, toward steadily increasing centralization of the coercive social order. We are entirely justified in calling the still decentralized coercive social order of primitive society "law," in spite of its rather crude techniques such as self-help; for this decentralized order constitutes the first step in an evolution which ultimately leads to the law of the State, to a centralized coercive order. As the embryo in the mother's womb is from the beginning a human being, so the decentralized coercive order of primitive self-help is already law, law *in statu nascendi.*

International Law as Primitive Law

. . . It is not a scientific but a political decision which gives preference to the *bellum iustum* theory. This preference is justified by the fact that only this interpretation conceives of the international order as law, although admittedly primitive law, the first step in an evolution which within the national community, the State, has led to a system of norms which is generally accepted as law. There can be little doubt that the international law of the present contains all the potentialities of such an evolution; it has even shown a definite tendency in this direction. Only if such an evolution could be recognized as inevitable would it be scientifically justified to declare the *bellum iustum* theory the correct interpretation of international law. Such a supposition, however, reflects political wishes rather than scientific thinking. From a strictly scientific point of view a diametrically opposite evolution of international relations is not absolutely excluded. That war is in principle a delict and is permitted only as a sanction is a possible interpretation of international relations, but not the only one.

51

Paul Ramsey
(1913–1988)

Nuclear Weapons and
Legitimate Defense

> This nation should announce that as a matter of policy we will never be the
> first to use nuclear weapons – *except* tactical ones that may and will be used,
> against forces only and not strategically against an enemy's heartland, to stop
> an invasion across a clearly defined boundary, our own or one we are pledged
> by treaty to defend.
>
> "The Limits of Nuclear War"

A Methodist theologian who taught for many years at Princeton University, Paul
Ramsey played a pivotal role in the recovery of the just war idea in the second half
of the twentieth century. The first half of the century had already been marked, it
is true, by a renewal of interest in just war thinking. Under the tutelage of James
Brown Scott, the Carnegie Institution (and later the Carnegie Endowment for
International Peace) published an impressive series of volumes which reproduced,
both in the original Latin and in English translation, some of the most important
writings in the just war tradition.[1] However, Scott's work as editor and author[2]
was primarily historical. Moreover, he viewed the leading figures of this tradition
(Vitoria, Suárez, and Grotius) first and foremost as initiators of the modern discipline
of international law.[3] Paul Ramsey, by contrast, appears to have had little interest

---

[1] The first volume in the series appeared in 1911 and the last in 1950, for a total of twenty-two
different titles (a full list of may be found at the end of no. 22, vol. 1, the English translation of
Grotius's *De iure praedae commentarius*). The series includes works by Grotius, Vitoria, Suárez,
Wolff, Vattel, and others. Reprints are available from William S. Hein and Co., Buffalo, New York.

[2] In 1934 he published *The Spanish Origin of International Law: Francisco de Vitoria and his Law of
Nations* (Oxford: Clarendon Press).

[3] This reading has been much criticized in recent years. See, for example, J. Muldoon, "The
Contribution of the Medieval Canon Lawyers to the Formation of international law," *Traditio*, 28

in the historical dimensions of just war theory, apart from St. Augustine, whom he often quoted. Nor was Ramsey much concerned with international law; rather, he worked from the perspective of systematic Christian ethics. His great contribution in the field of military ethics was to frame just war principles – especially the *ius in bello* principles of proportionality and discrimination – in relation to the burning moral issues of his day. Indeed, by his choice of methodology Ramsey brought new vigor to the just war tradition. In this respect his work has served as a model for a whole generation of later theorists.

The emerging moral debate on nuclear weapons constituted the main topic of Ramsey's *War and the Christian Conscience* (1961) and would remain a constant theme in his later writings on military ethics. It should be noted, however, that he also discussed a wide range of other topics, *inter alia*: intervention, counter-insurgency, chemical weapons, selective conscientious objection, the theory of statecraft, and the role of churches in the public debate on war. In his writings on nuclear deterrence, Ramsey sought innovatively to engage two very different sorts of readers. On the one hand, he attempted to dissuade his fellow Christians from adopting a stance of nuclear pacifism. On the other hand, he addressed the secular policy community ("whose moral discourse lacked a moral component"[4]) in order to indicate what moral limits should be placed on the Cold War strategy of deterrence by assured mutual destruction. Ramsey's arguments in the essay below are directed principally to this second audience.[5] He considers nuclear weapons on two levels: their *actual* use on the battlefield, and their *threatened* use within a strategy of deterrence. Regarding the first, Ramsey maintains (see the section entitled "Suggested Policy Decisions") that this would be morally licit only when directed against the military forces of an invading enemy. Any use of such weapons against civilian population centers he entirely rules out. With respect to the second level, Ramsey paints a considerably more nuanced picture. While an enemy's cities should never be directly threatened with nuclear retaliation, the prospect of massive *side-effect harm* to its civilian population, stemming from a direct nuclear attack upon its military forces, would nevertheless provide it with a powerful disincentive against ever initiating such an exchange in the first place. If this strategy of "indirect" deterrence should prove inadequate, however, a nation may legitimately maintain a "studied ambiguity" regarding its very possession of a nuclear arsenal. While denying that it would ever deliberately use these weapons

(1972), pp. 483–97; Peter Haggenmacher, "La place de Francisco de Vitoria parmi les fondateurs du droit international," in A. Truyol y Serra et al. (eds.), *Actualité de la pensée juridique de Francisco de Vitoria* (Brussels: Bruylant, 1986), pp. 27–80.

[4]   James Turner Johnson, "Paul Ramsey and the Recovery of the Just War Idea," *Journal of Military Ethics*, 1, 2 (2002), pp. 136–44, on p. 137. This article provides an overview of Ramsey's contribution to military ethics.

[5]   Thinkers such as Herman Kahn, Klaus Knorr, and Thomas Schelling. Ramsey's text is interspersed with many quotes from these (and similar) authors. In the interests of space these quotes have not been included here.

against civilians, a nation's adversaries could never be certain that its commitment in this regard was truly steadfast. Deliberately cultivated, this doubt would serve as a last firewall against the threat of first attack by a reckless enemy.

Unsurprisingly, given the very nature of the topic, Ramsey's views on the nuclear question have elicited much criticism. Some have argued that his moral teaching is far too permissive.[6] Others,[7] by contrast, have held that deterrence can be justified on grounds broader than even Ramsey was willing to concede. To his credit, however, it must be said that Ramsey did much to set the terms of a debate that since has produced a large literature.

From "The Limits of Nuclear War"[8]

This chapter defends the thesis that counter-force nuclear war is the upper limit of rational, politically purposive military action. Two ways are commonly taken to avoid this conclusion, and another uncommonly. Those who magnify the difficulty and undesirability of adopting a policy of making just war possible usually do so because:

1 they believe that general disarmament is about to be accomplished and therefore no plans should be made for the use of any weapons, nuclear or other; or else because

2 they believe that balanced deterrence can be stabilized and kept perfect enough to insure that nuclear weapons will never be used except in their non-use for deterrence.

In these two schools, extremes meet. They are brothers under the skin who believe so strongly in peace by disarmament (whether unilaterally or by treaty or by technical contrivance by which the weapons will neutralize themselves) that as a consequence they see no need for thinking about the upper limit of sanity in the actual use of nuclear weapons. . . .

Therefore, no steps *should* be taken to plan to fight war justly against forces if you believe that peace by deliberate disarmament can soon be achieved; and no

---

[6] This is the position articulated, e.g., by Michael Walzer (*Just and Unjust Wars* [New York: Basic Books, 1977], pp. 278–83); The National Conference of Catholic Bishops (*The Challenge of Peace*, see chap. 57, this volume); and J. Finnis, J. M. Boyle, Jr. and G. Grisez (*Nuclear Deterrence, Morality and Realism* [Oxford: Clarendon Press, 1987, especially pp. 161–3]).

[7] See in particular Gregory S. Kavka, *Moral Paradoxes of Nuclear Deterrence* (Cambridge: Cambridge University Press, 1987).

[8] This essay first appeared in a pamphlet published by The Council on Religion and International Affairs, 170 East 64th Street, New York, 1965. It later appeared as a chapter in Paul Ramsey, *The Just War: Force and Political Responsibility* (New York: Scribner, 1968; reprint, Lanham, MD: University Press of America, 1983). It is from the 1968/1983 edition that the extracts below are taken (with most of the footnotes omitted), pp. 215–16, 221–2, 224, 236–7, 242–3, 249–58.

such steps *need* be taken if you believe that weapons technology can keep the nations permanently disarmed and no future rational decision-maker need ever decide to fire these weapons. . . .

There is no way to avoid thinking about militarily feasible and politically purposive warfare. Against the first of these positions, it must be said that nuclear weapons and armaments in general are unlikely to be scrapped soon, if ever. Against the second, it must be said that "balanced" deterrence and invulnerable weapons systems do not preclude the need to think about believable fight-the-war plans. Instead, the opposite is the result. The more the great powers think they have achieved for the moment a nearly automatic neutralization of nuclear weapons, from bases it will take years to find a way of attacking, the more the world is prepared for local war, for conventional and unconventional war. The more, too, will it seem possible to make a controlled use of tactical nuclears, and after that to expand the war to controlled attacks upon an enemy's strategic forces and then to engage with him in a cold-blooded exchange of a few cities. . . .

War as a Test of Wills

Policies of extreme committal to irrational behavior are only one illustration of where one is driven when war is regarded as primarily or exclusively a trial of wills or a test of resolve. There is no end here, no limits. Limited strategic war involving controlled city exchanges or limited counter-city retaliation *as a bargaining tactic* offer another illustration of war in which the sides aim to "prevail" *primarily* by demonstrating resoluteness. This, too, is "unthinkable" in the sense that the more you think about it the more it will seem manifestly "un-do-able." But first, a word should be said about war as a trial of wills in contrast to war as a trial of strength. (War, of course, always involves both these encounters.)

In war as a trial of wills, what one side does is determined primarily by its calculation of what the other side expects of it, or what is required for its resolution to be broken. Analysts in our day have developed an entire science of purely voluntaristic games of strategy simply by abstracting the encounter of the wills and minds of the combatants (always a significant aspect of military engagements) from other factors. For purposes of analysis one sets aside any consideration of war as a resort to a controlled collision of bodily forces, war as a trial of physical strength, or war as the challenge and response of national entities each with concrete policies to be defended or effected. Where will and resolve are at issue, the question is not what would I do if I were the enemy seeking to enforce some definite national policy by possible resort to arms. The question is, rather, what would I do if I were he, wondering what he should do if he were wondering what I would do if I were he . . . ? In the determination of radically voluntaristic policy, the focal point is each side's expectation of what the other expects it to expect to be expected to do. Such is the result of our present-day attempt thoroughly to "spiritualize" the conduct of war. Such is the result of trying to elevate war from being mainly a trial of strength directed toward some controlling objective, and of transmuting it into a test of resolve which has no other purpose than to prove who wins in a battle of wills. There is no limit or end to this. . . .

Fighting a war has its obscure *ratio* only when the conduct of war is subordinated to the civil life and purposes of a nation, to its concrete civilization, values, and policy objectives. The will to fight and the manner of fighting must be governed and controlled by the preeminence of society, and the effectuation or defense of its policy, over the use of armaments. This relationship is lost sight of when war becomes a matter of one will "prevailing" over another, and the destruction of an entire city is made a mere means of "demonstrating" resolution, or is used to "symbolize" one side's willingness to go higher unless the other "chickens out." . . .

Suggested Policy Decisions

. . . This nation should announce that as a matter of policy we will never be the first to use nuclear weapons – *except* tactical ones that may and will be used, against forces only and not strategically against an enemy's heartland, to stop an invasion across a clearly defined boundary, our own or one we are pledged by treaty to defend. This would make it unambiguously clear that tactical nuclear weapons will be used if need be against any invasion, even by conventional forces. The threat would be believable, because of the clearly declared limits which state that the use of nuclear weapons will be defensive only and that not even in reply to an invasion will we first use nuclear weapons "offensively" against an enemy's territory or his strategic forces. . . . This proposal may be called the right of first defensive use of nuclear weapons against invading forces, or a commitment to use nuclear weapons first only over one's own territory. . . .

The more one thinks about a policy of using tactical nuclears defensively, and unilateral initiatives to try to govern war in this fashion, the more it seems a possible choice for the nations of the world for the entire age in which nuclear weapons have been invented. At least we are forced to ask whether it is only for the time being that security for the free world and the peace of the entire world could be based on this proposal. If this first use of nuclear arms can be tied to the resistance of aggression across well-understood and conventionally well-defended boundaries, will not free world security and world peace be less in danger? Will not this be better than an absolute distinction between conventional and nuclear explosives as a basis for the peace-keeping machinery of some future international organization? Or, on the contrary, ought we to begin now to strengthen conventional forces with a view to placing all nuclear weapons in a class by themselves as illegitimate weapons (like bacteriological weapons) which may be possessed to deter their use by an enemy but never used first even in self-defense? . . .

Nuclear capability must be maintained for use in counter-force strikes over an enemy's territory. These strikes would have a dual purpose: first, to prosecute the trial of strength and destroy or decrease an enemy's forces and the force he can muster on the battlefield; secondly, to punish any violation and thus to enforce if possible the rule which we declare by word and by action we have imposed on ourselves, namely, that while defensive first use of tactical nuclear weapons is legitimate, not even in answer to this will we tolerate the use of tactical nuclear weapons offensively over the territory of another nation. Both these purposes indicate that nuclear weapons over an enemy's territory should first be used against *tactical* objectives, munitions dumps, supply lines, bridges, etc. If *nuclear* weapons are used to do this, their use will both prosecute the war and be a signal that the right to do this was granted when the enemy first used nuclear power offensively across another nation's boundary. The reasons for the limitation of these retaliatory strikes to tactical targets, however, will have to be declared again and gain and communicated to both the enemy and neutral nations. . . .

The Justice of Deterrence

. . . Any politically viable solution of the problem of war today requires that we finally employ a distinction between the *possibility* and the *certainty* of illimitable city destruction, and in deterrence during the war that we carefully discriminate between the *appearance* and *actuality* of being partially or totally committed to go to city exchanges. . . . A nation ought never to be totally committed to action that is so irrational it can never be done by free, present decision; and even to *appear* to be totally committed may itself be altogether too dangerous. A nation ought not to communicate to an enemy that it might go to city exchanges without at the same time communicating some doubt about it, if it wants both to remain and to seem to remain a free agent with still some control over its destiny and the course of world politics. The *appearance* of *partial* commitment, or the *appearance* of *possible* commitment, may be enough of a commitment to deter an enemy. . . .

It is never right to do wrong that good may come of it. Nuclear weapons have only added to this perennial truth the footnote: it can never do *any good* to do wrong that good may come of it. Neither is it right to *intend* to do wrong that good may come of it. If deterrence rests upon genuinely intending massive retaliation, it is clearly wrong no matter how much peace results. If weapons systems deter city exchanges only because and so far as they are *intended* to be used against cities, then deterrence involves a "conditional willingness"[9] to do evil, and evil on a massive scale. Granting that deterrence deters before or during

---

[9] Walter Stein (ed.), *Nuclear Weapons and Christian Conscience* (London: Marlin Press, 1961), p. 23.

the war, and that it supports peace or the control of war, that alone cannot justify it. It would be justified "if, and only if, in employing this threat, we were not involved in . . . *immoral hypothetical decisions*."[10] The distinction between murder and killing in war, or between directly killing combatants and directly murdering non-combatants, posits an ethico-political principle that can only be violated, never abrogated. "Nothing, not even the alleged interests of peace, can save murderousness from evil,"[11] and nothing, not even the alleged interest in deterrence during war for the control of war can save the *intention* to commit murder from being evil. Does reliance on nuclear weapons for deterrence hypothetically commit us, here and now, to murder, there and then?[12] If so, such deterrence is wrong, and can never be anything but wickedness. This conclusion would seem to follow from the comparatively simple moral truth that "if an action is morally wrong, it is wrong to intend to do it."[13] . . .

The technical possibility of deterrence before and during war can now be indicated, as can its compatibility with the moral prohibition of both the use and the intention to use nuclear (or any other) weapons in direct attacks on centers of population.

(1) The collateral civilian damage that would result from counter-forces warfare in its maximum form may itself be quite sufficient to deter either side from going so high and to preserve the rules and tacit agreements limiting conflict in a nuclear age. In that case, deterrence during the war and collateral civilian damage are both "indirect effects" of a plan and action of war which would be licit or permitted by the traditional rules of civilized conduct in war. To say that counter-force strikes over an enemy's own territory are licit or permitted is to say that one can morally intend and be "conditionally willing" to engage in such a war. Whether one positively should ever do so depends on the conditions. Collateral civilian damage is certainly an unavoidable indirect effect and, in the technical sense, an "unintended" result of something a nation may and should make itself conditionally willing and ready to do. The deterrent effect, of which we are now speaking, is then, as it were, an indirect effect of the foreseeable indirect effects of legitimate military conduct.[14]

---

[10]   Ibid., p. 36 (italics mine).

[11]   Ibid., p. 36.

[12]   Ibid., p. 125.

[13]   Ibid., p. 71.

[14]   [*Editor's note:*] Upon first appearance of this essay, Ramsey was criticized for using the language of "double effect" when describing how side-effect harm to civilians could serve as an element in the strategy of deterrence. Conceding that he had indeed spoken of "collateral deterrence" improperly, Ramsey added the following note to the 1968 re-printing of this essay in *The Just War*, p. 252. "[This was a quite inadequate, indeed, an unfortunate, formulation of this first step in defense of the justice of deterrence. I should not have described 'collateral deterrence' as the 'indirect effect of foreseeable indirect effects' of legitimately targeted nuclear strikes. Instead, this deterrent effect should have been described as a *direct* and a *wanted* effect of the unwanted, indirect, collateral consequences of even a

One can certainly "intend" to deter in this fashion, and oneself be similarly deterred. Not knowing the tyrannies future history may produce one cannot say whether the one effect of successful resistance to them will justify the direct and the indirect costs. Still we foreknow that these costs may be very great indeed. This is to say that, at least to a very great degree, perhaps a sufficient degree, nuclear warfare is a design for war that is inherently self-limiting upon rational decisionmakers without their having to intend to use these weapons directly to murder cities and civilians. . . .

(2) In respect to the nature of the weapons we possess, there are two possible uses which cannot be removed from them. The dual use the weapons themselves have – the fact that they may be used either against strategic forces or against centers of population – means that *apart from intention* their capacity to deter cannot be removed from them. This means that there may be sufficient deterrence in the subjectively unintended consequence of the mere possession of these weapons. No matter how often we declare, and quite sincerely declare, that our targets are an enemy's forces, he can never be quite *certain* that in the fury or in the fog of war his cities may not be destroyed. This is so certainly the case that the problem of how to deter an enemy from striking our cities ought not for one moment to impede the shift to a counter-forces policy and to the actual intention to use nuclear weapons only against forces. We should declare again and again, and give evidence by what we do, that our targets are his forces rather than his cities. Since it is morally repugnant to wage war without renouncing morally repugnant means, this should be speedily done, and communicated as effectively as possible to the enemy. Still, without any hesitation or ambiguity on our part, the weapons themselves will continue to have deterrent effect because they have ambiguous uses. They always may be used over cities; and no enemy can *know* that this will not be done. . . .

. . . War being sufficiently threatening, a conclusive case can be made for the proposition that massive nuclear weapons should never be intended for use against societies. The nations of the world *should* and *can* devote all their attention and intention to making only just or counter-forces war possible. A single great power *can* and *should* do this, since the other ominous possibility will always remain in the background as a shared and unintended threat.

(3) Only now do we come again to the suggestion that the distinction between the *appearance* and the *actuality* of being partially or totally committed to go to city exchanges may have to be employed in deterrence policy. In that case, only the appearance should be cultivated. If the first two points above do not seem to

just use of nuclear weapons. For me to revise the language of the text above and remove this mistake would be to attribute to myself a prescience and an aptitude for words that I did not have. This would also prevent the reader from being drawn into the argument over the justice of deterrence as it unfolds in subsequent chapters. Therefore, in what follows this misleading wording will continue to be used until I was forced to supplant it by better wording for the same thought.]"

the military analyst sufficiently persuasive, or *able to be made so*, then an *apparent* resolution to wage war irrationally or at least an *ambiguity* about our intentions have to be our expressed policy. This is a matter, not of the nature of the weapons themselves, but of the manner in which we possess them – the "having" of them that might be necessary to sustain deterrence during justifiably conducted war. . . .

The crucial question for the moralist is whether deterrent effects that flow from a *specified kind* of studied ambiguity concerning the intention with which a nation holds nuclear weapons in reserve are *praeter intentionem* (besides or without the actual intention to attack cities) as surely as are the first two types of deterrent effects we have analyzed. To say and to act as if we might go to city exchanges is certainly a form of deception. But, if this can be done without intending to make irrational, immoral use of nuclear weapons, or even with the intention that our weapons be not so used and with the intention of revoking what had never even the appearance of total committal, such deception cannot be said to be based on the criminal intention or conditional willingness to do murder. The first thing to be said then, is that the intention to deceive is certainly a far cry from the intention to murder society, or to commit mutual homicide.

The second thing to be said is in connection with the moral problem of *deception* in politics and in wartime. A moralist need not slur over the fact that in all sorts of ways deception may be an evil, just as he need not slur over the fact that the killing of combatants is evil (though certainly not wicked). But having said this, it must then be pointed out that there are deceptions and deceptions. Or rather, the word "deception" ought perhaps to be reserved for any denial of the truth to someone to whom the truth is due, or permitting him to gather from you a false or inadequate impression concerning the exact truth which, in some sense, "belongs" to him. If this is a fair statement of the moral rule, then an experienced finding of fact must be that there are many situations in both private and public life when withholding the "truth" or even communicating an inadequate representation of the "truth" is not a lie. Relative to this, there is a teaching of long standing in the Western tradition about the virtues of a military commander, to the effect that there is nothing wrong with his having military secrets provided he does not pretend that he has none. It would be extremely difficult to support the judgment that an effective reservation about the use of the weapons we possess, or about our intention that they not be used over cities, in any sense belongs to an enemy, or that this information is due to be given him, if thereby deterrence will fail and war break out and go *whoosh!*

Finally, a moralist must raise the question of whether this truth is not owed to the people of an enemy nation, if not to their military commanders. In answer to this, it goes to the point to say that this may be necessary to save *their* lives as well as those of our own civilians. Or (worse than their death from the point of view of an ethics that does not place supreme value in mere physical existence) it may be necessary in order to save them (and ourselves) from a measure of complicity in their government's conditional or actual willingness to save them by doing mass murder, or from the *tragedy* (not the *wickedness*) of actually being saved by murderous intention (if a wrongly willed deterrent worked) and some of them from the tragedy of living on in a world in which their lives have been spared in the midst of the greatest possible wrong-*doing* by a government which in remote degrees of participation was still their own (if the shared intentional risk does not work). So the question resolves itself into the question whether it is ever right to withhold the truth in order to save life, to save from moral wrong-doing, to save from sheer tragedy. Does the truth that might well be "fatal" in all these senses "belong" to them? Is it "due" to be given if it can be? Do we "owe" them a true report that will unambiguously quiet their fears by effectively communicating to them (if this can ever be done) that we have no intention of engaging with their government in inter-society warfare under any circumstances? I am so far from believing that one ought readily to justify this deception that it seems to me that the first two types of deterrence must, if at all possible, be made to work. Still, if deterrence were based on a cultivated ambiguity about our real intentions, and if "deception" in an objectionable moral sense would thus in some measure be perpetrated, it would still be an intent to deceive and not an intent possibly to do murder.

Perhaps we should say that we ought to be conditionally willing to strive for this ingredient in deterrence, that is, on the condition that it is necessary to deter and to save life. I do not grant to a physician any right to withhold from a patient knowledge of his true condition; but then I also do not believe that learning the truth about his condition can be demonstrated to be so nearly fatal as, in our present supposition, it would be for an enemy government and population to learn that we do not intend to attack people. A better analogy might be the following one. If you were trying to save a man out on the ledge of a building, threatening to commit suicide and to take you with him, would you withhold from him, and have an obligation to withhold from him, any blandishments, including "daring" him to join you inside for a duel to the death by "Russian roulette" at three paces, with no intention of ever carrying out this dissuasive dare or threat?

. . . [T]his may be one of those customarily "unthinkable" things, which, the more you think about it, will prove to be technically and politically "do-able." If needed, it should be developed in many a scenario. It is on balance morally "do-able," as city-busting is not, however much you think about it. Whether this ingredient in deterrence can be adopted and exercised by a democratic society is, of course, a serious question. . . .

Then it may be possible to put, not nuclear weapons as such, but the inter-city use of nuclear weapons into a category by itself, so that, while the capability still exists, the intention to attack cities will recede into the background so far as not to have actuality. Things as strange have happened before in the history of warfare. Tribes living close to death in the desert have fought cruel wars. They even used poisoned arrows, and certainly to a limited extent they fought one another by means of direct attack upon women and children. But they knew *not to poison wells!* That would have been a policy of mutual homicide, and a form of society-*contra*-society warfare that would have removed the possibility of any more bloody cruel wars, not to mention peacetime pursuits. In refraining from massive well-poisoning, or in keeping that ambiguous, did these tribes, in any valid or censorable sense of the word, still "intend" to poison wells?

52

G. E. M. Anscombe (1919–2001)

The Moral Recklessness of Pacifism

> [P]acifism teaches people to make no distinction between the shedding of innocent blood and the shedding of any human blood. And in this way pacifism has corrupted enormous numbers of people who will not act according to its tenets . . . seeing no way of avoiding wickedness, they set no limits to it.
>
> "War and Murder"

For many students of philosophy, the name of Gertrude Elizabeth Margaret Anscombe is invariably connected with that of Ludwig Wittgenstein, one of the twentieth century's greatest philosophical minds. Her one-time teacher and close friend for the last decade or so of his life, he made her one of the executors of his literary estate. But in addition to editing and translating many of Wittgenstein's most famous works,[1] Anscombe was also the author of a substantial corpus of philosophical writings of her own, much of it on ethics and themes within Catholic thought. Her arguably most famous work, the short but intricate monograph *Intention*,[2] is regarded as the source of modern action theory, weaving together a complex web of influences spanning the full history of philosophy – from Aristotle, via Aquinas, to Wittgenstein. As we shall see, her theoretical work on intention and action is essential also to her work in applied ethics, and is especially apparent in the way she articulates the implications of the doctrine of double effect.

In this chapter we will be excerpting from three of her works: two self-published pamphlets and one scholarly article.[3] The first of these, "The Justice of the Present

---

[1] Notably *Philosophical Investigations* and *On Certainty*.

[2] Ithaca, NY: Cornell University Press, 1957; 2nd edn., Cambridge, MA: Harvard University Press, 2000.

[3] All have since been reprinted in volume 3 of her *Collected Philosophical Papers*, entitled *Ethics, Religion and Politics* (Oxford: Basil Blackwell, 1981, pp. 72–81, 62–71, and 51–61, respectively).

War Examined," co-authored with a student friend at the tender age of 20, launches a scathing critique of Great Britain's intentions for engaging in what was to become World War II, concluding that "we are fighting against an unjust cause, indeed; but not for a just one" ("The Justice of the Present War Examined," p. 75). The second, "Mr Truman's Degree," she published protesting Oxford University's awarding an honorary doctorate to Harry Truman, former US president, on account of his decision to employ atomic bombs over Hiroshima and Nagasaki. Finally, there is "War and Murder," which pulls together and provides theoretical back-up for her reflections in the two pamphlets. Here she works largely within the virtue-ethical tradition of Catholicism, thereby providing an interesting contrast to the more Kantian reflections evinced in our selections from Thomas Nagel (whom she very much inspired). Since the three writings largely overlap, we have chosen to proceed thematically rather than look at them one by one.

We ask the reader to take special note of Anscombe's comments from the fall of 1939. Here we have an author who clearly opposes Hitler and Nazism. Yet arguing neither from a pacifist nor from a strategic-realist standpoint, she nonetheless opposes the war as it had been initiated by Great Britain and France.

As is well known, most non-pacifists have later come to see the declaration of war against Germany in September 1939 as laudable, possibly even unavoidable. Against this background, understanding the grounds for the young Elizabeth Anscombe's *criticism* of the Allied policy is an interesting and challenging task.

Innocence and Immunity

Anscombe's immediate target in the last two articles is the notion that the nature of modern weaponry and the complexity of contemporary societies conspire to blur the distinction between civilians and soldiers in war. Originally forwarded by military strategists and apologists, this argument has since been adopted also by pacifists, aiming to bolster the notion that all wars are by nature unjust. Anscombe sees this as dangerous obscurantism, which threatens to erase perfectly clear and absolutely vital moral distinctions. As she starkly declares in "Mr Truman's Degree" (p. 69): "[Pacifism] is a factor in that loss of the conception of murder which is my chief interest in this pamphlet."

From "Mr Truman's Degree"[4]

For some time before war broke out [World War II], and more intensely afterwards, there was propaganda in this country on the subject of the "indivisibility" of modern war. The civilian population, we were told, is really as much combatant

---

[4] Ibid., p. 63.

as the fighting forces. The military strength of a nation includes its whole economic and social strength. Therefore the distinction between the people engaged in prosecuting the war and the population at large is unreal. There is no such thing as a non-participator; you cannot buy a postage stamp or any taxed article, or grow a potato or cook a meal, without contributing to the "war effort". War indeed is a "ghastly evil", but once it has broken out no one can "contract out" of it. "Wrong" indeed must be being done if war is waged, but you cannot help being involved in it. There was a doctrine of "collective responsibility" with a lugubriously elevated moral tone about it. The upshot was that it was senseless to draw any line between legitimate and illegitimate objects of attack. Thus the court chaplains of the democracy. I am not sure how children and the aged fitted into this story: probably they cheered the soldiers and munitions workers up.

From "War and Murder"[5]

Now pacifism teaches people to make no distinction between the shedding of innocent blood and the shedding of any human blood. And in this way pacifism has corrupted enormous numbers of people who will not act according to its tenets. They become convinced that a number of things are wicked which are not; hence seeing no way of avoiding wickedness, they set no limits to it. How endlessly pacifists argue that all war must be *à outrance*! that those who wage war must go as far as technological advance permits in the destruction of the enemy's people. As if the Napoleonic wars were perforce fuller of massacres than the French war of Henry V of England. It is not true: the reverse took place. Nor is technological advance particularly relevant; it is mere squeamishness that deters people who would consent to area bombing from the enormous massacres *by hand* that used once to be committed.

The policy of obliterating cities was adopted by the Allies in the last war [World War II]; they need not have taken that step, and it was taken largely out of a villainous hatred, and as corollary to the policy, now universally denigrated, of seeking "unconditional surrender". (That policy itself was visibly wicked, and could be and was judged so at the time; it is not surprising that it led to disastrous consequences, even if no one was clever and detached enough to foresee this at the time.)

Pacifism and the respect for pacifism is not the only thing that has led to a universal forgetfulness of the law against killing the innocent; but it has had a share in it.

In order to revive the "conception of murder" which she feels that realism and pacifism have jointly contributed to undermining, she stakes out and defends a

[5] Ibid., pp. 57–8.

notion of "innocence," defined as applying to the class of people not actively engaged in harming.[6]

From "War and Murder"[7]

What is required, for the people attacked to be non-innocent in the relevant sense, is that they should themselves be engaged in an objectively unjust proceeding which the attacker has the right to make his concern; or – the commonest case – should be unjustly attacking him. Then he can attack them with a view to stopping them; and also their supply lines and armament factories. But people whose mere existence and activity supporting existence by growing crops, making clothes, etc., constitute an impediment to him – such people are innocent and it is murderous to attack them, or make them a target for an attack which he judges will help him towards victory. For murder is the deliberate killing of the innocent, whether for its own sake or as a means to some further end.

Intention and Double Effect

Nonetheless, not even the prohibition on killing innocents is absolute, if it occurs as the unintended consequence of a legitimate action. Saying that x killed y in self-defense is to imply that x did not *choose* to kill y (for then it would be murder): rather, y's death occurred as an unintended, if foreseeable, consequence of x's legitimate intended aim, namely self-defense. This aim, moreover, is rendered legitimate by circumstances not of x's choosing, namely the threat posed by y. Although this notion of double effect is deeply ingrained in Christian thought, it is, as Anscombe points out, ill understood in contemporary legal practice.

From "War and Murder"[8]

In saying that a private man may not choose to kill, we are touching on the principle of "double effect". The denial of this has been the corruption of non-Catholic thought, and its abuse the corruption of Catholic thought. Both have disastrous consequences which we shall see. This principle is not accepted in English law: the law is said not usually to distinguish the foreseen and the intended consequences of an action. Thus, if I push a man over a cliff when he is menacing my life, his death is considered as intended by me, but the intention to be justifiable for the sake of self-defence. Yet the lawyers would hardly find the laying of poison tolerable as an act of self-defence, but only killing by a violent action in

---

[6]   In this, her usage of "innocence" is etymologically correct. The Latin *innocens* means "harmless."

[7]   Ibid., p. 53.

[8]   Ibid., pp. 54–5.

a moment of violence. Christian moral theologians have taught that even here one may not seek the death of the assailant, but may in default of other ways of self-defence use such violence as will in fact result in his death. The distinction is evidently a fine one in some cases: what, it may be asked, can the intention be, if it can be said to be absent in this case, except a mere wish or desire?

And yet in other cases the distinction is very clear. If I go to prison rather than perform some action, no reasonable person will call the incidental consequences of my refusal – the loss of my job, for example – intentional just because I knew they must happen. And in the case of the administration of a pain-relieving drug in mortal illness, where the doctor knows the drug may very well kill the patient if the illness does not do so first, the distinction is evident; the lack of it has led an English judge to talk nonsense about the administration of the drug's not having *really* been the cause of death in such a case, even though a post mortem shows it was. For everyone understands that it is a very different thing so to administer a drug, and to administer it with the intention of killing.

From "War and Murder"[9]

The distinction between the intended, and the merely foreseen, effects of a voluntary action is indeed absolutely essential to Christian ethics. For Christianity forbids a number of things as being bad in themselves. But if I am answerable for the foreseen consequences of an action or refusal, as much as for the action itself, then these prohibitions will break down. If someone innocent will die unless I do a wicked thing, then on this view I am his murderer in refusing: so all that is left to me is to weigh up evils. Here the theologian steps in with the principle of double effect and says: "No, you are no murderer, if the man's death was neither your aim nor your chosen means, and if you had to act in the way that led to it or else do something absolutely forbidden." Without an understanding of this principle, anything can be – and is wont to be – justified, and the Christian teaching that in no circumstances may one commit murder, adultery, apostasy (to give a few examples) goes by the board. These absolute prohibitions of Christianity by no means exhaust its ethic; there is a large area where what is just is determined partly by a prudent weighing up of consequences. But the prohibitions are bedrock, and without them the Christian ethic goes to pieces. Hence the necessity of the notion of double effect.

From "Mr Truman's Degree"[10]

Choosing to kill the innocent as a means to your ends is always murder. Naturally, killing the innocent as an end in itself is murder too; but that is no more than a

---

[9] Ibid., p. 58.
[10] Ibid., pp. 66–7.

possible future development for us: in our part of the globe it is a practice that has so far been confined to the Nazis. I intend my formulation to be taken strictly; each term in it is necessary. For killing the innocent, even if you know as a matter of statistical certainty that the things you do involve it, is not necessarily murder. I mean that if you attack a lot of military targets, such as munitions factories and naval dockyards, as carefully as you can, you will be certain to kill a number of innocent people; but that is not murder. . . .

It may be impossible to take the thing (or people) you want to destroy as your target; it may be possible to attack it only by taking as the object of your attack what includes large numbers of innocent people. Then you cannot very well say they died by accident. Here your action is murder. "But where will you draw the line? It is impossible to draw an exact line." This is a common and absurd argument against drawing any line; it may be very difficult, and there are obviously borderline cases. But we have fallen into the way of drawing no line, and offering as justifications what an uncaptive mind will find only a bad joke. Wherever the line is, certain things are certainly well to one side or the other of it.

Now who are "the innocent" in war? They are all those who are not fighting and not engaged in supplying those who are with the means of fighting. A farmer growing wheat which may be eaten by the troops is not "supplying them with the means of fighting". Over this, too, the line may be difficult to draw. But that does not mean that no line should be drawn, or that, even if one is in doubt just where to draw the line, one cannot be crystal clear that this or that is well over the line.

"But the people fighting are probably conscripts! In that case they are just as innocent as anyone else." "Innocent" here is not a term referring to personal responsibility at all. It means rather "not harming". But the people fighting are "harming", so they can be attacked; but if they surrender they become in this sense innocent and so may not be maltreated or killed.

However, it is essential that double-effect reasoning be tempered by considerations of proportionality, as Anscombe reminds us in the following section, arguing against the indiscriminatory means employed by the Allied forces against Germany even in the early days of World War II.

From "The Justice of the Present War Examined"[11]

No action can be excused whose consequences involve a greater evil than the good of the action itself, whether these consequences are accidental or not. Double effect therefore only excuses a grave incidental consequence where the balance of the total effects of an action is on the side of the good.

[11]   Ibid., pp. 78–9.

There is a great distinction between attacking a group of persons directly, and killing them accidentally in the course of attack on others. But yet another distinction must be made. It is a different thing, while making one group of persons a target, to kill others by accident, and to make a group of persons a target, in order – by attacking them all – to attack some members of the group who are persons who may legitimately be attacked. The first case involves no sin; the second involves murder and is not an example of double effect. It has been claimed as such by some who, defending blockade, allow that civilians are not a proper military target, but who argue that attack may be made on a whole group of persons which includes both civilians and combatants. This claim cannot be allowed.

From "The Justice of the Present War Examined"[12]

[U]njust deliberate killing is murder and this is a great sin which "cries to heaven for vengeance"; if, therefore, the warring state intends, under any circumstances, to commit it as a means of prosecuting the war, then the war is made wicked. As we have seen, our government does intend to do that which is unlawful, and it is already blockading Germany with intent to starve the national life. The present war is therefore wrong on account of means.

Right Intention and Conditions of Surrender

But questions of intention pertain not only to the *in bello* strategizing of state leaders and generals, but to the *ius ad bellum* as well: as we have seen empha- sized several times in this volume, it is a mainstay of the just war tradition that a legitimate war must be waged not only with a *just cause* but also with a *right intention*. As we mentioned, Anscombe addresses this issue in her 1939 pamphlet, where her condemnation of the Alliance's intention may serve as a reminder of the particular difficulty involved in applying just war categories to ongoing con- flicts. But more positively, she also connects the notion of right intention with the idea of declaring specific aims for the war effort. These aims constitute *conditions of surrender*, and without such conditions, even an initially limited war may easily slide toward totality. Significantly, also after World War II, Anscombe singled out the demand for unconditional surrender as the chief catalyst of the excesses com- mitted by the Allied forces during the war. As she says in her indictment of Harry Truman: "The connection between such a demand and the need to use the most ferocious methods of warfare will be obvious. And in itself the proposal of an unlimited objective in war is stupid and barbarous" ("Mr Truman's Degree," p. 62).

[12] Ibid., p. 79.

From "The Justice of the Present War Examined"[13]

Our policy, it might be said, is incomprehensible, except as a policy, not of opposing German injustice, but of trying to preserve the status quo and that an unjust one. Some of us may think the case clear enough; yet such argument is likely to lead us into endless controversy. It may be that we could not prove irrefutably that our government's aims are positively vicious. Some might say that the government is not clear enough about its aims for them to be vicious. Yet if this is so, the government's intention in fighting the war must still be condemned. For it is a condition of a just war that it should be fought with a just intention; not that it should not be fought with an unjust intention. If the government's intentions cannot be known to be unjust because they are vague, that vagueness itself vitiates them. But the case is even clearer than this. For the truth is that the government's professed intentions are not merely vague, but unlimited. They have not said: "When justice is done on points A, B and C, then we will stop fighting." They have talked about "sweeping away everything that Hitlerism stands for" and about "building a new order in Europe". What does this mean but that our intentions are so unlimited that there is no point at which we or the Germans could say to our government: "Stop fighting; for your conditions are satisfied."

---

[13] Ibid., pp. 74–5.

53

John Rawls (1921–2002)

The Moral Duties of Statesmen

The way a war is fought and the actions ending it endure in the historical memory of peoples and may set the stage for future war.

"Fifty Years after Hiroshima"

With his widely acclaimed work *A Theory of Justice* (1971), John Rawls almost single-handedly revived interest in – and set the stage for a vigorous debate about – liberal political philosophy. Developing and refining the social contract theories of Locke, Rousseau, and Kant, he set out to create a robust theory of just institutions, fair distributional schemes, and individual rights. It is indeed interesting to see how many of the concepts set out in *A Theory of Justice* have become commonplace in recent academic debate about liberal democracy: "justice as fairness" (the name Rawls gave to his theory), "the original position" (his name for the ideal initial-choice situation in social contract theory), "the veil of ignorance" (his description of our state of mind when we enter the original position), and "reflective equilibrium" (the dialectical process by which we reach an acceptable description of the original position), to name but a few. Responding in his later writings to criticism from communitarians, he famously described his position as being "political not metaphysical," and stressed that what one should seek in political philosophy is a workable "overlapping consensus" between various philosophical and religious viewpoints, rather than a comprehensive theory that can answer all of life's manifold challenges.[1]

---

[1] Aside from *A Theory of Justice* (Cambridge, MA: Harvard University Press, 1971), Rawls's most important work is *Political Liberalism* (New York: Columbia University Press, 1993), in which he seeks to downplay the comprehensive character of the liberalism of his former work. *Political Liberalism* can be seen as a reply to some of his communitarian critics, such as Michael Sandel, who had held that Rawls with his "original position" and "veil of ignorance" made misguided and ultimately wrongful claims about human beings and their lives in the world.

In spite of this wealth of concepts and ideas, it has often been remarked that Rawls in *A Theory of Justice* has little to say about international justice.[2] Indeed, critics have argued that his liberal principles are ill suited to addressing the international problems of war, poverty, commerce, or development.

Rawls eagerly wanted to correct this impression, and in later years – most famously in an Amnesty Lecture entitled "The Law of Peoples" in Oxford in 1993 – he set out to portray in greater detail the relevance of his contract theory for international affairs.[3] Although he also discussed just war principles in this context,[4] we here excerpt from another work dating from the same period, namely, a fifty-year retrospective on the bombing of Hiroshima and Nagasaki. While incorporating the typically Rawlsian emphasis on democratic justice and rights, the essay also brings out other points of crucial importance for the ethics of war: the responsibilities and characteristics of true statesmen, and the prudent and moral communication of values during wartime as an indispensable precondition for peaceful coexistence after war has ceased. Rawls insists that a coherent idea of *ius in bello* must also include a fair and thorough consideration of how one can bring about *ius post bellum*, justice *after* war.[5]

"Fifty Years after Hiroshima"[6]

The fiftieth year since the bombing of Hiroshima is a time to reflect about what one should think of it. Is it really a great wrong, as many now think, and many also thought then, or is it perhaps justified after all? I believe that both the fire-bombing of Japanese cities beginning in the spring of 1945 and the later atomic bombing of Hiroshima on August 6 were very great wrongs, and rightly seen as such. In order to support this opinion, I set out what I think to be the principles governing the conduct of war – *ius in bello* – of democratic peoples. These peoples[7]

---

[2]   For a good portrayal of this debate, see Patrick Hayden, *John Rawls towards a Just World Order* (Cardiff: University of Wales Press, 2002).

[3]   See John Rawls, "The Law of Peoples", in *On Human Rights: The Oxford Amnesty Lectures*, ed. Stephen Shute and Susan Hurley (New York: Basic Books, 1993), and John Rawls, *The Law of Peoples* (Cambridge, MA: Harvard University Press, 1999).

[4]   To a large extent, Rawls follows Michael Walzer and adds little that is original to just war theory as such, although the essay brings an important new dimension to Rawls's own theory.

[5]   Rawls himself does not use the term *ius post bellum*, which has recently been developed by several writers on just war, among them Brian Orend, who draws quite heavily on Rawls; see, for instance, Brian Orend, *Michael Walzer on War and Justice* (Cardiff: University of Wales Press, 2000).

[6]   From John Rawls, *Collected Papers*, ed. Samuel Freeman (Cambridge, MA: Harvard University Press, 1999), pp. 565–72. The essay is reproduced here in its entirety. It was originally published in the Summer 1995 issue of *Dissent*, pp. 323–7. Rawls acknowledges Burton Dreben, Thomas Nagel, and T. M. Scanlon for discussing the essay with him.

[7]   [*All the notes that follow are reproduced from Rawls's text:*] I sometimes use the term "peoples" to mean the same as nations, especially when I want to contrast peoples with states and a state's apparatus.

have different ends of war than nondemocratic, especially totalitarian, states, such as Germany and Japan, which sought the domination and exploitation of subjected peoples, and in Germany's case, their enslavement if not extermination.

Although I cannot properly justify them here, I begin by setting out six principles and assumptions in support of these judgments. I hope they seem not unreasonable; and certainly they are familiar, as they are closely related to much traditional thought on this subject.

1. The aim of a just war waged by a decent democratic society is a just and lasting peace between peoples, especially with its present enemy.

2. A decent democratic society is fighting against a state that is not democratic. This follows from the fact that democratic peoples do not wage war against each other;[8] and since we are concerned with the rules of war as they apply to such peoples, we assume the society fought against is nondemocratic and that its expansionist aims threatened the security and free institutions of democratic regimes and caused the war.[9]

3. In the conduct of war, a democratic society must carefully distinguish three groups: the state's leaders and officials, its soldiers, and its civilian population. The reason for these distinctions rests on the principle of responsibility: since the state fought against is not democratic, the civilian members of the society cannot be those who organized and brought on the war. This was done by its leaders and officials assisted by other elites who control and staff the state apparatus. They are responsible, they willed the war, and for doing that, they are criminals. But civilians, often kept in ignorance and swayed by state propaganda, are not.[10] And this is so even if some civilians knew better and were enthusiastic for the war. In a nation's conduct of war many such marginal cases may exist, but they are irrelevant. As for soldiers, they, just as civilians, and leaving aside the upper ranks of an officer class, are not responsible for the war, but are conscripted or in other ways forced into it, their patriotism often cruelly and cynically exploited. The grounds on which they may be attacked directly are not that they are responsible for the war but that a democratic people cannot defend itself in any other way, and defend itself it must do. About this there is no choice.

4. A decent democratic society must respect the human rights of the members of the other side, both civilians and soldiers, for two reasons. One is because they simply have these rights by the law of peoples. The other reason is to teach enemy soldiers and civilians the content of those rights by the example of how

---

[8] I assume that democratic peoples do not go to war against each other. There is considerable evidence of this important idea. See Michael Doyle's two-part article, "Kant, Liberal Legacies, and Foreign Affairs," *Philosophy and Public Affairs*, 12 (Summer/Fall 1983), pp. 205–35, 323–53. See especially his summary of the evidence in the first part, pp. 206–32.

[9] Responsibility for war rarely falls on only one side, and this must be granted. Yet some dirty hands are dirtier than others, and sometimes even with dirty hands a democratic people would still have the right and even the duty to defend itself from the other side. This is clear in World War II.

[10] Here I follow Michael Walzer's *Just and Unjust Wars* (New York: Basic Books, 1977).

they hold in their own case. In this way their significance is best brought home to them. They are assigned a certain status, the status of the members of some human society who possess rights as human persons.[11] In the case of human rights in war the aspect of status as applied to civilians is given a strict interpretation. This means, as I understand it here, that they can never be attacked directly except in times of extreme crisis, the nature of which I discuss below.

5. Continuing with the thought of teaching the content of human rights, the next principle is that just peoples by their actions and proclamations are to foreshadow during war the kind of peace they aim for and the kind of relations they seek between nations. By doing so, they show in an open and public way the nature of their aims and the kind of people they are. These last duties fall largely on the leaders and officials of the governments of democratic peoples, since they are in the best position to speak for the whole people and to act as the principle applies. Although all the preceding principles also specify duties of statesmanship, this is especially true of 4 and 5. The way a war is fought and the actions ending it endure in the historical memory of peoples and may set the stage for future war. This duty of statesmanship must always be held in view.

6. Finally, we note the place of practical means-end reasoning in judging the appropriateness of an action or policy for achieving the aim of war or for not causing more harm than good. This mode of thought-whether carried on by (classical) utilitarian reasoning, or by cost-benefit analysis, or by weighing national interests, or in other ways – must always be framed within and strictly limited by the preceding principles. The norms of the conduct of war set up certain lines that bound just action. War plans and strategies, and the conduct of battles, must lie within their limits. (The only exception, I repeat, is in times of extreme crisis.)

In connection with the fourth and fifth principles of the conduct of war, I have said that they are binding especially on the leaders of nations. They are in the most effective position to represent their people's aims and obligations, and sometimes they become statesmen. But who is a statesman? There is no office of statesman, as there is of president, or chancellor, or prime minister. The statesman is an ideal, like the ideal of the truthful or virtuous individual. Statesmen are presidents or prime ministers who become statesmen through their exemplary performance and leadership in their office in difficult and trying times and manifest strength, wisdom, and courage. They guide their people through turbulent and dangerous periods for which they are esteemed always, as one of their great statesmen.

The ideal of the statesman is suggested by the saying: the politician looks to the next election, the statesman to the next generation. It is the task of the student of philosophy to look to the permanent conditions and the real interests of a just and good democratic society. It is the task of the statesman, however, to discern these conditions and interests in practice; the statesman sees deeper and

---

[11]   For the idea of status, I am indebted to discussions of Frances Kamm and Thomas Nagel.

further than most others and grasps what needs to be done. The statesman must get it right, or nearly so, and hold fast to it. Washington and Lincoln were statesmen. Bismarck was not. He did not see Germany's real interests far enough into the future, and his judgment and motives were often distorted by his class interests and his wanting himself alone to be chancellor of Germany. Statesmen need not be selfless and may have their own interests when they hold office, yet they must be selfless in their judgments and assessments of society's interests and not be swayed, especially in war and crisis, by passions of revenge and retaliation against the enemy.

Above all, they are to hold fast to the aim of gaining a just peace, and avoid the things that make achieving such a peace more difficult. Here the proclamations of a nation should make clear (the statesman must see to this) that the enemy people are to be granted an autonomous regime of their own and a decent and full life once peace is securely reestablished. Whatever they may be told by their leaders, whatever reprisals they may reasonably fear, they are not to be held as slaves or serfs after surrender,[12] or denied in due course their full liberties; and they may well achieve freedoms they did not enjoy before, as the Germans and the Japanese eventually did. The statesman knows, if others do not, that all descriptions of the enemy people (not their rulers) inconsistent with this are impulsive and false.

Turning now to Hiroshima and the fire-bombing of Tokyo, we find that neither falls under the exemption of extreme crisis. One aspect of this is that since (let's suppose) there are no absolute rights – rights that must be respected in all circumstances – there are occasions when civilians can be attacked directly by aerial bombing. Were there times during the war when Britain could properly have bombed Hamburg and Berlin? Yes, when Britain was alone and desperately facing Germany's superior might; moreover, this period would extend until Russia had clearly beat off the first German assault in the summer and fall of 1941, and would be able to fight Germany until the end. Here the cutoff point might be placed differently, say the summer of 1942, and certainly by Stalingrad.[13] I shall not dwell on this, as the crucial matter is that under no conditions could Germany be allowed to win the war, and this for two basic reasons: first, the nature and history of constitutional democracy and its place in European culture; and second, the peculiar evil of Nazism and the enormous and uncalculable moral and political evil it represented for civilized society.

---

[12] See Churchill's remarks explaining the meaning of "unconditional surrender" in *The Hinge of Fate* (Boston: Houghton Mifflin, 1950), pp. 685–8.

[13] I might add here that a balancing of interests is not involved. Rather, we have a matter of judgment as to whether certain objective circumstances are present which constitute the extreme crisis exemption. As with any other complex concept, that of such an exemption is to some degree vague. Whether or not the concept applies rests on judgment.

The peculiar evil of Nazism needs to be understood, since in some circumstances a democratic people might better accept defeat if the terms of peace offered by the adversary were reasonable and moderate, did not subject them to humiliation, and looked forward to a workable and decent political relationship. Yet characteristic of Hitler was that he accepted no possibility at all of a political relationship with his enemies. They were always to be cowed by terror and brutality, and ruled by force. From the beginning the campaign against Russia, for example, was a war of destruction against Slavic peoples, with the original inhabitants remaining, if at all, only as serfs. When Goebbels and others protested that the war could not be won that way, Hitler refused to listen.[14]

Yet it is clear that while the extreme crisis exemption held for Britain in the early stages of the war, it never held at any time for the United States in its war with Japan. The principles of the conduct of war were always applicable to it. Indeed, in the case of Hiroshima many involved in higher reaches of the government recognized the questionable character of the bombing and that limits were being crossed. Yet during the discussions among allied leaders in June and July 1945, the weight of the practical means–end reasoning carried the day. Under the continuing pressure of war, such moral doubts as there were failed to gain an express and articulated view. As the war progressed, the heavy fire-bombing of civilians in the capitals of Berlin and Tokyo and elsewhere was increasingly accepted on the allied side. Although after the outbreak of war Roosevelt had urged both sides not to commit the inhuman barbarism of bombing civilians, by 1945 allied leaders came to assume that Roosevelt would have used the bomb on Hiroshima.[15] The bombing grew out of what had happened before.

The practical means–end reasons to justify using the atomic bomb on Hiroshima were the following:

The bomb was dropped to hasten the end of the war. It is clear that Truman and most other allied leaders thought it would do that. Another reason was that it would save lives where the lives counted are the lives of American soldiers. The lives of Japanese, military or civilian, presumably counted for less. Here the calculations of least time and most lives saved were mutually supporting. Moreover, dropping the bomb would give the Emperor and the Japanese leaders a way to save face, an important matter given Japanese samurai culture. Indeed, at the end a few top Japanese leaders wanted to make a last sacrificial stand but were overruled by others supported by the Emperor, who ordered surrender on August 12, having received word from Washington that the Emperor could stay provided it

---

[14] On Goebbels's and others' protests, see Alan Bullock, *Hitler: A Study in Tyranny* (London: Oldham's Press, 1952), chap. 12, section 5, pp. 633–44.

[15] For an account of events, see David M. McCullough, *Truman* (New York: Simon and Schuster, 1992), chap. 9, section IV, and chap. 10, pp. 390–464; and Barton Bernstein, "The Atomic Bombings Reconsidered," *Foreign Affairs*, 74 (Jan.–Feb. 1995), p. 1.

was understood that he had to comply with the orders of the American military commander. The last reason I mention is that the bomb was dropped to impress the Russians with American power and make them more agreeable with our demands. This reason is highly disputed but is urged by some critics and scholars as important.

The failure of these reasons to reflect the limits on the conduct of war is evident, so I focus on a different matter: the failure of statesmanship on the part of allied leaders and why it might have occurred. Truman once described the Japanese as beasts and to be treated as such; yet how foolish it sounds now to call the Germans or the Japanese barbarians and beasts![16] Of the Nazis and Tojo militarists, yes, but they are not the German and the Japanese people. Churchill later granted that he carried the bombing too far, led by passion and the intensity of the conflict.[17] A duty of statesmanship is not to allow such feelings, natural and inevitable as they may be, to alter the course a democratic people should best follow in striving for peace. The statesman understands that relations with the present enemy have special importance: for as I have said, war must be openly and publicly conducted in ways that make a lasting and amicable peace possible with a defeated enemy, and prepares its people for how they may be expected to be treated. Their present fears of being subjected to acts of revenge and retaliation must be put to rest; present enemies must be seen as associates in a shared and just future peace.

These remarks make it clear that, in my judgment, both Hiroshima and the fire-bombing of Japanese cities were great evils that the duties of statesmanship require political leaders to avoid in the absence of the crisis exemption. I also believe this could have been done at little cost in further casualties. An invasion was unnecessary at that date, as the war was effectively over. However, whether that is true or not makes no difference. Without the crisis exemption, those bombings are great evils. Yet it is clear that an articulate expression of the principles of just war introduced at that time would not have altered the outcome. It was simply too late. A president or prime minister must have carefully considered these questions, preferably long before, or at least when they had the time and leisure to think things out. Reflections on just war cannot be heard in the daily round of the pressure of events near the end of the hostilities; too many are anxious and impatient, and simply worn out.

Similarly, the justification of constitutional democracy and the basis of the rights and duties it must respect should be part of the public political culture and discussed in the many associations of civic society as part of one's education. It is

---

[16] See McCullough, *Truman*, p. 458, [for] the exchange between Truman and Senator Russell of Georgia in August 1945.

[17] See Martin Gilbert, *Winston Churchill: Never Despair*, vol. VIII (Boston: Houghton Mifflin, 1988), p. 259, reflecting later on Dresden.

not clearly heard in day-to-day ordinary politics, but must be presupposed as the background, not the daily subject of politics, except in special circumstances. In the same way, there was not sufficient prior grasp of the fundamental importance of the principles of just war for the expression of them to have blocked the appeal of practical means–end reasoning in terms of a calculus of lives, or of the least time to end the war, or of some other balancing of costs and benefits. This practical reasoning justifies too much, too easily, and provides a way for a dominant power to quiet any moral worries that may arise. If the principles of war are put forward at that time, they easily become so many more considerations to be balanced in the scales.

Another failure of statesmanship was not to try to enter into negotiations with the Japanese before any drastic steps such as the fire-bombing of cities or the bombing of Hiroshima were taken. A conscientious attempt to do so was morally necessary. As a democratic people, we owed that to the Japanese people – whether to their government is another matter. There had been discussions in Japan for some time about finding a way to end the war, and on June 26 the government had been instructed by the Emperor to do so.[18] It must surely have realized that with the navy destroyed and the outer islands taken, the war was lost. True, the Japanese were deluded by the hope that the Russians might prove to be their allies,[19] but negotiations are precisely to disabuse the other side of delusions of that kind. A statesman is not free to consider that such negotiations may lessen the desired shock value of subsequent attacks.

Truman was in many ways a good, at times a very good president. But the way he ended the war showed he failed as a statesman. For him it was an opportunity missed, and a loss to the country and its armed forces as well. It is sometimes said that questioning the bombing of Hiroshima is an insult to the American troops who fought the war. This is hard to understand. We should be able to look back and consider our faults after fifty years. We expect the Germans and the Japanese to do that – "*Vergangenheitsverarbeitung*," as the Germans say. Why shouldn't we? It can't be that we think we waged the war without moral error!

None of this alters Germany's and Japan's responsibility for the war nor their behavior in conducting it. Emphatically to be repudiated are two nihilist doctrines. One is expressed by Sherman's remark, "War is hell," so anything goes to get it over with as soon as one can. The other says that we are all guilty so we stand on a level and no one can blame anyone else. These are both superficial and deny all reasonable distinctions; they are invoked falsely to try to excuse our misconduct or to plead that we cannot be condemned.

The moral emptiness of these nihilisms is manifest in the fact that just and decent civilized societies – their institutions and laws, their civil life and background

---

[18] See Gerhard Weinberg, *A World at Arms* (Cambridge: Cambridge University Press, 1994), pp. 886–9.
[19] See ibid., p. 886.

culture and mores – all depend absolutely on making significant moral and political distinctions in all situations. Certainly war is a kind of hell, but why should that mean that all moral distinctions cease to hold? And granted also that sometimes all or nearly all may be to some degree guilty, that does not mean that all are equally so. There is never a time when we are free from all moral and political principles and restraints. These nihilisms are pretenses to be free of those principles and restraints that always apply to us fully.

54

Michael Walzer
(b. 1935)

Terrorism and Ethics

For we judge the assassin by his victim, and when the victim is Hitler-like in character, we are likely to praise the assassin's work, though we still do not call him a soldier.

Just and Unjust Wars

The American philosopher Michael Walzer has spent the bulk of his professional career as Professor of Social Science at the Institute for Advanced Study (Princeton, New Jersey) and as editor of the political journal *Dissent*. He is the author of several books, dealing with questions of distributive justice, multiculturalism, and toleration, but also with issues in the Jewish political tradition. Along with works by Alasdair MacIntyre, Michael Sandel, and Charles Taylor, his 1983 book *Spheres of Justice* ranks among the defining contributions to the then emerging "communitarian critique" of liberalism, instigating one of the most important debates in twentieth-century political philosophy.

In this chapter, we will be excerpting from his book *Just and Unjust Wars: A Moral Argument with Historical Illustrations.*[1] This was arguably one of the first, and by far the most influential, comprehensive non-religious expositions of just war theory. It still remains essential reading for anyone with an interest in the subject, and continues to shape much of the way in which the just war vocabulary is understood and employed in the mainstream political discussion.

It is impossible, however, to do full justice to a work of the breadth, depth, and originality of *Just and Unjust Wars* in a volume such as this. For this reason, we have chosen instead to reproduce one chapter in its entirety. Our choice – the chapter on terrorism – is obviously not arbitrary, and yet it might come as a small surprise to readers already familiar with Walzer's book. Its most famous sections, such as the opening chapter which argues against political realism, are attempts at

---

[1] New York: Basic Books, 1977; 2nd edn. 1992; 3rd edn. 2000.

establishing the viability of *any* conception of justice in war. In other, much dis-cussed sections of the book he turns to the details of the *ius ad bellum* – for instance, the definition of aggression, the principle of non-intervention, and the question of preemptive strikes. Yet strong and persuasive as he is on all these matters, Walzer's book is also remarkable, if not to say unique, for the attention it accords to questions of *ius in bello*. Most other authors seem to find little falling under that heading worthy of philosophical attention, and are happy to regard our moral intuitions as givens, and remaining questions of interpretation best left to scholars of international law. Yet as Walzer's work on the area shows – a full six chapters devoted to exploring various aspects of the war convention – there certainly are issues of moral principle to be raised also regarding the *ius in bello*. And even if, as Walzer insists, our judgments of the two sides of the just war coin are logically independent – just wars can be unjustly fought and vice versa – unless these complementary issues are raised and explored, our appreciation even of the restrictions of the *ius ad bellum* will likely remain one-sided.

The general argument of *Just and Unjust Wars* is premised, as is international law, on the notion that belligerent rights are possessed by states. In this chapter we will see him venturing into territory where that premise is challenged. Since the mid-nineteenth century, history has witnessed an upsurge of political violence committed by revolutionary groups. These groups typically act without state sponsorship, often attempting precisely to overthrow the reigning regime of the state in which they act. Yet they do claim to be involved in war of some kind, and certainly to be fighting with a just cause. Recently, the problem of understanding and morally assessing non-state-sponsored violence has come back to haunt us with a force that was hard to foresee while the Cold War was still raging.

Walzer's chapter about terrorism elaborates an informal parallel to the war con-vention, which he names "the political code." The political code enjoins, on analogy with the war convention's principle of non-combatant immunity,[2] a morally con-sequential distinction between selective assassinations and random murder. No matter what we otherwise think of the aims and methods of revolutionary violence, Walzer thus asks us to admit of a distinction between revolutionary groups targeting only representatives of the putatively oppressive regime and those targeting ordinary citizens living under that regime. Indeed, Walzer provides a chilling reminder that the blurring of the distinction, so common today, is a recent development: "terrorism in the strict sense, the random murder of innocent people, emerged as a strategy of revolutionary struggle only in the period after World War II, that is, only after it had become a feature of conventional war" (*Just and Unjust Wars*, p. 198). He adds later that "[o]ne might even feel easier about killing officials than about killing soldiers, since the state rarely conscripts its political, as it does its military agents; they have chosen officialdom as a career" (p. 200).

---

[2] See our chapters on Anscombe and Nagel (chaps. 52 and 55, this volume) for more on the philosophical implications of the principle of non-combatant immunity.

Still, while the analogy is a suggestive one, Walzer does point out a telling difference. Even if we do in some sense applaud terrorists who restrict their campaign to targeting only government officials, we will not admit them belligerent rights. While a revolutionary group naturally aims to implement a new conception of justice, in the interim they still remain tied to the civil legal order they wish to overturn.[3] Thus, revolutionary struggle remains a "civilian strategy" and civilians are, by definition not engaged in war. The killing of state officials in service of a revolutionary cause thereby remains a criminal activity, subject to the laws of the reigning regime.

From *Just and Unjust Wars*, chap. 12, "Terrorism"[4]

The Political Code

The word "terrorism" is used most often to describe revolutionary violence. That is a small victory for the champions of order, among whom the uses of terror are by no means unknown. The systematic terrorizing of whole populations is a strategy of both conventional and guerrilla war, and of established governments as well as radical movements. Its purpose is to destroy the morale of a nation or a class, to undercut its solidarity; its method is the random murder of innocent people. Randomness is the crucial feature of terrorist activity. If one wishes fear to spread and intensify over time, it is not desirable to kill specific people identified in some particular way with a regime, a party, or a policy. Death must come by chance to individual Frenchmen, or Germans, to Irish Protestants, or Jews, simply because they are Frenchmen or Germans, Protestants or Jews, until they feel themselves fatally exposed and demand that their governments negotiate for their safety.

In war, terrorism is a way of avoiding engagement with the enemy army. It represents an extreme form of the strategy of the "indirect approach."[5] It is so indirect that many soldiers have refused to call it war at all. This is a matter as much of professional pride as of moral judgment. Consider the statement of a British admiral in World War II, protesting the terror bombing of German cities: "We are a hopelessly unmilitary nation to imagine that we [can] win the war by

---

[3] Walzer elaborates a more general form of this thesis while discussing interventions in chap. 6 of *Just and Unjust Wars*.

[4] Michael Walzer, *Just and Unjust Wars*, pp. 197–206. All footnotes in the following are the author's own.

[5] But Liddell Hart, the foremost strategist of the "indirect approach," has consistently opposed terrorist tactics: see, for example, *Strategy* (2nd rev. edn., New York: Praeger, 1967), pp. 349–50 (on terror bombing).

bombing German women and children instead of defeating their army and navy."[6] The key word here is unmilitary. The admiral rightly sees terrorism as a civilian strategy. One might say that it represents the continuation of war by political means. Terrorizing ordinary men and women is first of all the work of domestic tyranny, as Aristotle wrote: "The first aim and end [of tyrants] is to break the spirit of their subjects."[7] The British described the "aim and end" of terror bombing in the same way: what they sought was the destruction of civilian morale.

Tyrants taught the method to soldiers, and soldiers to modern revolutionaries. That is a crude history; I offer it only in order to make a more precise historical point: that terrorism in the strict sense, the random murder of innocent people, emerged as a strategy of revolutionary struggle only in the period after World War II, that is, only after it had become a feature of conventional war. In both cases, in war and revolution, a kind of warrior honor stood in the way of this development, especially among professional officers and "professional revolutionaries." The increasing use of terror by far left and ultranationalist movements represents the breakdown of a political code first worked out in the second half of the nineteenth century and roughly analogous to the laws of war worked out at the same time. Adherence to this code did not prevent revolutionary militants from being called terrorists, but in fact the violence they committed bore little resemblance to contemporary terrorism. It was not random murder but assassination, and it involved the drawing of a line that we will have little difficulty recognizing as the political parallel of the line that marks off combatants from noncombatants.

The Russian populists, the IRA, and the Stern Gang

I can best describe the revolutionary "code of honor" by giving some examples of so-called terrorists who acted or tried to act in accordance with its norms. I have chosen three historical cases. The first will be readily recognizable, for Albert Camus made it the basis of his play *The Just Assassins*.

(1) In the early twentieth century, a group of Russian revolutionaries decided to kill a Tsarist official, the Grand Duke Sergei, a man personally involved in the repression of radical activity. They planned to blow him up in his carriage, and on the appointed day one of their number was in place along the Grand Duke's usual route. As the carriage drew near, the young revolutionary, a bomb hidden under his coat, noticed that his victim was not alone; on his lap he held two small children. The would-be assassin looked, hesitated, then walked quickly away. He would wait for another occasion. Camus has one of his comrades say, accepting

---

[6]   Rear Admiral L. H. K. Hamilton, quoted in David Irving, *The Destruction of Convoy PQ 17* (New York: Simon and Schuster, 1968), p. 44.

[7]   *Politics*, trans. Ernest Barker (Oxford: Oxford University Press, 1948), p. 288 (1314a).

this decision: "Even in destruction, there's a right way and a wrong way – and there are limits."[8]

(2) During the years 1938–9, the Irish Republican Army waged a bombing campaign in Britain. In the course of this campaign, a republican militant was ordered to carry a pre-set time bomb to a Coventry power station. He traveled by bicycle, the bomb in his basket, took a wrong turn, and got lost in a maze of streets. As the time for the explosion drew near, he panicked, dropped his bike, and ran off. The bomb exploded, killing five passers-by. No one in the IRA (as it was then) thought this a victory for the cause; the men immediately involved were horrified. The campaign had been carefully planned, according to a recent historian, so as to avoid the killing of innocent bystanders.[9]

(3) In November 1944, Lord Moyne, British Minister of State in the Middle East, was assassinated in Cairo by two members of the Stern Gang, a right-wing Zionist group. The two assassins were caught, minutes later, by an Egyptian policeman. One of them described the capture at his trial: "We were being followed by the constable on his motorcycle. My comrade was behind me. I saw the constable approach him . . . I would have been able to kill the constable easily, but I contented myself with . . . shooting several times into the air. I saw my comrade fall off his bicycle. The constable was almost upon him. Again, I could have eliminated the constable with a single bullet, but I did not. Then I was caught."[10]

What is common to these cases is a moral distinction, drawn by the "terrorists," between people who can and people who cannot be killed. The first category is not composed of men and women bearing arms, immediately threatening by virtue of their military training and commitment. It is composed instead of officials, the political agents of regimes thought to be oppressive. Such people, of course, are protected by the war convention and by positive international law. Characteristically (and not foolishly), lawyers have frowned on assassination, and political officials have been assigned to the class of nonmilitary persons, who are never the legitimate objects of attack.[11] But this assignment only partially represents our common moral judgments. For we judge the assassin by his victim, and when the victim is Hitler-like in character, we are likely to praise the assassin's work, though we still do not call him a soldier. The second category is less problematic: ordinary citizens, not engaged in political harming – that is, in

---

[8] *The Just Assassins*, in *Caligula and Three Other Plays*, trans. Stuart Gilbert (New York: Vintage Books, 1958), p. 258. The actual historical incident is described in Roland Gaucher, *The Terrorists: from Tsarist Russia to the OAS* (London: Secker and Warburg, 1965), pp. 49, 50 n.

[9] J. Bowyer Bell, *The Secret Army: A History of the IRA* (Cambridge, MA: MIT Press, 1974), pp. 161–2.

[10] Gerold Frank, *The Deed* (New York: Simon and Schuster, 1963), pp. 248–9.

[11] James E. Bond, *The Rules of Riot: Internal Conflict and the Law of War* (Princeton, NJ: Princeton University Press, 1974), pp. 89–90.

administering or enforcing laws thought to be unjust – are immune from attack whether or not they support those laws. Thus the aristocratic children, the Coventry pedestrians, even the Egyptian policeman (who had nothing to do with British imperialism in Palestine) – these people are like civilians in wartime. They are innocent politically as civilians are innocent militarily. It is precisely these people, however, that contemporary terrorists try to kill.

The war convention and the political code are structurally similar, and the distinction between officials and citizens parallels that between soldiers and civilians (though the two are not the same). What lies behind them both, I think, and lends them plausibility, is the moral difference between aiming and not aiming – or, more accurately, between aiming at particular people because of things they have done or are doing, and aiming at whole groups of people, indiscriminately, because of who they are. The first kind of aiming is appropriate to a limited struggle directed against regimes and policies. The second reaches beyond all limits; it is infinitely threatening to whole peoples, whose individual members are systematically exposed to violent death at any and every moment in the course of their (largely innocuous) lives. A bomb planted on a street corner, hidden in a bus station, thrown into a cafe or pub – this is aimless killing, except that the victims are likely to share what they cannot avoid, a collective identity. Since some of these victims must be immune from attack (unless liability follows from original sin), any code that directs and controls the fire of political militants is going to be at least minimally appealing. It is so much of an advance over the willful randomness of terrorist attacks. One might even feel easier about killing officials than about killing soldiers, since the state rarely conscripts its political, as it does its military agents; they have chosen officialdom as a career.

Soldiers and officials are, however, different in another respect. The threatening character of the soldier's activities is a matter of fact; the unjust or oppressive character of the official's activities is a matter of political judgment. For this reason, the political code has never attained to the same status as the war convention. Nor can assassins claim any rights, even on the basis of the strictest adherence to its principles. In the eyes of those of us whose judgments of oppression and injustice differ from their own, political assassins are simply murderers, exactly like the killers of ordinary citizens. The case is not the same with soldiers, who are not judged politically at all and who are called murderers only when they kill noncombatants. Political killing imposes risks quite unlike those of combat, risks whose character is best revealed by the fact that there is no such thing as benevolent quarantine for the duration of the political struggle. Thus the young Russian revolutionary, who eventually killed the Grand Duke, was tried and executed for murder, as were the Stern Gang assassins of Lord Moyne. All three were treated exactly like the IRA militants, also captured, who were held responsible for the deaths of ordinary citizens. That treatment seems to me appropriate, even if we share the political judgments of the men involved and defend their resort to violence. On the other hand, even if we do not share their judgments, these men are entitled to a kind of moral respect not due to terrorists, because they set limits to their actions.

The Vietcong assassination campaign

The precise limits are hard to define, as in the case of noncombatant immunity. But we can perhaps move toward a definition by looking at a guerrilla war in which officials were attacked on a large scale. Beginning at some point in the late 1950s, the NLF waged a campaign aimed at destroying the governmental structure of the South Vietnamese countryside. Between 1960 and 1965, some 7,500 village and district officials were assassinated by Vietcong militants. An American student of the Vietcong, describing these officials as the "natural leaders" of Vietnamese society, argues that "by any definition this NLF action . . . amounts to genocide."[12] This assumes that all Vietnam's natural leaders were government officials (but then, who was leading the NLF?) and hence that government officials were literally indispensable to national existence. Since these assumptions are not remotely plausible, it has to be said that "by any definition" the killing of leaders is not the same as the destruction of entire peoples. Terrorism may foreshadow genocide, but assassination does not.

On the other hand, the NLF campaign did press against the limits of the notion of officialdom as I have been using it. The Front tended to include among officials anyone who was paid by the government, even if the work he was doing – as a public health officer, for example – had nothing to do with the particular policies the NLF opposed.[13] And it tended to assimilate into officialdom people like priests and landowners who used their nongovernmental authority in specific ways on behalf of the government. They did not kill anyone, apparently, just because he was a priest or a landowner; the assassination campaign was planned with considerable attention to the details of individual action, and a concerted effort was made "to ensure that there were no unexplained killings."[14] Still, the range of vulnerability was widened in disturbing ways.

One might argue, I suppose, that any official is by definition engaged in the political efforts of the (putatively) unjust regime, just as any soldier, whether he is actually fighting or not, is engaged in the war effort. But the variety of activities sponsored and paid for by the modern state is extraordinary, and it seems intemperate and extravagant to make all such activities into occasions for assassination. Assuming that the regime is in fact oppressive, one should look for agents of

[12]   Douglas Pike, *Viet Cong: The Organization and Techniques of the National Liberation Front of South Vietnam* (Cambridge, MA: MIT Press, 1966), p. 248.

[13]   Jeffrey Race, *War Comes to Long An* (Berkeley: University of California Press, 1972), p. 83, which suggests that it was precisely the *best* public health officers, teachers, and so on who were attacked – because they constituted a possible anti-communist leadership.

[14]   Pike, *Viet Cong*, p. 250.

oppression and not simply for government agents. As for private persons, they seem to me immune entirely. They are subject, of course, to the conventional forms of social and political pressure (which are conventionally intensified in guerrilla wars) but not to political violence. Here the case is the same with citizens as with civilians: if their support for the government or the war were allowable as a reason for killing them, the line that marks off immune from vulnerable persons would quickly disappear. It is worth stressing that political assassins generally don't want that line to disappear; they have reasons for taking careful aim and avoiding indiscriminate murder. "We were told," a Vietcong guerrilla reported to his American captors, "that in Singapore the rebels on certain days would dynamite every 67th streetcar . . . the next day it might be every 30th, and so on; but that this hardened the hearts of the people against the rebels because so many people died needlessly."[15]

I have avoided noticing until now that most political militants don't regard themselves as assassins at all but rather as executioners. They are engaged, or so they regularly claim, in a revolutionary version of vigilante justice. This suggests another reason for killing only some officials and not others, but it is entirely a self-description. Vigilantes in the usual sense apply conventional conceptions of criminality, though in a rough and ready way. Revolutionaries champion a new conception, about which there is unlikely to be wide agreement. They hold that officials are vulnerable because or insofar as they are actually guilty of "crimes against the people." The more impersonal truth is that they are vulnerable, or more vulnerable than ordinary citizens, simply because their activities are open to such descriptions. The exercise of political power is a dangerous business. Saying this, I do not mean to defend assassination. It is most often a vile politics, as vigilante justice is most often a bad kind of law enforcement; its agents are usually gangsters, and sometimes madmen, in political dress. And yet "just assassinations" are at least possible, and men and women who aim at that kind of killing and renounce every other kind need to be marked off from those who kill at random – not as doers of justice, necessarily, for one can disagree about that, but as revolutionaries with honor. They do not want the revolution, as one of Camus' characters says, "to be loathed by the whole human race."

However the political code is specified, terrorism is the deliberate violation of its norms. For ordinary citizens are killed and no defense is offered – none could be offered – in terms of their individual activities. The names and occupations of the dead are not known in advance; they are killed simply to deliver a message of fear to others like themselves. What is the content of the message? I suppose it could be anything at all; but in practice terrorism, because it is directed against entire peoples or classes, tends to communicate the most extreme and brutal intentions – above all, the tyrannical repression, removal, or mass murder of the population under attack. Hence contemporary terrorist campaigns are most often

[15]   Ibid., p. 251.

focused on people whose national existence has been radically devalued: the Protestants of Northern Ireland, the Jews of Israel, and so on. The campaign announces the devaluation. That is why the people under attack are so unlikely to believe that compromise is possible with their enemies. In war, terrorism is associated with the demand for unconditional surrender and, in similar fashion, tends to rule out any sort of compromise settlement.

In its modern manifestations, terror is the totalitarian form of war and politics. It shatters the war convention and the political code. It breaks across moral limits beyond which no further limitation seems possible, for within the categories of civilian and citizen, there isn't any smaller group for which immunity might be claimed (except children; but I don't think children can be called "immune" if their parents are attacked and killed). Terrorists anyway make no such claim; they kill anybody. Despite this, terrorism has been defended, not only by the terrorists themselves, but also by philosophical apologists writing on their behalf. The political defenses mostly parallel those that are offered whenever soldiers attack civilians. They represent one or another version of the argument from military necessity. It is said, for example, that there is no alternative to terrorist activity if oppressed peoples are to be liberated. And it is said, further, that this has always been so: terrorism is the only means and so it is the ordinary means of destroying oppressive regimes and founding new nations.[16] The cases I have already worked through suggest the falsity of these assertions. Those who make them, I think, have lost their grip on the historical past; they suffer from a malign forgetfulness, erasing all moral distinctions along with the men and women who painfully worked them out.

Violence and Liberation

Jean-Paul Sartre and the Battle of Algiers

But there is another argument which, because of the currency it has gained, must be taken up here, even though it has no immediate analogue in wartime debates. It has been put forward in its starkest form by Sartre in a justification of FLN terrorism in Algeria, published as a preface to Frantz Fanon's *The Wretched of the Earth*. The summary lines of Sartre's argument are these:[17]

> To shoot down a European is to kill two birds with one stone, to destroy an oppressor and the man he oppresses at the same time: there remains a dead man and a free man.

[16] The argument, I suppose, goes back to Machiavelli, though most of his descriptions of the necessary violence of founders and reformers have to do with the killing of particular people, members of the old ruling class: see *The Prince*, chap. VIII, and *Discourses*, I:9, for examples.

[17] *The Wretched of the Earth*, trans. Constance Harrington (New York: Grove Press, 1968), pp. 18–19.

In his usual fashion, with a certain zest for Hegelian melodrama, Sartre is here describing what he takes to be an act of psychological liberation. Only when the slave turns on his master, physically confronts him and kills him, does he create himself as a free human being. The master dies; the slave is reborn. Even if this were a believable picture of the terrorist act, the argument is not persuasive; it is open to two obvious and crippling questions. First, is the one-to-one relation necessary? Did it take one dead European to make one free Algerian? If so, there were not enough Europeans living in Algeria; more would have had to be brought over if the Algerian people were to free themselves by Sartrean means. If not it must follow that some one else besides the man-who-kills can be liberated. . . . How? By watching? By reading about the murder in the newspaper? It is hard to see how vicarious experience can play an important part in a process of personal liberation (as described by an existentialist philosopher).

The second question raises more familiar issues: will any European do? Unless Sartre thinks all Europeans, including children, are oppressors, he cannot believe that. But if it is only liberating to attack and kill an agent of oppression, we are back with the political code. From Sartre's perspective, that cannot be right, since the men and women he is defending had explicitly rejected that code. They killed Europeans at random, as in the well-known scene from the (historically accurate) film *The Battle of Algiers*, in which a bomb is set off in a milk bar where French teenagers are drinking and dancing.[18]

MILK BAR. EXPLOSION. OUTSIDE. DAY.

The jukebox is flung into the middle of the street. There is blood, stripes of flesh, material . . . the white smoke and shouts, weeping, hysterical girls' screams. One of them no longer has an arm and runs around howling despairingly; it is impossible to control her . . . The sounds of sirens is heard . . . The ambulances arrive.

Such an event is not easily reconstructed as an existentialist encounter between masters and slaves.

Certainly, there are historical moments when armed struggle is necessary for the sake of human freedom. But if dignity and self-respect are to be the outcomes of that struggle, it cannot consist of terrorist attacks upon children. One can argue that such attacks are the inevitable products of oppression, and in a sense, I suppose, that is right. Hatred, fear, and the lust for domination are the psychological marks of oppressed and oppressor alike, and their acting out on either side, can be said to be radically determined. The mark of a revolutionary struggle against oppression, however, is not this incapacitating rage and random violence, but restraint and self-control. The revolutionary reveals his freedom in the same

---

[18] *Gillo Pontecorvo's The Battle of Algiers*, ed. PierNico Solinas (New York: Scribner, 1973), pp. 79–80.

way as he earns it, by directly confronting his enemies and refraining from attacks on anyone else. It was not only to save the innocent that revolutionary militants worked out the distinction between officials and ordinary citizens, but also to save themselves from killing the innocent. Whatever its strategic value, the political code is intrinsically connected to psychological liberation. Among men and women trapped in a bloody struggle, it is the key to self-respect. The same thing can be said of the war convention: in the context of a terrible coerciveness, soldiers most clearly assert their freedom when they obey the moral law.

55

Thomas Nagel (b. 1937)

The Logic of Hostility

> Once the door is opened to calculations of utility and national interest, the usual speculations about the future of freedom, peace, and economic prosperity can be brought to bear to ease the consciences of those responsible for a certain number of charred babies.
>
> "War and Massacre"

Thomas Nagel, professor at New York University's Faculties of Law and Philosophy, is among the most popular and widely read philosophers of his generation. Monographs and collections such *The Possibility of Altruism* (1970), *Mortal Questions* (1979), *The View from Nowhere* (1986), and *Equality and Partiality* (1991), connecting ethics and political philosophy with issues in epistemology and philosophy of mind, are read and cherished by specialists and the general audience alike.

In what follows we will be excerpting from his essay "War and Massacre,"[1] written, like Michael Walzer's *Just and Unjust Wars*, in response to American atrocities committed in Vietnam. Like the almost identically entitled article by his erstwhile teacher G. E. M. Anscombe, Nagel's article addresses the moral and practical implications of non-combatant immunity. Unlike Anscombe, however, who worked largely from within a virtue-ethical tradition looking back to Aristotle and Aquinas, Nagel takes up the problem from the particular vantage point provided by deontological ethics, drawing inspiration from the work of Immanuel Kant. Virtue ethics and deontology are alike, however, in opposing *consequentialism*, the notion that only the total outcome of an action is relevant to assessing its moral quality. Underlying the distinction, Nagel claims, is the perennial philosophical problem of means and ends. Consequentialism, taken to its logical extreme, holds that any

---

[1] Originally published in *Philosophy and Public Affairs*, 1 (Oxford: Basil Blackwell, 1972), pp. 123–44. Reprinted in *Mortal Questions* (Cambridge: Cambridge University Press, 1979), pp. 53–74. Page references are to this edition.

means whatsoever can be sanctioned by an important enough end. By contrast, Nagel's deontological *absolutism* holds that certain means are absolutely prohibited, no matter what the ends.

In this article, the specific means–ends problematic that Nagel has in mind is that of waging war on civilian populations with the aim of exerting indirect political pressure on governments. Here, what may at first blush appear to be a relatively anemic difference over philosophical principle, may turn out to have dramatic consequences in practice.

From "War and Massacre"[2]

The policy of attacking the civilian population in order to induce an enemy to surrender, or to damage his morale, seems to have been widely accepted in the civilized world, and seems to be accepted still, at least if the stakes are high enough. It gives evidence of a moral conviction that the deliberate killing of noncombatants – women, children, old people – is permissible if enough can be gained by it. This follows from the more general position that any means can in principle be justified if it leads to a sufficiently worthy end. Such an attitude is evident not only in the more spectacular current weapons systems but also in the day-to-day conduct of the nonglobal war in Indo-China: the indiscriminate destructiveness of antipersonnel weapons, napalm, and aerial bombardment; cruelty to prisoners; massive relocation of civilians; destruction of crops; and so forth. An absolutist position opposes to this the view that certain acts cannot be justified no matter what the consequences. Among those acts is murder – the deliberate killing of the harmless: civilians, prisoners of war, and medical personnel.

In the present war such measures are sometimes said to be regrettable, but they are generally defended by reference to military necessity and the importance of the long-term consequences of success or failure in the war. I shall pass over the inadequacy of this consequentialist defense in its own terms. (That is the dominant form of moral criticism of the war, for it is part of what people mean when they ask, 'Is it worth it?') I am concerned rather to account for the inappropriateness of offering any defense of that kind for such actions.

Still, in spite of its apparent clarity, Nagel warns us against expecting easy solutions from adopting an absolutist stance. We should emphatically not adopt absolutism on utilitarian grounds, as it were; indeed, absolutism can itself amount to a "paradoxical position".

[2]   Ibid., pp. 57–8.

From "War and Massacre"[3]

Once the door is opened to calculations of utility and national interest, the usual speculations about the future of freedom, peace, and economic prosperity can be brought to bear to ease the consciences of those responsible for a certain number of charred babies.

For this reason alone it is important to understand what is wrong with the frame of mind which allows such arguments to begin. But it is also important to understand absolutism in the cases where it genuinely conflicts with utility. Despite its appeal, it is a paradoxical position, for it can require that one refrain from choosing the lesser of two evils when that is the only choice one has. And it is additionally paradoxical because, unlike pacifism, it allows one to do horrible things to people in some circumstances but not in others.

These "horrible things" that even absolutism may come to allow are usually thought justified by reference to a principle of double effect, about which Nagel now pauses to express some concern. His claim is not that the doctrine of double effect is theoretically flawed, but rather that it is vulnerable to sophistical abuse on a case-by-case basis, introducing "uncertainty where there need not be uncertainty" (p. 60).

From "War and Massacre"[4]

Because of casuistical problems like this, I prefer to stay with the original, unanalyzed distinction between what one does to people and what merely happens to them as a result of what one does. The law of double effect provides an approximation to that distinction in many cases, and perhaps it can be sharpened to the point where it does better than that. Certainly the original distinction itself needs clarification, particularly since some of the things we do to people involve things happening to them as a result of other things we do. In a case like the one discussed, however, it is clear that by bombing the village one slaughters and maims the civilians in it. Whereas by giving the only available medicine to one of two sufferers from a disease, one does not kill the other or deliberately allow him to die, even if he dies as a result.

Having clarified these technicalities, Nagel moves to the core of his argument. Here the Kantian influence runs deeper than the *en passant* reference to the

---

[3] Ibid., p. 59.
[4] Ibid., p. 61.

principle of treating a person as "an end in himself" might suggest. At the heart of Nagel's argument is the notion that "hostility or aggression should be directed at its true object" ("War and Massacre," p. 66): one can subject a person to hostile treatment only because of something that person *does*; pertinently, carry a weapon and threaten its use. Moreover, the hostile treatment must be directed at the person *in virtue of the threat posed* – once the person is disarmed, hostile treatment must cease. Finally, it is *absolutely prohibited* to channel the hostile treatment through some third, innocent party, even where it is generally acknowledged that this would greatly facilitate the disarmament. This is not, Nagel adds, a moral principle applying exclusively, or even especially, to war; on the contrary, its force derives precisely from its being of perfectly general nature, applying to all forms of human interaction.

From "War and Massacre"[5]

Absolutist restrictions in warfare appear to be of two types: restrictions on the class of person at whom aggression or violence may be directed and restrictions on the manner of attack, given that the object falls within that class. These can be combined, however, under the principle that hostile treatment of any person must be justified in terms of something *about that person* which makes the treatment appropriate. Hostility is a personal relation, and it must be suited to its target. One consequence of this condition will be that certain persons may not be subjected to hostile treatment in war at all, since nothing about them justifies such treatment. Others will be proper objects of hostility only in certain circumstances, or when they are engaged in certain pursuits. And the appropriate manner and extent of hostile treatment will depend on what is justified by the particular case.

A coherent view of this type will hold that extremely hostile behavior toward another is compatible with treating him as a person – even perhaps as an end in himself. This is possible only if one has not automatically stopped treating him as a person as soon as one starts to fight with him. If hostile, aggressive, or combative treatment of others always violated the condition that they be treated as human beings, it would be difficult to make further distinctions on that score *within* the class of hostile actions. That point of view, on the level of international relations, leads to the position that if complete pacifism is not accepted, no holds need be barred at all, and we may slaughter and massacre to our hearts' content, if it seems advisable. Such a position is often expressed in discussions of war crimes.

But the fact is that ordinary people do not believe this about conflicts, physical or otherwise, between individuals, and there is no more reason why it should be true of conflicts between nations. There seems to be a perfectly natural conception of the distinction between fighting clean and fighting dirty. To fight dirty

---

[5] Ibid., pp. 64–5, 66–7.

is to direct one's hostility or aggression not at its proper object, but at a peripheral target which may be more vulnerable, and through which the proper object can be attacked indirectly. This applies in a fist fight, an election campaign, a duel, or a philosophical argument. If the concept is general enough to apply to all these matters, it should apply to war – both to the conduct of individual soldiers and to the conduct of nations. . . .

The importance of such restrictions may vary with the seriousness of the case; and what is unjustifiable in one case may be justified in a more extreme one. But they all derive from a single principle: that hostility or aggression should be directed at its true object. This means both that it should be directed at the person or persons who provoke it and that it should aim more specifically at what is provocative about them. The second condition will determine what form the hostility may appropriately take.

It is evident that some idea of the relation in which one should stand to other people underlies this principle, but the idea is difficult to state. I believe it is roughly this: whatever one does to another person intentionally must be aimed at him as a subject, with the intention that he receive it as a subject. It should manifest an attitude to *him* rather than just to the situation, and he should be able to recognize it and identify himself as its object. The procedures by which such an attitude is manifested need not be addressed to the person directly. Surgery, for example, is not a form of personal confrontation but part of a medical treatment that can be offered to a patient face to face and received by him as a response to his needs and the natural outcome of an attitude toward *him*.

Hostile treatment, unlike surgery, is already addressed to a person, and does not take its interpersonal meaning from a wider context. But hostile acts can serve as the expression or implementation of only a limited range of attitudes to the person who is attacked. Those attitudes in turn have as objects certain real or presumed characteristics or activities of the person which are thought to justify them. When this background is absent, hostile or aggressive behavior can no longer be intended for the reception of the victim as a subject. Instead it takes on the character of a purely bureaucratic operation. This occurs when one attacks someone who is not the true object of one's hostility – the true object may be someone else, who can be attacked through the victim; or one may not be manifesting a hostile attitude toward anyone, but merely using the easiest available path to some desired goal. One finds oneself not facing or addressing the victim at all, but operating on him – without the larger context of personal interaction that surrounds a surgical operation.

If absolutism is to defend its claim to priority over considerations of utility, it must hold that the maintenance of a direct interpersonal response to the people one deals with is a requirement which no advantages can justify one in abandoning. The requirement is absolute only if it rules out any calculation of what would justify its violation. I have said earlier that there may be circumstances so extreme that they render an absolutist position untenable. One may find then that one has no choice but to do something terrible. Nevertheless, even in such cases absolutism retains its force in that one cannot claim *justification* for the violation. It does not become *all right*.

The above reflections, though theoretically complex, enjoin relatively clear-cut restrictions on the class of allowable objects of attack, entailing an absolute prohibition on targeting civilian populations. But more originally, they also say something about *the manner* in which even appropriate targets may be attacked. Nagel speaks of "weapons [which] attack the men, not the soldiers" ("War and Massacre," p. 71), abandoning "any attempt to discriminate in their effects between the combatant and the human being" (p. 72). Certain weapons – for instance napalm, dum-dum bullets, and various poison gases – seek not only to disarm, but to dismember, disfigure, and disable. They thereby violate the absolutist restriction that hostile treatment, even of legitimate targets, must aim "specifically at what is provocative about them" (p. 66). Similar considerations also restrict the manner in which a country may be attacked: targets must be chosen in virtue of the specific threat posed. Nagel would thereby oppose the practice, apparently becoming more and more commonplace, of targeting infrastructural items such as power grids, water purification plants, and other facilities needed to sustain communal life.

From "War and Massacre"[6]

First let us see how it implies that attacks on some people are allowed, but not attacks on others. It may seem paradoxical to assert that to fire a machine gun at someone who is throwing hand grenades at your emplacement is to treat him as a human being. Yet the relation with him is direct and straightforward. The attack is aimed specifically against the threat presented by a dangerous adversary, and not against a peripheral target through which he happens to be vulnerable but which has nothing to do with that threat. For example, you might stop him by machine-gunning his wife and children, who are standing nearby, thus distracting him from his aim of blowing you up and enabling you to capture him. But if his wife and children are not threatening your life, that would be to treat them as means with a vengeance.

    This, however, is just Hiroshima on a smaller scale. One objection to weapons of mass annihilation – nuclear, thermonuclear, biological, or chemical – is that their indiscriminateness disqualifies them as direct instruments for the expression of hostile relations. In attacking the civilian population, one treats neither the military enemy nor the civilians with that minimal respect which is owed to them as human beings. This is clearly true of the direct attack on people who present

---

[6] Ibid., 69–70, 72.

no threat at all. But it is also true of the character of the attack on those who *are* threatening you, i.e., the government and military forces of the enemy. Your aggression is directed against an area of vulnerability quite distinct from any threat presented by them which you may be justified in meeting. You are taking aim at them through the mundane life and survival of their countrymen, instead of aiming at the destruction of their military capacity. And of course it does not require hydrogen bombs to commit such crimes. . . .

Finally, the same condition of appropriateness to the true object of hostility should limit the scope of attacks on an enemy country: its economy, agriculture, transportation system, and so forth. Even if the parties to a military conflict are considered to be not armies or governments but entire nations (which is usually a grave error), that does not justify one nation in warring against every aspect or element of another nation. That is not justified in a conflict between individuals, and nations are even more complex than individuals, so the same reasons apply. Like a human being, a nation is engaged in countless other pursuits while waging war, and it is not in those respects that it is an enemy.

56

James Turner Johnson (b. 1938)

Contemporary Just War

> To protect and preserve values is the only justifying cause for the use of force
> that is admitted in Western moral tradition.
> > "Does Defense of Values by Force Remain a Moral Possibility?"

The awesome technological advances in warfare during the twentieth century have led many thoughtful people to question whether the good achieved by resort to armed force can ever be made proportionate to the evils which inevitably follow in its wake. By contrast, other voices have argued for the continued relevance of the just war idea, not least among them James Turner Johnson, who for many years has been a professor at Rutgers University. In numerous writings, Johnson (who once studied under Paul Ramsey) has aimed to show how the most effective way to frame the questions that presently confront us is not by rejecting but rather by revisiting two thousand years of ethical reflection on war. Johnson has also done pioneering work on Christian and Islamic approaches to war, aiming to show that amid all the cultural and theological differences, several of the crucial questions and answers within the two faiths overlap and may even enrich each other.[1]

The two texts of Johnson's that we reproduce below deal with the relevance of just war theorizing in the face of (a) the nuclear threat and (b) the lack of discrimination between combatants and non-combatants in modern war. Refusing to move toward either a total pacifism or a resigned realism, Johnson defends the use of just war categories in both contexts.

---

[1] Johnson's most important works on the just war tradition and its relationship to other attitudes to the use of armed force are *Just War Tradition and the Restraint of War* (Princeton, NJ: Princeton University Press, 1981) and *The Quest for Peace* (Princeton, NJ: Princeton University Press, 1987). Among his contributions to the debate about Islam and Christianity, *The Holy War Idea in Islamic and Western Traditions* (University Park: Pennsylvania State University Press, 1997) should be mentioned.

Note that the line of argument employed in connection with nuclear war is to a significant degree directed against the argument made by the US Catholic Bishops (see chapter 57, this volume).

From "Does Defense of Values by Force Remain a Moral Possibility?"[2]

Two deep and broad streams of moral reflection on war run through Western history. These streams have their thematic origin in a single fundamental question: Is it ever morally allowable to employ force in the protection and preservation of values? The moral tradition of pacifism has resulted from a negative response to this question, given in various ways under various historical circumstances. A positive answer, given in ways no less conditioned by historical circumstance yet with a similar depth of underlying consistency and wholeness, has produced the other moral tradition on force and violence, which it is both convenient and proper to call by a familiar name: just war tradition.[3] We should note two characteristic facts about this tradition.

First, it is a moral response to the question of value and force that is not only historically deep but is a product of reflection and action across the whole breadth of this culture's experience. It is not a moral doctrine in the narrow sense, reflecting the attitudes only of those sectors of the culture, like religion, often conceived as having a specialized function of moralizing cut off from the rest of human existence. This tradition has often found expression, to be sure, in church law and theological reflection; yet it also appears in codifications and theories of international law, in military manuals on how rightly to conduct war, and, as Michael Walzer has shown in *Just and Unjust Wars*, in the judgments and reactions of common people. In short, this tradition encapsulates something of how we in this culture respond morally to the question of protection of value by force; it is not the only response, for pacifist rejection of force parallels it through history, but it is a fundamental one, revealing how we characteristically think about morality and war and defining the terms for our reflections in new or changing circumstances.

The second characteristic fact about just war tradition is that it preserves two kinds of moral response to the question of value and force, not merely one: limitation always accompanies justification. The response that says, yes, here are some conditions in which it is morally right to use force to protect value goes on

---

[2] From *The Parameters of Military Ethics*, ed. Lloyd J. Matthews and Dale E. Brown (Washington, DC: Pergamon-Brassey's, 1989), pp. 3–4. The article first appeared (with a slightly different title) in the spring 1985 issue of the journal *Parameters*.

[3] In other contexts, Johnson has also defined a third tradition of moral restraint, namely, the so-called perpetual peace idea which he finds in Immanuel Kant, with roots back to, among others, Dante Alighieri (see Johnson, *The Quest for Peace*).

to set limits to what may rightly be done toward that end. This second element in the response is determined by the nature of the value or values to be protected; thus the need for limitation is built into the need to protect value as a necessary correlate. This means in general that unlimited or even disproportionately large amounts of force are not what is justified when the use of force to protect values is itself justified. Just war tradition, as recognized by such contemporary commentators as Paul Ramsey, William V. O'Brien, and, as already mentioned, Walzer, is a moral tradition of justifiable and limited war. What has come to be known as the *ius ad bellum* has to do with the question of justification, while that of limitation is addressed by the *ius in bello*. These are interconnected areas, but the priority, logical as well as historical, is with the former: only after the fundamental question is answered about the moral justification of employing force to protect value does the second question, about the morally requisite limits governing the use of that force, in turn arise. Problems arising in the *ius in bello* context may cause us to want to reflect further about the nature of the values we hold, the threat against them, and the means we may use to defend them; yet such further reflection means only that we must again enter the arenas of the "war decision,"[4] the *ius ad bellum*.

It is often claimed that the development of nuclear weapons has made this traditional way of thinking about morality and war obsolete and irrelevant. From what I have said, it should be clear that I think this is not the case. . . . We do not do well to repudiate this tradition of moral reflection from the past; doing so merely isolates us from the wisdom of others surely no less morally or intellectually acute than we, who in their own historical context have faced problems analogous to our own about whether and how to employ force in the defense of values. It is thus better to use this tradition consciously, trying to learn from it and with it, even in the nuclear age, than it is to forget it and then have to reinvent it. . . .

To protect and preserve values is the only justifying cause for the use of force that is admitted in Western moral tradition. Classically the use of force in response to a threat to values was justified in four ways: to protect the innocent, to recover something wrongly taken, to punish evil, and to defend against a wrongful attack in progress.

Johnson next argues against the tendency, prevalent in the contemporary setting, to restrict the *ius ad bellum* to simple defense against attack. He maintains on the contrary that the other traditional rationales (discussed in the passage above) also maintain their relevance.

---

[4] [*Author's note:*] The term is William V. O'Brien's and is meant by him to emphasize the difference in order of priority between the *ius ad bellum* and the *ius in bello*, which has to do with "war-fighting" once the initial decision to make war has been made. See O'Brien, *The Conduct of Just and Limited War* (New York: Praeger, 1981), esp. chaps. 1–3.

From "Does Defense of Values by Force Remain a Moral Possibility?"[5]

[C]oncentrating solely on the rightness of defense against aggression, while admittedly a moral justification for the use of force, has led us to think of strategic nuclear deterrence by threat of catastrophe as morally right, while ruling out lesser levels of force as possible responses to threats to value, even while these latter are more justifiable from the broader perspectives of just war tradition.

In short, we would do well to remember what many in our present debate have either forgotten or systematically ignored: that circumstances may come into being in human history in which the use of force, at appropriate levels and discriminatingly directed, may be the morally preferable means for the protection and preservation of values. In forgetting or ignoring this, sometimes in the name of ostensibly moral considerations, those who would reject such a use of force are in fact choosing a less moral course than the one historically given form in the tradition which says that just war must also be limited war. . . .

May values ever be defended by forceful means? Answering this question requires us to think, first, about the nature of the values to be protected and the interrelation among values. We do this normally not by reflection but by affirmation. Hence the following from John Stuart Mill:

> War is an ugly thing, but not the ugliest of things. The decayed and degraded state of moral and patriotic feeling which thinks nothing *worth* a war, is worse. . . . A man who has nothing which he cares about more than he does about his personal safety is a miserable creature who has no chance of being free, unless made and kept so by the exertions of better men than himself.[6]

Mill in this context alludes to the values from which he speaks, but the salient fact about this statement is his ranking of relative values. He does not deny the value of personal safety; yet it is not for him the *highest* value. He does not deny the ugliness of war; he only affirms that in the ranking of priorities it is not the *worst* evil. Mill was, of course, a utilitarian in ethics; yet such priority ranking of values is not a feature unique to utilitarianism and to be dismissed by all non-utilitarians. Such ranking is indeed a feature of *any* ethic, for the service of one value often conflicts with the service of another, and there must be some way of deciding among them.

Johnson goes on to compare Mill's ranking of values with the one proposed by the famous humanist Erasmus, who situated war at the bottom of the value scale. (As

---

[5] Matthews and Brown (eds.), *The Parameters*, pp. 7–8.

[6] From John Stuart Mill, "The Contest in America," in *Dissertations and Discussions* (Boston: William V. Spencer, 1867), pp. 208–9.

Erasmus says: "Indeed, what realm . . . can be weighed against the life, the blood, of so many thousand men?"[7]). Johnson holds that the disagreement between the Erasmian and the Millian positions over the placing of war among human pursuits is crucial even to the present-day debate. Against those who follow Erasmus in all but rejecting war and thereby portraying war in itself as savage, gruesome, and utterly destructive, Johnson presents the following just war arguments.

From "Does Defense of Values by Force Remain a Moral Possibility?"[8]

First, while there is no need to deny the charm of an idealistic vision of world community, such a conception of an ideal that is not yet a reality (and may never become one) should not subtract from the quite genuine value to be found in the nation-state system or, more particularly, in a national community like our own. Historically the roots of the nation-state system are in the need to organize human affairs so as to minimize conflict while preserving the unique cultural identities of different peoples. It can be argued plausibly that it still fulfills these functions – imperfectly, to be sure, but with nothing better currently at hand. Likewise, the personal security, justice, freedom, and domestic peace provided in a liberal democratic nation-state like the United States are not to be dismissed lightly by reference to a utopian vision in which these and other values would all be present in greater measure. We must always, as moral beings, measure reality against our ideals; yet to reject the penultimate goods secured by the real because they do not measure up to the ultimate goods envisioned in the ideal is to ensure the loss of even the penultimate goods that we now enjoy. The ultimate would certainly be better; yet in the meantime, we have the obligation to hold as fast as possible to the values at hand, even though doing so must inevitably incur costs. A positive response to the original just war question recognizes this, as did Mill; Erasmus and his contemporary idealistic descendants have not.

Second, if force is to be used to protect values, it is not trivia that are to be protected but values of fundamental worth. . . . Equally, I believe, not to be reduced to the trivial or frivolous is Walzer's perception, expressed throughout *Just and Unjust Wars*, that the justification for fighting lies in the recognition of evil and revulsion against it. Walzer's negative way of putting the matter is important for another reason: it reminds us that we do not have to be able to give an extensive and comprehensive listing of all values that may be protected and in what ranking in order to know *that there are* such values; they will be apparent when they are violated or threatened with violation.

---

[7] From Desiderius Erasmus [Erasmus of Rotterdam], "Letter to Antoon van Bergen" (no. 288), in *The Conference of Erasmus, Letters 142 to 297*, trans. R. A. B. Minors and D. F. S. Thomson (Toronto: University of Toronto Press, 1975), lines 62–3.

[8] Matthews and Brown (eds.), *The Parameters*, pp. 10–11.

Third, knowing that some wars have resulted from the aggressively self-assertive characters of rulers does not mean that war may never be anything else. . . . In our own age we must surely make a distinction between, for example, the war made by Hitler and that made by Churchill; nor is it particularly useful to reduce the rise and fall of relations between the United States and the Soviet Union to the personalities of a Carter and a Brezhnev, an Andropov or Chernenko and a Reagan. A manichean dismissal of everything military as "militaristic" is also an uncalled-for reductionism that makes military preparedness itself an evil, not an instrument for good or ill in ways to be determined by human choices.

Finally, neither in Erasmus' time nor in our own is it right to represent war as the irreducible *summum malum.* . . . [Furthermore, it is wrong to assimilate] all contemporary war to catastrophic nuclear war. Let us dwell on this for a moment.

Who would want a nuclear holocaust? Yet the effort to avoid such a catastrophe is not itself justification for rejection of the possibility that lower levels of force may justifiably be employed to protect value. This is, nonetheless, the clear import of the argument when limited conventional war is collapsed into limited nuclear war by reference to the threat of escalation and nuclear war of any extent is collapsed into catastrophic holocaust on a global scale. Such an argument has the effect of making any contemporary advocate of the use of force to protect values an advocate instead of the total destruction of humankind or even of all life on earth. It should hardly need to be said that such rhetorical hyperbole is unjustified; no one who argues from just war tradition, with its strong emphasis on counting the costs and estimating the probability of success of any projected military action, should be represented as guilty of befriending the idea of nuclear holocaust.

Yet this collapsing of categories is also wrong historically. War in the nuclear age has not been global catastrophe but a continuation of conventional warfare limited in one or several ways – by geography, goals, targets, means. This arena of contemporary limited warfare is one in which traditional moral categories for judging war are very much at home, as such different writers as William V. O'Brien and Michael Walzer have, in their respective ways, both recognized. The issue, then, is not of the prohibition of all means of defense in the nuclear age, because the assimilation of all contemporary war to the *summum malum* of nuclear holocaust is invalid; it is rather the perennial question of when and how force may be used for the defense of values.

In the course of the twentieth century, civilian losses in war have grown dramatically. Claiming that such losses are inevitable in modern war, some military leaders have come to question the relevance of – or sometimes openly to disregard – the norm of non-combatant immunity. The refusal (or professed inability) to preserve the distinction between combatants and non-combatants has arisen most frequently in insurgency warfare, where the civilian population is often drawn into the conflict. While pacifist critics of war have argued against all use of armed force because of the severe and obvious dangers to civilians posed by modern warfare, Johnson, however, insists on the continuing applicability of the traditional *ius in bello* idea of discrimination:

From "Maintaining the Protection of Non-combatants"[9]

The increase in the magnitude, deliberateness, and variety of harm to non-combatants in present-day armed conflicts poses a special irony, since this same century has witnessed impressive developments in international law designed to protect non-combatants, as well as intense and sustained moral argument on behalf of such protection. Though I have focused on Western moral tradition in this article, concern to distinguish non-combatants from combatants and to protect them from harm during armed conflict is by no means unique to the West, but is recognized in the major moral traditions of other world cultures as well.[10] Nor is the rejection of such warfare limited to elites: media accounts and public consciousness react strongly to violence directed against non-combatants. The problem is not that the need for such protection is poorly realized and not widely accepted, or even that the protections due non-combatants are ill defined; indeed, the irony is that exactly the opposite is the case.

At the same time, however, . . . arguments persist that the combatant–non-combatant distinction is meaningless in modern warfare, or meaningless in wars over ideology, ethnicity, and religion, or cannot be made a standard for the actual conduct of war because of the great destructive power of modern weapons. If it were only war criminals who made these arguments, they would be of little account; yet, in fact, they are common among well-meaning, highly moral people who see them as supporting their principled opposition to all war. Modern war, they argue, cannot be conducted so as to honor moral distinctions and restraints; therefore war as such must be abolished. Such an argument does not explain why it is presumably possible to abolish war entirely, yet impossible to restrain it within moral limits. Whatever the long-term prospect, in the present day, war has not disappeared, and it does not seem likely to do so in the foreseeable future. This poses an immediate moral obligation: so long as there continue to be armed conflicts, there remains an urgent need to hold fast to the moral and legal restraints defining non-combatant status and seeking to protect non-combatants during such conflict. . . .

---

[9] From *Journal of Peace Research*, 37, 4 (2000), pp. 421–48; our excerpts are from pp. 444, 445–6, 447.

[10] [*Author's note:*] See, for example, John Kelsay, "Islam and the Distinction between Combatants and Noncombatants," in *Cross, Crescent, and Sword: The Justification and Limitation of War in Western and Islamic Tradition*, ed. James Turner Johnson and John Kelsay (New York: Greenwood Press, 1990).

[The distinction between non-combatants and combatants requires] active moral effort to identify *who* are non-combatants so as to spare them from direct, intentional harm. When the effort is made for exactly the opposite reason – to identify non-combatants as "soft targets" who can be attacked with impunity as a means of injuring the enemy's ability to fight – then this utterly reverses the moral purpose behind the combatant–non-combatant distinction. In . . . the conflicts in Rwanda–Zaire and the former Yugoslavia, there is evidence not only of a disregard of non-combatant status and protection, but also of an effort that is just the reverse of what it should be: to target non-combatants directly and intentionally *as non-combatants.*

As to whether the weapons of modern war make it inherently incapable of combatant–non-combatant discrimination, [it is useful to analyze the conflicts in Rwanda–Zaire and the former Yugoslavia] because these have *not* involved such weapons. In these conflicts, the weapons used – from sticks to knives to rifles to artillery fire – became indiscriminate in their effects only because the persons using them, or their commanders, made the conscious choice to use them in this way. That choice and the resulting action are immoral in any and every war in any and every time, past, present, or future. Of course, weapons of mass destruction are rightly rejected as *mala in se*; this is because their inherent purpose is to target non-combatants. But even clubs, knives, and bullets become weapons of mass destruction when they are used intentionally and directly to kill masses of people. The point of insisting on a distinction between non-combatants and combatants is exactly to avoid this.

Another justification for attacks against non-combatants is often offered in contemporary warfare and is involved directly in raising the question of genocide: all the members of the opposing group are equally enemies because of ideology, religious belief, ethnicity, or some other cultural factor, so that the combatant–non-combatant distinction does not matter in conflict with them. From the standpoint of moral tradition and international law on war, this is not so much a counter-argument as a denial of the fundamental perspective of both morality and law. This perspective holds that common moral rules apply even in war; the rejection consists in the claim that war is necessarily total. The rationale for distinguishing non-combatants and for treating them differently in war was well put by the eighteenth-century philosopher, diplomat, and jurist Emmerich [Emer] de Vattel, who spoke both for the just war tradition he had inherited and for the positive international law whose development he influenced:

> Women, children, the sick and aged, are in the number of enemies. And there are rights with regard to them as belonging to the nation with which one is at war, and the rights and pretensions between nation and nation affect all its members. *But these are enemies who make no resistance, and consequently give us no right to treat their persons ill, or use any violence against them, much less to take away their lives.*[11]

[11] Emmerich de Vattel, *The Law of Nations; or Principles of the Law of Nature* (London: publisher unknown, 1740), section 145, emphasis added.

In moral terms, the argument that allows warfare to be intentionally directed against ethnically or religiously different non-combatants in such conflicts as those in the former Yugoslavia and Rwanda–Zaire is simply wrong. Only what persons *do* makes them morally liable to have armed force used against them, not what they *believe* religiously or who they *are* ethnically or culturally.

Holding to the combatant–non-combatant distinction is basic to the moral conduct of war, but moral tradition and international law also seek to limit the means of war so that they do not cause destruction out of proportion to the justified goal. What is wrong to do to combatants certainly should never be done against non-combatants: the rule protecting the former also covers the latter. Consider some examples: combatants rendered helpless are to be made prisoners of war and treated humanely, not killed or tortured; non-combatants, by definition helpless, deserve no less. The use of poison gas or chemical or biological agents against combatants is prohibited in the law of armed conflicts and, more generally, poison is prohibited as *mala in se* in the moral tradition; thus, such means may also not be used against non-combatants. To use means calculated to cause unnecessary suffering against combatants is forbidden in the law of armed conflict; similarly, such means are forbidden in dealing with non-combatants. These are all examples of the principle of proportionality, and they apply apart from concerns having to do with the distinction between non-combatants and combatants. Moreover, proportionality imposes the positive obligation to seek to accomplish justified military objectives by the least destructive means overall. . . . [E]ven when non-combatants and combatants are inextricably mingled, or even when the idea of a distinction between them is denied, there remains the separate obligation imposed by proportionality: for example, not to destroy a town completely or drive all the inhabitants from an area in order to possess it. . . .

Thus, both because it is inherently wrong to make war on non-combatants and because of the goal of peace and stability in domestic and international affairs, it is vitally important to maintain the restraints on the conduct of war found in moral tradition and in international law on war. Doing so affects everyone, and so does failure to do so.

57

National Conference of Catholic Bishops (1983 and 1993)

A Presumption against War

> The task before us is not simply to repeat what we have said before; it is first to consider anew whether and how our religious-moral tradition can assess, direct, contain, and, we hope, help to eliminate the threat posed to the human family by the nuclear arsenals of the world.
>
> *The Challenge of Peace*, section 122

In 1983, the Roman Catholic Bishops of the United States issued a pastoral letter on the grave problems associated with nuclear war. The letter appeared at the very moment when the US and other NATO powers were engaged in a heated debate about whether or not to place tactical nuclear weapons in Western Europe. In addition to expressing strong reservations about any possible use of such weapons, the bishops also questioned the ethical foundations of the strategy of deterrence by assured mutual destruction. Immediately controversial, the letter was widely read, both within the Christian churches and by the secular policy community.

The letter opened with a summary of principles, in which the Catholic teaching was described as implying "a presumption against war." Particularly noteworthy was the rejection of any kind of offensive war, which marked a significant departure from the traditional just war doctrine of Aquinas, Vitoria, and Suárez.[1] Then, in the Introduction, the bishops made a similar move, modifying the standard presentation of the conditions of a just war by the postulation of a new criterion called "comparative justice."

---

[1] On the difference between the traditional Catholic teaching and the contemporary presumption view, see Gregory M. Reichberg, "Is There a 'Presumption Against War' in Aquinas's Ethics?" *The Thomist*, 66 (July 2002), pp. 337–67.

On the substantive moral questions relating to nuclear weapons, the bishops took two firm stands. First, appealing to "reasonable hope of success,"[2] "discrimination," "proportionality," and other such criteria, the bishops denied that there might be "any situation in which the deliberate initiation of nuclear warfare, on however restricted a scale [i.e. through the use of tactical nuclear weapons], can be . . . justified" (section 150). Second, on the question of deterrence, the bishops held that any targeting (direct or even indirect) of civilian population centers was morally unacceptable. In both respects the pastoral letter sharply contradicted the position that had earlier been articulated by the influential just war theorist Paul Ramsey (see chap. 51, this volume). While the bishops did allow for a strategy of nuclear deterrence in which military targets might be threatened with retaliatory attack, they emphasized that this strategy was only provisionally acceptable, under condition that it serve "as a step on the way toward progressive disarmament" (section 188).

From *The Challenge of Peace: God's Promise and Our Response*[3]

Summary

. . . I. Some principles, norms and premises of Catholic teaching

A: On war

1   Catholic teaching begins in every case with a presumption against war and for peaceful settlement of disputes. In exceptional cases, determined by the moral principles of the just-war tradition some uses of force are permitted.
2   Every nation has a right and duty to defend itself against unjust aggression.
3   Offensive war of any kind is not morally justifiable.
4   It is never permitted to direct nuclear or conventional weapons to "the indiscriminate destruction of whole cities or vast areas with their populations. . . ."[4] The intentional killing of innocent civilians or non-combatants is always wrong.

---

[2] The text also refers to this criterion as "probability of success."

[3] National Conference of Catholic Bishops, *The Challenge of Peace: God's Promise and Our Response*, A Pastoral Letter on War and Peace, May 3, 1983 (Washington, DC: Office of Publishing Services, United States Catholic Conference, 1983), pp. iii, 6–7, 28–31, 33–4, 39, 46–51, 56–9. The full text of this letter (yet without the opening summary) may be found online at http://www.osjspm.org/cst/cp.htm.

[4] Vatican II, *Pastoral Constitution on the Church in the Modern World* (hereafter cited as *Pastoral Constitution*), no. 80.

5   Even defensive response to unjust attack can cause destruction which violates
    the principle of proportionality, going far beyond the limits of legitimate
    defense. This judgment is particularly important when assessing planned use
    of nuclear weapons. No defensive strategy, nuclear or conventional, which
    exceeds the limits of proportionality is morally permissible. . . .

Introduction

. . . (16) Catholic teaching on peace and war has had two purposes: to help
Catholics form their consciences and to contribute to the public policy debate
about the morality of war. These two purposes have led Catholic teaching to
address two distinct but overlapping audiences. The first is the Catholic faithful,
formed by the premises of the Gospel and the principles of Catholic moral
teaching. The second is the wider civil community, a more pluralistic audience, in
which our brothers and sisters with whom we share the name Christian, Jews,
Moslems, other religious communities, and all people of good will also make
up our polity. Since Catholic teaching has traditionally sought to address both
audiences, we intend to speak to both in this letter, recognizing that Catholics
are also members of the wider political community. . . .

(84) The determination of *when* conditions exist which allow the resort to
force in spite of the strong presumption against it is made in light of *ius ad
bellum* criteria. The determination of *how* even a justified resort to force must be
conducted is made in light of the *ius in bello* criteria. We shall briefly explore the
meaning of both.[5]

Ius ad bellum

(85) Why and when recourse to war is permissible.

(86) (a) *Just Cause:* War is permissible only to confront "a real and certain
danger," i.e., to protect innocent life, to preserve conditions necessary for decent
human existence, and to secure basic human rights. As both Pope Pius XII and
Pope John XXIII made clear, if war of retribution was ever justifiable, the risks of
modern war negate such a claim today.

(87) (b) *Competent Authority:* In the Catholic tradition the right to use force
has always been joined to the common good; war must be declared by those with
responsibility for public order, not by private groups or individuals.

(88) The requirement that a decision to go to war must be made by competent authority is particularly important in a democratic society. It needs detailed
treatment here since it involves a broad spectrum of related issues. Some of the

---

[5]   For an analysis of the content and relationship of these principles cf.: R. Potter, "The Moral Logic
of war," *McCormick Quarterly* 23 (1970), pp. 203–33.

bitterest divisions of society in our own nation's history, for example, have been evoked over the question of whether or not a president of the United States has acted constitutionally and legally in involving our country in a *de facto* war, even if – indeed, especially if – war was never formally declared. Equally perplexing problems of conscience can be raised for individuals expected or legally required to go to war even though our duly elected representatives in Congress have, in fact, voted for war.

(89) The criterion of competent authority is of further importance in a day when revolutionary war has become commonplace. Historically, the just-war tradition has been open to a "just revolution" position, recognizing that an oppressive government may lose its claim to legitimacy. Insufficient analytical attention has been given to the moral issues of revolutionary warfare. The mere possession of sufficient weaponry, for example, does not legitimize the initiation of war by "insurgents" against an established government, any more than the government's systematic oppression of its people can be carried out under the doctrine of "national security."

(90) While the legitimacy of revolution in some circumstances cannot be denied, just-war teachings must be applied as rigorously to revolutionary–counterrevolutionary conflicts as to others. The issue of who constitutes competent authority and how such authority is exercised is essential.

(91) When we consider in this letter the issues of conscientious objection and selective conscientious objection, the issue of competent authority will arise again.

(92) (c) *Comparative Justice:* Questions concerning the *means* of waging war today, particularly in view of the destructive potential of weapons, have tended to override questions concerning the comparative justice of the positions of respective adversaries or enemies. In essence: which side is sufficiently "right" in a dispute, and are the values at stake critical enough to override the presumption against war? The question in its most basic form is this: do the rights and values involved justify killing? For whatever the means used, war, by definition, involves violence, destruction, suffering, and death.

(93) The category of comparative justice is destined to emphasize the presumption against war which stands at the beginning of just-war teaching. In a world of sovereign states recognizing neither a common moral authority nor a central political authority, comparative justice stresses that no state should act on the basis that it has "absolute justice" on its side. Every party to a conflict should acknowledge the limits of its "just cause" and the consequent requirement to use *only* limited means in pursuit of its objectives. Far from legitimizing a crusade mentality, comparative justice is designed to relativize absolute claims and to restrain the use of force even in a "justified" conflict.[6]

---

[6]   Paul Ramsey, *The Just War: Force and Political Responsibility* (New York: 1981); James T. Johnson, *Ideology, Reason and the Limitations of War* (Princeton: 1975); W. O'Brien, *The Conduct of Just and Limited War* (New York: 1981), pp. 13–30; A. Vanderpol, *La doctrine scolastique du droit de guerre* (Paris: 1911), p. 387ff.; J. C. Murray, "Theology and Modern Warfare," in W. J. Nagel (ed.), *Morality and Modern Warfare*, p. 80ff.

(94) Given techniques of propaganda and the ease with which nations and individuals either assume or delude themselves into believing that God or right is clearly on their side, the test of comparative justice may be extremely difficult to apply. Clearly, however, this is not the case in every instance of war. Blatant aggression from without and subversion from within are often enough readily identifiable by all reasonably fair-minded people.

(95) (d) *Right Intention:* Right intention is related to just cause – war can be legitimately intended only for the reasons set forth above as a just cause. During the conflict, right intention means pursuit of peace and reconciliation, including avoiding unnecessarily destructive acts or imposing unreasonable conditions (e.g., unconditional surrender).

(96) (e) *Last Resort:* For resort to war to be justified, all peaceful alternatives must have been exhausted. There are formidable problems in this requirement. No international organization currently in existence has exercised sufficient internationally recognized authority to be able either to mediate effectively in most cases or to prevent conflict by the intervention of United Nations or other peacekeeping forces. Furthermore, there is a tendency for nations or peoples which perceive conflict between or among other nations as advantageous to themselves to attempt to prevent a peaceful settlement rather than advance it.

(97) We regret the apparent unwillingness of some to see in the United Nations organization the potential for world order which exists and to encourage its development. Pope Paul VI called the United Nations the last hope for peace. . . .

(98) (f) *Probability of Success:* This is a difficult criterion to apply, but its purpose is to prevent irrational resort to force or hopeless resistance when the outcome of either will clearly be disproportionate or futile. The determination includes a recognition that at times defense of key values, even against great odds, may be a "proportionate" witness.

(99) (g) *Proportionality:* In terms of the *ius ad bellum* criteria, proportionality means that the damage to be inflicted and the costs incurred by war must be proportionate to the good expected by taking up arms. Nor should judgments concerning proportionality be limited to the temporal order without regard to a spiritual dimension in terms of "damage," "cost," and "the good expected." In today's interdependent world even a local conflict can affect people everywhere; this is particularly the case when the nuclear powers are involved. Hence a nation cannot justly go to war today without considering the effect of its action on others and on the international community.

(100) This principle of proportionality applies throughout the conduct of the war as well as to the decision to begin warfare. During the Vietnam war our bishops' conference ultimately concluded that the conflict had reached such a level of devastation to the adversary and damage to our own society that continuing it could not be justified.[7]

---

[7] United States Catholic Conference, *Resolution on Southeast Asia* (Washington, DC, 1971).

Ius in bello

(101) Even when the stringent conditions which justify resort to war are met, the conduct of war (i.e., strategy, tactics, and individual actions) remains subject to continuous scrutiny in light of two principles which have special significance today precisely because of the destructive capability of modern technological warfare. These principles are proportionality and discrimination. In discussing them here, we shall apply them to the question of *ius ad bellum* as well as *ius in bello*; for today it becomes increasingly difficult to make a decision to use any kind of armed force, however limited initially in intention and in the destructive power of the weapons employed, without facing at least the possibility of escalation to broader, or even total, war and to the use of weapons of horrendous destructive potential. This is especially the case when adversaries are "superpowers," as the council clearly envisioned:

> Indeed, if the kind of weapons now stocked in the arsenals of the great powers were to be employed to the fullest, the result would be the almost complete reciprocal slaughter of one side by the others not to speak of the widespread devastation that would follow in the world and the deadly after effects resulting from the use of such weapons . . .[8]

(105) When confronting choices among specific military options, the question asked by proportionality is: once we take into account not only the military advantages that will be achieved by using this means but also all the harms reasonably expected to follow from using it, can its use still be justified? We know, of course, that no end can justify means evil in themselves, such as the executing of hostages or the targeting of non-combatants. Nonetheless, even if the means adopted is not evil in itself, it is necessary to take into account the probable harms that will result from using it and the justice of accepting those harms. It is of utmost importance, in assessing harms and the justice of accepting them, to think about the poor and the helpless, for they are usually the ones who have the least to gain and the most to lose when war's violence touches their lives.

(106) In terms of the arms race, if the *real* end in view is legitimate defense against unjust aggression, and the means to this end are not evil in themselves, we must still examine the question of proportionality concerning attendant evils. Do the exorbitant costs, the general climate of insecurity generated, the possibility of accidental detonation of highly destructive weapons, the danger of error and miscalculation that could provoke retaliation and war – do such evils or others attendant upon and indirectly deriving from the arms race make the arms race itself a disproportionate response to aggression? Pope John Paul II is very clear in

---

[8]   *Pastoral Constitution*, no. 80.

his insistence that the exercise of the right and duty of a people to protect their existence and freedom is contingent on the use of proportionate means.[9]

(107) Finally, another set of questions concerns the interpretation of the principle of discrimination. The principle prohibits directly intended attacks on noncombatants and nonmilitary targets. It raises a series of questions about the term "intentional," the category of "noncombatant," and the meaning of "military." . . .

(110) These two principles, in all their complexity, must be applied to the range of weapons – conventional, nuclear, biological, and chemical – with which nations are armed today. . . .

II. War and Peace in the Modern World: Problems and Principles

(122) Both the just-war teaching and non-violence are confronted with a unique challenge by nuclear warfare. This must be the starting point of any further moral reflection: nuclear weapons particularly and nuclear warfare as it is planned today, raise new moral questions. No previously conceived moral position escapes the fundamental confrontation posed by contemporary nuclear strategy. Many have noted the similarity of the statements made by eminent scientists and Vatican II's observation that we are forced today "to undertake a completely fresh reappraisal of war." The task before us is not simply to repeat what we have said before; it is first to consider anew whether and how our religious-moral tradition can assess, direct, contain, and, we hope, help to eliminate the threat posed to the human family by the nuclear arsenals of the world. . . .

Moral principles and policy choices

(146) In light of these perspectives we address the questions more explicitly: (1) counterpopulation warfare; (2) initiation of nuclear war; and (3) limited nuclear war.

1. Counterpopulation warfare

(147) Under no circumstances may nuclear weapons or other instruments of mass slaughter be used for the purpose of destroying population centers or other predominantly civilian targets. Popes have repeatedly condemned "total war" which implies such use. For example, as early as 1954 Pope Pius XII condemned nuclear warfare "when it entirely escapes the control of man," and results in "the pure and simple annihilation of all human life within the radius of action."[10] The condemnation was repeated by the Second Vatican Council:

[9] John Paul II, "World Day of Peace Message 1982," no. 12.
[10] Pius XII, "Address to the VIII Congress of the World Medical Association," in *Peace and Disarmament: Documents of the World Council of Churches and the Roman Catholic Church* (Geneva and Rome, 1982), p. 131.

Any act of war aimed indiscriminately at the destruction of entire cities or of extensive areas along with their population is a crime against God and man itself. It merits unequivocal and unhesitating condemnation.[11]

(148) Retaliatory action whether nuclear or conventional which would indiscriminately take many wholly innocent lives, lives of people who are in no way responsible for reckless actions of their government, must also be condemned. This condemnation, in our judgment, applies even to the retaliatory use of weapons striking enemy cities after our own have already been struck. No Christian can rightfully carry out orders or policies deliberately aimed at killing non-combatants . . .[12]

2. The initiation of nuclear war

(150) We do not perceive any situation in which the deliberate initiation of nuclear warfare, on however restricted a scale, can be morally justified. Non-nuclear attacks by another state must be resisted by other than nuclear means. Therefore, a serious moral obligation exists to develop nonnuclear defensive strategies as rapidly as possible.

(151) A serious debate is under way on this issue.[13] It is cast in political terms, but it has a significant moral dimension. Some have argued that at the very beginning of a war nuclear weapons might be used, only against military targets, perhaps in limited numbers. Indeed it has long been American and NATO policy that nuclear weapons, especially so-called tactical nuclear weapons, would likely be used if NATO forces in Europe seemed in danger of losing a conflict that until then had been restricted to conventional weapons. Large numbers of tactical nuclear weapons are now deployed in Europe by the NATO forces and about as many by the Soviet Union. Some are substantially smaller than the bomb used on Hiroshima, some are larger. Such weapons, if employed in great numbers, would totally devastate the densely populated countries of Western and Central Europe.

(152) Whether under conditions of war in Europe, parts of Asia, or the Middle East, or the exchange of strategic weapons directly between the United States and the Soviet Union, the difficulties of limiting the use of nuclear weapons are immense. A number of expert witnesses advise us that commanders operating under conditions of battle probably would not be able to exercise strict control; the number of weapons used would rapidly increase, the targets would be expanded beyond the military, and the level of civilian casualties would rise enormously.[14]

---

[11] *Pastoral Constitution*, no. 80.

[12] Ibid.

[13] M. Bundy et al., "Nuclear Weapons," cited; K. Kaiser, G. Leber, A. Mertes and F. J. Schulze, "Nuclear Weapons and the Preservation of Peace," *Foreign Affairs* 60 (1982): 1157–70; cf. other responses to Bundy article in the same issue of *Foreign Affairs*.

[14] Testimony given to the National Conference of Catholic Bishops Committee during preparation of this pastoral letter.

No one can be certain that this escalation would not occur, even in the face of political efforts to keep such an exchange "limited." The chances of keeping use limited seem remote, and the consequences of escalation to mass destruction would be appalling. Former public officials have testified that it is improbable that any nuclear war could actually be kept limited. Their testimony and the consequences involved in this problem lead us to conclude that the danger of escalation is so great that it would be morally unjustifiable to initiate nuclear war in any form. The danger is rooted not only in the technology of our weapons systems but in the weakness and sinfulness of human communities. We find the moral responsibility of beginning nuclear war not justified by rational political objectives.

(153) This judgment affirms that the willingness to initiate nuclear war entails a distinct, weighty moral responsibility; it involves transgressing a fragile barrier – political, psychological, and moral – which has been constructed since 1945. We express repeatedly in this letter our extreme skepticism about the prospects for controlling a nuclear exchange, however limited the first use might be. Precisely because of this skepticism, we judge resort to nuclear weapons to counter a conventional attack to be morally unjustifiable.[15] Consequently we seek to reinforce the barrier against any use of nuclear weapons. Our support of a "no first use" policy must be seen in this light. . . .

3. Limited nuclear war

(157) It would be possible to agree with our first two conclusions and still not be sure about retaliatory use of nuclear weapons in what is called a "limited exchange." The issue at stake is the *real* as opposed to the *theoretical* possibility of a "limited nuclear exchange."

(158) We recognize that the policy debate on this question is inconclusive and that all participants are left with hypothetical projections about probable reactions in a nuclear exchange. While not trying to adjudicate the technical debate, we are aware of it and wish to raise a series of questions which challenge the actual meaning of "limited" in this discussion.

(a) Would leaders have sufficient information to know what is happening in a nuclear exchange?

(b) Would they be able under the conditions of stress, time pressures, and fragmentary information to make the extraordinarily precise decision needed to keep the exchange limited if this were technically possible?

(c) Would military commanders be able, in the midst of the destruction and confusion of a nuclear exchange, to maintain a policy of "discriminate

---

[15] Our conclusion and judgments in this area, although based on careful study and reflection of the application of moral principles, do not have, of course, the same force as the principles themselves and therefore allow for different versions.

targeting"? Can this be done in modern warfare, waged across great distances by aircraft and missiles?

(d) Given the accidents we know about in peacetime conditions, what assurances are there that computer errors could be avoided in the midst of a nuclear exchange?

(e) Would not the casualties, even in a war defined as limited by strategists, still run in the millions?

(f) How "limited" would be the long-term effects of radiation, famine, social fragmentation, and economic dislocation?

(159) Unless these questions can be answered satisfactorily, we will continue to be highly skeptical about the real meaning of "limited." One of the criteria of the just-war tradition is a reasonable hope of success in bringing about justice and peace. We must ask whether such a reasonable hope can exist once nuclear weapons have been exchanged. The burden of proof remains on those who assert that meaningful limitation is possible.

(160) A nuclear response to either conventional or nuclear attack can cause destruction which goes far beyond "legitimate defense." Such use of nuclear weapons would not be justified. . . .

Deterrence in principle and practice

(162) The moral challenge posed by nuclear weapons is not exhausted by an analysis of their possible uses. Much of the political and moral debate of the nuclear age has concerned the strategy of deterrence. Deterrence is at the heart of the US–Soviet relationship, currently the most dangerous dimension of the nuclear arms race.

1. The concept and development of deterrence policy

(163) The concept of deterrence existed in military strategy long before the nuclear age, but it has taken on a new meaning and significance since 1945. Essentially, deterrence means "dissuasion of a potential adversary from initiating an attack or conflict, often by the threat of unacceptable retaliatory damage."[16] In the nuclear age, deterrence has become the centerpiece of both US and Soviet policy. Both superpowers have for many years now been able to promise a retaliatory response which can inflict "unacceptable damage." A situation of stable deterrence depends on the ability of each side to deploy its retaliatory forces in ways that are not vulnerable to an attack (i.e., protected against a "first strike"); preserving stability requires a willingness by both sides to refrain from deploying weapons which appear to have a first strike capability. . . .

[16] W. H. Kincade and J. D. Porro, *Negotiating Security: An Arms Control Reader* (Washington, DC, 1979).

2. The moral assessment of deterrence

...(178) Targeting doctrine raises significant moral questions because it is a significant determinant of what would occur if nuclear weapons were ever to be used. Although we acknowledge the need for a deterrent, not all forms of deterrence are morally acceptable. There are moral limits to deterrence policy as well as to policy regarding use. Specifically, it is not morally acceptable to intend to kill the innocent as part of a strategy of deterring nuclear war. The question of whether US policy involves an intention to strike civilian centers (directly targeting civilian populations) has been one of our factual concerns.

(179) This complex question has always produced a variety of responses, official and unofficial in character. The NCCB Committee has received a series of statements of clarification of policy from US government officials.[17] Essentially these statements declare that it is not US strategic policy to target the Soviet civilian population as such or to use nuclear weapons deliberately for the purpose of destroying population centers. These statements respond, in principle at least, to one moral criterion for assessing deterrence policy: the immunity of non-combatants from direct attack either by conventional or nuclear weapons.

(180) These statements do not address or resolve another very troublesome moral problem, namely, that an attack on military targets or militarily significant industrial targets could involve "indirect" (i.e., unintended) but massive civilian casualties. ...

(181) While any judgment of proportionality is always open to differing evaluations, there are actions which can be decisively judged to be disproportionate. A narrow adherence exclusively to the principle of noncombatant immunity as a criterion for policy is an inadequate moral posture, for it ignores some evil and unacceptable consequences. Hence, we cannot be satisfied that the assertion of an intention not to strike civilians directly, or even the most honest effort to implement that intention, by itself constitutes a "moral policy" for the use of nuclear weapons.

(182) The location of industrial or militarily significant economic targets within heavily populated areas or in those areas affected by radioactive fallout could well

---

[17] Particularly helpful was the letter of January 15, 1983, of Mr. William Clark, national security adviser, to Cardinal Bernardin. Mr Clark stated: " For moral, political and military reasons, the United States does not target the Soviet civilian population as such. There is no deliberately opaque meaning conveyed in the last two words. We do not threaten the existence of Soviet civilization, by threatening Soviet cities. Rather, we hold at risk the war-making capability of the Soviet Union – its armed forces, and the industrial capacity to sustain war. It would be irresponsible for us to issue policy statements which might suggest to the Soviets that it would be to their advantage to establish privileged sanctuaries within heavily populated areas, thus inducing them to locate much of their war-fighting capability within those urban sanctuaries." A reaffirmation of the administration's policy is also found in Secretary Weinberger's *Annual Report to the Congress* (Casper Weinberger, *Annual Report to the Congress*, February 1, 1983, p. 55): "The Reagan Administration's policy is that under no circumstances may such weapons be used deliberately for the purposes of destroying populations."

involve such massive civilian casualties that, in our judgment, such a strike would be deemed morally disproportionate, even though not intentionally indiscriminate.

(183) The problem is not simply one of producing highly accurate weapons that might minimize civilian casualties in any single explosion, but one of increasing the likelihood of escalation at a level where many, even "discriminating," weapons would cumulatively kill very large numbers of civilians. Those civilian deaths would occur both immediately and from the long-term effects of social and economic devastation. . . .

(186) These considerations of concrete elements of nuclear deterrence policy, made in light of John Paul II's evaluation, but applying it through our own prudential judgments, lead us to a strictly conditioned moral acceptance of nuclear deterrence. We cannot consider it adequate as a long-term basis for peace. . . .

(188) *On the basis of these criteria we wish now to make some specific evaluations*:

1   If nuclear deterrence exists only to prevent the *use* of nuclear weapons by others, then proposals to go beyond this to planning for prolonged periods of repeated nuclear strikes and counter-strikes, or "prevailing" in nuclear war, are not acceptable. They encourage notions that nuclear war can be engaged in with tolerable human and moral consequences. Rather, we must continually say "no" to the idea of nuclear war.

2   If nuclear deterrence is our goal, "sufficiency" to deter is an adequate strategy; the quest for nuclear superiority must be rejected.

3   Nuclear deterrence should be used as a step on the way toward progressive disarmament. Each proposed addition to our strategic system or change in strategic doctrine must be assessed precisely in light of whether it will render steps toward "progressive disarmament" more or less likely.

(189) Moreover, these criteria provide us with the means to make some judgments and recommendations about the recent direction of US strategic policy. Progress toward a world freed of dependence on nuclear deterrence must be carefully carried out. But it must not be delayed. There is an urgent moral and political responsibility to use the "peace of a sort" we have as a framework to move toward authentic peace through nuclear arms control, reductions, and disarmament. Of primary importance in this process is the need to prevent the development and deployment of destabilizing weapons systems on either side; a second requirement is to insure that the more sophisticated command and control systems do not become mere hair triggers for automatic launch on warning; a third is the need to prevent the proliferation of nuclear weapons in the international system. . . .

In 1993, ten years after *The Challenge of Peace*, the US Catholic Bishops issued a new pastoral letter, *The Harvest of Justice is Sown in Peace*. The letter reiterated many of the core presuppositions of the 1983 document, which it sought to apply in a post-Cold War context. Particularly striking was the letter's emphasis on peacemaking and strategies of non-violent change, while still remaining within a non-pacifist, just war framework. The letter also invoked the idea of a "global common good" (an expansion of the classical idea of the "common good") asserting that this, rather than the single nation-state, should serve as the main referent for any legitimate warmaking authority.

From *The Harvest of Justice is Sown in Peace*[18]

Peace does not consist merely in the absence of war, but rather in sharing the goodness of life together. In keeping with Pope John [XXIII]'s teaching [from his encyclical letter *Pacem in Terris*, 1963], the Church's positive vision of a peaceful world includes the following: (a) the primacy of the global common good for political life; (b) the role of social and economic development in securing the conditions for a just and lasting peace; and (c) the moral imperative of solidarity between affluent industrial nations and poor, developing ones.

. . . A key element in Pope John's conception of a peaceful world is a global order oriented to the full development of all peoples, with governments committed to the rights of citizens, and a framework of authority that enables the world community to address fundamental problems that individual governments fail to resolve. In this framework, sovereignty is in the service of people. All political authority has as its end the promotion of the common good, particularly the defense of human rights. When a government clearly fails in this task or itself becomes a central impediment to the realization of those rights, the world community has a right and a duty to act where the lives and the fundamental rights of large numbers of people are at serious risk. . . .

An essential component of a spirituality for peacemaking is an ethic for dealing with conflict in a sinful world. The Christian tradition possesses two ways to address conflict: non-violence and just war. . . .

Throughout history there has been a shifting relation between the two streams of the tradition that always remain in tension. Like Christians before us who have sought to read the signs of the times in light of this dual tradition, we today struggle to assess the lessons of the nonviolent revolutions in Eastern Europe in 1989 and the former Soviet Union in 1991, on the one hand, and of the conflicts in Central America, the Persian Gulf, Bosnia, Somalia, Lebanon, Cambodia, and Northern Ireland on the other.

---

[18] National Conference of Catholic Bishops, *The Harvest of Justice is Sown in Peace*, reprinted in *Origins*, 23, 26 (1993), pp. 449–64; these excerpts are from pp. 452–4. The full text is available online at www.nccbuscc.org/sdwp/harvest.htm

The devastation wrought by these recent wars reinforces and strengthens for us the strong presumption against the use of force, which is shared by both traditions. Overall, the wars fought in the last 50 years show a dramatic rise in the proportion of noncombatant casualties. This fact points to the need for clear moral restraints both in avoiding war and in limiting its consequences. The high level of civilian deaths raises serious moral questions about the political choices and military doctrines which have had such tragic results over the last half century. The presumption against the use of force has also been strengthened by the examples of the effectiveness of non-violence in some places in Eastern Europe and elsewhere. . . .

. . . National leaders bear a moral obligation to see that nonviolent alternatives are seriously considered for dealing with conflicts. New styles of preventative diplomacy and conflict resolution ought to be explored, tried, improved, and supported. As a nation we should promote research, education, and training in nonviolent means of resisting evil. Nonviolent strategies need greater attention in international affairs.

Such obligations do not detract from a state's right and duty to defend against aggression as a last resort. They do, however, raise the threshold for the recourse to force by establishing institutions which promote non-violent political commitment to solutions of disputes and nuturing such efforts. In some future conflicts, strikes and people power could be more effective than guns and bullets.

58

Kofi Annan (b. 1938)

Toward a New Definition of Sovereignty

> When we read the Charter today, we are more than ever conscious that its aim
> is to protect individual human beings, not to protect those who abuse them.
>
> "Two Concepts of Sovereignty"

The rapid fragmentation of the Eastern Bloc, culminating in the dissolution of the Soviet Union in 1991, signaled the end of an era during which the study of international politics and diplomacy had been largely devoted to a single aim: that of maintaining the balance of power between two opposing blocs of nations – a precarious system of mutual deterrence designed to keep us, or so it seemed, indefinitely on the brink of a cataclysmic nuclear war.

However, the international community's sigh of relief would prove short-lived. For it quickly became apparent that while the United Nations had focused on quelling conflicts between sovereign states, wars were still taking place, not between but within such states. Indeed, while the total number of armed conflicts has declined since the end of the Cold War, the ferocity and brutality of civil wars have not abated.

In dealing with civil wars, the legal and institutional framework of the United Nations seemed to provide not an aid, but an obstacle, as the legal map of the Charter could not be made to match the new political landscape. Indeed, citing the Charter's concern for international peace and stability, many held that the policies of governments toward dissidents and minorities were, in the words of Article 2.7, a matter "essentially within the domestic jurisdiction of any state." Such policies were therefore not a fit target for international sanction, let alone for military intervention. As public awareness of the massive humanitarian disasters caused by such conflicts increased, the call for a new balance between the rights of peoples and the rights of states appeared to place the UN in a tragic dilemma, jeopardizing its authority and tearing at the fabric of the international system.

Humanitarian intervention was the concept that came to epitomize this dilemma. "Intervention" had been the euphemism of choice among the old imperial powers and their superpower descendants seeking to "maintain their interests" abroad. Adding to this term the adjective "humanitarian" still seems to many to have the makings of an oxymoron, yet for its proponents, it serves as a reminder that such measures, even when justifiable, must remain occasional and exceptional – for no matter what its aim is, it remains intervention: an infringement of state sovereignty whose legal, political, and moral status remains to be clarified.

Not that such interventions were unheard of even in the Cold War period: India's intervention in Pakistan in 1971 was frequently cited as a precedent as the debates raged in the 1990s, as were Vietnam's intervention in Cambodia in 1978 and Tanzania's intervention in Uganda in 1979. It is telling, however, that while the humanitarian credentials of these operations were never in serious dispute, these were never the terms under which the states in question sought to justify them. Instead, they all spoke, and quite tenuously so, in terms of self-defense under the Charter's Article 51, thereby saving the UN from having to take a principled stand on the underlying issue.[1]

In a series of writings and addresses toward the end of the 1990s, UN Secretary-General Kofi Annan sought to raise the question of the limits of state sovereignty and the place of human rights in international politics.[2] These were prompted by the Security Council impasse over the Kosovo crisis, which culminated with the unauthorized NATO intervention in March 1999. Kosovo, however, was certainly not the UN's first encounter with the problem, nor was it Annan's. Situations in Sudan, Sierra Leone, and Indonesia, to name but a few, had made painfully apparent the inability of the UN to deal quickly and effectively with humanitarian crises. Further, Annan's appointment to the position of Secretary-General was initially shrouded in controversy: as Head of the UN Department of Peacekeeping Operations, he was in charge when the UN in 1994 had failed to respond to the atrocities in Rwanda, ultimately resulting in the most appalling outbreak of genocidal violence since World War II.

Still, while it is unanimously agreed today that the international community failed in not intervening to prevent the slaughter of the Tutsis, it remains a serious

---

[1] It is worth noting that such hesitation around matters of principle persists even today. For instance, British Prime Minister Tony Blair, speaking shortly after the onset of the NATO campaign in Kosovo in 1999, urged first that "[t]his is a just war, based not on any territorial ambitions but on values. We cannot let the evil of ethnic cleansing stand," only to add that "[w]hen oppression produces massive flows of refugees which unsettle neighbouring countries, they can properly be described as 'threats to international peace and security'" (Tony Blair, "Doctrine of the International Community," Speech to the Economic Club of Chicago, Hilton Hotel, Chicago, USA, Thursday April 22, 1999).

[2] His predecessor Boutros Boutros-Ghali also had touched in the issue, claiming that "[t]he time of absolute and exclusive sovereignty . . . has passed; its theory was never matched by reality" (Boutros-Ghali, *An Agenda for Peace*, 2nd edn. [New York: United Nations, 1995], p. 44).

question whether, in general, blunt military force is a suitable tool in service of humanitarian ideals. The first selection reproduced below is from Kofi Annan's much-cited article "Two Concepts of Sovereignty." Here he addresses this problematic, and reminds us that intervention, properly conceived, encompasses a larger array of options than just military force, including economic sanctions and targeted aid. Indeed, it is one of the tragic consequences of the received view of state sovereignty that the international community is rarely willing to contemplate any such measures until it is too late and military force is the only option that remains.

From "Two Concepts of Sovereignty"[3]

The tragedy of East Timor, coming so soon after that of Kosovo, has focused attention once again on the need for timely intervention by the international community when death and suffering are being inflicted on large numbers of people, and when the state nominally in charge is unable or unwilling to stop it.

In Kosovo a group of states intervened without seeking authority from the United Nations Security Council. In Timor the council has now authorised intervention, but only after obtaining an invitation from Indonesia. We all hope that this will rapidly stabilise the situation, but many hundreds – probably thousands – of innocent people have already perished. As in Rwanda five years ago, the international community stands accused of doing too little, too late.

Neither of these precedents is satisfactory as a model for the new millennium. Just as we have learnt that the world cannot stand aside when gross and systematic violations of human rights are taking place, we have also learnt that, if it is to enjoy the sustained support of the world's peoples, intervention must be based on legitimate and universal principles. We need to adapt our international system better to a world with new actors, new responsibilities, and new possibilities for peace and progress.

State sovereignty, in its most basic sense, is being redefined – not least by the forces of globalisation and international cooperation. States are now widely understood to be instruments at the service of their peoples, and not vice versa. At the same time individual sovereignty – by which I mean the fundamental freedom of each individual, enshrined in the charter of the UN and subsequent international treaties – has been enhanced by a renewed and spreading consciousness of individual rights. When we read the charter today, we are more than ever conscious that its aim is to protect individual human beings, not to protect those who abuse them.

These changes in the world do not make hard political choices any easier. But they do oblige us to think anew about such questions as how the UN responds to

---

[3] Kofi Annan, "Two Concepts of Sovereignty," *The Economist*, 352 (September 18, 1999), pp. 49–50.

humanitarian crises; and why states are willing to act in some areas of conflict, but not in others where the daily toll of death and suffering is as bad or worse. From Sierra Leone to Sudan, from Angola to Afghanistan, there are people who need more than words of sympathy. They need a real and sustained commitment to help end their cycles of violence, and give them a new chance to achieve peace and prosperity.

The genocide in Rwanda showed us how terrible the consequences of inaction can be in the face of mass murder. But this year's conflict in Kosovo raised equally important questions about the consequences of action without international consensus and clear legal authority.

It has cast in stark relief the dilemma of so-called "humanitarian intervention". On the one hand, is it legitimate for a regional organisation to use force without a UN mandate? On the other, is it permissible to let gross and systematic violations of human rights, with grave humanitarian consequences, continue unchecked? The inability of the international community to reconcile these two compelling interests in the case of Kosovo can be viewed only as a tragedy.

To avoid repeating such tragedies in the next century, I believe it is essential that the international community reach consensus – not only on the principle that massive and systematic violations of human rights must be checked, wherever they take place, but also on ways of deciding what action is necessary, and when, and by whom. The Kosovo conflict and its outcome have prompted a debate of worldwide importance. And to each side in this debate difficult questions can be posed.

To those for whom the greatest threat to the future of international order is the use of force in the absence of a Security Council mandate, one might say: leave Kosovo aside for a moment, and think about Rwanda. Imagine for one moment that, in those dark days and hours leading up to the genocide, there had been a coalition of states ready and willing to act in defence of the Tutsi population, but the council had refused or delayed giving the green light. Should such a coalition then have stood idly by while the horror unfolded?

To those for whom the Kosovo action heralded a new era when states and groups of states can take military action outside the established mechanisms for enforcing international law, one might equally ask: Is there not a danger of such interventions undermining the imperfect, yet resilient, security system created after the Second World War, and of setting dangerous precedents for future interventions without a clear criterion to decide who might invoke these precedents and in what circumstances? Nothing in the UN charter precludes a recognition that there are rights beyond borders. What the charter does say is that "armed force shall not be used, save in the common interest." But what is that common interest? Who shall define it? Who shall defend it? Under whose authority? And with what means of intervention? In seeking answers to these monumental questions, I see four aspects of intervention which need to be considered with special care.

First, "intervention" should not be understood as referring only to the use of force. A tragic irony of many of the crises that go unnoticed or unchallenged in the world today is that they could be dealt with by far less perilous acts of intervention than the one we saw this year in Yugoslavia. And yet the commitment of the world to peacekeeping, to humanitarian assistance, to rehabilitation and reconstruction varies greatly from region to region, and crisis to crisis. If the new commitment to humanitarian action is to retain the support of the world's peoples, it must be – and must be seen to be – universal, irrespective of region or nation. Humanity, after all, is indivisible.

Second, it is clear that traditional notions of sovereignty alone are not the only obstacle to effective action in humanitarian crises. No less significant are the ways in which states define their national interests. The world has changed in profound ways since the end of the Cold War, but I fear our conceptions of national interest have failed to follow suit. A new, broader definition of national interest is needed in the new century, which would induce states to find greater unity in the pursuit of common goals and values. In the context of many of the challenges facing humanity today, the collective interest *is* the national interest.

Third, in cases where forceful intervention does become necessary, the Security Council – the body charged with authorising the use of force under international law – must be able to rise to the challenge. The choice must not be between council unity and inaction in the face of genocide – as in the case of Rwanda – and council division, but regional action, as in the case of Kosovo. In both cases, the UN should have been able to find common ground in upholding the principles of the charter, and acting in defence of our common humanity.

As important as the council's enforcement power is its deterrent power, and unless it is able to assert itself collectively where the cause is just and the means available, its credibility in the eyes of the world may well suffer. If states bent on criminal behaviour know that frontiers are not an absolute defence – that the council will take action to halt the gravest crimes against humanity – then they will not embark on such a course assuming they can get away with it. The charter requires the council to be the defender of the "common interest". Unless it is seen to be so – in an era of human rights, interdependence and globalisation – there is a danger that others will seek to take its place.

Fourth, when fighting stops, the international commitment to peace must be just as strong as was the commitment to war. In this situation, too, consistency is essential. Just as our commitment to humanitarian action must be universal if it is to be legitimate, so our commitment to peace cannot end as soon as there is a ceasefire. The aftermath of war requires no less skill, no less sacrifice, no fewer resources than the war itself, if lasting peace is to be secured.

This developing international norm in favour of intervention to protect civilians from wholesale slaughter will no doubt continue to pose profound challenges to the international community. In some quarters it will arouse distrust, scepticism, even hostility. But I believe on balance we should welcome it. Why? Because, despite all the difficulties of putting it into practice, it does show that humankind today is less willing than in the past to tolerate suffering in its midst, and more willing to do something about it.

A fuller exposition of the Secretary-General's thoughts on the question of intervention can be found in his 1998 Ditchley Foundation Lecture. Debating the status of the Universal Declaration of Human Rights vis-à-vis the principle of state sovereignty, he reminds us that "[t]he Charter . . . was issued in the name of 'the peoples,' not the Governments, of the United Nations." He further emphasizes the fundamental commitment that while military force must remain a last resort, it is a resort that the international community must stand prepared to use when the need arises. Finally, he addresses the important issue of Security Council reforms.

From the 1998 Ditchley Foundation Lecture: "Intervention"[4]

I expect some of you are surprised by the title I have chosen for my talk. Or if not, you may think I have come to preach a sermon against intervention. I suppose that would be the traditional line for a citizen of a former British colony to take, in an address to senior policy makers and diplomats of the former imperial Power. And some people would also expect a sermon on those lines from the United Nations Secretary-General, whatever his country of origin. The United Nations is, after all, an association of sovereign States, and sovereign States do tend to be extremely jealous of their sovereignty. Small States, especially, are fearful of intervention in their affairs by great Powers. And indeed, our century has seen many examples of the strong "intervening" – or interfering – in the affairs of the weak, from the Allied intervention in the Russian civil war in 1918 to the Soviet "interventions" in Hungary, Czechoslovakia and Afghanistan. Others might refer to the American intervention in Viet Nam, or even the Turkish intervention in Cyprus in 1974. The motives, and the legal justification, may be better in some cases than others, but the word "intervention" has come to be used almost as a synonym for "invasion".

The Charter of the United Nations gives great responsibilities to great Powers, in their capacity as permanent members of the Security Council. But as a safeguard against abuse of those powers, Article 2.7 of the Charter protects national sovereignty even from intervention by the United Nations itself. I'm sure everyone in this audience knows it by heart. But, let me remind you – just in case – that Article forbids the United Nations to intervene "in matters which are essentially within the domestic jurisdiction of any State".

---

[4] Available from http://www.un.org/News/Press/docs/1998/19980626.sgsg6613.r1.html.

That prohibition is just as relevant today as it was in 1945: violations of sovereignty remain violations of the global order. Yet, in other contexts the word "intervention" has a more benign meaning. We all applaud the policeman who intervenes to stop a fight, or the teacher who prevents big boys from bullying a smaller one. And medicine uses the word "intervention" to describe the act of the surgeon, who saves life by "intervening" to remove malignant growth, or to repair damaged organs. Of course, the most intrusive methods of treatment are not always to be recommended. A wise doctor knows when to let nature take its course. But, a doctor who never intervened would have few admirers, and probably even fewer patients.

So it is in international affairs. Why was the United Nations established, if not to act as a benign policeman or doctor? Our job is to intervene: to prevent conflict where we can, to put a stop to it when it has broken out, or – when neither of those things is possible – at least to contain it and prevent it from spreading. That is what the world expects of us, even though – alas – the United Nations by no means always lives up to such expectations. It is also what the Charter requires of us, particularly in Chapter VI, which deals with the peaceful settlement of disputes, and Chapter VII, which describes the action the United Nations must take when peace comes under threat, or is actually broken.

The purpose of Article 2.7, which I quoted just now, was to confine such interventions to cases where the international peace is threatened or broken, and to keep the United Nations from interfering in purely domestic disputes. Yet even that article carries the important rider that "this principle shall not prejudice the application of enforcement measures under Chapter VII". In other words, even national sovereignty can be set aside if it stands in the way of the Security Council's overriding duty to preserve international peace and security. On the face of it, there is a simple distinction between international conflict, which is clearly the United Nations business, and domestic disputes, which are not. The very phrase "domestic dispute" sounds reassuring. It suggests a little local difficulty which the State in question can easily settle, if only it is left alone to do so.

We all know that in recent years it has not been like that. Most wars nowadays are civil wars. Or at least that is how they start. And these civil wars are anything but benign. In fact they are "civil" only in the sense that civilians – that is, non-combatants – have become the main victims. In the First World War, roughly 90 per cent of those killed were soldiers, and only 10 per cent civilians.

In the Second World War, even if we count all the victims of Nazi death camps as war casualties, civilians made up only half, or just over half, of all those killed. But in many of today's conflicts, civilians have become the main targets of violence. It is now conventional to put the proportion of civilian casualties somewhere in the region of 75 per cent. I say "conventional" because the truth is that no one really knows. Relief agencies such as the Office of the United Nations High Commissioner for Refugees (UNHCR) and the Red Cross rightly devote their resources to helping the living rather than counting the dead.

Armies count their own losses, and sometimes make boasts about the number of enemies they have killed. But, there is no agency whose job is to keep a tally of civilians killed. The victims of today's brutal conflicts are not merely anonymous, but literally countless. Yet so long as the conflict rages within the borders of a single State, the old orthodoxy would require us to let it rage. We should leave it to "burn itself out", or perhaps to "fester". (You can choose your own euphemism.) We should leave it even to escalate, regardless of human consequences, at least until the point when its effects begin to spill over into neighbouring States so that it becomes, in the words of so many Security Council resolutions, "a threat to international peace and security".

In reality, this "old orthodoxy" was never absolute. The Charter, after all, was issued in the name of "the peoples", not the Governments, of the United Nations. Its aim is not only to preserve international peace – vitally important though that is – but also "to reaffirm faith in fundamental human rights, in the dignity and worth of the human person". The Charter protects the sovereignty of peoples. It was never meant as a licence for governments to trample on human rights and human dignity. Sovereignty implies responsibility, not just power.

This year we celebrate the fiftieth anniversary of the Universal Declaration of Human Rights. That declaration was not meant as a purely rhetorical statement. The General Assembly which adopted it also decided, in the same month, that it had the right to express its concern about the apartheid system in South Africa. The principle of international concern for human rights took precedence over the claim of non-interference in internal affairs.

And the day before it adopted the Universal Declaration, the General Assembly had adopted the Convention on the Prevention and Punishment of the Crime of Genocide, which puts all States under an obligation to "prevent and punish" this most heinous of crimes. It also allows them to "call upon the competent organs of the United Nations" to take action for this purpose.

Since genocide is almost always committed with the connivance, if not the direct participation, of the State authorities, it is hard to see how the United Nations could prevent it without intervening in a State's internal affairs.

As for punishment, a very important attempt is now being made to fulfil this obligation through the Ad hoc International Criminal Tribunals for the former Yugoslavia and Rwanda. And 10 days ago in Rome, I had the honour to open the Conference which is to establish a permanent international criminal court. Within a year or two, I sincerely hope, this court will be up and running, with competence to try cases of war crimes and crimes against humanity wherever, and by whomsoever, they are committed.

State frontiers, ladies and gentlemen, should no longer be seen as a watertight protection for war criminals or mass murderers. The fact that a conflict is "internal" does not give the parties any right to disregard the most basic rules of human conduct. . . .

And yet the most effective interventions are not military. It is much better, from every point of view, if action can be taken to resolve or manage a conflict before it reaches the military stage. Sometimes this action may take the form of economic advice and assistance.

In so many cases, ethnic tensions are exacerbated by poverty and famine, or by uneven economic development which brings wealth to one section of a community while destroying the homes and livelihood of another. If outsiders can help avert this by suitably targeted aid and investment, by giving information and training to local entrepreneurs, or by suggesting more appropriate State policies, their "intervention" should surely be welcomed by all concerned.

That is why I see the work of the United Nations Development Programme, and of our sister "Bretton Woods" institutions in Washington, as organically linked to the United Nations work on peace and security. In other cases, what is most needed is skilful and timely diplomacy. . . .

We must assume, however, that there will always be some tragic cases where peaceful means have failed: where extreme violence is being used, and only forceful intervention can stop it. Even during the Cold War, when the United Nations' own enforcement capacity was largely paralysed by divisions in the Security Council, there were cases where extreme violations of human rights in one country led to military intervention by one of its neighbours. In 1971 Indian intervention ended the civil war in East Pakistan, allowing Bangladesh to achieve independence. In 1978 Viet Nam intervened in Cambodia, putting an end to the genocidal rule of the Khmer Rouge. In 1979 Tanzania intervened to overthrow Idi Amin's erratic dictatorship in Uganda.

In all three of those cases the intervening States gave refugee flows across the border as the reason why they had to act. But what justified their action in the eyes of the world was the internal character of the regimes they acted against. And history has by and large ratified that verdict. Few would now deny that in those cases intervention was a lesser evil than allowing massacre and extreme oppression to continue. Yet at the time, in all three cases, the international community was divided and disturbed. Why? Because these interventions were unilateral. The States in question had no mandate from anyone else to act as they did. And that sets an uncomfortable precedent.

Can we really afford to let each State be the judge of its own right, or duty, to intervene in another State's internal conflict? If we do, will we not be forced to legitimize Hitler's championship of the Sudeten Germans, or Soviet intervention in Afghanistan?

Most of us would prefer, I think – especially now that the Cold War is over – to see such decisions taken collectively, by an international institution whose authority is generally respected. And surely the only institution competent to assume that role is the Security Council of the United Nations. The Charter clearly assigns responsibility to the Council for maintaining international peace and security. I would argue, therefore, that only the Council has the authority to decide that the internal situation in any State is so grave as to justify forceful intervention.

As you know, many Member States feel that the Council's authority now needs to be strengthened by an increase in its membership, bringing in new permanent members or possibly adding a new category of member. Unfortunately a consensus on the details of such a reform has yet to be reached.

This is a matter for the Member States. As Secretary-General I would make only three points. First, the Security Council must become more representative in order to reflect current realities, rather than the realities of 1945. Secondly, the Council's authority depends not only on the representative character of its membership but also on the quality and speed of its decisions. Humanity is ill served when the Council is unable to react quickly and decisively in a crisis. Thirdly, the delay in reaching agreement on reform, however regrettable, must not be allowed to detract from the Council's authority and responsibility in the meanwhile.

The Council in its present form derives its authority from the Charter. That gives it a unique legitimacy as the linchpin of world order, which all Member States should value and respect. It also places a unique responsibility on Council members, both permanent and non-permanent – a responsibility of which their governments and indeed their citizens should be fully conscious.

Of course the fact that the Council has this unique responsibility does not mean that the intervention itself should always be undertaken directly by the United Nations, in the sense of forces wearing blue helmets and controlled by the United Nations Secretariat. No one knows better than I do, as a former Under-Secretary-General in charge of peacekeeping, that the United Nations lacks the capacity for directing large-scale military enforcement operations.

At least for the foreseeable future, such operations will have to be undertaken by Member States, or by regional organizations. But they need to have the authority of the Security Council behind them, expressed in an authorizing resolution. That formula, developed in 1990 to deal with the Iraqi aggression against Kuwait, has proved its usefulness and will no doubt be used again in future crises. But we should not assume that intervention always needs to be on a massive scale.

There are cases where the speed of the action may be far more crucial than the size of the force. Personally, I am haunted by the experience of Rwanda in 1994: a terrible demonstration of what can happen when there is no intervention, or at least none in the crucial early weeks of a crisis. General Dallaire, the commander of the United Nations mission, has indicated that with a force of even modest size and means he could have prevented much of the killing. Indeed he has said that 5,000 peacekeepers could have saved 500,000 lives. How tragic it is that at the crucial moment the opposite course was chosen, and the size of the force reduced.

Surely things would have been different if the Security Council had at its disposal a small rapid reaction force, ready to move at a few days' notice. I believe that if we are to avert further such disasters in the future we need such a capacity; that Member States must have appropriately trained stand-by forces immediately available, and must be willing to send them quickly when the Security Council requests it.

Some have even suggested that private security firms, like the one which recently helped restore the elected President to power in Sierra Leone, might play a role in providing the United Nations with the rapid reaction capacity it needs. When we had need of skilled soldiers to separate fighters from refugees in the Rwandan refugee camps in Goma, I even considered the possibility of engaging a private firm. But the world may not be ready to privatize peace.

In any case, let me stress that I am not asking for a standing army at the beck and call of the Secretary-General. The decision to intervene, I repeat, can only be taken by the Security Council. But at present the Council's authority is diminished, because it lacks the means to intervene effectively even when it wishes to do so.

Let me conclude by coming back to where I started. The United Nations is an association of sovereign States, but the rights it exists to uphold belong to peoples, not governments. By the same token, it is wrong to think the obligations of United Nations membership fall only on States. Each one of us – whether as workers in government, in intergovernmental or non-governmental organizations, in business, in the media, or simply as human beings – has an obligation to do whatever he or she can to correct injustice. Each of us has a duty to halt – or, better, to prevent – the infliction of suffering.

Index